한 달만에 끝내는

스파르타 토익 800

RC

English&북스

한 달만에 끝내는

스파르타 토익 800 RC

NEW EDITION

개정판 1쇄 발행 2019년 7월 1일
개정판 6쇄 발행 2024년 1월 24일

저 자 피터, 박선영
펴낸이 박성호
펴낸곳 잉글리쉬앤 (주)

편 집 박고우니, 장서원
영업마케팅 여주형, 김성윤, 방성출, 박훈효, 조민형, 이달님, 강정구, 이진희, 조병운 변중구, 정노을, 조예선, 조광민, 이현정, 김정민, 최희성, 최인태, 윤종철 엄주아, 이가은, 신현수, 오지현

주 소 서울 특별시 관악구 쑥고개로 67-1
대표전화 (02) 878-1945
출판등록 2002년 3월 3일 제 320-2002-00045호

ISBN 978-89-6715-128-7 13740

* 가격은 표지에 있습니다. 잘못된 책은 바꾸어 드립니다.
www.english.co.kr

Preface

스파르타 토익 800 RC 개정판을 내면서

2016년 첫 출간 이후 독자 여러분께 꾸준히 사랑을 받아온 토익 종합서 베스트셀러인 스파르타 토익 800 RC가 새롭게 개정판을 출간합니다.

어떻게 하면 단기간에 토익 고득점에 꼭 필요한 내용만 효율적으로 학습할 수 있을까? 토익을 준비하는 모든 수험생들의 한결같은 질문일 것입니다.

이미 많은 고득점자들이 증명한 대로 토익은 단기간에 집중적으로 공부해서 끝내야 합니다. 토익은 한정된 유형이 반복 출제되기 때문에 무엇을 어떻게 학습하는지가 고득점의 관건이라고 할 수 있습니다.

스파르타 토익 800 RC 개정판은 기출 문제를 기반으로 토익 고득점 점수에 도달할 수 있도록 안내하는 중급용 전략서입니다. 본 교재에는 저자진이 15년 이상 현장에서 집중 훈련을 통해 고득점자를 배출한 전략 및 노하우가 모두 응축되어 있습니다. 토익 유형을 완벽히 분석하여, 이에 맞는 문제 풀이 전략과 다양한 실전 문제들로 구성하였습니다.

토익 공부를 어떻게 시작해야 할지 막막한 학습자, 목표 점수가 나오지 않아 고민인 학습자들을 위해 스파르타 토익 800 RC 개정판이 토익 고득점으로 향하는 지름길을 제시하고자 합니다. 그리고 그 길을 함께하며 여러분을 항상 응원하겠습니다.

Contents

PART 5&6

PART 7

토익 소개

토익이란?

Test Of English for International Communication의 약자로, 영어가 모국어가 아닌 사람들의 일상생활이나 국제업무 등에 필요한 실용 영어 능력을 평가하는 국제 평가 시험

▶ 시험 구성

<table>
<tr><th>구성</th><th>Part</th><th colspan="2">유형</th><th colspan="2">문항 수</th><th>시간</th><th>배점</th></tr>
<tr><td rowspan="4">듣기(LC)</td><td>1</td><td colspan="2">사진 묘사</td><td>6</td><td rowspan="4">100</td><td rowspan="4">45분</td><td rowspan="4">495점</td></tr>
<tr><td>2</td><td colspan="2">질의 응답</td><td>25</td></tr>
<tr><td>3</td><td colspan="2">대화문</td><td>39</td></tr>
<tr><td>4</td><td colspan="2">담화문</td><td>30</td></tr>
<tr><td rowspan="4">읽기(RC)</td><td>5</td><td colspan="2">단문 공란 채우기</td><td>30</td><td rowspan="4">100</td><td rowspan="4">75분</td><td rowspan="4">495점</td></tr>
<tr><td>6</td><td colspan="2">장문 공란 채우기</td><td>16</td></tr>
<tr><td rowspan="2">7</td><td rowspan="2">지문 독해</td><td>단일 지문</td><td>29</td></tr>
<tr><td>복수 지문</td><td>25</td></tr>
<tr><td>TOTAL</td><td colspan="3">7 Parts</td><td colspan="2">200문항</td><td>120분</td><td>990점</td></tr>
</table>

▶ 시험 내용

Part	유형	유형 내용
1	사진 묘사	제시된 사진을 알맞게 설명하는 보기 고르기
2	질의 응답	질문을 듣고 알맞은 대답 고르기
3	대화문	대화를 듣고 질문에 알맞은 내용 고르기
4	담화문	담화를 듣고 질문에 알맞은 내용 고르기
5	단문 공란 채우기	빈칸에 맞는 내용을 골라 문장 완성하기
6	장문 공란 채우기	빈칸에 맞는 내용을 골라 장문 완성하기
7	지문 독해	단일 지문 또는 이중 · 삼중 지문을 읽고 문제에 맞는 내용 고르기

접수 방법은?

▶ 한국 토익 위원회 사이트 혹은 앱으로 접수 ➔ www.toeic.co.kr
▶ 인터넷 접수할 때 시험일, 고사장, 개인 정보 등을 입력 (증명사진 필요)
※ 접수 마감일 이후 추가 접수일에 접수 시 추가 비용 발생

응시 준비물은?

▶ 규정 신분증 (주민등록증, 운전면허증, 기간 만료 전의 여권, 중고등학생만 학생증 인정)
▶ 연필, 지우개 (볼펜이나 사인펜은 사용 금지)
▶ 아날로그 시계 (전자 시계 불가)

시험 진행은?

▶ **시험 시간이 오전일 경우** 오전 9:20까지 입실 (오전 9:50 이후 입실 불가)
▶ **시험 시간이 오후일 경우** 오후 2:20까지 입실 (오후 2:50 이후 입실 불가)

오전 시험	오후 시험	시험 진행
오전 9:30 ~ 9:45 (15분)	오후 2:30 ~ 2:45 (15분)	답안지 작성에 관한 오리엔테이션
오전 9:45 ~ 9:50 (5분)	오후 2:45 ~ 2:50 (5분)	수험자 휴식 시간
오전 9:50 ~ 10:05 (15분)	오후 2:50 ~ 3:05 (15분)	신분 확인
오전 10:05 ~ 10:10 (5분)	오후 3:05 ~ 3:10 (5분)	문제지 배부, 파본 확인
오전 10:10 ~ 10:55 (45분)	오후 3:10 ~ 3:55 (45분)	듣기 평가(LC)
오전 10:55 ~ 12:10 (75분)	오후 3:55 ~ 5:10 (75분)	읽기 평가(RC)

※ 읽기 평가(RC) 시간에 2차 신분 확인 실시

성적 확인은?

▶ 시험일로부터 약 2주 후에 토익 위원회 사이트(www.toeic.co.kr)에서 확인 가능
▶ 온라인 출력과 우편 수령은 1회 무료, 이후에는 유료 발급

파트별 유형 및 전략

PART 5

단문 공란 채우기 30문제

파트 5는 문장 안에 있는 빈칸에 적절한 단어나 어구를 채워 넣는 파트이다. 총 30문항이 출제되며, 문법 문제와 어휘 문제가 등장한다. 문제 유형에 따라 풀이 방식이 다르므로 이를 가장 먼저 파악하는 것이 중요하다.

| 핵심 전략 |

- ✚ 문제를 풀기 전, 보기를 통해 문제 유형을 파악하는 연습을 한다.
- ✚ 문법 문제는 문장 구조나 빈칸 주변의 문법을 통해 문제를 풀어야 한다. 문법 문제를 단시간에 풀기 위해서 명사, 동사, 형용사 등의 기본적인 문법을 확실히 익혀 두도록 하자.
- ✚ 어휘 문제는 해석을 통해 문맥에 가장 적절한 단어를 선택해야 한다. 가능한 한 많은 어휘를 암기하고, 예문을 통해 어휘가 어떻게 사용되는지를 이해하자.
- ✚ 자주 함께 쓰이는 단어 및 표현들을 숙지하여 빠른 시간 내에 문제를 풀어야 한다.

| 문제 형태 |

101 Sky Motors offers a variety of training programs to help enhance ------- in the workplace.

(A) productivity
(B) produce
(C) productive
(D) productively

102 The fundraising event recorded such high ------- that the proceeds will be higher than expected.

(A) representative
(B) consultation
(C) safety
(D) attendance

PART 6

장문 공란 채우기 16문제

파트 6는 지문 안에 있는 4개의 빈칸에 알맞은 보기를 선택하는 파트이다. 문법, 어휘, 문장을 넣는 문제가 등장하며, 총 16문항이 출제된다. 문맥에 맞는 문장을 고르는 문제는 각 지문마다 1개씩 출제된다.

| 핵심 전략 |

- 전체 문맥을 이해해야 풀 수 있는 문법 및 어휘 문제가 나오므로 지문의 흐름을 놓치지 않는 것이 중요하다.
- 빈칸에 알맞은 문장을 넣는 문제는 빈칸 앞뒤와 전체 맥락을 파악하여 정답을 골라야 하므로 전반적인 독해력을 늘려야 한다.
- 지문을 읽으면서 흐름상 다음에 나와야 할 내용을 예측하면 정답을 쉽게 찾을 수 있다.

| 문제 형태 |

Questions 135-138 refer to the following notice.

Important Notice about Hatter Industries

Please note that the contact information for Hatter Industries changed on March 21. Due to the closure of our Dabbley office and the ------- (135) of our operations in Buena, all correspondence concerning our products and services should now be sent to the following address: Hatter Industries, 642 Mandela Lane, Buena, CA. Our employees' e-mail addresses, as well as our Web site's address, www.hatterindustries.com, remain ------- (136). However, we are still waiting for our new telephone and fax numbers. ------- (137) will be updated on our Web site as soon as the new numbers are assigned as of March 25.

------- (138)

135 (A) decision
(B) relocation
(C) suspension
(D) result

136 (A) assigned
(B) even
(C) formal
(D) unchanged

137 (A) Yours
(B) Another
(C) These
(D) Theirs

138 (A) We apologize for any inconvenience and thank you for your understanding.
(B) Refer to the side of the packet for full details of instructions before applying.
(C) Her office location will also remain the same.
(D) For more information about the forthcoming event, visit www.lizard.org.br/events.

PART 7

지문 독해 54문제

파트 7은 지문을 읽고 지문과 관련된 문제 2~5개를 푸는 파트이다. 총 54문항이 출제되며, 지문은 편지, 문자 메시지, 광고, 공지문 등 다양한 유형으로 나온다. 단일 지문 10개, 이중 지문 2개, 삼중 지문 3개의 세트가 등장한다.

| 핵심 전략 |

- ✚ 지문의 종류와 제목, 키워드를 파악하여 내용을 미리 예측하고 정답 단서를 찾는다.
- ✚ 지문의 단서가 보기에는 다르게 패러프레이징될 수 있으므로, 단어를 암기할 때 동의표현을 함께 익힌다.
- ✚ 복수 지문에서는 2개 이상의 지문을 연계하여 풀어야 하는 문제들이 출제되므로, 지문간의 관계를 파악하는 연습을 해야 한다.

| 문제 형태 |

Questions 162-164 refer to the following advertisement.

ACCOUNT SERVICE DIRECTOR WANTED

A leading financial service bank is looking for an account services director. —[1]—. He or she will be responsible for reclassifying income payment to ensure the accurate reporting of tax payments. —[2]—. Validating tax related information, determining reclassification amounts, processing reclassifications using various internal systems, and performing quality-control checks relevant to all tax-reporting processes will be some of the other responsibilities. —[3]—. In order to qualify, the candidate must have a college degree and previous tax or brokerage experience along with strong analytical skills. —[4]—.

If you are interested, please send your résumé to:

Rosabeth Moss Kanter / Lawrence Financial, Inc.
985, Andrew Park Avenue / Houston, TX 48954

162 What position is being advertised?

(A) Public official
(B) Real estate agent
(C) Accountant
(D) Financial consultant

163 Which of the following is required for the position?

(A) Communication skills
(B) A license approved by a related organization
(C) Background knowledge of Lawrence Financial, Inc.
(D) A college education

164 In which of the positions marked [1], [2], [3], and [4] does the following sentence best belong?

"They must also be able to work overtime and weekends when required."

(A) [1]
(B) [2]
(C) [3]
(D) [4]

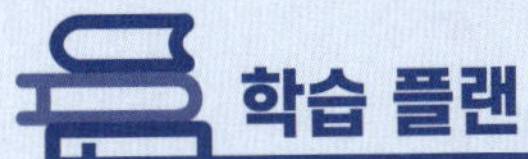

학습 플랜

> 2주 완성

	Day 1	Day 2	Day 3	Day 4	Day 5
1 week	UNIT 01-02 & UNIT 19	UNIT 03-05 & UNIT 20	UNIT 06 & UNIT 21	UNIT 07-08 & UNIT 22	UNIT 09 & UNIT 23-24
2 week	UNIT 10-12 & UNIT 25-26	UNIT 13-14 & UNIT 27	UNIT 15-16 & UNIT 28	UNIT 17 & UNIT 29	UNIT 18 & 실전모의고사

> 4주 완성

	Day 1	Day 2	Day 3	Day 4	Day 5
1 week	UNIT 01-02	UNIT 03-05	UNIT 06	UNIT 07-08	UNIT 09
2 week	UNIT 10-12	UNIT 13-14	UNIT 15-16	UNIT 17	UNIT 18
3 week	UNIT 19	UNIT 20	UNIT 21	UNIT 22	UNIT 23-24
4 week	UNIT 25-26	UNIT 27	UNIT 28	UNIT 29	실전모의고사

PART
5&6

UNIT 01 명사

명사는 토익에서 매월 평균 2~3문제가 출제된다. 명사는 ① 명사 자리 문제, ② 명사 어휘 문제, ③ 가산명사와 불가산명사 구분 문제, ④ 사람명사와 사물명사 구분 문제, ⑤ 복합명사 문제로 출제된다.

Preview

01 I 명사의 역할

주어 **Production** will be increased next year. 내년에는 생산(량)이 늘어날 것이다.

목적어 I got **a refund** on this item. 나는 이 물건에 대한 환불을 받았다.

보어 He became **an accountant**. 그는 회계사가 되었다.

02 I 가산명사와 불가산명사

가산명사 **(셀 수 있는 명사)**	사람이나 물건과 같이 기준이 명확하여 누가 세더라도 그 숫자가 분명한 것 employee 직원 customer 고객 document 서류 fee 수수료 price 가격 item 물품
불가산명사 **(셀 수 없는 명사)**	세는 기준이나 단위가 모호하여 셀 수 없는 것 information 정보 equipment 장비 furniture 가구 luggage 수하물 advice 조언

03 I 사람을 나타내는 명사

-er/or	employer 고용주 consumer 소비자 manager 관리자 advisor 고문 investor 투자자
-ant	applicant 지원자 accountant 회계사 consultant 상담가 defendant 피고 tenant 세입자
-ee	attendee 출석자 employee 직원 interviewee 면접 대상자 trainee 연습생
-ist	economist 경제학자 journalist 기자 tourist 관광객 chemist 화학자 specialist 전문가

04 I 혼동하기 쉬운 명사

-tive	objective 목적 representative 대표, 직원 executive 중역 alternative 대안 incentive 장려금 initiative 계획, (불) 적극성 relative 친척
-al	renewal 갱신 approval 승인 proposal 제안 arrival 도착 professional 전문가
-ing	funding 자금지원 ticketing 발권 seating 좌석 housing 주택 advertising 광고(업) processing 처리 clothing 의류 training 훈련 meeting 회의 lodging 숙박 accounting 회계 planning 기획 opening 공석, 개장 financing 자금조달

05 I 특정 의미로서 반드시 복수로 쓰고 복수 취급하는 명사

-s	clothes 옷 goods 상품, 물품 savings 저금, 저축액 belongings 소지품 earnings 소득, 수익 surroundings 주변환경 means 수단 valuables 귀중품 proceeds 수익금 findings 조사결과 authorities 당국, 관계자 details 세부 사항 proceedings 회의(의사)록

POINT 1 명사의 역할과 위치

01 | 명사는 주어 역할을 한다.

The [acquisition / ~~acquired~~] of three businesses helped to boost the Novartis Company's revenue last year. 3개 사업체의 인수는 작년에 Novartis 사의 매출을 높이는 데 도움이 되었다.

02 | 명사는 목적어 역할을 한다.

Belt Co. **enhanced** [collaboration / ~~collaborate~~] among its staff members by developing new strategies.
Belt 사는 새로운 전략을 개발함으로써 직원들 사이에 협력을 강화했다. ▶ 타동사의 목적어

Upgrading the existing machine will result in a sustainable improvement **in** [efficiency / ~~efficient~~].
기존의 기계를 업그레이드하면 효율성이 지속해서 향상된다. ▶ 전치사의 목적어

+TIP 명사는 준동사인 to부정사나 동명사의 목적어 역할을 할 수 있다.

After careful consideration, I have decided **to accept** the job offer.
신중하게 고려한 후에, 나는 그 일자리 제안을 받아들이기로 결정했다.

03 | 명사는 보어 역할을 한다.

Sun Motors **has become a** [leader / ~~leading~~] in the car manufacturing business.
Sun 자동차는 자동차 제조업에서 선두주자가 되었다. ▶ 주격 보어

The board of directors **considered** Mr. Anderson **a competent** [employee / ~~employs~~].
이사회는 앤더슨 씨를 능력이 있는 직원으로 여겼다. ▶ 목적격 보어

04 | 명사는 한정사의 수식을 받는다.

He had made **an important contribution** to **the company's** [success / ~~succeed~~].
그는 회사의 성공에 아주 중요한 공헌을 하였다.

The controversial [issue / ~~issued~~] of additional vacation time for first-year employees was settled at yesterday's board meeting. 논란이 되고 있는 신입 사원들을 위한 추가 휴가 시간 문제는 어제 이사회에서 해결되었다.

+TIP 한정사란?

the, a(an), my, this, some, either, every, enough, several 같이 명사 혹은 명사구를 수식하면서 그 의미를 한정하는 역할을 한다.

SPARTA Check-UP! 1

해설 p. 322

1 The ------- on Mr. Henson's résumé show that he will be a valued member of our team.
(A) accomplished
(B) accomplishes
(C) accomplishments
(D) accomplishing

2 Ms. Lucy called earlier today for ------- that the package she sent on Monday had been received.
(A) confirm
(B) confirms
(C) confirmation
(D) confirmed

3 When you place an order, be sure to include your ------- at the bottom of the order form.
(A) to sign
(B) signature
(C) signed
(D) sign

POINT 2 가산명사와 불가산명사

01 | 가산명사는 반드시 앞에 관사를 붙이거나 복수형으로 써야 한다.

You can ask for [a refund / ~~refund~~] if your order is not delivered within 10 business days.
영업일 기준 10일 이내에 주문한 물건이 도착하지 않으면 환불을 요청할 수 있다.

Some [applicants / ~~applicant~~] have extensive experience in the medical industry.
일부 지원자들은 의료 분야에서 아주 많은 경험을 가지고 있다.

+ VOCABULARY | 빈출 가산명사

돈	fund 자금 fee 수수료 refund 환불 price 가격 profit 수익 cost 비용 discount 할인
시간	day 날 week 주 month 월 year 년
서류	letter 편지 report 보고서 proposal 제안서 estimate 견적서 statement 진술서
사람	employee 직원 applicant 지원자 candidate 후보자 representative 대표
규칙	regulation 규정 procedure 절차 standard 기준 measure 조치 direction 지시사항

02 | 불가산명사는 앞에 부정관사(a, an)를 붙이거나 복수형으로 쓸 수 없다.

[Productivity / ~~Productivities~~] during the first quarter exceeded the 5-percent growth many analysts had forecast. 1분기 동안의 생산성이 많은 분석가가 예상했던 5퍼센트 성장을 넘어섰다.

+ VOCABULARY | 빈출 불가산명사

clothing 의류
access 접근, 이용
luggage/baggage 짐
productivity 생산성
furniture 가구
attention 주의
advice 충고
employment 고용
negligence 부주의
information 정보
knowledge 지식
assistance 도움
efficiency 효율성
progress 진보
merchandise 상품
use 사용, 이용

+TIP 혼동하기 쉬운 가산명사와 불가산명사

가산명사	불가산명사
a plan 계획	planning 계획
a ticket 티켓	ticketing 발권
a price 가격	pricing 가격 책정
a certificate 자격증	certification 인증

가산명사	불가산명사
a seat 좌석	seating 좌석(배치)
an account 계좌	accounting 회계
a fund 기금, 자금	funding 자금 지원
a permit 허가증	permission 허가

SPARTA Check-UP! 2

| 해설 p. 322

1 Mr. Gabrawy will check the storage cabinet before he orders more office -------.
(A) supplies
(B) supplying
(C) supply
(D) supplied

2 JC Soft is looking for a marketing manager with a high ------- of expertise in the field.
(A) level
(B) levels
(C) leveled
(D) being leveled

3 ------- to the management workshops have been sent to all the department managers.
(A) Invite
(B) Inviting
(C) Invitation
(D) Invitations

POINT ③ 사람명사와 사물명사의 구분

01 | 명사 자리에는 사람명사나 사물명사가 쓰일 수 있는데, 각기 다른 의미를 가지므로 문맥에 맞게 써야 한다.

The safety [**inspection** / ~~inspector~~] of all facilities is scheduled for next week.
모든 시설의 안전 점검이 다음 주로 일정이 잡혀 있다.

The company's financial problem is largely due to poor [**management** / ~~manager~~].
회사의 재정 문제는 주로 형편없는 경영 때문이다.

All passengers are required to present a boarding pass to the airline [**attendant** / ~~attention~~].
모든 승객은 승무원에게 탑승권을 제시해야 한다.

All [**visitors** / ~~visit~~] to the Suntech Solar Plant must report to the security desk immediately upon arrival. Suntech 태양열 발전소의 모든 방문객들은 도착하는 즉시 보안 데스크에 보고해야 합니다.

+ VOCABULARY | 빈출 사람명사 vs. 사물명사

사람명사	사물명사
accountant 회계사	accounting 회계(학)
attendee 참석자/출석자	attendance 출석/참석
contributor 기부자	contribution 공헌/기부
competitor 경쟁자	competition 경쟁/대회
donator/donor 기부자	donation 기부/기증
employee 직원	employment 고용
evaluator 평가자	evaluation 평가
critic 비평가	criticism 비평
recipient 수령인/영수인	receipt 영수증/수령
supervisor 감독관	supervision 감독
architect 건축가	architecture 건축

사람명사	사물명사
advertiser 광고업자	advertisement 광고
applicant 지원(신청)자	application 지원/신청(서)
consultant 상담자	consultation 상담
consumer 소비자	consumption 소비
distributor 배급업자	distribution 분배/배급
producer 생산자	productivity 생산성
interpreter 통역사	interpretation 통역
negotiator 협상가	negotiation 협상
subscriber 구독자	subscription 구독
resident 거주자/주민	residence 거주, 거주지
authority 권위자/권한	authorization 허가

SPARTA ☑ Check-UP! ③

| 해설 p. 322

1 Holland & Barrett is the only ------- of premium dairy products in the Tiaren Lakes region.
(A) distributed
(B) distributing
(C) distribution
(D) distributor

2 The seminar ------- must register by phone at least two weeks in advance.
(A) attendance
(B) attends
(C) attention
(D) attendees

3 Generally speaking, doctors need written ------- in order to release patients' medical records.
(A) authorized
(B) authorizes
(C) authorization
(D) authority

POINT 4 복합명사

01 | 두 개 또는 두 개 이상의 명사로 이루어진 복합명사는 한 단어로 취급한다.

The new **safety** [regulations / ~~regulated~~] regarding the use of the office computer will take effect on November 1. 사내 컴퓨터 사용에 대한 새로운 안전규정이 11월 1일부로 효력을 발휘하게 될 것이다.

You are not allowed to wear casual clothes in accordance with the **company dress** [code / ~~to code~~]. 당신은 회사 복장 규정에 따라 캐주얼 의상을 입을 수 없습니다.

+ VOCABULARY | 빈출 복합명사

safety feature 안전 사양
registration form 등록 양식
enrollment fee 등록비
expiration date 만기일
production line 생산 라인
meal preference 선호 식단
attendance record 출석률
time management 시간 관리
transportation system 교통 체계
job openings 공석, 일자리
office supplies 사무용품
safety regulations 안전 규정
complaint form 불만신고 양식
satisfaction guarantee 만족 보장
submission deadline 제출 마감일
account information 계좌 정보
communication skill 의사소통기술
baggage allowance 수하물중량 제한

+TIP 복합명사의 복수형은 뒤의 명사에 -s를 붙인다.

- **a** registration form 등록 양식 → registration form**s**
- **an** interest rate 이자율 → interest rate**s**

+TIP 일부 복합명사는 앞에 오는 명사를 항상 복수형으로 쓴다.

award**s** ceremony 시상식
earning**s** growth 수입 증대
benefit**s** package 복리 후생 제도
oversea**s** investment 해외 투자
sale**s** strategy 영업 전략
sale**s** figure 판매 수치
custom**s** office 세관
saving**s** plan 예금 상품

This year's [awards / ~~awarded~~] **ceremony** for the best employee will begin at approximately 6 P.M.
올해의 우수사원 시상식은 저녁 6시쯤에 시작할 것이다.

SPARTA Check-UP! 4

| 해설 p. 322

1 Hyper Ltd. has become an industry ------- in digital audio production.
(A) leader
(B) leadership
(C) leading
(D) leads

2 The Dmitri Glass Factory recently issued an important update to its ------- regulations.
(A) safe
(B) safety
(C) safeties
(D) safely

3 The Radisson Hotel requires that guests present a major credit card to complete the ------- process.
(A) registers
(B) registered
(C) register
(D) registration

PRACTICE

해설 p. 323

▪ 괄호 안의 보기 중 알맞은 단어를 고르세요.

1 The board members have indicated their **[approval / approves]** of the expansion of the facility.

2 A team of **[inspectors / inspections]** regularly checks the quality of all products.

3 The consultant conducted an analysis of our **[perform / performance]**.

4 It is mandatory for all employees to attend the **[safety / safely]** training on Friday.

5 Each visitor must pick up a **[secure / security]** pass from the receptionist at the main entrance.

6 I want to work for a leading **[company / companies]** in the financial industry.

7 Ms. Boniadi will continue working at Maruti Holdings until her **[replacing / replacement]** arrives.

8 The PR manager position requires a candidate with outstanding communication **[skill / skills]**.

9 The Lowell Group has increased its employee productivity by offering **[lecture / lectures]** on time management.

10 **[Applicants / Applications]** are required to provide at least two references from previous employers.

11 The next **[edits / edition]** of the travel guide will include information about hiking and biking trails.

12 The senior media **[director / direction]** for the SSI Group coordinates the planning of all promotional campaigns.

13 Employees are asked to call the help desk at extension 130 for **[assistance / assistant]** with any technical difficulties.

14 **[Employees / Employment]** who wish to telecommute should discuss the matter with their immediate supervisor.

15 Basic **[safety / safely]** precautions should be observed when removing computer parts.

1 To make your next ------- with Dr. Horton, please call his office during business hours today.

(A) appointed (B) appoint
(C) appointment (D) appoints

2 After a close ------- of the current fire danger conditions by the fire chief, the decision was made to cancel the 25th annual Malibu Concert.

(A) evaluate (B) evaluated
(C) evaluates (D) evaluation

3 All job ------- are asked to bring an essay explaining how they would feel about working for a small business.

(A) applicants (B) applications
(C) apply (D) applied

4 If our maintenance team can be of any further ------- or should you have any questions, please feel free to contact us directly.

(A) assist (B) assists
(C) assisted (D) assistance

5 Robert Brown, the chairman of Landstar Electronics Co., emphasized the ------- of software technologies, a talented workforce, and patents in a keynote speech.

(A) important (B) most important
(C) importantly (D) importance

6 The employees are authorized to use company credit cards while on official business but may not use them for personal -------.

(A) expends (B) expenses
(C) expended (D) expensive

7 This season's special tour package at Five Star Tour Agency features attractive ------- such as exclusive discount rates at high-class hotels and a continental breakfast.

(A) benefit (B) benefits
(C) beneficial (D) beneficially

8 Starting in May, customer service ------- will be trained to respond properly to various issues.

(A) representatives (B) representational
(C) represent (D) represents

9 Travel agencies are required to regularly review ------- of tourist attractions in order to learn about new sites to introduce.

(A) journalists (B) journals
(C) journalism (D) journalistic

10 Thompson Virtual College is recruiting ------- capable of teaching African history and languages for its distance learning courses.

(A) instruction (B) instructors
(C) instructed (D) instructive

11 Thanks to careful -------, the construction of the new train station in Gastown will cause very little inconvenience to the community.

(A) plan (B) planner
(C) planning (D) planned

12 A revised schedule for completing the state-of-the-art production plant has been proposed as an ------- to the one currently in place.

(A) alternative (B) alternatively
(C) alternatives (D) alternativeness

Questions 13-16 refer to the following memo.

From: Elizabeth Manning
To: Robert Jenkins
Subject: Promotion
Date: April 21

Dear Mr. Jenkins,

This is Elizabeth Manning from the Human Resources Department. I would like to inform you that your promotion has been ------- (13.) by our department. Effective May 1, your new title will be director of sales, and you will be transferred to our headquarters in Salt Lake City. ------- (14.). I will send you an e-mail with an attached file which includes the official description of your new ------- (15.) as the director of sales.

I will be more than happy to answer any questions you may have, so please don't hesitate to contact me. We look forward to the additional ------- (16.) you will be making to our company.

Sincerely,

Elizabeth Manning
Director, Human Resources

13 (A) notified
(B) applied
(C) approved
(D) cited

14 (A) It will be held at 1 P.M. at the Emerald Country Club.
(B) This year, we will be celebrating the achievements of Mr. Jenkins, the director of advertising.
(C) Beginning on May 25, your paycheck will reflect a 15-percent pay raise.
(D) We are asking each associate to contribute $25 for a goodbye gift.

15 (A) examples
(B) responsibilities
(C) foundation
(D) knowledge

16 (A) contributions
(B) contributors
(C) contributed
(D) contributes

UNIT 02 대명사

대명사는 매월 출제된다. 대명사 문제 유형은 ① 인칭대명사의 수와 격의 일치 ② 재귀대명사의 강조 용법과 재귀 용법 ③ 지시대명사 ④ 부정대명사 순이다. 특히, 명사 앞 소유격 문제와 재귀대명사의 강조 용법 문제가 자주 출제된다.

Preview

01 | 인칭대명사의 역할과 종류

인칭	인칭대명사				소유대명사	재귀대명사
	주격		소유격	목적격		
1인칭 단수	I		my	me	mine	myself
1인칭 복수	we		our	us	ours	ourselves
2인칭 단수	you		your	you	yours	yourself
2인칭 복수	you		your	you	yours	yourselves
3인칭 단수	남성	he	his	him	his	himself
	여성	she	her	her	hers	herself
	중성	it	its	it	-	itself
3인칭 복수	they		their	them	theirs	themselves

대명사는 명사를 대신하는 말로서 언급된 명사를 반복하지 않고 좀 더 간결한 문장을 만드는 데 사용된다. 따라서 명사와 같이 문장에서 주어, 목적어, 보어의 역할을 한다.

We have already told **him** that several times. 우리는 그에게 그것을 이미 여러 차례 말했다.
주어 - 주격 대명사 목적어 - 목적격 대명사

02 | 재귀대명사

재귀대명사는 주어나 목적어를 강조하는 강조 용법과 주어가 타동사의 목적어나 전치사의 목적어와 같을 때 쓰는 재귀 용법이 있다.

I **myself** wrote this book. (= I wrote this book **myself**.) 내가 직접 이 책을 썼다. ▶ 강조 용법

She describes **herself** as a singer. 그녀는 자신을 가수라고 말한다. ▶ 재귀 용법(주어=목적어)

03 | 지시대명사

이미 나온 명사의 반복을 피하기 위해 that(앞의 명사가 단수) 또는 those(앞의 명사가 복수)를 쓴다.

The size of the parking lot is bigger than **that** (= **the size**) of the stadium near the town.
주차장의 크기가 마을 근처에 있는 운동장의 그것(크기)보다 더 크다.

04 | 부정대명사

막연한 사물이나 사람을 가리킬 때 쓰며 some(일부), a few(소수), most(대다수), all(전부) 등이 있다.

Some of the information is quite technical. 그 정보 중 일부는 상당히 기술적이다.

POINT 1 인칭대명사의 역할

01 | 주어 자리에 인칭대명사가 올 때는 주격을 쓴다.

[We / ~~Our~~] believe that **he** is the most qualified for this position.
우리는 그가 이 직책에 가장 적격이라고 생각한다.

I would appreciate it if [you / ~~your~~] could forward me the contract.
계약서를 제게 전송해 주시면 감사하겠습니다.

02 | 명사 앞에 인칭대명사가 올 때는 소유격을 쓰며, 명사를 수식하는 역할을 한다.

If you need further help, you can call [my / ~~me~~] **direct line**.
도움이 더 필요하시면, 제 직통 전화로 전화 주십시오.

After the changes are made to [your / ~~you~~] **reservation**, I will send you a confirmation e-mail.
귀하의 예약이 변경된 후에, 확인 이메일을 보내드리겠습니다.

03 | 타동사의 목적어나 전치사의 목적어 자리에는 목적격을 쓴다.

Please do not hesitate to **contact** [me / ~~my~~] at your earliest convenience.
주저하지 마시고 편하신 가장 빠른 시일 내에 제게 연락 주시기 바랍니다.

If you have a problem, we will provide a full refund **to** [you / ~~your~~].
만약 문제가 생기면 당신에게 전액 환불을 해 드리겠습니다.

04 | 소유대명사는 '소유격+명사'를 대신한 것으로, '~의 것'의 의미이다.

주어 Steven will stay in my house while [his / ~~he~~] is being renovated.
(=his house)
Steven은 그의 집이 보수공사가 진행되는 동안 내 집에서 머무를 것이다.

목적어 Mr. Boyle received his evaluation, but I'm still waiting for [mine / ~~me~~].
(=my evaluation)
Boyle 씨는 그의 평가를 받았지만, 나는 아직도 내 것을 기다리는 중이다.

보어 I mistakenly thought Mr. Hoffman's report was [mine / ~~me~~].
(=my report)
나는 실수로 Hoffman 씨의 보고서가 내 것이라고 생각했다.

▶ 소유대명시 문제는 보통 be동사 뒤에 빈칸을 둔 형태로 출제된다.

SPARTA Check-UP! 1

해설 p. 325

1 ------- can reserve a flight at a discounted price by calling our travel agency at least 24 hours in advance.
(A) Your
(B) Yours
(C) You
(D) Yourself

2 Mr. Felton has been selected as the employee of the month by ------- co-workers.
(A) he
(B) his
(C) him
(D) himself

3 The clerk collects packages from each department twice a day and takes ------- to the mailroom.
(A) they
(B) theirs
(C) their
(D) them

POINT 2 재귀대명사의 용법과 관용표현

01 | 재귀 용법

타동사의 목적어나 전치사의 목적어가 주어와 같을 때 재귀대명사를 쓰며, 이때의 재귀대명사는 문장의 필수 성분이므로 생략 불가!

We should try to adapt [**ourselves** / ~~us~~] to the new economic environment.
우리는 새로운 경제 환경에 우리 자신을 적응시키도록 노력해야 한다.

All personnel are asked to take care of [**themselves** / ~~them~~] in case of a fire.
모든 직원들은 화재 시에 그들 스스로를 챙기라는 지시를 받았다.

+TIP 재귀대명사는 주어 자리에 쓰지 않는다.

When [**you** / ~~yourself~~] have completed the form, hand it in at the desk.
양식을 완성하시면, 접수원에게 건네주세요.

02 | 강조 용법

주어나 목적어를 강조할 때 '직접'이라는 뜻으로, 강조하고자 하는 단어 뒤나 문미에 사용한다. 이때의 재귀대명사는 문장의 필수 성분이 아니므로 생략 가능!

The CEO [**himself** / ~~him~~] welcomed our group when we visited the company.
우리가 회사를 방문했을 때 사장이 직접 우리를 환영해 주었다.

The CEO will interview at least 50 candidates for the research position [**herself** / ~~her~~].
사장이 직접 최소 50명의 연구직 후보들을 인터뷰할 것이다.

03 | 관용 표현

by oneself (=on one's own=alone) 혼자서, 직접	for oneself 혼자 힘으로, 자신을 위해
to oneself 혼자만, 마음속으로	of itself 저절로
in itself (=naturally) 본래, 그 자체로	in spite of oneself (=unconsciously) 자기도 모르게

All employees are expected to complete their assignments **by** [**themselves** / ~~their own~~].
모든 직원들은 스스로 그들의 업무를 완수할 것으로 기대된다. = on their own

Because his colleagues were out sick, Tony had to finish the report on [**his own** / ~~himself~~].
동료들이 아파서 결근했기 때문에 토니는 혼자서 보고서를 끝내야만 했다.

SPARTA Check-UP! 2

해설 p. 325

1 Ms. Lin will try the new accounting software ------- before commenting on it.
(A) she
(B) her
(C) hers
(D) herself

2 At the end of the meeting, we found ------- looking over the documents in detail again and again.
(A) we
(B) our
(C) ours
(D) ourselves

3 Although teamwork is emphasized, many employees at PT Industries still prefer to do things on -------.
(A) their
(B) themselves
(C) them
(D) their own

POINT 3 지시대명사 that/those의 구별

01 | 일반대명사는 앞에 언급된 명사 자체를 가리키는데, that과 those는 앞에서 언급된 것과 다른 것을 가리킨다. 명사 반복을 피하기 위해 쓰이며 of 이하의 전치사구를 이끈다.

Our computers will meet your needs, or you can return [**them** / ~~that~~].
우리 컴퓨터들은 귀하의 요구에 맞을 것이며, 그렇지 않으면 그것들을 반품하셔도 됩니다.

▶ 앞에서 언급한 '우리 컴퓨터들(our computers)'을 반품해 준다는 의미이므로 일반대명사 them으로 받는다.

Our computers are cheaper and more reliable than [**those** / ~~it~~] **of** our competitors.
우리 컴퓨터들은 경쟁사들의 그것(컴퓨터들)보다 더 싸고 더 신뢰할 만하다.

▶ 동일한 컴퓨터가 아니라 앞에 언급된 명사 computers를 대신하여 지시대명사 those로 받는다.

02 | 앞에 나온 명사가 단수이면 that, 복수이면 those를 쓴다.

His salary as a bus driver is much higher than [**that** / ~~this~~] of a teacher.
버스 기사로서의 그의 봉급은 교사의 그것(봉급)보다 훨씬 더 많다.

My views differ considerably from [**those** / ~~these~~] of my parents.
나의 견해는 부모님의 그것들(견해)과 상당히 다르다.

03 | those who(~하는 사람들)과 anyone who(~하는 사람은 누구든지)

[**Those** / ~~They~~] **who** would like to go on a trip should put their business cards in the box.
여행을 가고자 하는 사람들은 그들의 명함을 상자 안에 넣어야 한다.

[**Those** / ~~They~~] **who are** interested in the position must submit a completed form before May 30.
= [**Those** / ~~They~~] interested in the position must submit a completed form before May 30.
그 직책에 관심이 있는 사람들은 5월 30일 전에 완성된 서류를 제출해야 한다.

[**Anyone** / ~~Them~~] **who is** wishing to attend next week's workshop must register by this Friday.
= [**Anyone** / ~~Them~~] wishing to attend next week's workshop must register by this Friday.
다음 주 워크숍을 참여하고 싶은 사람은 이번 주 금요일까지 등록해야 한다.

▶ '주격 관계대명사+be동사'는 생략이 가능하며, 이때 <those / anyone + 분사>의 형태가 올 수 있다. 여기서 those와 anyone은 분사의 수식을 받기 때문에 인칭대명사가 대신할 수 없다.

SPARTA ☑ Check-UP! 3

| 해설 p. 326

1 Jim's sales experience and ------- of his colleagues allowed them to join the international sales team.

(A) it
(B) there
(C) that
(D) his

2 Most companies use their own brand names to distinguish their products from ------- of other companies.

(A) it
(B) that
(C) them
(D) those

3 ------- who want to participate in the workshop on March 11 must contact Ms. Daiso by Monday.

(A) Those
(B) Them
(C) They
(D) Herself

POINT 4 부정대명사의 용법 1

01 | 부정대명사 one은 앞에 나온 명사와 같은 종류의 다른 것을 나타낼 때 쓴다.

The old fax machine in the office has been replaced with **a new** [one / ~~it~~].
사무실에 있던 낡은 팩스기가 새것으로 교체되었다.

▶ one은 앞에 나온 명사와 동일한 것이 아닌, 같은 종류이지만 다른 것을 나타낼 때 쓴다.

All of the facilities in the building have been replaced with **new** [ones / ~~another~~].
건물 안에 있던 시설물 모두가 새것들로 교체되었다.

▶ one의 복수형은 ones를 쓰며, 정해지지 않은 복수명사를 대신한다.

02 | 부정대명사 another는 불특정 대상 중 이미 언급된 것 외에 '또 다른 하나'를 의미한다.

You can transfer money from **one account** to [another / ~~one~~] by using our online banking service.
저희 온라인 금융 서비스를 이용하여 한 계좌에서 또 다른 계좌로 돈을 이체하실 수 있습니다.

03 | 둘 이상의 정해진 대상 중 '나머지 하나'를 가리킬 때 the other을 쓰며, 셋 이상의 정해진 대상 중 '나머지 전부'를 가리킬 때 the others를 쓴다. others는 막연히 '다른 사람[것]들'을 가리킬 때 쓴다.

She is holding a ball in **one hand** and a racket in [the other / ~~others~~].
그녀는 한 손에는 공을, 다른 한 손에는 라켓을 들고 있다.

Of the ten applicants, only **Steven** arrived on time as [the others / ~~any other~~] were late for the interview. 10명의 지원자들 중 Steven만 정시에 도착했고, 나머지는 모두 면접에 늦었다.

Please be considerate of [others / ~~the other~~] when parking near an intersection.
교차로 부근에 주차할 때 다른 사람들을 배려해 주세요.

04 | 부정대명사 관용표현

each other (둘 사이) 서로	**one another** (셋 이상 사이) 서로

The two firms are under contract to share technology with [each other / ~~another one~~].
두 회사는 서로의 기술을 공유하기 위한 계약 하에 있다.

The program will give **attendees** a good opportunity to meet [one another / ~~other one~~].
프로그램은 참석자들이 서로를 만날 좋은 기회를 제공할 것입니다.

SPARTA Check-UP! 4

해설 p. 326

1 The contact module helps people get in touch with -------.
(A) one another
(B) another
(C) the other
(D) other

2 If your washing machine malfunctions, you may replace it with ------- or get a full refund.
(A) another
(B) one another
(C) one
(D) other

3 The weekly rail pass from Edmonton to Toronto is the most economic option for commuters, but ------- are also available.
(A) one
(B) other
(C) another
(D) others

POINT 5 부정대명사의 용법 2

05 | 수량을 나타내는 부정대명사는 정해지지 않은 사람이나 사물의 수와 양을 나타낼 때 쓴다.

수	수 / 양	양
many 많은 수 (a) few 적은 수 both 둘 다 either 둘 중 어느 하나 neither 둘 다 아님 another 다른 것	some 몇몇, 일부 any 어느 (것), 어떤 (것) none 아무(것)도 (아님) all 모두 a lot 많은 수 / 양 most 대부분	much 많은 양 (a) little 적은 양

[Many / ~~Much~~] **of the customers** were confused about Olly Kitchen's new shipping policy.
고객들 많은 수가 Olly Kitchen 사의 새로운 배송 정책에 혼란스러워했다.

[All / ~~Many~~] **of the merchandise** in the catalogue can be ordered over the Internet.
카탈로그에 있는 모든 상품들은 인터넷으로 주문할 수 있다.

+TIP 일부 부정대명사는 부정 형용사로 쓸 수 있다.

Please forward all **customer complaints** to the customer service center.
모든 고객 불만사항들은 고객 서비스 센터로 넘겨 주세요.

Some **stress** is necessary for change and personal mental growth.
어느 정도의 스트레스는 변화와 개인의 정신적 발전을 위해 필요하다.

+TIP all, both, half는 중간의 of를 생략할 수 있지만, 그 외의 부정대명사들은 of를 생략할 수 없다.

all **(of)** the employees 직원들 전부
both **(of)** the employees 직원들 둘 다
half **(of)** the employees 직원들 중 절반

none **of** the employees 직원들 중 아무도 (아닌)
many **of** the employees 직원들 중 많은 사람들
some **of** the employees 직원들 중 일부

SPARTA Check-UP! 5

해설 p. 326

1 ------- the technical staff members are encouraged to attend the international computer conference.
(A) Each
(B) Every
(C) Most
(D) All

2 ------- of our twenty branch offices around the country has its own warehouse serving as the distribution center for the allocated area.
(A) Most
(B) All
(C) Every
(D) Each

3 The general manager expressed his gratitude to ------- of the dedicated and loyal employees.
(A) all
(B) every
(C) ones
(D) much

POINT 6 주의해야 할 대명사

01 | 재귀대명사와 목적격 인칭대명사의 구분

1) 재귀대명사가 들어가는 경우

The banquet was canceled, so **the delegates** were left to [**themselves** / ~~them~~] for the rest of the evening. 연회가 취소되어서 대표들은 그날 저녁 내내 그들끼리 남아 있었다.

▶ '연회가 취소되어서 대표들은 그날 저녁 내내 그들끼리 남았다'이므로, 주어(delegates)와 동일인인 'themselves'가 적절하다.

2) 목적격 인칭대명사가 들어가는 경우

The president of the company introduced the new sales manager, who was sitting next to [**him** / ~~himself~~]. 회사 사장은 자신 옆에 앉아 있는 새로운 영업 부장을 소개했다.

▶ 관계대명사 who를 빼면 "the new sales manager was sitting next to himself"가 되며 '새 영업 부장이 자기 자신 옆에 앉아 있다' 라는 어색한 문장이 된다. 따라서 전치사(next to)의 목적어로 president를 대신하는 대명사 him이 적절하다.

02 | all/every/each의 차이점과 공통점

1) all / every의 차이점 : all은 복수 가산명사, every는 단수 가산명사와 결합한다.

[**All** / ~~Every~~] **applicants** were asked to fill out an application form.
모든 지원자는 지원서를 작성하도록 요청 받았다.

[**Every** / ~~All~~] **applicant** was asked to fill out an application form.
모든 지원자는 지원서를 작성하도록 요청 받았다.

2) every / each의 공통점 : 모두 단수 가산명사와 결합한다.

[**Every** / **Each**] **applicant** was asked to fill out an application form.
[모든 / 각] 지원자들은 지원서를 작성하도록 요청 받았다.

3) every / all / each의 차이점 : every는 형용사로만 쓰고, all / each는 형용사, 대명사로 쓰인다.

[**All** / ~~Every~~] **of the applicants** were asked to fill out an application form.
지원자 모두는 지원서를 작성하도록 요청 받았다.

[**Each** / ~~Every~~] **of the applicants** was asked to fill out an application form.
지원자 각자는 지원서를 작성하도록 요청 받았다.

SPARTA Check-UP! 6

| 해설 p. 326

1 I can assure ------- that I will be able to make a big contribution to your Sales Department.

(A) you
(B) your
(C) yourself
(D) yours

2 Through his excellent risk-management work, Mr. Lee has shown ------- to be a future executive.

(A) he
(B) him
(C) himself
(D) his

3 Mr. Hoffman received a letter inviting ------- to take the branch manager position.

(A) he
(B) him
(C) his
(D) himself

PRACTICE

해설 p. 327

▪ 괄호 안의 보기 중 알맞은 단어를 고르세요.

1 You should make compromises between your needs and **[that / those]** of your partner.

2 **[Each / Every]** of the articles was corrected by the end of the month.

3 **[No / None]** of the employees said they were unsatisfied with their job.

4 Please contact Ms. Bell and Mr. Corden and ask if **[themselves / they]** are available next Monday.

5 TJ International has established **[it / itself]** by producing the best-quality products.

6 Ms. Irvin's work skills are so efficient that she could do all the work by **[her / herself]**.

7 Brian talked so persuasively that all the directors agreed with **[him / himself]**.

8 Paula's work as a student volunteer at a hospital made **[her / herself]** interested in becoming a nurse.

9 **[Them / Those]** interested in the advertisement should contact Ms. Allen in the Personnel Department.

10 Working people should prepare for their retirement by saving at least 20 percent of **[their / them]** monthly income.

11 The American standard of living is still higher than **[that / those]** of other countries in the world.

12 AP Computers will release its new model soon, but we have not yet finished designing **[us / ours]**.

13 **[Some / Each]** of the local farmers have decided to combine their efforts to face competition from foreign agricultural producers.

14 The company is searching for more qualified market analysts to compete against **[other / others]**.

15 At **[it / its]** 10th anniversary celebration, Timeline unveiled some ambitious projects for the next 10 years.

1 Loudoun County encourages residents to volunteer in ------- communities through cooperation with local civil servants.

(A) them (B) they
(C) their (D) theirs

2 When Charlotte goes to Kyoto next month, ------- will stay at the Lake View Hotel.

(A) hers (B) her
(C) she (D) herself

3 Andrew Harley volunteered to coordinate several activities ------- for the upcoming company workshop.

(A) he (B) him
(C) himself (D) his

4 Now that ------- of our offices have been rewired, our electric bill is considerably lower.

(A) all (B) little
(C) every (D) each

5 The capacity of an average-sized modern oil tanker is larger than ------- of the largest cargo ship made 10 years ago.

(A) that (B) this
(C) these (D) those

6 ------- using climbing equipment is personally responsible for learning how to use it correctly.

(A) Anyone (B) Whoever
(C) Some (D) Them

7 Goldfields Logistics will purchase ------- chief competitor, Snyman Transport, on September 17.

(A) itself (B) them
(C) its (D) themselves

8 As Mr. Penna's assistant, Ms. Kravitz is in charge of briefing ------- on the latest financial news.

(A) him (B) himself
(C) he (D) his

9 Mr. Kim completed his budget report ahead of schedule, and he offered to help Jessica finish -------.

(A) hers (B) her
(C) herself (D) she

10 Members of the parent-teacher association will decide among ------- who will coordinate the upcoming conference.

(A) themselves (B) they
(C) itself (D) yourself

11 The product descriptions the company provided to customers were so obscure that customers had to struggle to determine which products ------- wanted to buy.

(A) they (B) you
(C) he (D) we

12 Alternative treatments for the disease, including ------- employed by acupuncturists and herbalists, are reviewed on our Web site.

(A) them (B) this
(C) that (D) those

해설 p. 328

Questions 13-16 refer to the following letter.

Mr. and Mrs. Smith
1534 Oxford Street
Philadelphia, PA 19121

Dear Mr. and Mrs. Smith,

We received your letter concerning your recent stay at Motawi Bungalow by the seashore. We sincerely regret that the suite you reserved last month was ------- (13.) at the time of your confirmation call, and we thank you for agreeing to the alternative accommodations that we arranged for you. ------- (14.). It is ------- (15.) way of saying sorry for the inconvenience that we caused you and extending gratitude to you for your understanding. When booking a room on our Web site, ------- (16.) any of our Motawi locations and enter the code number stated on the coupon in the Payment Option section.

We look forward to greeting you again in the future.

Sincerely,

Felicity O'Dell
Customer Service Department

13 (A) occupied
(B) continued
(C) misplaced
(D) intended

14 (A) Detach the coupon and return it as soon as possible.
(B) Please attach the coupon to the front of your letter.
(C) Unfortunately, we cannot be held responsibility for what happened.
(D) Please accept the enclosed 50-percent discount coupon for your next visit.

15 (A) your
(B) our
(C) her
(D) their

16 (A) selected
(B) selecting
(C) selects
(D) select

UNIT 03 형용사

형용사 문제는 토익에서 매월 평균 2문제 이상 출제된다. 문제 유형은 ① 형용사의 자리 문제 ② 수량/부정 형용사 ③ 혼동되는 형용사 어휘 문제로 나눌 수 있다.

Preview

01 | 일반 형용사의 형태

-able/-ible	considerable 상당한 predictable 예상할 수 있는 profitable 수익성 있는 possible 가능한
-ive	creative 창조적인 defective 결함 있는 impressive 인상적인 sensitive 민감한
-ar	regular 정기적인 similar 유사한 popular 유명한 particular 특별한
-al	additional 추가적인 beneficial 유익한 professional 전문적인 industrial 산업의
-ic	economic 경제적인 enthusiastic 열정적인 specific 명확한 politic 현명한
-ous	ambitious 야심 찬 cautious 조심스러운 famous 유명한 conscious 의식 있는
-ant/-ent	important 중요한 significant 상당한 different 다른 consistent 일관된
-ful	beautiful 아름다운 successful 성공적인 wonderful 훌륭한 useful 유용한

02 | 형용사의 한정적 용법 : 명사 앞/뒤에서 수식

전치 수식 He offered her **a** good **position**. 그는 그녀에게 좋은 직책을 제안하였다.

후치 수식 He used every **means** possible. 그는 가능한 모든 수단을 썼다.

03 | 형용사의 서술적 용법 : 명사의 상태 설명

주격 보어 **Their prices** are very competitive. 그들의 가격은 매우 경쟁력이 있다. ▶ 주어의 상태 설명

목적격 보어 I found **the book** very informative. 나는 그 책이 매우 유익하다는 것을 알게 되었다. ▶ 목적어의 상태 설명

04 | 수량형용사 : 명사의 수나 양 표시

Many **candidates** applied for the internship. 많은 후보자들이 인턴십에 지원했다.

The office photocopier takes up too much **space**. 사무실 복사기가 너무 많은 공간을 차지한다.

05 | 부정형용사 : 범위가 정해지지 않은 명사 표시

The handbook outlines some **rules** for healthy weight and fat loss.
안내서는 적정 체중과 체지방 감소를 위한 일부 규칙들을 설명하고 있다.

Another **new shopping center** in the same area is not a good idea.
같은 지역에 또 다른 새로운 쇼핑센터가 생기는 것은 좋은 생각이 아니다.

Gold is often used to protect other **metals** from corrosion.
금은 다른 금속들을 부식으로부터 보호하기 위해 자주 사용된다.

POINT 1 형용사의 역할과 위치

01 | 명사 수식: 형용사+명사/명사+형용사

There has been [tremendous / ~~tremendously~~] **growth** in the service sector in the last ten years.
지난 10년간 서비스 분야에서 상당한 성장이 있었다.

All meetings are scheduled for **a time** [acceptable / ~~acceptably~~] to the club members.
모든 회의는 클럽 회원들에게 받아들여질 수 있는 시간에 일정이 잡힌다.

▶ 뒤따르는 전치사와 의미 단위를 형성하는 형용사는 명사 뒤에서 수식한다.

We will make every **effort** [possible / ~~possibly~~] to keep to the scheduled timetable.
우리는 예정된 시간표를 지키기 위하여 가능한 모든 노력을 다할 것이다.

02 | 주격 보어: 주어+be/become/remain/stay/seem/look+형용사

be ~이다	become ~이 되다	remain 계속 ~이다	stay 그대로 ~이다
seem ~처럼 보이다	look ~처럼 보이다	appear ~인 것 같다	prove ~임이 드러나다

Their services **are** inexpensive and [efficient / ~~efficiently~~]. 그들의 서비스는 저렴하고 효율적이다.

The new factory will **become** [operational / ~~operationally~~] next month. 새 공장은 다음 달에 가동될 것이다.

The office will **remain** [open / ~~opening~~] during the weekend. 사무실은 주말 동안 문을 열 것이다.

03 | 목적격 보어: 주어+consider/find/keep/make+목적어+형용사

consider + 목적어 + 목적격 보어 ~을 …으로 여기다	keep + 목적어 + 목적격 보어 ~을 …한 상태로 유지하다
find + 목적어 + 목적격 보어 ~이 …임을 알게 되다	make + 목적어 + 목적격 보어 ~을 …으로 만들다

Some people **consider** electric cars [impractical / ~~impractically~~].
어떤 사람들은 전기 자동차를 비실용적인 것으로 여긴다.

Most participants **found** the seminar [useful / ~~usefully~~].
대부분의 참석자들은 세미나가 유익했음을 알게 되었다.

Lawyers must **keep** their clients' files [confidential / ~~confidentially~~].
변호사들은 그들의 고객 파일을 비밀로 유지해야 한다.

▶ 5형식 문장의 목적격 보어는 명사, to부정사, 동사원형, 분사, 그리고 형용사가 올 수 있다.

+TIP 5형식에서 목적어와 목적격 보어가 동격인 경우 명사를 목적격 보어로 취한다.

We consider **our manager** a very competent person.
우리는 매니저를 매우 능력 있는 사람이라고 생각한다.

our manager = a very competent person이므로 목적격 보어로 명사가 쓰였나.

SPARTA Check-UP! 1

해설 p. 329

1 If you reserve an airplane ticket two months before departing, you will get a ------- discount.
(A) subsidy
(B) substantial
(C) substance
(D) substantially

2 Though Mr. Ana considered it ------- to finish the report by the deadline, he managed to hand it in on time.
(A) difficult
(B) difficulty
(C) difficultly
(D) difficultness

3 It is not ------- to discuss confidential information outside the company.
(A) appropriateness
(B) appropriate
(C) appropriately
(D) most appropriately

POINT 2 수량형용사와 부정형용사

01 | a(an)/another/each/every/this/that+단수 가산명사

There is enough office space for [each / ~~few~~] **manager** to have a private room.
각 과장들이 전용 사무실을 갖기에 충분한 사무 공간이 있다.

Our engineers have taken the necessary steps to prevent [another / ~~several~~] **system failure**.
우리 기술자들은 또 다른 시스템 오작동을 피하기 위해서 필요한 조치들을 취했다.

+TIP every/another+기수+복수명사

every+기수+복수명사 ~마다	ex) **every** two days 이틀마다
another+기수+복수명사 ~만큼 더	ex) **another** three hours 3시간 더

02 | (a) few/several/many/numerous/a number of/these/those+복수 가산명사

[Many / ~~Every~~] **people** have left the city since the automotive plant closed.
자동차 공장이 문을 닫은 후에 많은 사람들이 도시를 떠났다.

Despite [a few / ~~little~~] **negative comments** from our competitors, our new sedan is selling well.
경쟁사들로부터의 몇몇 부정적인 평에도 불구하고, 우리의 신형 세단은 잘 팔리고 있다.

03 | (a) little/much/an amount of/a great deal of+불가산명사

The office desks and cabinets take up too [much / ~~many~~] **space**.
사무실 책상과 캐비닛이 너무 많은 공간을 차지한다.

Clean-Your-Car detergent allows you to wash your car with only [a little / ~~few~~] **water**.
Clean-Your-Car 세제는 약간의 물로도 당신의 차를 닦을 수 있도록 합니다.

04 | other/a lot of/lots of/plenty of/all/some/more/most+복수 가산명사/불가산명사

We need [other / ~~another~~] **suppliers** to secure a supply of our product parts.
우리 제품의 부품 공급을 확실할 수 있도록 다른 공급업체들이 필요하다.

You should wear a hat or [other / ~~another~~] **clothing** designed to reduce sun exposure.
햇빛 노출을 줄이기 위해 고안된 모자나 다른 의복을 착용해야 한다.

SPARTA Check-UP! 2

해설 p. 329

1 ------- international passengers must arrive at the airport at least two hours before their departure time.
(A) Much
(B) How
(C) Who
(D) All

2 You should inspect the contents of ------- package to ensure that the shipment is in good condition.
(A) few
(B) each
(C) many
(D) whichever

3 Due to Time Delivery's rising rates, we are looking for ------- delivery company.
(A) some
(B) another
(C) others
(D) other

POINT ③ 주의해야 할 형용사 1

01 | 유사 형태 형용사의 의미 구별

informative 유익한	informed 잘 아는, 정통한	dependable 믿을 수 있는	dependent (on) 의존하는
comparable 비슷한	comparative 비교의	reliable 믿을 수 있는	reliant (on) 의존하는
confident 자신 있는	confidential 기밀의	economic 경제의	economical 검소한
considerable 상당한	considerate (of) 사려 깊은	impressed 감명받은 (*사람만 수식)	impressive 인상적인
responsible (for) 책임 있는	responsive (to) 반응하는	argumentative 논쟁적인	arguable 주장할 수 있는
successful 성공적인	successive 연속적인	operating 경영상의	operational 가동 준비가 된
respectful 공손한	respective 각각의	late 늦은	latest 최신의

Valu Soft announced an [impressive / ~~impressed~~] new product lineup for this summer.
Valu Soft 사는 이번 여름을 위한 인상적인 신제품 구성을 발표했다.

02 | 명사+-ly = 형용사 : -ly 형태의 형용사

costly	costly products 값비싼 제품들	**lovely**	lovely weather 매우 좋은 날씨
timely	in a timely manner 시기적절하게	**orderly**	in an orderly fashion 질서 정연하게
friendly	friendly person 친절한 사람	**likely**	be likely to ~할 가능성이 있다

The audience came out of the concert hall **in an** [orderly / ~~order~~] **fashion**.
관객들은 질서 정연하게 공연장을 빠져 나왔다.

The company policy states that supervisors must review vacation requests **in a** [timely / ~~times~~] **manner**. 회사의 정책은 관리자들이 반드시 휴가 요청을 시기적절하게 검토해야 함을 명시한다.

daily, weekly, monthly, quarterly, yearly는 형용사와 부사로 쓰인다.

There will be **a** monthly **meeting** tomorrow. 내일 월간 회의가 있을 것이다. ▶ 명사를 수식하는 형용사

The sales meeting **is held** monthly. 영업 회의는 매달 열린다. ▶ 동사를 수식하는 부사

SPARTA ☑ Check-UP! ③

해설 p. 330

1 The ------- audiovisual equipment is available to help make events such as conferences and seminars run smoothly.
(A) late
(B) lately
(C) later
(D) latest

2 All employees should be ------- of their colleagues by speaking softly in the office.
(A) considerable
(B) considerate
(C) consideration
(D) considerably

3 A good coordinator must remain calm at all times and avoid becoming ------- with representatives of other firms.
(A) argumentative
(B) argument
(C) arguable
(D) argue

POINT 4 주의해야 할 형용사 2

01 | be+형용사+to부정사

be (un)able to ~할 수 있다(없다)	be eager to 간절히 ~하고 싶어 하다	be likely to ~할 것 같다
be liable to ~하기 쉽다	be willing to 기꺼이 ~하다	be proud to ~을 자랑스럽게 여기다
be reluctant to ~하기를 꺼리다	be scheduled to ~하기로 예정되다	be unwilling to ~하기를 꺼리다
be supposed to ~하기로 되어 있다	be sure[certain] to 확실히 ~할 것이다	be due to ~하기로 되어 있다
be ready to ~할 준비가 되다	be anxious to ~을 몹시 하고 싶다	be eligible to ~할 자격이 있다
be entitled to ~할 자격이 있다	be difficult to ~하기 어렵다	be easy to ~하기 쉽다

All full-time staff members are [eligible / ~~eligibly~~] to **enroll** in the fitness program at the company's gym. 모든 정규직 직원들은 회사 체육관의 운동 프로그램에 등록할 자격이 있다.

02 | (be동사)+형용사+전치사

to	be close to ~에 가깝다/거의 ~하다 be similar to ~와 비슷하다 be comparable to ~에 필적하다 be dedicated to ~에 전념하다 be known to ~에게 알려지다	be subject to ~에 영향받기 쉽다 be equal to ~와 똑같다 be responsive to ~에 반응하다 be used to ~에 익숙하다 be attached to ~에 첨부되다	be assigned to ~에 할당되다 be related to ~와 관련되어 있다 be committed to ~에 전념하다 be accustomed to ~에 익숙하다 be attributed to ~의 덕/탓이다
for	be famous for ~로 유명하다 be responsible for ~을 책임지다	be known for ~로 유명하다 be eligible for ~에 자격이 있다	be noted for ~로 유명하다 be suitable for ~에 적합하다
with	be content with ~에 만족하다 be compatible with ~와 호환되다 be familiar with ~을 잘 알다	be concerned with ~에 관련되다 be faced with ~에 직면하다 be equipped with ~을 갖추고 있다	be consistent with ~와 일치하다 be finished with ~을 끝내다 be acquainted with ~를 알다
of	be aware of ~을 잘 알다	be full of ~로 가득 차다	be capable of ~할 수 있다
from	be absent from ~에 불참하다	be different from ~과 다르다	be exempt from ~에서 면제되다
on	be dependent on ~에 의존하다	be reliant on ~에 의존하다	be based on ~에 근거하다

We at the DHF Delivery Center are [committed / ~~based~~] to **providing** quick and safe delivery services. 저희 DHF Delivery Center는 빠르고 안전한 배달 서비스를 제공하는 것에 전념합니다.

SPARTA Check-UP! 4

해설 p. 330

1 If you are over 18 years old, you are ------- to enter the International Peace Poster Contest.
(A) eligibility
(B) eligibleness
(C) eligible
(D) eligibly

2 We are sorry to let you know that Pacific Airways is not ------- for any lost luggage.
(A) responsive
(B) responsible
(C) respond
(D) response

3 Mr. Jones cannot attend the conference, but Mr. Park will be able ------- the company there.
(A) representing
(B) represented
(C) to representing
(D) to represent

 PRACTICE

해설 p. 330

▪ 괄호 안의 보기 중 알맞은 단어를 고르세요.

1 Evans Consulting earned the **[complete / completion]** trust of its clients through its thorough analysis.

2 The medical building will be **[ready / readily]** for use by the end of the month.

3 Investors remain **[optimistic / optimistically]** about the stock price.

4 It seems **[evident / evidently]** that Mr. Anderson is the most qualified person for the job.

5 The publishers are **[hopeful / hopefully]** that the book will be ready for distribution before the new year.

6 Many staff **[member / members]** have to work on the weekend to meet the deadline.

7 Mr. Dalton's team simply needed **[a little / a few]** encouragement to improve its sales results.

8 The board of directors has shown little **[interest / interests]** in increasing investments.

9 Please ensure that **[all / every]** mobile electronic devices are turned off during presentations.

10 Computer users are supposed to change passwords **[all / every]** 30 days.

11 When S-Cable went out of business, all its customers were forced to use **[another / other]** cable providers.

12 The Web site provides tourism, travel, and **[another / other]** information about New Zealand.

13 The improvement in sales figures had a **[beneficial / benefitted]** effect on the company as a whole.

14 The city of Toronto is **[responsive / responsible]** for the general maintenance and repair of the sports complex.

15 With the **[economic / economical]** indicators looking slightly better than last quarter, consumer confidence is up a certain degree.

1 The towns of Sontag and Washok have recently united in a ------- effort to address transportation-related issues.

(A) collaborate (B) collaborates
(C) collaborative (D) collaboratively

2 The innovative house is an experiment in using a ------- variety of materials and structural solutions.

(A) widen (B) width
(C) wide (D) widely

3 With ------- service and formula, Ms. Lynn has lifted Walter, Inc.'s revenues from last year's $10 million to $15 million.

(A) relied (B) reliably
(C) reliable (D) rely

4 MVI General Manager Don Magnuson told company stockholders that he believed the newly launched products would be very -------.

(A) profitable (B) profitably
(C) profited (D) profits

5 Most applicants who were interviewed had more than ten years of ------- experience in the field of public health.

(A) manages (B) manageably
(C) managerially (D) managerial

6 Review the assembly manual carefully to ensure that ------- steps have been carried out in the proper order.

(A) almost (B) most of
(C) all (D) much

7 Mr. Brown was commended for organizing an ------- meeting on contracts and copyright law for authors.

(A) informative (B) informing
(C) informed (D) informally

8 To build a revolving house is ------- in cost to building a conventional house.

(A) comparable (B) comparably
(C) comparison (D) comparing

9 The dormitory policy states that supervisors must acknowledge receipt of accommodation requests to students in a ------- manner.

(A) time (B) timing
(C) timely (D) timer

10 Customers can reschedule for another date at ------- extra cost if they do so at least 48 hours before their check-in date.

(A) no (B) not
(C) none (D) never

11 Christine Olson, one of the stockholders, is very ------- of the plan to reorganize the company.

(A) criticize (B) critic
(C) critical (D) critically

12 Two or three staff members at our information desk are available to take customers' calls ------- weekend from 10:00 A.M. to 2:30 P.M.

(A) every (B) much
(C) under (D) few

해설 p. 331

Questions 13-16 refer to the following announcement.

For those of you who ------- (13.) in the Service Department, please be aware the 20% off discount coupons are set to ------- (14.) tomorrow.

Under no circumstances will there be any exceptions, and you are to politely tell customers that the coupons have expired and that we will have new coupons in two weeks.

We also have Milo Sarcav, the president of Pocket Outlets, visiting us to check on the store next Wednesday, so those of you that park in the back, please leave one ------- (15.) spot for the president. He will be touring the outlet and will let us know what he wants done around the place. ------- (16.). The more cons he mentions, the harder our work is going to be in the future, so please have your area cleaned. I know I don't need to remind you guys of this, but please be respectful. Without him, we wouldn't have our jobs. Thank you.

13 (A) is working
(B) is worked
(C) has been worked
(D) are working

14 (A) return
(B) expire
(C) submit
(D) violate

15 (A) delicate
(B) adequate
(C) vacant
(D) block

16 (A) He will let us know the pros and cons about how our outlet is being run right now.
(B) I sincerely hope that we can accommodate all employees' schedules.
(C) Unfortunately, he will not be able to give his presentation as planned.
(D) Milo Sarcav will give instructions to new employees about their jobs.

UNIT 04 부사

부사 관련 문제는 매월 2~3문제가 출제된다. 문제 유형은 ① 부사의 자리 문제 ② 부사의 어휘 문제 ③ 부사의 용법 문제로 나눌 수 있다. 부사는 다른 문장 성분 또는 문장 전체를 수식하는 역할을 한다. 문장 내에 부사가 올 수 있는 자리와 자주 출제되는 부사 어휘들을 익혀 두면 어렵지 않게 해결할 수 있다. 부사 어휘만 익히면 정확성이 떨어지기 때문에 어울리는 표현들도 함께 익혀 두도록 하자.

Preview

01 | 부사의 형태

본래 부사	often 종종 well 잘, 제대로 very 매우 now 지금, 이제 yet 아직 soon 곧			
'형용사+ly' 부사	clearly 분명하게 easily 쉽게 successfully 성공적으로 closely 면밀하게			
의미가 달라지는 -ly 부사	late 늦게	high 높게	hard 열심히	near 가까이
	lately 최근에	highly 매우	hardly 거의 ~않다	nearly 거의
형용사와 형태가 같은 부사	early 형 이른 부 일찍	right 형 바른 부 바르게, 즉시	late 형 늦은 부 늦게	
	fast 형 빠른 부 빨리	only 형 유일한 부 오직	high 형 높은 부 높게	

02 | 부사의 역할

동사 수식 The economy **grew steadily**. 경제가 꾸준히 성장했다.

형용사 수식 The project was **extremely successful**. 그 프로젝트는 매우 성공적이었다.

부사 수식 She speaks four languages **very fluently**. 그녀는 4개 국어를 아주 유창하게 한다.

문장 전체 수식 **Fortunately, they found the way to solve the problem.**
다행히도, 그들은 그 문제를 해결할 방법을 찾아냈다.

03 | 부사의 종류

시간부사	already 이미, 벌써 still 아직 yet 아직 ago 전에 once 한때 soon 곧 later 이후에 lately 최근에 recently 최근에
빈도부사	always 항상 usually 보통 often 종종 almost 거의 frequently 자주 sometimes 때때로 hardly 거의 ~않다 seldom 좀처럼 ~않다 never 결코 ~않다
정도부사	very 매우 quite 꽤 greatly 크게 dramatically 급격하게 considerably 상당히 remarkably 두드러지게 significantly 상당히
강조부사	just 단지 only 오직 well 아주, 훨씬 right 바로 even ~조차
접속부사	therefore 그러므로 moreover 더욱이 however 그러나 besides 게다가 nevertheless 그럼에도 불구하고 otherwise 그렇지 않으면 meanwhile 그동안

POINT 1 부사의 역할과 위치 1

01 | 주어+동사+(목적어)+부사 : 자·타동사 뒤, 문장 뒤에서 동사 수식

Now that the Christmas season has ended, sales **are decreasing** [rapidly / ~~rapid~~].
크리스마스 시즌이 끝났기 때문에 매출이 급속히 감소하고 있다.

Employees at Credle, Inc. **handle** every customer inquiry [carefully / ~~careful~~].
Credle 사의 직원들은 모든 고객의 문의 사항을 주의 깊게 다룬다.

02 | 주어+부사+동사 : 주어와 일반 동사 사이에서 동사 수식

Mr. Kevin [enthusiastically / ~~enthusiastic~~] **approved** of Mike's new design.
Kevin 씨는 Mike의 새로운 디자인을 열렬히 찬성했다.

We [sincerely / ~~sincere~~] **regret** any inconvenience that the production delay has caused.
저희는 생산 지체가 야기한 모든 불편한 점에 대해 진심으로 사과드립니다.

03 | 주어+조동사+부사+동사 : 조동사와 동사 사이에서 동사 수식

Bach Industries **will** [shortly / ~~short~~] **be** prepared to expand its manufacturing facilities in Chester.
Bach 산업은 곧 체스터에서 자사의 제조 시설을 확장할 준비가 될 것입니다.

To stay competitive, McGill Electronics **will** [occasionally / ~~occasional~~] **lower** the prices of its products. 경쟁력을 유지하기 위해, McGill 전자는 가끔 자사 제품의 가격을 낮출 것이다.

04 | 부사+형용사/분사 : 형용사 또는 분사 앞에서 수식

Finishing the project on time seemed [extremely / ~~extreme~~] **difficult**.
프로젝트를 제시간에 마치는 것은 매우 힘들어 보였다.

A [thoughtfully / ~~thoughtful~~] **designed** work environment can increase productivity.
주의 깊게 설계된 업무 환경은 생산성을 증가시킬 수 있다.

It is important to **be** [suitably / ~~suitable~~] **dressed** for a job interview.
취업 인터뷰를 위해서는 적절하게 옷을 차려입는 것이 중요하다.

The due date for applying for a World Trade Center internship **is** [rapidly / ~~rapidity~~] **approaching**. 세계 무역 센터의 인턴십 지원 마감일이 빠르게 다가오고 있다.

SPARTA ☑ Check-UP! 1

해설 p. 333

1 Before signing a contract, Mr. Hopkins ------- questions his lawyer about potential problems.
(A) thoroughness
(B) thorough
(C) thoroughly
(D) most thorough

2 Technological changes are happening much more slowly than ------- predicted.
(A) origin
(B) originally
(C) original
(D) originated

3 The project manager was ------- proud of his team for completing the proposal successfully.
(A) extreme
(B) extremes
(C) extremely
(D) extremity

POINT 2 부사의 역할과 위치 2

01 | 부사+주어+동사 : 문장 전체 수식

[Normally / ~~Normal~~], diners at Ryan's tip the servers 20 to 30 percent.
보통, Ryan's의 식사 손님들은 종업원들에게 20~30%의 팁을 준다.

+ VOCABULARY | 시험에서 문두에 나와 자주 정답이 되는 부사

regrettably / unfortunately 유감스럽게도
normally 보통, 일반적으로
presumably / probably 아마도
obviously / definitely 분명히

02 | to부정사+부사 / to부정사+목적어+부사 : to부정사 수식

In order to function [properly / ~~proper~~], this machine must be serviced at regular intervals.
제대로 작동하기 위해서, 이 기계는 정기적으로 정비를 받아야 합니다.

Luna County requires local restaurant owners **to renew** their business licenses [annually / ~~annual~~].
Luna County는 지역 식당 주인들에게 그들의 사업자 등록증을 매년 갱신하라고 요구한다.

03 | 전치사+부사+동명사 : 동명사 수식

The AG Consultant suggested an idea **for** [successfully / ~~successful~~] **implementing** our business model. AG Consultant 사는 우리의 사업 모델을 성공적으로 시행하기 위한 아이디어를 제안했다.

04 | 부사+전치사+명사구 : 전명구 수식

When reviewing your contract, you can make changes [directly / ~~directed~~] **on the first draft**.
계약서를 검토하실 때, 당신은 원고 초안을 직접 수정하실 수 있습니다.

+TIP 시험에 자주 나오는 <부사+전치사구> 표현

currently under discussion 현재 토론 중인
only for 3 weeks 3주 동안만
promptly at 11 정확히 11시에
right after the meeting 회의 직후에
especially in the winter 특히 겨울에
directly to the director 이사에게 바로
even during the slow season 비수기조차도
largely[mostly] due to 주로 ~때문에

The film's success **was** [largely / ~~large~~] **due to** positive reviews from viewers.
이 영화의 성공은 대체로 관객들의 긍정적인 평 때문이었다.

SPARTA Check-UP! 2

해설 p. 333

1 It is very important to ------- review all the terms of the contract before you sign it.
(A) care
(B) carefully
(C) careful
(D) carefulness

2 After ------- interviewing highly qualified applicants, Nano Tech, Inc. finally decided to hire over 10 individuals this year.
(A) carefully
(B) to care
(C) most careful
(D) careful

3 Employees wishing to receive the samples immediately may submit a request ------- to the production manager.
(A) directing
(B) direction
(C) directive
(D) directly

POINT ❸ 부사의 용법 3

01 | still (아직, 여전히) vs. yet (아직)

The experts [still / ~~yet~~] do **not** understand the reason the market has been quite volatile.
전문가들은 시장이 상당히 불안정한 이유를 아직 이해하지 못하고 있다.

▶ still이 부정문에 쓰일 경우 부정어 앞에 위치한다.

The disagreement between the two opposing sides has **not** [yet / ~~still~~] been resolved.
두 반대 당 사이의 의견 충돌이 아직 해결되지 않았다.

▶ yet은 보통 부정문에 쓰이며, 부정어 뒤에 위치한다.

02 | late (형 늦은 / 부 늦게) vs. lately (부 최근에)

Employees are asked to contact their supervisors if they anticipate being [late / ~~lately~~] to work.
직원들은 그들이 직장에 늦을 것으로 예상되면 상급자에게 연락하도록 요청 받는다.

Due to the low quality of the product, the manufacturer has received many complaints [lately / ~~hardly~~]. 제품의 낮은 품질 때문에 제조사는 최근에 많은 불평을 들었다.

▶ 빈도 부사 hardly는 be동사나 조동사 뒤, 일반동사 앞에 온다.

+ VOCABULARY | 주의해야 할 빈출 부사

free	형 자유로운, 무료의 / 부 무료로	freely	부 자유롭게
late	형 늦은 / 부 늦게, 늦게까지	lately	부 최근에
near	형 가까운 / 부 가까이에 / 전 ~근처에	nearly	부 거의 (= almost)
hard	형 어려운, 딱딱한 / 부 열심히	hardly	부 거의 ~하지 않다
high	형 높은 / 부 높이	highly	부 대단히, 매우 (= very, much)
most	형 가장 많은, 대부분의 / 부 가장	mostly	부 대체로, 주로 (= largely)
close	형 가까운, 면밀한 / 부 (거리상) 가깝게	closely	부 밀접하게, 면밀하게, 친밀하게
right	형 올바른 / 부 바로, 바르게	rightly	부 공정하게

03 | only (오직 ~만), just (불과 ~만) : 명사구나 전치사구 강조

Because of space constraints, the airline allows [only / ~~even~~] **two suitcases** per passenger.
공간의 제약으로 항공사는 일인당 오직 두 개의 여행 가방만을 허용한다.

Our new software produces complex statistical tables from sales data [just / ever] **in a few seconds**. 우리의 새로운 소프트웨어는 불과 몇 초 만에 매출 데이터에서 복잡한 통계표를 뽑아낸다.

SPARTA ☑ Check-UP! ❸

| 해설 p. 333

1 The Research Department ------- has a considerable amount of work to do on the new design before the monthly meeting next week.
(A) still
(B) always
(C) yet
(D) shortly

2 Rumors about the health of the president have been circulating -------.
(A) late
(B) later
(C) latest
(D) lately

3 Mr. Simpson made it clear that ------- the landowner may authorize improvements to the property.
(A) only
(B) once
(C) ever
(D) still

POINT 4 부사의 용법 4

01 | very (매우)

The customer **was** [very / ~~so~~] **pleased** with the dress, but she requested that the length be shortened. 고객은 드레스에 매우 만족해했지만, 길이를 줄여 달라고 요청했다.

▶ very는 동사를 수식할 수 없다. 단 감정 동사 amused, disappointed, excited, interested, pleased, surprised 등은 과거분사이지만 형용사화되어 very의 수식을 받을 수 있다. 따라서 감정 동사의 수동태<be + --- + p.p.>에서 very는 가능하다.

02 | already (이미, 벌써)

Ms. Tanuki **has** [already / ~~ago~~] **begun** working on resolving the problems with the customers.
Tanuki 씨는 고객들과의 문제를 해결하는 일을 벌써 시작했다.

▶ ago는 '기간+ago' 형태로 쓰이며, 과거시제 동사와 어울려 쓰인다.

03 | ever (이제껏, 지금까지) : 최상급 표현을 이끎

Lake Grill is **the largest** restaurant [ever / ~~well~~] to be built along the shores of Lake Swan.
Lake Grill은 Lake Swan 호숫가를 따라 지어진 역대 가장 큰 식당이다.

▶ well은 '잘'이라는 뜻으로 p.p.가 뒤에 나온다.

04 | enough (충분히) : 형용사/부사+enough+to부정사

The room for the July 1 meeting is large [enough / ~~already~~] to **accommodate** 20 individuals.
7월 1일 회의를 위한 방이 20명 수용하기에 충분히 넓다.

▶ enough는 형용사로 쓰이면 '충분한', 부사로 쓰이면 '충분히'라는 의미를 나타내며 명사 앞 또는 형용사/부사 뒤에 위치한다.

05 | have yet to+동사원형 (아직 ~하지 못했다)

Germany's two major airlines have [yet / ~~still~~] to **finalize** the details of their cooperative effort to increase tourism. 독일의 두 주요 항공사들은 관광업을 증진시키기 위한 그들의 협력 사항들을 아직 마무리짓지 못했다.

+TIP not yet은 '아직 ~하지 않다'라는 뜻이며, 이때 yet은 not 바로 뒤나 문장 끝에 올 수 있다.

I have not yet paid my annual membership fee.
= I have not paid my annual membership fee yet.
나는 연회비를 아직 지불하지 않았습니다.

SPARTA Check-UP! 4

해설 p. 333

1 The new financial incentive plan for sales representatives proved to be ------- profitable for some employees.
(A) enough
(B) too much
(C) very
(D) well

2 Ms. Swan had planned to leave for Singapore on Sunday, but the flight was ------- fully booked.
(A) already
(B) well
(C) soon
(D) never

3 The Sun Corporation's annual earnings were not impressive ------- to attract more investors.
(A) fully
(B) quite
(C) enough
(D) rather

POINT 5 시험에 자주 출제되는 부사 표현 1

01 | 증감동사 수식 부사

증감동사			부사
increase 증가하다	decrease 감소하다	+	dramatically / drastically 급격히
rise 증가하다	decline 감소하다		considerably / significantly / substantially 상당히
raise 인상하다	drop / fall 떨어지다		tremendously / greatly 엄청나게
hike (up) 대폭 인상하다	reduce 줄이다		sharply / suddenly 급격히, 갑자기
surge / soar 급등하다	plunge 급락하다		rapidly / quickly 빠르게
expand 확대하다	shrink / wane 줄어들다		slowly / gradually / progressively 느리게, 서서히, 점차
improve 개선하다	dwindle (점점) 줄다		noticeably / remarkably / markedly 현저히
grow 성장하다	worsen 악화되다		consistently / continuously / steadily 지속적으로, 꾸준히
recover 회복하다	regress 퇴보하다		slightly / somewhat 약간, 조금

Sales of TV sets **increased** [dramatically / ~~nearly~~] after the manufacturer dropped the price by 25 percent. 제조업자가 가격을 25% 인하한 후에 TV 세트의 매출액이 급격하게 증가했다.

▶ nearly는 '거의'라는 뜻의 부사로 숫자 등의 수식 대상이 뒤에 나온다.

02 | 숫자 수식 부사

exactly 정확히	approximately / roughly / about / around 대략
nearly / almost 거의	over / more than ~ 이상
at least 최소한, 적어도	just / only 단지

[Approximately / ~~By~~] **ten percent** of the auto parts produced by our supplier are faulty.
우리의 납품업체에서 생산된 자동차 부품 중 대략 10%가 불량품이다.

▶ by는 전치사로, 주어 자리에 '전치사+명사'의 전치사구를 쓸 수 없다.

03 | (be) ---- located[situated / placed] 사이에 자주 출제되는 부사

(be) +	conveniently 편리한 곳에 / agreeably 좋은 곳에 / perfectly 완벽히 / centrally 중앙에	+ located(= situated / placed) ~에 위치한

There are a variety of restaurants [conveniently / ~~convenient~~] **located** on the same street as the shopping mall. 다양한 식당들이 그 쇼핑몰과 같은 거리에 편리하게 위치해 있다.

SPARTA Check-UP! 5

해설 p. 334

1 By hiring a public relations firm, Zuno Technologies expects sales to rise ------- over the next two quarters.
(A) dramatize
(B) dramatically
(C) dramatist
(D) dramatic

2 According to the recent report, ------- 20,000 commuters will benefit from the addition of 16 new bus lines throughout the state.
(A) approximate
(B) approximated
(C) approximately
(D) approximation

3 The large bookstore chain is considering renovating the old store ------- located in the newly developed area.
(A) conveniently
(B) correctly
(C) greatly
(D) widely

POINT 6 시험에 자주 출제되는 부사 표현 2

04 | '몇 시 정각에'라는 의미를 나타내는 부사

promptly / exactly / precisely at 정각 ~시에

The training class on Internet security begins [**promptly** / ~~prompt~~] **at 9 A.M.**
인터넷 보안 강좌가 오전 9시 정각에 시작한다.

▶ promptly, exactly, precisely는 <at+----+시각>나 <at+시각+---->에도 놓일 수 있다.

05 | 시간이나 기간을 나타내는 전치사/접속사와 자주 어울리는 부사

right / just / soon / promptly / shortly / immediately	+ before / prior to ~하기 직전에 + after / following ~한 직후에

▶ before/after는 전치사와 접속사 둘 다 가능하며 뒤에 '명사' 또는 '(주어+)동사'가 온다. prior to/following은 전치사로 뒤에 명사가 온다.

- **immediately after** graduating 졸업 직후에
- **shortly before** they arrive 그들이 도착하기 직전에
- **soon after** the launch 출시 후 얼마 지나지 않아
- **just before** you came 당신이 오기 직전에

Reimbursements for medical expenses will be paid [**shortly** / ~~short~~] **after** all required forms have been received. 의료 비용 상환은 필요한 모든 서류가 수령된 직후에 지급될 것이다.

06 | 주로 형용사/부사만을 수식하는 부사(동사 수식 불가)

so 그렇게	very 대단히, 매우	too 너무, 지나치게
extremely 아주, 대단히	relatively 비교적	quite 꽤

Mr. James has been an [**extremely** / ~~extreme~~] **valuable** member of the sales team for five years.
제임스 씨는 5년 동안 영업 팀의 매우 중요한 멤버였다.

07 | 특정 전치사나 접속사와 어울리는 부사

1) 접속사 though / although / even though / even if, 전치사 despite / in spite of와 어울리는 still

Although Mr. Carter was transferred, we [**still** / ~~seldom~~] have chosen no one to replace him.
카터 씨가 전근을 갔지만, 우리는 아직까지 그의 후임자를 결정하지 못했다.

▶ seldom은 '좀처럼 ~않다'라는 뜻으로 부정의 의미를 가지고 있기에 부정어와 같이 쓸 수 없다.

2) 전치사/접속사(after)와 어울리는 finally

After(= Following) careful consideration, we [**finally** / ~~so~~] decided to offer you the job.
우리는 세심히 숙고한 후, 마침내 당신을 그 자리에 모시기로 결정했습니다.

SPARTA Check-UP! 6

| 해설 p. 334

1 Every employee at the Stellar Technical Institute should sign a nondisclosure agreement ------- after joining the company.
(A) immediately
(B) extremely
(C) numerously
(D) previously

2 ------- after becoming CEO of the Brezet Company, Mahat M. Ali expanded the Marketing Department by 10 percent.
(A) How
(B) Ever
(C) Often
(D) Soon

3 The staff meeting is scheduled to start ------- at 10 A.M. on Monday, so all members have to attend without exception.
(A) promptly
(B) soon
(C) sometime
(D) presently

SPARTA PRACTICE

해설 p.334

▪ 괄호 안의 보기 중 알맞은 단어를 고르세요.

1 The workshop was **[original / originally]** scheduled to begin at 9 A.M.

2 Many of our new employees have not yet been trained **[adequate / adequately]**.

3 Solar power is an energy source that is **[economic / economically]** beneficial.

4 Due to insufficient staffing, it is becoming **[increasing / increasingly]** difficult to serve clients.

5 The entire division worked very **[hard / hardly]** to complete the assignment on time.

6 The copy machine looks new because it has **[hard / hardly]** been used.

7 The proposal could not be accepted because it was submitted **[late / lately]**.

8 **[Regrettable / Regrettably]**, there will be no school festival this year because of lack of funds.

9 Although Mr. Gonzales has been working as a trader for **[already / only]** three months, he is highly regarded by his clients.

10 Employees who have not **[still / yet]** signed and returned a copy of the company security policy are instructed to do so immediately.

11 Aron Airlines has expanded its operations **[very / substantially]** by acquiring additional aircraft.

12 Department managers submit expense reports **[directly / directed]** to Helen Mirren rather than to her assistant.

13 According to the *Cosmopolitan News*, Tower Records will soon be opening a store **[correctly / conveniently]** located on Piccadilly Avenue.

14 It will take **[enough / approximately]** 20 minutes to drive from headquarters to the Missouri Conference Center.

15 Because the banquet will begin **[promptly / occasionally]** at 7 P.M., all catering staffers are asked to arrive at 5 P.M.

1 The Nova Vista Resort is ------- located, providing the best walking access to major tourist attractions, restaurants, and souvenir shops.

(A) centrally (B) center
(C) central (D) centered

2 Ashely Lee, the newly hired fashion editor, seemed ------- excited to be at Isaac Mizzoni's runway show, which featured the new line of clothes reflecting this year's trends.

(A) truly (B) true
(C) truthful (D) truthfulness

3 Primex Electronics is planning to launch more ------- priced products compared to those sold last year.

(A) competitively (B) competitive
(C) competed (D) competition

4 Applicants applying to the degree program should arrange for at least three letters of recommendation to be sent ------- to the administration office.

(A) directive (B) directing
(C) directly (D) direction

5 To ensure that services are being performed to our high standards, Celebrity Cleaning, Inc.'s supervisors ------- check every jobsite they are in charge of.

(A) period (B) periodic
(C) periodical (D) periodically

6 Although Dr. Jenkins asserted his rights ------- to retain his experiment, the Tess Academy of Medical Science refused to fund him.

(A) forced (B) forcing
(C) forceful (D) forcefully

7 Metropolitan Motor Inns are ------- located near over 20 major highways across the country.

(A) consistently (B) heavily
(C) frequently (D) conveniently

8 The receptionists at Cosa Vueno will distribute name tags and place cards to the participants ------- before the opening ceremony.

(A) shorten (B) shorter
(C) short (D) shortly

9 Because of the new censorship laws, alcoholic beverage advertisements are ------- ever shown in the media.

(A) hard (B) harder
(C) hardly (D) hardest

10 Due to the recent switched delivery incident, the manager's admonition lasted for ------- an hour.

(A) variously (B) nearly
(C) finely (D) openly

11 Before further investigation could be carried out, Mr. Kim had ------- been found guilty of misappropriating public funds.

(A) later (B) already
(C) soon (D) eventually

12 Icarus Airlines will not let you board a plane if you do not have an appropriate visa, which ends up being ------- inconvenient for some passengers.

(A) extremely (B) extreme
(C) extremes (D) extremist

해설 p. 335

Questions 13-16 refer to the following letter.

15471 South First Street
Vanderbilt TN 38358

Dear Mr. Hagiwara,

I'm sorry that it has taken so long to ------- the details of your trip to China in December.
13.
-------. In the meantime, here is your tentative schedule.
14.

- December 15: You will arrive in Beijing in the evening. Mr. Henry Hu will meet you and take you ------- to your hotel.
15.

- December 16: You will visit three different factories between 9 A.M. and 2 P.M.

- December 17: Mr. Henry Hu will pick you up at 7 A.M., and you will fly to Guangzhou. Our branch manager, Richard Grant, is planning the Guangzhou events, so he will send you the details about that part of the trip at a ------- time.
16.

- December 18: You will fly home from Guangzhou.

Sincerely,

Mary Molliconi

13 (A) finalize
(B) terminate
(C) discontinue
(D) close

14 (A) Immediately proceed to the branch office for a briefing on the week's itinerary.
(B) We will send you the details about that part of the trip by the end of December.
(C) But I'm glad to report that I will have a detailed itinerary by the end of the week.
(D) However, this schedule is subject to change.

15 (A) directly
(B) direct
(C) directing
(D) direction

16 (A) latest
(B) lately
(C) lateness
(D) later

UNIT 05 전치사

전치사 문제는 전치사의 고유 의미를 묻거나 명사, 동사, 형용사 등과 함께 쓰는 전치사 관용 표현 문제가 주를 이룬다. 먼저 전치사의 의미와 역할을 이해하고 혼동되는 전치사의 정확한 용법을 숙지해야 한다. 특정 동사나 명사, 형용사와 함께 쓰이는 전치사는 덩어리째 암기하는 것이 효과적이다.

Preview

01 | 전치사의 역할

1) 전치사는 명사, 대명사, 동명사 등의 앞에 쓰여 연결고리 역할을 한다.

Put it in **the drawer**. 그것을 서랍장 안에 두세요.

Please send the contract to **me**. 계약서를 제게 보내 주세요.

She showed her appreciation by **sending** flowers. 그녀는 꽃을 보내 감사를 표시했다.

2) 전치사는 시간, 장소, 위치, 방향, 이유, 양보 등의 의미를 전달한다.

We arrived late at **the airport**. 우리는 공항에 늦게 도착했다. ▶ 장소

They meet on **every Monday** of the month. 그들은 매달 월요일에 만난다. ▶ 시간

3) 전치사구(전치사+명사)는 명사 뒤에서 형용사나 부사 역할을 한다.

Our Web site provides **information** on the issue. 우리 웹 사이트는 그 사안에 대한 정보를 제공한다. ▶ 형용사 역할

Leave the documents in the meeting room. 그 서류들을 회의실에 두세요. ▶ 부사 역할

+TIP 전치사 뒤에는 절이 올 수 없다. 절은 접속사가 연결한다.

[Although / ~~Despite~~] there is a recession, we decided to raise employee salaries.
불경기이긴 하지만, 우리는 직원 임금을 올리기로 결정했다.

02 | 전치사의 위치

명사+전치사+명사	We determined **the title** of **the book**. 우리는 책의 제목을 결정했다.
형용사+전치사+명사	He is **responsible** for **this accident**. 그는 이번 사건에 책임이 있다.
동사+전치사+명사	Please **turn** on **the TV**. TV를 켜 주세요.

03 | 전치사의 종류

일반 전치사	in, on, at, to, from, for, by, over, since, about, before, after
구 전치사	according to ~에 따르면 in case of ~의 경우에 on account of ~ 때문에
분사형(-ing형) 전치사	including ~을 포함하여 excluding ~을 제외하고 regarding ~에 관하여

POINT 1 시간을 나타내는 전치사

01 | 시간

in + 월/연도/계절 (~에)	in March 3월에 in 2019 2019년에 in the spring 봄에
on + 요일/날짜 (~에)	on Monday 월요일에 on March 2 3월 2일에
at + 시각 (~에)	at 9 A.M. 오전 9시에 at noon 정오에 at the moment 지금

The meeting with Marketing Director John Howard will take place [at / ~~on~~] **3 P.M.**
마케팅 부장인 John Howard와의 회의가 오후 3시에 있을 것이다.

02 | 시점

by + 시점 ~까지 (완료)	by the end of this month 이달 말까지
until + 시점 ~까지 (계속)	until the end of this year 올해 말까지
before/prior to + 시점 ~전에	before the deadline 마감일 전에
after + 시점/기간 ~후에	after the renovations 개조 후에
since + 시점 ~이후로	since last week 지난주 이후로 since the election 선거 이후로
toward + 시점 ~쯤, 무렵에	toward the end of the negotiation 협상 끝 무렵에

Research proposals must be submitted [by / ~~until~~] **next Friday.**
연구 제안서가 다음 주 금요일까지 제출되어야 한다.
▶ by는 '특정 시점까지 완료되어야 함'을 의미. complete, submit, register, pay 등의 일회성 완료 동사와 함께 쓰인다.

The sales meeting originally scheduled for next Monday has been postponed [until / ~~by~~] **next Friday.**
원래 다음 주 월요일로 잡혀 있던 영업 회의가 다음 주 금요일까지 연기되었다.
▶ until은 '특정 시점까지 상태가 지속됨'을 의미. remain, stay, continue, postpone, last, wait 등의 상태 동사와 함께 쓰인다.

The computers in the office have not been working [since / ~~by~~] **7:00 this morning.**
사무실 컴퓨터가 아침 7시 이후로 작동하지 않고 있다.
▶ since는 '~이래로, 이후로'를 의미. 현재완료 시제와 함께 쓰며, since 뒤에는 과거 시점이 온다.

03 | 기간

for + 숫자로 표현된 기간 ~동안	for 10 years 10년 동안
during + 기간 ~동안	during the performance 공연 동안 during business hours 업무 시간 동안
over + 기간 ~동안, ~이상	over the last two years 지난 2년 동안 over five years 5년 이상
through(out) + 기간 ~동안 내내	through(out) the workday 근무 시간 내내
within + 기간 ~이내에	within two weeks 2주 이내에
in + 기간 ~이후에, ~ 동안	in 30 minutes 30분 후에 in the past three years 지난 3년 동안

To receive a refund, customers must return the product [within / ~~during~~] **30 days of purchase.**
환불을 받기 위해, 고객들은 반드시 제품을 구매 30일 이내에 반품해야 합니다.

SPARTA Check-UP! 1

해설 p. 337

1 Customers who order a 3D music system ------- November 30 will receive a 20-percent discount.
(A) at
(B) in
(C) within
(D) before

2 ------- her time at Sierra University, Jane Novak made a positive impression on the humanities professors.
(A) Into
(B) During
(C) Upon
(D) About

3 Sales personnel should complete their weekly quota ------- the fourth day of the five-day period.
(A) until
(B) by
(C) between
(D) under

POINT ② 장소를 나타내는 전치사

01 | 장소

in+넓은 공간 ~(안)에서	in the complex 단지 안에서 in Manila 마닐라에서
on+장소 ~(위)에서	on the table 탁자 위에 on the first floor 1층에
throughout+장소 ~전체에	throughout the plant 공장 전체에
within+장소 ~내부에, 이내에	within a radius of the plant 공장 반경 내에

Dr. Lee's new office is located [on / ~~in~~] **the second floor** of the Sun Building in Seattle.
Lee 박사의 새로운 사무실은 시애틀에 있는 Sun 빌딩 2층에 있다.

02 | 위치

at+지점 ~에서	at the counter 카운터에서
above / over ~위에	above sea level 해수면 위[해발] over the river 강 위로
below / under / beneath ~아래에	below sea level 해수면 아래[해저] under the bridge 다리 아래
beside / next to / by / alongside ~옆에	beside / next to / by the door 문 옆에
along ~을 따라	along the road 도로를 따라
around ~ 주위에; (지역) 모든 곳에서	around the table 탁자 주위에 around the world 전 세계에서
opposite ~맞은편에	opposite the building 건물 맞은편에
between (둘) 사이에	between A and B A와 B 사이에
among (셋 이상) 사이에, 중에	among the applicants 지원자들 중에

The keynote speaker explained the differences [between / ~~among~~] the individual activities and the group activities at the resort. 기조 연설자가 리조트에서 개인 활동과 단체 활동 간의 차이점을 설명했다.

03 | 방향

to+목적지/대상 ~에게, ~으로	return to the office 사무실로 돌아가다
from+출처 ~로부터	return from the office 사무실에서 돌아오다
into ~안으로 ↔ **out of** ~밖으로	into the office 사무실 안으로 out of the office 사무실 밖으로
through ~을 통과하여	through the tunnel 터널을 통과하여
across ~을 가로질러; ~전체에	across the road 도로를 가로질러 across Europe 유럽 전체에
toward ~쪽으로, ~을 향하여	toward the shore 해안 쪽으로

Tour Today offers many interesting articles [to / ~~toward~~] **its readers**.
<Tour Today>는 많은 흥미 있는 기사들을 독자들에게 제공한다.

SPARTA Check-UP! 2

| 해설 p. 337

1 The search function in Word Soft allows users to search for words ------- a file very easily.
(A) where
(B) while
(C) within
(D) wherever

2 The changes occurring ------- the financial industry show efforts to control fluctuations in the financial market.
(A) into
(B) throughout
(C) during
(D) as

3 Coogie, Inc. holds seminars regularly to promote better communication ------- its staff members.
(A) under
(B) past
(C) among
(D) behind

POINT 3 기타 전치사

01 | 이유, 양보, 목적·용도, 수단

이유	**due to / because of / owing to** ~ 때문에 **on account of** ~ 때문에 **thanks to** ~덕분에	due to a power failure 정전 때문에 thanks to their support 그들의 지원 덕분에
양보	**despite / in spite of** ~에도 불구하고	despite the bad weather 나쁜 날씨에도 불구하고
목적·용도	**for** ~을 위해서, ~용으로	for future use 추후 사용을 위해 items for sale 판매용 물건
수단	**through** ~로, ~을 통해 **with+도구** ~로 **by+교통수단** ~로, ~를 타고	through the Internet 인터넷을 통해 with pencil 연필로 by train/bus 기차/버스로 *cf.* on foot 도보로

02 | 화제, 정도, 제외, 부연, 대체

화제	**on/about/concerning/regarding/ as to/pertaining to** ~에 관하여	concerning the schedule 일정에 관하여 on business ethics 기업 윤리에 관하여
정도	**beyond** ~를 넘어서, ~이상으로 **above** ~이상으로	beyond repair/control 수리가/통제가 불가능한 beyond/above expectation 기대 이상으로
제외	**except (for)** ~을 제외하고 **without** ~없이 **barring** ~이 없다면	except legal holidays 법정 공휴일을 제외하고 without consent/notice 동의/통보 없이 barring further delays 더 이상의 지연이 없다면
부연	**besides/in addition to** ~외에도	besides competitive salaries 좋은 급여 외에도
대체	**instead of** ~대신에	instead of waiting for approval 승인을 기다리는 대신에

03 | 소유, 소지, 자격, 비교

소유	**of** ~의, ~을 가진, ~중에	the number of guests 손님들의 수
소지	**with/alongside** ~와 함께	the meeting with Mr. Son Son 씨와 회의
자격	**as** ~로서	as a vice president 부사장으로서
비교	**like** ~처럼, ~와 미찬기지로 ↔ **unlike** ~와 달리 **regardless of** ~에 상관없이	unlike other competitors 다른 경쟁사와는 달리 regardless of age 나이에 상관없이

SPARTA Check-UP! 3

| 해설 p. 337

1 ------- technical problems, the launch of the new office software will not be delayed.
(A) Prior to
(B) Due to
(C) Despite
(D) Yet

2 ------- waiting for reports, the director himself called each of the branch managers.
(A) According to
(B) Further
(C) Instead of
(D) However

3 As the director ------- the Personnel Department, Mr. Philippe is in charge of hiring new employees.
(A) on
(B) of
(C) to
(D) by

POINT ④ 전치사 관용표현 1

01 | 자동사+전치사

deal with ~을 다루다, 취급하다	dispose of ~을 처리하다
agree with[to/on/about] ~에 동의하다	depend[rely] on[upon] ~에 의지하다, ~에 달려 있다
ask for ~을 요청하다	enroll in, register for ~에 등록하다
benefit from ~로부터 혜택을 얻다	interfere with ~을 방해하다
cooperate[collaborate] with ~와 협력하다	look into ~을 조사하다 look for ~을 찾다
cooperate[collaborate] on ~에 대해 협력하다	object to ~에 반대하다
compete with[against] ~와 경쟁하다	participate in ~에 참가하다
compete for ~을 위해 경쟁하다	proceed with ~을 진행하다
comply with ~에 따르다, 준수하다	react to ~에 반응하다
consist of ~로 구성되다	refrain from ~을 삼가다
contribute to ~에 기여하다	succeed in ~에 성공하다

02 | 명사+전치사

access to ~의 접근, 이용	dependence[reliance] on[upon] ~에 대한 의존
advance in ~의 발전	effect[impact/influence] on ~에 대한 영향
concern over[about] ~에 대한 우려/걱정	opposition to ~에 대한 반대
confidence in ~에 대한 자신감	problem[trouble] with ~에 대한 문제
decrease[increase] in ~의 감소/증가	qualification for ~에 대한 자격
dispute over ~에 대한 논쟁	solution to ~에 대한 해결책

03 | (be)+형용사+전치사

(be) associated with/related to ~와 관련되다	(be) pleased[satisfied] with ~에 만족하다
(be) aware of ~을 알다	(be) responsible for ~을 책임지다
(be) capable of ~을 할 수 있다	(be) responsive to ~에 반응하다
(be) compatible with ~와 호환되다	(be) similar to ~와 유사하다
(be) eligible for ~에 대해 자격이 있다	(be) involved in ~에 관련되다, 연루되다
(be) suitable for ~에 적합하다	(be) familiar with ~에 익숙하다, ~를 잘 알다
(be) exempt from ~을 면제 받다	(be) ideal for ~에 이상적이다

SPARTA Check-UP! 4

해설 p. 337

1 Ms. Baker agreed ------- the idea of hiring 200 new assembly line workers.
(A) toward
(B) with
(C) onto
(D) from

2 Local residents have voiced concern ------- the proposal to build a parking lot on 4th Street.
(A) over
(B) around
(C) along
(D) into

3 In the hospitality business, it is especially important to be responsive ------- guests' needs.
(A) from
(B) on
(C) of
(D) to

POINT 5 전치사 관용표현 2

04 | 전치사+명사

in	in detail 상세히 in duplicate 복사본 2부로 in writing 서면으로 in a timely manner 적시에	in demand 수요가 있는 in time 제때 in advance 미리, 사전에 in alphabetical order 알파벳순으로
on / upon	on/upon arrival[departure] 도착[출발]하자마자 on time 정각에/정시에 on the market 시중에 나와 있는 on the phone 통화 중인	upon request 요청 시 on schedule 예정대로 on the radio 라디오에서 on the Internet 인터넷에서
under	under control 통제되는 under a new policy 새로운 정책 하에 under the supervision of ~의 감독 하에	under construction 공사 중인 under new management 새 경영체제 하에 under the direction of ~의 지시 하에
at	at the rate of ~의 (비율)속도로 at no extra charge[cost] 추가 비용 없이 at the cost[price/expense] of ~의 비용으로 at a low[affordable] price 싼 가격으로 at all times 항상 at least 적어도, 최소한	at a fast pace 빠른 속도로 at full speed 전속력으로 at one's expense ~의 비용으로 at the beginning[end] of the month 월초(말)에 at your earliest convenience 가급적 신속히 at the latest 늦어도
without	without written consent 서면 동의 없이 without prior notification 사전 통보 없이 without a parking permit 주차 허가증 없이	without hesitation 주저 없이 without exception 예외 없이 without careful planning 신중한 계획 없이
within	within 30 days 30일 이내에 within the company 회사 내에 within budget 예산 내에서	within the guidelines 규정을 어기지 않고 within the warranty period 보증기간 내에 within walking distance 걸어 갈 만한 거리에 있는

SPARTA Check-UP! 5

해설 p. 338

1 The Grand Hotel requires that all guests check in at the front desk ------- arrival.

(A) ever
(B) upon
(C) into
(D) as

2 The new restaurant serves exotic food from around the world ------- reasonable prices.

(A) by
(B) on
(C) at
(D) from

3 ------- new management, the company's profits have doubled since last year.

(A) At
(B) To
(C) Under
(D) Out of

POINT 6 전치사 관용표현 3

05 | 전치사+명사+전치사

as a result of ~의 결과로	in exchange for ~와 교환하여
at the beginning[end] of ~의 시작[끝]에	in favor of ~에 지지하여/찬성하여
at the risk of ~의 위험을 무릅쓰고, ~을 희생하여	in honor of ~을 기념하여/축하하여
at the cost[rate/speed] of ~의 비용[비율/속도]로	in light of ~에 비추어, ~을 고려하여
by means of ~의 도움으로, ~을 써서	in line with ~와 함께, ~에 따라
in observance of ~에 따라, ~을 준수하여	in addition to ~ 이외에도, ~에 더하여
in compliance with ~에 따라, ~을 준수하여	in place of ~ 대신에
in accordance with ~에 따라, ~을 준수하여	in response to ~에 반응하여, ~에 따라
in case of / in the event of ~의 경우에	in time for ~의 시간에 맞추어
in celebration of ~을 축하하여	on account of ~ 때문에
in charge of ~을 책임지는	on behalf of ~을 대표/대신하여
in comparison with ~와 비교하여	with the exception of ~을 제외하고

06 | 분사형 전치사

regarding ~에 관하여	regulations regarding the labeling of food 식품의 라벨링에 관한 규정
concerning ~에 관하여	questions concerning the report 그 보고서에 관한 질문들
barring ~이 없으면	barring any further delays 더 이상의 지연이 없다면 (일어나지 않는다면)
considering ~을 고려하면	considering his lack of experience 그의 경험 부족을 고려하면
excepting ~을 빼고	excepting the weather 날씨 빼고
pending ~하는 동안에	pending the negotiation 협상 동안에
including ~을 포함하여	twenty people including children 아이들을 포함해서 20명
excluding ~을 제외하고	excluding (= except for) airfares 항공 요금을 제외하고
following ~이후에	following a long debate 오랜 논쟁 이후(끝)에
notwithstanding ~에도 불구하고	notwithstanding the heavy rain 폭우에도 불구하고

SPARTA Check-UP! 6

해설 p. 338

1 ------- the service cost and other service policies, customers can contact us by telephone or e-mail, whichever they prefer.
(A) Regard
(B) Regards
(C) Regarded
(D) Regarding

2 All haircare products will be 20 percent off next week ------- celebration of Hugo Cosmetics' 10th anniversary.
(A) of
(B) under
(C) at
(D) in

3 ------- the news report, Nelson Bank posted a net profit of 100 million dollars.
(A) According to
(B) Nevertheless
(C) Even though
(D) As if

 PRACTICE

해설 p.338

▪ 괄호 안의 보기 중 알맞은 단어를 고르세요.

1 Mr. Ogawa will not be able to return from his business trip **[within / before]** October 1.

2 Mr. Barnett wishes to travel to Barcelona **[at / with]** the rest of the marketing team.

3 Recently introduced models can be purchased **[about / from]** any of our dealers nationwide.

4 **[Regardless / Despite]** price cuts, Pattice, Inc. has improved its pre-tax profits by 30%.

5 Our sales growth is 2 percent this quarter, which is **[less / below]** last year's rate of 5 percent.

6 Customers are supposed to keep store receipts **[as / through]** proof of purchase.

7 High interest rates have adversely affected the housing industry **[on / throughout]** the region.

8 The proceeds from the concert will be used **[for / of]** the renovation of St. Mary Music School.

9 We've trained all of the new recruits **[over / since]** the past three months, but all have failed to show any kind of enthusiasm.

10 **[Because of / In case of]** the publicity campaign, Ocean City residents expect an increase in tourism.

11 If you want your laundry to be delivered **[by / until]** tomorrow morning, a 20% extra charge will be added to your bill.

12 If you don't **[comply / observe]** with the local traffic regulations, you may be fined or even jailed for up to a month.

13 Requests for further information **[concerning / relating]** the conference schedule will be fulfilled as soon as the schedule is completed.

14 Every international sales representative should behave in **[accordance / result]** with local customs.

15 Success in this industry depends on the ability to introduce new products to the market in a timely **[basis / manner]**.

1 Sales of the Antivirus 3.7 software have tripled ------- the last six months.

(A) in (B) on
(C) at (D) of

2 Trains delayed by heavy snowfall in Minsk have been rescheduled to depart ------- the next three hours.

(A) of (B) to
(C) from (D) within

3 The first half of the Thompson Business School live meeting will be led ------- Irene McDonell later today.

(A) up (B) by
(C) on (D) as

4 ------- a close inspection, the technician was able to figure out the cause of the malfunction of the microwave oven.

(A) Toward (B) Onto
(C) Through (D) About

5 ------- the extraordinary success of the publication *Town & Around*, we have been prompted to provide readers with an online version of magazine.

(A) According to (B) Similarly
(C) Unless (D) Due to

6 Members of the jury are asked to complete questionnaires ------- the duration of the trial.

(A) between (B) behind
(C) upon (D) throughout

7 People who are over 65 years old and are eligible for an age exemption should contact the town treasury ------- further instructions.

(A) onto (B) within
(C) along (D) for

8 ------- the Great Little Trading Company, we value joint effort and strive to provide the best working conditions possible.

(A) On (B) At
(C) Of (D) To

9 Mr. Ford sent an e-mail requesting all staffers to register ------- one of our presentation skill sessions for free.

(A) as (B) near
(C) about (D) for

10 ------- better warning systems at weather forecast stations, this year's tornado season has been the worst in decades.

(A) Even if (B) While
(C) Despite (D) Although

11 The article in the *Deccan Herald* clearly stated that the cruise ship *Blue Rush* was not fully ------- international maritime safety regulations.

(A) complied (B) complying
(C) in compliance (D) compliant with

12 The Web programmer position requires extensive computer experience ------- vast knowledge in a related field.

(A) otherwise (B) in addition to
(C) meanwhile (D) even though

Questions 13-16 refer to the following e-mail.

To: Goranka Lazovic <lazovic@nus.edu>
From: Tracy Lopez <lopez@limebooks.com>
Date: July 24
Subject: The rare book you're looking for

I am writing in response to your e-mail yesterday. -------. **13.**
However, we will be able to order the book for you from the publisher ------- **14.** the next week.

If this ------- **15.** interests you, please reply to this e-mail and provide us with your telephone number.

We will ------- **16.** you when the item becomes available for delivery.

I look forward to your response.

Regards,

Tracy Lopez
Customer Service
Lime Books

13 (A) A replacement charge will be charged for each item that is returned in damaged condition.
(B) I am sorry to inform you that the book you are interested in purchasing is not currently in stock.
(C) I am very sorry to hear that you have not received your order.
(D) The books you ordered will be delivered free of charge.

14 (A) when
(B) between
(C) within
(D) since

15 (A) moment
(B) author
(C) advantage
(D) option

16 (A) notify
(B) noticeably
(C) notification
(D) noticeable

UNIT 06

동사의 종류

동사는 종류가 매우 다양해서 자동사와 타동사를 다시 세분화하여 다섯 개의 형식으로 나눈 것이 문장의 5형식이다. 이 장에서는 문장의 1형식부터 5형식의 기본 구조를 익히고 각 형식에 해당하는 동사의 특징을 숙지해야 한다. 특히 2형식과 5형식 관련 문제는 자주 출제되고 있으니 더욱 주의를 기울여야 한다.

Preview

01 | 1형식 문장 : 주어+동사 (S+V)

1형식에 쓰이는 동사는 완전 자동사로서 목적어나 보어가 필요하지 않다. 1형식의 문장이라고 '주어+동사'만으로 쓰이는 문장은 별로 없으며, 대개는 여러 가지 수식어가 따르게 된다.

He **has** just **arrived.** 그는 막 도착했다.

The company **should comply** with safety regulations. 회사는 안전 규칙을 따라야 한다.

02 | 2형식 문장 : 주어+동사+주격 보어 (S+V+S.C)

2형식에 쓰이는 동사는 불완전 자동사로서 목적어는 쓰이지 않지만, 주어를 설명해 주는 주격 보어가 필요하다. 보어 자리에는 명사나 형용사, 또는 명사나 형용사 역할을 하는 어구가 올 수 있다.

Tom **remained** calm without saying a word. Tom은 한마디도 하지 않고 조용히 있었다.

The new accounting program **became** available. 그 새로운 회계 프로그램이 이용 가능했다.

03 | 3형식 문장 : 주어+동사+목적어 (S+V+O)

3형식에 쓰이는 동사는 완전 타동사로서 동작의 대상이 되는 목적어가 뒤따르게 된다. 목적어로는 명사나 대명사, 또는 부정사, 동명사, 명사구와 같은 명사 상당어구가 쓰인다.

Let's **discuss** the problem. 그 문제를 논의합시다.

You can't **access** the building without a permit. 당신은 허가증 없이 건물에 들어갈 수 없습니다.

04 | 4형식 문장 : 주어+동사+간접 목적어+직접 목적어 (S+V+I.O+D.O)

4형식에 쓰이는 동사는 수여동사라고 하는데, 수여동사 뒤에는 '~에게'라는 의미를 갖는 간접 목적어가 오고, 그 뒤에 '~을[를]'이라는 의미를 갖는 직접 목적어가 뒤따르게 된다.

They **offered** me a chance to transfer to the Hong Kong office. 그들은 내게 홍콩 사무소로 전근할 기회를 제의했다.

She **sent** her boss the letter by airmail. 그녀는 그녀의 사장에게 그 편지를 항공 우편으로 보냈다.

05 | 5형식 문장 : 주어+동사+목적어+목적격 보어 (S+V+O+O.C)

5형식에 쓰인 동사는 불완전 타동사라 하는데, 불완전 타동사는 뒤에 목적어와 그 목적어를 설명하는 목적격 보어를 필요로 한다. 목적격 보어로는 명사, 형용사, to부정사, 분사, 동사원형이 올 수 있다.

We **elected** him (as) chairperson. 우리는 그를 의장으로 선출했다.

Staff members have to **keep** the file room locked at all times. 직원들은 항상 서류실을 잠가 두어야 한다.

POINT 1 1형식 동사 : 완전 자동사

01 | 주어+완전 자동사+(부사구) : 자동사는 목적어를 취할 수 없다.

The refrigerator's warranty date [expired / ~~finished~~] (last month).
냉장고의 보증 기간은 (지난달) 만기되었다.

▶ 타동사 finish는 뒤에 목적어가 필요하고, 자동사 expire는 뒤에 목적어가 올 수 없다.

The entire department worked [collaboratively / ~~collaboraton~~] to finish the inventory on time.
전체 부서는 재고 조사를 제때 끝내기 위해서 협력하여 일했다.

▶ 완전 자동사는 뒤에 명사가 올 수 없고, 단독으로 사용되거나 부사, 부사구, 전명구가 오게 된다.

02 | 자동사는 수동태(be+p.p.)가 될 수 없다.

The overseas sales manager has just [arrived / ~~been arrived~~] at the airport.
해외영업부 과장이 방금 공항에 도착했다.

Retail sales in apparel [declined / ~~was declined~~] in August after a significant increase in July.
의류 분야의 소매 판매는 7월의 현저한 증가 이후 8월에 감소하였다.

03 | 자동사+전치사 : 타동사로 혼동하기 쉬운 자동사

abide by ~을 준수하다	comply with ~을 준수하다	proceed with ~을 계속하다
account for ~을 설명하다	consent to ~을 승낙하다, ~에 동의하다	react to ~에 반응하다
adhere to ~를 고수하다/준수하다	participate in ~에 참석하다	enroll in ~에 등록하다
agree with ~에 동의하다	contribute to ~에 기여하다	refrain from ~을 삼가다
apologize for ~에 대해 사과하다	deal with ~을 다루다, 처리하다	respond to ~에 답하다
apply for ~을 신청하다	depend on ~에 의존하다/달려 있다	talk about ~에 대해 이야기하다
approve of ~에 찬성하다	insist on ~을 고집하다	think of ~을 떠올리다
benefit from ~에서 이득을 얻다	interfere with ~을 방해하다	subscribe to ~을 구독하다
compete with ~와 경쟁하다	object to ~을 반대하다	wait for ~을 기다리다

Temporary workers [dealt with / ~~dealt~~] increased workloads. 임시직 직원들은 증가된 업무량을 처리했다.

Ms. Weinstein [contributes to / ~~contributes~~] the development of social organizations.
Weinstein 씨는 사회 조직의 발전에 기여하고 있다.

SPARTA Check-UP! 1

| 해설 p. 341

1 If Mr. Albert ------- at the office on time, he could get his daily tasks done by the end of each day.
(A) sent
(B) arrived
(C) delayed
(D) examined

2 The manager posted a notice demanding that all staff members ------- in Wednesday's meeting.
(A) arrive
(B) attend
(C) belong
(D) participate

3 All new workers can ------- in the computer programs during the next five days.
(A) admit
(B) apply
(C) enroll
(D) subscribe

POINT ❷ 2형식 동사 : 불완전 자동사

01 | 주어+불완전 자동사+보어 : 불완전 자동사 뒤에는 보어로서 명사나 형용사가 온다.

불완전 자동사 +	명사	Each summer, the Cayman Islands become **a popular tourist destination.** 매년 여름, Cayman 섬은 인기 있는 관광지가 된다.
	형용사	The Cluster Building remains **empty** after the accident. Cluster 건물은 사고 후에 비어 있는 상태이다.
	to부정사	The new copy machine seems **to work faster than the old one.** 새 복사기는 전에 사용하던 것보다 더 빠르게 작동하는 것 같다.
	전치사구	Construction work to restore the historic bridge is **under way.** 역사적인 다리를 재건하기 위한 공사 작업이 진행 중이다.
	명사절	What I've learned is **that the electricity bill was overcharged this month.** 내가 알게 된 것은 전기료 고지서 금액이 이번 달에 너무 많이 나온 것이다.

+ VOCABULARY | 불완전 자동사의 종류

상태	be ~이다 continue 계속하다 remain 계속 ~이다 stay ~한 상태로 유지하다, 그대로 있다
결과	become ~이 되다 get ~이 되다 prove ~임이 드러나다, 판명되다
감각	look ~처럼 보이다 appear ~처럼 보이다 seem ~인 것 같다 feel ~인 것 같다

I regret to inform you that your present prices are not competitive in this market.
당신의 현재 가격은 지금 시장에서 경쟁력이 없다는 것을 알려드리게 되어 유감입니다.

The company's new product has become popular.
회사의 신제품은 인기 상품이 되었다.

Many people still feel uneasy about making online purchases.
많은 사람들이 아직 온라인상에서 물건 구매하는 것을 불안해한다.

SPARTA ☑ Check-UP! ❷

| 해설 p. 341

1 The manager finally decided to fire the salesman when he became ------- with a long-time client.

(A) argue
(B) argumentative
(C) argumentatively
(D) argument

2 The owner of the Blue Sky Restaurant was ------- that it had received a negative review in the local newspaper.

(A) disappoint
(B) disappointment
(C) disappointed
(D) disappointingly

3 For our guests' convenience, a hotel manager is ------- at the front desk from 7:00 A.M. to midnight seven days a week.

(A) probable
(B) eligible
(C) considerable
(D) available

POINT 3 3형식 동사 : 완전 타동사

01 | 주어+완전 타동사+목적어 : 타동사 뒤에는 전치사 없이 바로 목적어를 취한다.

The building managers should [discuss / ~~talk~~] **how to minimize inconveniences during the renovation process.** 건물 관리자들은 개조 과정 동안에 일어날 문제들을 어떻게 최소화할지를 논의해야 한다.

▶ 타동사 discuss는 뒤에 목적어가 필요하고, 자동사 talk는 바로 뒤에 목적어를 쓸 수 없다.

+ VOCABULARY | 자동사로 혼동하기 쉬운 빈출 타동사

access 접속하다, 접근하다
acquire 취득하다, 인수하다
appreciate 감사하다
approve 승인하다
mention 언급하다
discuss 의논하다
express 표현하다
indicate 나타내다
reach ~에 이르다, 도달하다
return 돌려주다
approach 접근하다
inspect 조사하다

02 | 'A(사람)에게 B(사물)를 말하다'를 뜻하는 3형식 타동사

announce (to 사람) that S+V	(사람에게) S가 V하다는 것을 발표하다
introduce (to 사람) that S+V	(사람에게) S가 V하다는 것을 소개하다
explain (to 사람) that S+V	(사람에게) S가 V하다는 것을 설명하다
suggest (to 사람) that S+V	(사람에게) S가 V하다는 것을 제안하다
recommend (to 사람) that S+V	(사람에게) S가 V하다는 것을 권하다

Fashion Trend [announced / ~~informed~~] **to reporters that it will reduce its staff by as much as 40 percent.** Fashion Trend 사는 기자들에게 직원들을 40%만큼 줄이겠다고 발표했다.

+ VOCABULARY | 'A(사람)에게 B(사물)를 말하다'를 뜻하는 4형식 타동사

동사 + 목적어(사람) + that절	
inform/notify 사람 that S+V	사람에게 S가 V하다는 것을 알리다
advise 사람 that S+V	사람에게 S가 V하다는 것을 충고하다
remind 사람 that S+V	사람에게 S가 V하다는 것을 상기시키다
convince 사람 that S+V	사람에게 S가 V하다는 것을 확신시키다

SPARTA Check-UP! 3

해설 p. 341

1 After our class, let's ------- our plan to study together for the midterm exams.
(A) talk
(B) speak
(C) discuss
(D) remark

2 The Harrison Corporation is pleased to ------- to you that your promotion has been approved.
(A) tell
(B) inform
(C) convince
(D) announce

3 SpeedMax Shipping ------- all clients that oversized or heavy items may require additional delivery time.
(A) announces
(B) explains
(C) advises
(D) introduces

POINT 4 3형식 동사 : 빈출 타동사 패턴

01 | A가 ~하는 것을 막다

prevent / keep / stop / discourage / prohibit + A from -ing

Corporate policy discourages **staff members** [from / ~~in~~] **conducting personal business during working hours.** 회사 정책은 직원들이 업무 시간 동안 개인적인 일을 하지 못하도록 막는다.

02 | A(사람)에게 B(사물)를 제공하다

provide / equip / furnish / supply + A with B [B to A]

Customers should [provide / ~~offer~~] **us** with **a proper document to request a refund or replacement.** 고객들은 환불이나 교체를 요청하기 위해서 우리에게 적절한 서류를 제출해야 한다.

03 | A를 B에 ~하다

concentrate[focus] A on B A를 B에 집중시키다	spend A(시간/돈/에너지) on B A를 B에 소비하다
apply A to B A를 B에 적용하다	escort A to B A를 B로 안내하다

The company has been focusing **all its efforts** [on / ~~from~~] **the upcoming launch of its new product.** 그 회사는 다가오는 신제품의 출시에 모든 노력을 집중하고 있다.

04 | A를 B로 바꾸다

replace A with B A를 B로 대체하다	substitute A for B B 대신 A를 쓰다
exchange A for B A를 B로 교환하다	trade A for B A를 B로 교환하다

They replaced **the old control system** with **a new one.** 그들은 오래된 통제관리 시스템을 새것으로 교체했다.
= **The old control system** was replaced with **a new one.** ▶ 수동태 표현

05 | 자주 쓰이는 타동사 관용 표현

make	make a request 요청하다 make a reservation 예약하다 make a decision 결정하다 make a presentation 발표하다 make a commitment 헌신하다 make an effort 노력하다
take	take measures[steps/actions] 조치를 취하다 take precautions 예방조치를 취하다
give / play	give a speech 연설하다 play a role in ~에서 역할을 하다

Ms. Lahinaiken has gone to Prague to [give / ~~take~~] a speech on foreign exchange procedures.
Lahinaiken 씨는 외환 절차에 대해 연설하기 위해 프라하로 갔다.

SPARTA Check-UP! 4

해설 p. 341

1 Visitors to the Donald Museum are prohibited ------- taking photographs or making video recordings of our exhibits.
(A) by
(B) away
(C) under
(D) from

2 We need to understand how they were able to replace the old system ------- a new one without losing any sales.
(A) of
(B) on
(C) with
(D) by

3 Some measures have been ------- by the National Bank of Pakistan to solve the liquidity problem in the banking sector.
(A) had
(B) played
(C) given
(D) taken

POINT 5 4형식 동사 : 수여동사

01 | 주어+수여동사+A(사람: 간접 목적어)+B(사물: 직접 목적어) : A에게 B를 주다

give 주다	forward 전송하다	offer 제공하다	send 보내다	grant 수여하다, 승인해 주다	
issue 발행해주다	award 수여하다	lend 빌려주다	show 보여주다	sell 팔다	buy 사주다

The doctor gave **Brandon**(사람) **a prescription**(사물) after a thorough physical examination.

의사는 철저한 검진 이후에 Brandon에게 처방전을 주었다.

Mr. Brian sent **every member of the Sales Department**(사람) **the presentation handouts**(사물).

Brian 씨는 모든 영업부서의 직원에게 발표용 자료를 보냈다.

The *Metro Herald*, the city's leading newspaper, is offering **new customers**(사람) **a ten-percent discount**(사물).

시의 선두 신문인 <Metro Herald>는 신규 고객들에게 10퍼센트 할인을 제공하고 있다.

02 | 주어+수여동사+B(사물)+전치사+A(사람) : 4형식 → 3형식

4형식 Critics gave **the director of the play**(사람) **outstanding reviews**(사물).

3형식 Critics gave **outstanding reviews**(사물) to **the director of the play**(사람).

비평가들은 연극 감독에게 좋은 평을 내렸다.

4형식 They offered **me**(사람) **a transfer**(사물) to the New York branch.

3형식 They offered **a transfer**(사물) to **me**(사람) to the New York branch.

그들은 내게 뉴욕 지사로 전근을 제의했다.

+TIP 4형식 동사 → 3형식 동사

give, send, offer, bring 등 거의 모든 4형식 동사는 give B to A, send B to A, offer B to A, bring B to A로 바꿔 쓸 수 있다. 예외로 buy, make를 buy B for A, make B for A로, ask를 ask B of A로 바꿔 쓸 수 있다.

SPARTA Check-UP! 5

해설 p. 341

1 Mr. Johnson in Accounting ------- everyone in his department the e-mail he received from the vice president of the company.
(A) spoke
(B) received
(C) announced
(D) forwarded

2 After several requests, Luxar Incorporated will ------- the HR manager a company card but will hold him responsible if he loses it.
(A) agree
(B) grant
(C) complete
(D) arrange

3 This afternoon, I sent an e-mail ------- you with an attached invoice for the order.
(A) to
(B) by
(C) at
(D) with

POINT 6 5형식 동사 : 불완전 타동사

01 | 주어+불완전 타동사+목적어+목적격 보어

make keep find leave consider

The repeated failure of the test made **the researchers** [upset / ~~upsets~~].
거듭된 실험의 실패가 연구원들의 마음을 상하게 했다. ▶ 목적어의 상태 설명

Staff members have to keep **the file room** [locked / ~~locking~~] at all times.
직원들은 항상 서류 보관실을 잠가 두어야 한다. ▶ 목적어와 수동적 관계

02 | 목적격 보어로 to부정사를 취하는 동사 : 목적어와 능동적 관계

권고	encourage, convince, cause, persuade, teach, urge	+목적어+to부정사
요구	ask, force, instruct, require, request, get	
허락	permit, allow, enable	
기대	expect, want, wish, intend, would like	
통보	advise, recommend, remind, warn	

The Royal Bank encourages **staff members** [to attend / ~~attending~~] evening courses in work-related fields of study. Royal Bank는 직원들에게 업무와 관련된 분야의 저녁 수업 과정에 참석할 것을 권장한다.

A new computer system would enable **the Research Department** [to complete / ~~completed~~] projects much faster. 새로운 컴퓨터 시스템은 연구부서가 프로젝트를 훨씬 더 빨리 끝낼 수 있도록 할 것이다.

03 | 목적격 보어로 동사원형을 취하는 사역동사

let, have, make+사람+동사원형	목적어(사람)와 능동적 관계
have, make, get+사물+과거분사	목적어(사물)와 수동적 관계
help+사람/사물+동사원형/to부정사	목적어(사람/사물)와 능동적 관계

Mr. McCormic made **his secretary** [confirm / ~~confirmed~~] his hotel reservation.
McCormic 씨는 그의 비서에게 그의 호텔 예약 상황을 확인하도록 했다.

The favorable benefits helped **the textile company** [attract / ~~attracted~~] the best production workers in the industry. 유리한 혜택은 섬유 회사가 산업의 최고 생산 근로자들을 끌어들이도록 도왔다.

SPARTA Check-UP! 6

해설 p. 342

1 Mr. Chang's report has ------- managers aware of hiring needs for the coming year.
(A) made
(B) become
(C) brought
(D) given

2 HDC Financial expects its employees ------- themselves in a professional manner when speaking with customers.
(A) conduct
(B) conductor
(C) conducting
(D) to conduct

3 Our online service ------- you to view your account, pay bills, and even transfer funds from one account to another.
(A) allowance
(B) allows
(C) allowing
(D) allowable

PRACTICE

해설 p. 342

▪ 괄호 안의 보기 중 알맞은 단어를 고르세요.

1 Food prices **[rose / raised]** because of the bad harvest last year.

2 A friend of mine **[offered / is offered]** me the most important position in the company.

3 Whenever he is late for appointments, it makes me **[angry / angrily]**.

4 The new director **[let / got]** the administrative assistant to take care of all the paperwork.

5 During the conference on organizational effectiveness, the keynote speaker **[talked / discussed]** the merits of mentoring programs for new employees.

6 The SW 47 vacuum cleaner uses advanced filter technology to keep carpets **[clean / cleanly]** and looking like new.

7 The financial director **[went / took]** the new high-speed train to Monday's board meeting.

8 Please **[explain / notify]** Ms. Lee that her package will be delivered to her office by Friday.

9 These stories have **[given / been given]** them enormous pleasure over the years.

10 We have done significant research on the real estate market to help us **[choose / choosing]** the best home for our family.

11 The property management program has **[expected / made]** our staff become more aware of our surroundings.

12 The furniture **[arrived / was arrived]** yesterday, and we were very pleased with the way it looked in our office.

13 The police chief told the detective to **[proceed / decide]** with the investigation after the evidence had been gathered.

14 Due to the decreased price of fuel, long car trips are once again becoming **[afford / affordable]** for most people.

15 The GUID system **[allows / allowing]** our clients to save money on development costs and to unify data from various sources.

1 The executives at Titan Chemicals have ------- a commitment to increase research and development spending.

(A) made (B) faced
(C) showed (D) complied

2 If any problems with the server occur, please ------- promptly to inquiries from customers.

(A) answer (B) inquire
(C) respond (D) request

3 Great pitching and some timely hitting made yesterday's ballgame quite -------.

(A) excitement (B) exciting
(C) excitedly (D) excitable

4 When the company announced its success in the European market, it ------- all of its employees to have a one-week vacation as a reward.

(A) let (B) had
(C) allowed (D) made

5 When its office lease -------, EK Investment will relocate to the downtown area.

(A) expires (B) expiring
(C) expiration (D) is expired

6 After the implementation of some key changes, our company will be able to ------- customers improved prices and services.

(A) make (B) control
(C) offer (D) restore

7 The sales manager and his team finally managed to get the project ------- on schedule.

(A) complete (B) completing
(C) completed (D) to complete

8 The public images of most industries remain quite ------- to what they were a year ago, except for those in the drug and oil industries.

(A) close (B) closely
(C) closing (D) closes

9 Textile products shipped overseas must ------- to international labeling requirements.

(A) update (B) comply
(C) confront (D) conform

10 When attaching company contracts to an e-mail, keep these documents ------- by password-protecting them.

(A) secure (B) security
(C) securely (D) securing

11 All requests for new office supplies must be ------- in writing to the appropriate department supervisor.

(A) caused (B) made
(C) called (D) asked

12 If you want to improve your computer skills, please ------- the Baton Career Center to learn about our low-cost courses.

(A) contact (B) speak
(C) touch (D) connect

Questions 13-16 refer to the following e-mail.

To: subscriptions@gardener.com
From: Hboyd@naoro.co.kr
Subject: Subscription #364954

To Whom It May Concern,

I would like to ------- (13.) my subscription to *Gardener's Secret*. While your articles and photo essays are always informative and interesting, I no longer have the time to enjoy them.

In fact, almost all of the last six months' issues have been put aside, ------- (14.) unread. -------. (15.) If your records ------- (16.) that this is correct, please send me a refund of $75, which is half of what I paid for my subscription.

Thank you in advance for your prompt attention to this matter.

Sincerely,

Harold Boyd

13 (A) confirm
(B) renew
(C) receive
(D) cancel

14 (A) still
(B) once
(C) hardly
(D) enough

15 (A) You will receive our special anniversary issue.
(B) There are some serious problems with your order processing.
(C) I believe that my subscription is active until next May.
(D) I am really disappointed with your customer service.

16 (A) indication
(B) indicate
(C) indicating
(D) indicates

UNIT 07 수 일치

동사의 수 일치 문제는 매월 평균 1~2 문제가 꾸준히 출제된다. 단, 수 일치를 포함한 관련 문제 개수는 6문제 이상이 된다. 문제 유형은 ① 주어를 제시하고 동사의 수를 일치시키는 유형, ② 동사를 제시하고 동사의 수에 주어를 일치시키는 유형으로 출제된다. 이 장에서 수 일치 관련 기본 문법뿐만 아니라 단수동사/복수동사와 결합하는 특정 주어의 형태도 익혀 둔다.

Preview

01 | 하나의 문장에는 하나의 주어와 하나의 동사가 존재한다.

The guide (주어) **includes** (동사) useful information.
안내서에는 유용한 정보들이 포함되어 있다.

The new expense report format (주어) **was** (동사) simple and accurate.
새로운 비용 보고서 형태는 단순하고 정확했다.

02 | 주어와 동사의 수를 일치시킨다.

Our new products (복수주어) **are** (복수동사) currently available on the market.
우리의 신상품들을 현재 시장에서 이용하실 수 있습니다.

Tom and his friends (복수주어) **visit** (복수동사) their parents regularly.
Tom과 그의 친구들은 그들의 부모들을 정기적으로 방문한다.

03 | 주어와 동사 사이의 수식어를 구별해야 한다.

His report (on the company's current status) **was** highly regarded.
(회사의 현 상태에 대한) 그의 보고서는 높은 평가를 받았다.

The technician (with whom I work) **is** very skillful.
(나와 함께 일하는) 기술자는 매우 솜씨가 좋다.

04 | 주어가 생략된 명령문과 조동사 뒤의 동사는 원형을 사용한다.

Please **accept** our apology for the late delivery of your order.
귀하의 주문 배달이 늦어진 점에 대해 저희 사과를 받아 주세요.

You **may request** a refund or a replacement for any damaged item.
파손된 물건에 대해 환불이나 교환을 요구하실 수 있습니다.

POINT 1 주어와 동사의 수 일치

01 | 단수주어+단수동사

1) 단수명사+단수동사

Our Web site [provides / ~~provide~~] you with information about hotels and transportation.
저희 웹 사이트는 여러분께 호텔과 교통에 대한 정보를 제공해 드립니다.

2) 3인칭 단수 인칭대명사(he/she/it)+단수동사

She [is / ~~are~~] a special customer who is allowed to give her orders directly to our manufacturer.
그녀는 우리의 제조공장으로 직접 주문하는 것이 허락된 특별 고객이다.

3) 동명사+단수동사

Limiting the use of the air-conditioning system in the office [reduces / ~~reduce~~] the morale of employees. 사무실에서 냉방 시스템의 사용을 제한하는 것은 직원들의 사기를 감소시킨다.

4) to부정사+단수동사

To meet the deadline for an assigned project [is / ~~are~~] a basic obligation of an office worker.
지정된 프로젝트의 마감일을 맞추는 것은 직장인의 기본적인 의무이다.

5) 명사절+단수동사

What I heard on the news [was / ~~were~~] about a new medical breakthrough.
뉴스에서 내가 들은 것은 의학의 새로운 발전에 관한 것이었다.

02 | 복수주어+복수동사

1) 복수명사+복수동사

Invitations to the workshop [have / ~~has~~] **been sent** to all department supervisors.
워크숍의 초대장이 모든 부서장들에게 보내졌다.

2) 복수 인칭대명사(you/we/they)+복수동사

They [have / ~~has~~] agreed to come to the office to conduct special classes.
그들은 특별 수업을 위해 사무실로 오는 것에 동의했다.

3) 복수 대명사(many 많은 사람들, few 소수, both 둘 다)+복수동사

Many (people) [hesitate / ~~hesitates~~] to book flights in other countries because of communication problems. 많은 사람들이 의사소통 문제 때문에 다른 나라 항공편을 예약하는 것을 망설인다.

SPARTA ☑ Check-UP! 1

해설 p. 344

1 Application forms for the training seminar ------- to be submitted to the Personnel Department by the end of next month.
(A) need
(B) needs
(C) to need
(D) needing

2 ------- advise companies to allocate costs for consumer security and to treat online privacy with the utmost importance.
(A) Analysis
(B) Analyze
(C) Analyst
(D) Analysts

3 The customer service center should give written notice to customers within 15 days of the date the ------- is received.
(A) complaint
(B) complain
(C) complains
(D) complaining

POINT ❷ 단수 수량표현 주어의 수 일치

01 | every/each+단수명사+단수동사

Every employee [has / ~~have~~] the right to receive at least one month's notice of dismissal.
모든 직원은 해고 통보를 최소 한 달 전에 받을 권리가 있다.

Each office in the building [is / ~~are~~] equipped with a radio system.
건물 내 각 사무실은 라디오 시스템을 구비하고 있다.

02 | one/each+of the+복수명사+단수동사

One of the most important factors in achieving success at any company [is / ~~are~~] having team spirit. 어떤 회사에서든 성공을 이루는 데 가장 중요한 요소 중 하나는 협동심을 갖는 것이다.

03 | the number of+복수명사+단수동사

The number of freelance journalists [has / ~~have~~] increased rapidly in recent years.
프리랜서 기자들의 수가 최근 몇 년간 급속히 증가했다.

04 | 부정대명사+단수동사

anybody	everybody	nobody	somebody	+단수동사
anyone	everyone	no one / none	someone	
anything	everything	nothing	something	

No one from the Marketing Department [was / ~~were~~] able to attend the meeting this morning.
마케팅 부서에서는 아무도 오늘 아침 회의에 참석할 수 없었다.

Before reversing your vehicle, please be certain that **nothing** [obstructs / ~~obstruct~~] your view.
당신의 차량을 후진하기 전에, 반드시 아무것도 당신의 시야를 가리지 않도록 하세요.

SPARTA Check-UP! 2

해설 p. 344

1 Each of my colleagues ------- over 5 years of experience in computer systems and architectural design.
(A) has
(B) had
(C) have
(D) having

2 A free bicycle lock is available to anyone who ------- our bike before July 1.
(A) purchase
(B) purchaser
(C) purchases
(D) purchasing

3 Everyone in the company ------- that an opportunity like this doesn't come along very often.
(A) realizing
(B) realize
(C) realizes
(D) realization

POINT 3 복수 수량표현 주어의 수 일치

01 | a series of/a variety of/a group of/a range of/several (of)+복수명사+복수동사

A series of lectures [are / ~~is~~] taking place on February 5 at Morristown Community College.
일련의 강의들이 2월 5일 Morristown Town Community College에서 열린다.

A variety of small businesses [are / ~~is~~] making successful changes to computerized accounting systems. 여러 중소기업들이 전산화된 회계 시스템으로 성공적으로 전환하고 있다.

A group of inspectors [report / ~~reports~~] on the local factory conditions to the government once a year. 조사단은 지역의 공장 상태를 일 년에 한 번씩 정부에 보고한다.

02 | -(e)s가 붙지 않는 복수명사+복수동사

People who [have / ~~has~~] high-blood pressure should get a doctor's permission before starting an exercise regimen. 고혈압이 있는 사람들은 운동 요법을 시작하기 전에 의사의 허락을 받아야 한다.

Children [are / ~~is~~] admitted into the stadium only when accompanied by a paying adult.
아이들은 비용을 지불하는 성인과 동반될 때만 경기장에 입장이 허용된다.

+TIP 회사 이름 등의 고유명사는 복수형이더라도 단수형 동사를 써야 한다.

영어로 된 회사명은 복수형으로 표시되는 경우가 많다. 예를 들어 Adams & Associates, Wesson Broders 등인데, 자세히 보면 대문자로 시작됨을 알 수 있다. 이와 같이 고유명사 주어가 오면 동사는 단수형을 써야 한다.

Western Enterprises [has / ~~have~~] announced that it will hire 100 people over the next three months. Western Enterprises 사는 앞으로 3개월 기간에 걸쳐 100명을 채용하겠다고 발표했다.

03 | a number of+복수명사+복수동사

A number of milk producers [are / ~~is~~] against lowering the costs of milk production.
많은 우유 생산업자들이 우유 생산 비용을 낮추는 것에 맞서고 있다.

SPARTA Check-UP! 3

해설 p. 345

1 Only a small group of medical professionals in the country truly ------- how to diagnose and treat autism.
(A) known
(B) knows
(C) know
(D) knowing

2 Even though the neighborhood looks small in size, a variety of businesses ------- interspersed throughout the area.
(A) is
(B) are
(C) will
(D) can

3 Solomon Brothers ------- a great reputation as a quality auto-service provider.
(A) enjoying
(B) enjoys
(C) to enjoy
(D) enjoy

POINT 4 그 밖에 수 일치

01 | 상관접속사의 수 일치

either A or B	동사는 B와 수 일치	both A and B	동사는 반드시 복수동사
neither A nor B	동사는 B와 수 일치	not A but B	동사는 B와 수 일치
not only A but also B	동사는 B와 수 일치	B as well as A	동사는 B와 수 일치

Neither Mr. Chang nor his co-workers [have / ~~has~~] heard about the notice.
Chang 씨와 그의 동료들 모두 그 통보를 듣지 못했다.

Rising oil prices **as well as the unstable stock market** [are / ~~is~~] the main reason for the global recession. 불안정한 주식 시장뿐만 아니라 오르고 있는 유가는 세계 경기침체의 주요 원인이다.

02 | A and B+복수동사 / each and every+단수명사+단수동사

Mr. Jackson and Ms. Ciccone [were / ~~was~~] invited to a luncheon.
Jackson 씨와 Ciccone 씨는 오찬에 초대 받았다.

Each and every job application [was / ~~were~~] reviewed with careful consideration.
모든 채용 지원서는 신중하게 고려하여 검토되었다.

03 | There is[was/has been]+단수명사 (주어) / There are[were/have been]+복수명사 (주어)

There [are / ~~is~~] **five clerical support workers** in the field office.
그 현장 사무소에는 5명의 사무지원 직원들이 있다.

+TIP 부분이나 전체를 나타내는 표현은 of 뒤의 명사에 수 일치 시킨다.

all 모든 most 대부분 half 부분 any 어떤 ~이든지 a lot(lots) 많은 some 몇몇의 the rest 나머지 the majority 과반수의 숫자+percent 몇 퍼센트	of the/소유격	+단수명사+단수동사 +복수명사+복수동사

All of the employees [are / ~~is~~] encouraged to attend the workshop on Sunday.
모든 직원들은 일요일에 있는 워크숍에 참석하도록 권장된다.

SPARTA Check-UP! 4

해설 p. 345

1 The manager together with twenty workers ------- care of all of the orders incoming from overseas by e-mail.
(A) take
(B) to take
(C) taken
(D) takes

2 At the city's children's hospital, either the doctor or the nurses ------- overnight at least three times a week.
(A) works
(B) working
(C) to work
(D) work

3 There ------- several new lamp posts installed along the freeway, which has always been an accident-prone area.
(A) its
(B) is
(C) was
(D) were

PRACTICE

해설 p. 345

▪ 괄호 안의 보기 중 알맞은 단어를 고르세요.

1 Powell Electronics **[does / do]** not offer refunds on products returned without the original receipts.

2 Accounting figures completed by Morgan Stanley Co. **[is / are]** expected to be available soon.

3 The furniture that you ordered **[is / are]** scheduled to be delivered on May 11.

4 Savings **[bank / banks]** across the country have begun to recover from the economic downturn.

5 He was hired by a law firm that **[specialize / specializes]** in business disputes.

6 The number of new employees who **[require / requires]** extensive training has declined.

7 A variety of responsibilities, including managing budgets, **[have / has]** been given to the manager.

8 The number of doctors hired by Central Hospital **[is / are]** relatively small.

9 A number of employees **[is / are]** interested in attending the securities trading seminar.

10 The electric company, along with several other energy providers, **[is / are]** lowering its rates.

11 The team manager together with coworkers **[work / works]** overtime every day.

12 A letter containing the schedule for the annual summer events **[are sent / will be sent]** to the new supervisor.

13 To prepare for its expansion plans, the electronics company has recruited employees from several of its **[competitor / competitors]**.

14 With Mr. Temple in charge of Highlander Asset Management, many **[predicts / predict]** the firm will focus on the debt side of the business.

15 Membership in the DK Club includes a range of **[benefit / benefits]** such as use of sports facilities and member discounts on meals at the club's award-winning restaurants.

SPARTA ACTUAL TEST

1 Discount ------- for Thursday evening's jazz concert are available in Ms. Klein's office.

(A) ticket (B) tickets
(C) ticketing (D) ticketed

2 The weather ------- expects rain this afternoon, so the cancer foundation has decided to postpone its fundraiser.

(A) forecast (B) forecasts
(C) to forecast (D) will forecast

3 Timely completion of next month's marketing proposals ------- clear communication between the marketing staff and sales personnel.

(A) require (B) requires
(C) requiring (D) to require

4 The use of disposable items such as paper bags and diapers ------- to be reduced for the sake of the environment.

(A) have (B) has
(C) having (D) been

5 Drivers are reminded that parking ------- for visitors are limited to the green-colored areas.

(A) space (B) spaces
(C) special (D) specialized

6 ------- who wish to reschedule an appointment should contact our receptionist by this afternoon.

(A) Those (B) Anyone
(C) Yourself (D) They

7 The firm's new human resources policy ------- employees from transferring to another position if they are not performing well in their current role.

(A) restricts (B) restricting
(C) restrict (D) was restricted

8 Managers of the nuclear power plant ------- to be notified ahead of time by the plant's safety inspector in case any suspicious signs are detected.

(A) expect (B) expecting
(C) expectation (D) expects

9 Recreational facilities within walking distance of the Luxor Hotel ------- a swimming pool and a spacious park with picnic tables.

(A) include (B) is including
(C) including (D) includes

10 Each of the employees ------- to providing the highest level of service to our customers.

(A) is dedicated (B) dedicate
(C) to dedicate (D) dedicating

11 Copies of personal information ------- not distributed to the staff without prior authorization.

(A) are (B) is
(C) was (D) being

12 The news that savings banks across the country have already begun to recover from the long economic recession ------- many companies to increase investments.

(A) encourages (B) encourage
(C) encouragement (D) encouraging

해설 p. 346

Questions 13-16 refer to the following letter.

Customer Service
Correia Appliances
32 Juan Avenue
Fairfield, Australia

Dear Customer Service:

I recently ordered a digital camera from your online shop. But when I received it yesterday, I found that there were small cracks on the lenses as well as scratches on the viewing screen. According to your Web site, your company ------- (13.) items in the best possible condition. If there are any faults with an item, it will be replaced with a new one. -------, (14.) I request an immediate exchange of this item for another.

The maker is MacCom, and the model number is I-3935. I have attached the invoice. Please send the new item to the address ------- (15.) on it. Since I'm returning a defective item, I expect you to cover the shipping charges. -------. (16.)

Please pay immediate attention to my request.

Thanks very much.

Sincerely,

Ketan Chauhan

13 (A) deliver
(B) delivery
(C) deliverable
(D) delivers

14 (A) In addition
(B) Therefore
(C) However
(D) Instead

15 (A) writing
(B) written
(C) wrote
(D) write

16 (A) I hope to receive the new item as soon as possible.
(B) I am quite satisfied with this recent incident.
(C) Please call Mirah Rahman at Customer Service for more information.
(D) To apply for a Gold card, call the company's customer service hotline at 1-800-555-3266.

UNIT 08 태

능동태와 수동태를 구분하는 유형의 문제는 매월 1~2문제, 동사와의 결합 형태를 포함하면 4문제 정도 출제된다. 주어가 수동적 입장이면 수동태를 써야 하고, 자동사는 수동태가 불가능하다는 점이 출제 대상이 된다.

Preview

01 | 능동태의 목적어가 수동태의 주어가 된다.

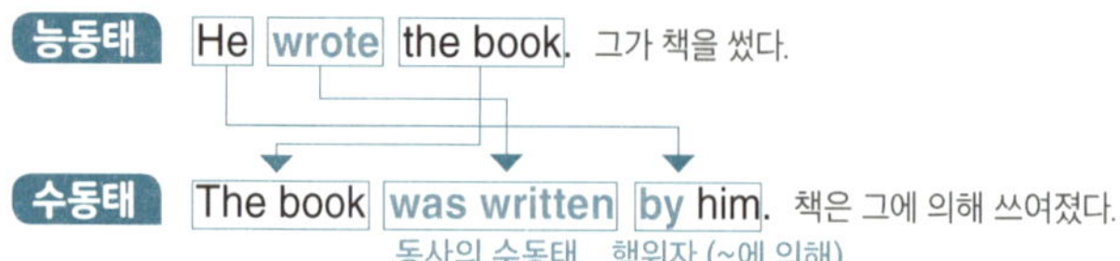

능동태 He wrote the book. 그가 책을 썼다.
수동태 The book was written by him. 책은 그에 의해 쓰여졌다.
동사의 수동태
행위자 (~에 의해)

능동태를 수동태로 바꾸는 3단계

❶ 능동태의 목적어(the book)를 수동태의 주어로 보낸다.

❷ 능동태의 동사(wrote)를 <be+p.p.>인 was written으로 바꾼다.

❸ 능동태의 주어(He)를 <by+목적격>에 맞게 by him으로 바꾼다.

02 | 수동태의 시제와 형태

시제	능동태	수동태
현재시제	현재동사	am[is/are]+p.p.
과거시제	과거동사	was[were]+p.p.
미래시제	will+동사원형	will+be+p.p.
진행시제	be+-ing	be+being+p.p.
완료시제	have[has]+p.p.	have[has]+been+p.p.
조동사(may, can, should 등)	조동사+동사원형	조동사+be+p.p.

The reports **are checked** by experienced technicians. 보고서들은 경험이 많은 기술자들에 의해 확인된다.

The sales meeting **will be held** next week. 영업 회의가 다음 주에 열리게 될 것이다.

03 | 자동사는 목적어를 취하지 못하므로 수동태로 쓸 수 없다.

Unemployment [**has risen** / ~~has been risen~~] by 30,000 this year. 실업자 수가 올해 3만 명이나 늘었다.

The financial briefing [**will begin** / ~~will be begin~~] at 10 A.M. on Thursday.
재무 브리핑은 목요일 오전 10시에 시작될 것입니다.

POINT 1 목적어가 있는 능동태

01 | 조동사의 능동태 : 조동사+동사원형+목적어

All staff members **should** [use / ~~be used~~] **the employee parking lot** at the rear of the building.
모든 직원들은 건물의 뒤쪽에 있는 직원 전용 주차장을 사용하셔야 합니다.

If we receive the related documents, we **will** [process / ~~be processed~~] **your application**.
관련 서류를 받으면 저희는 귀하의 신청서를 처리할 것입니다.

02 | 진행시제의 능동태 : be동사+현재분사(-ing)+목적어

Mr. Parkman [is making / ~~is made~~] **a purchase contract** for a new order of supplies.
Parkman 씨는 새로운 물품 주문을 위한 구매 계약서를 작성하고 있다.

When I visited him, Mr. Wilson [was interviewing / ~~was interviewed~~] **applicants**.
내가 방문했을 때 Wilson 씨는 지원자들 면접을 보고 있었다.

03 | 완료시제의 능동태 : have+p.p.+목적어

Residents of the Leeds area [have proposed / ~~have been proposed~~] **developing** a lot that has been unused for many years.
Leeds 지역의 주민들은 수년간 사용되지 않았던 부지를 개발할 것을 제안했다.

Since being employed a year ago, Ms. Andy [has impressed / ~~has been impressed~~] **her supervisors** by her faithfulness.
일 년 전에 고용된 이래로, Andy 씨는 성실성으로 그녀의 상사들을 감명시켜 왔다.

04 | to부정사의 능동태 : to+동사원형+목적어

It is necessary for all participants at the seminar to [complete / ~~be completed~~] **the evaluation form.** 세미나의 모든 참석자들은 평가서 작성을 마쳐야 한다.

The Thai restaurant **has decided** to [add / ~~be added~~] **several new items** to its already popular breakfast menu.
그 태국 식당은 이미 인기 있는 아침 메뉴에 몇몇 새로운 항목들을 추가하기로 결정했다.

SPARTA Check-UP! 1

| 해설 p. 347

1 The personnel manager ------- company policies to the new members of the staff.
(A) explaining
(B) are being explained
(C) had been explained
(D) explained

2 The staff will ------- the unused equipment and either dispose of it or donate it to charity.
(A) collecting
(B) collect
(C) collection
(D) be collected

3 Charlotte Foods ------- yesterday that it will release many new items in the coming year.
(A) announcing
(B) is announced
(C) announced
(D) have announced

POINT 2 목적어가 없는 수동태

01 | 조동사의 수동태 : 조동사+be+p.p. (+전치사구)

The order form **should** [be submitted / ~~submit~~] to the office to process your order.
당신의 주문을 처리하기 위해서 주문서가 사무실로 제출되어야 한다.

The air conditioner **will** [be delivered / ~~deliver~~] to your office no later than tomorrow.
에어컨은 늦어도 내일까지 당신의 사무실로 배달될 것이다.

02 | 진행시제의 수동태 : be동사+being+p.p. (+전치사구)

Low interest rates [are being offered / ~~are offering~~] by credit card companies.
낮은 이자율이 신용 카드 회사에 의해 제공되고 있다.

03 | 완료시제의 수동태 : have 동사+been+p.p. (+전치사구)

The employment contract form [has been approved / ~~has approved~~] by the Rockland County Association. 고용 계약서가 Rockland County 협회에 의해 승인되었다.

04 | to부정사의 수동태 : to be+p.p. (+전치사구)

The hiring director expects the résumés of the applicants **to** [be submitted / ~~submit~~] by the end of this month. 채용 담당이사는 지원자들의 이력서가 이달 말까지 제출되기를 바란다.

+ VOCABULARY | 수동태로 사용할 수 없는 자동사

exist 존재하다	happen(= occur) 일어나다	take place 개최되다, 일어나다	expire 만기가 되다
proceed 나아가다	talk 말하다	arrive 도착하다	wait 기다리다
rise 오르다	decline 감소하다	function 작동하다	travel 여행하다
remain 남다, 머무르다	consist 구성되다	participate 참여하다	respond 대답하다
react 반응하다	reply 대답하다	succeed 성공하다	specialize 전문으로 하다
stay 머무르다	work 효과가 있다	emerge 출현하다	last 지속되다

+TIP <자동사+전치사>가 하나의 의미 단위를 나타내는 타동사구가 되면 수동태로 표현할 수 있다.

deal은 자동사이지만 deal with은 타동사구가 되어 '~을 다루다'라는 의미가 된다. 이런 타동사구에는 comply with / fill in(out) / carry out / refer to 등이 있다. (p.82 참조)

능동태 **He** will deal with **the problem** as soon as possible. 그는 조속히 문제를 해결할 것이다.

수동태 **The problem** will be dealt with as soon as possible **by him**. 문제는 그에 의해 조속히 해결될 것이다.

SPARTA Check-UP! 2

| 해설 p. 347

1 All orders for office supplies must be ------- to Ms. Weaton before 6 P.M. in order to receive the products the following day.
(A) submitting
(B) submitted
(C) submit
(D) submission

2 The parameters of the project have to be completely ------- because we now have less time, money, and personnel.
(A) revised
(B) revising
(C) revise
(D) revises

3 The payment of the most recent shipment is due and must ------- within a week.
(A) received
(B) to receive
(C) receive
(D) be received

✎ POINT ③ 4·5 형식의 수동태

01 | 두 개의 목적어를 갖는 4형식 동사는 수동태 뒤에도 목적어가 올 수 있다.

능동태 The Plaza Hotel [sent / ~~was sent~~] **Mr. Ibsen a check for $2,000 dated June 12**.
Plaza 호텔에서 6월 12일 날짜로, 2,000달러에 해당하는 수표를 Ibsen 씨에게 보냈다.

수동태 **Mr. Ibsen** [was sent / ~~was sending~~] **a check for $2,000 dated June 12**.
Ibsen 씨는 6월 12일 날짜로 2,000달러에 해당하는 수표를 받았다.

수동태 **A check for $2,000 dated June 12** [was sent / ~~sent~~] to **Mr. Ibsen**.
6월 12일 날짜로 2,000달러에 해당하는 수표가 Ibsen 씨에게 보내졌다.

02 | 5형식 동사의 수동태는 수동태 뒤에 목적격 보어가 온다.

1) 목적격 보어에 명사가 오는 경우의 수동태

능동태 Many people [consider / ~~are considered~~] the Crop Boutique **the most renowned souvenir shop** in the area. 많은 사람들이 Crop Boutique를 그 지역에서 가장 유명한 기념품 가게라고 여긴다.

수동태 The Crop Boutique [is considered / ~~considers~~] **the most renowned souvenir shop** in the area (by many people). Crop Boutique는 지역에서 가장 유명한 기념품 가게로 여겨진다.

▶ 수동태 <be+p.p.> 뒤에 명사가 남는 경우, 이 명사를 목적어로 착각하지 않도록 주의해야 한다.

2) 목적격 보어에 to부정사가 오는 경우의 수동태

능동태 We [asked / ~~were asked~~] all of the employees **to comply** with the new regulations.
우리는 모든 직원들에게 새로운 규정을 따를 것을 요구했다.

수동태 All of the employees [were asked / ~~asked~~] **to comply** with the new regulations (by us).
모든 직원들은 새 규정을 따를 것을 요청 받았다.

▶ '주어+동사+목적어+to부정사'의 구조를 갖는 동사들은 수동태가 되면 '주어+be p.p.+to부정사'의 구조를 갖게 된다.

+ VOCABULARY | be p.p.+to부정사 빈출표현

be asked to ~하라고 요청 받다
be required to ~하라고 요구 받다
be expected to ~하도록 기대되다
be allowed to ~하도록 허용되다
be reminded to ~하라는 말을 듣다
be advised to ~하라는 충고를 듣다
be intended to ~을 위한 목적이다
be encouraged to ~하라고 권고 받다

SPARTA ☑ Check-UP! ③

해설 p. 348

1 Our clients ------- given access to all of the appropriate information needed for them to make the best decisions possible.
(A) is
(B) have
(C) are
(D) being

2 All visitors ------- to report to the main college reception area in the new red-brick Millennium Building.
(A) asks
(B) asking
(C) is asking
(D) are asked

3 Employees are ------- to call Mr. Tomson in the Personnel Department a day in advance if they want to call in sick.
(A) requiring
(B) requirement
(C) required
(D) requires

POINT 4 다양한 전치사를 쓰는 수동태 표현

01 | by 이외의 전치사를 쓰는 수동태

We **are dedicated** [to / ~~by~~] helping young entrepreneurs find success in business.
우리는 젊은 사업가들이 사업에 성공할 수 있도록 도와주는 데 전념한다.

+ VOCABULARY | be+p.p.+전치사 빈출표현

be satisfied with ~에 만족하다
be pleased with ~을 기뻐하다
be equipped with ~을 갖추고 있다
be associated with ~와 관련되다
be surprised at ~에 놀라다
be disappointed at ~에 실망하다
be shocked at ~에 충격을 받다
be known as ~으로 알려지다 (자격)
be known for ~으로 유명하다 (이유)
be related to ~와 관계가 있다
be dedicated to ~에 헌신하다, 전념하다
be devoted to ~에 헌신하다
be worried about ~을 걱정하다
be interested in ~에 관심이 있다
be involved in ~에 관여하다
be based on ~에 근거하다
be composed of ~로 구성되다
be filled with ~로 가득 차다

02 | 자동사+전치사의 수동태

능동태	수동태	능동태	수동태
deal with ~을 처리하다	be dealt with ~이 처리되다	carry out ~을 수행하다	be carried out ~이 수행되다
put off ~을 연기하다	be put off ~이 연기되다	fill in ~을 작성하다	be filled in ~이 작성되다
enroll in ~에 등록하다	be enrolled in ~에 등록되다	pay for ~을 지불하다	be paid for ~이 지불되다

능동태 Due to a scheduling conflict, we [put off / ~~were put off~~] the board meeting until next week.
일정이 겹쳐서 우리는 이사 회의를 다음 주로 연기했다.

수동태 Due to a scheduling conflict, the board meeting was [put off / ~~putting off~~] until next week.
일정이 겹쳐서 이사 회의가 다음 주로 연기되었다.

SPARTA Check-UP! 4

| 해설 p. 348

1 Industrial psychologists in the United States have become increasingly involved ------- the issue of flight safety.
(A) in
(B) with
(C) from
(D) by

2 It has been reported that HR Mortgage is closely ------- with the bank, which is under investigation.
(A) associate
(B) associating
(C) associates
(D) associated

3 Any employees who are ------- in attending the business workshops should contact Mr. Besson, who is the chief of the Personnel Department.
(A) enclosed
(B) interested
(C) hopeful
(D) listed

해설 p. 348

▪ 괄호 안의 보기 중 알맞은 단어를 고르세요.

1 To be a member, you have to **[recommend / be recommended]** by a current club member.

2 Contrary to our expectations, the unemployment rate **[has / was]** risen three quarters in a row.

3 We **[pleased / are pleased]** to receive your letter answering our advertisement for electric heaters and have enclosed with this letter a copy of our latest catalog.

4 All employees are strongly **[encouraging / encouraged]** to familiarize themselves with the new procedures manual as soon as they can.

5 Fortunately, it was not yet too late to correct the mistake before the price list **[sent / was sent]** out.

6 All candidates are **[planning / planned]** to attend the orientation session, which will begin at 8 A.M. on Monday with a catered continental breakfast.

7 A social event for residents of the community will **[take / be taken]** place Friday afternoon in our spacious activity room.

8 The Hannel Banquet Hall **[has reserved / has been reserved]** for the September 12 employee appreciation dinner.

9 Now that the capacity of the main memory storage of our computers **[is enhancing / has been enhanced]**, we expect a 15% increase in sales.

10 Once we heard that the departing flight would **[delay / be delayed]** for several hours, we exercised by walking around the baggage claim area.

11 He **[hired / was hired]** by Advance Data Technology, Inc., but the firm went bankrupt early in December, leaving him jobless.

12 The general manager was quite impressed when he **[saw / was seen]** the improved production at the assembly lines.

13 One of the biggest complaints we received from our survey **[was / has]** that customers do not like to wait for their deliveries.

14 Product competitiveness is the most important aspect that the Sales Department **[is concentrated / has been concentrating]** its attention on in recent months.

15 If Mr. Lee **[applies / is applied]** for the job at the accounting firm, he is likely to get it because he is well-qualified.

1 All user's manuals must be ------- in order to make sure customers understand how to use the device.

(A) format (B) formatted
(C) formatting (D) formats

2 All new employees should be ------- to show their driver's licence and social security card to the director of Human Resources as proof of citizenship.

(A) prepare (B) preparation
(C) prepared (D) prepares

3 Under the new plan, a total of 3.5 million square meters of land ------- for the construction of universities.

(A) reserves
(B) was reserving
(C) to be reserved
(D) has been reserved

4 Hardwood for furniture production must be ------- two months in advance in order to arrive at the factory in time.

(A) order (B) ordering
(C) ordered (D) orders

5 If you are a new employee, you will be ------- for an ID card, which will include your name, photo, and ID number.

(A) photographs (B) photograph
(C) photography (D) photographed

6 Surprisingly, the patient ------- from the hospital after only two hours without receiving proper treatment.

(A) released (B) releasing
(C) was released (D) has release

7 The annual report should ------- to the manager of the Sales Department by e-mail tomorrow morning.

(A) send (B) sent
(C) be sent (D) to send

8 Until the new rechargeable battery ------- in the electric car, please keep driving the minimum speed limit.

(A) were installing
(B) would be installing
(C) to be installed
(D) has been installed

9 Once the Internet laws and regulations -------, there will be a noticeable decrease in cyber crimes, and online users will be more aware of netiquette.

(A) are approved (B) has approved
(C) approved (D) will approve

10 Financial analysts at Face to Face Holdings in Chicago ------- the effects on shareholder value when a company sells parts of its assets.

(A) researches (B) have researched
(C) researching (D) will be researched

11 Dr. Orenstein ------- to join the newly established economic planning council and accepted the offer without hesitation.

(A) was invited (B) invited
(C) inviting (D) had invited

12 Thousands of commuters must use alternative routes into and out of town while the tunnel -------.

(A) repairs (B) is repairing
(C) has repaired (D) is being repaired

Questions 13-16 refer to the following announcement.

To: All employees
Subject: Security Upgrades

Edmonton-Hewitt is ------- working on updating our entire security system.
13.
As one of the steps to make our system better, we will be creating new identification cards for all employees. -------.
14.

Next Monday, all employees should receive their new identification cards from the security manager, Ted Hargraves. The system is ------- on the following day of distribution.
15.

-------, as our system gradually changes over to the new system, you should be aware that some
16.
problems could arise. If you notice any such issues or have any concerns about the transition, please visit the security office on the third floor.

13 (A) currently
(B) recently
(C) previously
(D) shortly

14 (A) However, these machines often malfunctioned as they were quite old and out of date.
(B) All employees are assigned a staff identification number on their first day of work.
(C) As of October 4th, your current cards will no longer be usable at any place in the building.
(D) Badges must be worn at all times while in the building from now on.

15 (A) servicing
(B) to be serviced
(C) will service
(D) being servicing

16 (A) However
(B) Likewise
(C) Indeed
(D) Since

UNIT 09 시제

시제 문제는 매월 평균 Part 5에서 1~2문제, Part 6에서 1~2문제로 총 3~4문제가 출제된다. Part 5에서는 시제와 다른 문법(태, 수 일치)을 동시에 묻는 유형이 출제되며, Part 6에서는 문맥상 적절한 시제를 선택하는 문제가 출제된다. 기본 시제별 개념 및 특정 시제와 어울려 쓰이는 시간부사를 익히도록 한다.

Preview

01 | 영어의 기본 12시제

시제	현재	과거	미래
단순	I **live** in Korea.	I **lived** in Korea.	I **will live** in Korea.
진행	I **am living** in Korea.	I **was living** in Korea.	I **will be living** in Korea.
완료	I **have lived** in Korea.	I **had lived** in Korea.	I **will have lived** in Korea.
완료진행	I **have been living** in Korea.	I **had been living** in Korea.	I **will have been living** in Korea.

02 | 각 시제와 어울리는 시간 부사구

현재	always 항상 frequently/often 자주 usually 보통 every/each+시점 매~, ~마다
과거	once 한때 last+시간 지난 ~ 시간+ago ~전에 after+과거 ~한 후에 yesterday 어제
미래	next+시간 다음 ~에 as of+시간 ~부로 tomorrow 내일 in the future 미래에
현재완료	over/in/for/during+the past+기간 지난 ~동안 since+과거시점 ~한 이후에 so far 지금까지

현재시제 The meeting **is** usually **held** on the last Saturday of every month.
(usually: 현재시제 단서)
모임은 보통 매달 마지막 토요일에 열린다.

과거시제 Mr. Kim **joined** the firm as a public relations manager two years ago.
(two years ago: 과거시제 단서)
Kim 씨는 2년 전 회사에 홍보부장으로 입사했다.

미래시제 The secretary **will write** the details of the meeting tomorrow.
(tomorrow: 미래시제 단서)
비서가 내일 있을 회의에 대한 세부 사항을 적을 것이다.

현재완료 The Morgan Company **has provided** office supplies for 10 years.
(for 10 years: 현재완료시제 단서)
Morgan 사는 10년 동안 사무용품을 제공해 오고 있다.

과거완료 When I arrived, the annual conference **had finished**.
(When I arrived: 과거완료시제 단서)
내가 도착했을 때, 연례 회의는 끝난 후였다.

POINT 1 단순시제 : 과거/현재/미래

01 | 현재시제는 일반적인 사실 또는 습관이나 반복되는 행위를 나타낸다.

Mr. O'Connel **always** [forgets / ~~forgot~~] what he's going to say halfway through his presentation.
O'Connel 씨는 항상 그의 발표 도중 말하려는 것을 잊어버린다.

Staff members in the PT Office Tower **usually** [eat / ~~are eating~~] lunch in the outdoor area.
PT Office Tower에서 근무하는 직원들은 보통 밖에서 점심을 먹는다.

• 정답의 단서가 되는 현재 시간부사

always 항상 frequently/often 자주 usually 보통 generally 일반적으로 regularly 정기적으로

+TIP 시간이나 조건 부사절에서는 현재가 미래를 대신한다.

시간 접속사 (as soon as, after, before, when, until ...)
조건 접속사 (if, unless, in case, once ...)
+주어+동사(현재) ~, 주어+동사(미래)

If your application [arrives / ~~will arrive~~] after the deadline, it will not be considered.
당신의 지원서가 마감 날짜 이후에 도착하면 지원서는 고려되지 않을 것입니다.

02 | 과거시제는 과거에 일어난 사실을 나타낸다.

The salesman [demonstrated / ~~has demonstrated~~] the amazing features of the newly released cellphone **yesterday**. 판매원은 어제 새로 출시된 휴대폰의 놀라운 특성들의 시범을 보였다.

• 정답의 단서가 되는 과거 시간부사(구)

yesterday 어제 ~ ago ~전에 last 지난 ~에 recently 최근에 in+과거년도 ~년에 previously 이전에

03 | 미래시제는 앞으로 일어날 일을 나타낸다.

The office [will close / ~~closed~~] for the holiday at 4:30 P.M. tomorrow.
휴일이라서 사무실은 내일 오후 4시 30분에 닫을 것이다.

The reception [will begin / ~~will be beginning~~] promptly **after** the conclusion of the awards ceremony. 환영회는 시상식 종료 직후에 시작될 예정이다.

• 정답의 단서가 되는 미래 시간부사(구)

tomorrow 내일 in+기간 (기간) 후에 next 다음 ~에 later+시점 ~말에

SPARTA Check-UP! 1

해설 p. 351

1 It only ------- a few months for large-scale layoffs to seriously impact a company.
(A) has taken
(B) has been taking
(C) takes
(D) is taking

2 The board of directors and management ------- sometime next week to talk about the restoration of the IMK Building.
(A) will convene
(B) convened
(C) to convene
(D) convening

3 The CEO and many other executives recently ------- a one-month tour of their new satellite offices in Europe.
(A) will conduct
(B) to conduct
(C) conducted
(D) conduct

POINT 2 진행 시제 : 과거진행/현재진행/미래진행

01 | 과거진행시제 [was/were+-ing] : 과거의 특정 시점에 진행 중이던 일을 나타낸다.

The director [was attending / ~~attends~~] the conference in Singapore **when the annual sales meeting was held.** 연례 영업 회의가 열렸을 때 부장은 싱가포르에서 총회에 참석하고 있는 중이었다.

02 | 현재진행시제 [am/is/are+-ing] : 현재 진행 중인 일을 나타낸다.

The committee [is considering / ~~considers~~] the feasibility of upgrading the current computer system **now.** 이사회는 현재 컴퓨터 시스템을 업그레이드하는 것에 대한 가능성을 고려 중이다.

• **정답의 단서가 되는 현재진행 시간부사(구)**

now 지금 currently 현재 at the moment (= right now) 바로 지금

+TIP 현재진행시제는 아주 가까운 미래를 나타낼 때도 쓰인다.

Mr. Simmons is leaving for New Zealand **tonight** with a tentative itinerary from Gullivers Travel. Simmons 씨는 Gullivers 여행사에서 받은 임시 여행 일정표를 가지고 오늘 밤 뉴질랜드로 떠날 것이다.

03 | 미래진행시제 [will be+-ing] : 미래에 진행 예정인 일을 나타낸다.

All supervisors at the production facilities [will be attending / ~~were attending~~] safety workshops **next Thursday.** 생산 시설의 모든 감독관들은 다음 주 목요일에 안전 워크숍에 참가하고 있을 것이다.

▶ 미래진행시제는 미래의 특정 순간을 강조하지만 단순미래 시제와 의미 차이는 없다.

04 | 감정이나 상태를 나타내는 동사는 진행형으로 사용할 수 없다.

감정	believe 믿다	prefer 선호하다	like 좋아하다	hate 미워하다	surprise 놀라게 하다
상태	know 알다	include 포함하다	consist 구성되다	seem ~처럼 보이다	exist 존재하다
소유	have 가지다	possess 소지하다	own 소유하다	belong ~에 속하다	

Ms. Yuki [believes / ~~is believing~~] that she will need about $2,000 a month for daily expenses after retirement. Yuki 씨는 은퇴 후 생활비로 한 달에 약 2,000달러가 필요할 것이라고 생각한다.

SPARTA Check-UP! 2

해설 p. 351

1 The product development team ------- the feasibility of new ideas at the moment.
(A) discussing
(B) to discuss
(C) is discussing
(D) discusses

2 We are pleased to announce that Ms. Kate, the new vice president, ------- her position on November 1.
(A) has been starting
(B) will be starting
(C) is started
(D) is being started

3 Mr. Yoon ----- from jet lag when he returned on Friday, so the meeting has been postponed until next week.
(A) suffers
(B) will suffer
(C) will have suffered
(D) was suffering

POINT 3 완료 시제 : 과거완료/현재완료/미래완료

01 | 과거완료시제 [had+p.p.] : 과거의 두 시점 중 더 먼저 일어난 일을 나타낸다.

Before Ms. Kim joined Office Decor, Inc., she [**had worked** / ~~works~~] in the field of interior design for many years already.
Kim 씨가 Office Decor 회사에 입사하기 전에, 그녀는 이미 수년 동안 인테리어 분야에서 일한 경력이 있었다.

02 | 현재완료시제 [have+p.p.] : 과거의 일이 현재까지 지속되거나 현재에 영향을 주는 일, 과거에 시작되어 방금 완료된 일을 나타낸다.

지속 **For the past two years**, Mr. Proctor [**has been** / ~~was~~] the head of the International Department. 지난 2년 동안 Proctor 씨가 국제부 부장이었다.

경험 **Since he graduated from college**, Mr. Lee [**hasn't had** / ~~hadn't had~~] many chances to go skiing. 대학을 졸업한 이래로, Lee 씨는 스키 타러 갈 기회가 많지 않았다.
▶ since가 이끄는 절에는 과거시제(graduated)를, 주절에는 현재완료시제(hasn't had)를 쓴다.

완료 The Fletcher Corporation [**has** / ~~was~~] **recently negotiated** a contract for the exclusive rights to distribute its new software in the city of Brenton.
Fletcher 사는 최근에 브렌튼 시에 그들의 새로운 소프트웨어 유통 독점권을 위한 계약을 성사시켰다.

• 정답의 단서가 되는 현재완료시제 시간부사(구)

for / in / over / during+the past/last+기간 지난 ~동안	recently(= lately) 최근에
since+주어+과거동사 / since+과거시점 ~이래로, 이후로	until now / so far 과거부터 지금까지

03 | 미래완료시제 [will have+p.p.] : 미래의 특정 시점까지 계속되어 그 시점에서 완료되는 일을 나타낸다.

By next May, Mr. Leigh [**will have worked** / ~~will work~~] for the company for ten years.
오는 5월이면 Leigh 씨는 그 회사에서 10년째 근무한 것이 된다.

+TIP By the time과 관련된 시제

By the time + 주어 + 현재시제, 주어 + **will have p.p.** ~할 때쯤, ~일 것이다/~했을 때 ~했을 것이다
By the time + 주어 + 과거시제, 주어 + **had p.p.** ~했을 때, 이미 ~했었다

By the time the technicians solve the computer problems, **several files will have been erased** already. 기술자들이 컴퓨터 문제를 해결했을 즈음엔, 이미 몇 개의 파일들이 지워져 있을 것이다.

SPARTA Check-UP! 3

해설 p. 351

1 Many employees at Central Waste Removal ------- an important part of the service industry in this community for the last ten years.
(A) will be
(B) shall be
(C) are
(D) have been

2 Before the workers arrived at the construction site, the materials -------.
(A) are disappearing
(B) will have disappeared
(C) disappear
(D) had disappeared

3 By the time the Town Village Center store opens, hundred of customers ------- for store membership cards.
(A) will have signed up
(B) will be signed up
(C) signed up
(D) sign up

POINT 4 동사원형을 쓰는 경우

01 | 주장·요구·명령·제안 동사+that+주어+(should)+동사원형

주장, 명령, 제안, 요구 등의 동사가 주절에 쓰였을 때는 that절의 동사는 <(should)+동사원형>의 형태로 나타낸다.

의미	동사	구조 *당위성을 나타냄
주장	insist / maintain / assert / urge	+that+S+(should)+[not]+동사원형
요구	require / request / ask / demand	
명령	order / command	
제안	suggest / recommend / propose	
기타	(충고의) advise / (결정의) decide	

The chief engineer **insists that** the brake system (**should**) [**be redesigned** / ~~is redesigned~~].
수석 엔지니어는 브레이크를 재설계해야 한다고 주장한다.

+TIP 당위성 구조임에도 that 절의 동사가 동사원형이 되지 않는 경우

The report **suggests that** the company's revenue **has fallen** over the last five years.
보고서는 회사의 수익이 지난 5년 동안 하락했음을 시사한다.

▶ 동사가 suggest인데 that절의 동사는 동사원형으로 쓰지 않았다. that절이 '주어가 ~해야 한다'는 의미일 때만 that절의 동사를 원형으로 쓸 수 있다. 여기서 suggest는 '제안하다'가 아닌 '시사하다'라는 뜻을 나타낸다.

02 | It is[was]+이성적 판단의 형용사+that+주어+(should)+동사원형

가주어 진주어로 이루어진 구문<It is[was]+형용사 that S+V>에서 형용사가 '의무'를 나타낼 때 that 절의 동사는 <(should)+동사원형>의 형태로 나타낸다.

구조	이성적 판단의 형용사	구조
It is[was]	important / crucial (중요한)	+that+S+(should)+[not]+동사원형
	imperative / necessary / essential	

It is imperative that Ms. Swanson (**should**) [**contact** / ~~is contacting~~] us by the end of the day.
Swanson 씨는 퇴근 시간까지 우리에게 반드시 연락해야 한다.

SPARTA ☑ Check-UP! 4

해설 p. 351

1 Mr. Raymond wasn't able to attend the annual staff meeting and requested that the minutes ------- to his office.
(A) send
(B) be sent
(C) had sent
(D) has been sent

2 It is ------- that every applicant submit a résumé promptly to the Human Resources Department.
(A) necessity
(B) necessitate
(C) necessary
(D) necessarily

3 The marketing director asked that the consulting firm ------- the data and report on the most promising market segments.
(A) analyzed
(B) analysis
(C) analytical
(D) analyze

 PRACTICE

해설 p. 352

▪ 괄호 안의 보기 중 알맞은 단어를 고르세요.

1 Pat Louis usually **[works / worked]** out at a fitness club with his wife whenever he has time.

2 High-quality laser printers **[started / have started]** to gain popularity a year ago.

3 As soon as they **[have finished / will finish]** packing, they will move into the house.

4 Due to recent networking problems, repairs **[will be made / has been made]** to our servers tomorrow between 2 P.M. and 4 P.M.

5 Next month, our marketing division **[will relocate / relocated]** to a new office with ample space.

6 The recent increase in accidents means that safety inspections **[had to be / will have to be]** increased over the next two weeks.

7 Mr. Phoenix **[served / has served]** as chief financial officer at Grobal Network Inc. for the last 10 years.

8 It is important that all staff members of the sales team **[attend / attended]** today's meeting.

9 Sales of Keen Rock products **[was increased / have increased]** substantially in the past year.

10 Jane **[signed / has signed]** a formal contract to hire Ms. Bork as an assistant to help her work last week.

11 Before he left the company, Mr. Letscher **[had hired / will hire]** a suitable replacement to fill his position.

12 Edward Duran **[writes / wrote]** sports articles for several magazines and newspapers until his retirement last year.

13 The president will talk about it at the conference when our clients **[arrive / will arrive]** this afternoon.

14 Mr. Wilson requests that this month's sales report **[submits / be submitted]** by the end of the month.

15 After the current year, the automobile manufacturer **[will discontinue / discontinued]** manufacturing all four-door sedans and introduce a new line of sports cars.

1 The chief marketing officer ------- the proposal before it was submitted for approval last week.

(A) is revising (B) will revise
(C) revises (D) revised

2 Ms. White ------- at Hampshire University three years ago and may return again next semester.

(A) teaches (B) is teaching
(C) taught (D) has taught

3 Last week, the Canadian Embassy in Dublin ------- new visa application procedures.

(A) implemented (B) implements
(C) implementing (D) implement

4 The HR Department announced that Ms. Vieri ------- her new job as an assistant director as of Friday, July 14.

(A) has been starting (B) will be starting
(C) is started (D) is being started

5 Mr. McKay says that our total exports ------- by over forty percent by this time next year.

(A) increased
(B) had increased
(C) will increase
(D) will have increased

6 Every year since he ------- mayor, he has recommended rebuilding the city's shopping district, but the public has shown little interest in that.

(A) had elected (B) is electing
(C) was elected (D) will elect

7 Mr. Hyde learned when he was a mountain climber many years ago that water ------- at a lower temperature at high altitudes.

(A) is boiling (B) boils
(C) boiled (D) had boiled

8 As soon as the house ------- examined for fire risks, you may resume your usual activities without any special restrictions.

(A) is (B) was
(C) had been (D) will be

9 Many suppliers ------- in the program recently, and they feel that it is reliable.

(A) were participated
(B) have been participating
(C) are to be participating
(D) will have been participating

10 Jeff Rouse ------- his career as a film director even before he graduated from San Diego Art School.

(A) has begun (B) will begin
(C) is beginning (D) had begun

11 By the time Ms. Quinn joined our firm as a Web designer, she ------- in the Web-design field for many years already.

(A) works (B) will work
(C) has worked (D) had worked

12 Since Ace Electronics ------- its new product, its total sales figures have increased noticeably.

(A) releases (B) released
(C) was released (D) has released

해설 p. 352

Questions 13-16 refer to the following letter.

Inspection of Ventilation System at Charring Cross Station
by Juno Electrical Service

On June 10, Juno Electrical Service ------- the ventilation system at Charring Cross Station in London.
13.

Based on this inspection, Juno Electrical Service discovered that the building's ventilation system needs extensive repairs, including the replacement of some parts.

-------. This ------- covers both parts and labor costs.
14. **15.**

The changes we recommended will guarantee you more comfortable and pleasant working conditions.

As shown on our Web site, Juno ------- seeks ways to eliminate unnecessary costs and to meet the customers' needs.
16.

Thank you.

13 (A) is inspecting
(B) inspected
(C) will inspect
(D) inspect

14 (A) No bids will be accepted without a written estimate of the construction costs.
(B) The estimated cost to complete this work is £1,700.
(C) The final touches on the house are expected to be completed shortly.
(D) Appliances can be repaired by our maintenance staff free of charge.

15 (A) connection
(B) procedure
(C) problem
(D) figure

16 (A) actively
(B) lately
(C) decreasingly
(D) apparently

UNIT 10 to부정사

to부정사는 매월 평균 1~2문제가 출제된다. 문제 유형은 ① to부정사를 목적어로 취하는 동사, ② 명사를 수식하는 형용사적 용법의 to부정사, ③ 목적의 to부정사, ④ to부정사를 목적격 보어로 취하는 5형식 동사를 묻는 문제로 출제된다. 특히, to부정사가 쓰인 숙어 표현은 출제 빈도가 높은 편이므로 교재에 제시된 표현은 모두 암기해야 한다.

Preview

01 | to부정사(to+동사원형)는 문장에서 명사 역할을 할 수 있다.

주어 To find the right person for this job **is** very important.
이 일에 적임자를 찾는 것은 매우 중요하다.

목적어 The committee **agreed** to invest in the company.
위원회는 그 회사에 투자하는 것에 동의했다.

주격 보어 Your job **is** to deal with customer complaints promptly.
당신의 일은 고객의 불만사항들을 신속히 처리하는 것이다.

목적격 보어 I **want** you to do your homework right now.
나는 당신이 지금 바로 숙제를 하기를 원한다.

02 | to부정사는 명사를 수식하는 형용사 역할을 할 수 있다.

Two factories were closed in **an attempt** to cut costs.
비용을 삭감하려는 시도로 공장 두 군데가 문을 닫았다.

The ability to interact effectively with others is of great importance for managers.
다른 사람들과 효율적으로 상호작용할 수 있는 능력은 매니저에게 매우 중요하다.

03 | to부정사는 형용사·부사·동사·문장 전체를 수식하는 부사 역할을 할 수 있으며, 목적, 감정의 원인, 조건, 결과 등을 나타낸다.

목적 They left ahead of schedule to avoid the heavy traffic.
그들은 심한 교통체증을 피하기 위해 예정보다 일찍 출발했다.

원인 I'm pleased to hear the news that you got a promotion.
나는 당신이 승진했다는 소식을 들어서 기쁘다.

조건 I would be very glad to be of service to you.
내가 당신에게 어떠한 도움이라도 줄 수 있다면 기쁠 것이다.

POINT 1 to부정사의 명사적 용법 1

01 | to부정사가 명사적 용법으로 사용되면 '~하는 것'으로 해석된다.

주어 [To respond / ~~Response~~] promptly to customer's complaints at all times **is** important.
고객들의 불만사항에 항상 즉시 응답하는 것은 중요하다.

목적어 Ms. Jackson says she would **prefer** [to work / ~~worked~~] on the report by herself.
Jackson 씨는 그녀 혼자서 보고서를 작성하는 것을 선호한다고 말한다.

주격 보어 The first step in developing effective advertising **is** [to understand / ~~understood~~] its concept. 효과적인 광고를 개발하는 것의 첫 단계는 광고의 컨셉을 이해하는 것이다.

목적격 보어 We **require** all managers [to submit / ~~submitting~~] proposals by the end of the month.
우리는 모든 매니저들이 월말까지 제안서를 낼 것을 요구한다.

02 | to부정사의 의미상 주어는 일반적으로 to부정사 앞에 <for+목적격>으로 나타낸다.

It is necessary [for / ~~that~~] you **to carry** a valid photo ID during your visit.
방문 중에는 사진이 부착된 유효한 신분증을 반드시 지니고 다녀야 합니다.

+TIP 의미상 주어가 일반인일 경우나 주어와 to부정사의 의미상 주어가 같을 때는 흔히 생략한다.

It is good (for [people / us]) **to exercise** every morning. ▶ 일반적인 사람
매일 아침 운동하는 것은 좋다.

(You) Make sure (for you) **to turn off** the light when you leave. ▶ 문장 주어와 같은 경우
나갈 때 불을 확실히 꺼라.

+TIP

감정이나 사람에 대한 평가를 나타내는 형용사(kind / nice / wise / considerate / generous)가 나올 경우, <of+목적격>으로 의미상 주어를 만든다.

It is very **kind** of you to explain the details of the incident.
사건의 세부사항을 설명해 주셔서 정말 감사합니다.

It is **wise** of her to use discount coupons when buying groceries at Well Mart.
그녀가 웰마트에서 식료품을 구매할 때 할인쿠폰을 이용하는 것은 현명하다.

SPARTA Check-UP! 1

해설 p. 354

1 The Howell Consulting Company decided ------- the operating system in order to increase productivity.
(A) to change
(B) changing
(C) change
(D) changed

2 Mountain hikers are encouraged to ------- long pants throughout the year to protect their legs from thorns.
(A) wearing
(B) wear
(C) wore
(D) worn

3 It is important for managers ------- make sure employees follow safety precautions to minimize the risk of injuries.
(A) to
(B) should
(C) that
(D) upon

POINT ② to부정사의 명사적 용법 2

01 | to부정사는 진주어로 사용된다.

It is mandatory [to write / ~~for writting~~] the article in accordance with the newspaper's guidelines.
신문사 지침에 따라 기사를 쓰는 것이 의무적이다.

▶ to부정사를 주어 자리에 쓰는 경우도 있지만, 그보다는 가주어 it을 세우고 to부정사구는 뒤로 빼는 경우가 일반적이다. 따라서 [It + is/was + 형용사 + to부정사]의 가주어/진주어 패턴에 익숙해지는 것이 좋다.

To write the article in accordance with the newspaper's guidelines (주어) is **mandatory**. ▶ 강조 표현

= It (가주어) is **mandatory** to write the article in accordance with the newspaper's guidelines (진주어). ▶ 일반 표현

▶ <It+is/was+형용사+to부정사>의 패턴으로 자주 쓰이는 형용사로 easy / hard / difficult / (im)possible / necessary / convenient / mandatory 등이 있다.

02 | to부정사는 진목적어로 사용된다.

The decrease in gasoline prices made **it** possible for the company to lower its delivery costs.
휘발유 가격의 하락은 회사가 그들의 배송비를 낮추는 것을 가능하게 했다.

▶ 5형식 동사 find, make, think 등의 타동사 뒤에 목적어가 긴 경우는 목적어 자리에 it을 세우고 진목적어인 to부정사를 문장 뒤로 보낸다.

The decrease in gasoline prices made to lower its delivery costs (목적어) **possible** (목적격 보어) for the company. (x)

The decrease in gasoline prices made it (가목적어) **possible** for the company to lower its delivery costs (진목적어). (o)

+TIP 가목적어가 자주 쓰이는 패턴

find it 목적격 보어 to do	~하는 것이 ~임을 알게 되다/~라고 여기다
think it 목적격 보어 to do	~하는 것을 ~라고 생각하다
consider it 목적격 보어 to do	~하는 것을 ~라고 생각하다(여기다)
leave it 목적격 보어 to do	~하는 것을 ~로 남기다
make it 목적격 보어 to do	~하는 것을 ~하게 만들다

SPARTA Check-UP! 2

해설 p. 354

1 It is not possible for Ms. Knightley ------- finish the statistical analysis by herself.
(A) to
(B) for
(C) in
(D) that

2 We have launched an online marketing Web site, making ------- possible for consumers to purchase groceries via the Internet.
(A) them
(B) that
(C) it
(D) if

3 It is ------- for us to finalize our strategy to meet the new deadline.
(A) important
(B) importation
(C) importance
(D) importantly

POINT 3 to부정사의 부사적·형용사적 용법

01 | 부사적 용법

1) to부정사는 목적(~하기 위하여)을 나타낸다.

Some clothes at this store are often sold at a discount to [make / ~~making~~] room for new products.
이 상점의 일부 옷들은 종종 신상품들을 위한 공간을 만들기 위해서 할인 가격에 판매된다.

This information is provided by the public education center [to improve / ~~improving~~] the computer skills of the students. 이 정보는 학생들의 컴퓨터 실력을 향상시키기 위해서 공공교육센터로부터 제공된다.

2) 목적의 의미를 강조하는 in order to부정사 (= so as to부정사)

You should return the merchandise within 7 days in order [to receive / ~~receiving~~] a full refund.
전액 환불을 받기 위해서는 7일 내로 상품을 반품해야 합니다.

So as to **be** able to respond promptly to road hazards, drivers are advised to avoid using cellphones while driving. 도로 위험에 즉각적으로 대응할 수 있도록, 운전자들은 운전하는 동안 휴대폰 사용을 피하도록 권고 받는다.
▶ so as라는 표현은 없으므로 시험에서 보기에 제시될 경우 오답이 된다.

3) to부정사는 원인(~하게 되어서), 이유(~하기 때문에), 결과(~해서 ~하다)를 나타낸다.

I am pleased [to announce / ~~announcing~~] that our sales figures have dramatically increased in the second quarter. 저는 2분기에 우리의 매출액이 급격히 신장되었음을 알리게 되어 기쁩니다. ▶ 원인

It is not surprising that he grew up [to become / ~~becoming~~] one of the most influential people in the IT industry. 그가 자라서 IT 산업에서 가장 영향력 있는 인물 중 하나가 된 것은 놀랄 일이 아니다. ▶ 결과

02 | 형용사적 용법

to부정사는 앞의 명사를 수식하는 형용사적 용법으로 사용된다.

Employees will have **an opportunity** [to show / ~~showing~~] their knowledge of our products during the product demonstrations. 직원들은 제품설명회 동안 우리 제품에 대한 그들의 지식을 보여줄 기회를 갖게 될 것이다.

We reserve **the right** [to cancel / ~~canceling~~] the order if you fail to keep the delivery date.
만일 상품의 배송일을 지키지 못할 경우, 우리는 주문을 취소할 수 있는 권리를 가지고 있습니다.

SPARTA Check-UP! 3

해설 p. 355

1 We removed this vending machine from the premises today ------- perform regular maintenance.
(A) so as
(B) as if
(C) despite
(D) in order to

2 The retailer reserves the right ------- all prices listed in the company catalogue without notice.
(A) alter
(B) to alter
(C) altering
(D) altered

3 ------- research in nanotechnology, the government has offered to pay up to 50 percent of the cost to build the Nano Technology Institute.
(A) To promote
(B) For the promotion
(C) By promoting
(D) As a promotion

POINT 4 to부정사와 같이 사용하는 어휘

01 | to부정사를 목적어로 취하는 동사

afford to부정사 ~할 경제적 여유가 있다	hesitate to부정사 ~하려는 것을 주저하다
agree to부정사 ~할 것에 대해 동의하다	intend to부정사 ~하려고 의도하다
ask to부정사 ~해 줄 것을 부탁하다	manage to부정사 그럭저럭 ~해내다
attempt to부정사 ~하려고 시도하다	plan to부정사 ~하려고 계획하다
choose to부정사 ~할 것을 선택하다	prefer to부정사 ~하는 것을 선호하다
decide to부정사 ~하려고 결심하다	promise to부정사 ~할 것을 약속하다
expect to부정사 ~할 것을 기대[예상]하다	refuse to부정사 ~할 것을 거절하다
fail to부정사 ~하려던 것을 하지 못하다	tend to부정사 ~하는 경향이 있다 / ~하기 쉽다

Mr. Kirby decided [to reserve / ~~reserving~~] a private room in case the restaurant was noisy.
Kirby 씨는 식당이 시끄러운 경우를 대비해서 개인실을 예약하기로 결심했다.

02 | to부정사와 함께 사용하는 명사

the plan to부정사 ~할 계획	the ability to부정사 ~할 수 있는 능력
the right[authority] to부정사 ~할 권리/권한	the opportunity[chance] to부정사 ~할 기회
the way[means] to부정사 ~할 방식/방법	the effort to부정사 ~하려는 노력
the decision to부정사 ~하려는 결정	the attempt to부정사 ~하려는 시도

In an effort [to provide / ~~providing~~] better banking service, Apex Bank invites customers to make comments. 보다 나은 은행 서비스를 제공하기 위한 노력의 일환으로, Apex 은행은 고객이 의견을 제시하도록 요청합니다.

03 | to부정사와 함께 사용하는 구문

be (un)able to부정사 ~할 수 있다[없다]	be likely[liable] to부정사 ~할 것 같다
be eager to부정사 간절히 ~하고 싶어 하다	be proud to부정사 ~을 자랑스럽게 여기다
be sure[certain] to부정사 반드시 ~하다	be scheduled to부정사 ~하기로 예정되어 있다
be willing to부정사 기꺼이 ~하다	be supposed to부정사 ~하기로 되어 있다
be reluctant to부정사 ~하기를 꺼려하다	be eligible to부정사 ~할 자격이 있다

All employees at our company are eligible [to enter / ~~entering~~] the management training course.
우리 회사의 전 직원은 경영 훈련 과정에 참가할 자격이 있다.

SPARTA Check-UP! 4

해설 p. 355

1 Management would like ------- employees and their families to attend the annual company picnic next Friday.
(A) invite
(B) to invite
(C) invitation
(D) invitingly

2 Many foreign companies hope to ------- their business in Japan once deregulation is carried out.
(A) expansion
(B) expanding
(C) expand
(D) expansive

3 Although there was some controversy over the qualifications of the winning contestant, the judges allowed their decisions -------.
(A) stands
(B) standing
(C) stand
(D) to stand

해설 p. 355

- 괄호 안의 보기 중 알맞은 단어를 고르세요.

1 When the economy is performing poorly, companies tend **[postpone / to postpone]** upgrading their software.

2 We need **[to receive / receiving]** instructions from the client directly in order to provide personal financial advice.

3 In the event that you decide **[to change / changing]** the banquet menu, you must consult with the reception committee at least 10 days prior to the event.

4 All staff members are required **[adhere / to adhere]** to the regulations stated in the safety manual while they work in the field.

5 One of Mr. Cramer's best qualities is his ability **[work / to work]** on several complex problems at the same time.

6 Tom expressed to me that he doesn't feel that you have the right **[criticism / to criticize]** his project when you haven't even read the literature pertaining to it.

7 I regret that I have another engagement at that time and will not be able to **[attend / attendance]**.

8 Investors are eager to **[establish / establishing]** a company office in Mumbai, the country's largest city.

9 Our products allow users of digital equipment **[to transmit / transmitting]** computer data over analog networks.

10 The Highway Safety Board would like to remind you to **[take / taking]** the following precautions this holiday season.

11 George Frankman is expected to **[announce / announcing]** his retirement at the meeting tomorrow.

12 The Thomson & Thomson Corporation would like all staff members **[will work / to work]** together to complete the project by the due date.

13 It will be necessary to use tissue paper **[to wrap / wrapped]** fragile items to keep them from breaking.

14 Travelers are advised to call the airline **[to / for]** confirm flights at least two days prior to their departure.

15 Only the company's employees are allowed **[for entering / to enter]** rooms that are designated with a "Staff Only" sign.

1 The budget changes are unlikely ------- by the board of directors.

(A) to pass (B) to be passed
(C) passing (D) by passing

2 The sales manager promised ------- sales volume by more than 50%.

(A) increasing (B) to increase
(C) to increasing (D) increases

3 The reasonable price of our LCD monitor encourages customers ------- our products.

(A) buy (B) to buy
(C) buying (D) bought

4 In order to ------- how the company operates, employees should have some knowledge of the management structure.

(A) understand (B) understanding
(C) understandable (D) understood

5 Chris Cunningham, the vice president of Hanson Motors, will soon have a chance ------- the new branch offices in the Middle East.

(A) to visit (B) visiting
(C) visit (D) to visiting

6 The president would like all staff members ------- together to develop innovative strategies.

(A) works
(B) be working
(C) to work
(D) will work

7 Our company policy requires employees ------- in accordance with federal safety regulations at all times.

(A) acting (B) acted
(C) are acting (D) to act

8 Job descriptions enable both prospective and current employees ------- what is expected of them.

(A) of knowing (B) know
(C) and know (D) to know

9 When you call an airline ------- find out a flight's departure time, make sure to have the flight number at hand.

(A) for (B) so
(C) to (D) when

10 The right ------- bail is a constitutional right of the court, especially in cases where a judge considers the accused unfit to make rational decisions.

(A) refuse (B) to refuse
(C) refusing (D) refused

11 To fully ------- our overseas clients, the Green Hotel is providing free international calls to Europe and Asia for all guests.

(A) accommodate (B) accommodation
(C) accommodates (D) accommodating

12 The salespeople do not want long breaks during the brainstorming sessions, so they often order lunch ------- delivered.

(A) will be (B) to be
(C) has been (D) was

Questions 13-16 refer to the following notice.

TO: All Newly Promoted Managers

This is to let you ------- (13.) that the orientation session for new managers will take place on Tuesday, September 8.

All recently promoted managers are ------- (14.) to attend unless they have made other arrangements. The orientation will address topics ------- (15.) benefits, the performance-review process, and confidential policies.

A new employee ID and a parking permit will be provided. Please come to conference room 5 on the twelfth floor of the Jefferson Building by 10:00 A.M. ------- (16.).

You are welcome to contact me if you have any questions.

Sincerely,

Emily Burris
Human Resources

13 (A) know
(B) to know
(C) knowing
(D) known

14 (A) required
(B) compared
(C) included
(D) reported

15 (A) so that
(B) besides
(C) likewise
(D) such as

16 (A) The orientation schedule is as follows:
(B) The manger suffered a heart attack and is recovering in the hospital.
(C) The session will improve your understanding of the managerial position.
(D) There is a sign-up sheet in the break room next to the water cooler.

UNIT 11 동명사

동명사 문제는 매달 1~2문제 정도 출제된다. 문제 유형은 ① 주어 역할을 하는 동명사, ② 동명사를 목적어로 취하는 동사, ③ 전치사와 목적어 사이에 명사와 동명사의 구별, ④ 동명사 관용어구를 묻는 문제 유형으로 구분해 볼 수 있다. 특히 전치사와 명사 사이가 빈칸으로 제시되었을 때 동명사가 정답이 되는 유형이 가장 많이 출제된다.

Preview

01 | 동명사(동사+-ing)는 문장에서 주어, 목적어, 보어, 전치사의 목적어 역할을 한다.

주어 Supporting them **requires** a large amount of budget.
그들을 후원하는 것은 큰 예산을 요구한다.

목적어 I **am considering** going to Canada to study more.
나는 더 많이 공부하기 위해 캐나다로 가는 것을 고려하고 있다.

보어 One of my hobbies **is** taking pictures.
내 취미 중 하나는 사진을 찍는 것이다.

전치사의 목적어 Thank you **for** answering my questions.
제 질문에 답변해 주셔서 감사드립니다.

02 | 동명사의 수동형은 <being+p.p.>, 완료형은 <having+p.p.>로 나타낸다.

These forms must be filled out completely before being submitted.
이 양식들은 제출되기 전에 완전하게 작성되어야 한다.

▶ forms(양식들)가 스스로 제출하는(submit) 것이 아니라 제출되는 것이므로 동명사를 수동태(being+p.p.)로 쓴다.

03 | 동명사는 명사와는 달리 목적어와 보어를 취할 수 있다.

[Developing / ~~Development~~] **a new car** is absolutely necessary. ▶ a new car가 developing의 목적어
새로운 차를 개발하는 것은 분명히 필요하다.

Please read it carefully before [signing / ~~sign~~] **the contract**. ▶ the contract가 signing의 목적어
계약서에 서명하기 전에 주의 깊게 읽으십시오.

The furniture has the distinction of [being / ~~be~~] **easy** to clean. ▶ easy가 being의 보어
그 가구는 쉽게 닦을 수 있다는 특징이 있다.

POINT 1 동명사의 역할

01 | 동명사+목적어+동사+보어

주어

[Establishing / ~~Establishment~~] **marketing strategies** is **one of the most demanding tasks** at the company. 마케팅 전략을 수립하는 것은 회사에서 가장 까다로운 업무 중 하나다.

▶ marketing strategies는 동명사(establishing)의 목적어로 쓰였다.

+TIP 동명사가 문장의 주어로 올 때, 동사는 단수동사를 쓴다.

Borrowing **library materials** without the necessary identification **is** not allowed.
동명사: 단수 / 단수 동사
필요한 신분증 없이 도서관 자료를 빌리는 것은 허용되지 않는다.

02 | 동사+동명사+목적어 / 전치사+동명사+목적어

타동사의 목적어 / 전치사의 목적어

The responsibilities for this position include [inspecting / ~~to inspect~~] **our assembly line** regularly.
이 직책의 업무는 우리의 조립라인을 정기적으로 점검하는 것을 포함한다.

Durban Shipping hopes to expand into South America and Africa by [opening / ~~open~~] **new offices**.
Durban Shipping 사는 새로운 사무소들을 개장함으로써 남미와 아프리카로 사업을 확대하기를 바라고 있다.

+TIP 자주 쓰이는 전치사 + V-ing

without+V-ing ~하지 않고
instead of+V-ing ~하는 대신
in addition to+V-ing ~하는 것뿐만 아니라
on/upon+V-ing ~하자마자
in+V-ing ~함에 있어서
by+Ving ~함으로써

03 | 동명사의 의미상 주어는 동명사 앞에 소유격으로 표시한다.

동명사는 동사의 성질을 그대로 가지고 있다. 그래서 동사처럼 목적어나 보어를 가질 수 있으며 경우에 따라서는 주어도 가질 수 있다. 이때의 주어를 의미상의 주어라고 한다.

[Your / ~~You~~] **informing** us of any errors in the system will help us provide better service to our customers. 당신이 우리에게 시스템상의 오류를 알려주는 것은 우리가 고객들에게 더 나은 서비스를 제공하는 데 도움을 줍니다.

Mr. Brown said that there was no chance of [his / ~~him~~] **accepting** a takeover offer.
Brown 씨는 자신이 그러한 인수 제안을 수락할 가능성은 전혀 없었다고 말했다.

SPARTA Check-UP! 1

해설 p. 358

1 The biggest complaint about the new S2O batteries is that ------- them takes more time than other brands.
(A) recharge
(B) recharger
(C) recharged
(D) recharging

2 The Accounting Department delayed the project by ------- additional funding.
(A) withhold
(B) withheld
(C) withholds
(D) withholding

3 Mr. Carey suggests ------- an e-mail to applicants immediately after their insurance policy is approved.
(A) sends
(B) sending
(C) sent
(D) would send

POINT 2 동명사와 명사의 구분

01 | 동명사는 준동사로, 명사와는 달리 목적어를 가질 수 있다.

Reed-Winton Machines is currently considering [**developing** / ~~development~~] **a new refrigerator brand.** Reed-Winton Machines 사는 현재 새로운 종류의 냉장고를 개발하는 것을 고려하고 있다.

cf. Although the new design is innovative, it would be too costly to proceed with [**development** / ~~developing~~]. 비록 그 디자인이 혁신적이긴 하지만, 개발을 진행하기에는 비용이 너무 많이 든다.

02 | 동명사는 관사와 함께 사용할 수 없다.

After **the** [**retirement** / ~~retiring~~] of Mr. Valdes, the company launched a search for a new CEO.
Valdes 씨의 퇴직 후 회사는 새로운 CEO를 찾기 시작했다.

The changes to the original phone design represent **an** [**improvement** / ~~improving~~] in quality and convenience.
기존 전화기 디자인의 변경사항들은 품질과 편의성의 개선을 보여준다.

▶ 동명사 뒤에는 목적어가 올 수 있지만 명사 뒤에는 목적어가 올 수 없다. 관사(a/an/the) 뒤에 동명사가 올 수 없다.

+ VOCABULARY | 시험에 자주 출제되는 명사화된 동명사

advertising 광고, 광고업	belongings 소지품	dining 식사, 정찬
covering 덮개	cleaning 청소	opening 빈자리(공석), 개업
funding 자금 조달	monitoring 감시, 통제	warning 경고
processing 처리	founding 창립	understanding 이해
planning 기획, 입안	outing 야유회	packaging 포장
seating 좌석 수용(력)	publishing 출판업	rising 상승
staffing 채용	spending 지출	listing 목록, 명단
ticketing 발권	setting 설정, 설치	sightseeing 관광

Gate, Inc. has announced **a** full-time [**opening** / ~~openness~~] for a financial advisor in the Birmingham office.
Gate 사는 버밍햄 지사의 재정 고문 정규직 채용을 공고했다.

SPARTA Check-UP! 2

| 해설 p. 358

1 ------- an improved method of quality control will lead to greater profitability in the long run.
(A) Develop
(B) Developing
(C) Developed
(D) Development

2 Many companies are going through the process of ------- their employees to meet the standards of global competition.
(A) retrain
(B) retrained
(C) retraining
(D) retrainable

3 Thanks to careful ------- and consistent product quality, the newly established Kolof Bakery, Inc. has quickly become a leader in the market.
(A) planner
(B) plan
(C) planning
(D) planned

POINT ③ 주의해야 할 동명사 용법

01 | 명사는 형용사의 수식을 받고, 동명사는 부사의 수식을 받는다.

One of the keys to [successfully / ~~successful~~] **launching** a new product is thorough market research.
신상품을 성공적으로 출시하는 비결 중 하나는 철저한 시장 조사이다.

▶ 동명사는 동사를 명사화한 것으로 문장 안에서 동사가 될 수는 없으나, 동사의 성질을 여전히 가지고 있어 부사의 수식을 받을 수 있다.

02 | 동명사는 to부정사와는 달리 전치사 뒤에 쓸 수 있다.

We look forward to [hearing / ~~hear~~] from you soon. 우리는 당신으로부터 곧 소식을 듣기를 고대합니다.

I am used to [making / ~~make~~] speeches in public. 나는 대중 앞에서 연설하는 것에 익숙하다.

▶ 전치사 to 뒤에는 (동)명사가 오고 to부정사의 to 뒤에는 동사가 와야 한다.

+TIP be used to부정사 : ~하기 위하여 사용되다

The open access database can be used to [search / ~~searching~~] for job opportunities at Tozer Publishing. 오픈 데이터베이스는 Tozer Publishing 사에 일자리를 검색하는 데 사용될 수 있다.

전치사는 목적어로 to부정사를 쓸 수 없으며, 반드시 명사 또는 동명사를 써야 한다. 단, 전치사 to와 to부정사의 to를 혼동할 수 있으므로 전치사 to를 동반한 빈출 표현을 따로 외워 두어야 한다.

Shoppers are encouraged to pay for their purchases by [using / ~~to use~~] credit cards.
쇼핑객들은 신용 카드를 사용하여 물건 값을 지불하도록 권장 받는다.

The organization is committed to [finding / ~~find~~] new methods **of improving** public health.
조직은 공중위생을 개선할 새로운 방법을 찾는 데 전념한다.

+TIP to부정사 vs. 전치사 to

• to부정사의 형태 : to+동사원형
• 전치사 to의 형태 : to+명사(구)

to부정사 관련 표현	전치사 to 관련 표현
be scheduled to V ~할 예정이다 would like to V ~하고 싶다 hesitate to do ~하기를 주저하다	be opposed to V-ing ~에 반대하다 look forward to V-ing ~를 기대하다 object to V-ing ~에 반대하다

SPARTA Check-UP! ③

해설 p. 358

1 Several services on the Internet are helpful at ------- books that are hard to find or out of print.
(A) located
(B) locating
(C) will locate
(D) to locate

2 After ------- himself to the audience, Mr. Canet, who wrote many articles for *Able Magazine*, started to deliver his talk.
(A) introduce
(B) introducing
(C) introduced
(D) to introduce

3 After ------- reviewing your résumé, we have unfortunately decided to reject your application.
(A) thorough
(B) thoroughly
(C) thoroughness
(D) most thorough

POINT 4 동명사의 관용 표현

01 | 동명사가 사용된 관용 표현

be used[accustomed] to -ing ~하는 데 익숙해지다	be capable of -ing ~할 수 있다
be worth -ing ~할 가치가 있다	be busy -ing ~하느라 바쁘다
cannot help -ing ~하지 않을 수 없다	have trouble[difficulty] -ing ~하는 데 어려움을 겪다
be committed[dedicated] to -ing ~하는 데 헌신적이다	spend+시간/돈+-ing ~하는 데 시간/돈을 소비하다

Mr. Watanabe **was capable of** [solving / ~~solved~~] the problem with the Fiantze 145 software.
Watanabe 씨는 Fiantze 145 소프트웨어에 대한 문제를 해결할 수 있었다.

02 | 동명사를 목적어로 받는 동사

제안 / 고려	suggest 제안하다 consider 고려하다 recommend 추천하다
부정 / 거부	dislike 싫어하다 deny 거부하다 mind 꺼리다 avoid 피하다
중지 / 연기	finish 끝내다 discontinue 중단하다 postpone/delay 연기하다
인정 / 허용	admit 받아들이다 permit 허용하다 allow 허락하다
기타	enjoy 즐기다 keep 계속하다 include 포함하다 involve 필요로 하다

The new mayor strongly **recommended** [rebuilding / ~~to rebuild~~] the city's shopping district.
새로운 시장은 시의 쇼핑 구역을 재건축할 것을 강력히 제안했다.

03 | to부정사와 동명사를 모두 목적어로 취하는 동사

need to부정사 ~할 필요가 있다	need -ing ~될 필요가 있다
remember to부정사 ~할 것을 기억하다	remember -ing ~했던 것을 기억하다
forget to부정사 ~할 것을 잊다	forget -ing ~했던 것을 잊다
stop to부정사 ~하려고 멈추다	stop -ing ~하는 것을 멈추다
continue to부정사/-ing 계속해서 ~하다	start to부정사/-ing ~하기 시작하다

Passengers should **remember** [to reconfirm / ~~reconfirming~~] their flight reservation 72 hours before the scheduled departure time. 승객들은 예정된 출발 72시간 전에 비행기 예약을 재확인할 것을 기억해야 한다.

Ms. Stein **remembered** [getting / ~~to get~~] the notice of the staff recognition banquet last week.
Stein 씨는 지난주에 직원 격려 파티의 공지를 받았던 것을 기억했다.

SPARTA Check-UP! 4

| 해설 p. 358

1 Amplipiers' Production Department spent half its budget ------- new audio equipment.
(A) developed
(B) developing
(C) to develop
(D) develops

2 A survey technician finished ------- the property lines at 5501 Marcus Avenue last Wednesday.
(A) map
(B) to map
(C) mapped
(D) mapping

3 Until the new payroll system has been fully implemented, please continue ------- the old reporting method.
(A) usage
(B) using
(C) useful
(D) used

PRACTICE

해설 p. 359

▪ 괄호 안의 보기 중 알맞은 단어를 고르세요.

1 **[Maintenance / Maintaining]** exceptional service to its customers is the top priority at Dudley Holdings.

2 Due to an error in the most recent software, please refrain from **[schedule / scheduling]** any new events on the online calendar until further notice.

3 You will receive your computer within a week of **[place / placing]** your order online.

4 After **[careful / carefully]** interviewing ten candidates for the managerial position, the boss himself chose Mr. Koepp.

5 Staff members now send travel requests electronically **[because of / instead of]** submitting a paper form.

6 Because the price is expected to fall further, I recommend **[to postpone / postponing]** the purchase for another few weeks.

7 Spike Jonze, the new CEO of Gold Post, suggested **[modifying / being modified]** the company's investment strategies.

8 Although Ms. Steil began **[working / to working]** at Wilton Shop in May, she was already named assistant manager by July.

9 Malcolm, Inc. plays a critical role in **[helping / help]** our company achieve its goals on every project.

10 Residents of Queens have proposed **[development / developing]** the lot that has been unused for many years.

11 A team of meteorologists led by Andrew Jackson is dedicated to **[provide / providing]** accurate weather forecasts to the local community.

12 Dreamworks focuses on providing business solutions with a commitment to **[enhance / enhancing]** a company's competitive advantage.

13 If notification is given in **[written / writing]** at least 30 days in advance, policyholders may discontinue their policy at any time.

14 Forbes management is **[scheduled / committed]** to working cooperatively with surrounding communities to reduce recycling costs.

15 We look forward to **[find / finding]** out more about the company during the next shareholders' meeting.

1 Ziatech has been working continuously on ------- new ways to synthesize chemical products.

(A) development (B) developing
(C) develop (D) developed

2 Mr. Turner suggested ------- until midnight in order to get the project done by the deadline.

(A) working (B) to work
(C) worked (D) of working

3 The hotel policy requires that all restaurant workers put on hats and wash their hands before ------- the kitchen and food storage rooms.

(A) to enter (B) enter
(C) entered (D) entering

4 ------- a balance between state general fund allocations and student tuition is an ongoing challenge and one of our most important responsibilities.

(A) Maintain (B) Maintenance
(C) Maintaining (D) Maintained

5 The Greensboro National Museum has increased its visitor traffic by ------- updating its Web site.

(A) regular (B) regularity
(C) regularize (D) regularly

6 Mr. Roberts is an amateur writer who enjoys spending his free time ------- novels.

(A) composes (B) composed
(C) composing (D) composer

7 Telecommunication companies cannot change contracts without first ------- customers.

(A) notifies (B) notified
(C) notifying (D) notification

8 Safety protocols at the Vector power plant were modified last month in order to ------- with new standards.

(A) comply (B) compliance
(C) complying (D) complied

9 By introducing up-to-date equipment and technology, GoodFuels has shown its commitment to ------- the risk of radiation leaks at all nuclear power plants.

(A) lower (B) low
(C) lowered (D) lowering

10 In addition to ------- the company's budget, Mr. Washock organizes a number of meetings with local subcontractors.

(A) manage (B) manages
(C) manageable (D) managing

11 Tony Goldwyn, the CEO of Power Electronics, is eagerly awaiting ------- reports from all divisions.

(A) earn (B) earned
(C) to earn (D) earnings

12 Because of Mike Waters's success in ------- the new company divisions, management has decided to hire him as a full-time consultant.

(A) organization (B) organizer
(C) organize (D) organizing

Questions 13-16 refer to the following letter.

Bayonne Plaza Apartments
C-205 Atlantic Street, Neptune City
New Jersey 95124

Dear New Residents,

Congratulations on your recent ------- (13.) to rent an apartment at Bayonne Plaza. ------- (14.). We trust that you will enjoy coming home to our newly renovated building located on the Atlantic side of the city. You will enjoy the wonderful ocean view and the convenience of living ------- (15.) walking distance of some of the finest restaurants and historical landmarks in the city.

As a tenant, you are responsible for the activation of electricity and telephone service by your move-in date. Should any maintenance issues arise, an on-site facilities technician is available twenty-four hours a day.

We look forward to serving you. Thank you for ------- (16.) at Bayonne Plaza.

With best wishes,

Mark Smith

13
(A) decision
(B) decide
(C) decides
(D) decisive

14
(A) This letter confirms that your rental contract has been reviewed and signed.
(B) You are notified that your rental contract is terminated for your failure to pay rent.
(C) You are ordered to surrender tenancy of the premises by the termination date.
(D) You are required to surrender the premises by delivering the key to the landlord.

15
(A) until
(B) within
(C) from
(D) since

16
(A) visiting
(B) going
(C) hearing
(D) renting

UNIT 12 분사

분사 문제는 크게 ① 명사 앞·뒤에서 현재분사와 과거분사를 구별하는 문제, ② be동사 뒤에 나올 현재분사와 과거분사를 구별하는 문제, ③ 분사구문 관련 문제로 구분할 수 있으며, 매월 평균 1~2문제가 출제된다.

Preview

01 | 현재분사(동사+-ing) : 진행형에서 쓰이거나 형용사로 사용한다.

진행형	be동사+현재분사(V -ing) → 주어와 능동 관계 He **is** playing soccer with his friends. 그는 친구들과 함께 축구를 하고 있다.
명사 수식	분사가 단독으로 쓰여 명사를 앞에서 수식 He is **a** demanding **supervisor**. 그는 까다로운 상사이다.
	분사가 다른 어구를 동반하여 명사를 뒤에서 수식 **The man** playing soccer is my brother. 축구를 하고 있는 그 남자는 내 형이다.
보어	주격 보어 또는 목적격 보어로 사용 The rules **made** the game **exciting**. 규칙이 경기를 흥미롭게 만들었다. ▶ the game과 exciting은 능동 관계

02 | 과거분사(동사+-ed) : 수동태로 쓰이거나 형용사로 사용한다.

수동태	be동사+과거분사(V -ed) → 주어와 수동 관계 People **are** interested in the game. 사람들은 게임에 관심이 있다. ▶ 사람(People)은 감정(interest)을 느끼는 대상이므로 수동 관계
명사 수식	명사 앞 또는 뒤에서 수식 **The car** repaired by that mechanic is mine. 정비공이 수리한 차는 내 차이다.
보어	주격 보어 또는 목적격 보어로 사용 I **found** teenagers **interested** in the game. 나는 십대들이 게임에 흥미 있어 하는 것을 알게 되었다. ▶ 사람(teenagers)은 감정(interest)을 느끼는 대상이므로 수동 관계

03 | 분사구문 : '부사절 접속사+주어+동사'로 된 절을 구로 만든 것

	부사절을 분사구문으로 바꾸는 순서
1	부사절의 접속사를 생략한다.
2	부사절의 주어가 주절의 주어와 같을 경우 부사절의 주어를 생략한다. (다를 경우에는 생략 불가)
3	부사절의 동사에 -ing를 붙인다.
4	-ing 요소가 being 또는 having been일 경우는 생략이 가능하다.

If you practice writing English every day, you will be able to improve your writing skills.
= **Practicing writing English every day**, you will be able to improve your writing skills.
매일 영어쓰기 연습을 한다면, 당신의 작문실력을 향상시킬 수 있을 것이다.

POINT 1 분사의 역할과 형태

01 | 분사는 명사의 앞 또는 뒤에서 명사를 수식한다.

Car sales have decreased due to the [increasing / ~~increases~~] **cost** of gasoline.
증가하는 휘발유 가격으로 자동차 판매가 감소했다.

The Statue of Liberty is one of the most [visited / ~~visits~~] **tourist attractions** in America.
자유의 여신상은 미국에서 가장 많이 방문하는 관광 명소 중 하나이다.

Anyone [interested / ~~interesting~~] in the seminar is asked to contact Matthew Beard first.
세미나에 관심이 있는 누구든 매튜 비어드 씨에게 먼저 연락해야 한다.

Employees [remaining / ~~remained~~] in the office after 7:00 P.M. should notify the general manager in advance.
저녁 7시 이후에 사무실에 남아 있는 사원들은 총지배인에게 미리 알려야 한다.

▶ 자동사의 형용사형은 p.p. 형태로 쓰지 못한다. 예를 들어 '남겨진 직원들'은 의미상 p.p. 형태인 remained가 적절해 보이지만, remain은 자동사이므로 remaining이 되어야 한다.

02 | 분사는 주격 보어 또는 목적격 보어로 사용된다.

All of the employees did their best, but the results **were** [disappointing / ~~disappointment~~].
모든 직원들이 최선을 다했지만 결과는 실망스러웠다.

▶ be동사와 같은 2형식 동사 뒤 주격 보어 자리에 분사를 쓸 수 있다. 주어와 주격 보어의 능동/수동 관계에 주목한다.

The rules they created last year **made** the game [exciting / ~~excited~~].
그들이 작년에 만든 규칙이 경기를 흥미롭게 만들었다.

▶ 동사 keep, find, consider와 같은 5형식 동사는 목적격 보어 자리에 분사를 쓸 수 있다. 목적어와 목적격 보어의 능동/수동 관계에 주목한다.

03 | 능동의 의미로 명사를 수식할 때는 현재분사, 수동의 의미로 명사를 수식할 때는 과거분사 형태가 된다.

We are so pleased with the [overwhelming / ~~overwhelmed~~] **response** to this exhibition.
저희는 이번 전시회의 엄청난 반응에 기뻐하고 있습니다.

There is now an [updated / ~~updating~~] **version** of the software program available on the distributor's Web site.
현재 판매자의 웹사이트에서 최신 버전의 소프트웨어 프로그램을 이용할 수 있다

SPARTA Check-UP! 1

해설 p. 361

1 The ------- tax project would make states impose taxes on products purchased over the Internet.
(A) streamline
(B) streamlining
(C) streamlines
(D) streamlined

2 The parking area behind the NK Building will remain ------- until the west side of the parking lot is full.
(A) closing
(B) closes
(C) closed
(D) closure

3 A concourse ------- the hotel to the conference center is available for use by our guests.
(A) connects
(B) connected
(C) is connecting
(D) connecting

✎ POINT ❷ 감정동사의 분사

01 | 수식을 받는 대상이 사물이면 현재분사를 쓴다.

amusing 재미있는	satisfying 만족스러운	fascinating 매력적인	interesting 흥미로운
confusing 혼동시키는	disappointing 실망스러운	worrying 걱정스러운	frustrating 불만스러운
encouraging 고무적인	exciting 흥미진진한	surprising 놀라운	shocking 충격적인
tiring 피곤하게 하는	exhausting 지치게 하는	irritating 짜증 나게 하는	embarrassing 당황스러운

Every customer can enjoy [satisfying / ~~satisfied~~] **dishes** which are sold at very affordable prices at Lucy's Kitchen. 모든 손님은 Lucy's Kitchen에서 매우 저렴한 가격에 판매되는 만족스러운 음식들을 즐길 수 있습니다.

Due to the [disappointing / ~~disappointed~~] **returns** last year, the budget will be reduced by 50 percent this year. 지난해의 실망스러운 수익 때문에, 올해 예산은 50%까지 줄어들 것이다.

02 | 수식을 받는 대상이 사람이면 과거분사를 쓴다.

amused 재미있어하는	satisfied 만족하는	fascinated 매료된	interested 관심 있는
confused 혼란스러운	disappointed 실망한	worried 걱정하는	frustrated 불만스러워하는
encouraged 고무된	excited 신이 난	surprised 놀란	shocked 충격을 받은
tired 피곤한	exhausted 지친	irritated 짜증 난	embarrassed 당황한

Lean Green Construction has served hundreds of [satisfied / ~~satisfying~~] **customers** over the years. Lean Green 건설사는 지난 수년 동안 많은 만족하는 고객들을 위하여 일해 왔다.

The massage service at the Comfort Hotel is recommended for [exhausted / ~~exhausting~~] **guests** in need of physical relief. 신체적 휴식을 필요로 하는 지친 손님들을 위해 Comfort 호텔의 마사지 서비스를 추천합니다.

+TIP 목적격 보어에 감정동사의 능동과 수동 구분

The goal of our company is to keep **our employees** [satisfied / ~~satisfying~~].
우리 회사의 목표는 우리 직원들을 계속 만족하게 하는 것이다.

▶ 목적어가 감정을 주는 원인(보통 사물)이면 현재분사, 감정을 느끼는 대상(사람, 단체)이면 과거분사를 쓴다.

SPARTA ☑ Check-UP! ❷

해설 p. 361

1 Although critics found Ms. Crew's artwork at the exhibition -------, it hasn't attracted many visitors.

(A) fascinating
(B) fascinated
(C) fascinate
(D) fascination

2 Biogen Science made an ------- recovery by posting incredible profits after three consecutive quarters of losses.

(A) amazing
(B) amazement
(C) amaze
(D) amazingly

3 The number of investors ------- in residential real estate is not growing at all because of the economic depression.

(A) interesting
(B) to interest
(C) interest
(D) interested

POINT 3 분사구문

01 | 분사구문은 시간·원인·양보·조건·연속 동작 등을 나타낸다.

분사구문은 [접속사+주어+동사]의 부사절을 축약한 형태로, 접속사는 생략될 수 있으며, 생략된 접속사는 문맥을 통해 판단한다.

시간 Completing the survey, please return it to our customer service department.
= **When you complete** the survey, please return it to our customer service department.
설문조사를 완료한 다음, 그것을 우리 고객 서비스 부서로 보내주세요.

원인 Damaged during delivery, the microwave oven was replaced immediately.
= **Because it had been damaged** during delivery, the microwave oven was replaced immediately.
배달 도중 손상이 되어서, 전자레인지는 즉시 교체되었다.

양보 Having made an obvious mistake in the report, Ms. Lee still refused to admit it.
= **Although she had made** an obvious mistake in the report, Ms. Lee still refused to admit it.
보고서에 명백한 실수가 있었지만, Lee 씨는 여전히 인정하지 않았다.
▶ 완료분사 구문<having+p.p.>은 분사구문의 시제가 주절의 시제보다 앞설 때 사용한다.

조건 Unless delivered within a week, orders are fully refundable.
= **Unless they are delivered** within a week, orders are fully refundable.
만약 주문품들이 일주일 이내에 배달되지 않으면, 전액 환불될 수 있습니다.

연속 동작 We purchased TG Technology, confirming our plans to expand into the European market.
우리는 유럽 시장으로 확장할 계획을 확인하면서, TG Technology 사를 인수했다.

02 | 분사구문에서 현재분사와 과거분사의 구별

**생략된 주어와 분사가 능동 관계이면 현재분사, 수동 관계이면 과거분사를 쓴다.
분사구문에서 뒤에 목적어가 있으면 현재분사, 목적어가 없으면 과거분사를 쓴다.**

After [reviewing / ~~reviewed~~] **the complaint report**, the company decided to put one more worker on the assembly line. 불만 사항 보고서를 검토한 뒤, 회사는 직원 한 사람을 조립 라인에 더 투입시키기로 결정했다.
▶ 분사구문의 의미를 더욱 정확하게 전하기 위해 접속사는 그대로 두는 경우도 있다. 단, 접속사 Because, As(이유), Although는 분사구문 앞에 쓰지 않는다.

[Impressed / ~~Impressing~~] **with Joan's qualifications**, Kevin scheduled the interview right after he read her résumé. Joan의 자격요건에 깊은 인상을 받았기 때문에, Kevin 씨는 그녀의 이력서를 본 직후 면접 일정을 잡았다.

SPARTA Check-UP! 3

| 해설 p. 362

1 When ------- announcements for the bulletin board, we recommend that you follow the format shown in this sample.
(A) prepared
(B) preparing
(C) to prepare
(D) prepare

2 ------- successfully finished the project, all team members received an unexpected bonus.
(A) Had
(B) Having
(C) To have
(D) Having been

3 ------- to sign a contract with A&C, the manager of the Sales Department was dismissed yesterday.
(A) Fail
(B) Have failed
(C) Having failed
(D) Failed

POINT 4 현재분사와 과거분사의 관용 표현

01 | 현재분사+명사

existing equipment	기존 장비	**misleading information**	잘못된 정보
lasting impression	지속적인 인상	**mounting pressure**	증가하는 압력
leading company	선두 기업	**deteriorating economy**	악화되는 경제
promising candidates	유망한 후보	**disappointing revenues**	실망스러운 수입
increasing demand	증가하는 수요	**remaining inventory**	남아 있는 재고
opening remarks	개회사	**demanding supervisor**	까다로운 상사
presiding officer	사회자	**missing baggage**	분실된 짐

02 | 과거분사+명사

revised procedure	개정된 절차	**attached document**	첨부된 서류
written consent	서면 동의	**updated manual**	최신의 설명서
finished product	완제품	**enclosed brochure**	동봉된 소책자
detailed information	자세한 정보	**unlimited guarantee**	무제한 보장
discounted price	할인된 가격	**recognized organization**	인정 받는 기관
preferred means	선호되는 수단	**informed decision**	잘 알고 내린 결정
damaged luggage	파손된 수하물	**designated area**	지정된 구역
reserved seat	지정석	**restricted area**	제한 구역

+TIP 분사구문의 관용적 표현(as p.p.)

as discussed 논의된 대로	as notified 공지된 대로	as planned 계획대로
as noted 언급된 대로	as mentioned 언급된 대로	as scheduled 일정대로
as requested 요청한 대로	as indicated 지시한 대로	as projected 예상한 대로

All applicants must meet our requirements, as [outlined / ~~outlining~~] in the application form.
모든 지원자들은 지원서에 요약된 대로 우리가 원하는 조건을 갖추어야 한다.

SPARTA Check-UP! 4

해설 p. 362

1 The vacuum cleaner was sent back to the manufacturer because the attachments arrived in ------- condition.
(A) damage
(B) damaging
(C) damages
(D) damaged

2 Please place your payment in the ------- postage-paid envelope and mail it to Deron Electronics by December 15.
(A) enclosure
(B) enclosed
(C) enclosing
(D) enclose

3 As -------, operating costs at the factory will increase by 20 percent by the end of the month.
(A) projects
(B) projected
(C) projecting
(D) to project

PRACTICE

해설 p. 362

▪ 괄호 안의 보기 중 알맞은 단어를 고르세요.

1 The company increased its profits by reducing the time **[requiring / required]** to assemble the parts.

2 A free sample will be provided with every purchase of $30 or more for a **[limiting / limited]** period of time.

3 The new package tour includes the area's most **[celebration / celebrated]** tourist attractions.

4 After **[repeating / repeated]** requests by local residents, the city council finally agreed to erect a town monument.

5 Please accept the **[enclosing / enclosed]** coupon that guarantees you 10% off your entire purchase on your next visit to our store.

6 To place an order, simply complete the attached order form and send it along with your payment in the reply envelope **[providing / provided]** in your booklet.

7 The plant manager was asked to present the **[opposing / opposed]** point of view on the plan to construct a new parking lot.

8 T&T Software offers the widest range of applications and operating systems, **[will allow / allowing]** customers to take full advantage of the new era of e-business.

9 Individuals who have not turned in their **[revising / revised]** monthly reports should meet with their immediate supervisor as soon as possible.

10 Due to sagging exports and a steep decline in corporate facility investment, the economy grew at a far slower rate than **[expect / expected]** in the latter half of this year.

11 Employees **[seek / seeking]** reimbursement for business-related expenses should submit all the receipts to the Accounting Department.

12 The profits at Thomson Electronics rose to 500 million dollars last year, **[reconfirming / reconfirmed]** its status as a leader in the field.

13 Travelers **[use / using]** the local airport in Hopkins complain that the security checkpoints take too much time.

14 A thunderstorm **[will accompany / accompanied]** by gusty winds is expected to affect the entire region.

15 We want an **[experienced / experiencing]** and energetic senior executive to develop our corporate culture to allow us to meet our goals more effectively.

1 Advanced Data Technology has a large number of highly ------- researchers in the engineering field.

(A) experienced (B) experiencing
(C) experience (D) experiences

2 The CEO found the analysis of the financial report which is presented by the head of management -------.

(A) satisfy (B) to satisfy
(C) satisfying (D) satisfied

3 In a ------- interview with reporter Harold Gilliam, world-famous actress Michelle Beasley spoke candidly about the emptiness of fame in the entertainment industry.

(A) fascinating (B) fascinate
(C) fascination (D) fascinated

4 The funds ------- by the community will be used to refurbish a number of the exhibits within the museum.

(A) donate (B) donated
(C) donating (D) donation

5 We offer flexible program formats to fit the needs of individuals or groups of professionals ------- the class.

(A) attends (B) attended
(C) attending (D) attendance

6 The airline is not responsible for any lost jewelry or cash ------- in checked or unchecked luggage.

(A) containing (B) container
(C) contain (D) contained

7 When ------- the new contract on Thursday, we need to keep in mind the terms and conditions and copy the old contract just in case.

(A) renegotiate (B) to renegotiate
(C) renegotiated (D) renegotiating

8 The International Monetary Fund was established to provide loans to countries having temporary difficulties ------- their financial obligations to other countries.

(A) to meet (B) meeting
(C) met (D) meet

9 ------- in 1971, the Bluewave Company employs over 31,000 employees in six countries.

(A) Founded (B) Founding
(C) Been founded (D) Having founded

10 As ------- at the meeting this afternoon, we will launch the new product no later than May 8.

(A) discuss (B) discussion
(C) discussing (D) discussed

11 Management has been ------- employees in the Marketing Department to come up with good ideas for the new project.

(A) encourage (B) encouraged
(C) encouraging (D) encouragement

12 The first year's sales of the new refrigerator were so ------- that the company made a decision to withdraw the model from the market.

(A) discouraging (B) discourage
(C) discouraged (D) discouragingly

Questions 13-16 refer to the following advertisement.

JOB OPENING

Job Title : Software Engineer
Company : M2M Solutions
Location : San Jose
Salary : $60,000+

M2M Solutions is a growing company that has already built a ------- (13.) for creating imaginative and effective solutions to a variety of customers' computer needs.

We are currently looking for talented computer professionals to join our team. Candidates should have 3-6 years of experience in an engineering or programming field and must have a working knowledge of C++ and Unix. We are looking for people with imagination who can not only work on a team but also have the self-confidence to act on their own -------. (14.)

Benefits include : 12 days paid vacation, a company car, and the paying of relocation expenses.

Furthermore, all employees are ------- (15.) to an annual profit-sharing bonus after their first year of employment.

Please e-mail your résumé to our personnel manager, Minka Jenkins, at minkaj@m2msolutions.net.

-------. (16.)

13 (A) excellence
(B) character
(C) value
(D) reputation

14 (A) initial
(B) initiation
(C) initiative
(D) initially

15 (A) enabled
(B) encouraged
(C) enlarged
(D) entitled

16 (A) Those who have extensive experience in the service industry are welcome to apply.
(B) Qualified applicants must be proficient in both English and French.
(C) She will contact you to arrange an interview.
(D) Access to this information is limited to authorized personnel.

UNIT 13 등위접속사와 상관접속사

등위접속사 문제는 ① 앞뒤 의미를 파악하여 의미상 알맞은 등위접속사를 골라야 하는 문제, ② 등위접속사 다음 빈칸을 두어 알맞은 형태를 고르는 문제로 출제된다. 상관접속사 문제는 보통 접속사 and, but (also), or, nor나 부사 both, either, neither 중 한 곳을 비워두고 어울리는 짝을 묻는 문제로 출제된다.

Preview

01 | 등위접속사

등위접속사는 단어와 단어, 구와 구, 절과 절을 대등한 관계로 이어준다. 즉, 등위접속사의 앞뒤는 동일한 문장 구조를 취함으로써 병렬 구조가 맞아야 한다.

- **and : 대등한 관계로 연결하는 순접의 접속사**

  We have to improve **quality** (목적어) and **productivity** (목적어). 우리는 품질과 생산성을 향상시켜야 한다.

- **but : 반대나 대조의 의미를 나타내는 역접의 접속사**

  He bought a car (절), but **he doesn't drive it at all** (절). 그는 자동차를 샀지만 그 차를 전혀 운전하지 않는다.

- **or : 선택의 의미를 나타내는 접속사**

  Keep the documents **in the file folder** (부사구) or **in the cabinet** (부사구). 서류들을 파일철이나 캐비닛에 보관하세요.

- **yet : but과 같은 역접의 접속사**

  He said that he would pay (절), yet **he didn't** (절). 그는 돈을 지불하겠다고 말했으나 아직 갚지 않았다.

- **so : 결과의 내용을 연결하는 접속사**

  I was getting tired (절), so **I came home early** (절). 나는 피곤해서 일찍 집에 돌아왔다.

02 | 상관접속사

상관접속사는 짝을 이루어 쓰이며, 등위접속사와 마찬가지로 단어와 단어, 구와 구, 절과 절을 연결한다.

both	**A**	**and**	**B**	A와 B 모두, A와 B 양쪽 다
either		**or**		A 혹은 B, A B 둘 중 하나
neither		**nor**		A도 B도 아닌
not only		**but (also)**		A뿐만 아니라 B도 (= B as well as A)
not		**but**		A가 아니라 B

The company intends to relocate its global headquarters to either **France** or **Italy**.
회사는 본사를 프랑스나 이탈리아로 이전하려 한다.

Neither **you** nor **he** knows the fact that they were not involved in the case.
당신도 그도 그들이 그 사건에 연루되지 않았다는 사실을 모르고 있다.

POINT 1 등위접속사

01 | 등위접속사의 종류와 의미

and 그리고(추가)　or 또는(선택)　but / yet 그러나, 하지만(반대)　so 그래서(결과)

Please call [or / ~~yet~~] e-mail Mr. Kim as soon as the fax comes in.
팩스가 도착하는 대로 Kim 씨에게 전화나 이메일 주세요.

The interview was supposed to be on Monday at 3:00, [but / ~~and~~] Ms. Davis wants to know if you can meet her at 2:00 instead.
면접은 월요일 3시로 예정이었지만 Davis 씨는 그 대신 2시에 만날 수 있을지 알고 싶어 합니다.

Tom is being transferring to New York, [so / ~~therefore~~] his colleagues will throw him a farewell party. Tom은 뉴욕으로 전근을 가게 되어, 그의 동료들이 그를 위해 송별회를 열 것이다.
▶ 등위접속사 so가 문장과 문장을 연결하고 있다. therefore는 부사이기 때문에 뒤에 절(문장)을 연결할 수 없다.

02 | 등위접속사 앞뒤는 같은 품사나 구조가 병렬된다.

Cracked **or** [damaged / ~~damagingly~~] orders must be returned within 30 days of the purchase date.
금이 가거나 손상된 주문품은 구매일로부터 30일 이내에 반품되어야 합니다.

The workshop will help restaurant owners evaluate their ability to effectively [recruit / ~~recruiting~~] **and** train staff.
워크숍은 식당 주인들이 직원을 효과적으로 모집하고 훈련시킬 수 있는 그들의 능력을 평가하는 데 도움이 될 것입니다.

+TIP so는 앞뒤에 모두 완전한 문장이 와야 한다.

and, but(= yet), or는 문장 및 그 외의 대등한 단위를 연결할 수 있는 반면, so는 문장들만 연결할 수 있다.

Max City **has the largest port on the coast** [and / ~~so~~] **is a major exporter of goods**.
Max City는 해안에 가장 큰 항구가 있고, 주요 상품 수출국이다.
▶문장과 문장을 연결하는 것이 아니므로 and를 써야 한다.

+TIP 등위접속사는 문두에 올 수 없다.

[Because / ~~And~~] the landlord offered a discount, the Dell Group chose to lease the office space. 임대인이 할인을 제공했기 때문에 Dell Group은 사무실 공간을 임대하기로 결정했습니다.

SPARTA Check-UP! 1

| 해설 p. 365

1 The CEO wants the employees to have commitment to their work ------- expertise in their field.
(A) as
(B) and
(C) after
(D) since

2 Mr. Hart will be away on a business trip next week ------- can be reached by e-mail in his absence.
(A) so
(B) nor
(C) but
(D) then

3 The company parking area will be repaved next week, ------- employees are advised to use public transportation during the week.
(A) except
(B) if
(C) so
(D) because

POINT 2 상관접속사

01 | 상관접속사의 종류와 의미

Jeff Catering has been providing excellence in dining for **both casual [and / ~~or~~] formal** events.
Jeff Catering 사는 비공식 및 공식 행사 모두에 탁월한 서비스를 제공해 왔습니다.

Hotel guests who stay 10 nights a year will be entitled to [either / ~~neither~~] **one free night or a room upgrade**.
1년에 10박을 하는 호텔 투숙객들에게는 1박 무료 또는 객실 업그레이드가 제공됩니다.

Neither **Ms. Pedrad** [nor / ~~and~~] **Ms. Magnussen** received the e-mail outlining the project proposal.
Pedrad 씨나 Magnussen 씨 둘 다 프로젝트 제안서를 요약한 이메일을 받지 못했습니다.

Mr. Ritchie's shop is known not only **for its fine products** (A) but (also) **its knowledgeable staff** (B).

= Mr. Ritchie's shop is known for **its knowledgeable staff** (B) as well as **its fine products** (A).

Ritchie 씨의 상점은 훌륭한 제품들뿐만 아니라 박식한 직원들로도 유명합니다.

▶ as well as : 앞뒤에 명사, 형용사 등 다양한 형태가 올 수 있지만 <주어+동사> 형태의 절은 올 수 없다. as well as 바로 뒤에는 동사원형이 올 수도 있다.

02 | 상관접속사가 문장의 주어일 때 동사의 수 일치

either A or B	동사는 B와 수 일치	**both A and B**	동사는 반드시 복수동사
neither A nor B	동사는 B와 수 일치	**not A but B**	동사는 B와 수 일치
not only A but (also) B	동사는 B와 수 일치	**B as well as A**	동사는 B와 수 일치

Both the supervisor **and** his assistant [have / ~~has~~] already arrived.
관리자와 보조원 둘 다 벌써 도착했다.

Not only the report **but also** the graphs [were / ~~was~~] produced by Ms. Hiben.
보고서뿐만 아니라 그래프들까지 Hiben 씨에 의해 제작되었다.

SPARTA Check-UP! 2

| 해설 p. 365

1 The sales manager said that neither high prices ------- a lack of effort was a factor in losing customers.
(A) nor
(B) yet
(C) so
(D) but

2 The governor believes that his program will not only clean up the environment ------- will also create many meaningful, well-paid jobs.
(A) and
(B) but
(C) however
(D) also

3 Both Ms. Suto and her associate ------- to be able and honest in their dealing with clients.
(A) has proved
(B) have proved
(C) proves
(D) proving

▪ 괄호 안의 보기 중 알맞은 단어를 고르세요.

1 We will issue you a refund check **[or / yet]** credit it to your account.

2 The cruise ship includes space for 500 passengers **[and / but]** entertainment areas.

3 We are waiting for the results of the last board meeting, **[but / or]** they have not arrived yet.

4 Employees' responses to this questionnaire are needed for our files **[and / but]** will help us make our company a better place to work.

5 Before applying for a **[license / licensed]** or construction permit, developers must conduct a specific environmental impact assessment.

6 As of next month, tickets to the concert can be purchased by either e-mail **[and / or]** phone.

7 All the recent automobile models produced by Worthington Motors are made of heavier materials; **[yet / thus]** they typically offer better gas mileage than their counterparts.

8 Because neither the union **[or / nor]** management requested mediation by the government, union officials are expected to map out their protest plan this month.

9 Admission tickets can be purchased **[either / neither]** online or at the ticket office beside the entrance.

10 In the event that a customer receives a broken product, we will send a replacement **[or / nor]** give the customer a full refund.

11 In order to register with the organization, the man knew he had to show either his driver's license **[or / also]** his birth certificate.

12 The carrier is responsible for proper loading, the vessel, and storage and discharging procedures **[but / also]** not for the packaging of the goods.

13 The company's directors opposed the compensation package **[whether / not only]** because of the high salary but also because of the standard it would set.

14 **[Whether / Both]** Mr. McDonnell and Ms. Douglas will work overtime to help their supervisor prepare for a big presentation.

15 The reason why this merchandise is not selling well is not because its price is high **[but / and]** because its quality is bad.

1 Mr. Lee almost always goes to meetings late, ------- he doesn't seem to care much about it.

(A) and (B) or
(C) which (D) although

2 Both the press ------- the local community enthusiastically applauded the governor's new policy on supporting the old.

(A) but (B) or
(C) nor (D) and

3 If you have not yet renewed your subscription to our monthly magazine, you should ------- sign up online today or visit the nearest distribution center in person.

(A) neither (B) either
(C) yet (D) nor

4 The weather forecaster today said there was a 60-percent chance of rain, ------- in fact, the temperature remained high all day with clear skies.

(A) and (B) or
(C) but (D) if

5 Withdrawals over $1,000 a day must be signed by ------- the account holder and the authorized signatory.

(A) both (B) whether
(C) either (D) not only

6 Juno Apartment Complex security officers not only frequently monitor the resident parking area ------- ticket unidentified vehicles in the area.

(A) therefore (B) and then
(C) however (D) but also

7 New employees receive a benefits package offering ------- health and dental insurance or health and vision insurance.

(A) either (B) not only
(C) both (D) whether

8 Maria really likes her job at the shoe store, ------- she wishes that it could be more exciting.

(A) and (B) so
(C) but (D) then

9 The stock market across Asia remains stable compared to that of last month, ------- all is not as it seems.

(A) but (B) also
(C) nor (D) despite

10 Coachella Valley Music Festival tickets ------- the performers' albums are on sale at the Columbus Civic Center box office.

(A) either (B) and
(C) that (D) so

11 Diane Nicholls was offered the international marketing job last week ------- has still not responded.

(A) although (B) but
(C) unless (D) nor

12 Please indicate on the envelope whether you would prefer regular ------- deluxe photo processing as well as the size of the prints for each photograph.

(A) nor (B) so
(C) or (D) and

Questions 13-16 refer to the following memo.

Memorandum

Date: July 5
From: Jeffrey Pfeffer, Director, Data Management Research
To: Aaron Bernstein, Director, Research Programs
Subject: Commendation-Charles Perrow-Customer Virus Project

Charles has been working on the special assignment with the Customer Virus Project team for the past five months. I would like to take this time ------- (13.) him for his exceptional contribution to the CVP throughout the assignment.

I want to make sure that he gets some recognition for his hard work and contributions to the project now that he is about to return to his part of the organization. His great enthusiasm as a project manager played a vital role in the entire project ------- (14.) as a programmer but also as a colleague and project team member. -------. (15.)

I strongly believe that the organization should recognize his ------- (16.) performance.

13 (A) to commend
(B) commending
(C) commendation
(D) commend

14 (A) therefore
(B) and
(C) or
(D) not only

15 (A) Please contact me as soon as possible to discuss this matter.
(B) Last year, we also celebrated the achievements of Charles Perrow.
(C) The annual employee luncheon will be held at 1 P.M. at the Emerald Club.
(D) In addition, he is one of the most productive programmers that I have ever worked with.

16 (A) excepting
(B) except
(C) exceptional
(D) exception

UNIT 14 관계대명사

관계대명사 문제는 ① 관계대명사의 격을 묻는 문제와 ② 주격 관계대명사 절의 동사와 선행사의 수 일치 문제가 출제되고 있다. 특히 주격 관계대명사와 소유격 관계대명사가 자주 출제된다.

Preview

01 | 관계대명사의 역할

관계대명사는 접속사와 대명사의 기능을 가지며, 선행사(명사)를 수식하는 형용사절이다.

문장 1 Our company is looking for **a person.** 우리 회사는 사람을 찾고 있다.

문장 2 **The person** can speak both English and French. 그 사람은 영어와 불어를 모두 할 수 있다.

문장 1 + 문장 2 Our company is looking for **a person** who can speak both English and French.
우리 회사는 영어와 불어를 모두 할 수 있는 사람을 찾고 있다.

02 | 관계대명사의 종류와 격 변화

주격	주격 관계대명사 뒤에는 주어가 없는 불완전한 문장이 온다.
소유격	소유격 관계대명사 다음에는 완전한 문장이 나오며, 뒤에 항상 명사를 수반한다.
목적격	목적격 관계대명사 뒤에는 타동사의 목적어가 없거나, 전치사의 목적어가 없는 불완전한 문장이 온다.

관계대명사는 수식을 받는 선행사가 사람인지 사물인지에 따라 달라지며 주격, 소유격, 목적격으로 나뉜다.

선행사	주격 관계대명사	소유격 관계대명사	목적격 관계대명사
사람	who	whose	who / whom
사물	which	whose / of which	which
사람/사물	that	-	that

The president was unable to remember the name of **the agent** who(= **that**) visited him yesterday.
사장은 어제 그를 방문한 대리인의 이름을 기억할 수 없었다.

I work for **an LED company** whose president is in his early 30s.
나는 LED 회사에서 일하는데, 그 회사의 사장님은 30대 초반이다.

Through the Internet, we can learn various **things** that(= **which**) we cannot actually experience.
인터넷을 통해서 우리는 실제로 경험할 수 없는 여러 가지 것들을 배울 수 있다.

POINT 1 관계대명사의 역할

01 | 관계대명사 = 접속사+대명사

The company is looking for **a motor designer**. **The motor designer** has a master's degree.
→ The company is looking for **a motor designer** who has a master's degree.
그 회사는 석사 학위를 지닌 자동차 디자이너를 찾고 있다.

02 | 관계대명사는 선행사를 수식하는 형용사절이다.

AD-Net is **an international advertising firm** [that / ~~when~~] specializes in the food and beverage industry. AD-Net은 식음료 산업을 전문으로 하는 국제 광고 회사입니다.

The department heads whom I met were all very friendly. 내가 만났던 부서장들은 모두 아주 친절했다.

03 | 관계대명사는 선행사의 종류에 따라 달라진다.

Customers [who / ~~which~~] make cash withdrawals frequently may be interested in the lower fees of a high-volume account. 현금 인출을 자주 하는 고객들은 거래량이 많은 계좌에 매기는 더 낮은 수수료에 관심이 있을 것이다.
▶ 선행사가 사람일 때 관계대명사는 who나 that을 쓴다.

I have enclosed **my résumé**, [which / ~~that~~] gives more details about my working history and my educational background.
저의 경력과 학력에 대한 자세한 정보를 제공하는 이력서를 동봉했습니다.
▶ 선행사가 사물일 때 관계대명사는 which나 that을 쓴다. 단, that은 콤마 뒤에는 사용할 수 없다.

At the monthly meeting, Ms. Scott frequently offers **tips** [that / ~~who~~] help maintenance staff members perform their duties better.
월례 회의에서 Scott 씨는 정비 직원들이 직무를 더 잘 수행할 수 있도록 도와주는 팁을 자주 제시한다.
▶ that은 선행사가 사람, 사물일 때 모두 쓸 수 있다.

+TIP 주격 관계대명사 바로 다음에 나오는 동사의 경우 선행사에 수 일치를 시킨다.

Customers who [want / ~~wants~~] a refund must return with the merchandise and the receipt within 30 days of purchase. 환불을 원하는 고객은 30일 이내에 상품과 영수증을 가지고 와야 한다.
▶ 선행사 Customers에 수 일치를 시켜 wants가 아닌 want를 써야 한다.

SPARTA Check-UP! 1

해설 p. 368

1 The number of healthcare providers ------- use electronic devices capable of sharing data is increasing.
(A) who
(B) which
(C) whom
(D) where

2 You will receive a document detailing all of the issues ------- will be discussed during the meeting.
(A) who
(B) that
(C) what
(D) it

3 Car Life Insurance offers policies which ------- full coverage of most vehicle repair bills.
(A) provide
(B) providing
(C) was provided
(D) provides

POINT 2 관계대명사의 역할

01 | 주격 관계대명사 : 주격관계대명사 뒤에는 주어가 없다.

Shoppers [who / ~~whom~~] **join the Gatsby's Mart Bargain Club** will receive a $10 discount coupon.
Gatsby's Mart Bargain Club에 가입하는 쇼핑객들은 10달러 할인쿠폰을 받을 것이다.

The Rosenberg Group is seeking skilled workers for its hotel project [which / ~~whose~~] **is supposed to begin next year**.
Rosenberg 그룹은 다음 해에 시작될 예정인 호텔 프로젝트에 참여할 숙련된 직원들을 구하고 있다.

02 | 목적격 관계대명사 : 목적격 관계대명사 뒤에는 목적어가 없다.

Mr. Russell talked about the TNA Development Plan, [which / ~~who~~] **he will announce next month**.
러셀 씨는 다음 달에 발표할 TNA 개발 계획에 관해 이야기했다.

The business team must meet its deadline for arranging all the meetings [that / ~~whose~~] **its supervisor has ordered**.
경영 팀은 매니저가 지시한 모든 회의 준비 마감 기한을 반드시 지켜야 한다.

03 | 소유격 관계대명사 : 소유격 관계대명사는 완전한 문장이 뒤따르며, 바로 뒤에 명사가 온다.

It is the Human Resources manager [whose / ~~who~~] job **is to evaluate and keep or terminate employees**.
직원을 평가하거나 해고하는 것은 인적자원부 부장의 일이다.

We are still looking for a candidate [whose / ~~which~~] qualifications **meet the requirements for the senior editor position**.
우리는 자격 요건이 선임 편집장의 조건을 충족시키는 지원자를 아직도 찾고 있다.

▶ 관계대명사 문제에서 빈칸 뒤에 명사가 연결되어 있으면 소유격 관계대명사를 선택한다.

SPARTA Check-UP! 2

해설 p. 368

1 The civil service organization is composed of various offices and the employees ------- run them.
(A) they
(B) what
(C) which
(D) who

2 Fine Arts is an organization ------- mission is to support public art projects in the Lena Rivers area.
(A) that
(B) what
(C) which
(D) whose

3 We're sorry that the item ------- you ordered is currently out of stock.
(A) whose
(B) who
(C) that
(D) what

POINT ③ 관계대명사의 생략

01 | 주격 관계대명사+be동사의 생략

The new auditor **who is joining** our department next week is known for his outstanding experience.
→ The new auditor [**joining** / ~~joins~~] our department next week is known for his outstanding experience. 다음 주에 우리 부서로 합류할 신임 감사관은 탁월한 경력으로 유명하다.

You should be aware of the expertise **which is needed** for this engineering position.
→ You should be aware of the expertise [**needed** / ~~was needed~~] for this engineering position.
당신은 이 기술직에 필요한 전문지식에 대하여 알고 있어야 한다.

02 | 목적격 관계대명사의 생략

The replacements **which your company ordered** will be shipped by next week at the latest.
→ The replacements **your company** [**ordered** / ~~was ordered~~] will be shipped by next week at the latest. 당신의 회사가 주문한 교체품들이 늦어도 다음 주에 배송될 것이다.
▶ which는 생략 가능하며, 생략하더라도 ordered의 목적어 역할을 한다.

03 | 관계대명사가 생략된 구조의 판단

1) 빈칸 뒤에 명사 목적어가 있으면 능동태 구조의 축약으로 현재분사(-ing)를 선택한다.

Employees [**seeking** / ~~are seeking~~] **reimbursement** for travel expenses should submit an application form to Mr. Simpson. 출장비를 상환 받으려는 직원들은 Simpson 씨에게 신청서를 제출해야 한다.

2) 빈칸 뒤에 목적어가 없으면 수동태 구조의 축약으로 과거분사(p.p.)를 선택한다.

It is imperative that all employees attend the sales meeting [**scheduled** / ~~was scheduled~~] **for June 11**. 모든 직원들은 반드시 6월 11일로 예정된 영업 회의에 참석해야 합니다.

+TIP remain, work, stay 등의 자동사는 항상 현재분사로 쓴다는 점에 유의한다.

Guests [**staying** / ~~stayed~~] at Marada Inn were asked to rate the quality of their accommodations.
Marada Inn에 머무르는 투숙객들은 숙박 시설을 평가해 달라는 요청을 받았습니다.

SPARTA Check-UP! 3

해설 p. 369

1 There are a variety of charges ------- with taking out a home loan.
(A) associate
(B) associated
(C) association
(D) associating

2 Of the three candidates we ------- for the position, Mr. Pere appears to know the most about the energy campaign.
(A) interviewee
(B) interviewed
(C) interviewing
(D) were interviewed

3 Workers ------- in Kolache factory will receive a one-month paid vacation at the end of the year.
(A) working
(B) worked
(C) will work
(D) are worked

POINT 4 그 밖에 주의해야 할 관계대명사

01 | 관계대명사 what : 선행사와 관계대명사가 합쳐진 것으로 <~ 것>, <무엇>으로 해석한다.

1) 관계대명사 what(= the thing which)은 선행사를 포함한 관계대명사로 명사절을 이끈다.

We want to know [**what** / ~~that~~] our competitors are trying to accomplish.
= the thing which
우리는 경쟁사들이 무엇을 이루기 위해 애쓰고 있는지 알기 원한다.

2) 관계대명사 what 다음에는 주어나 목적어가 없는 불완전한 문장이 온다.

[**What** / ~~That~~] **is important** is how we should cope with the problem.
→ 주어가 없는 불완전한 문장
중요한 것은 우리가 어떻게 그 문제를 처리해 나가야 하는가이다.

The merchandise is [**what** / ~~that~~] **I purchased through the Internet yesterday**.
→ 타동사(purchased)의 목적어가 없는 불완전한 문장
그 상품은 내가 어제 인터넷을 통해 산 것이다.

02 | 관계대명사의 that과 명사절 접속사의 that

The company hired a new manager [**that** / ~~while~~] **has a lot of experience**.
→ 주어가 없는 불완전한 절로 명사 뒤에서 명사를 수식한다.
그 회사는 경험이 많은 새 매니저를 고용했다.

Southeast Airlines announced [**that** / ~~what~~] **the flight would be delayed**.
→ 완전한 문장을 갖춘 채 문장에서 목적어 역할을 한다.
사우스이스트 항공사는 비행기가 연착될 것이라고 발표했다.

03 | 전치사+목적격 관계대명사

The project [**that** / ~~whose~~] Mr. Kim is working **on** is supposed to be completed this week.
The project **on** [**which** / ~~that~~] Mr. Kim is working is supposed to be completed this week.
김 씨가 작업 중인 프로젝트는 이번 주에 마무리될 예정이다.

▶ 목적격 관계대명사는 that으로 바꾸어 쓸 수 있지만, 전치사 다음에 오는 경우에는 that으로 바꾸어 쓸 수 없다.

SPARTA Check-UP! 4

해설 p. 369

1 The business consultant explains ------- you need to know about trading to become profitable in your business.
(A) what
(B) which
(C) where
(D) how

2 ------- impresses stockholders the most is that the Melcam Company has boosted international recognition of its brand this year.
(A) Which
(B) What
(C) Nothing
(D) Neither

3 Restaurant management announced ------- the restaurant would be closed for renovations for three weeks.
(A) that
(B) where
(C) who
(D) what

SPARTA PRACTICE

해설 p. 369

▪ 괄호 안의 보기 중 알맞은 단어를 고르세요.

1 The company is seeking an interior designer **[who / which]** has a master's or doctor's degree.

2 Ms. Diaz predicts **[that / what]** Kodic's latest camera will be a great success in the retail marketplace.

3 I'm sorry, but we can't reimburse you for a product **[who / which]** has been damaged or purchased more than 15 days ago.

4 If there is any copy paper **[who / that]** is left in the storage room, please bring it to Ms. Park.

5 Please present the complimentary dining coupon **[you / your]** received with the purchase of our product.

6 I would like to thank Dr. Nelson, **[who / which]** has agreed to deliver an address at the 10th annual conference this coming Saturday.

7 The interviewer was most impressed by Sandra, **[who / that]** established her own company shortly after graduating from university.

8 The person **[who / whose]** job is to process new applications is Peter Kim, the Human Resources manager.

9 The HR Department has been recording all of the expenses **[for / by]** which you have requested reimbursement.

10 The names of the department managers to **[whom / which]** the monthly account statements should be mailed are located on the manual.

11 Applicants are required to submit documentation **[verifying / verified]** their eligibility for the position.

12 I subscribe to the *Times Journal*, **[distributing / distributed]** monthly by the American Medical Society.

13 All new employees should attend the orientation sessions the company **[will be held / will be holding]** next month.

14 In many years, airline mileage **[incurred / incurring]** for business purposes is a tax-deductible expense.

15 Interested applicants should submit their résumé and cover letter by the date **[writing / written]** on the application form.

1 The bus line, ------- has been operating since last week, stops at each bus stop every 7 minutes.

(A) which (B) whom
(C) who (D) what

2 Subscribers ------- are experiencing IPTV connection problems should call the help desk, which is available around the clock.

(A) which (B) who
(C) what (D) whose

3 Trevor Satchell, ------- shareholders have expressed concern about the financial crisis, has postponed the quarterly meeting on stockholder equity until next week.

(A) whatever (B) whose
(C) which (D) who

4 The seminar will examine the many factors ------- affect the costs of raw materials in the automotive industry.

(A) that (B) where
(C) who (D) what

5 All advertisements must arrive a minimum of 15 days prior to the release date of the issue in ------- you expect it to be displayed.

(A) who (B) which
(C) that (D) what

6 Delly Catering Service, a catering company ------- the region for ten years, is currently offering a 30-percent discount for any events in the area.

(A) serve (B) serving
(C) served (D) to serve

7 Employees should report to the boardroom at 7:30 A.M., after ------- there will be a short information session to introduce new employees and to review policies.

(A) while (B) which
(C) where (D) what

8 The personnel change form includes a section for those employees ------- personal status has changed.

(A) whom (B) which
(C) that (D) whose

9 Unfortunately, after some discussion, it seems that there are ------- will probably not respect the accountant's decision.

(A) those who (B) whatever
(C) of which (D) of whom

10 The Nutty Company apologizes for any problems ------- by the noise from the construction on the second floor.

(A) cause (B) causes
(C) causing (D) caused

11 Attach the shipping label ------- with your original order if you wish to get a refund.

(A) provides (B) provided
(C) is provided (D) providing

12 A hotel in Miami decided to offer free movie tickets to customers ------- longer than one week.

(A) will stay (B) stayed
(C) have stayed (D) staying

해설 p. 370

Questions 13-16 refer to the following advertisement.

JUNIOR ACCOUNTS ASSISTANT WANTED

Maidstone Education Services is a professional education company ------- (13.) on financial markets, life sciences, computer literacy, and the public sector.

------- (14.). Reporting to the financial controller, the junior accounts assistant will play a significant ------- (15.) within the Finance Department by focusing his or her primary responsibilities on the management of debtors, creditors, banks, and expenses.

The successful candidate will be a flexible team player ------- (16.) can meet strict deadlines. A minimum of 1-2 years' experience in a similar field would be an advantage. Knowledge of accounting software is required. If you are interested in working in an enjoyable, highly innovative environment with an extensive international client base, Maidstone Education Services would like to hear from you.

To apply for this position, please send your résumé to:
Human Resources Department, Maidstone Education Services P.O. BOX 4059, N.Y.

13
(A) focuses
(B) has focused
(C) will focus
(D) focusing

14
(A) Two accounts assistants were hired in preparation of the firm's expansion.
(B) We are pleased to announce your promotion to the position of financial controller.
(C) We are currently looking for talented individuals for the position of junior accounts assistant.
(D) You are being considered for a promotion to the position of financial controller.

15
(A) lead
(B) job
(C) post
(D) role

16
(A) which
(B) what
(C) who
(D) whom

UNIT 15 명사절과 명사절 접속사

명사절 접속사는 자주 출제되는 유형은 아니지만, 문장 구조의 이해를 위해서 반드시 알아 두어야 하는 부분이다. 빈출 문제는 ① [----+문장]+동사, ② 동사+[----+문장] 형태로 출제되며, 특히 that, what, whether, how가 정답이 되는 문제가 많이 출제된다.

01 | 명사절은 문장에서 주어, 목적어, 보어 역할을 한다.

주어 That he has known the confidential information **is** obvious.
주어 / 동사 / 보어
그가 그 기밀 정보를 알고 있음이 분명하다.

목적어 The president **said** that the rumor was true.
주어 / 동사 / 목적어
사장은 그 소문이 사실이라고 말했다.

보어 My idea **is** that we should have a promotional campaign.
주어 / 동사 / 보어
내 생각은 우리가 홍보 캠페인을 해야 한다는 것이다.

02 | 명사절 접속사 if, whether(~인지 아닌지)는 불확실한 의문을 나타낼 때 사용한다.

I will check if(= whether) **tickets are still available.**
표를 아직도 구할 수 있는지 확인해 보겠다.

Let me know whether **you will accept our offer or not.**
우리의 제안을 받아들일 것인지 아닌지 알려주세요.

03 | It ~ that 구문에서 that은 명사절 접속사로 절을 이끌며, 진주어로 쓰인다.

That the company should hire more employees is necessary.
= **It** is necessary that the company should hire more employees.
회사가 더 많은 직원을 고용하는 것은 꼭 필요하다.

▶ that절이 주어일 경우 보통 문장의 맨 뒤에 위치하고 가주어 it이 대신할 수 있다.

POINT 1 명사절 접속사의 역할

01 | 명사절은 주어, 목적어, 보어 역할을 한다.

1) 주어

[That / ~~While~~] **the concert was sold out two weeks ago** suggests that the singer is very popular with local residents.
콘서트가 2주 전에 매진되었다는 것은 가수가 지역 주민들에게 매우 인기가 있음을 보여준다.

2) 목적어

The Cotta Company announced that it is contemplating [whether / ~~because~~] **it will place all production on standby.** Cotta 사는 모든 생산을 대기 상태로 둘지 고려중이라고 발표했다.

3) 보어

One of the advantages at Kelip is [that / ~~although~~] **employees are entitled to two days off every four days.**
Kelip 사의 혜택들 중 한 가지는 근무자가 4일 근무 후 이틀을 쉴 수 있다는 점이다.

▶ '접속사+주어+동사'로 이루어진 덩어리가 문장에서 주어나 목적어 또는 보어의 역할을 할 때 명사절이라고 부른다.

02 | 명사절 접속사의 자리에 관계대명사나 부사절 접속사는 올 수 없다.

It is essential [that / ~~which~~] **the results of the research study remain confidential.**
조사 연구의 결과는 기밀 상태로 유지하는 것이 필수적이다.

The survey reports [that / ~~because~~] **the amount of spending on food is about the same as last year.** 설문조사는 음식에 소비하는 총액이 지난해와 비슷할 것이라고 전한다.

03 | 명사절과 관계사절의 구별

Mervin Software **announced** (동사) [that / ~~whereas~~] **it is planning to expand into India** (명사절 (생략할 수 없음)).
Mervin Software 사는 인도로 사업을 확장할 계획이라고 발표했다.

▶ that 이하 명사절이 announce의 목적어 역할을 하고 있다. whereas는 '~인 반면에'라는 의미의 부사절 접속사다.

I bought **three art magazines** (선행사) [that / ~~whether~~] **were recommended by experts** (형용사절 (생략할 수 있음)).
나는 전문가들이 추천한 예술 잡지 세 권을 샀다.

▶ that 이하 관계대명사절이 앞에 선행사(명사)를 수식하고 있다. whether 명사절은 선행사를 수식할 수 없다.

SPARTA Check-UP! 1

해설 p. 372

1 No one told us ------- there was a complaint filed against our department, so we need some time to look into it.
(A) what
(B) that
(C) which
(D) who

2 One of the good aspects of this new machine is ------- it is clearly designed to conserve energy.
(A) than
(B) that
(C) what
(D) because

3 When asked ------- he will retire next year, Mr. Frederic said that he will never quit working.
(A) while
(B) whereas
(C) whenever
(D) whether

POINT ② 명사절 접속사 that

01 | that절을 목적어로 자주 취하는 동사

suggest ~을 제시하다, 나타내다	explain ~를 설명하다	say ~을 말하다
show ~을 보여주다, 입증하다	report ~를 보고하다	ensure ~을 보증하다
indicate ~을 알리다, 나타내다	state ~라고 진술하다	believe ~라고 믿다, 생각하다
announce ~를 발표하다	think ~라고 생각하다	note ~에 주목[주의]하다

The director has suggested [that / ~~before~~] **the workshop be postponed until next week.**
이사는 워크숍이 다음 주까지 연기되어야 한다고 제안했다.

02 | that절을 자주 취하는 형용사

be aware that ~을 알고 있다	be sure that ~이 확실하다	make sure that 확실히 ~하다
be confident that ~에 자신 있다	be certain that ~임이 확실하다	be hopeful that ~을 기대하다
be likely that ~일 것 같다	be pleased that ~이 기쁘다	be delighted that ~이 기쁘다

Please be aware [that / ~~since~~] **some Web pages may work incorrectly.**
일부 웹 페이지가 제대로 작동하지 않을 수 있습니다.

03 | 동격의 명사절 접속사 that

the fact that ~라는 사실	the rumor that ~라는 소문
the truth that ~라는 사실	the opinion that ~라는 의견
the news that ~라는 뉴스	the idea that ~라는 의견
the statement that ~라는 진술, 성명	the claim that ~라는 주장

Everyone knows the fact [that / ~~where~~] **the meeting has been canceled.**
모든 사람들은 회의가 취소되었다는 사실을 알고 있다.

SPARTA Check-UP! 2

해설 p. 372

1 The findings from the report indicate ------- shoppers prefer ordering online to visiting the actual store.
(A) that
(B) which
(C) those
(D) what

2 The supervisor of the Marketing Department made sure ------- everything was perfect for the summer tourism campaign.
(A) that
(B) what
(C) how
(D) which

3 Due to the fact ------- Pannel's flat-screen televisions are already discounted, they will not qualify for this weekend's sale.
(A) what
(B) who
(C) which
(D) that

POINT ❸ 명사절 접속사 whether과 if

01 | 명사절 접속사 if(~인지 아닌지)는 타동사의 목적어로만 쓸 수 있다.

[Whether / ~~If~~] **the company should follow its corporate lawyer's advice** has been controversial with management since last month.
회사가 기업 변호사들의 자문을 따를지 여부는 지난달 이후부터 경영진에게 논란이 분분한 문제였다.

02 | 타동사의 목적어로 쓰이는 경우 whether과 if 둘 다 가능하다.

Please call Tom by 6 P.M. on Friday to let him know [whether / if] **you will be able to attend the meeting**.
당신의 회의 참석 여부를 알 수 있도록, 금요일 오후 6시까지 Tom에게 전화해 주세요.

03 | 뒤에 to부정사가 오는 경우 if를 쓸 수 없다.

The recommendation from the planning board will determine [whether / ~~if~~] (**or not**) **to relocate** the firm.
= The recommendation from the planning board will determine [whether / ~~if~~] **to relocate** the firm (**or not**).
전략기획 위원회의 권고는 회사의 이전 여부를 결정할 것이다.

04 | 뒤에 A or B가 오는 경우는 if를 쓸 수 없다.

Sally hasn't decided [whether / ~~if~~] she should apply for a job **in administration or in accounting**.
Sally는 그녀가 관리부서에 지원해야 할지 회계부서에 지원해야 할지 결정하지 못했다.

+TIP 명사절 접속사 whether나 if를 목적어로 자주 취하는 동사

ask	물어보다	see	확인하다	decide	결정하다	determine	결정하다
tell	구별하다	don't know	모른다	wonder	궁금하다	find out	알아내다

SPARTA ☑ Check-UP! ❸

| 해설 p. 372

1 The question in the air this summer is ------- people will be listening to the new Anna Lopez CD.
(A) what
(B) those
(C) that
(D) whether

2 Once Arizona Microtek, Inc. decides ------- or not it wants to continue manufacturing the MSL, we will know what assignment we'll be working on next.
(A) if
(B) whether
(C) that
(D) what

3 Brian Cox, president of Ace Electronics, is considering ------- to renew the contract with Max Express.
(A) whether
(B) If
(C) what
(D) so

POINT 4 의문사와 복합관계대명사

01 | 의문사는 명사절 접속사로 사용한다.

who 누가 when 언제 where 어디서 what 무엇을 how 어떻게 which 어떤(것)

1) who / what / which + 불완전한 절

After reviewing the résumés, supervisors will decide [who / ~~whose~~] **is eligible for the position**.
이력서들을 검토한 후에 감독관들은 누가 직책에 적합한지를 결정할 것이다.

2) whose / what / which + 명사 + 완전한 절

We have to decide [whose / ~~who~~] **résumés are the best written** and most clearly organized among all of them. 우리는 모든 이력서 중 누구의 이력서가 가장 잘 쓰였고 가장 알기 쉽게 정리되어 있는지 결정해야 한다.

3) when / where / how / why + 완전한 절

The travel agency will notify you [when / ~~what~~] **the airline tickets are ready for delivery**.
여행사는 당신에게 비행기 티켓이 언제 준비될지 알려드릴 겁니다.

02 | 복합관계대명사(선행사를 포함한 관계대명사)는 명사절 접속사로 사용한다.

whoever (= anyone who) 누구든지	whomever (= anyone who) 누구든지	whichever (= anything which) 어느 것이든지	whatever (= anything which) 무엇이든지

1) whoever + 동사

[Whoever / ~~Who~~] **comes** here before 8:00 A.M. can get a free ticket.
(= Anyone who)
여기에 오전 8시 전에 오는 누구든지 공짜 표를 받을 수 있다.

2) whomever / whichever / whatever + (주어) + 동사

You can read [whatever / ~~whoever~~] **attracts** your interest in the library.
(= anything which)
당신은 도서관에서 관심을 끄는 무엇이든 읽을 수 있다.

SPARTA Check-UP! 4

해설 p. 372

1 Managers will be asked to contribute ideas on ------- the company can continue to minimize expenses.
(A) who
(B) whom
(C) how
(D) what

2 ------- model you choose, both the air-conditioning and audio system will be installed in the vehicle free of charge.
(A) Whichever
(B) Whomever
(C) Whoever
(D) That

3 We assure you that ------- you choose will be able to be delivered by this weekend.
(A) whoever
(B) whenever
(C) whichever
(D) however

PRACTICE

해설 p. 373

▪ 괄호 안의 보기 중 알맞은 단어를 고르세요.

1 He ensured **[that / what]** all the doors were locked before he left his apartment.

2 The Human Resources director has indicated **[that / these]** the company hiring policy will change starting in May.

3 They guarantee **[that / what]** your catalogue order will arrive within three business days.

4 **[That / What]** seats are small is a frequent complaint of air travelers.

5 The analyst predicted **[that / what]** the company would not go bankrupt and might even show a profit.

6 It is well known **[that / what]** the governor did to reduce the budget.

7 Performance evaluations are used as a way of letting employees know **[that / what]** needs to be improved.

8 Northlake Holdings President Sean Bean is hopeful **[whether / that]** the construction deadline can be met this fall.

9 The last quarterly report showed **[which / that]** Global Electronics' earnings were lower than anticipated.

10 Everybody is aware **[that / so]** the new dress code will take effect as of tomorrow.

11 One of the desk clerk's responsibilities is to make sure **[that / what]** outgoing packages are addressed correctly.

12 The project is a huge undertaking, and I doubt **[whether / what]** he will be able to do all the work by himself.

13 I asked Nick **[whether / if]** or not he had finished the research project funded by the government.

14 **[Whoever / Anyone]** ordered the sample had better pick it up from the Shipping Department before the end of the day.

15 In such a case just contact us by telephone or e-mail, and we will send a replacement or a refund, **[whichever / however]** you prefer.

1 We ask ------- you please refrain from eating food and drinking beverages in the meeting room.

(A) that (B) so that
(C) what (D) unless

2 Whether you work in our stores, corporate offices, or distribution centers, there is no limit on ------- you can achieve at the IMP Group.

(A) that (B) how
(C) what (D) whoever

3 ------- clients retain a company's services will depend more on the quality of help the company provides than on its fees.

(A) Which (B) Whether
(C) Whoever (D) Although

4 Please be advised ------- we wish to place an order with your company for five color printers for our office.

(A) that (B) what
(C) which (D) whom

5 Comfort Airline wishes to inform customers ------- there will be limited service from now until January 1 due to scheduled repairs.

(A) this (B) these
(C) what (D) that

6 Government officials quarreled over ------- or not to pass the bill.

(A) whether (B) when
(C) and (D) that

7 Customers should be careful because computer software products are not refundable, ------- opened or not.

(A) neither (B) whether
(C) unless (D) besides

8 To compete effectively, the company should be aware of ------- competitors in the industry are trying to accomplish.

(A) that (B) whether
(C) what (D) how

9 A nationwide survey suggests ------- the government has lost the battle to win the hearts and minds of the Iraqi people.

(A) if (B) on
(C) that (D) for

10 You can enroll in next week's workshop on expanding market share, ------- you are a new employee or a current staff member.

(A) between (B) neither
(C) nor (D) whether

11 Customers are invited to tour the Birmingham factory to see ------- our office furniture is made.

(A) whom (B) during
(C) about (D) how

12 It is not yet clear how -------- Ms. Harper was in her presentation to the Walton Motors executives.

(A) persuade (B) persuasiveness
(C) to persuade (D) persuasive

Questions 13-16 refer to the following instructions.

Around 70 people ------- to attend the community barbecue that is being held tomorrow.
13.

Let's see ------- we can do in 4 hours. We have a lot of bread we need to make, so let's get started right away.
14.

Here are the steps to making good bread. -------.
15.

First, put the flour mixture and water in the bowl. We have already made the flour bread mixture, so all we have to do is to mix it with water. Sprinkle salt ------- on top of the dough and bake it at 375 degrees for eight minutes or until the bread rises.
16.

There we have it. We have bread. As you know, other groups are in charge of meats and pastas, so our group has it easy.

13 (A) expected
(B) is expecting
(C) expects
(D) are expected

14 (A) that
(B) which
(C) when
(D) what

15 (A) You can easily find recipes for quick dinners and party foods.
(B) Please leave your name and number on our beeper at 555-1272.
(C) Margarine can be substituted for butter in the recipe.
(D) Please read carefully as the smallest mistake can result in bad bread.

16 (A) slightly
(B) slight
(C) slightness
(D) slighting

UNIT 16 부사절과 부사절 접속사

부사절 접속사는 주로 ① 문맥상 어울리는 접속사를 선택하는 문제, ② 의미가 같은 접속사와 전치사를 구분하는 문제가 등장하며, 매월 평균 1~2문제 출제된다. 이 장에서는 자주 등장하는 부사절 접속사의 종류를 알아보고, 관계부사와 복합관계부사 및 부사절의 축약 구조에 대해 학습한다.

Preview

01 | 부사절 접속사의 종류

부사절을 이끄는 접속사는 시간, 조건, 양보, 이유 등을 나타낸다.

시간	when, as, after, before, while, as soon as ...
조건	if, unless, only if ...
양보	although, though, even though, even if ...
이유	as, because, since, now that ...

02 | 부사절의 형태

부사절은 <접속사+주어+동사>의 형태로 문장 내에서 부사 역할을 하여 주절의 내용을 추가 설명하는 절이다. 부사절은 종속절로서 문장의 수식 성분이므로 단독으로 쓰일 수 없다.

Customers will receive an invoice when they place a new order.
주절 / 부사절 : 부사절 접속사 + 주어 + 동사 (완전한 문장)
고객들이 새로운 주문을 할 때 청구서를 받게 된다.

03 | 부사절의 자리

주절의 앞이나 뒤에 오며, 주절의 앞에 올 때는 부사절 뒤에 쉼표(,)를 반드시 붙여야 한다.

1) 부사절이 주절 앞에 온 경우

When you make a decision on a job, consider the salary and benefits.
직업 결정을 내릴 때, 급여 및 복리후생을 고려하십시오.

2) 부사절이 주절 뒤에 온 경우

Earnings significantly increased **after the company was restructured**.
회사의 구조 조정이 이루어진 후 수익이 상당히 높아졌다.

POINT 1 시간, 이유, 양보의 부사절 접속사

01 | 시간을 나타내는 접속사

when ~할 때	as ~할 때	at the time ~할 때	by the time ~할 때쯤
after ~한 후에	until ~까지	since ~이래로	each(every) time ~할 때마다
before ~전에	while ~하는 동안	once ~하자마자	as soon as ~하자마자

No one is allowed to enter the conference room [while / ~~during~~] **a meeting is ongoing.**
회의가 진행 중인 동안 아무도 회의실에 들어갈 수 없다.
▶ 시간 접속사 while은 뒤에 완전한 절이 오며, 전치사 during 뒤에는 명사구가 온다.

[Since / ~~When~~] **Mr. Brandin became the sales manager**, sales figures have increased by 30 percent.
Brandin 씨가 영업 과장이 된 이후로, 판매수치가 30% 만큼 상승했다.
▶ since가 시간 접속사로 사용되는 경우에 since절에는 과거시제를, 주절에는 현재완료시제를 쓴다.

02 | 이유를 나타내는 접속사

because / since / as / now that ~때문에

[Because / ~~Even if~~] **our CFO is away on business,** the budget meeting has been rescheduled for Friday.
우리의 재무 최고 책임자가 출장 중이기 때문에, 예산 회의 일정이 금요일로 변경되었습니다.

Mr. King has to miss the meeting tomorrow [since / ~~except that~~] **he is supposed to be out of the office.**
King 씨는 외근을 하기로 돼 있어 내일 회의에 빠져야 한다.
▶ since가 이유 접속사로 사용되는 경우에는 문맥에 맞는 시제를 사용한다.

03 | 양보를 나타내는 접속사

although / even though / even if / though / while ~에도 불구하고, ~지만

[While / ~~Despite~~] **our company welcomes all applicants,** we particularly prefer those with accounting experience.
우리 회사는 모든 지원자들을 환영하지만 특히 회계 경험을 가진 사람들을 선호한다.
▶ while은 부사절 접속사로서 뒤에 완전한 절을 이끌고, despite는 전치사이므로 명사(구)가 온다.

The meeting began on time [though / ~~unless~~] **several staff members were late due to heavy traffic.**
몇몇 직원들이 교통체증 때문에 지각했지만 회의는 정각에 시작되었다.
▶ 두 개의 절이 대조를 이루고 있으므로 though를 쓴다. unless가 이끄는 조건 부사절은 주절에 명령문 또는 미래동사와 어울린다.

SPARTA Check-UP! 1

해설 p. 375

1 ------- the meeting began late, we were able to come to an agreement before it was over.
(A) Although
(B) Nevertheless
(C) Still
(D) However

2 Computer access will be suspended ------- the maintenance is finished.
(A) whereas
(B) as long as
(C) up to
(D) until

3 ------- he was assigned to the new sales team, Mr. Gleeson hasn't won any contracts.
(A) Since
(B) If
(C) When
(D) While

POINT 2 조건, 목적, 결과의 부사절 접속사

01 | 조건을 나타내는 접속사

if ~이라면	in the event (that) ~한 경우에는	given (that) ~을 고려해 볼 때
unless ~이 아니라면	in case (that) ~한 경우를 대비하여	except when ~일 때를 제외하면
once 일단 ~하면	considering (that) ~을 고려하면	except (that) ~을 제외하면
as far as ~하는 한	as long as ~하기만 한다면	on condition that ~라는 조건으로
provided (that) / providing (that) ~이라 가정하면		only if ~하는 경우에만

[If / ~~Unless~~] **you finish the work within the contracted period,** a bonus of 10% will be paid.
만약 당신이 계약기간 이내에 일을 끝낸다면, 10% 보너스가 지급될 것이다.

A new secretary will be hired to replace Sophia [once / ~~in case of~~] **the manager gives his approval**.
일단 관리자가 승인하면 소피아를 대신할 새로운 비서가 고용될 것이다.

▶ once는 부사절 접속사로서 뒤에 완전한 절을 이끌고, in case of는 전치사로서 뒤에 절이 올 수 없다.

02 | 목적을 나타내는 접속사

so that+주어+can	in order that+주어+may	~하기 위해서, ~하도록

Please don't leave any questions blank [so that / ~~because~~] **we can process** your application form efficiently.
저희가 당신의 신청서를 효율적으로 처리할 수 있도록 양식의 어떤 질문도 빈칸으로 남겨 두지 마세요.

03 | 결과를 나타내는 so ~ that, such ~ that 구문

so+형용사/부사+that	such (a)+형용사+명사+that	너무 ~해서 …하다

The Nukuda Company is [so / ~~such~~] **confident** in the reliability of its personal computers that it offers a three-year warranty on its latest models.
Nukuda 사는 개인용 컴퓨터의 안정성에 자신이 있어서 최신 모델에 대해 3년간의 품질보증을 하고 있다.

It took [such / ~~so~~] **a long time** for Supplies Limited to process our orders that we decided to stop dealing with the company.
Supplies Limited 사가 우리의 주문을 처리하는 데 시간을 너무 오래 지체하였기 때문에 이 회사와 거래를 중단하기로 했다.

▶ so ~ that 구문과 such ~ that 구문의 뜻은 같지만 so 뒤에는 형용사가 오고 such 뒤에는 명사가 오는 점이 다르다.

SPARTA ☑ Check-UP! 2

| 해설 p. 375

1 ------- our present supplier agrees to give us a discount, we will have to find another supplier who can give us a better deal.
(A) Unless
(B) Because
(C) When
(D) As if

2 The system administrator manipulated ------- important records that it had a significant influence on the company's annual financial report.
(A) too
(B) such
(C) very
(D) so

3 The demanding supervisor made us stay late ------- we could submit the report by the next morning.
(A) so that
(B) however
(C) moreover
(D) in case that

POINT 3 부사절 접속사 vs. 전치사

01 | 부사절 접속사 자리에는 전치사가 올 수 없다.

접속사	전치사(구)	의미
because, since, as, now that	because of, due to, owing to	~때문에
though, although, even though, even if	in spite of, despite	~에도 불구하고
while	during	~하는 동안에
in case (that), in the event (that)	in case of, in the event of	~한 경우에
except that	except (for), excluding	~을 제외하고

[Although / ~~In spite of~~] **its profits have considerably decreased,** HUO, Inc. will continue aggressive promotions.
비록 수익이 상당히 감소해 왔지만 HUO 사는 공격적인 홍보를 계속할 것이다.

[Because / ~~Due to~~] **the banquet will begin promptly at 6:00,** all catering employees are requested to arrive at 5:30.
연회가 6시 정각에 시작할 것이기 때문에, 모든 음식 공급업체 직원들은 5시 반까지 도착할 것이 요구된다.

02 | 부사절/형용사절/명사절 접속사를 구별해야 한다.

All workers should follow the safety rules [so that / ~~what~~] **they can use the equipment safely**.
모든 직원들은 장비를 안전하게 사용하기 위해서 안전 수칙을 따라야 한다.
▶ 부사절 : 문장을 품은 채 부사 역할을 한다. 따라서 생략할 수 있다.

All the paintings [which / ~~when~~] **are displayed at the art center** may not be sold without consent.
예술 센터에 전시된 모든 그림들은 동의 없이 판매될 수 없다.
▶ 형용사절 : 문장을 품은 채 명사를 수식하는 형용사 역할을 한다. 따라서 생략할 수 있다.

[What / ~~Now that~~] **you want to know about our company** is explained in this brochure.
여러분이 저희 회사에 대해 알고 싶어 하는 것은 이 안내서에 설명되어 있습니다.
▶ 명사절 : 문장을 품은 채 문장에서 주어, 목적어, 보어 역할을 한다. 따라서 생략할 수 없다.

SPARTA Check-UP! 3

| 해설 p. 375

1 ------- a new computer seemed like a good investment for their company, they decided not to buy one.
(A) Because of
(B) Due to
(C) Despite
(D) Although

2 ------- we require in order to boost sales of the product is more active promotional activities.
(A) Although
(B) What
(C) Why
(D) Because

3 ------- it is getting colder, it is necessary that you keep office doors closed and turn heaters on during work hours.
(A) However
(B) Now that
(C) Whatever
(D) Because of

POINT 4 부사절의 축약

01 | 부사절의 축약 구조

1) 능동태 문장 : 접속사+주어+동사+목적어 → 접속사+V-ing+목적어

When [preparing / ~~prepared~~] **announcements** for the bulletin board, we recommend that you follow the format shown in this sample.

= **When** you prepare **announcements** for the bulletin board, we recommend that you follow the format shown in this sample.
당신이 게시판에 게시할 공고문을 준비할 때 우리는 이 견본에 나와 있는 구성을 따를 것을 권고합니다.

▶ 부사절의 주어와 주절의 주어가 동일할 때 부사절의 주어를 생략하고 동사를 현재분사(-ing)로 바꾼다.
▶ 빈칸 앞에 생략된 주어와 분사가 능동 관계이며, 빈칸 뒤에 목적어가 있으므로 현재분사를 쓴다.

2) 수동태 문장 : 접속사+주어+be p.p. → 접속사+p.p.

As [noted / ~~notes~~] in our rental agreement, rental cars should be returned to the original rental location with a full tank of gas.

= **As** it is noted in our rental agreement, rental cars should be returned to the original rental location with a full tank of gas.
저희 임대 계약서에 명시된 바와 같이, 렌터카는 연료 탱크를 가득 채워서 차량을 렌트하셨던 장소에 반환해야 합니다.

▶ 부사절의 주어와 주절의 주어가 동일할 때 부사절의 주어와 be동사를 생략하고 과거분사(p.p.)만 남긴다.
▶ 'as+p.p.' 관용 표현에는 as stated, as requested, as discussed, as mentioned 등이 있다. (p.114 참고)

02 | 축약 구조의 접속사 선택

[Since / ~~While~~] **launched** last quarter, Telesat's latest computer model has been widely advertised.

= **Since it was launched** last quarter, Telesat's latest computer model has been widely advertised.
그것이 지난 분기에 도입된 후로 Telesat의 최신 컴퓨터 모델은 널리 광고되어 왔다.

[When / ~~Unless~~] **returning** any merchandise, please indicate your account number on the return form.

= **When you return** any merchandise, please indicate your account number on the return form.
물건을 반환하실 때 반환 신청서에 계좌 번호를 기입해 주세요.

▶ 축약 구조의 접속사 자리에 빈칸을 제시한 문제가 출제되는 경우 의미 해석을 통해 풀어야 한다.

SPARTA Check-UP! 4

해설 p. 375

1 When ------- the agreement, Angela Winkler will be accompanied by her secretary.
(A) sign
(B) signing
(C) to sign
(D) signed

2 Once ------- by the board of directors, the new project will be implemented as of November 21.
(A) approval
(B) approved
(C) approving
(D) to approve

3 ------- receiving notice that Elton will retire, Mr. Craig has been searching for a replacement.
(A) Because
(B) As
(C) Since
(D) While

POINT 5 관계부사와 복합관계부사

01 | 관계부사는 형용사절을 이끌며 부사를 대신하므로 생략될 수 있으며, 뒤에는 완전한 절이 온다.

의미	선행사		관계부사	전치사 + 관계대명사
시간	the time, the day, the year 등		when	in / on / at which
장소	the place, the area, the site 등	+	where	in / on / at which
이유	the reason		why	for which
방법	the way(*the way와 how 둘 중 하나만 씀)		how	in which

관계부사는 <전치사+관계대명사>로 바꾸어 사용할 수 있다.

The city council proposed developing a new residential **area** [where / ~~when~~] the sugar factory used to be.
= in which

시의회는 설탕 공장이 있던 구역에 새 주택가를 개발하자는 제안을 했다.

The price of heating oil peaked in **November** [when / ~~where~~] suppliers were unable to meet demand.
= in which

공급업자들이 수요를 충족시키지 못했던 11월에 난방유의 가격이 최고조에 달했다.

02 | 복합관계부사는 부사절을 이끈다.

복합관계부사	의미	구조
whenever	~할 때마다	whenever(= no matter when)+주어+동사
wherever	어디에나, 어디든지	wherever(= no matter where)+주어+동사
however	아무리 ~해도	however(= no matter how)+형용사/부사+주어+동사

An alarm rings at Johansson Laboratories [whenever / ~~whichever~~] **a visitor enters** a restricted area.
= no matter when

Johansson Laboratories에서는 방문객들이 출입 금지 구역에 들어갈 때마다 경보기가 울린다.

▶ whichever는 복합관계대명사로 뒤에 불완전한 문장이 온다.

[However / ~~whenever~~] **uncomfortable they may be**, helmets must be worn by anyone entering the construction zone.
= No matter how

아무리 불편하더라도, 공사 지역을 출입하는 사람은 누구든지 헬멧을 꼭 착용해야 한다.

SPARTA Check-UP! 5

해설 p. 376

1 Several local universities will hold a job fair ------- many students will have chances to meet recruiters.
(A) which
(B) where
(C) that
(D) whose

2 ------- you plan to go for your vacation, you can rely on Top World Travel for the lowest airfares.
(A) Wherever
(B) Whichever
(C) However
(D) Whoever

3 No matter ------- strict the dress code is, you can always find a way to express your individuality.
(A) how
(B) who
(C) where
(D) what

POINT 6 접속부사

01 | 접속부사

접속부사는 부사이므로 한 문장 안에서 두 절을 연결할 수 없다. 따라서 문장을 연결할 때는 접속사나 세미콜론(;)을 쓴다.

양보	however 하지만, 그러나 nevertheless 그럼에도 불구하고 nonetheless 그럼에도 불구하고
대조	on the other hand 다른 한편으로, 반면에 in contrast 대조적으로
결과	therefore 그러므로 thus 이와 같이 as a result 결과적으로 consequently 결과적으로
시간	meanwhile 그 동안에 at the same time 그와 동시에
부연 설명	furthermore 더욱이 moreover 게다가, 더욱이 in addition 게다가 besides 게다가

Our favorite soccer team's game was canceled; [therefore / ~~because~~], we decided to go to a movie.
우리가 좋아하는 축구팀의 경기가 취소되어서 영화를 보러 가기로 했다.

02 | 접속부사의 자리

틀린 예	옳은 예
접속부사+주어+동사, 주어+동사	주어+동사. **접속부사**, 주어 +동사 / 주어+동사, **접속부사**, 주어 +동사
주어+동사 **접속부사** 주어+동사	주어+동사: **접속부사**, 주어 +동사 / 주어+동사; **접속부사**, 주어 +동사

+TIP 의미가 유사한 접속사와 (접속)부사를 구별해야 한다.

의미	부사절 접속사	접속부사
원인 / 이유	because, since, as, now that	therefore, thus
대조 / 양보	though, although, even though, even if	however, otherwise, nevertheless, nonetheless
기간	while	meanwhile, meantime

+TIP 자주 출제되는 <접속사 + 부사>

and then 그러고 나서 and also 또한 and therefore 그러므로
Modern digital devices are more efficient **and therefore** cost much less to run.
현대식 디지털 장치는 더 효율적이므로 실행 비용도 훨씬 적다.

SPARTA Check-UP! 6

해설 p. 376

1 The company provides us with dormitories; -------, they are not totally free of charge.
(A) thus
(B) however
(C) then
(D) therefore

2 I will be away until next Tuesday, ------- if any of my friends call me, please tell them I will get back to them as soon as possible.
(A) but
(B) so
(C) otherwise
(D) furthermore

3 The company is located in the center of the city; -------, it is very near some subway stations.
(A) meantime
(B) otherwise
(C) however
(D) besides

해설 p. 376

▪ 괄호 안의 보기 중 알맞은 단어를 고르세요.

1 **[If / Although]** you plan to get to the conference via the highway, make sure you check ahead of time that there are no traffic problems.

2 **[Although / Despite]** I was unable to reach one of your references, all of the others spoke so warmly about you that I've decided to add you to the team.

3 **[During / While]** Mr. Pierce is at the conference, please direct all calls to his administrative assistant.

4 **[After / Meanwhile]** Victoria returned from vacation, she noticed that she had missed several calls from a very important client.

5 Employees are asked to contact their immediate supervisor **[or / if]** they anticipate arriving late to work.

6 The annual meeting has been rescheduled **[since / so]** that tomorrow's visitors from foreign countries can attend.

7 **[Although / So that]** the accountants are requested to work on the premises, the company may allow them to work at home in special cases.

8 Mr. Benjamin will be arriving early for the important meeting with his clients at the CA Hotel, so be sure that everything is fully ready **[before / since]** he checks in.

9 **[However / Although]** we requested that the new machine parts be sent immediately, we were informed that they could not arrive before the end of the month.

10 **[Except / Unless]** something is done about the construction zones, traffic congestion will continue to worsen.

11 **[Although / Despite]** production figures are better than they were last year, there is still some room for improvement.

12 Customers should be reminded to call the manufacturer **[why / if]** problems with the product are not resolved by the wholesaler.

13 After **[finishing / finished]** lunch, Ms. Smith decided to go shopping at Sam's Club.

14 If **[submitting / submitted]** by the tenth of this month, the application will be reviewed.

15 After **[reviewing / reviewed]** the complaint thoroughly, the company decided to put one more worker on the assembly line.

1 No orders of any kind are processed ------- we have your final approval and the inventory is verified.

(A) until (B) even
(C) just (D) which

2 Ben Gardiner was employed as a replacement for the former sales representative ------- he was the most qualified for the job.

(A) until (B) because
(C) not only (D) so that

3 ------- customers may be contacted by several service providers, there is no requirement that they respond to any solicitation that they may receive.

(A) Anyone (B) Something
(C) Although (D) Whenever

4 I didn't know that Julie was married ------- she seldom talks about herself.

(A) between (B) unlike
(C) so that (D) since

5 Shock Snow Boarding employees are asked to work overtime during the winter months ------- manufacturing orders usually surge during this time.

(A) as (B) if
(C) once (D) whether

6 ------- often a person visits the Tunnel Museum, there is always some new exhibit to attract the viewer's interest.

(A) Whichever (B) Whenever
(C) However (D) Whomever

7 It will be easier to place an order for office supplies ------- Office Max starts offering an online payment option on its Web site.

(A) instead (B) after
(C) during (D) beyond

8 ------- Mr. Harley has not yet finished preparing his presentation, he will complete it in time to lead the monthly sales meeting.

(A) In order that (B) Even though
(C) When (D) Until

9 If the language courses you've signed up for are not recorded correctly on our electronic register, please contact us ------- we may rectify the error.

(A) so that (B) if
(C) which (D) due to

10 Electricity use during peak hours has declined 4% in the six months ------- customers began receiving monthly statements illustrating their time-of-day consumption patterns.

(A) despite (B) since
(C) even (D) besides

11 Marissa was assigned to monitor the operations of the Taiwan headquarters in Taipei ------- the regional director went on a business trip to India.

(A) due to (B) while
(C) once (D) except for

12 It is mandatory for employees to take 15-minute breaks every three hours, ------- busy they are.

(A) no matter how (B) so far as
(C) nevertheless (D) in order that

Questions 13-16 refer to the following letter.

Tracy Jakes
3100 Timmons Lane
Houston, Texas 77027

Dear Ms. Jakes,

I appreciate your recent ------- (13.) from the Williams Plumbing & Heating Inc. We are pleased that you have chosen this new heating equipment for your office.

Sam Dumiak from our Maintenance Department will call you tomorrow ------- (14.) the installation process of the equipment. -------. (15.) No additional heaters will be necessary ------- (16.) the installation has been successfully done.

Mr. Dumiak will talk about detailed information with you and answer any questions you might have when he calls.

Sincerely,

Karen Chitty, Manager
Williams Plumbing & Heating Inc.

13 (A) donation
(B) visit
(C) purchase
(D) article

14 (A) will discuss
(B) to discuss
(C) discussion
(D) discusses

15 (A) The office heating system has not been running properly.
(B) Residents pay only small electric fees due to their effective use of solar panels.
(C) Soon, the demand for heating oil will decrease sharply.
(D) This apparatus is designed to maximize the efficiency of the heating process.

16 (A) once
(B) afterward
(C) following
(D) upon

UNIT 17 원급, 비교급, 최상급

비교 관련 문제는 ① 원급/비교급(짝을 이루는 문제), ② 비교급 강조부사 선택, ③ 최상급 표현을 묻는 문제가 주로 출제된다. 원급, 비교급, 최상급 관련 문제는 어려운 문제가 출제되지 않으므로 기본 원리를 잘 이해하고 빈출 유형만 잡으면 문제를 푸는 데 큰 어려움은 없다.

Preview

01 | 원급, 비교급, 최상급 비교 구문

1) 원급: 동등하거나 비슷한 성질, 상태를 비교한다.

This computer is just as **reliable** as the previous model. 이 컴퓨터는 이전 모델만큼 믿을 만하다.

2) 비교급: 서로 다른 둘의 성질, 상태를 비교한다.

This computer is more expensive than yours. 이 컴퓨터는 당신 것보다 더 비싸다.

3) 최상급: 서로 다른 셋 이상을 비교한다.

She is the greatest of all the politicians in our country. 그녀는 우리나라에 있는 모든 정치인들 중 가장 훌륭하다.

02 | 규칙 변화

1) 1음절 형용사나 부사는 원급에 -(e)r, -(e)st를 붙여서 비교급과 최상급을 만드는 것이 원칙이다.

- old — older — oldest
- fast — faster — fastest

2) [단모음+단자음]으로 끝나는 말은 그 어미의 자음을 겹치고 -er, -est를 붙인다.

- hot — hotter — hottest
- big — bigger — biggest

3) [자음+y]로 된 말은 y를 i로 고치고 -er, -est를 붙인다.

- easy — easier — easiest
- early — earlier — earliest

4) 대다수의 2음절과 3음절 이상의 형용사나 부사는 more, most를 붙인다. 단, 부사의 최상급 앞에는 the를 생략할 수 있다.

- useful — more useful — most useful
- quickly — more quickly — (the) most quickly

03 | 불규칙 변화

원급	비교급	최상급
good / well	better	best
bad / ill	worse	worst
old	older / elder	oldest / eldest
late (늦은, 나중의)	later (더 나중의) / latter (순서가 더 늦은)	latest (최신의) / last (마지막의)

POINT 1 원급

01 | as+형용사/부사의 원급+as : ~만큼 …한

Customers did not find the new product [as / ~~enough~~] attractive as they had expected.
고객들은 신상품이 그들이 기대했던 것만큼 매력적이지 않음을 알게 되었다.

▶ 주어진 문장에서 as를 보고 as ~ as 구문임을 파악할 수 있다.

Many readers do not rate Internet journals as [highly / ~~higher~~] as print publications.
많은 독자들은 인터넷 신문을 출판 발행물만큼 높이 평가하지 않는다.

▶ as ~ as 원급 비교 구문에 비교급 또는 최상급 표현을 쓸 수 없다.

+TIP as ~ as 사이에 들어갈 품사 문제는 as, as를 걷어내고 문장 구조를 확인하면 쉽게 알 수 있다.

Our new refrigerator is ~~**as**~~ [reliable / ~~reliably~~] ~~**as** the previous model despite its lower price~~.
우리의 새로운 냉장고는 더 낮은 가격에도 불구하고 이전 모델만큼 믿을 만하다.

02 | as+many/much+명사+as : ~만큼이나 많은

1) as+many+복수 가산명사+as

Night-shift workers are likely to make five times as [many / ~~much~~] **mistakes** as their colleagues on the day shift. 야간근무 직원들은 주간에 일하는 동료들보다 다섯 배나 실수할 경향이 높다.

2) as+much+불가산명사+as

Before a job interview, it's important to find out as [much / ~~many~~] **information** as you can about the company. 채용면접에 앞서, 그 회사에 대한 최대한 많은 정보를 알아보는 것이 중요하다.

03 | the same (+명사)+as : ~와 같은

There are a variety of restaurants conveniently located on the same **street** [as / ~~than~~] the convention center. 다양한 레스토랑이 컨벤션 센터와 같은 거리에 편리하게 위치해 있다.

+TIP 원급 비교구문의 부정은 not as ~ as, not so ~ as (~만큼 ~하지 않은)으로 표현한다.

Sleeping on the sofa is not as **comfortable** as sleeping on a bed.
소파에서 자는 것은 침대에서 자는 것만큼 안락하지 않다.

SPARTA Check-UP! 1

| 해설 p. 379

1 The upgraded desktop units will enable us to perform our work as ------- as possible.
(A) efficient
(B) efficiently
(C) efficiency
(D) more efficient

2 They are ------- efficient as the other researchers, but a careful analysis indicates they could produce more than the others and get better results.
(A) the most
(B) most
(C) more
(D) as

3 In these days of rising fuel costs, it is important for everyone to try to conserve ------- much energy as possible.
(A) as
(B) more
(C) than
(D) very

POINT ② 비교급

01 | 형용사/부사의 비교급+than+비교 대상

두 개의 대상을 서로 비교하여, 한쪽이 다른 쪽보다 <더/덜 ~한(형용사)> 또는 <더/덜 ~하게(부사)>라는 뜻을 나타낸다.

1) 우등 비교 : 두 대상 중 한쪽이 우월할 때 <형용사/부사의 비교급+than>을 쓴다.

Producing high-quality products is **more** [**important** / ~~importantly~~] **than** making a profit.
양질의 제품을 생산하는 것이 이익을 내는 것보다 더 중요하다.

▶ be동사의 보어 자리이므로 more ~ than 사이에는 주어의 상태를 서술하는 형용사가 들어간다.
▶ 비교급 뒤에 'than+비교 대상'을 쓴다는 것에 유의한다.

2) 열등 비교 : 두 대상 중 한쪽이 열등할 때 <less+형용사/부사+than>을 쓴다.

We are using recyclable materials **less** [**efficiently** / ~~efficient~~] **than** our competitors.
우리는 경쟁사들보다 재활용할 수 있는 물건들을 덜 효율적으로 사용한다.

▶ <주어+동사+목적어>가 있는 완전한 문장이므로 less ~ than 사이에는 동사 are using을 수식하는 부사가 들어간다.

02 | 비교급 강조 부사

비교급 앞에서 비교급을 강조하며 '훨씬, 상당히'로 해석한다.

훨씬	far, much, even, still, a lot, a great deal	+ 비교급
상당히	substantially, considerably, significantly	

The demand for our new SUV is [**much** / ~~very~~] **higher than** we expected.
우리의 새로운 SUV 차량에 대한 수요는 우리가 기대했던 것보다 훨씬 높다.

03 | 비교급 앞에 the를 쓰는 경우

1) the+비교급 ~, the+비교급 ... : ~하면 할수록 더 …하다

The more expensive the product, **the** [**more** / ~~most~~] **likely** it will be to sell quickly.
물건이 비싸면 비쌀수록 더 빨리 팔리는 것 같다.

2) of the two 복수명사, the+비교급 ~ : 둘 중에서 더 ~한

Of these two applicants, Mr. Smith is [**the better** / ~~best~~] qualified for the sales position.
두 명의 후보들 중에서, Smith 씨가 영업직에 더 자격 있는 후보이다.

SPARTA ☑ Check-UP! 2

해설 p. 379

1 The problem with the housing market may be stronger and more persistent ------- economists had foreseen.
(A) than
(B) onto
(C) within
(D) there

2 Our policy of decentralizing acquisitions allows for even ------- flexibility on the part of each branch.
(A) great
(B) greater
(C) greatest
(D) greatly

3 Of these two applicants, Mr. Park is the ------- qualified to work on the payroll update project.
(A) better
(B) much
(C) too
(D) well

POINT 3 최상급

01 | 형용사/부사의 최상급

Of the subway lines that stop in the central business district, the green line is [the easiest / ~~easier~~] to get to the Franklin Building.
중앙 상업 지구에 정차하는 모든 지하철 노선 중에서, 녹색 노선이 Franklin Building으로 가기 가장 수월하다.

The trainers who will run next year's seminar are the [most highly / ~~higher~~] regarded in the fields of sales and marketing.
다음 해 세미나를 진행할 트레이너들은 영업과 마케팅 분야에서 가장 높이 평가받고 있다.

02 | 최상급 패턴 : 셋 이상을 비교하며 최고, 최상의 의미를 나타낸다.

1) the+최상급+of (all the)+복수명사/불가산명사 : … 중에 가장 ~한

The attorneys at LW Firm remain committed to providing our clients with the [highest / ~~most highly~~] **level of service** possible.
LW Firm의 변호사들은 우리 고객들에게 가능한 한 최상의 서비스를 제공하는 데 헌신한다.

2) the+최상급+(in) 장소/범위 부사구 : …에서 가장 ~한

According to a customer survey, Debbie Shrimp Delight offers the [highest / ~~higher~~] **quality seafood** in **Monroe City**.
고객 설문에 의하면, Debbie Shrimp Delight는 Monroe 시에서 가장 높은 품질의 해산물 요리를 제공한다.

3) the+최상급+명사+(that) ~ ever : 지금까지 … 중에서 가장 ~한

Sorin's Lakeview Grill is the [largest / ~~larger~~] **restaurant** ever to be built along the shores of Lake Swensen. Sorin's Lakeview Grill은 Swensen 호수가에 지금까지 세워진 레스토랑 중 가장 규모가 크다.

03 | 최상급 강조부사

최상급을 강조할 때는 by far, quite, single, ever, possible, the very(단연코)를 쓴다.

Purchasing a home is the [single / ~~extremely~~] **largest** investment most of us will ever make.
내 집 마련은 일생일대의 가장 큰 투자이다.

SPARTA Check-UP! 3

해설 p. 380

1 Although we at K-Dex Express make every effort to provide the ------- delivery available in the country, we cannot guarantee shipping on the same day.
(A) more speed
(B) speediest
(C) speedily
(D) most speed

2 The Stomach Cancer Foundation will gather some of the ------- highly regarded scientists in stomach cancer research for the scientific presentation.
(A) most
(B) so
(C) such
(D) much

3 Extensive on-the-job training is ------- the best method of ensuring high levels of productivity.
(A) much
(B) still
(C) by far
(D) very

POINT 4 그 밖에 주의해야 할 비교급

01 | 라틴계 비교급

비교급 than 대신 to를 쓴다는 점에 유의한다. 라틴계 비교급은 prior to가 출제된 적이 많다.

prior to ~에 앞서	posterior to ~보다 이후에
superior to ~보다 우수한	inferior to ~보다 열등한

- prefer A to B B보다 A를 더 좋아한다 A, B는 명사나 동명사 (to: 전치사)
- prefer to A rather than B B보다 A를 더 좋아한다 A, B는 동사원형 (to: 부정사)

This high-tech equipment is superior [to / ~~than~~] old equipment. 이 첨단 장비는 예전 장비보다 뛰어나다.

Prior [to / ~~than~~] becoming an accountant, he worked as a financial secretary.
회계사가 되기 전에, 그는 회계 비서로 일했다.

02 | 비교구문의 관용 표현

1) as soon as possible (one can) : 가능한 한 빨리

We regret to inform you that the items you ordered are presently out of stock, but we will do our best to restock them [as soon as / ~~whenever~~] **we can.**
주문하신 제품이 현재 재고가 없다는 걸 알려드리게 되어서 유감입니다만, 가능한 한 빨리 최선을 다해서 재고를 확보해 놓겠습니다.

2) no longer = not any ~ longer : 더 이상 ~않다

Please note that all billing questions will no [longer / ~~later~~] be handled by the Customer Service Department. 청구서에 관한 모든 문의들이 더 이상 고객 서비스 부서에서 취급되지 않는다는 것을 주의하세요.

3) more than (~ 이상의) / less than (~ 미만의)

It will take [more than / ~~more~~] a month for the city to recover from the damage that the storm caused. 도시가 태풍으로 인한 피해로부터 복구되는 데 한 달 이상의 시간이 걸릴 것이다.

4) rather than : ~ 라기보다, ~ 대신에

Some tourists prefer to travel by themselves rather [than / ~~to~~] with a tour group.
몇몇 관광객들은 단체로 여행하는 것보다 오히려 그들 혼자 여행하는 것을 더 선호합니다.

5) no later than : 늦어도 ~까지

We have to submit the report no [later / ~~lately~~] than September 15.
늦어도 9월 15일까지 보고서를 제출해야 한다.

SPARTA Check-UP! 4

해설 p. 380

1 Passengers whose flights are delayed more ------- five hours may qualify for a 30% discounted ticket.
(A) from
(B) than
(C) as
(D) of

2 The advertisement stated that all office furniture is on sale for 35 percent off ------- the actual discount of 15 percent.
(A) even though
(B) regardless of
(C) rather than
(D) since

3 I regret to inform you that our company ------- longer requires your services as a sales representative.
(A) any
(B) seldom
(C) no
(D) none

PRACTICE

해설 p. 380

▪ 괄호 안의 보기 중 알맞은 단어를 고르세요.

1 Of all of our employees, Paul Nicholls is the **[more / most]** responsible.

2 Aluminum products are **[light / lighter]** than glass and may be recyclable.

3 **[More of / The greater]** the offer, the more pressure we'll have to face.

4 Housing loans used to be obtained more **[easy / easily]** in the past than now.

5 SDI's major objective has been to establish even **[strong / stronger]** ties between its domestic and international divisions.

6 Between the two applicants, Mr. Sampson is the **[better / most]** qualified for that position.

7 Of the two consultants, I'd have to say that Mr. Wilkinson is the **[better / best]** one at this stage of his career.

8 What really impressed me was that the sales team paid much **[close / closer]** attention to detail than other teams did.

9 Of the different paths, the green line is the **[easiest / most easily]** to walk to the Cicada Building.

10 We went to a seminar on the environment last night and that was the **[more / most]** interesting discussion I have attended in years.

11 According to the report, the Research and Development Department spent **[very / a lot]** more than usual on courier services last month.

12 The Chinese economy is expected to be the **[large / largest]** in the world within the next half-century.

13 The higher our efficiency rating is at the end of this year, the **[greater / greatest]** the sizes of our bonuses will be.

14 We have to proceed **[more quickly / most quickly]** than before if we want to get the letter delivered on time.

15 One of the **[many / most]** important qualifications for this job is that the applicant must be able to speak English as a foreign language.

1 We ensure that our customers' sensitive financial data is more ------- than ever before.

(A) secure (B) securer
(C) security (D) securely

2 In the third quarter of the fiscal year, the Franklin Corporation succeeded in reaching sales figures that were ------- than average.

(A) high (B) highest
(C) highly (D) higher

3 Health insurance premiums rose ------- faster than earnings over the last five years.

(A) many (B) more
(C) most (D) much

4 The new innovative diesel engine works ------- than the engines of other companies.

(A) quiet (B) quietly
(C) more quiet (D) more quietly

5 According to company insiders, the financial condition of Manutek, Inc. is ------- than recent news reports have indicated.

(A) weaker (B) weak
(C) weakest (D) weakness

6 The Peach Health Medical Center offers the most ------- cancer research facilities in the country.

(A) comprehend (B) comprehension
(C) comprehensive (D) comprehensively

7 Montaz Motorcycles wants to make the partnership between the Product and Research departments -------.

(A) strength (B) strengthens
(C) stronger (D) strengthening

8 For consumers, the prime advantage of Internet telephones is that they are ------- cheaper than conventional phone service.

(A) even (B) many
(C) that (D) very

9 If your service is not as ------- as your competitors, you will lose many valued customers.

(A) reliably (B) reliant
(C) reliability (D) reliable

10 The sooner the building is finished, ------- the companies will be able to open their new offices.

(A) quickly (B) the faster
(C) the better (D) soon

11 Department managers submit expense reports directly to Marc Platt ------- than to their assistants.

(A) few (B) most
(C) less (D) rather

12 Our Allegro office earned the ------- ratings for customer satisfaction in a recent corporate survey.

(A) higher (B) highest
(C) more highly (D) most highly

해설 p. 381

Questions 13-16 refer to the following letter.

Dear Mr. Eldridge,

------- (13.) one of our frequent flier VIP customers, we would like to invite you to join our Platinum Club.

With this membership, you will have exclusive access to Falcon Air suites and lounges across the globe. You will also be given preferential upgrades on all flights over 2 hours in length as well as complimentary meals and beverages before and after your flights.

We will provide you with the ------- (14.) care and service at all times while traveling with us.

Falcon Air has a special branch of customer service representatives who ------- (15.) 24/7 for our Platinum Club members.

-------. (16.)

Sincerely,

Gail Pembridge
Human Relations & VIP Division
Falcon Airlines International

13 (A) For
(B) During
(C) As
(D) Because

14 (A) most expensive
(B) most luxurious
(C) finest
(D) largest

15 (A) are on call
(B) are calling
(C) have been calling
(D) are being called

16 (A) We wish to show you just how much we appreciate your patronage.
(B) The failure was caused by work on an upgrade to the ticketing Web site.
(C) We apologize for any inconvenience caused to our passengers.
(D) No single baggage item may exceed the 24kg weight limit.

UNIT 18 가정법과 도치

가정법 관련 문제나 도치 구문 문제는 출제 빈도가 매우 낮아 1년에 1~2문제가 출제되거나 출제되지 않은 적도 있다. 가정법 빈출 유형으로는 ① 가정법 과거완료의 형태, ② 가정법 미래와 과거완료의 도치를 묻는 문제이다. 이 장에서는 시제별 가정법과 가정법의 도치 및 일반 도치구문의 유형을 학습한다.

Preview

01 | 가정법 미래

미래에 실현 가능성이 희박한 일을 가정할 때 사용되나 정중한 요청이나 제안하는 경우에도 사용되며, 이 경우 명령문과 함께 잘 쓰인다.

구조	If+주어+should+동사원형 ~, ┌ 주어+will [can / may / shall]+동사원형 └ (please) 동사원형
의미	(그럴 가능성은 적지만) 혹시라도 ~한다면, ~할 것이다.

If you should have any questions, please contact us at any time.
혹시 문의 사항이 있으시면 언제든 저희에게 연락하세요.

02 | 가정법 과거

현재 사실과 반대되는 상황을 가정하며, 현재의 의미로 해석한다.

구조	If+주어+동사의 과거형 ~, 주어+would [could / might / should]+동사원형
의미	만일 ~한다면, ~할 텐데.

If I had a lot of money, **I** could buy a car. 만약 내가 많은 돈을 가지고 있다면, 그 차를 살 수 있을 텐데.

If I were you, **I** would attend the conference. 만약 내가 너라면 회의에 참석했을 텐데.

03 | 가정법 과거완료

과거 사실과 반대되는 가정, 소망, 상상 등을 나타낸다. 시험에서 출제 빈도 1순위 가정법 표현이다.

구조	If+주어+had+p.p. ~, 주어+would [could / might / should]+have+p.p.
의미	만일 ~하였다면[했었다면], ~했을 텐데.

If he had followed the security rules, **he** would not have been fired.
그가 보안정책을 준수했더라면, 그는 해고되지 않았을 텐데.

POINT 1 가정법 if

01 | 시제별 가정법의 형태

1) 가정법 미래 : If + 주어 + should + 동사원형 ~, 주어 + will/would + 동사원형

If **it** [should / ~~would~~] rain, **we** will have to postpone the company picnic.
만약 비가 온다면, 우리들은 회사 야유회를 연기해야 할 것이다.

2) 가정법 과거 : If + 주어 + were/동사의 과거형 ~, 주어 + 조동사의 과거형 + 동사원형

If **it** [were / ~~was~~] not for his help, **they** wouldn't finish the project.
그의 도움이 없다면 그들은 프로젝트를 못 끝냈을 것이다.

▶ if절의 동사가 be동사인 경우 주어의 단/복수와 상관없이 were를 쓴다.

3) 가정법 과거완료 : If + 주어 + had p.p. ~, 주어 + 조동사의 과거형 + have p.p.

If **she** had made a flight reservation earlier, **Ms. Ashton** [could have attended / ~~could attend~~] the conference.
만약 더 일찍 비행기 예약을 했었더라면, Ashton 씨가 회의에 참석할 수 있었을 것이다.

+TIP 가정법 if와 조건절 if의 구분

가정법은 '사실과 다른 내용을 가정'할 때 쓰는 반면, 조건절 if는 '실현될 가능성'이 있을 때 쓴다.

1) 가정법에서는 if절과 주절의 동사 시제가 다르다. 주절의 동사는 if절의 동사보다 한 단계 앞선 시점의 시제를 쓴다.

If Mr. Johnson **had remained** in the race, he **would have won** the election easily.
Johnson 씨가 경쟁에 계속 남아 있었다면, 그는 선거에서 쉽게 당선되었을 것이다.

2) if절이 조건을 나타낼 때는 상황에 따라 적절한 시제를 쓴다.

If employees **anticipate** arriving late to work, they **will contact** their immediate supervisor.
만약 직원들이 직장에 늦게 도착할 것을 예상한다면, 그들은 직속 상관에게 연락을 취할 것이다.

SPARTA Check-UP! 1

해설 p. 383

1 If Ms. Kim decides to retire early, management ------- a junior member of her department to fill the void.
(A) promote
(B) promoted
(C) would have promoted
(D) will promote

2 If she had completed the report yesterday, she ------- a new project today.
(A) could start
(B) start
(C) could have started
(D) had started

3 If the project had started with our international partners, some of these cost overruns would certainly -------.
(A) eliminate
(B) was eliminated
(C) have been eliminated
(D) had been eliminated

POINT 2 가정법 도치와 without 가정법

01 | 가정법 도치 : if를 생략시키고 if절의 조동사 또는 be동사가 주어 앞으로 온다.

1) 가정법 미래의 도치

If you should have any questions or concerns, please feel free to contact me at your convenience.
→ [Should / ~~Before~~] **you** have any questions or concerns, please feel free to contact me at your convenience.
혹시라도 질문이나 염려가 생긴다면, 언제든지 편하신 시간에 연락하세요.

2) 가정법 과거의 도치

If it were not for the employees' commitment, we wouldn't be here celebrating the company's 30th anniversary.
→ [Were / ~~If~~] **it** not **for** the employees' commitment, we wouldn't be here celebrating the company's 30th anniversary.
직원들의 헌신이 없으면, 우리는 회사의 30주년 기념일을 이 자리에서 축하할 수 없을 겁니다.

3) 가정법 과거완료의 도치

If Ms. Deschanel had known that one of the guests was a vegetarian, she would have prepared a dish without meat for the luncheon.
→ [Had / ~~Should~~] **Ms. Deschanel** known that one of the guests was a vegetarian, she would have prepared a dish without meat for the luncheon.
Deschanel 씨가 손님 중 한 명이 채식주의자인 것을 알았더라면, 오찬을 위해 고기가 없는 요리를 준비했을 것이다.

02 | 가정법은 if 대신 without, but for, barring 등으로 나타낼 수 있다.

If it had not been for the contributions of Ken Johnson, the problems with the design of the new motorcycle could not have been solved.
→ [Without / ~~Within~~] the contributions of Ken Johnson, the problems with the design of the new
(= But for, Barring)
motorcycle could not have been solved.
Ken Johnson의 헌신이 없었다면, 새로운 오토바이의 디자인 문제는 해결될 수 없었을 것이다.

SPARTA Check-UP! 2

| 해설 p. 383

1 ------- Mr. Peters need anything during his visit to the factory floor, please contact Jane Kim in the main office.
(A) Perhaps
(B) Whether
(C) May
(D) Should

2 Had the financial advisor released his findings earlier, we ------- to the changes in the market.
(A) react
(B) could react
(C) can react
(D) could have reacted

3 Had Mr. Roy ------- the 7 A.M. train, he might have been on time for the weekly department meeting.
(A) catch
(B) been caught
(C) caught
(D) being caught

POINT 3 도치구문

01 | 보어+동사+주어

The copy of your original purchase order is **included** with the shipment.
→ [**Included** / ~~Inclusion~~] with the shipment is **the copy** of your original purchase order.
최초 주문증 사본이 주문품에 포함되어 있습니다.

+TIP 빈칸에 명사가 오려면 주어와 보어가 동격이어야 한다.

> [**Attached** / ~~Attachment~~] to the letter is **a tentative schedule** for the monthly meeting.
> 월례 회의의 임시 일정표가 이 편지에 첨부되어 있습니다.

02 | only+부사구/부사절+조동사+주어+동사

[**Only** / ~~Soon~~] **after you've written and sent the article will we pay** you the agreed amount.
당신이 기사를 작성하고 보낸 후에나 우리는 합의한 금액을 지불할 것입니다.

Only when complaints are received in writing [**does** / ~~do~~] **North Airlines reimburse** passengers for damaged baggage. 불만이 서신으로 접수되었을 때만 North 항공사는 승객들에게 손상된 화물에 대해 배상을 해준다.

03 | 부정어(never/nor/neither/hardly/rarely/seldom)+조동사+주어+동사

[**Never** / ~~Always~~] **had Ms. Hall seen** such high ratings of the IMT Broadcast Studio's sitcom before.
Hall 씨는 IMT방송국의 이토록 높은 시트콤의 시청률을 이전에 본 적이 없다.

Companies are not permitted to sell personal information about their customers, [**nor** / ~~so~~] **can they share** it. 기업은 고객에 대한 신상 정보를 팔거나 공유하도록 허용되지 않는다.

[**Hardly** / ~~Ever~~] **had the new *Thunder Bird* video games been displayed** on the store shelves for ten minutes before they sold out. 새로운 Thunder Bird 비디오 게임이 가게 선반에 진열된 지 10분도 안 되어 품절되었다.

SPARTA Check-UP! 3

해설 p. 383

1 Had Mr. Freeman contacted the repair company when the problem started, he ------- in this predicament now.
(A) won't be
(B) wouldn't have been
(C) wasn't
(D) wouldn't be

2 Never ------- I think that Paramount would announce the bankruptcy of its parent and subsidiary companies at the same time.
(A) does
(B) did
(C) am
(D) will

3 Not ------- does the business trip to Europe take place on a national holiday, but it also conflicts with my wife's vacation plans.
(A) along
(B) rarely
(C) hardly
(D) only

POINT 4 혼합 가정법과 그 밖에 주의해야 할 가정법 구문

01 | 혼합 가정법

가정법 과거완료와 가정법 과거가 혼합된 형태로 과거의 사실을 후회하면서 '주어가 ~했었더라면, 현재 …일 텐데'라는 의미의 표현이다. 과거의 사실을 후회하면서 현재의 결과를 이야기하기 때문에 today, now, this year 같은 시간 부사구를 함께 써 주는 것이 일반적이다.

구조	If+주어+had p.p. ~, 주어+would [could / might / should]+동사원형+today[now/this year]
의미	만일 ~했었다면, 오늘[지금/올해] ~할 텐데

If **you** had studied hard, **you** [would / ~~will~~] not have a hard time finding a job now.
당신이 열심히 공부를 했더라면, 지금 일자리 찾는 데 어려움을 겪지 않을 것이다.

+TIP 주의해야 할 가정법

1) I wish (that) 주어+동사의 과거형 : ~라면 좋을 텐데 (현재 사실에 반대되는 소망을 나타냄)

I wish I **could be** with you all the time.
항상 당신과 함께 할 수 있길 바랍니다.

2) I wish (that) 주어+had p.p. : ~였더라면 좋을 텐데 (과거 사실에 반대되는 소망을 나타냄)

I wish I **had studied** management in college.
대학에서 경영학을 공부했었다면 좋았을 텐데.

3) 주어+동사+as if+주어+동사의 과거형 : 마치 ~인 것처럼

Suits are displayed in a window as if they **were** works of art.
양복들은 마치 예술작품인 것처럼 진열장에 전시되어 있다.

4) 주어+동사+as if+주어+had p.p. : 마치 ~였던 것처럼

The next day, he pretended as if nothing **had happened**.
다음 날, 그는 아무 일도 없었다는 듯이 행동했다.

SPARTA Check-UP! 4

해설 p. 383

1 If we had followed the management consultant's advice, we ------- in this financial crisis now.

(A) would not be
(B) would be
(C) would have been
(D) would not have been

2 Had our company invested money in employee benefits, we ------- such a high turnover of staff now.

(A) will not be
(B) would not had
(C) would not have
(D) would not have been

3 Even though the due date for the proposal was tight, Mr. Benshaw acted as if he still ------- time.

(A) have
(B) had
(C) has
(D) will have

PRACTICE

해설 p. 384

▪ 괄호 안의 보기 중 알맞은 단어를 고르세요.

1 If I were not busy now, I **[will / would]** help you out with the assignment.

2 If interest rates were lowered, we **[will / would]** achieve our sales goals.

3 If our company **[reduces / reduced]** its deficit by half, our competitiveness would be stronger than before.

4 Had the rumor not spread, she might not **[leave / have left]**.

5 **[Had / Should]** management acted sooner, the strike wouldn't have happened.

6 Had he **[took / taken]** more time, the results would have been better.

7 If the plant **[were / had]** not been damaged by the fire, the order would have been completed by the end of the year.

8 Had we **[knew / known]** that the company was suffering from financial difficulties, we would not have signed the contract with them.

9 If you **[will / should]** need any help, please feel free to call me.

10 Should you **[arrive / arrived]** before the office is open, the security guard will not let you in.

11 **[Had / Should]** you need any help with your research, feel free to call me at any time.

12 Basically, if the design team **[spent / had spent]** more time on this online game, it would have been an almost perfect game.

13 If the yield had gone up over 10 percent, it **[would be / would have been]** the highest average yield since 1990.

14 Should you **[have / had]** any problems with the product, contact your local repairman.

15 Had we known in advance that the monthly meeting had been canceled, we **[could leave / could have left]** early last night.

1 If procedures had been taken to break up the monopoly, the competition certainly -------.

(A) had eliminated
(B) eliminates
(C) would have been eliminated
(D) would eliminate

2 Should our Invoicing Department ------- any difficulties, please call me.

(A) had experienced (B) experiences
(C) experience (D) experiencing

3 ------- the vacuum cleaner not work properly, please contact our customer service center, and we'll exchange it for another or refund your money.

(A) Won't (B) Can
(C) Might (D) Should

4 If the features of our product were emphasized in our advertisement, customers ------- our products much more than they do now.

(A) would buy (B) bought
(C) have bought (D) buy

5 If the company ------- its interviews last month, it would have likely filled the position.

(A) conducting (B) had conducted
(C) will be conducting (D) would conduct

6 If drinking water ------- the standards of quality set by the law, that means the water is considered safe and drinkable.

(A) meet (B) to meet
(C) had met (D) meets

7 Had we not implemented significant reforms over the past two years, our company ------- from severe fiscal pressure and possible bankruptcy.

(A) suffered (B) suffer
(C) would have suffered (D) was suffering

8 The supervisor commented that the manual could ------- better had the company hired an editor to go over the material before it was printed.

(A) organize
(B) be organized
(C) have organized
(D) have been organized

9 Mr. Powell ------- never have succeeded at making a profit for his division without his staff's expertise and work ethic.

(A) can (B) would
(C) must (D) need

10 If he had studied harder in university, he ------- easily won admission to medical school.

(A) could (B) must have
(C) would have (D) have

11 ------- the workers known the safety regulations before entering the chemical factory, the accident could have been avoided.

(A) Have (B) Had
(C) Would (D) Should

12 ------- the staff's sincere devotion to the project, this remarkable report would not have been possible.

(A) Provided (B) Only
(C) Without (D) For

해설 p. 385

Questions 13-16 refer to the following information.

Dear Customer,

Thank you for patronizing Astica Sambo Furniture!

The receipt you were issued when you made your purchase provides details of our free delivery service. On the receipt, we ------- (13.) the time and date of your delivery. ------- (14.).

------- (15.) there be a delay, we will contact you in advance. Someone over the age of 18 needs to be at the designated location to sign for your merchandise.

Please ------- (16.) your receipt for your records. If you have any questions or need to reschedule your delivery, call our Customer Service Department at 800-555-1096.

13 (A) have indicated
(B) would indicate
(C) are indicated
(D) will indicate

14 (A) In the meantime, I hope you'll accept this tentative schedule.
(B) The local government did not agree to our proposed deadline.
(C) Our Delivery Department will make every effort to adhere to this schedule.
(D) As the schedule is set, the Delivery Department will design a poster for the conference.

15 (A) Had
(B) Should
(C) As though
(D) Whether

16 (A) sustain
(B) assign
(C) retain
(D) apply

PART 7

UNIT 19 주제 / 목적 (General Questions)

주제(topic)란 글의 핵심 내용을 의미하며, 이것이 드러나 있는 핵심 문장을 주제문(topic sentence)이라고 한다. 모든 글에는 주제가 있으며 전반적인 내용과 글을 쓴 목적을 알 수 있다. 주제 관련 문제는 거의 모든 지문의 첫 문제로 자주 출제된다.

■ 빈출 문제 유형

What is the topic of this memo? 이 회람의 주제/쟁점은 무엇인가?

What is the text message about? 이 문자메시지는 무엇에 관한 것인가?

What is mainly discussed in this online chat discussion? 이 온라인 채팅에서 주로 무엇이 논의되고 있는가?

What is the problem[change]? 문제점[변경 사항]이 무엇인가?

What is the purpose of this notice? 이 공지의 목적이 무엇인가?

For whom is this letter intended? 이 편지는 누구를 대상으로 하고 있는가?

Where would this advertisement most likely be found? 이 광고는 어디에서 보게 될 것 같은가?

■ 주제를 알려주는 표현

① 편지/이메일 주제

I'm writing to~ ~하기 위하여 이 글을 씁니다.

We are very sorry to inform you that~ ~을 알려 드리게 되어 유감입니다.

② 구인/상품 광고 주제문

We are looking for[searching for/seeking]~ 우리 회사는 ~를 찾고 있습니다.

We are giving you a special opportunity to~ 우리 회사는 당신에게 ~할 특별한 기회를 드립니다.

③ 공지/회람 주제문

Please be informed that~ ~을 알아 주십시오.

I want to remind you that~ ~을 당신에게 상기시켜 드리고 싶습니다.

고득점 SOLUTION

① 주제가 제목에 확실히 드러나지 않는 경우에는
글을 작성한 사람과 읽는 사람의 관계에 집중하여 글의 목적을 파악한다.
ex 편지의 경우 쓴 사람의 회사나 직책명에 집중한다.

② 주제문이 확실하지 않은 경우에는
글의 중간에 나온 세부 내용을 참고하여 주제문을 역으로 추론한다.
ex 세부 내용에 통제된 도로명이 나왔다면 글의 주제는 행사 소개가 아니라 '교통 통제'에 대한 공지이다.

③ 주제를 찾는 문제를 자주 틀린다면
주제문(topic sentence)에서 답을 찾는 연습을 반복한다.

POINT 1

Question 1 refers to the following letter. ---- 1 글의 종류를 확인한다.

Dear Mr. Johnson: ---- 2 'We would like to inform you that ~'으로 시작하는 주제문을 정독으로 찾는다.

We would like to inform you that we are currently unable to process your visitor tax refund application because you did not submit documentation proving that the computer you bought was purchased in Canada.

Proof of export is required for you to receive a sales tax rebate on high-value items.

We are sending you a visitor tax rebate application form and the original receipt for the item. So please submit a completed application form, the original receipt, the proof of export, and a copy of this letter. ---- 세부 내용

Yours truly,

Tedd Marshall

Q1 Why was this letter written? ---- 3 주제를 묻는 문제로, 정독으로 파악한 주제문에서만 답을 찾는다.

(A) To remind Mr. Johnson of the date of a payment
(B) To notify Mr. Johnson of the rejection of an application ---- 4 '방문자 세금 환급 신청'을 포괄적으로 표현한 '신청 거부를 알리기 위해'인 (B)가 정답이다.
(C) To suggest that Mr. Johnson set up a meeting
(D) To ask Mr. Johnson to save a document

존슨 씨에게:
귀하가 산 컴퓨터가 캐나다에서 구입한 것임을 입증하는 문서를 제출하지 않으셨기 때문에 현재 귀하의 방문자 세금 환급 신청을 진행할 수 없음을 알려드립니다.
고가제품의 판매세 환급을 받기 위해서 반출 증명서류가 요구됩니다.
방문자 세금 환급 신청서와 제품에 대한 원본 영수증을 보내드립니다. 따라서 작성한 신청서, 원본 영수증, 반출 증명서류와 이 서신의 사본을 제출해 주십시오.
존경을 표하며,
테드 마샬

Q1. 이 편지는 왜 쓰였는가?
(A) Johnson 씨에게 지불 날짜를 상기시키기 위해
(B) Johnson 씨에게 신청 거부를 알리기 위해
(C) Johnson 씨에게 회의 준비를 제안하기 위해
(D) Johnson 씨에게 서류를 보존하라고 요청하기 위해

패러프레이징 표현

1	annual conference 연례 회의	session once a year/ yearly conference 연 1회의 회의
2	get reimbursed 상환 받다	be paid back 환급 받다 be granted compensation 보상 지급 받다
3	need a receipt 영수증이 필요하다	request an official proof of purchase 공식적인 구매 증빙을 요청하다
4	express our appreciation to you 당신에게 감사를 표하다	thank all of our staff members 우리의 모든 직원들에게 감사하다
5	turn in a completed form 작성된 양식을 제출하다	submit an application 신청서를 제출하다
6	Some of the parts failed to be delivered. 부품의 일부가 배송되지 않았다.	Some orders are missing. 주문품이 일부 누락되었다
7	effective as of April 1 4월 1일부터 효력이 발생하는	start on April 1 4월 1일에 시작하다
8	return a piece of merchandise 상품 한 점을 반품하다	get a refund 환불 받다
9	cut down on expenses 비용을 절감하다	cut[reduce] costs 경비를 줄이다
10	Registration is required in advance. 미리 등록해야 한다.	Prior enrollment is necessary. 사전 등록은 필수이다.
11	complete the online survey 온라인 설문지를 작성하다	fill in the form on the Web site 웹 사이트에서 양식을 기입하다
12	estimated 견적의, 추산된	expect the value to rise/fall 가치가 올라갈/떨어질 것으로 예상하다
13	lay off some employees 몇몇 직원들을 해고하다	fire[dismiss] some employees 몇몇 직원들을 해고하다
14	have knowledge of marketing 마케팅에 대해 알다	be familiar with marketing 마케팅에 정통하다
15	drop off the documents at my office 내 사무실에 서류를 갖다놓다	leave materials 자료를 두다

패러프레이징 연습

Paraphrasing

해설 p. 387

▪ 다음 문장 또는 지문과 의미상 일치하는 것을 고르세요.

1

> The changed policy on parking will be effective as of November 11. Employees who work overtime should be approved to park their cars in designated areas.

(A) The new policy on parking for the night shift will begin on November 11.
(B) All employees should be allowed to park their vehicles.

2

> If you wish to return a defective product, you need to provide the receipt as proof of purchase within a month of buying the item.

(A) Any merchandise with a malfunction can be replaced with new one.
(B) In order to get a refund, a document must be provided.

3

> We would like to express our appreciation for your hard work in achieving your sales goal this year although there is continuing severe recession due to rapidly changed trends in the industry.

(A) We want to thank staff members who have struggled to overcome the economic downturn.
(B) Sales figures this year are higher than ever before.

4

> We placed an order on your online store 3 days ago, and the products were delivered yesterday. However, we would like to inform you that some of the items were not included in the package.

(A) We will cancel this transaction.
(B) Part of the shipment is missing.

해설 p. 387

Notice

The annual human resources seminar by the Personnel Department will take place on September 21 at 10 A.M. in Meeting Room 22 on the first floor across from the mail room.

Q1 What is the purpose of this notice?

(A) To encourage some employees to attend a seminar
(B) To notify some employees of a change in a schedule
(C) To encourage some employees to submit a report
(D) To notify some employees of the new theme of a seminar

Dear Ms. Peterson,

We are very sorry to hear that two of the Lilly collection plates in your recent order were cracked when you received them. We at Flower Fine China & Glass, Inc. take pride in our customer service, and we are pleased to send you replacements. We have enclosed a return kit for your damaged items. So you only need to pack the item and call Deliver Courier Service at 0232-512-2446. Upon receipt of the returned items, we will send the plates free of charge.
Once again, we apologize for the inconvenience. Thank you very much for your business.

Sincerely yours,

Dennis Klein,
Customer Service Manager
Flower Fine China & Glass, Inc.

Q2 What is mainly discussed in the letter?

(A) A misplaced order
(B) Missing merchandise
(C) An unavailable product
(D) A solution to a problem

해설 p. 387

Questions 1-2 refer to the following e-mail.

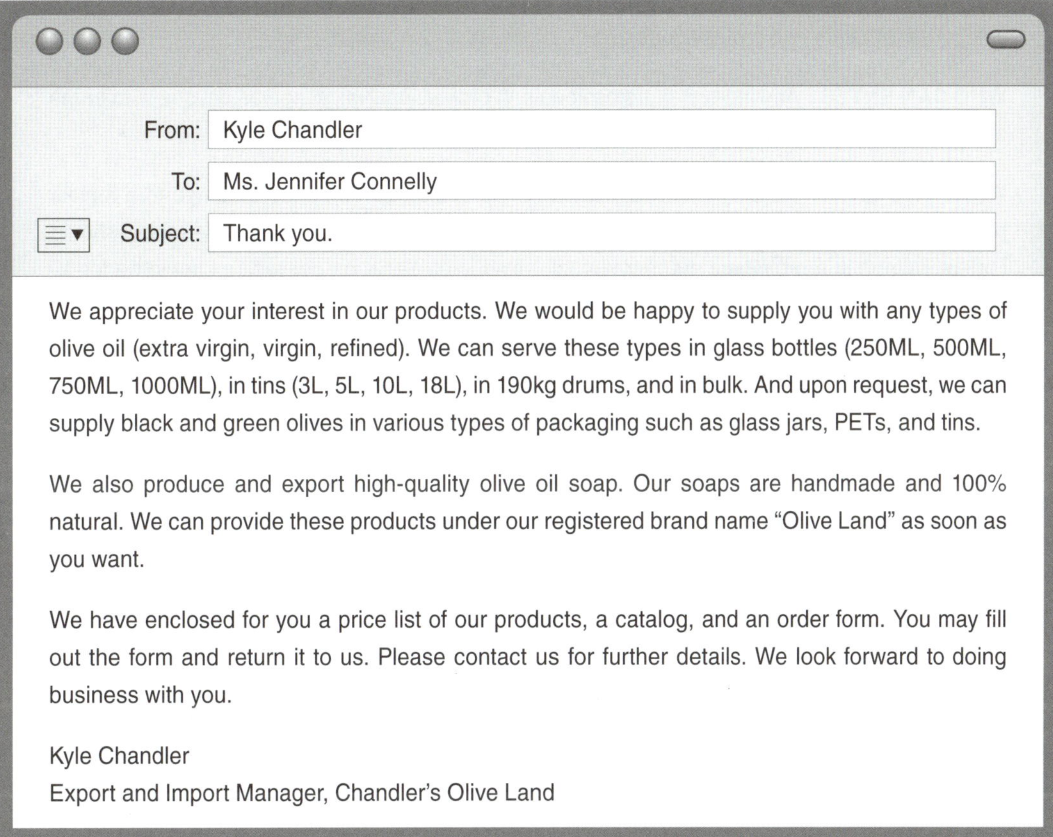

From: Kyle Chandler

To: Ms. Jennifer Connelly

Subject: Thank you.

We appreciate your interest in our products. We would be happy to supply you with any types of olive oil (extra virgin, virgin, refined). We can serve these types in glass bottles (250ML, 500ML, 750ML, 1000ML), in tins (3L, 5L, 10L, 18L), in 190kg drums, and in bulk. And upon request, we can supply black and green olives in various types of packaging such as glass jars, PETs, and tins.

We also produce and export high-quality olive oil soap. Our soaps are handmade and 100% natural. We can provide these products under our registered brand name "Olive Land" as soon as you want.

We have enclosed for you a price list of our products, a catalog, and an order form. You may fill out the form and return it to us. Please contact us for further details. We look forward to doing business with you.

Kyle Chandler
Export and Import Manager, Chandler's Olive Land

1 Why was this e-mail written?

(A) To promote items to a potential buyer
(B) To acknowledge the receipt of a parcel
(C) To request a quote
(D) To thank Ms. Jennifer Connelly

2 What is the e-mail about?

(A) Descriptions of products for sale
(B) Kinds of olive oil
(C) A manufacturing technique
(D) The capacities of containers

Questions 3-5 refer to the following notice.

> We want to know how the best cooks in the world prepare British Columbia's favorite fish, salmon. And we want to recognize the work of both home and working chefs, so this cook-off has two entry categories: amateur and professional.
>
> **WHO CAN ENTER :** Amateurs and professionals. A professional is defined as anyone who earns any part of his or her income from cooking. All entrants must be at least 18 years old.
>
> **WHAT THE ENTRY MUST INCLUDE :** Each recipe submission must be attached to a legible hand-printed or typed entry form (see below); the form can be photocopied. The recipe should feature salmon in a prominent manner (1/4 kilo minimum). Servings per recipe should be for 10 people or fewer. Contestants must warrant that the recipe is original. For each recipe submission, please tell us, in 50 words or fewer, how you created the recipe.
>
> **THE PRIZES :** Fifty semifinalists will receive merit certificates. Eight finalists (four in each category) will win a trip, including airfare and one night's lodging, to *ABC Magazine* headquarters in Vancouver. The finalists' recipes will be published in the forthcoming cookbook *A Taste of British Columbia*.

3 What is the notice about?

(A) The promotion of a publication
(B) A review of a restaurant
(C) Ways to learn new recipes
(D) A description of a competition

4 Who is most likely writing this notice?

(A) The Pelagic Fishery Association
(B) A publisher of periodicals
(C) A senior chef
(D) A catering service

5 Who will most likely be interested in this notice?

(A) Owners of restaurants
(B) Both amateur and professional cooks
(C) Columnists
(D) Researchers in the restaurant business industry

Questions 6-8 refer to the following article.

The stock exchange announced yesterday that it has reached an agreement to sell the Beauty & Trend Trade Corporation as a part to concentrate on a smaller number of services. The announcement comes before the publication later this week of the "*Financial Report*."

Beauty & Trend, a company that produces small items such as rings, earrings, and bracelets, has been sold to Party 'n Crafts, a rival company that owns a confirmation system called Steady 'n Co. The president of Party 'n Crafts has promised that it will not combine with Beauty & Trend yet but will eventually merge the two into one company.

The terms of the acquisition were not disclosed although Beauty & Trend has been losing money, and Mr. Riley, the president and CEO of Party 'n Crafts, said the deal would reduce uncertainty for shareholders.

6 What is mainly discussed in this article?

(A) A huge loss at the confirmation system
(B) The publication of a new book
(C) A settlement of selling a company
(D) Electronic confirmation of stock trading

7 Which of the following is NOT likely to be sold at Party 'n Crafts?

(A) A diamond ring
(B) An earring
(C) A bracelet
(D) A watch

8 What is Beauty & Trend?

(A) A jewelry store
(B) An accessory company
(C) A financial program
(D) A plastic knife

세부 내용 (Specific Questions)

주제문을 설득력 있게 뒷받침하는 세부 내용에 관한 문제 유형이다. 가장 빈번히 출제되는 문제 유형으로 세부 내용 확인, 진위 내용 확인과 추후 일정 및 당부 사항 확인 문제로 구분된다. 주제문을 확인한 후 글의 전반적인 흐름에 따라 속독하다가 문제에서 확인해 두었던 핵심어가 나타나면 바로 그 주변 맥락에서 답을 찾으면 된다. 신속하게 처리해야 하는 문제 유형이며, 핵심어가 패러프레이징 되었더라도 정확히 알 수 있도록 철저한 훈련이 필요하다.

■ 빈출 문제 유형

① 세부 내용 확인

What is Mr. Ayer scheduled to present? 에이어 씨는 무엇을 발표할 예정인가?

Who should be contacted to confirm the reservation? 예약을 확인하기 위해 누구에게 연락해야 하는가?

② 진위 내용 확인

What is NOT a requirement of the job opening? 공석의 자격요건이 아닌 것은 무엇인가?

Which of the following is NOT stated about the supervisor? 감독관에 대해 언급되지 않은 것은 무엇인가?

What is true about the identification? 신분증에 관해 사실인 것은 무엇인가?

What is mentioned[indicated/stated] in the notice? 공지에서 언급된 것은 무엇인가?

③ 추후 일정 및 당부 내용 확인

What are employees asked[suggested/recommended/instructed/encouraged/invited] to do?
직원들은 무엇을 하라고 요청[제안/추천/지시/장려/요구]되는가?

What will the editor do next? 편집자는 이후에 무엇을 할 것인가?

What will Ian's Bistro offer to do? 이안 비스트로는 무엇을 해 주겠다고 할 것인가?

How should passengers buy tickets online? 승객들은 온라인으로 어떻게 티켓을 구매할 수 있는가?

When will the workshop be held? 워크숍은 언제 열릴 예정인가?

■ 세부 내용을 알려주는 표현

Please~ ~해 주세요.

Would[Could] you~? ~해 주시겠습니까?

You can[should/have to/may/will]~ 당신은 ~할 겁니다.

Why don't you~? ~하지 않으실래요?

I ask[suggest/recommend/instruct/encourage/invite/want/would like/expect/need] you to do~
저는 당신이 ~하길 바랍니다.

고득점 SOLUTION

진위 내용 확인 문제 유형에서 문제 푸는 시간이 오래 걸린다면

지문과 대조해야 할 실제 핵심어(key word)는 문제가 아니라 보기에 있다. 그러므로 문제와 대조할 때보다 보기 4개와 대조하는 시간이 더 걸릴 수밖에 없다. 이러한 문제의 특성을 잘 이해하여 보기의 핵심어를 미리 표시해 두고 지문과 대조하여 한 번에 진위 파악을 해결하도록 한다.

POINT 1

Question 1 refers to the following advertisement. ---- **1** 글의 종류를 확인한다.

Megatech International is looking for a corporate communications manager with the following qualifications: ---- **2** 주제문을 정독으로 찾고 이후 흐름을 추측한다.

- Must have (A) **a master's degree** in business management/administration
- Excellent communication skills both (C) **in writing and speaking**
- At least eight years of experience in various communication disciplines, preferably gained from a multinational and/or multi-cultural organization
- Strong computer skills
- Adept in projects and events management
- A good personality with a broad understanding of global and local business issues
- Must be very (D) **competitive** but at the same time be a (D) **team player**
- Should be able to manage and cope with unexpected changes and/or conflicts

---- **5** 문제 핵심어인 'requirement'까지 속독으로 찾아간다. 그 이후에는 미리 찾아 두었던 보기의 핵심어의 진위를 한번에 대조하여 판단한다. (보기의 핵심어 (B) personal은 보이지 않으므로 거짓 정보로 확인한다. 그러므로 정답은 (B)이다.)

Please e-mail your application letter and your comprehensive résumé to hr@megatech.com. If you would like more information, please contact us at 899-4759. ---- 추후 당부 사항

Q1 Which is NOT a requirement for being accepted as a corporate communications manager? ---- **3** 문제의 핵심어를 파악한다. (자격요건 중에 아닌 것을 찾아야 하므로 아래 보기에서 핵심어를 미리 찾아 둔다.)

(A) **A master's degree** in business management
(B) A broad understanding of personal issues
(C) The ability to communicate well both **in writing and speaking**
(D) **Competitiveness** and the ability to work on a **team**

---- **4** 지문과 바로 대조할 핵심어를 찾아둔다.

Megatech International은 다음의 자격을 갖춘 기업 홍보 부장을 모집합니다.

- 기업 경영/관리 분야의 석사 학위 소지 필수
- 탁월한 서면, 구두 의사소통능력
- 최소 8년 이상의, 특히 다국적, 다문화 기구에서의 얻은 다양한 의사소통 관련 업무 경험
- 뛰어난 컴퓨터 사용능력
- 프로젝트와 행사 관리에 능숙함
- 좋은 성품과 세계, 지역 경제 정세에 대한 폭넓은 식견
- 경쟁심이 있는 동시에 팀 플레이어인 사람
- 예측 불허의 변화나 갈등에 대한 대처능력

당신의 지원서와 이력서를 hr@megatech.com로 메일을 보내주시기 바랍니다. 문의 사항은 899-4759로 전화 주시기 바랍니다.

Q1. 기업 홍보 부장이 되기 위한 자격 조건이 아닌 것은?
(A) 기업 경영 분야의 석사 학위
(B) 개인 문제에 대한 폭넓은 이해
(C) 서면, 구두 의사소통 능력
(D) 경쟁심과 팀으로 일할 수 있는 능력

패러프레이징 표현

1	make an appointment 약속하다	arrange an appointment 약속을 정하다
2	refer to a source 자료를 참고하다	consult materials 자료를 참고하다
3	dining area 식당	bistro 작은 식당
4	register for a course 수업에 등록하다	join a class 수업에 참여하다
5	refurbished property 재단장한 건물	renovated building 개조된 건물
6	send a form online 온라인으로 양식을 보내다	submit an application electronically 온라인으로 신청서를 제출하다
7	modified regulation 수정된 규정	revised provision 개정된 규정
8	damaged merchandise 손상된 제품	cracked product 금이 간 상품
9	visit an office directly 사무실로 직접 방문하다	in person here 여기로 직접
10	get together every Sunday 매주 일요일에 모이다	meet once a week 일주일에 한 번 만나다
11	affordable price 알맞은 가격	cost-competitive 가격 경쟁력 있는
12	allocated responsibilities 할당된 책임	assigned duties 배정된 임무
13	sold out 품절된	unavailable 구할 수 없는
14	It is essential to speak English. 영어 말하기는 필수적이다.	Fluency in English is a requisite. 영어의 유창성은 필수조건이다.
15	review about a performance 공연에 대한 평론	feedback on a play 연극에 대한 피드백

패러프레이징 연습

해설 p. 389

- 다음 문장 또는 지문과 의미상 일치하는 것을 고르세요.

1

> When completing this document, you had better consult some materials in Vancouver Public Library, which holds a plenty of historical materials.

(A) It is important to submit a report about a historical library.
(B) It is a good idea to refer to some historical books for an assignment.

2

> If you need to take this class, all you have to do is visit the receptionist directly and fill out a registration form. Due to the limited class size, we suggest that you do not hesitate.

(A) It is better to make a plan carefully in advance.
(B) You should register for a course at the front desk in person to secure a seat.

3

> According to the modified regulations, we are scheduled to change the design of the exterior of the premises.

(A) We are supposed to change some parts of this building design to comply with the revised building regulations.
(B) The exterior of this property is out of harmony with other places in the city.

4

> I would like to make an appointment to consult with Ms. Davis on purchasing raw materials in bulk. What should I do?

(A) I need to arrange an appointment to talk with Ms. Davis about some business matters.
(B) I want to ask a question about distributing merchandise internationally.

해설 p. 389

The winning name will be chosen by a panel of judges made up of a famous advertising agent, the president of Kramer Beverages, well-known sports figure John Hawkes, and Mike McGlone, the head of the Creative Department at Goldson and Harper. The contest will be canceled if no suitable name is found. The winner will receive $1,000 in cash.

Q1 How many judges will decide the winner?

(A) Two (B) Three (C) Four (D) Five

Apartment Management

A full-time manager is needed immediately.
600 unit complex in midtown Detroit. Desirable, safe neighborhood.

Duties: answer phone, show apartments to prospective tenants, schedule and manage maintenance staff, respond to on-line inquires, maintain newspaper ads, and hire and train administrative assistants.

Q2 What is NOT mentioned about the apartment complex?

(A) It has 600 units.
(B) It is in a secure neighborhood.
(C) The cost of rent is below average for the city.
(D) The complex is in a metropolis.

Because this is a very important discussion about how we will conduct meetings with other branches in the future, I want all of you who are attending the meeting to contact the employees at other branches and to discuss any special needs or ideas they may have prior to the meeting.

Q3 Who must attendees contact prior to the meeting?

(A) In-house employees
(B) Their fellow managers
(C) Staff members at other offices
(D) Clients they wish to have a conference with

해설 p. 390

Questions 1-3 refer to the following advertisement.

Do you spend too much of your day driving to work?
Are you tired of being held up in traffic every day?

Adventure Bicycle Shop has the perfect solution: a bicycle.

From now until July 15, all of our models are being offered for 20% off their regular prices. We are also offering bicycle equipment and tools at a discount of 40%. Finally, get the finest brand names in biking apparel for 50% off and purchase tires and bicycle seats for 60% off their sticker prices.

Adventure has been in the business of selling bicycles for over 30 years. It was our founder's belief that "There's no better way to get there than on a bicycle."

Adventure makes sure to hire only the most knowledgeable staff members. Our employees are here to serve your needs. Thanks to our loyal customers, we're the most popular bicycle shop in the state. Come down to 140 Bernard Street and check us out. We'll find the perfect bike for you in no time.

At Adventure, you're guaranteed a good set of wheels!

1 What advantage of cycling is mentioned in this advertisement?

(A) Having shorter commuting times
(B) Becoming healthier
(C) Being able to enjoy nature
(D) Saving money by not driving

2 How much of a discount is being offered on clothing?

(A) 20%
(B) 40%
(C) 50%
(D) 60%

3 What is mentioned about Adventure Bicycle Shop?

(A) It has a convenient location downtown.
(B) It has just opened a store in a new location.
(C) It always sells its products at discounted prices.
(D) Its employees know a lot about their products.

Questions 4-6 refer to the following e-mail.

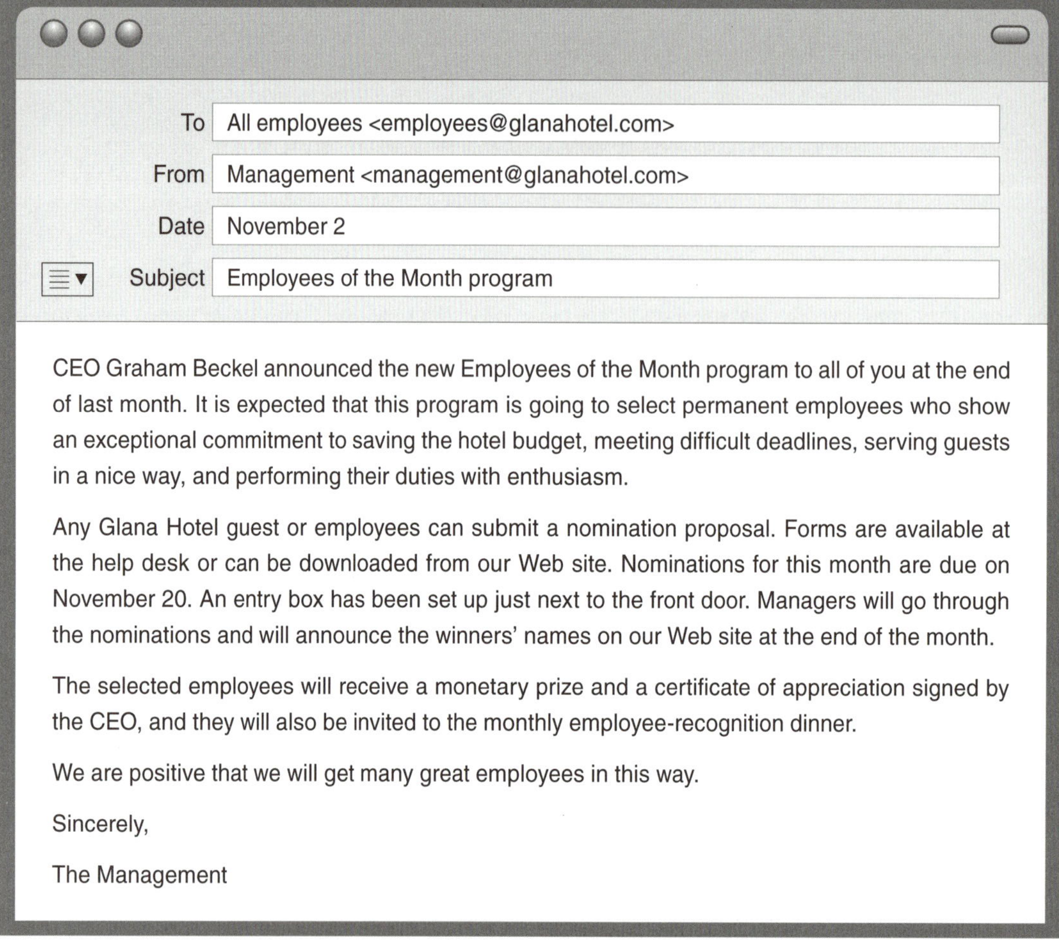

To: All employees <employees@glanahotel.com>

From: Management <management@glanahotel.com>

Date: November 2

Subject: Employees of the Month program

CEO Graham Beckel announced the new Employees of the Month program to all of you at the end of last month. It is expected that this program is going to select permanent employees who show an exceptional commitment to saving the hotel budget, meeting difficult deadlines, serving guests in a nice way, and performing their duties with enthusiasm.

Any Glana Hotel guest or employees can submit a nomination proposal. Forms are available at the help desk or can be downloaded from our Web site. Nominations for this month are due on November 20. An entry box has been set up just next to the front door. Managers will go through the nominations and will announce the winners' names on our Web site at the end of the month.

The selected employees will receive a monetary prize and a certificate of appreciation signed by the CEO, and they will also be invited to the monthly employee-recognition dinner.

We are positive that we will get many great employees in this way.

Sincerely,

The Management

4 Where can nomination forms be submitted?

(A) In the manager's office
(B) On the hotel Web site
(C) By the main entrance
(D) At the reception desk

5 What is indicated about the selected employees?

(A) They may bring their family members to the monthly dinner.
(B) They will be awarded with money.
(C) They have worked at the hotel for at least six months.
(D) They will be selected on November 20.

6 What is stated about Mr. Beckel?

(A) He will sign the certificates of appreciation.
(B) He knows all his employees' names.
(C) He sent the e-mail to management.
(D) He meets with his managers every month.

Questions 7-9 refer to the following notice.

Security Rules

All personnel are obliged to conform to some specific rules while in this workroom.

- Safety apparel, including body, hand, face, and eye wear, is required whenever in the workroom and should be disposed of in the antechamber near the doorway.
- Before exiting the workroom, remove safety attire in the antechamber and deposit it in the containers labeled "safety garments".
- Tag cylinders, dishes, and canisters appropriately prior to stowing them in cold storage and cupboards.
- To avert splatters, all receptacles must be moved on wagons with safety hampers. Ensure that covers have proper seals to avoid seepage.
- If a leak occurs, carry out the protocol for decontamination displayed in each work area. If you require help from service personnel, communicate with Mr. Allen at extension 320.

The foregoing rules are in place for your safety. Personnel who ignore the rules will receive a letter of caution from their manager.

7 What is the reason for the notice?

(A) To apprise personnel of safety rules
(B) To inform personnel of uniform changes
(C) To acknowledge a staff grievance
(D) To provide guidelines for using new gear

8 Where should personnel in the workroom deposit their safety apparel?

(A) On wagons
(B) In containers
(C) In cupboards
(D) In work areas

9 Why does the notice suggest that staff members should contact Mr. Allen?

(A) In case they require help cleaning up a spill
(B) In case they need to buy extra cylinders and dishes
(C) In case they need to advise management of missing instrument
(D) In case they need to get authorization for lab tests

PART 7

UNIT 21 동의어 / 추론

동의어와 추론 문제는 전체적인 맥락을 정확히 인지하는 종합적 사고능력을 필요로 하는 고득점 유형이다. 그러므로 이 유형의 문제는 반드시 주제문을 중심으로 전반적인 흐름에 집중하여 해결해야 한다.

■ 빈출 문제 유형

① 동의어 찾는 문제

The word "concern" in paragraph 1, line 5, is closest in meaning to
첫 단락, 다섯 번째 줄의 단어 "concern"과 의미상 가장 가까운 것은

② 추론 문제

What can be inferred from this text-message chain?
이 문자 메시지에서 무엇을 추론할 수 있는가?

What does the announcement imply about the community?
안내문은 그 단체에 대해 무엇을 암시하는가?

What is suggested about the schedule?
일정표에 대해 무엇이 암시되는가?

For whom is this advertisement intended?
이 광고는 누구를 대상으로 한 것인가?

Where would this notice most likely appear?
이 공지는 어디에 게시될 것 같은가?

When would the workshop probably be canceled?
워크숍은 아마도 언제 취소될 것 같은가?

고득점 SOLUTION

① 맥락에 알맞은 동의어를 찾기 힘들다면
사전적 의미에 의존하지 말아야 하며, 일단 문제의 어휘를 찾아 지문에 표시해 두고 그것이 비어 있다고 생각하자. 그리고 독해를 하다가 보기 중에서 가장 맥락을 자연스럽게 이어 주는 어휘를 선택하면 된다.

② 추론 문제에서 정답에 관한 정확한 근거를 찾기 힘들다면
추론 문제는 지문 속의 특정 근거를 가지고 답을 바로 찾을 수 있는 문제로는 거의 출제되지 않는다. 지문 전반에 흩어져 있거나 암시된 근거를 종합해서 풀어야 하는 유형이 대부분이다. 이 문제에 효과적으로 접근하려면, 글의 전반 내용을 포괄하는 주제문에서 일단 잠정적인 답변을 고르고, 지문 전체를 다 읽은 후 다시 한번 문제의 답을 확정하는 이중의 풀이 과정이 필요하다. 또한 지문 전체를 읽어도 문제의 단서가 충분치 않은 경우에는 보기 중 가장 합당한 답(the best answer)을 찾기 위해 소거의 전략도 적절히 활용하여야 한다.

✎ POINT ❶ 동의어 찾는 문제

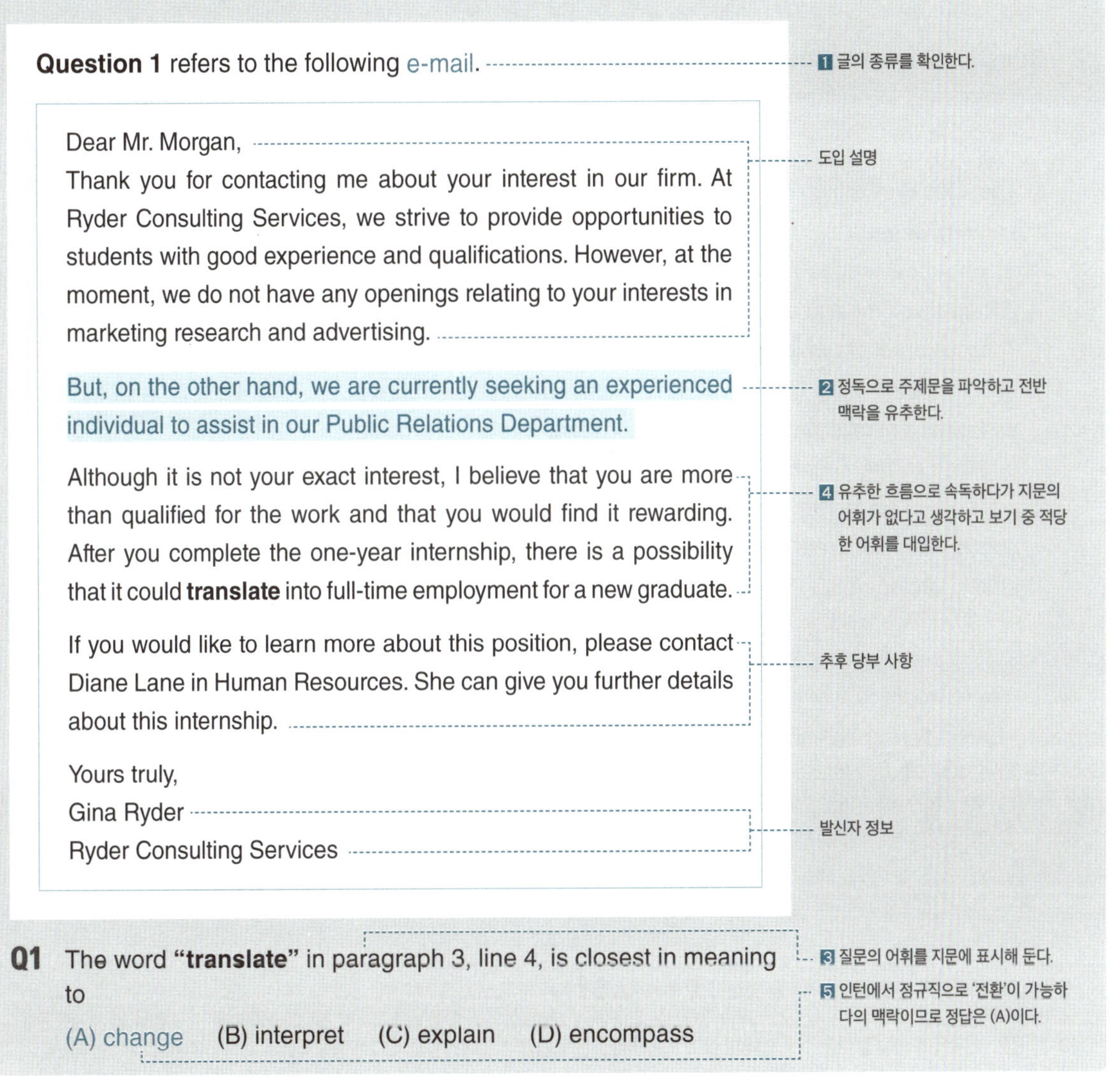

Question 1 refers to the following e-mail. ― ❶ 글의 종류를 확인한다.

Dear Mr. Morgan,
Thank you for contacting me about your interest in our firm. At Ryder Consulting Services, we strive to provide opportunities to students with good experience and qualifications. However, at the moment, we do not have any openings relating to your interests in marketing research and advertising. ― 도입 설명

But, on the other hand, we are currently seeking an experienced individual to assist in our Public Relations Department. ― ❷ 정독으로 주제문을 파악하고 전반 맥락을 유추한다.

Although it is not your exact interest, I believe that you are more than qualified for the work and that you would find it rewarding. After you complete the one-year internship, there is a possibility that it could **translate** into full-time employment for a new graduate. ― ❹ 유추한 흐름으로 속독하다가 지문의 어휘가 없다고 생각하고 보기 중 적당한 어휘를 대입한다.

If you would like to learn more about this position, please contact Diane Lane in Human Resources. She can give you further details about this internship. ― 추후 당부 사항

Yours truly,
Gina Ryder
Ryder Consulting Services ― 발신자 정보

Q1 The word **"translate"** in paragraph 3, line 4, is closest in meaning to ― ❸ 질문의 어휘를 지문에 표시해 둔다.

(A) change (B) interpret (C) explain (D) encompass ― ❺ 인턴에서 정규직으로 '전환'이 가능하다의 맥락이므로 정답은 (A)이다.

Morgan 씨께,
우리 회사에 대한 귀하의 관심에 대해 문의해 주셔서 감사합니다. Ryder Consulting Services는 좋은 경력과 요건을 갖춘 학생들에게 기회를 주고자 힘쓰고 있습니다. 그러나 현시점에서 마케팅 조사와 광고에 대한 귀하의 관심과 관련된 일자리가 없는 상황입니다.
그러나 한편으로 저희는 현재 홍보부서에서 일할 경험 있는 인물을 모집하고 있습니다.
비록 귀하의 정확한 관심 분야는 아니지만, 귀하께서 그 업무에 대한 자격을 충분히 갖추고 있으며 그 일이 보람된 일임을 알게 되실 거라 믿습니다. 1년간의 인턴 과정을 마치면, 새로운 졸업생들에 대한 정규직 전환이 가능할 수도 있습니다.
이 직책에 대해 좀 더 알고 싶으시면, 인사부의 Diane Lane에게 문의하시기 바랍니다. 이 인턴 과정에 대한 보다 상세한 정보를 알려 줄 수 있을 것입니다.
진심으로,
Gina Ryder / Ryder Consulting Services

Q1. 세 번째 단락, 네 번째 줄의 "translate"와 의미상 가장 가까운 것은
(A) 바꾸다 (B) 해석하다 (C) 설명하다 (D) 포함하다

POINT 2 추론 문제

Question 2 refers to the following notice. ❶ 글의 종류를 확인한다.

CUSTOMS ❷ 제목을 확인한다.

The following limits on personal effects apply to all visitors entering Canada. ❸ 정독으로 주제문을 파악하고 전반 맥락을 유추한다.

Alcoholic beverages **brought into** the country may not exceed 2 liters in volume and must be carried by persons aged 21 or over. Tobacco products weighing not over 300 grams **may be brought in** by persons aged 18 or over. Live plants are prohibited. Pets and other animals **must pass** through quarantine before being admitted to the country. Those found transporting illegal drugs will be prosecuted to the full extent of the law. Ivory and other goods manufactured from rare and endangered species are strictly forbidden. ❺ 세부 사항을 속독하며 흐름을 파악한다. 이때 추론 문제의 근거가 있으면 표시해 둔다.

Q2 Where would this notice **most likely** be found? ❹ 추론 문제임을 확인하고 주제문을 통해 잠정적으로 정답을 찾는다.

(A) On a form given to airline passengers ❻ 지문 독해가 끝난 후 근거를 통합하여 정답을 찾는다. (캐나다로 들어오는 모든 관광객들에게 적용되는 사유물의 규제사항을 얘기하는 공고임을 알 수 있으므로 (A)가 답으로 적절)
(B) On a United States tax form
(C) At an overseas duty-free shop
(D) In a Canadian embassy

세관

소지품에 대한 아래의 규제가 캐나다에 들어오는 모든 관광객들에게 적용됩니다.
국가로 들여온 알코올 음료는 양으로 2리터를 초과해서는 안 되며, 21세 이상의 사람들이 소지해야 합니다. 300g을 넘지 않는 담배 제품들은 18세 이상의 사람들에 의해 들여올 수 있습니다. 살아 있는 식물들은 금지됩니다. 애완동물과 다른 동물들은 국가에서 수용되기 전 검역소를 거쳐야 합니다. 불법 약물을 운반하다가 적발된 사람들은 법에 의해 기소될 것입니다. 상아와 다른 희귀하고 멸종 위기에 처한 종들로부터 만들어진 제품들은 엄격히 금지됩니다.

Q2. 이 공고는 어디서 발견될 것인가?
(A) 항공기 승객들에게 주어진 양식에서
(B) 미국 납세 신고서에서
(C) 해외 면세점에서
(D) 캐나다 대사관에서

패러프레이징 표현

1	**comply with / observe** (법규나 명령 따위)를 따르다, 준수하다 Construction companies in this region should **[comply with / observe]** safety standards. 이 지역의 건축회사들은 안전규정을 준수해야 한다.
2	**continually / constantly** 계속, 끊임없이 We plan to update our Web site **[continually / constantly]**. 우리는 웹 사이트를 지속해서 갱신할 계획이다.
3	**conditions / terms** 계약 조건 We need you to look over the **[conditions / terms]** carefully. 우리는 당신이 계약 조건을 꼼꼼히 살펴보길 바랍니다.
4	**complement / enhance** ~을 보완하다, 향상시키다 We are going to have the efficiency of the machine **[complemented / enhanced]** by the end of this year. 우리는 올해 말까지 이 기계의 성능을 보완(향상)시킬 예정이다.
5	**exclusively / only / solely** 독점적으로, 유일하게 This vehicle is designed **[exclusively / only / solely]** for disabled drivers. 이 차량은 장애인 운전자들만을 위해 디자인되었다.
6	**verify / confirm** 입증하다, 확인하다 These figures **[verify / confirm]** that our sales goal this quarter was achieved. 이 수치는 이번 분기의 우리 판매 목표가 달성되었음을 입증합니다.
7	**maintain / keep up** 유지하다 You should **[maintain / keep up]** a balanced diet for overall health. 당신은 전반적인 건강을 위한 균형 잡힌 식단을 유지해야 합니다.
8	**rectify / remedy** 고치다, 시정하다 Mr. Declan tried to **[rectify / remedy]** the shortcomings of his communication skills. 디클랜 씨는 그의 소통기술의 약점을 고치기 위해 노력했다.
9	**assume / take on** 떠맡다 The team **[assumed / took on]** a large number of responsibilities for this project. 팀은 이 프로젝트를 위한 많은 업무를 떠맡았다.
10	**oversee / supervise / lead** 감독하다, 총괄하다 The committee is scheduled to **[oversee / supervise / lead]** a fundraising campaign. 위원회가 모금 운동을 총괄하기로 예정되어 있다.

The exhibition, which will run from December 1st to January 30th, features some of the most fascinating architectural pieces from the Classical Period of the 5th century B.C. to the end of the 2nd century B.C. There will be a number of special events to complement the exhibit, including lectures by scholarly experts.

Q1 The word "complement" in line 3 is closest in meaning to

(A) enhance (B) obtain (C) select (D) describe

Information to subscribers

Requests for subscription renewals are sent automatically one week prior to your current subscription's expiration date, subject to the conditions below.

Q2 The word "conditions" in line 3 is closest in meaning to

(A) ends (B) proposals (C) terms (D) names

Joe Reed, the director of the Leisure Department, stated that the money received from a variety of events held this time of the year plays an important role in maintaining amenities and leisure facilities throughout the year.

Q3 The word "maintaining" in line 2 is closest in meaning to

(A) keeping up (B) defending (C) declaring (D) looking out

When I was organizing my company's holiday party last year, the service and quality you provided were excellent. I trust that you will rectify this situation and offer me a refund for the flowers that I didn't receive and for those that came in wrong color. If not, I may take my business elsewhere when it comes time for my company's holiday party this December 5th.

Q4 The word "rectify" in line 2 is closest in meaning to

(A) remedy (B) eliminate (C) simplify (D) consolidate

Finally, I want to let you know that while I was at work today, I overheard some people talking about the flyer you posted here at the gym. They were talking about how much they love your restaurant and how they wouldn't miss the anniversary party. I think you will have a great turnout!

Q5 What is suggested about the writer?

(A) He works at a restaurant.
(B) He works at a gym.
(C) He is the organizer of a party.
(D) He will bartend at a party.

The renovated Auckland Art House will debut with a gala dinner this Thursday. Invited guests will attend the exhibition, which will feature approximately thirty new works by acclaimed painter Stephen Schwartz. This event will then be open to the public on March 2 for about 3 weeks from Tuesday through Sunday from 10:00 A.M. to 7:00 P.M.

Q6 On what day of the week is the Auckland Art House probably closed?

(A) Monday
(B) Thursday
(C) Saturday
(D) Sunday

John Constable, the owner and head chef of Constable Bistro, spent a year restoring this historic building. The location boasts lovely surroundings at the intersection of King Street and 2nd Street across from Oracle Park. "It's such a fabulous space, with arched doors and big classical murals", Mr. Constable said.

Q7 What is implied about the location of Constable Bistro?

(A) It is next to ancient ruins.
(B) It is located on a corner.
(C) It is surrounded by several parks.
(D) It is within a block of other restaurants

Questions 1-2 refer to the following e-mail.

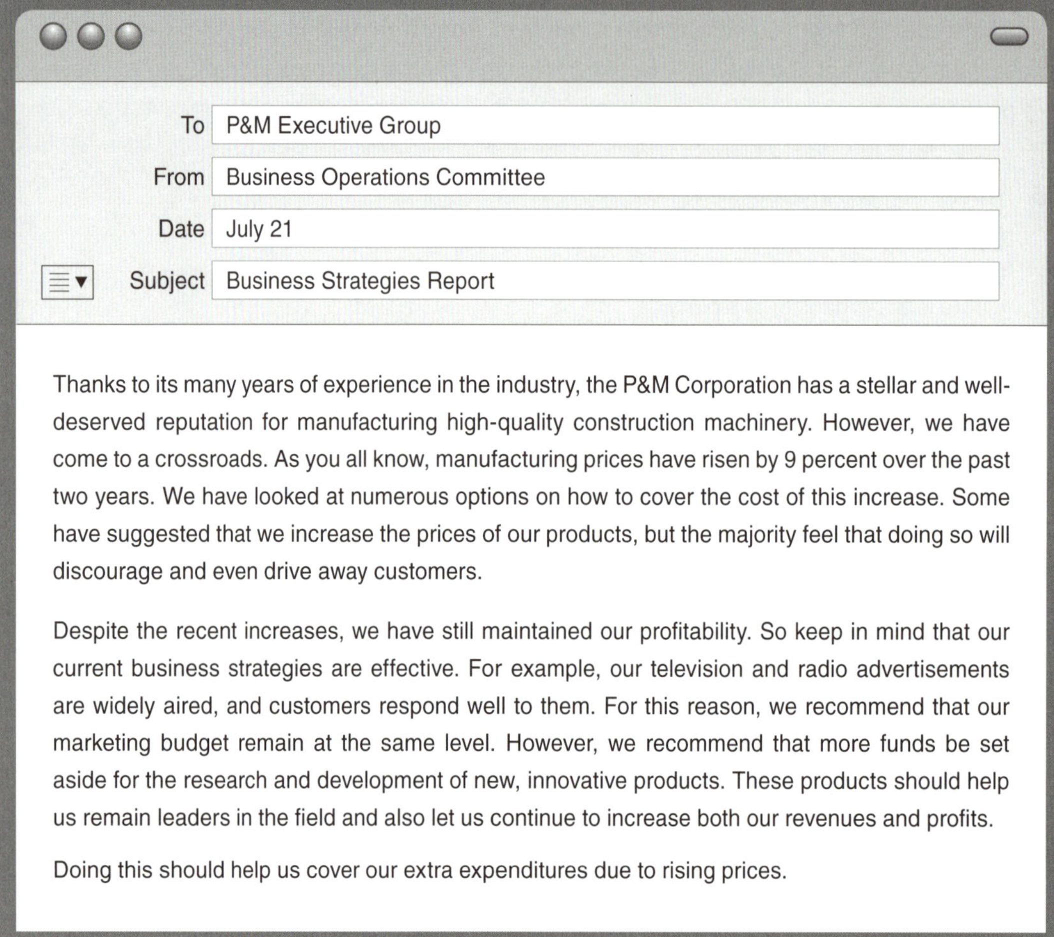

To: P&M Executive Group
From: Business Operations Committee
Date: July 21
Subject: Business Strategies Report

Thanks to its many years of experience in the industry, the P&M Corporation has a stellar and well-deserved reputation for manufacturing high-quality construction machinery. However, we have come to a crossroads. As you all know, manufacturing prices have risen by 9 percent over the past two years. We have looked at numerous options on how to cover the cost of this increase. Some have suggested that we increase the prices of our products, but the majority feel that doing so will discourage and even drive away customers.

Despite the recent increases, we have still maintained our profitability. So keep in mind that our current business strategies are effective. For example, our television and radio advertisements are widely aired, and customers respond well to them. For this reason, we recommend that our marketing budget remain at the same level. However, we recommend that more funds be set aside for the research and development of new, innovative products. These products should help us remain leaders in the field and also let us continue to increase both our revenues and profits.

Doing this should help us cover our extra expenditures due to rising prices.

1 What is implied about the P&M Corporation?

(A) Its advertisements are not popular.
(B) Few of its business strategies have been effective.
(C) The quality of its products has decreased.
(D) It effectively covered extra expenses in the first half of the year.

2 The word "cover" in paragraph 1, line 4, is closest in meaning to

(A) decrease
(B) pay for
(C) conceal
(D) reach for

Questions 3-5 refer to the following review.

June 5th

A Taste of India

On Saturday evening, I dined at Kashmir's, Brightwell's new Indian restaurant. I have reviewed almost every restaurant in Brightwell, and I can honestly say that dining at Kashmir's was one of the best dining experiences I've ever had. The food was fantastic, the ambience was cultural and decorative, and the service was impressive and efficient. To celebrate the restaurant's grand opening this past Saturday, Mr. Sidiqui offered all guests a complimentary drink with the purchase of a main course.

As you would expect at an Indian restaurant, the menu includes items intended to appeal to a wide variety of tastes.

Main courses include delicious biryani, tandoori, and tikka dishes. All menu items are freshly prepared daily and reasonably priced.

Kashmir's is offering various menu items at reduced prices from June 6th through June 10th. All main courses are served with rice, sweet and spicy sauces, and naan bread. Kashmir's is located on Brightwell's High Street. It is open 7 days a week from 11 A.M to 10 P.M. The restaurant can also cater for events of all sizes.

Raza Suleman
Brightwell Daily Report

3 Who most likely is Raza Suleman?
(A) A food critic
(B) A journalist
(C) A chef
(D) A restaurant owner

4 What is indicated about Kashmir's?
(A) It is located on Kashmir Avenue.
(B) It is open for breakfast.
(C) It is moderately priced.
(D) It is closed on Mondays.

5 The word "ambience" in paragraph 1, line 3, is closest in meaning to
(A) arrangement
(B) atmosphere
(C) lighting
(D) selection

Questions 6-9 refer to the following letter.

Dear Ms. Fogel,

We've been pleased to work with Ms. Kate McKinnon here at Geneva Electronics for the past five years. She began as a junior sales representative, and after only two years of outstanding work, Ms. McKinnon was promoted to a senior sales associate. In both positions, she consistently exceeded her yearly sales targets.

I joined Geneva Electronics as a sales manager in the second half of last year and was fortunate to have her on my team from that very moment. Her ability to understand her customers is distinguished, and she always has a positive attitude. She works well on a team in a very busy environment, which reflects her natural leadership skills.

Having held a position as a customer service representative before joining Geneva Electronics, Ms. McKinnon also has a superior ability to handle customer complaints. Her exceptional performance on the team let me offer her more responsibilities.

Accordingly, I heartily recommend Ms. McKinnon for the position she is applying for, and I have no doubt that she will be a tremendous asset to your company.

Sincerely,

Justin Theroux
Sales Manager
Geneva Electronics

6 Why did Mr. Theroux write the letter?

(A) To offer Ms. McKinnon a promotion
(B) To request information about Ms. McKinnon
(C) To nominate Ms. McKinnon for an award
(D) To help Ms. McKinnon to get a new job

7 What is suggested about Ms. McKinnon?

(A) She has not always worked in sales.
(B) She has never been a supervisor.
(C) She learned about Geneva Electronics from Mr. Theroux.
(D) She held three different positions while at Geneva Electronics.

8 What is NOT stated as one of Ms. McKinnon's qualifications?

(A) Leadership skills
(B) A positive attitude
(C) The ability to solve problems
(D) A willingness to go on business trips

9 The word "reflects" in paragraph 2, line 4, is closest in meaning to

(A) influences
(B) considers
(C) realizes
(D) shows

UNIT 22

맥락 완성

전반적인 맥락을 논리적으로 이해하는 능력이 필요하다. 특히 맥락을 따라가다가 흐름이 이상하거나 비약이 있는 부분, 혹은 논리적으로 공백이 있는 부분에 집중하면 정답을 쉽게 찾을 수 있다.

■ 빈출 문제 유형

In which of the positions marked [1], [2], [3], and [4] does the following sentence best belong?

"Still, some transportation workers are skeptical."

(A) [1]
(B) [2]
(C) [3]
(D) [4]

지문에 표시된 [1], [2], [3], 그리고 [4] 중에서 다음의 문장이 들어가기에 가장 좋은 위치가 어디인가?
"여전히, 일부 대중교통 종사자들은 회의적이다."
(A) [1]
(B) [2]
(C) [3]
(D) [4]

고득점 SOLUTION

① 정답이 되는 자리를 찾을 수 없어 여러 번 다시 읽게 된다면

지문 속에서 주어진 문장의 적절한 자리를 효과적으로 찾으려면, 반드시 글의 전반적인 흐름에 집중하여야 한다. 그러므로 주제문을 찾은 후, 그 내용이 지문에 드러나 있는지 확인하는 방식으로 속독하는 기법이 필요하다. 이렇게 확인하다가 논리적 흐름에 비약이나 공백이 있다면, 그 자리에 주어진 문장을 삽입하면 된다. 주제문과 비롯된 글 전반의 논리적인 흐름에 집중해야 해결할 수 있는 유형이다.

② 계속 오답을 찾게 된다면

맥락의 흐름을 나타내는 표시어에 유의해 보도록 한다. 맥락의 흐름 표시어는 접속사, 접속부사, 대명사, 지시어 등을 말한다. 이 품사들은 주제문을 중심으로 글을 논리적으로 전개하기 위해 문장과 문장을 하나의 유기적인 맥락으로 연결하는 역할을 한다. 그러므로 표시어를 잘 활용하면 맥락의 논리적 흐름에 집중할 수 있어서 맥락의 논리적 공백이나 비약을 효과적으로 파악할 수 있다. 표시어를 학습할 때에는 단순히 사전적인 의미에 집중하기보다는 실제 예문이나 맥락을 활용하도록 한다.

Question 1 refers to the following announcement.

1 글의 종류를 확인한다.

We are currently looking for an experienced, creative, and dedicated environmental expert to work in our office in Vienna, Austria. —[1]—.
With employees from all **over the world**, the FOE is a **linguistically diverse community**. —[2]—. Applicants **must also possess** a degree in environmental science, hydrology, or biology and have at least three years of international work experience. —[3]—.
Please e-mail your application with a current résumé, a letter of recommendation, and a writing sample to Clifford Samuelson by September 30. —[4]—.

2 정독으로 주제문을 파악하고 전체 맥락을 유추한다.

4 유추한 전체 맥락을 따라 속독하다가 접속부사에 유의하며 문장이 들어갈 만한 적절한 자리를 찾는다.

추후 당부 사항

Q1 In which of the positions marked [1], [2], [3], and [4] does the following sentence best belong?
"**However**, **English** is the working **language of the organization,** and fluency in written and spoken English **is a must**."
(A) [1] (B) [2] (C) [3] (D) [4]

3 문제를 읽고 전반적인 맥락 속에 어디에 위치하는 게 좋은지 유추한다. (이때, 접속부사 같은 흐름 표시어를 잘 활용한다.)

5 적절한 자리의 번호를 정답으로 선택한다.

현재 오스트리아 빈에 위치한 우리 사무실에서 근무할 경험 있고, 창조적이며, 헌신적인 환경 전문가를 찾고 있습니다.
전 세계 출신 직원들과 함께 FOE는 다양한 언어가 사용되는 단체입니다. 하지만 영어가 조직에서 통용되는 언어이므로 반드시 문어와 구어로 영어를 유창하게 구사할 수 있어야 합니다. 지원자들은 또한 환경 과학, 수질학, 또는 생물학에 학위를 소지하고 있어야 하고, 최소 3년 이상의 국제 업무 경험도 가지고 있어야 합니다.
최근에 작성된 이력서와 추천서 한 부, 그리고 작문 샘플 한 부를 9월 30일까지 신청서와 함께 Clifford Samuelson에게 이메일로 보내 주십시오.

Q1. 지문에 표시된 [1], [2], [3], 그리고 [4] 중에서 다음의 문장이 들어가기에 가장 좋은 위치가 어디인가?
"하지만 영어가 조직에서 통용되는 언어이므로 반드시 문어와 구어로 영어를 유창하게 구사할 수 있어야 합니다."
(A) [1] (B) [2] (C) [3] (D) [4]

해설

삽입할 문장을 보면 However를 중심으로 앞에 반대되는 내용이 언급됨을 알 수 있다. [2] 앞에 '이 단체는 언어적으로 다양한 집단이다'라고 했고, 삽입할 문장 '하지만 영어를 반드시 구사해야 한다'는 내용이 뒤를 잇는 것이 적합하다. 또한 [2] 뒤의 also로 내용을 덧붙여 주고 있는 것도 확인할 수 있다.

맥락 완성 관련 표현

① 접속부사란?

접속부사는 접속의 의미가 있는 부사를 의미하며, 수식어로서 맥락을 연결하고 의미를 매끄럽게 하는 기능이 있다. 접속부사를 충분히 활용하여 글의 흐름이 논리적으로 전개되고 있는지 그리고 문장들이 서로 유기적으로 연결되어 있는지 확인하도록 한다.

양보	nevertheless=nonetheless 그럼에도 불구하고 however 그러나
대조	on the other hand 반면에 in contrast=on the contrary 그와 반대로
결과	therefore 그러므로 consequently 결과적으로 hence 그러므로 thus 그러므로 as a result 결과적으로
가정	otherwise 그렇지 않으면 then 그렇다면, 그때, 그 다음에
부연 설명	in addition=additionally 게다가 also 또한 furthermore 더욱이 besides 게다가 moreover 더욱이
예시	for example=for instance 예를 들면
요약	in conclusion 마지막으로 finally 끝으로 in short 요컨대
일반화	in general=generally 일반적으로 on the whole 대체로

② 지시어란?

지시어는 이미 언급된 내용을 다시 언급할 때 본문의 맥락이 매끄럽게 이어지도록 하는 역할을 한다. 지시어를 해석하기에 앞서 글의 주제문에 대한 이해가 없으면 지시어가 맥락 내에서 무엇을 의미하는지 알 수 없으므로 글 전체의 윤곽을 잡기가 매우 어려워진다. 그러므로 문장 삽입 문제를 성공적으로 풀려면 항상 주어진 지문 내에서 주제문을 바탕으로 지시어를 해석해야 하고, 그 활용을 철저히 연습해야 한다.

인칭대명사	1인칭	I we	my our	me us	mine ours	myself ourselves
	2인칭	you	your	you	your	yourselves
	3인칭	he she it they	his her its their	him her it them	his hers - theirs	himself herself itself themselves
지시대명사	this these that those					
부정대명사	one another some any most all none (a) few (a) little					

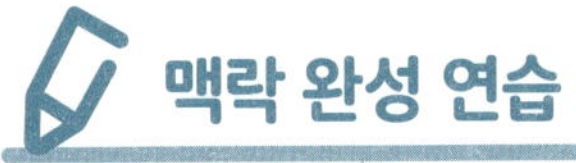

맥락 완성 연습

해설 p. 395

▪ 다음 문장 또는 지문과 의미상 일치하는 것을 고르세요.

1

We are now working under the new name of Bansum-Holden Insurance. Your claims account will not be altered. -------, you can expect the variety of services that we can provide you to improve.

(A) For instance (B) However (C) In short (D) Therefore

2

The exhibition will be open to anyone interested from March 1 to August 31 this year. -------, on the night of Wednesday February 20, there will be a rehearsal which will include the staff members of the art center.

(A) In addition (B) Instead (C) Specifically (D) As a result

3

I work for a company called Heughan Studios, and we are currently seeking locations for interviews with new movie stars. We thought your place would be perfect for shooting a broadcast. One of our cinematographers will be in ------- establishment today. Please let me know your availability.

(A) my (B) your (C) its (D) his

4

Thanks for your suggestion regarding the implementation of an employee wellness program. The goals and objectives you laid out seem exceptionally reasonable both financially and logistically. The research you provided on why the program would be good for us was also persuasive. I've decided to go ahead with -------.

(A) I (B) you (C) it (D) them

해설 p. 395

—[1]—. We apologize for the missing enclosure in your coffee table order. —[2]—. The assembly toolkit is being mailed to you today by overnight express mail for arrival by tomorrow. —[3]—. I apologize for the inconvenience of not having the assembly toolkit required for your coffee table. Krog looks forward to your continued patronage. —[4]—.

Q1 In which of the positions marked [1], [2], [3], and [4] does the following sentence best belong?
"We have also included, along with the kit, a 20% discount card for your next Krog Furniture purchase."

(A) [1]
(B) [2]
(C) [3]
(D) [4]

To: Tech Support Staff
From: Willem Dafoe
Date: September 7
Subject: New Telephone Extensions

To make internal communications easier, a new telephone extension numbering system has been devised. —[1]—. The number "1" identifies you as being on the Tech Support Team. The "0" is used because an extension must have at least 3 numbers. —[2]—. The last digit is the number of your cubicle. —[3]—. Cubicles are numbered consecutively in the room. —[4]—. As long as you know where a staff member sits, you should be able to determine his or her telephone extension even when you don't have the extension key with you.

Q2 In which of the positions marked [1], [2], [3], and [4] does the following sentence best belong?
"Attached, you will find your new extensions."

(A) [1]
(B) [2]
(C) [3]
(D) [4]

Questions 1-3 refer to the following letter.

February 17

Dear Mr. Reddick,

Thank you for your interest in FC Bank. We received your online application and résumé for the branch manager position in Heidelburg. —[1]—. Unfortunately, we require 2 years of previous managerial experience for that position. —[2]—. We currently have a need for one at our Deer Park branch. —[3]—. I forwarded your résumé to the district manager of that branch, but you also need to submit a new application online. —[4]—. You should expect to hear from that manager within a week. Thank you again for your application. I hope this opportunity is of interest to you.

Sincerely,

Bridget Regan

FC Bank
Human Resources Representative

1 What is the main purpose of the letter?

(A) To inform an applicant that he failed to meet the qualifications for a position
(B) To let an applicant know that the job he applied for is no longer vacant
(C) To arrange an interview with an applicant
(D) To ask an applicant to provide additional information

2 What does Ms. Regan suggest that Mr. Reddick do?

(A) Apply in person at the Deer Park branch
(B) Fill out a new application
(C) Send an e-mail to the hiring manager at the Deer Park branch
(D) Enroll in FC Bank's management training program

3 In which of the positions marked [1], [2], [3], and [4] does the following sentence best belong?

"However, I was impressed with your résumé and think that you would be a good candidate for an assistant branch manager position."

(A) [1]
(B) [2]
(C) [3]
(D) [4]

Questions 4-7 refer to the following article.

Oklahoma (29 October) — Business has been booming at Joe's Addiction, a local café serving snacks and a variety of beverages. —[1]—. While the establishment has mainly served local residents, owner Joe Mendes said that she has seen more businesspeople from other cities coming through the doors. She believes the main reason is that some new office complexes were recently built nearby.

"All the changes in the area have certainly led to our surge in business," Ms. Mendes said. "We have always offered services at reasonable prices, and we're now seeing a lot of businesspeople who visit us during busy lunchtime.—[2]—."

Starting next month, the restaurant is adding a special salad bar to provide healthy food. —[3]—. "We strive to provide various menu options based on locally grown fruits and vegetables, and seasonal ingredients," Ms. Mendes said, "I sincerely appreciate that some regular customers have been coming to us for ten years." Ms. Mendes is also considering opening the café for lunch on weekends and holidays. —[4]—. If you are interested, check out Joe's Addiction, located on Southeastern Avenue.

4 According to the article, why has Joe's Addiction seen an increase in business?

(A) It renovated its dining area.
(B) It reduced its service prices.
(C) It has developed a good reputation.
(D) It is close to many additional offices.

5 What does Ms. Mendes plan to do shortly?

(A) Open a new location
(B) Obtain additional financing
(C) Hire more chefs
(D) Expand the menu offerings

6 What is NOT mentioned about Joe's Addiction?

(A) It offers lunch on Saturdays.
(B) It has been in business for over a decade.
(C) It is owned by an individual.
(D) It provides inexpensive meal.

7 In which of the positions marked [1], [2], [3], and [4] does the following sentence best belong?

"Some of them even stop by several times a week."

(A) [1]
(B) [2]
(C) [3]
(D) [4]

Questions 8-10 refer to the following recommendation.

To Whom It May Concern:

We benefited immensely from the employment of Youjeong Kang as a marketing advisor. —[1]—. Most of our clients are satisfied with our innovative and informative training systems for local small businesses. However, due to the online training services of several competitors that can be offered with more affordable options, our sales dropped dramatically. —[2]—. Because I was seriously worried about lowering our service prices to compete with other businesses, Ms. Kang strived to solve the problem by suggesting strategies for retaining existing clients and for attracting new ones.

First of all, I implemented one of her suggestions to create promotional materials to focus on the unique aspects of our own. In addition, we emphasized our professional consulting service and our in-depth financial analysis of each business. —[3]—. We are now steadily improving, and I know that this is possible due to Ms. Kang's efforts. —[4]—. I highly recommend her!

Sincerely,

Jordan Peele
Jordan Peele Owner
Peele Center

8 What did Mr. Peele hire Ms. Kang to do?

(A) Provide business advice
(B) Analyze financial strategies
(C) Gather customer feedback
(D) Create marketing materials

9 What is suggested about the Peele Center?

(A) It doesn't offer online services.
(B) It has multiple branches.
(C) It provides consulting for the lowest prices in the area.
(D) It changes the titles of its classes regularly.

10 In which of the positions marked [1], [2], [3], and [4] does the following sentence best belong?

"Making differences became an important part of our marketing, and it actually paid off."

(A) [1]
(B) [2]
(C) [3]
(D) [4]

UNIT 23 편지 / 이메일

편지(letter)와 이메일(e-mail)은 가장 많이 출제되는 지문 유형이다. 내용은 주로 공적으로 글을 쓴 용건이 뚜렷하게 드러나 있기 때문에 비교적 쉽게 정답을 찾을 수 있다.

■ 빈출 문제 유형

[전반적인 내용] Why was this letter written? 이 편지는 왜 쓰였나?
What is the topic of this e-mail? 이메일의 주제는 무엇인가?
To whom is this letter addressed? 이 편지는 누구에게 보내는 것인가?
Where does Mr. Peterson most likely work? Peterson 씨는 어디에서 일할 것 같은가?

[동봉 사항] What is enclosed[included/attached] with this letter? 편지에 무엇이 동봉되어 있는가?

[추후 당부 내용] What is Ms. Wright being asked to do? Wright 씨는 무엇을 하라고 요청 받는가?

■ 빈출 지문 내용

- 고객과 고객관리부서 직원 간의 서비스 관련 문의 내용 편지
- 회사 간의 비즈니스 업무 처리 관련 이메일
- 회사 동료들 간의 업무 관련 이메일
- 회사나 단체의 공지가 목적인 이메일
- 특정 상품이나 서비스를 광고하는 이메일

■ 편지 / 이메일 빈출 표현

① 주제문

I'm writing to inform you that~ ~을 알리기 위해 편지(이메일)를 씁니다.
We are very happy to offer~ ~을 제공하게 되어 기쁩니다.
We are very sorry to say that~ ~을 알리게 되어 유감입니다.
This e-mail is to notify you of~ ~을 통보하기 위한 이메일입니다.

② 동봉 사항

Enclosed[Attached/Included] is~ ~이 첨부되어 있습니다.
We are forwarding this letter with~ 우리는 ~과 함께 편지를 발송합니다.

고득점 SOLUTION

① 편지/이메일의 주소가 없어 회사나 직책을 파악할 수 없을 경우에는
지문 속에 발신자와 수신자를 나타내는 I, we 그리고 you와 같은 표현 부분에서 그들의 업무가 무엇인지 파악하면 편지를 쓴 목적을 쉽게 파악할 수 있다.

② 이메일에서 상단에 주제(subject)가 누락되어 확인하기 어려운 경우에는
이메일 주소에 드러난 회사의 이름을 통해 이들의 용건을 파악하여 주제를 유추하도록 한다.

POINT 1 편지

Question 1 refers to the following letter. ---- 글의 종류

101 Main Street
Nashville, Tennessee
November 19th ---- 발신자 정보

Jin Ho Seo
Department of Languages
GNFS Mang Gok, Hong Kong
101616 Hong Kong ---- 수신자 정보

Dear Mr. Seo,

I am writing to you to find out more information about the Morgan Conference that will be held in Hong Kong this winter. ---- 주제문

Please send me more information regarding the attendees, times, and costs. I saw an ad for the conference in a magazine, and I am very interested in attending it. ---- 세부 내용 (추후 당부 내용)

I am enclosing along with this letter my business card that has my name, home phone number, cell phone number, e-mail address, and home address. ---- 동봉 사항

Thank you for your time. I will look forward to hearing from you.

Sincerely,
Dr. Paleja ---- 발신자 이름

Q1 What did Dr. Paleja send with the letter?

(A) A business card
(B) A paycheck
(C) A brochure
(D) Documents and applications

101 메인 거리 / 테네시주, 네쉬빌 / 11월 19일

서진호 / Department of Languages
홍콩, 망 곡, GNFS / 101616 홍콩

친애하는 서 씨에게,

이번 겨울에 홍콩에서 열리는 모르간 컨퍼런스에 관한 정보를 조금 더 알고 싶어서 당신에게 편지를 씁니다.

참석자, 주제 그리고 비용에 대해 추가 정보를 보내주세요. 잡지에서 회의 광고를 봤고, 저는 정말 참석하고 싶습니다.

제 이름, 집 전화, 휴대폰 번호 그리고 이메일 주소와 제 집 주소가 있는 명함을 편지와 함께 동봉했습니다.

시간을 내주셔서 감사합니다. 소식을 기다리겠습니다.

친애하는, / 닥터 팔레야로부터

Q1. 팔레야 씨는 편지와 함께 무엇을 보냈는가?

(A) 명함
(B) 급료
(C) 책자
(D) 서류와 지원서

해설

마지막 문단에 "I am enclosing along with this letter my business card ~" 나와 있듯이 명함을 동봉한다고 했으므로 답은 (A)이다.

POINT ② 이메일

Question 2 refers to the following e-mail. ------ 글의 종류

From: MMR Vaccines Customer Service <mvservice1@mvmedicals.com>
To: Thomas Wright <thomas2@digitalppl.net> ------ 수신자와 발신자 정보
Date: Tuesday, Dec 10, 14:27
Subject: Your antivirus software subscription program ------ 제목/주제

Welcome to MMR Vaccines! Thank you for your subscription with our company. As a new customer, you may be interested in registering to receive regular updates to the software. ------ 주제문

Our automatic daily update system ensures the full protection of your computer against viruses and spyware. ------ 세부 내용

To register, simply click on the "Register Now" button on our Web site at www.mmrvaccine.com. You will be asked to enter your subscription number, which is 1038939. ------ 추후 당부 내용

MMR Vaccines Customer Service ------ 발신자 정보

Q2 Why did the company contact Mr. Wright?

(A) To notify him of the change in the operating hours of the Customer Service Department
(B) To inform him of a new version of a protection program
(C) To suggest that he register to receive updates for a product
(D) To remind him of his subscription number

발신: MMR 백신 고객 서비스 <mvservice1@mvmedicals.com>
수신: 토마스 라이트 <thomas2@digitalppl.net>
날짜: 12월 10일, 화요일, 오후 2시 27분
제목: 당신의 바이러스 방어 소프트웨어 구독 프로그램

MMR 백신에 오신 것을 환영합니다! 우리 회사에 서비스 구독을 해 주셔서 감사합니다. 신규 고객으로서, 귀하께서는 소프트웨어 정기 업데이트를 등록하는 데 관심이 있으실 것입니다.
저희의 자동 매일 업데이트 시스템은 바이러스와 스파이웨어로부터 완벽한 보호를 보장합니다.
등록하시려면, 저희 웹사이트 www.mmrvaccine.com에 있는 '지금 등록' 버튼을 클릭하시기만 하면 됩니다. 고객님의 가입번호 1038939를 입력하셔야 합니다.

MMR 백신 고객 서비스

Q2. 회사가 라이트 씨에게 연락한 이유는?
(A) 그에게 고객 서비스 부서의 운영 시간 변경을 알리기 위해
(B) 그에게 보안 프로그램의 새로운 버전을 알리기 위해
(C) 제품 업데이트를 받기 위해 등록할 것을 권장하기 위해
(D) 그에게 구독 번호를 상기시키기 위해

해설

문제에서 company는 발신을, Mr. Wright는 수신을 하고 있으므로 이 문제는 편지를 쓴 목적을 묻는 문제이다. 그러므로 서식 상단에 있는 subject와 이것이 드러난 주제문에서 'As a new customer, you may be interested in registering to receive regular updates to the software.' 답을 찾도록 한다. 그러므로 정답은 (C)이다.

편지 / 이메일 관련 빈출 어휘

① 금융 거래 관련

account 계좌	deduct 공제하다
collection notice 징세 통지	credit rating 신용 등급
creditor 채권자	credit limit 신용 한도
utility bill 공과금	delinquent 미납의
bank statement 은행거래기록	accumulation 축적, 누적
clause (계약) 조항	sum 총액

② 유통 거래 관련

distribution 유통	comment 의견, 논평
promotional material 판촉물	subcontractor 하청업체
sensational 선풍적인	exclusive benefit 특별 혜택
stability 안정성	savings certificate 저축 채권
net price 정가	consignment 배송(물)
in hand 가지고 있는	freight 화물
commodity 상품	warehouse 창고
resource 자원	logistics 물류, 택배

③ 개인 거래 관련

giveaway 증정품	warranty 보증
expire 기간이 만료되다	manual 설명서
mark down 가격 인하하다	affordable (가격이) 알맞은
refund policy 환불 정책	carry 운반하다, 취급하다
in transit 운송 중에	defect 결함
terms and conditions 이용약관	voucher 할인권

④ 거주지 관련

occupant 입주자	tenure 거주권, 사용권
inhabitant, resident 거주자	furnished 가구를 갖춘
outskirt 교외의	rent 임대
premises 부동산, 건물	valuation 견적가격
landlord 집주인	tenant 세입자

From: Jake McLaughlin, Manager
To: Shaine Jones

Dear Shaine,

You asked in yesterday's e-mail what the procedure for writing a report on our newest products is. The purpose of the report is to make an accurate prediction for our shareholders of this product's sales potential.

Q1 What is the purpose of this e-mail?

(A) To make a sales prediction
(B) To ask a question
(C) To provide instructions
(D) To demonstrate a new product

Minoki Travel Agency
4-7-1 Matogaoka, Meguro-ku
Tokyo, 152-8799
Tel: (03) 5487-5561
Fax: (03) 5487-5562

Edward Olson
September 10
2-1-3 Nomizu, Chofu-Shi
Tokyo, 182-8799

Dear Mr. Olson:

Thank you for choosing the Minoki Travel Agency. Your reservations for your upcoming trip have been confirmed. Note that we were able to obtain direct flights in both directions. Please review the following itinerary. If any changes need to be made, please notify me by October 15.

Q2 What is the purpose of the letter?

(A) To advertise a vacation package
(B) To announce a change in an itinerary
(C) To request payment for tickets
(D) To confirm upcoming travel plans

Q3 What is indicated about Mr. Olson?

(A) He will take a direct flight to Tokyo.
(B) He will fly in first class.
(C) He is a frequent customer.
(D) He is traveling for business.

해설 p. 398

Questions 1-3 refer to the following letter.

December 11

Dear Seegene Supplies:

I was referred to your company by one of my colleagues at the Macquaint Medical Group when I was searching for a new supplier. He recommended your company as he has been enjoying your services for the last 10 years. When I mentioned some problems I had been experiencing with my current vendor, he emphasized that your staff is very courteous and attentive to customers.

I have already found what he said to be true. When I was trying to place an order online, a technical error occurred, and I called your Customer Care Department. I got an immediate response from one of the representatives, Isha. She also suggested placing my order by fax instead of waiting for the Web site to go back online. I am amazed by how efficiently and calmly she directed me through the final step of placing the order. Now that I am done with it, I'm submitting the brief feedback as requested.

Despite the initial technical problem, I am very pleased with the customer service, and I am looking forward to doing business with your company in the future.

Thanks for your kind and professional assistance.

Yours sincerely,

Serge Houde
KPC Professional Associates

1 What is suggested about Seegene Supplies?

(A) It specializes in selling office stationery.
(B) It has been in business for more than a decade.
(C) Its customer service staff provides feedback.
(D) Its online service has been unavailable for about a week.

2 What is implied about Mr. Houde's previous supplier?

(A) Its customer service was not good.
(B) Its Web site was difficult to use.
(C) Its delivery times were unreasonable.
(D) Its prices were too expensive.

3 How did Mr. Houde submit his order to Seegene Supplies?

(A) By e-mail
(B) By fax
(C) By telephone
(D) By mail

Questions 4-7 refer to the following e-mail.

To	tdament@gantengineering.com
From	rrcross@GPSwebdesign.com
Subject	August 29
Date	Your Inquiry

Dear Mr. Dament,

Thank you for contacting GPS Web Design online. I am writing in response to your inquiry about your company, Gant Engineering, and how we can help enhance media coverage for your product lines.

GPS Web Design was established 15 years ago. We have served as a design consultant for many major organizations both domestically and internationally. Our clients include CFC Manufacturing of Manila, the Freezer Corporation in New York, and UK Automation in London. Working with us, organizations can benefit from increased global coverage on the Internet and more efficient leads from their online media presence.

Should you choose to work with GPS Web Design, we can assure you that you will not be disappointed. Our company has an enviable reputation for completing projects on time and under budget. I am confident that you will see highly encouraging results.

Please contact me directly at 864-555-5142 to arrange a meeting during which we can talk about your requirements in greater depth. I look forward to hearing from you.

Sincerely,

Roger R. Cross
Communications Representative, GPS Web Design

4 Why did Ms. Cross send the e-mail?

(A) To confirm a prearranged meeting at Gant Engineering
(B) To describe how to establish a business proposal
(C) To give information about commencing a new project
(D) To reply to Mr. Dament's question

5 What does Gant Engineering most likely want to do?

(A) Increase its media presence
(B) Construct a new operating facility
(C) Raise the price of its services
(D) Improve its production line output

6 What is mentioned about GPS Web Design?

(A) It recently hired several new staff members.
(B) Its fees are more competitive than those of other consulting firms.
(C) It operates in more than one country.
(D) Its headquarters are in Kuala Lumpur.

7 The word "assure" in paragraph 3, line 1, is closest in meaning to

(A) claim
(B) soothe
(C) promote
(D) promise

Questions 8-10 refer to the following letter.

February 11
Mr. Camille Atebe
562 Drivers Place
Pretoria, South Africa 1294

Dear Mr. Atebe,

We at the Mining Industry of South Africa received your application regarding the position that was advertised last week in the *Cape Town Times* for a mining assistant. We are sorry to inform you that this position has already been filled. Nevertheless, we are planning to begin mining in another location in July, and we believe that you would be suitable for this position. With your permission, we would like to keep your details on file. The location is not far from our main production facilities in Johannesburg, but it will require some travel to Cape Town, Botswana, and other African countries. Please keep checking our Web site for any future vacancies that may arise in our organization. We wish you luck with your job search.

Kind regards,

Darien Provost, Personnel Supervisor

8 What is the main purpose of the letter?

(A) To let an applicant know that he failed to meet the qualifications for a position
(B) To ask an applicant for further details about his career
(C) To arrange an interview with an applicant
(D) To inform an applicant that the position he applied for is no longer available

9 Where are the main facilities of the Mining Industry of South Africa located?

(A) In Cape Town
(B) In Johannesburg
(C) In Pretoria
(D) In Botswana

10 What does Mr. Provost suggest that Mr. Atebe do?

(A) Check a Web site for additional job openings
(B) Send more information about his qualifications
(C) Contact the main facility for employment
(D) Read the job advertisements in the newspaper

PART 7

UNIT 24 광고

광고(advertisement)는 크게 구인 광고와 상품 광고 2가지 유형으로 분류되며 꾸준히 출제되고 있다. 구인 광고는 제목에 드러난 구인 직책(job position)을 파악하면 쉽게 흐름을 파악할 수 있다. 반면, 상품 광고는 제목에 소비자의 관심을 끌어올리기 위해 주로 광고 카피를 보여 준다. 따라서 광고하는 상품이나 서비스를 일컫는 고유명사에 집중하여 정확하게 흐름을 파악하도록 한다.

■ 빈출 문제 유형

① 구인 광고

[구인 직종] What position is being advertised? 어떤 직책이 광고 중인가?

[자격 요건] What is NOT a requirement for the position? 이 직책의 자격요건이 아닌 것은 무엇인가?

[지원 요령] How should applicants apply for the job opening?
이 직책에 지원하려면 지원자들은 어떻게 해야 하는가?

② 상품 광고

[광고 상품] What product is being advertised? 어떤 제품이 광고 중인가?

[상품 특징] What is mentioned as a feature of the service? 서비스의 특징으로 무엇이 언급되고 있는가?

[구매 방법] How are members asked to buy the program?
회원들에게 프로그램을 어떻게 구입하라고 요청하고 있는가?

③ 빈출 지문 내용

- 회사나 단체에서 필요한 직책의 사람을 구하는 광고
- 제조 상품과 서비스(식당, 대중교통 수단, 교육기관, 청소대행 업체 등)을 판매하는 광고

■ 광고 빈출 표현

① 주제문

We are looking for[searching for/seeking]~ 우리 회사는 ~를 구하고 있습니다

We are launching[offering]~ 우리 회사는 ~을 출시[제공]합니다

② 세부 사항

The ideal applicant must have~ 이상적인 지원자는 반드시 ~을 가져야 합니다

Preferred requirements are~ 우대되는 자격요건은 ~입니다

You can also receive~ 당신은 또한 ~을 받을 수 있습니다

Please visit our Web site to learn more about~ ~에 관해 더 알고 싶으시면 웹 사이트를 방문해 주세요

고득점 SOLUTION

① 광고의 주제문이 잘 보이지 않는다면
구인 광고와 상품 광고 모두 일반적으로 회사 소개가 먼저 나오고 그 뒤에 주제문이 나온다. 그러므로 회사 소개가 끝난 후 주제문을 찾도록 한다.

② 상품 광고에서 광고되는 제품(주제)을 찾기 어렵다면
상품 광고에는 소비자의 관심을 끌기 위한 광고 카피가 많아 광고의 주제인 상품명을 찾기가 힘들다. 그러므로 광고되는 상품명이 고유명사로 나오는 문장을 찾도록 한다.

POINT 1 구인 광고

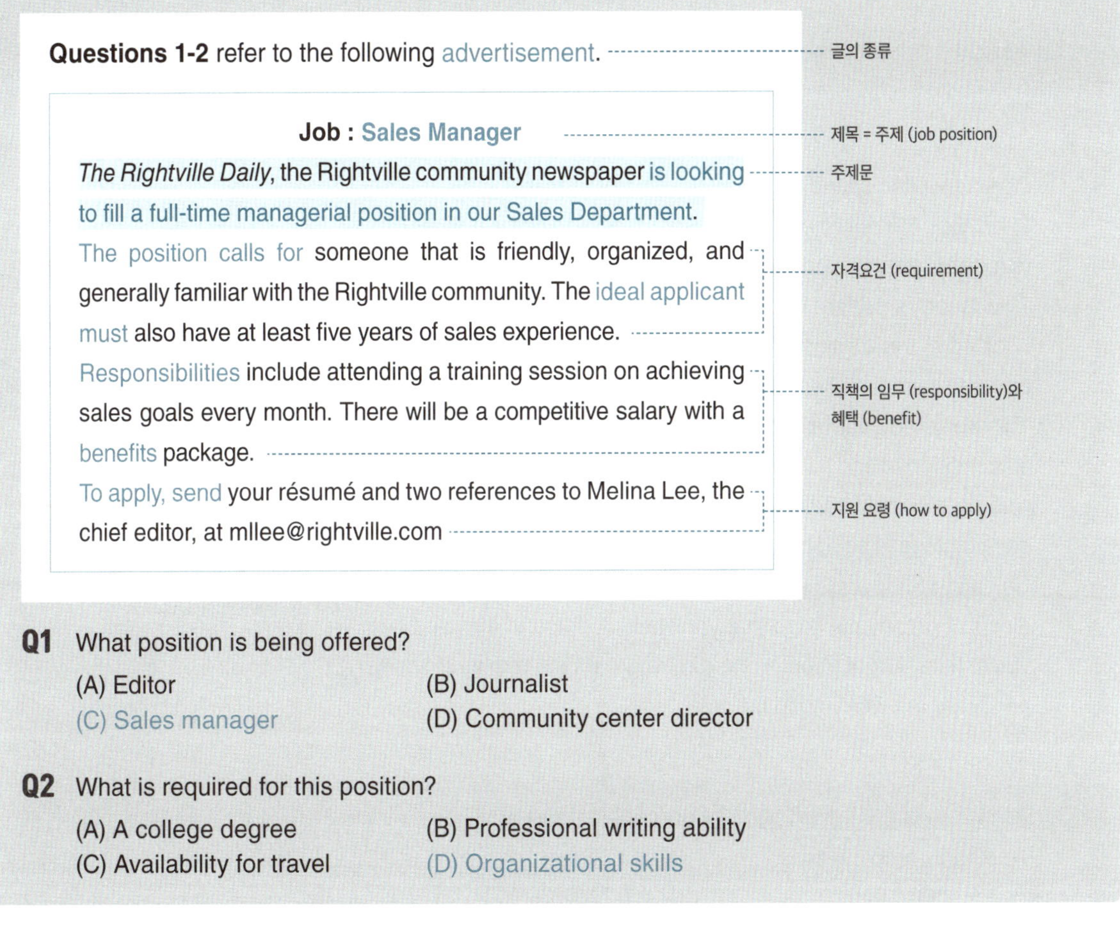

Questions 1-2 refer to the following advertisement.

Job : Sales Manager

The Rightville Daily, the Rightville community newspaper is looking to fill a full-time managerial position in our Sales Department.

The position calls for someone that is friendly, organized, and generally familiar with the Rightville community. The ideal applicant must also have at least five years of sales experience.

Responsibilities include attending a training session on achieving sales goals every month. There will be a competitive salary with a benefits package.

To apply, send your résumé and two references to Melina Lee, the chief editor, at mllee@rightville.com

Q1 What position is being offered?

(A) Editor
(B) Journalist
(C) Sales manager
(D) Community center director

Q2 What is required for this position?

(A) A college degree
(B) Professional writing ability
(C) Availability for travel
(D) Organizational skills

일자리 : 영업팀 부장

라이트빌 지역 신문인 <라이트빌 데일리>의 영업팀에서 정규직으로 근무할 부장을 찾고 있습니다. 직책이 요구하는 지원자는 친절하고, 기획력이 있으며, 라이트빌 지역사회에 대해 잘 알고 있어야 합니다. 또한 최소한 5년의 영업 경력이 있어야 합니다.
매달 판매 목표 달성을 위한 훈련에 참석하는 것이 업무에 포함됩니다. 업계 경쟁력 있는 급여와 복지혜택을 제공할 것입니다.
지원하시려면 이력서와 두 장의 추천서를 편집장인 멜리나 리에게 mllee@rightville.com으로 보내주십시오.

Q1. 어떤 일자리를 제안하고 있는가?
(A) 편집자 (B) 기자 (C) 영업팀 부장 (D) 커뮤니티 센터 국장

Q2. 이 직업의 자격요건은 무엇인가?
(A) 학사 학위 (B) 전문가 수준의 작문 능력 (C) 출장 가능 여부 (D) 기획 능력

해설

Q1. 첫 번째 줄에서 looking to fill a full-time managerial position in our Sales Department라고 언급하고 있으므로 이들은 영업부서에서 일할 부장을 찾고 있다. 정답은 (C).

Q2. 자격요건이 언급된 부분은 두 번째 문단에서 The position calls ~ community이다. 이 중 organized에 해당하는 것으로 정답은 (D)이다.

POINT 2 상품 광고

Question 3 refers to the following advertisement. ---- 글의 종류

Only for You and Your Family ---- 제목

Do you want to spend quality time with your family? ---- 도입 문장
Then visit the Excellent Valley Resort and think of nothing but relaxation, satisfaction, and pleasure. ---- 주제 (상품의 이름) 주제문
This resort is perfect for those who are looking for a great time. Located in the outskirts of the city, one can either take a bus or drive to reach Excellent Valley.
This weekend getaway boasts cozy cottages, all of which are fully air conditioned and have two bedrooms and a spacious bathroom with hot and cold showers. Outside, your family can grill food as each cottage is equipped with its own barbecue pit. ---- 상품의 특징 (features)
Call 451-5896, and you will immediately receive a five-percent discount on any package that you want. A piece of advice: while you're here, forget about work, have a great time with your family, and leave the worrying to us. ---- 구매 요령 (how to buy)

Q3 For whom is the advertisement primarily intended?

(A) Resort employees (B) Families
(C) TV repairmen (D) Plumbers

오직 당신과 당신의 가족만을 위해

가족들과 알찬 시간을 보내고 싶으신가요?
그럼, Excellent Valley Resort에 방문하셔서 아무 생각 없이 휴식과 만족, 즐거움을 얻으세요.
이곳 휴양지는 즐거운 휴일을 보내고 싶은 사람에게는 최적의 장소입니다. 도시 외곽에 위치하여 버스를 타거나 직접 운전해서 Excellent Valley에 올 수 있습니다.
이 주말 휴양지는 에어컨이 완비되어 있고 두 개의 침실이 있으며 냉수 및 온수 시설이 완비된 넓은 샤워 공간이 마련된 안락한 오두막을 자랑거리로 합니다. 각각의 오두막마다 마당에 바비큐 시설이 있기 때문에 가족들이 음식을 구울 수 있습니다.
451-5896번으로 전화 주시면 여러분께서 원하시는 패키지를 5% 할인해 드립니다. 한 가지 팁을 드리자면 이곳에 계시는 동안 모든 일상은 잊고 가족들과 함께 즐겁게 지내시면서 걱정은 저희에게 맡겨 주시기 바랍니다.

Q3. 이 광고의 대상은 주로 누구인가?
(A) 휴양지 직원 (B) 가족 (C) TV 수리공 (D) 배관공

해설

첫 문장 "Do you want to spend quality time with your family? Then visit the Excellent Valley ~ pleasure."를 통해 휴가를 즐기고 싶은 가족들에게 자신의 리조트를 소개하는 글임을 알 수 있다. 그러므로 정답은 (B)이다.

광고 관련 빈출 어휘

PART 7

① 구인 광고 관련

job vacancy 공석	employ/hire 고용하다
job opening 공석	recruit 고용하다
skillful 숙련된	cover letter 자기소개서
experienced 경험이 많은	reference letter 추천서
competent 능력 있는	diploma 졸업증명서
qualified 자격을 갖춘	degree 학위
qualification 지원자격	prerequisite 필수조건
proficient 능숙한	preferred 우대되는
applicant 지원자	reliable 신뢰할 만한
candidate 지원자	dependable 믿을 만한
employment 고용	professional 전문의
communication skills 의사소통 기술	amateur 비전문의

② 상품 광고 관련

commercial 광고	estimated 추산된
promotion 판촉, 승진	highly-rated 높은 평가를 받은
campaign 광고	user-friendly 사용자 친화적인
customized/tailored 소비자 주문에 맞춘	environmentally friendly 환경친화적인
business hours 영업시간, 근무시간	in bulk 대량으로
client 의뢰인	transaction 거래
sales representative 영업 직원	withdraw 철회하다, 인출하다
valid 유효한	come with a warranty 보증서가 딸려오다
expired 만료된	for your safety 고객의 안전을 위해
place an order 주문하다	be paid in full 전액 지불되다
in stock 재고가 있는	be designed to ~하기 위해 만들어지다
out of stock 재고가 없는	at the time of purchase 구매한 시점에서
track an order 주문을 조회하다	establish a record of ~의 기록을 세우다
invoice 청구서, 송장	earn recognition 인성을 받나
appreciate 인정하다, 평가하다	outstanding quality 뛰어난 품질

해설 p. 401

Accounting Director Needed

The Bland Corporation is seeking highly skilled and motivated professionals to apply for the position of accounting director for the northeast division. Applicants must have an MBA, be certified CPAs, have a minimum of 10 years' experience working in the accounting field, and have 5 years' management experience. The job will include roughly 20 days of travel a year to domestic and international locations. A very hardworking attitude is a requirement in this position. Benefits include full medical and dental family coverage, a six-figure salary, and an end-of-contract bonus as well as a substantial retirement pension, depending on how many years of service the successful applicant provides. Please send your résumé and cover letter to Ruth Jucinia at ruthjuice@bland.com.

Q1 Which of the following is required from applicants?

(A) A minimum of 5 years of experience in accounting field
(B) A willingness to travel
(C) A sense of humor
(D) A history of earning a high salary

Do you have a heart or blood pressure problem? Are you interested in eating healthy food but don't have time to cook it yourself? Try the Healthy Food Program where you will receive seven days worth of healthy meals in the mail at the beginning of each week. Meals are delivered frozen to your door, and you simply cook them in the microwave for a delicious, healthy dinner within minutes! A study involving 500 participants found that after 10 weeks on our low-fat, low-sodium meal plan, 73% of people recorded a drop in their cholesterol levels, and 75% showed a drop in blood pressure. Almost everyone reported feeling healthier and even lost some weight. So what are you waiting for? We at Healthy Food know this program is not a total cure for people's health problems, but we maintain that our meals will offer a start at learning how to manage health problems. Plus, this is the answer for those of you who simply don't have time to cook. We provide breakfast, lunch, and dinner. Call today for more information.

Q2 Who is NOT mentioned as someone who would want the meals?

(A) Someone with high blood pressure
(B) Someone who has little time to cook
(C) Someone who has high cholesterol
(D) Someone who is over the age of 55

Questions 1-3 refer to the following advertisement.

- **What** : 5 bedrooms, 3 bathrooms in 4,460 square feet on three-quarters of an acre.
- **Where** : Boston, Massachusetts, 16 miles from Logan International Airport.
- **Amenities** : Home ownership in Desert Ranch Estates includes a membership in the Desert Ranch Health Resort, which has fitness classes, tennis courts, and swimming pools. The monthly dues are $450 while the gated community's monthly association fee is $185.
- **Notes** : This 1994-style home is built around a courtyard with a fountain and a corner fireplace.

Desert Ranch Estates has 25 homes with seven more under construction. Since the community was established in 1989, there have been eight resales of properties. The most expensive sale there was $1,450,000 for a 4,750-square-foot furnished home that was listed at $1.5 million. In all of Massachusetts, four homes have sold for more than $1 million during the first six months of this year, including a 5,600-square-foot home on one acre listed at $1.85 million that sold for $1.6 million.

1 How far is Massachusetts from an airport?

(A) 3 miles
(B) 5 miles
(C) 16 miles
(D) 25 miles

2 Which of the following is an advertised feature of the house?

(A) A fireplace
(B) A hot tub
(C) A deluxe kitchen
(D) Four bedrooms

3 What is NOT true according to the advertisement?

(A) This five-bedroom house is in Boston, Massachusetts.
(B) This 1994-style home is built around a courtyard.
(C) There is no ongoing house construction in Desert Ranch Estates.
(D) The community was established in 1989.

Questions 4-6 refer to the following advertisement.

Flatiron Building Supply, Inc.

Weekend shifts required where indicated.

Loss-prevention Manager
Must have a university degree and good communication, leadership, and people skills. Prefer at least 2 years of loss-prevention experience. Basic working knowledge of retail policies and procedures required. Some weekend work is required for this position.

Delivery Driver
Must have a commercial driver's license and be able to read maps and follow specific directions and delivery instructions. Must be able to handle and move items weighing up to 30kg without assistance. Requires availability 7 days a week.

Customer Service Coordinator
Must have at least one year of call center or customer service experience. Associate's degree preferred. Computer knowledge and proficiency required. Weekend work is required.

Administrative Assistants
Must have strong written and verbal communication skills, organizational skills, and the ability to multi-task. Computer knowledge and proficiency required.

Please send résumé to : Human Resources
Flatiron Building Supply, Inc.
655 Bremo Road
Marietta, GA 78240

No phone calls or e-mails, please.

4 What is a requirement for the loss-prevention manager position?
(A) Excellent accounting experience
(B) A willingness to work at night
(C) A degree in communications
(D) Some knowledge of retail procedures

5 What position does NOT involve weekend shifts?
(A) Loss-prevention manager
(B) Delivery driver
(C) Customer service coordinator
(D) Administrative assistant

6 How can candidates apply for a position?
(A) Online
(B) By telephone
(C) By mail
(D) In person

Questions 7-9 refer to the following advertisement.

Manager Wanted for Golden Opportunity

Get in on the ground floor of the fastest-growing market in the world. Ortiz Telecommunications, a leader in international discount telecommunications, is looking for an experienced manager and technical support employees. Ortiz customers can save 40% or more on their international calls. In addition, they can enjoy substantial savings on their fax and Internet services. Moreover, with innovative features such as return call, our customers can utilize services unavailable with other carriers.

But as the demand for our services grows, so does our need for effective and aggressive action in the market. Ortiz Telecommunications offers a lucrative commission schedule and 3 weeks of vacation per year with every Saturday and Sunday off. This offer is an outstanding opportunity for engineers with people skills to work as a manager for a very good salary.

For more information, call us at 901-222-1111 or visit our Web site at www.ortiz.org.

7 What feature does Ortiz Telecommunications offer?

(A) Text messages
(B) Fast Internet
(C) Cheap international calls
(D) Voice mail

8 What does a customer NOT receive savings on?

(A) Internet services
(B) Fax services
(C) Cable television
(D) International calls

9 What is mentioned about the schedule for working times?

(A) Employees have every weekend off.
(B) Employees get 2 weeks of vacation each year.
(C) Employees get 3 weeks of vacation every 6 months.
(D) Employees can take 2 days off anytime during the week.

UNIT 25 공지 / 회람

공지(notice/announcement)와 회람(memo)은 다수의 사람들에게 공적인 내용을 통지하는 것이 목적이다. 그러므로 맥락이 뚜렷하고 일관되게 구현되어 매우 구조적인 것이 특징이다. 특히 공지는 대부분 첫 문장에 주제문을 제시한다. 또한 회람은 효율적인 공지를 위해 서식 상단에 수신인, 발신인, 주제가 별도로 제시되는 것이 특징이다.

■ 빈출 문제 유형

[글의 목적] Why was this memo written? 이 회람은 왜 쓰였는가?

[글이 게시된 곳] Where is this notice most likely posted? 이 공지는 어디에 게시되어 있을 것 같은가?

[글의 대상] For whom is this notice intended? 이 공지의 대상은 누구인가?

[추후 당부 내용] What are employees asked[recommended/suggested] to do?
직원들은 무엇을 하라고 요청[추천/제안] 받는가?

■ 빈출 지문 내용

• 지역 주민들에게 지역 내의 행사나 공사 같은 주요 일정을 알리는 공지

• 새로운 상품의 출시를 알리거나 구인을 하는 성격의 공지

• 사내에서 결정된 사안을 통보하는 회람

• 각종 행사의 참여를 요청하는 회람

■ 공지 / 회람 빈출 표현

① 주제문

We are happy[pleased] to announce that~ ~을 알리게 되어 기쁩니다

We regret to inform you that~ ~을 알리게 되어 유감입니다

We would like to give you a reminder that~ ~을 다시 알려 드리고 싶습니다

Please be informed that~ ~을 알아 두십시오

② 추후 당부 사항

We ask[suggest/recommend/instruct/expect/want/need/would like] to~ ~하길 바랍니다

You can[should/have to/may/will]~ ~하길 바랍니다

고득점 SOLUTION

① 공지에서 첫 문장이 주제문이 아니라면
세부 내용을 읽고 주제문을 역으로 추론하도록 한다.

② 회람의 상단 서식(수신인, 발신인, 주제)이 생략되어 전반적인 내용 파악이 어렵다면
회람도 공지의 성격이 있기 때문에 첫 문장이 주제문일 확률이 높다. 하지만 정확한 파악을 위해, 지문 속에 드러난 수신인(you)과 발신인(we, I)의 역할을 이용해 주제를 찾도록 한다.

POINT 1 공지

Questions 1-2 refer to the following notice. ---- 글의 종류

Notice ---- 제목

The annual human resources **seminar** led by the Personnel Department will take place on September 21 at 10 A.M. in meeting room 22 on the first floor across from the mail room. ---- 주제문

The theme of the seminar, "Improving Our Efficiency", should be particularly relevant considering the recent rise in competition in the market. ---- 세부 내용

All senior executives are required to attend. Junior managers are also welcome. Please be on time! ---- 추후 당부 내용

PART 7

Q1 What is the purpose of this notice?

(A) To encourage some employees to attend a seminar
(B) To notify some employees of a change in a schedule
(C) To encourage some employees to submit a report
(D) To notify some employees about the new theme of a seminar

Q2 Who is welcome to attend the seminar according to the notice?

(A) Employees in the Personnel Department
(B) Salespeople
(C) All employees
(D) Junior managers

공지

인사부의 인사 관련 연례 세미나가 오는 9월 21일 오전 10시에 1층 우편실 맞은편의 회의실 22호에서 열립니다.
최근 시장 경쟁이 격화하고 있는 점을 고려하면, "노동효율 향상"이라는 회의의 주제가 매우 뜻깊을 것입니다.
중견 간부들은 전원 참석해 주십시오. 하급 관리자 또한 환영합니다. 시간을 엄수해 주실 것을 부탁드립니다!

Q1. 이 공지의 목적은 무엇인가?
(A) 몇몇 직원들에게 세미나에 참석하도록 권장하기 위해 (B) 몇몇 직원들에게 일정 변경을 공지하기 위해
(C) 몇몇 직원들이 보고서를 제출하도록 하기 위해 (D) 몇몇 직원들에게 세미나의 새로운 주제를 공지하기 위해

Q2. 공지에 따르면 누가 세미나에 참석하는 것이 환영되는가?
(A) 인사과 소속 직원들 (B) 영업 사원들 (C) 모든 직원들 (D) 하급 관리자

해설

Q1. 'The annual human resources seminar ~ in meeting room 22'에서 세미나 관련 안내 및 참석할 것을 당부하는 공지임을 알 수 있다. 그러므로 정답은 (A)이다.

Q2. 'All senior executives are required to attend. Junior managers are also welcome.'에서 신참 관리자(junior manager)의 참석이 환영된다는 것을 알 수 있다. 그러므로 정답은 (D)이다.

POINT ❷ 회람

Question 3 refers to the following memo. ------ 글의 종류

From: System Manager
To: All employees ------ 발신자 / 수신자 정보
Subject: OS Upgrade ------ 주제
Date: June 18 ------ 작성 날짜

At 8:00 A.M. on July 1, our network will be shut down for the installation of an upgraded operating system. ------ 주제문

The system will be shut down all day, so please plan accordingly. To install the new OS, we will first make a backup copy of all files, and then all files on the system will be deleted. The data files will be reinstalled from the backups. ------ 세부 내용

There is a chance that data may be lost in the process, so we ask all employees to erase any unnecessary files from the system and to back up important files on a data storage device. ------ 추후 당부 내용

Q3 What action are employees asked to take?

(A) Change their passwords
(B) Make copies of important files
(C) Avoid using the system on July 1
(D) Delete all confidential files from the system

발신: 시스템 관리자
수신: 전 직원
주제: 운영체계 업그레이드
날짜: 6월 18일

7월 1일 오전 8시에 업그레이드된 운영체계를 설치하기 위해 네트워크가 사용 중지될 것입니다.
시스템은 하루 종일 사용 중지될 것이니 이에 맞추어 계획하시기 바랍니다. 새로운 운영체계를 설치하기 위해 우리는 먼저 모든 파일의 백업 복사본을 만들 것이고, 그런 다음 시스템 상에 있는 모든 파일들은 삭제될 것입니다. 데이터 파일들은 백업 파일들로부터 다시 설치될 것입니다.
이 과정 중에 정보가 분실되는 경우도 있습니다. 그래서 우리는 전 직원들이 시스템으로부터 불필요한 파일들을 지우고 중요한 파일들을 데이터 저장 장치에 백업해 두길 요청하는 바입니다.

Q3. 직원들에게 어떤 행동을 취하라고 요청되었는가?
(A) 암호를 바꾼다
(B) 중요한 파일들의 복사본을 만든다
(C) 7월 1일에 시스템 사용을 피한다
(D) 기밀 파일들을 시스템에서 삭제한다

해설

메모 중반에 'so we ask all employees to erase any unnecessary files from the system and to back up important files on a data storage device.'에서 직원들에게 중요한 파일을 데이터 저장 장치에 저장하라고 권고하고 있음을 알 수 있다. back up이 Make copies로 패러프레이징되었다. 따라서 정답은 (B)이다.

공지 / 회람 관련 빈출 어휘

① 공지 관련

reminder 상기시키기 위한 것	go through 겪다
eligible ~할 자격이 있는	curtail (기간을) 단축하다
withdrawal 출금, 철회	temporarily 임시로, 일시적으로
deposit 예금, 보증금	thanks to ~덕분에, ~때문에
benefit package 복리후생 제도	grant 보조금
contribution 공헌, 기부	foundation 재단
profitable 수익성이 있는	improvement 개선
exhibit 전시회	enlarge 확장하다
trade fair 무역 박람회	involve 포함하다, 수반하다
celebrate 축하하다	as a result of ~의 결과로
host 주최하다, 개최하다	relocate 이전시키다
conflict 충돌, 대립	resume 다시 시작하다
arise 발생하다	post 게시하다
display 전시, 게시	execute 실행하다, 수행하다
over the past few years 지난 수년에 걸쳐서	track out 탐지하다
operate 경영하다, 작동하다	inspection 정밀 검사
renovated 개조된	productivity 생산성

② 회람 관련

replacement 후임자	comply (규칙, 관례 등을) 따르다
code 규약, 관례	property 대지, 건물
cut back 삭감하다	align 정렬시키다
resignation 사직	discourage 단념시키다
retirement 은퇴	finalization 최종 승인, 마무리
training session 훈련	outcome 결과, 성과
assign 할당하다	modification 변경
contractor 하청업자	intermission (공연 중에) 휴식 시간
under construction 공사 중인	consult (자료 등을) 참고하다
urgent 긴급한	remind 상기시키다
regular business hours 정규 근무/영업 시간	time-consuming 시간이 걸리는
manage 관리하다	affiliate 계열사
appropriate 적절한	immediate supervisor 직속 상관

PART 7

- **Notice** -

May 20, 2020

The company announces that Kevin Brennan will resign as the finance director at the company on May 31, 2020, to pursue interests elsewhere. The directors thank him for his contributions to the company over the past three and a half years and wish him well in the future.

We are pleased to announce that Joy Kocay will join the company as the new finance director on June 2, 2020. Joy Kocay is a qualified accountant who graduated from the Business School of New York City College. He has been in resource banking for 14 years and is currently with the ING Capital Group in New York.

Kimberly Jones
Personnel Department Manager

Q1 What is the topic of this notice?

(A) A job offer
(B) A strategy proposal
(C) A personnel changes
(D) A company merger

MEMO

RE : New Telephone System
To : All staff
From : Dylan Walsh
Date : September 30, 2019

Our new telephone system will be completely installed this weekend rather than over a period of three weeks as was originally planned. It will be operational by Monday morning. Each staff member will continue to have individual voice mail, allowing callers to leave personal voice messages.

There will be a twenty-minute introduction to the system in Conference Room 3 on Monday at 10:00 A.M., 11:00 A.M., and 1:30 P.M. Please plan to attend one of these sessions so that you will be able to make full use of the features of our new phone system.

Q2 What are employees asked to do?

(A) Attend one of the introductory sessions
(B) Select an extension
(C) Call Dylan Walsh
(D) Read a manual about the new phone system

해설 p. 404

Questions 1-3 refer to the following memorandum.

To: All Employees
From: Chief Director of the supply section
Subject: Cartridge Recycling Program

It is estimated that over 100 million used cartridges will pollute our landfills this year. This can create a serious environmental problem in the future. Now we can all help reduce that number by selling our used cartridges!

In an effort to conserve and protect our vital natural resources, our company, in conjunction with TRC, has begun a cartridge recycling program. TRC covers the cost of shipping used cartridges from our location to theirs. In addition, they pay us quite a bit for every re-usable cartridge we save and send them. This money will be donated to company social clubs, local charities, or the children's hospital. Please do not throw away any used cartridges. Please address any questions you may have to me. I hope that everybody cooperates and helps make this successful. Do your part to help us create a clean and green future.

1 What is the main purpose of the cartridge recycling program?

(A) To make a profit
(B) To protect natural resources
(C) To donate commodities to charity
(D) To keep offices clean

2 According to the memorandum, where will some money be donated?

(A) To many social clubs in the local community
(B) To national charities
(C) To social clubs in the company
(D) To the women's hospital

3 What are employees asked to do?

(A) Throw away used cartridges
(B) Make contributions to the children's hospital
(C) Sell used cartridges individually
(D) Participate in a program

Questions 4-7 refer to the following notice.

Dear Visitors,

In recent years, the town of Eastlake has continued to grow, and Eastlake Hospital has experienced tremendous growth in patient volume. Therefore, Eastlake Hospital has decided to make some upgrades to our facilities. One of these projects consists of building a new entrance to the emergency room as well as a new parking lot for emergency room patients. The aim is to make the entrance to the ER safer and more convenient for our patients and staff. During construction, the ER entrance will be for ambulances only. All other visitors to the ER are asked to use the east entrance, which is located between the Pediatric Department and the cafeteria. Throughout the construction period, parking will be limited near the east entrance, so we ask that only visitors to the ER park in the east lot. We apologize for the inconvenience, but believe these improvements will greatly improve our ER services. To view more detailed information regarding the upcoming construction project, visit our Web site at www.westlakehospital.org.
Thank you for your cooperation.

4 What is the purpose of this notice?

(A) To ask for donations for the hospital renovations
(B) To announce the building of a new hospital
(C) To inform the public of upcoming renovations at the hospital
(D) To report a delay in the hospital's construction schedule

5 What prompted Eastlake Hospital to plan the construction project?

(A) The deterioration of the facilities
(B) Changes in management
(C) An increase in the number of patients
(D) An increase in the types of services offered

6 The word "volume" in line 2, is closest in meaning to

(A) sound
(B) quantity
(C) injury
(D) information

7 What will the public be unable to do while the project is underway?

(A) Enter through the emergency room entrance
(B) Visit patients in the Pediatric Department
(C) Buy food and beverages in the cafeteria
(D) Park their cars in the emergency room parking lot

Questions 8-11 refer to the following memo.

Dear employees,

As most of you are aware, medical costs have skyrocketed in the past few years. Despite the continued success of our business, the increasing cost of providing medical insurance has become a problem that we can no longer ignore. In an effort to address this situation, we have decided to make certain changes in the medical coverage that we offer. We have also altered the sick leave policy. We have tried very hard to be fair while at the same time being fiscally responsible.

We recognize that these changes are a serious matter that affects everyone, so we have arranged special meetings to go over the details and to answer any questions that may arise.

Please note the time of your meeting as listed below:
3rd week, May
Sales - Monday 9:00 A.M.
Accounting - Monday 2:00 P.M.
Production - Tuesday 9:00 A.M.
Customer Service - Wednesday 2:00 P.M.
General Office - Thursday 4:00 P.M.

8 What is the purpose of this memo?
(A) To announce changes in health benefits
(B) To announce the restructuring of departments
(C) To announce reduced healthcare costs
(D) To announce that sales have skyrocketed

9 Why have the meetings been arranged?
(A) To assign employees new tasks
(B) To solicit opinions on medical insurance
(C) To answer employees' questions
(D) To make plans for sick leave

10 Who should attend the Monday afternoon meeting?
(A) Sales staff members
(B) Bookkeeping staff members
(C) Reception staff members
(D) Customer Service staff members

11 What is mentioned in the memo?
(A) The company has continued to succeed.
(B) Medical costs have dramatically increased since last year.
(C) The meetings will be held at the beginning of this month.
(D) The sick leave policy is not changing.

UNIT 26 기사

기사(article)는 두괄식 구성의 지문이기 때문에 주제문이 대부분 첫 문장에 드러나 있다. 하지만 다른 지문과는 달리 예측 가능한 글의 구조 패턴이 없어 속독하기가 어렵다. 그러므로 충분히 시간을 안배하여 속독과 정독의 중간 속도로 정확히 읽어 내려가는 연습을 하도록 한다.

■ 빈출 문제 유형

[글의 주제] What is the issue[topic] of this article? 이 기사의 쟁점[주제]가 무엇인가?

[글의 목적] Why was this article written? 이 기사는 왜 쓰였는가?

[글의 대상] Who would most likely be interested in this article? 누가 이 기사에 관심이 있을 것 같은가?

[세부 내용] Which party has a positive[negative] opinion? 어떤 단체가 긍정적인[부정적인] 의견을 가지는가?

What is Winston Tech reported to have done? 윈스턴 테크 사는 무엇을 했다고 보도되고 있는가?

What is suggested about Mr. Crawford? 크로포드 씨에 대해 무엇이 암시되고 있는가?

What is NOT featured on the Web site? 웹 사이트에서 포함되어 있지 않은 것은 무엇인가?

■ 빈출 지문 내용

- 사회의 사건 사고에 대한 보도
- 정부나 단체, 기업의 향후 계획이나 결정된 사안에 대한 보도
- 특정 행사나 상품에 대한 평가나 보도 내용에 대한 다양한 사람들의 인터뷰
- 시사성이 있는 문제나 사회의 관심거리 등에 대해 평한 기사

■ 기사 빈출 표현

① 주제문

In the press release, the company announced that~ 기자회견에서 회사는 ~이라고 발표했다

The organization has completed~ 단체는 ~을 완료하였다

A survey revealed that~ 한 조사는 ~라는 것을 보여 준다

A new movie will be released~ 신작 영화가 ~에 개봉할 예정입니다

② 세부 사항

The spokesman said that~ 대변인이 ~라고 말했다

The group agreed that~ 단체는 ~을 동의했다

고득점 SOLUTION

① 기사문을 읽기 어렵다면
문항에 드러난 핵심어를 통해 기사문의 줄거리를 역으로 추론하여 읽는다.

② 기사의 인터뷰 내용 파악이 어렵다면
인터뷰를 하는 사람의 직책과 인터뷰 내용의 핵심이 되는 곳에 표시하여, 필요할 때 바로 확인할 수 있도록 한다.

Question 1 refers to the following article. ---- 글의 종류

Pasco to Purchase Atom's Supermarkets ---- 제목

Atom's Supermarkets, a family-owned chain that became a local institution and industry icon, announced that the company is being acquired by the Pasco Group for $150 million. ---- 주제문

Pasco Group is a Dutch-owned retail conglomerate that operates grocery stores in the United States under the name Dream Food. The transaction will include 25 stores, inventory, equipment, and lease agreements. Atom's has estimated annual sales of about $600 million. "The Atom's brand is a well-recognized and well-known brand", said Frank Herrion, the president of Pasco. "We look forward to building on that brand".

Pasco operates 149 stores in Virginia, Maryland, and North Carolina under the Dream Food banner. The deal is expected to close in the first quarter of next year. ---- 세부 내용

Q1 What is the purpose of this article?

(A) To announce the hiring of a president
(B) To discuss the opening of a family business
(C) To report a business acquisition
(D) To recommend a store

패스코가 애텀 슈퍼마켓을 매입하다

지역회사 및 산업의 상징이 된 가족 소유 체인점인 애텀 슈퍼마켓을 패스코 그룹에서 1억 5천만 달러에 인수를 진행하고 있다고 오늘 애텀 슈퍼마켓이 말했다.

패스코그룹은 드림 푸드란 이름으로 미국에서 식료품점을 운영하고 있는 네덜란드 국적의 대기업형 소매 기업이다. 이 거래는 25개의 상점, 재고, 장비 그리고 임대 계약까지를 포함하는 것이다. 애텀은 연 6억 달러의 매출을 예상하는데 패스코의 사장인 프랭크 해리언은 "애텀의 브랜드는 인지도가 높고 유명한 상표입니다."라고 말했다. "그 브랜드를 기반으로 해서 쌓아가기를 기대합니다."

패스코는 버지니아, 매릴랜드, 노스캐롤라이나에서 드림푸드란 이름을 내걸고 149개의 매장을 운영하고 있다. 이 거래는 내년 1분기에 완료될 것 같다.

Q1. 이 기사의 목적은?

(A) 사장 채용을 공고하기 위해
(B) 가족 사업 시작을 의논하기 위해
(C) 기업 인수 보도를 위해
(D) 상점 추천을 위해

해설

이 기사 제목(Pasco to Purchase Atom's Supermarkets) 및 지문의 첫 문장(Atom's Supermarkets ~ is being acquired by the Pasco Group)에서 알 수 있다. 패스코 그룹에서 지역의 오래된 기업인 애텀 슈퍼마켓 체인을 인수하기로 했다는 것이 기사의 핵심 내용이다. 그러므로 정답은 (C)이다.

POINT 2

Question 2 refers to the following article. ------ 글의 종류

According to a report released last week by the Bureau of Labor, wages increased by an average of just 3.1% in 2018, down from 3.8% the previous year, and the third-lowest rate of increase since records began in 1960. ------ 주제문

The lowest pay increase on record was 2.5% in 1990. The survey conducted in October showed an average pay hike of just $18.95. Construction workers received the largest wage increase, averaging $25.15, closely followed by utility employees at $23.15, and wholesale-retail employees received an extra $20.10 while service sector employees received the smallest increase, just $14.95. ------ 세부 내용 (글의 마지막에 추후 당부 사항이 없을 수도 있다.)

Q2 Which group of workers fared best in this year's wage hikes?

(A) Service sector employees
(B) Wholesale-retail employees
(C) Utility employees
(D) Construction workers

노동청이 지난주에 발표한 보고서에 의하면, 2018년에 평균 임금 인상률은 3.1%에 불과했다. 이 수치는 그 전해의 3.8%보다 낮은 것으로 1960년에 기록을 시작한 이후로 세 번째로 낮은 수치다.
기록에 의하면, 1990년에 제일 낮은 2.5%의 임금 인상률을 기록했다. 10월에 실시한 조사에 의하면 평균 임금 인상이 18.95달러에 불과했다. 건축 근로자들이 제일 많은 평균 25.15달러가 인상되었고, 전기 가스 수도 사업 종사자들이 다음으로 23.15달러, 도소매업 사업 종사자들이 20.10달러, 그리고 서비스 분야 근로자들이 가장 적게 인상되어 14.95달러였다.

Q2. 어떤 분야 근로자들의 임금이 제일 많이 올랐나?
(A) 서비스업 근로자들
(B) 도소매업 근로자들
(C) 공공사업 근로자들
(D) 건축근로자들

해설

지문 후반에서 건축 근로자들의 임금이 가장 많이 올랐다고 하므로 'Construction workers received the largest wage increase, averaging $25.15, closely followed by utility employees at $23.15, ~' 정답은 건축 근로자들임을 알 수 있다. 그러므로 답은 (D)이다.

기사 관련 빈출 어휘

① 기업 관련

unanimous 만장일치의	as a whole 총체적으로
tentative 잠정적인	unemployment rate 실업률
trade corporation 무역회사	statistics 통계 (자료)
merge 합병하다	labor 노동력
terms of an acquisition 인수조건	investor 투자자
reach an agreement 합의에 이르다	stock exchange 증권거래소
terminate 파기하다	come to an end 끝나다
commitment 약속, 책무	contribute to ~의 원인이 되다
negotiation 협상	strategy 전략
publish 공개하다, 출판하다	mutually beneficial 서로에게 이익이 되는
crucial 결정적인, 중대한	favorable 호의적인

② 경제 관련

put aside ~을 저축하다	bankrupt 파산한
chamber of commerce 상공회의소	fluctuate 변동하다
fiscal year 회계 연도	market share 시장 점유율
downsize 축소하다	prosperity 번영
sustainable 지속할 수 있는	surge 급등하다
barometer (여론의 동향을 나타내는) 지표	overhead cost 간접 비용
interest rate 이자율	dividend 배당금
recession 경기 불황	audit 회계감사
sluggish 경기가 부진한	margin 수익
stagnation 침체	extend 연장하다
stabilize 안정시키다	commitment 책무

③ 개인 관련

circumstance 환경	provisions 규정, 조항
conserve 보존하다	declare 신고하다
disposal 처분	duty 세금

PART 7

해설 p. 406

Jacob D. Dumelle, the chief designer of the Claude Forbes House of Fashion, has been named the designer of the year by the Young Designers Guild. Mr. Dumelle has been recognized because of his cutting-edge designs and innovative use of different materials for his fall 2019 collection. He was selected for the award by his peers in the guild through a secret ballot done during the guild's 10th anniversary in late September. "His designs show so much potential, and I expect to see a lot of what he still has to offer in the years to come", said last year's designer of the year, Lynn Collins.

Q1 Who is Ms. Collins?

(A) She was the chief designer of Claude Forbes in 2018.
(B) She was the winner of the designer of the year award in 2018.
(C) She is the president of the Young Designers Guild.
(D) She is Mr. Dumelle's mentor.

Yesterday at its annual shareholders' meeting, Urban Shipping announced that it will centralize its freight control operations near company headquarters in Singapore. Previously, Urban Shipping operated several localized freight control centers throughout Asia. However, improvements in communications technology and an increasingly competitive marketplace combined to motivate Urban Shipping to centralize its operations. The new operations center will be housed in Kon Towers and will utilize state-of-the-art technology to track the locations of shipments and to manage numerous shipping schedules. The operations center staff will also track weather conditions and chart alternate shipping routes by using new technology.

Q2 According to the article, what will the operations staff be responsible for?

(A) Monitoring weather conditions
(B) Rotating staff schedules
(C) Issuing billing statements
(D) Keeping track of efficiency measures

Q3 According to the article, why did the company centralize its control operations?

(A) It decided to reduce its staff in Singapore.
(B) It invented a new type of communications technology.
(C) It chose to sell one of its divisions.
(D) It wanted to make its operations more efficient.

해설 p. 406

Questions 1-3 refer to the following article.

Petersburg

Located in the Atrium Shopping Center on Broad Street, A Taste of Italy opened five years ago and quickly became a popular South Side restaurant. As its name implies, it features a traditional selection of homemade Italian dishes. A Taste of Italy was recently closed for two months while going through a change in management. It reopened its doors last weekend. The new chef, Kevin Brennan, has created an extensive menu that includes hearty salads, brick-oven pizzas, and enticing entrées. Some of his specialties include excellent pasta dishes, such as linguini with sauteed jumbo shrimp served in a spicy red sauce and spaghetti cacciatore with green peppers, mushrooms, sausage, and tomatoes. Be sure to save room for his signature dessert, homemade tiramisu. With so many delicious items to choose from, A Taste of Italy is sure to reclaim its popularity with Petersburg residents.

1 What is the purpose of the article?

(A) To review a restaurant
(B) To advertise cooking lessons
(C) To compare two restaurants
(D) To announce a change in location

2 What is mentioned about Mr. Brennan?

(A) He is skilled at making pasta dishes.
(B) He only uses organic ingredients.
(C) He renovated a restaurant.
(D) He started working at A Taste of Italy two months ago.

3 What is implied about the restaurant?

(A) Its management replaced most of the staff.
(B) It serves an excellent dessert.
(C) Its most popular dish is the linguini.
(D) It moved to a new location.

Questions 4-7 refer to the following article.

Perth – Over the past few years, Perth has been named one of the fastest-growing cities for tourist attractions in the country. It seems like that trend will continue.

Although other cities are still considered tourist hubs in the region, Perth's Swan River and valley have caught the attention of both national and international corporations, particularly those in the tourist industry and related fields. Some have already relocated their operations to Perth to preoccupy the market. As a result, job opportunities in the city have soared.

Resident Helen Leathers, formerly an architect, returned to Perth three years ago to get an advanced degree in tourism and hospitality administration. While she had difficulty finding a job in the construction industry, she had no such problems in her current field. "I received several job offers as soon as I graduated," Leathers said. "I could choose the company I wanted to work for."

For the last eighteen months, opportunities in related fields have continued to grow. Saito Tourist, one of the companies that relocated to Perth, is an example of that growth. John Gambino, a recruitment manager at Saito, said, "In the beginning, we started with 5 full-time agents, all of which quickly were added. And I'm planning to fill at least another 5 positions by the end of the year." The more businesses consider the possibility of relocating to Perth, the more demand for the jobs has in the field has increased.

To meet the demand, Western Australia University recently increased the number of students it admits, especially in tourism and related fields. Sarah Armstrong the program coordinator at Western Australia University, encourages graduating high school students to consider careers in tourism. "In addition to expert knowledge, successful businesspeople should possess the ability to analyze and handle difficult situations. They should be able to find creative solutions to problems," she added. "If they can do that so well, the field is suitable for them."

4 According to the article, why have some companies moved to Perth?

(A) It has development potential.
(B) It has a lot of qualified workers.
(C) It is a center of industry in its region.
(D) It has access to public transportation.

5 Why most likely did Ms. Leathers change her profession?

(A) Because she wanted to go back to school
(B) Because the number of jobs in the field of architecture was limited
(C) Because Ms. Armstrong recruited her
(D) Because she recently relocated to Perth

6 What is implied about Saito Tourist?

(A) It is expanding its workforce.
(B) It has offices all over the country.
(C) It mainly offers part-time positions.
(D) It is one of the newest companies in Perth.

7 What is probably true about Ms. Armstrong?

(A) She is employed by a university.
(B) She owns a recruiting company.
(C) She used to work at Saito Tourist.
(D) She teaches at a local high school.

Questions 8-10 refer to the following article.

A police officer on the streets typically feels a high degree of psychological stress and insecurity. A look at statistics will explain why. In 2018, a total of 201 police officers were killed on the streets. Over half of them died while making arrests, 25% while responding to calls for help, and 14% while making routine traffic stops.

One element which intensifies the sense of insecurity for the police officer is that he has no way to tell a likely cop killer from ordinary, law-abiding citizens. FBI experts have come up with detailed profiles of a number of felons, including the serial killer and rapist. Yet they have failed to provide characteristics of cop killers. All the experts can say is that they may be the last person a police officer perceives to be a threat.

An important source of stress to police officers is the growing number of cases to handle and the lack of manpower or time to handle them. There were 29 million crime victims in 2018. That figure grew by 12% the following year and has been rising ever since. In the meantime, police forces have not expanded their numbers, with the policeman-to-citizen ratio staying at two to 1,000. Faced with the increased incidence of crime and escalated degrees of violence in crime, police officers simply cannot fulfill the ideal role of active prevention of crime. They can only passively respond to it, and barely, at that.

8 What is the article mainly about?

(A) Sources of stress and insecurity for police officers
(B) Crime statistics and control for 2018
(C) Worsening security on the streets of the U.S.
(D) The serious shortage of police officers

9 What is NOT true of police fatality statistics for 2018?

(A) 201 policemen were killed on the streets.
(B) Over 100 policemen died while trying to arrest suspects.
(C) More than 40 had received calls for help.
(D) Most were killed while making traffic stops.

10 What is suggested as the ideal role of police officers?

(A) The immediate reaction to crime
(B) The protection of political liberty
(C) The active prevention of crime
(D) The enforcement of punishment

UNIT 27 온라인 대화문

온라인 대화문은 온라인 통신장비의 사용이 급격히 증가하면서 이를 이용한 수험생들의 실질적인 의사소통 능력을 평가하기 위한 유형이다. 문자 메시지(text-message chain)와 온라인 채팅 대화문(online chat discussion) 등이 독해 지문으로 등장한다. 또한 다자간의 대화문 형식도 출제되므로 대화에 참여한 화자 모두에게 집중하여 줄거리의 전반적인 흐름을 찾는 것이 중요하다.

■ 빈출 문제 유형

[전반 내용] What is the purpose of the text-message chain? 이 문자 메시지 대화문의 목적이 무엇인가?

What problem is mentioned in the online chat discussion?
이 온라인 대화문에서 언급되는 문제점이 무엇인가?

What is suggested about Jennifer? 제니퍼에 대해 무엇이 암시되는가?

[의도 찾기] At 2:19 P.M., what does Patrick mean when he writes, “How brave of you”?
오후 2시 19분에 패트릭이 쓴 “용감하다”는 무엇을 의미하는가?

[추후 당부] What is Mr. Bolton recommended to do during the conference call?
볼튼 씨는 화상회의에서 무엇을 하라고 추천 받는가?

What is Milo instructed to do? 마일로는 무엇을 하라고 지시 받는가?

■ 빈출 지문 내용

- 사내 동료들끼리 업무를 위한 대화문
- 고객과 고객센터 직원의 문제 해결을 위한 대화문
- 간단한 문의를 위한 대화문

■ 온라인 대화문 빈출 표현

① 주제문

I really want to know~ ~를 알고 싶습니다

I am sending a message to~ ~하기 위해 메시지를 보냅니다

I am looking for~ ~를 찾고 있습니다

I have some trouble~ ~에 문제가 생겼습니다

Are there any changes~? 혹시 ~에 변경사항이 있습니까?

② 추후 당부 사항

Why don't you[we]~? ~하지 않으실래요?

You'd better~ ~하는 게 좋아요

고득점 SOLUTION

① 숨은 의도를 찾는 문제가 어렵다면
문제로 출제된 표현이 지문 속에 없다고 생각하고 맥락을 이어주는 적절한 표현을 보기에서 고르도록 한다.

② 대화 지문의 주제 찾기가 어렵다면
지문의 초반에 드러난 화자들을 지칭하는 표현(I/we/you/here/there)에 집중하여 이들의 관계를 파악하도록 한다. 이 관계에서 드러난 용건이 곧 대화 지문의 주제가 된다.

✎ POINT ❶ 온라인 채팅 대화문

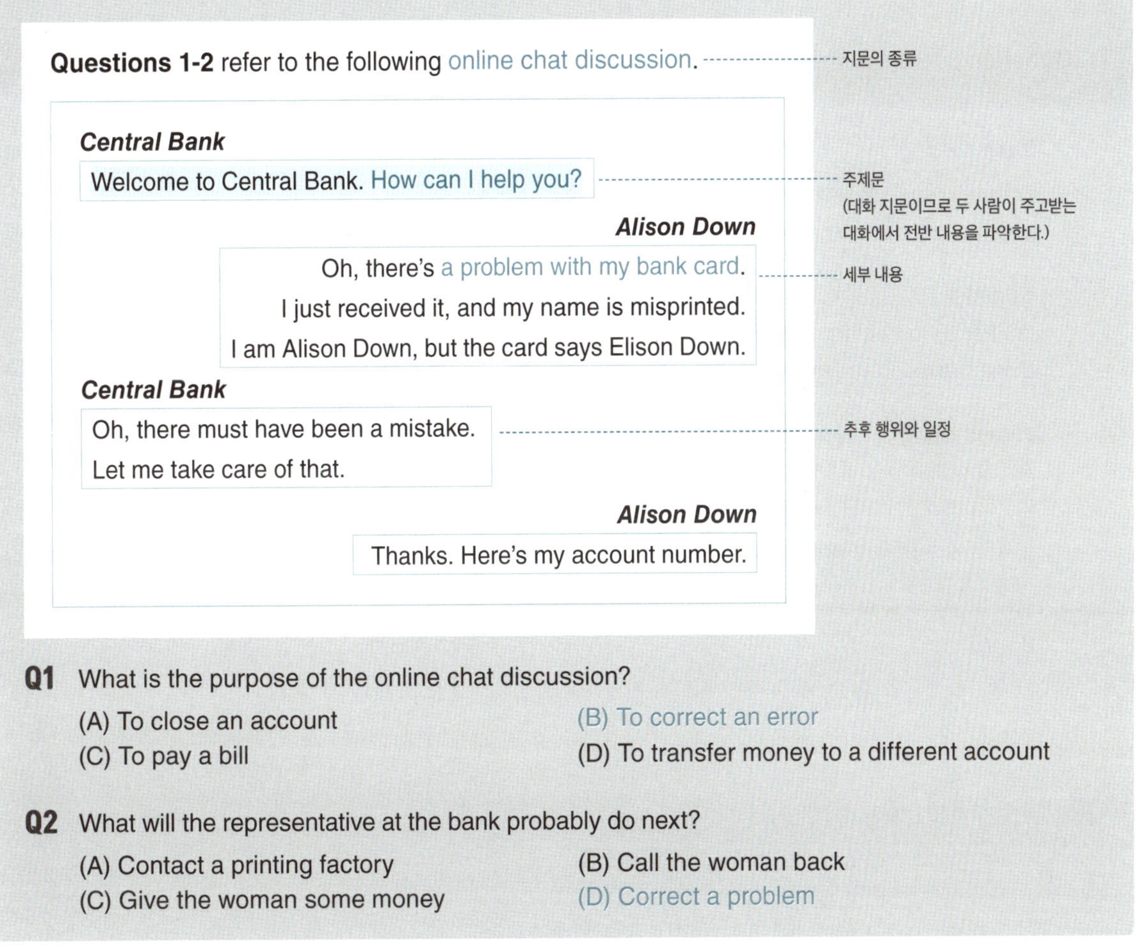
Questions 1-2 refer to the following online chat discussion. ------ 지문의 종류

Central Bank
Welcome to Central Bank. How can I help you? ------ 주제문 (대화 지문이므로 두 사람이 주고받는 대화에서 전반 내용을 파악한다.)

Alison Down
Oh, there's a problem with my bank card. ------ 세부 내용
I just received it, and my name is misprinted.
I am Alison Down, but the card says Elison Down.

Central Bank
Oh, there must have been a mistake. ------ 추후 행위와 일정
Let me take care of this.

Alison Down
Thanks. Here's my account number.

Q1 What is the purpose of the online chat discussion?

(A) To close an account
(B) To correct an error
(C) To pay a bill
(D) To transfer money to a different account

Q2 What will the representative at the bank probably do next?

(A) Contact a printing factory
(B) Call the woman back
(C) Give the woman some money
(D) Correct a problem

센트럴 은행: 센트럴 은행에 오신 것을 환영합니다. 어떻게 도와드릴까요?
앨리슨 다운: 아, 제 은행 카드에 문제가 있어요. 방금 받았는데, 제 이름이 잘못 인쇄되어 있네요. 저는 Alison Down인데, 카드에는 Elison Down으로 나왔어요.
센트럴 은행: 아, 실수가 있었나 보군요. 제가 처리해 드리겠습니다.
앨리슨 다운: 고마워요. 여기 제 계좌번호요.

Q1. 이 온라인 대화문의 목적은 무엇인가?
(A) 거래를 종료하기 위해 (B) 오류를 고치기 위해 (C) 청구서를 지불하기 위해 (D) 다른 계좌로 돈을 송금하기 위해

Q2. 은행 직원은 아마도 다음으로 무엇을 할 것인가?
(A) 인쇄 공장에 연락한다 (B) 여자에게 다시 전화한다 (C) 여자에게 돈을 준다 (D) 문제를 고친다

해설

Q1. '어떻게 도와 드릴까요'라는 말에 앨리슨은 'Oh, there's a problem with my bank card.'라며, 카드에 이름이 잘못되었다고 하므로 정답은 (B)이다.

Q2. 앨리슨의 은행 카드에 문제가 있음을 듣고 은행 직원은 'Let me take care of that.'이라며 자신이 처리하겠다고 말하고 있다. 즉, 그 문제를 바로잡을 것임을 알 수 있으므로 답은 (D)이다.

POINT ② 문자 메시지 대화문

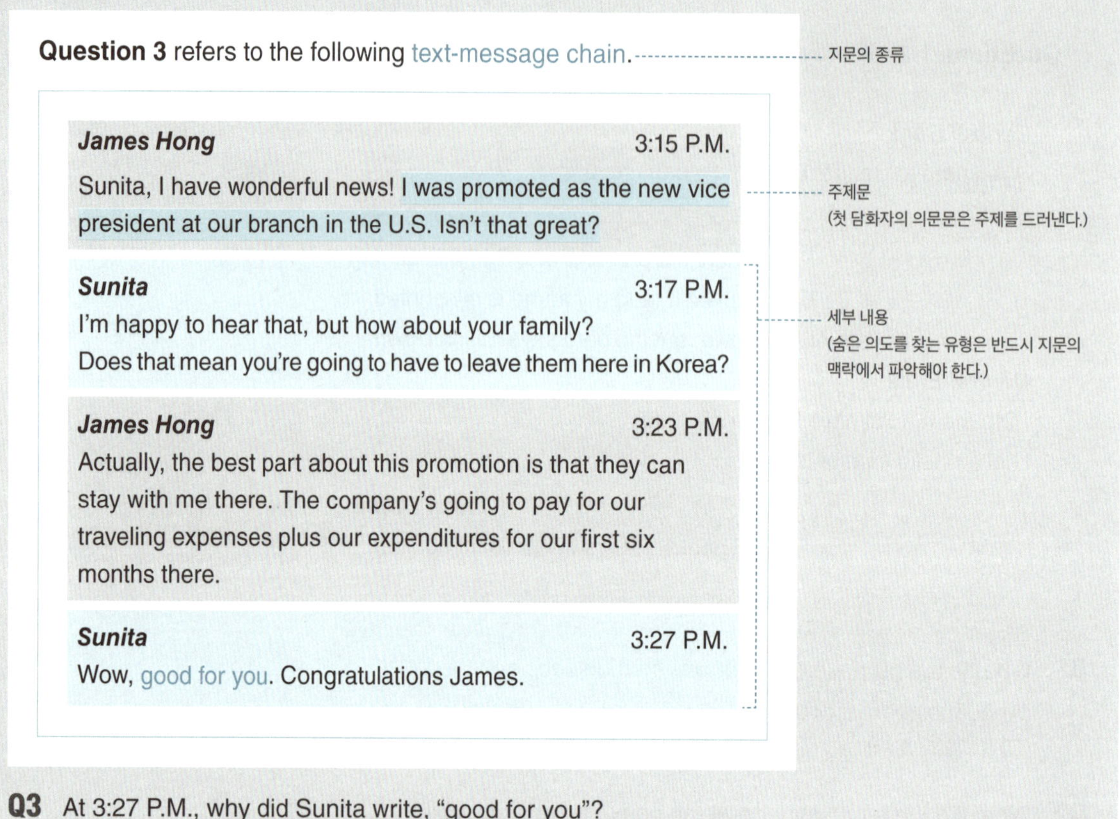

Question 3 refers to the following text-message chain. ---- 지문의 종류

James Hong 3:15 P.M.
Sunita, I have wonderful news! I was promoted as the new vice president at our branch in the U.S. Isn't that great?

---- 주제문
(첫 담화자의 의문문은 주제를 드러낸다.)

Sunita 3:17 P.M.
I'm happy to hear that, but how about your family? Does that mean you're going to have to leave them here in Korea?

---- 세부 내용
(숨은 의도를 찾는 유형은 반드시 지문의 맥락에서 파악해야 한다.)

James Hong 3:23 P.M.
Actually, the best part about this promotion is that they can stay with me there. The company's going to pay for our traveling expenses plus our expenditures for our first six months there.

Sunita 3:27 P.M.
Wow, good for you. Congratulations James.

Q3 At 3:27 P.M., why did Sunita write, "good for you"?

(A) Mr. Hong can work as a CEO in the U.S.
(B) Mr. Hong can take his family abroad with him.
(C) The company paid for Mr. Hong's retirement plan.
(D) The company will pay for Mr. Hong's expenses until he retires.

제임스 홍 (오후 3시 15분)	수니타, 좋은 소식이 있어요! 제가 우리 회사의 미국 지부 부사장으로 승진되었어요. 놀랍지 않아요?
수니타 (오후 3시 17분)	기쁜 소식이네요, 그런데 당신 가족은 어떻게 하고요, 그 말은 당신이 가족들을 이곳 한국에 두고 갈 것이란 말인가요?
제임스 홍 (오후 3시 23분)	사실, 이번 승진이 가장 좋은 점은 가족들이 그곳에서 나와 함께 머무를 수 있다는 점이에요. 회사에서 여행비를 포함하여 처음 6개월간의 경비를 지급해 주기로 하였어요.
수니타 (오후 3시 27분)	와, 정말 잘됐네요! 축하해요, 제임스.

Q3. 오후 3시 27분에 수니타가 쓴 "잘됐다"는 무엇을 의미하는가?
(A) 홍 씨는 미국에서 최고경영자로 일하게 되었다.
(B) 홍 씨는 가족들을 해외로 함께 데려갈 수 있게 되었다.
(C) 회사는 홍 씨의 퇴직에 대한 비용을 지불했다.
(D) 회사에서 홍 씨가 퇴직할 때까지 그의 경비를 부담할 것이다.

해설

제임스는 그가 가족들을 해외에 데려갈 수 있으며, 처음 6달간의 경비를 회사에서 지급해 준다는 것에 기뻐하고 있다. 따라서 수니타는 이것을 듣고 잘됐다고 말하고 있으므로 정답은 (B)가 된다.

온라인 대화문 관련 빈출 어휘

① 업무 관련

temporary position 비정규직	establishment 설립물, 시설
predecessor 전임자	take a day off 하루 휴가 내다
promote 승진시키다	maternity leave 출산휴가
replace (직책을) 대신하다	on a business trip 출장 중인
replacement 후임자	extension 내선
performance appraisal 업무 평가	return one's call 답신 전화를 하다
obliged 책임을 진	persuade 설득하다
settlement 분쟁 해결	voice mail 음성 메시지
strike 파업하다	run out of ~을 다 써버리다
convention 집회	installation 설치
enroll 등록하다	commercial 상품 광고
call off 취소하다	deadline extension 마감일 연장
accommodate (의견을) 수용하다	workforce 인력
retreat 야유회	surplus 흑자
come up with (아이디어 등을) 내놓다	deficit 적자

② 일상생활 관련

opening hour 개점 시간	itinerary 일정표
patron 단골고객	lodge 숙박하다
prohibit 금지하다	confirmation 확정
out of stock 품절된	traffic congestion 교통체증
back order 이월 주문하다	be stuck in traffic 차가 밀리다
proceed 처리하다	commute 통근하다
line up 제품군	detour 우회하다
get a full refund 전액 환불 받다	culinary 음식의
reasonable (가격이) 적절한	seasoning 조미료
customize ~을 주문 받아 만들다	caterer 출장 음식 제공업체
waive a fee 수수료를 면제하다	grocery store 식료품점
register for 신청하다	portable 휴대 가능한
available 이용 가능한	durable 견고한
admission 입장료	questionnaire 설문지
remains 유물	break down 고장 나다

해설 p.408

Kathy Bates

Hi, Mr. Smith! Have you seen Mr. Knepper? I've been looking for him all morning.

Jaden Smith

Yes, I saw him go to the conference room with Mr. Reed and a client. Why are you looking for him?

Kathy Bates

He left his cell phone on the table in the cafeteria. So I could return it to him.

Jaden Smith

Well, I suggest you just wait until they're done. It seems to be a very important meeting, and I don't think they'd like to be interrupted.

Q1 What will most likely Ms. Bates do next?

(A) Go to the conference room
(B) Return a phone after a meeting
(C) Continue looking for Mr. Knepper
(D) Leave the phone on a table in the cafeteria

Joshep

Do you have any software that will let me keep track of our expenses in all of our European divisions? Of course, safety and privacy are the first consideration.

Pass Mark Software Rep

You don't have to worry. Some programs boast high speed with a few errors. And some programs are a little bit slow, but their accuracy is 100% guaranteed. Would you like me to e-mail you the information?

Joshep

That would be great. Thank you.

Q2 What is the text-message chain about?

(A) An inquiry about the expenses of the European divisions
(B) An inquiry about financial software
(C) An inquiry about the warranty for some software
(D) An inquiry about an online service

Q3 What does the representative mean when he writes, "You don't have to worry"?

(A) Security is a major issue when choosing a product.
(B) Any information on the products can be e-mailed.
(C) One of the software programs is totally correct.
(D) His company has a variety of progarms.

해설 p. 409

Questions 1-2 refer to the following text-message chain.

Danny DeVito **9:10 A.M.**
Hi, Sharon. I received a call from Newsroom 24 last night. They're interested in interviewing someone from our research team today.

Sharon Rooney **9:11 A.M.**
About what?

Danny DeVito **9:13 A.M.**
About the public reaction to the current city project we're working on. They want to broadcast a segment tonight. I'd recommend Seth, but he is out of the office right now. So would you like to meet them?

Sharon Rooney **9:14 A.M.**
Sure. I'm almost done analyzing the votes on what you asked me to. It would be a good time for the interview.

Danny DeVito **9:21 A.M.**
Okay. I just talked to Ian Chen from Newsroom 24. He should arrive in about an hour. He suggested you leave the report out.

Sharon Rooney **9:23 A.M.**
That sounds good. Well, I'll submit it and report on it to you after the interview.

1 What is suggested about Mr. DeVito?
(A) He is Ms. Rooney's supervisor.
(B) He is interviewing someone today.
(C) He is changing his work schedule today.
(D) He is meeting Ms. Rooney on the second floor.

2 At 9:21 A.M., what does Mr. DeVito most likely mean when he writes, "He suggested you leave the report out"?
(A) The results will be finalized by analyzing the data.
(B) Seth may need to use the feedback.
(C) The survey report might be filmed for tonight's news.
(D) The documents will not be stolen.

Questions 3-6 refer to the following text-message chain.

Lupita Nyong'o [7:30 P.M.]
Hi, all. When I went to work 30 minutes ago, all the air conditioners on the 7th floor were on. Does anyone know how that happened?

Winston Duke [7:33 P.M.]
Right before I left the office this evening, they were turned off at 6:00 P.M.

Elisabeth Moss [7:35 P.M.]
Yes. When I went up there again to take my briefcase around 6:30 P.M., the air conditioners were off.

Lupita Nyong'o [7:37 P.M.]
Okay. I think there's definitely a problem given that this also happened last Thursday.

Winston Duke [7:42 P.M.]
I agree. The air conditioners must be turned on again before someone goes to work. I'll tell Mr. Choi, the building supervisor, to fix them when I get to work for my shift.

Lupita Nyong'o [7:48 P.M.]
Why don't we contact the company that did the installation? I think that would be a better idea.

Winston Duke [7:51 P.M.]
Will do.

3 What is most likely true about Ms. Nyong'o?
(A) She works in a maintenance office.
(B) She works the night shift.
(C) She lives near her workplace.
(D) She has a part-time job.

4 Who was the last person to see that the air conditioners were off?
(A) Ms. Nyong'o
(B) Mr. Duke
(C) Ms. Moss
(D) Mr. Choi

5 At 7:42 P.M., what does Mr. Duke most likely mean when he writes, "I agree"?
(A) He believes that the air conditioner needs to be repaired.
(B) He plans to follow Ms. Nyong'o's requests.
(C) He thinks that maintenance service will be provided promptly.
(D) He knows that Mr. Choi saw him turn off the air conditioners.

6 What will Mr. Duke most likely do next?
(A) Report the problem to the manager
(B) Turn on the air conditioner
(C) Fill out some paperwork
(D) Call another company

Questions 7-10 refer to the following online chat discussion.

Parker Sevak 9:45 A.M.

Everyone, good news! The new machines for the highly effective automatical inspection system have arrived at our facility. We have already used the system, so we expect it to considerably cut down on the time needed to complete large jobs. We will also notice a dramatic increase in productivity.

9:48 A.M. **Michael Chernus**

Yeah, that's right. When I inspected some products this week, the machines ran so smoothly and fast that I myself saw a huge difference. These machines are nearly twice as quick as the older ones. As you know, they hardly ever break down, too.

Samrat Chakrabarti 9:51 A.M.

Great to hear, Michael. I really hope to try them out soon!

9:51 A.M. **Sara Colangelo**

Are they only for your factory? We've never changed machines here since I was hired five years ago.

Parker Sevak 9:53 A.M.

I heard that the head office has decided to purchase them for all our facilities, Sara. Plymouth and Bristol will install their own on September 1 and October 14, respectively.

9:55 A.M. **Maggie Gyllenhaal**

Actually, no. Now that the plan was rescheduled, they will be delivered this Friday around 11:00 A.M. instead of the time listed on the original schedule. They will probably take a day to be installed, and you need to notify the staff members to make rooms for the machine in advance.

7 What is mainly being discussed?

(A) Plans to open new facilities
(B) An equipment upgrade
(C) The efficiency of a machine
(D) An upcoming conference

8 At 9:48 A.M., what does Mr. Chernus most likely mean when he writes, "Yeah, that's right"?

(A) He has completed a job in time.
(B) He accepted a suggestion regarding an installation.
(C) New machines will allow employees to be more productive.
(D) The updated newsletter is better than the previous version.

9 What is suggested about Ms. Colangelo?

(A) She is a new supervisor.
(B) She hopes to visit headquarters soon.
(C) She does not work in the same place as Mr. Sevak.
(D) She needs to repair an old machine.

10 Why does Ms. Gyllenhaal send a message to the discussion?

(A) To reschedule a delivery
(B) To make a recommendation
(C) To inform her colleagues of a change
(D) To request some help

UNIT 28 이중 지문

이중 지문은 한 세트당 5문제씩 구성되어, 총 2세트로 10문제가 출제된다. 이중 지문은 읽어야 할 양이 많기 때문에 자칫 맥락을 놓치기 쉽다. 그러나 첫 지문에서 정확히 주제문을 찾아 파악해 두면 두 번째 지문에서도 그 내용이 동일하게 반복됨을 알 수 있다. 후속 지문도 첫 지문과 동일한 맥락으로 두 지문을 하나의 지문처럼 읽을 수 있다. 또한 한 세트당 마킹 포함 5분의 시간을 정확히 안배하여 성공적인 문제 풀이가 가능하도록 철저한 훈련이 필요하다.

■ 빈출 지문 내용

[e-mails]	회사 동료들끼리 공통 주제를 가지고 주고받는 이메일
[advertisement & letter]	구인 광고와 구직을 위한 편지
[advertisement & e-mail]	상품 광고와 구입 문의 혹은 배송 문제 해결을 위한 이메일
[memo & e-mail]	회람에 대한 추후 당부, 목적 달성을 위한 이메일
[notice & review]	행사 공지와 그 행사에 대한 평가
[article & letter]	기사와 그 내용을 바탕으로 한 편지
[form & e-mail]	설문지, 스케줄, 청구서 등의 양식과 이에 대한 문의, 요청을 위한 이메일

■ 빈출 문제 유형

What is the main purpose of the first letter? 첫 번째 편지의 주요 목적이 무엇인가?

What is indicated in the second form? 두 번째 양식에서 무엇을 언급하고 있는가?

Why is Kelly the most qualified applicant? 켈리는 왜 가장 자격을 갖춘 지원자인가?

On what day does the trade fair need two more staff members? 무역 박람회에서 언제 직원 2명이 더 필요한가?

According to the first advertisement, what will Mr. McRyan do next week?
첫 번째 광고에 따르면 맥라이언 씨는 다음 주에 무엇을 할 것인가?

■ 이중 지문 접근 전략

① 첫 번째 지문의 주제문을 파악하여 맥락을 유추한다.

② 첫 번째 지문에 해당하는 문제를 읽는다.

③ 첫 번째 지문을 속독하며 문제의 답을 찾는다.

④ 첫 번째 지문의 마지막 부분의 추후 당부 내용을 반드시 파악한다.

⑤ 첫 번째 지문의 추후 당부 내용을 두 번째 지문의 주제문에 연결해 두 지문을 하나의 지문처럼 파악한다.

⑥ 두 번째 지문에 해당하는 문제를 읽는다.

⑦ 두 지문의 흐름을 연결해 남은 부분을 속독하며 문제의 답을 찾는다.

고득점 SOLUTION

① 지문의 양 때문에 전체적인 맥락을 파악하기 어렵다면

첫 번째 지문의 끝부분에 나오는 추후 당부 사항은 두 번째 지문이 생성되는 근거를 제공한다. 그러므로 이 부분에서 첫 번째 지문과 두 번째 지문을 이어 붙이는 연결고리를 찾아 하나의 글처럼 읽어서 전체적인 맥락을 파악하도록 한다.

② 문제 푸는 시간이 부족하다면

이중 지문과 삼중 지문의 문항 수가 총 25개이므로 마킹을 포함한 문제 풀이를 위해 적어도 25분의 시간을 확보하도록 한다. 그리고 LC 방송이 종료된 직후에 RC 시간이 시작되면, 다중 지문 25문항을 집중하기에 제일 좋은 시간대를 확보하여 전략적으로 시간을 안배하는 연습도 반드시 필요하다. 이러한 연습을 통해 본인이 가장 효율적으로 다중 지문을 풀 수 있는 전략을 확인하고, 꾸준한 훈련을 통하여 실전에 대비하여야 한다. (다중 지문은 지문의 양에 비해 문제의 난이도가 높지 않기 때문에 초반에 푸는 것도 효과적이다.)

③ 통합 지문 문제의 해결이 어렵다면

이중 지문은 서로 연계되어 있기 때문에 첫 번째 지문의 내용이 두 번째 지문에도 거의 반복된다. 다만, 이것을 동의어로 바꾸어 놓기 때문에 자칫하면 다른 정보로 인식할 수 있다. 그러므로 독해를 할 때는 주제문을 중심으로 전반적인 맥락에 집중해야 하며, 주요 핵심어에는 따로 표시해 두어 필요할 때 연결해서 생각할 수 있도록 미리 준비해야 한다.

POINT 1

Question 1 refers to the following advertisement and e-mail. 지문의 종류

Job openings at Matrix Technologies

1 제목을 통해 지문의 전반적인 내용을 추론한다.

Position: Senior Financial Consultant
Requirement: Candidates should have a strong background in accounting, budgeting, and finance management. At least 7 years of related experience required.

4 모리슨 씨가 갖추어야 할 자격요건을 찾는다.

Position: Security Director
Requirement: Candidates should have a good understanding of security policies and risk assessment. Must be willing to move to new locations on new projects when required. At least 5 years of related experience necessary.

Position: Human Resources Officer
Requirement: Strong communication skills are required. Please enclose a writing sample with the application. At least 6 years of related experience is necessary.

Position: Project Manager
Requirement: A university degree in mechanical engineering or electrical engineering. Candidates must have experience supervising large-scale operations.

How to apply: Send a cover letter and a résumé by e-mail to Dylan Walsh at Jobs@matrixtech.com. Please mention the position being applied for in the cover letter and include a list of recent references in your résumé.
Qualified applicants will be invited for an interview.

To: Dylan Walsh (jobs@matrixtech.com)
From: Tina Morrison
Date: January 14
Subject: Position at Matrix Technologies

Dear Mr. Walsh,

I'm writing in response to your job advertisement for the position of senior financial consultant.

3 모리슨 씨가 원하는 직책이 드러나 있다.

I have 8 years of experience in the field and have worked extensively in budgeting and accounting. In the position of senior manager at my previous job, I led several financial projects and initiatives. Earlier, I also worked as a reporter with a reputed financial magazine.
I am interested in this opening in your company and would appreciate an opportunity to discuss it further. I have included my résumé and a list of references for your review.
Thank you. I look forward to hearing from you.

Tina Morrison

Q1 What is a requirement of the position mentioned in the e-mail? ---------- 2 문제의 핵심어를 파악한다. (모리슨 씨가 쓴 두 번째 지문과 첫 지문에 언급된 'a requirement'를 통합한다.)

(A) A willingness to relocate
(B) A background in accounting
(C) Good communication skills
(D) Experience supervising project

PART 7

매트릭스 테크놀로지 구인

직책: 선임 금융 컨설턴트
요구사항: 지원자는 회계와 예산, 금융 관리에 확실한 지식을 가지고 있어야 합니다. 적어도 7년간의 관련 업무 경험이 요구됩니다.

직책: 보안 감독관
요구사항: 지원자는 보안 정책과 위험 관리에 대한 훌륭한 이해가 있어야 합니다. 필요 시 새로운 프로젝트에 의해 새로운 위치로 옮겨 다닐 수 있어야 합니다. 적어도 5년간의 관련 업무 경험이 필요합니다.

직책: 인사부 사무원
요구사항: 뛰어난 의사소통 능력이 필요합니다. 지원서에 서면 샘플을 첨부하세요. 관련 경력이 최소 6년 필요합니다.

직책: 프로젝트 담당자
요구사항: 기계 공학 또는 전기 공학 학사 학위. 지원자는 대규모 운영 감독 경험이 있어야 합니다.

지원 방법: 딜런 월시에게 이력서와 자기소개서를 이메일 Jobs@matrixtech.com으로 보내주십시오. 자기소개서에는 지원하는 직책에 대해 언급해 주시기 바라며, 이력서에는 최근 추천인 명단이 포함되어야 합니다.
적합한 지원자에게는 인터뷰가 안내될 것입니다.

수신: 딜런 월시 (jobs@matrixtech.com)
발신: 티나 모리슨
날짜: 1월 14일
제목: 매트릭스 테크놀로지의 직책

월시 씨께,

저는 귀사의 선임 금융 컨설턴트직에 관한 광고를 보고 지원하려고 합니다.
저는 예산과 회계 업무에 관한 8년간의 업무 경험이 있습니다. 지난 직장에서 선임 매니저 직책으로 일하면서 여러 가지 금융 프로젝트와 설계를 이끌었습니다. 그 전에, 명성 있는 금융 잡지에서 기자로 활동하기도 했습니다.
저는 귀사의 이번 채용에 관심이 있으며, 더 이야기할 기회를 갖고 싶습니다. 면접을 위한 제 이력서와 추천인 명단을 보실 수 있도록 첨부합니다.
감사합니다. 좋은 소식 기대하겠습니다.

티나 모리슨

Q1. 이메일에서 언급한 직책의 요구사항은 무엇인가?
(A) 재배치를 기꺼이 받아들임
(B) 회계에 대한 지식
(C) 좋은 커뮤니케이션 기술
(D) 프로젝트 감독 경험

해설

두 번째 지문, 첫 번째 문장에서 'I'm writing in response to your job advertisement for the position of senior financial consultant.'에서 지원하고 싶은 직책은 '선임 금융 컨설턴트'이다. 따라서 첫 번째 지문 '선임 금융 컨설턴트'의 요구사항을 보면 '확실한 회계 지식'(a strong background in accounting)이라고 했으므로 정답은 (B)이다.

Questions 1-5 refer to the following notice and e-mail.

Ana de Armas to Become Director of Client Services

The vice president's office is pleased to announce that Ana de Armas has accepted the position of director of client services and will officially begin this role on August 14th.

Ms. de Armas began her career with Presidium as a marketing associate 12 years ago. Her knowledge, skills, and ability were apparent, and 5 years later, she was asked to join the client services division as an associate director. She has excelled in that role for the past 7 years and is now more than ready to take over as the director of client services, which was made vacant because of Roberta Paquette's retirement.

Ms. de Armas will be reporting directly to senior vice president Peter McCarthy, who said, "Ana's expertise in marketing and far-reaching industry relationships will be a tremendous asset to Presidium and all of our clients. She will be instrumental in expanding and strengthening our client services."

Congratulations to Ms. de Armas. We wish her all the best in her new position.

To: Ana de Armas
From: Barry Allen
Date: Tuesday, August 2
Subject: Congratulations!

Dear Ms. de Armas,

We are all delighted that you are staying with us and look forward to your continued leadership.

I wanted to invite you to a formal luncheon that the client services division is hosting for some of our top clients. It will be tomorrow from 11:30 A.M. to 1:30 P.M. in Room 210 in the Reynolds Building.

Even though this takes place before you officially start your new position, it will be a good chance to introduce yourself to some of our clients that you may not have met yet. Plus, your new boss will be making a speech!

Please let me know if you are able to attend.

Barry Allen

Q1 Where would the notice most likely appear?

(A) In a business journal
(B) In a company newsletter
(C) In a city newspaper
(D) In a company financial report

Q2 What does the notice suggest about Ms. de Armas?

(A) She was recruited from another company.
(B) She has received several promotions.
(C) She will work for Ms. Paquette.
(D) She will take on a new role temporarily.

Q3 In the notice, the word "apparent" in paragraph 2, line 2, is closest in meaning to

(A) interim
(B) sincere
(C) ambiguous
(D) evident

Q4 Who will be speaking at the luncheon?

(A) Peter McCarthy
(B) Roberta Paquette
(C) Barry Allen
(D) Ana de Armas

Q5 What is indicated about the luncheon?

(A) It is for company employees.
(B) It requires a ticket to attend.
(C) It takes place before August 14.
(D) It will be at a restaurant.

Questions 1-5 refer to the following article and e-mail.

Renovations for the Blackberry Hill Region

May 7

Howard City—Since the city's museum has decided to relocate across town to a more spacious building on Bainford Street, the city council has been accepting bids for the use of the museum's space on Blackberry Hill. Many proposals have been submitted by local and national developers. Two proposals in particular have emerged as strong contenders.

One promising bid coming from Lean Construction suggests building an office complex on the hill. This project could serve to attract new businesses and to provide jobs for local residents over the next five years. However, such an ambitious project would take almost three years to complete. Additionally, these business tenants would require full-day parking privileges for their employees, and the parking problem in the area could be even more pronounced than its already high level. The three-year-old firm is currently undertaking similar building projects in London and Paris.

Another competing bid has come from Maverick Industries, a commercial developer with experience in the city. The company is planning an elaborate new shopping area. This project would provide residents with department stores, restaurants, and movie theaters. It is an attractive option for the city because this would provide residents with the shopping and entertainment areas that they lack. Maverick Industry, you may recall, was in charge of renovating the waterfront district.

In a poll conducted by the *Howard City Herald*, residents were asked which plan they prefer. The results indicated slightly stronger support for the Maverick development scheme. Although residents generally agree that either plan will have a positive effect on the city's economy, one outspoken interest group strongly opposes any commercial development of an area that once offered public service and is collecting signatures to petition the city to set aside the space for a community park.

by Brent Ackerly
Eagle Eye Daily

해설 p. 412

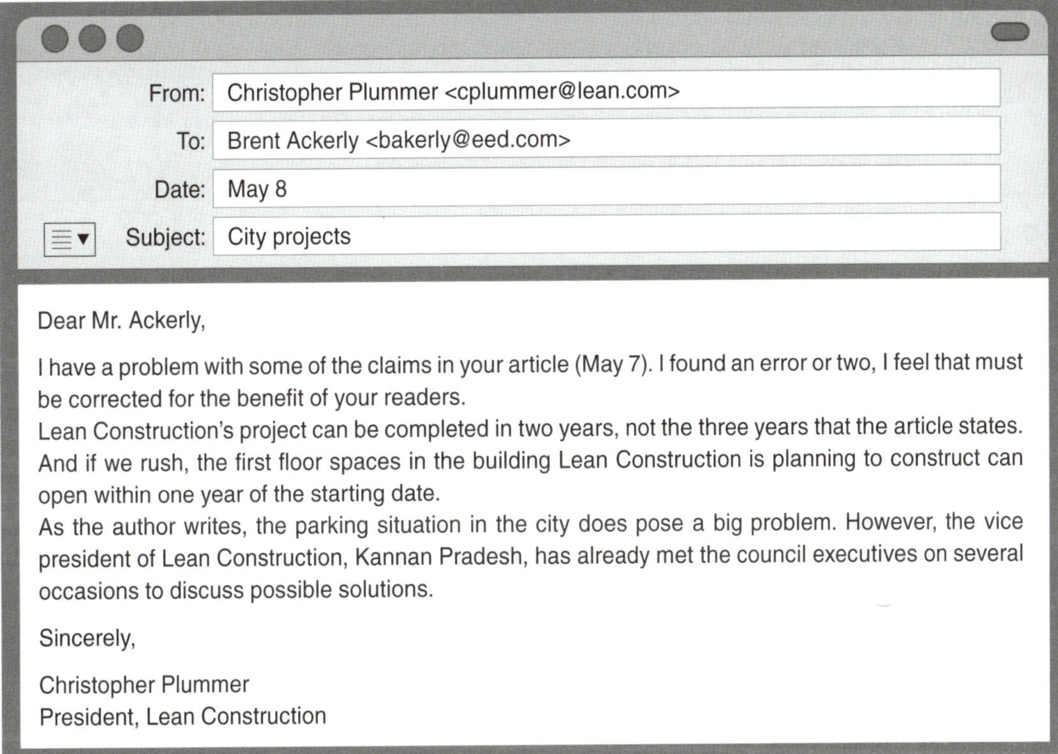

From: Christopher Plummer <cplummer@lean.com>
To: Brent Ackerly <bakerly@eed.com>
Date: May 8
Subject: City projects

Dear Mr. Ackerly,

I have a problem with some of the claims in your article (May 7). I found an error or two, I feel that must be corrected for the benefit of your readers.
Lean Construction's project can be completed in two years, not the three years that the article states. And if we rush, the first floor spaces in the building Lean Construction is planning to construct can open within one year of the starting date.
As the author writes, the parking situation in the city does pose a big problem. However, the vice president of Lean Construction, Kannan Pradesh, has already met the council executives on several occasions to discuss possible solutions.

Sincerely,

Christopher Plummer
President, Lean Construction

1 What is the main purpose of the article?
(A) To inform the public about possible renovations
(B) To give a history of two development companies
(C) To ask for reader feedback on construction proposals
(D) To announce the new location of the city's museum

2 What do most residents think about the two proposals?
(A) They will cause too many parking problems.
(B) They will benefit the economy.
(C) They see commercial development as harmful.
(D) They are poor replacements for a museum.

3 What is implied about Howard City?
(A) Its regions need improvement.
(B) It has hired Lean Construction in the past.
(C) It has too many entertainment areas.
(D) Parking is a big problem there.

4 According to the e-mail, what is Mr. Plummer's main complaint about the article?
(A) The author inaccurately projects the construction time.
(B) It takes Kannan Pradesh's statements out of context.
(C) It skews the statistics of the poll.
(D) It is one-sided in its presentation.

5 What is suggested about Mr. Plummer?
(A) He lives in Howard City.
(B) He recently built a condominium.
(C) He has worked with Howard City before.
(D) He has worked in Europe.

Questions 6-10 refer to the following e-mail and survey.

To	Joe Cortese <jcortese@gletter.com>
From	Customer Service <cservice@amazonsupplies.com>
Date	December 11
Subject	Your recent order

Dear Mr. Cortese,

It is our aim at Amazon Supplies to provide superior products and customer services. So we routinely ask our customers to find out how we are doing. According to our sales records, you made a purchase on December 7. If you let us know about your purchase experience at amazonsupplies.com, we would appreciate it, and we can continue to maintain our high level of customer satisfaction. You can complete the survey in only about 10 minutes. So please respond by the end of this month and receive a 20-percent discount coupon next month.

Click on the link at amazonsupplies.com/survey to begin your survey.

Thank you.

---

www.amazonsupplies.com/survey

Thank you for participating in the survey. Please, select the answers you think best match your most recent online shopping experience at amazonsupplies.com.

1. The date of last purchase : ***December 7***
2. How often do you visit the www.amazonsupplies.com Web site?

   _____ Daily _____ Weekly _____ Monthly _X_ Quarterly _____ Yearly
3. I found a good selection of merchandise available on the Web site.

   _X_ Strongly agree _____ Agree _____ Disagree _____ Strongly disagree
4. I found the Web site easy to navigate.

   _____ Strongly agree _X_ Agree _____ Disagree _____ Strongly disagree
5. What was your last purchase?

   _X_ Printer _____ Stationery product _____ Desk accessory

   _____ Office furniture _____ Computer _____ Computer accessory

Comments :

My purchase at the beginning of this month was highly satisfactory. I regularly place orders for paper supplies to make copies every few months. Unfortunately, the printer in my office broke suddenly, and it needed to be replaced with a new one immediately. I spoke with your sales representative, who recommended a different model from the one we had, given the volume of work our office does. So far it has been working well in our busy office. I really appreciated the recommendation and expedited next-day delivery.

6 What is indicated about Amazon Supplies?

(A) It provides merchandise at low prices.
(B) It has several international branches.
(C) It periodically requires feedback from customers.
(D) It recently expanded its selection of products.

7 In the e-mail, the word "aim" in paragraph 1, line 1, is closest in meaning to

(A) requirement
(B) direction
(C) result
(D) intention

8 What is implied about Mr. Cortese?

(A) He purchased an item from Amazon Supplies for the first time.
(B) He had a problem with the delivery.
(C) He changed his personal information.
(D) He will probably receive a discount next year.

9 What does Mr. Cortese suggest about his latest purchase?

(A) The delivery took much longer than expected.
(B) He was pleased with the advice.
(C) A defective product was sent.
(D) It was delivered for free.

10 What does Mr. Cortese usually purchase?

(A) Stationery supplies
(B) Copy machines
(C) Desk accessories
(D) Computers

Questions 11-15 refer to following article and e-mail.

Philadelphia (Oct 1) — America's Best-loved Story Society (ABSS) has selected 7 promising budding writers as finalists in a competition for a $50,000 grant. The prize, which has been awarded yearly over the past 3 years, is intended to assist new artists with costs related to their writing.

Previously, only nonfiction works, which are about real people and events, were eligible for the award. However, starting this year, when the competition is in its fourth year, the ABSS has decided to expand eligibility to historical fiction novels.

"Various novel concepts and styles considerably impressed us, and that reached a peak this year", said Anna Boden, the director of ABSS, "Since all of the entries are about various topics and focus on different periods, they also provided more unique and various perspectives on historical events. Therefore, it was so difficult for us to narrow down the finalists to seven writers."

The seven entries met with ABSS's board of directors a month ago to answer questions concerning their production goals and writing motivation. The winner, who will be determined by a panel, will be announced next month. If you want to know more about them, visit the Web site at www.abssmoviefestival.com.

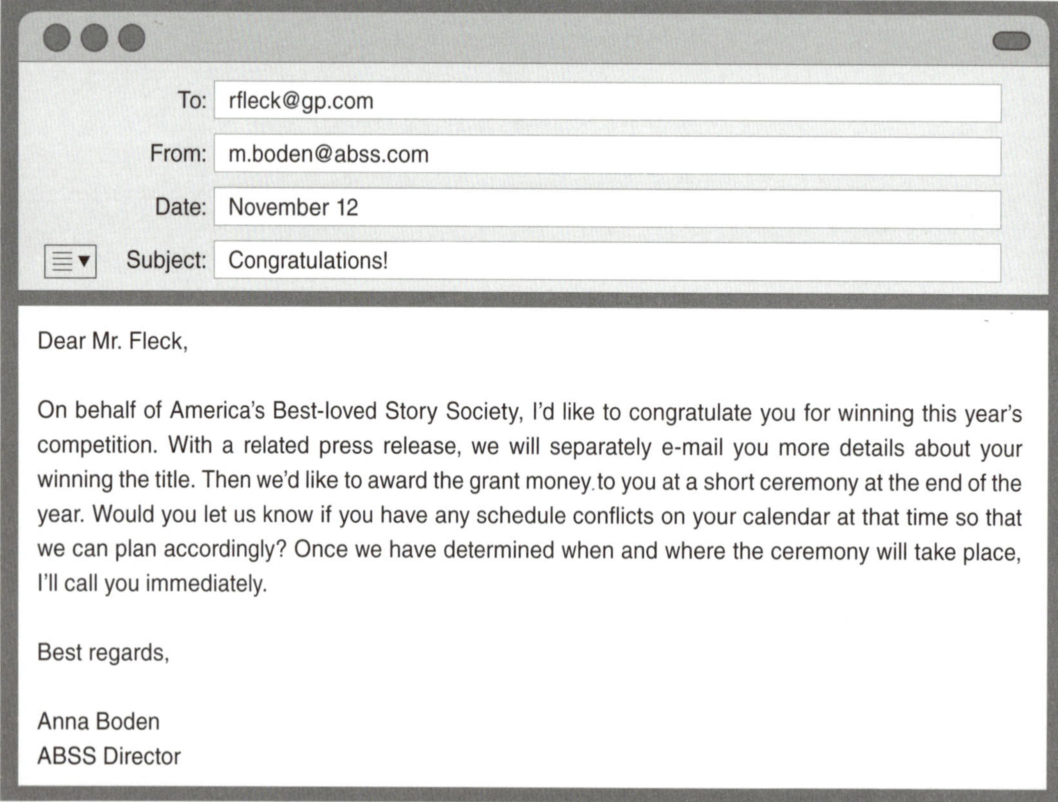

To: rfleck@gp.com
From: m.boden@abss.com
Date: November 12
Subject: Congratulations!

Dear Mr. Fleck,

On behalf of America's Best-loved Story Society, I'd like to congratulate you for winning this year's competition. With a related press release, we will separately e-mail you more details about your winning the title. Then we'd like to award the grant money to you at a short ceremony at the end of the year. Would you let us know if you have any schedule conflicts on your calendar at that time so that we can plan accordingly? Once we have determined when and where the ceremony will take place, I'll call you immediately.

Best regards,

Anna Boden
ABSS Director

11 How does this year's competition differ from previous ones?

(A) It allows other types of novels.
(B) Several winners will be selected.
(C) More grant money will be awarded.
(D) It is being promoted internationally.

12 In the article, the word "considerably" in paragraph 3, line 1, is closest in meaning to

(A) artistically
(B) substantially
(C) emotionally
(D) historically

13 According to the article, what can readers do online?

(A) Read about judges
(B) View application guidelines
(C) Vote for candidates
(D) Watch videos for previews

14 What is implied about Mr. Fleck?

(A) He was interviewed in September.
(B) He works with Ms. Boden.
(C) He created a movie.
(D) He won a grant three years ago.

15 In the e-mail, what is Mr. Fleck asked to do?

(A) Make a reservation for the awards ceremony
(B) Make an announcement in a press release
(C) Confirm his availability
(D) Serve as a member of a panel

UNIT 29 삼중 지문

삼중 지문은 이중 지문에서 나왔던 세부 내용의 일부를 발췌하여 제3의 시각 자료로 제시한 형태로, 다중 지문의 통합적 파악 능력을 평가하고자 하는 유형이다. 정보들이 구조화되어 표나 그래프와 같은 서식으로 주어지기 때문에 오히려 지문 독해에 대한 부담은 줄었다고 볼 수 있다. 다만 동의어로 패러프레이징된 표현이 늘어나 주제와 전반적인 맥락에 대한 이해가 없으면 이해하기 어려울 수 있다. 그러므로 유의어와 동의어를 통한 어휘 학습과 첫 지문에서 마지막 지문까지 흐름을 잡는 주제문 찾기 연습을 꾸준히 해야 한다. 또한 표나 그래프 같은 형식에 익숙할 수 있게 다양한 서식을 확인할 필요가 있다.

■ 빈출 지문 내용

[advertisement & invoice & letter]	상품 광고 + 주문서/청구서 + 문제 해결을 위한 고객의 편지
[notice & form & e-mail]	공지 + 공지사항을 다룬 표 + 문의를 위한 이메일
[advertisement & letter & résumé]	구인 광고 + 구직자의 지원 편지 + 첨부된 이력서
[invitation & report & article]	행사 초대장 + 행사 보고서 + 기사
[e-mail & itinerary & e-mail]	일정 확인 요청 이메일 + 출장 일정표 + 일정 확정 이메일

■ 삼중 지문 빈출 문제 유형

How much was the shipping charge for Mr. Sato's order? 사토 씨 주문의 배송료는 얼마였는가?
What actor does Ms. Rivera refer to in review? 리베라 씨는 논평에 어떤 배우를 언급하고 있는가?
According to the information, what is necessary? 정보지에 따르면 무엇이 필수적인가?
What is NOT mentioned in the invoice? 청구서에 언급되지 않은 것이 무엇인가?
What is the model number Mr. Benton purchased? 벤톤 씨가 구입한 상품 번호는 무엇인가?
How many sessions are scheduled on October 29? 10월 29일에 몇 개의 회의가 예정되어 있는가?
Which item is NOT included in the deposit? 어떤 항목이 계약금에 포함되지 않은가?
What is the changed function of TZ-035? TZ-035의 변경된 기능은 무엇인가?

■ 삼중 지문 접근 전략

① 첫 번째 지문의 주제문을 파악하여 맥락을 유추한다.

② 두 번째 지문의 주제문을 파악하여 맥락을 유추한다.

③ 세 번째 지문의 주제문을 파악하여 맥락을 유추한다.

④ 세 개의 지문에 대한 유추 내용을 토대로 각 문항을 지문별로 분류하며 핵심어를 정리해 둔다.

⑤ 지문별 문제의 핵심어를 토대로 각 지문을 속독하며 답을 찾는다.

고득점 SOLUTION

① 세 지문의 방대한 분량에 압도된다면

삼중 지문의 모든 내용은 서로 논리적으로 연계되어 있기 때문에 결국 하나의 지문을 세 개로 분리해 놓았다고 볼 수 있다. 이 점을 절대 잊지 말고 첫 지문의 주제문과 맥락을 철저히 파악하여 세 지문의 유기적 연관성을 파악하는 연습을 한다.

② 세 지문에 분산된 정보가 통합되지 않는다면

삼중 지문에서는 첫 번째 지문의 일부 세부 내용을 두 번째 지문의 표와 항목으로 따로 분리하거나, 혹은 간략하게 요약을 해 놓는다. 그러므로 이때 첫 번째 지문의 세부 내용을 두 번째 지문의 표에 기재된 수치나 고유명사 등으로 바꾸어 표현하는 게(paraphrasing) 일반적이다. 어차피 동일한 정보를 분산시켜 놓은 것이기 때문에, 이것을 하나의 정보로 식별이 가능하게 정보를 분류하여 표시해 두는 것도 좋은 전략이 될 수 있다. 따라서 삼중 지문을 통합하는 문제가 나올 때 이를 종합하여 판단할 수 있는 훈련을 한다.

Questions 1-2 refer to the following letter, comment card, and e-mail.

To Whom It May Concern,
I have always enjoyed staying at Koh-i-Noor whenever I visit Dubai. Your staff is unfailingly courteous and obliging.

5 라오 씨에 관해 함축된 Q1의 정답이 드러나 있다.

However, I was a little disappointed on my last visit.

1 지문의 전반적인 내용을 추론한다.

The television in my room did not work satisfactorily. The telephone lines were unclear, particularly while making overseas calls. Your swimming pool is excellent, but I found I couldn't use it in the mornings since it opens only after 11:00 A.M. I hope you can make some improvements before I return for my next stay.
Sincerely, / Vani Rao

Koh-i-Noor Hotel Customer Comment Card

2 지문의 전반적인 내용을 추론한다.

Name: Vani Rao
Day(s) of stay: November 2 - November 8

8 라오 씨가 1주일을 머물렀음을 알 수 있다.

Please rate the following:

	Excellent	Good	Average	Poor
Atmosphere/Ambience of Property	X			
Cleanliness		X		
Menu/Meals	X			
Service/Friendliness of Staff	X			
In-Room Services (Telephone/TV/Cable)			X	
Gym/Spa/Swimming Pool		X		

To: Vani Rao <vrao@remiss.net>
From: Faisal al Fahd <faisal@kohinnorhotel.com>
Date: November 23
Re: Your stay

3 지문의 전반적인 내용을 추론한다.

Dear Ms. Rao,

Thank you for the comments regarding your stay with us. I'm very sorry about the inconveniences you faced this time.
To apologize, I am attaching a 15% discount coupon you can use when making a reservation with same conditions you did this month. The coupon is valid for one year. You will be pleased to know that the swimming pool now opens at 6:00 A.M. We hope you enjoy using it when you come the next time.

7 Q2의 할인 조건이 드러나 있다. (라오 씨가 이번 달에 서비스를 이용했던 동일한 조건으로 예약해야 함)

Sincerely,
Faisal al Fahd / Manager / Koh-i-Noor Hotel

Q1 What is implied about Ms. Rao?

(A) She is a resident of Dubai.
(B) She has won a free stay at the hotel.
(C) She is an old customer.
(D) She will make another visit shortly.

4 라오 씨가 쓴 첫 지문을 토대로 답을 찾도록 한다.

Q2 How can Ms. Rao get a discount for the next visit?

(A) By submitting feedback
(B) By staying for a week or longer
(C) By visiting the hotel in advance
(D) By staying with a group of at least 4 people

6 라오 씨가 작성한 첫 지문과 두 번째 지문을 토대로 세 번째 지문에서 호텔 측이 언급한 할인 내용을 통합하여 답을 찾도록 한다.

PART 7

관계자분께,

저는 제가 두바이에 방문할 때마다 코-이-누어에 즐겁게 묵었습니다. 귀하의 직원들은 항상 예의바르고 친절했습니다. 하지만 지난번 방문에는 약간 실망했습니다. 제 방의 TV는 만족스럽게 작동하지 않았습니다. 전화 연결은 특히 해외 전화를 걸 때 깨끗하지 않았습니다. 수영장은 훌륭하지만 오전 11시 이후에 열기 때문에 저는 아침에 사용할 수 없었습니다. 제가 다시 방문하기 전에 이런 점들이 개선되길 희망합니다.

진심으로, / 바니 라오

코-이-누어 호텔 고객 평가 카드

이름: 바니 라오
숙박 기간: 11월 2일 ~ 11월 8일
다음 사항에 점수를 매겨 주십시오.

	탁월함	우수	양호	불량
분위기/건물의 주변 환경	X			
청결도		X		
메뉴/식사	X			

	탁월함	우수	양호	불량
직원의 서비스와 친절도	X			
룸서비스 (전화/TV/케이블)			X	
체육관/온천/수영장		X		

수신: 바니 라오 <vrao@remiss.net>
발신: 파이잘 알 파드 <faisal@kohinoorhotel.com>
날짜: 11월 23일
제목: 귀하의 숙박

라오 씨께,

저희 호텔의 숙박에 대해 의견을 주셔서 감사합니다. 이번에 겪으신 불편함에 대해 사과드립니다. 사과하는 의미로, 이번 달과 동일한 조건으로 예약하실 경우 사용할 수 있는 15%를 할인 쿠폰을 첨부합니다. 쿠폰의 유효 기간은 1년입니다. 이제 수영장이 오전 6시에 연다는 사실을 들으시면 좋아하실 거라고 생각합니다. 다음에 오셔서 즐겁게 이용하시길 바랍니다.

진심으로, / 파이잘 알 파드 / 코-이-누어 호텔 관리자

Q1. 라오 씨에 관해 암시된 것은?
(A) 두바이에 살고 있다. (B) 호텔의 무료 숙박권을 얻었다. (C) 오랜 단골이다. (D) 곧 방문할 것이다.

Q2. 라오 씨는 다음 방문 시에 어떻게 할인을 받을 수 있을 것인가?
(A) 피드백을 제출함으로써 (B) 1주 이상을 머무름으로써
(C) 사전에 호텔에 방문함으로써 (D) 적어도 4명의 그룹으로 숙박함으로써

해설 Q1 추론 유형

첫 번째 지문, 첫 문장에서 'I have always enjoyed staying at Koh-i-Noor whenever I visit Dubai'에서 그녀가 호텔에 처음 방문한 것이 아니라는 것을 추측할 수 있다. 따라서 정답은 (C)가 된다.

Q2 통합 지문 유형

세 번째 지문, 두 번째 문단, 첫 문장에서 '~ a 15% discount coupon you can use when making a reservation with same conditions ~'에서 할인 쿠폰을 사용하려면 지난 예약 조건을 동일하게 유지해야 함을 언급하고 있다. 이에 두 번째 지문에서 라오가 머물렀던 날짜는 11월 2일에서 8일로 약 1주일의 숙박 기간이 할인 조건이 될 수 있으므로 정답은 (B)이다.

SPARTA PRACTICE

Questions 1-5 refer to the following flyer, Web page, and table.

For Sale: EXcopy T-2000 color printer

I recently purchased the EXcopy T-2000 to print daily reports and other company documents. At the time, I did not realize that it can only print a small number of pages and is insufficient for my purposes. I am now planning to purchase a EXcopy printer with a printing capacity of 100 pages per minute.

The EXcopy T-2000 is perfect for printing small projects as it can print 50 pages per minute and 30 double-sided pages. The printer is unused and still in its original factory packaging. EXcopy promises to provide replacement parts for the life of all of its machines. Therefore, you will have no problems finding replacement parts in the future even though this model has been discontinued as of last week. In light of this recent development, I am only asking $50 for the machine although I originally paid $75 for it. If interested, please contact me at the mobile phone number below. I am not in the office every day, but I can arrange a time for you to come by to look at the machine.

Jason Wells
023-453-4032

http://www.excopy.com/machine_models

EXcopy printers

EXcopy machines suit many different project demands, enabling you to print proposals, pamphlets, and other professional documents within minutes! All machines are compatible with most standard paper formats including letter, legal, and A4. This quick comparison chart will help you select the product that is right for your needs. Complete product specifications can be found at excopy.com/printer_specs.

Model #	Maximum printing capacity (single side)	Maximum printing capacity (double side)	Price
T-1500	30	15	$65
T-2000	50	30	$75
M-1500	80	50	$120
M-2000	100	80	$165

Q1 What reason does Mr. Wells want to sell the EXcopy T-2000?

(A) It is too big for his office.
(B) It cannot handle large projects.
(C) He no longer needs a printer.
(D) He wants a machine that is easier to operate.

Q2 According to the flyer, why is the price of the machine relatively low?

(A) It is a used machine.
(B) It needs replacement parts.
(C) It is part of a factory clearance sale.
(D) It is a model that is no longer available.

Q3 Where can interested buyers see the machine?

(A) In Mr. Wells's office
(B) In the factory showroom
(C) At an office supply store
(D) At an EXcopy dealership

Q4 According to the Web page, what do all EXcopy machines have in common?

(A) They are lightweight.
(B) They come in a range of colors.
(C) They accommodate various paper sizes.
(D) They include sample project instructions.

Q5 What EXcopy model will Mr. Wells likely buy to replace the T-2000?

(A) T-1500
(B) T-2000
(C) M-1500
(D) M-2000

Questions 1-5 refer to the following letters and information.

Dear Mr. Roeder,

I am writing to inquire about your new line of commercial kitchen appliances. I work for Mezzanine Restaurant, a new establishment in Brussels, Belgium. We are looking to purchase some kitchen equipment soon as we expect to be open in about 90 days. We were referred to your company by the manager of Acacia Bistro. He mentioned that you have a new line of high-end commercial appliances and that you are currently offering discounted international shipping rates.

We are also looking to purchase a commercial grade gas range with six burners and a freezer with at least 15 cubic feet of storage capacity. Please send me a product list with descriptions and pricing information as well as your international shipping rates.

Sincerely,

Roy Lee

Dear Mr. Lee,

Thank you for your interest in our products. We are sending this letter with the information you requested.
We at Falcon Equipment Commercial Appliances handle a variety of merchandise which all kinds of restaurants need. As you know, we are presently providing customers with a special opportunity to celebrate our 10th anniversary. If you place an order for 2 or more appliances during the sales promotion, you are entitled to get a 10-percent discount on shipping. Don't miss this chance.

Roeder
Falcon Equipment

Falcon Equipment Commercial Appliances	
Stainless Steel Commercial Refrigerator 19.5 Cu. Ft. Capacity Heavy-duty cooling system Dynamic condenser improves performance in high-temperature environments Sealed cabinet interior for easy cleaning	£1,595
48 Commercial Style Dual Fuel Range with oven Dual fuel range offers the precision of a gas cooking surface with an electric oven Six 20k BTU gas burners Even heat convection system	£2,470
Under Counter Ice Machine Produces up to 50lbs of ice in 24 hours Stores up to 25 pounds of ice at one time	£945
13.8 Cu. Ft. Capacity Frost-Free Freezer Holds approximately 483lbs of frozen food 5 door shelves	£685

Shipping Rate : Domestic £100 International £130
(Special discounts offered only for 10 days)

1 According to the first letter, why is Mr. Lee interested in Falcon Equipment's appliances?

(A) They are available in a local store.
(B) They are reasonably priced.
(C) They were recommended by a colleague.
(D) They were reviewed in a magazine.

2 Why does Mezzanine Restaurant need appliances?

(A) It is preparing to open for business.
(B) It has just expanded.
(C) Its current equipment needs to be replaced.
(D) Its equipment is too old.

3 What product will Mr. Lee most likely order?

(A) Refrigerator
(B) Range
(C) Ice machine
(D) Freezer

4 What is NOT an advertised feature of the commercial refrigerator?

(A) It is easy to clean.
(B) It is energy efficient.
(C) It is made of stainless steel.
(D) It has a strong condenser.

5 If he is given a discount, how much will Roy Lee most likely pay for a shipping cost?

(A) £130
(B) £117
(C) £100
(D) £90

Questions 6-10 refer to the following guidelines, form, and e-mail.

Equipment Use Guidelines

The medical Technology Association operates, maintains advanced medical equipment and offers professional advice to support research and development activities in the medical industry. We rent lots of hospitals and medical device companies the equipment. An equipment reservation form must be completed in advance for all equipment requests. Experienced and expert specialists at the association hold tutorials and can assist individuals in using the equipment for professional and specific projects.

The guidelines for equipment reservations are as follows:

A. If it takes longer than 24 hours to rent equipment or the rental cost exceeds $130, the request must be approved by the applicant's department supervisor.

B. If requested equipment is designated as high sensitivity, it can only be used:

(1) When a specialist of our association is available to operate the equipment, or

(2) after the user has completed the operation and safety training session we regularly hold and submitted the training certificate.

EQUIPMENT RESERVATION FORM	
Request Number	#8232
Date	January 29
Employee Name	Jessica Dinnage
Department	Anatomy
Department Head	Johan Olsen
Ext.	6819
Equipment Code/Name	GFP-775 4F/ Optical Microscope
Rate (per day)	$178
High-Sensitivity Equipment?	■ **Yes** □ **No**
High-Sensitivity Equipment Training?	□ **Yes** ■ **No**
Date(s)/Time(s) Requested	February 5, 9:00 A.M. - 3:00 P.M.
Intended Use	Observing hydrated surface of biological samples
Attachment of Training Certificate	None

Employee Signature

Jessica Dinnage

Department Head Approval

(if required)

Johan Olsen

To	Jessica Dinnage
From	Gustav Moller
Date	January 30
Subject	Equipment Request #8232

Dear Mr. Dinnage:

I received your request form this morning. Unfortunately, the instrument you reserved is being rented by another establishment, and I don't think it will be available until February 7. Moreover, the specialist for your requested high-sensitivity instrument, Dr. Mary Lohmann, will be participating in a seminar next week and will be out of the office until February 10. I would like to reschedule the reservation to a date after Dr. Lohmann comes back. Please call or e-mail me to decide on a date. I apologize for the inconvenience.

Sincerely,

Gustav Moller
Medical Technology Association

6 Who is most likely interested in the guidelines?

(A) Device manufacturers
(B) Sales managers
(C) Technological firms
(D) Researchers

7 In the guidelines, the word "support" in paragraph 1, line 2, is closest in meaning to

(A) lift
(B) aid
(C) hold
(D) fund

8 Why did the reservation form require Mr. Olsen's signature?

(A) Because Ms. Dinnage will be using the equipment for longer than 24 hours
(B) Because the equipment requested is classified as high sensitivity
(C) Because Ms. Dinnage must attend a conference
(D) Because the rental fee is very high

9 What is suggested about Dr. Lohmann?

(A) She is Ms. Dinnage's supervisor.
(B) She will be unavailable throughout February.
(C) She is giving a presentation at a conference.
(D) She must be available during the operating of equipment.

10 What information will Ms. Dinnage mention to Mr. Moller?

(A) The type of equipment she needs to use
(B) The date when she will return to the association
(C) An alternate date when she wants to rent the equipment
(D) Contact information where she can be reached

Questions 11-15 refer to the following letter, instruction, and e-mail.

Sign Up for GoodFCU E-Statements or E-Notices
and Be Entered to Win a $100 Gas Card!

Dear Mr. HUSH,

Since you currently receive GoodFCU account E-statements, you know they offer you a fast and easy solution for viewing your monthly/quarterly account statement at Computer Line. Other E-notices that you may find useful are VISA E-statements, transaction notices, and loan billing notices.

Sign up for E-statements or E-notices from now until July 31 and be entered to win one of three $100 mobile gas cards. That would be perfect for your summer travels!

- **VISA E-statements** work just like your GoodFCU account E-statements. You receive an e-mail notifying you that your VISA E-statement is ready to be viewed in ComputerLine. In addition, with VISA E-statements, a link is provided to make an online payment.
- **Transaction Notices** are sent via e-mail and inform you if you have an overdraft transfer from one account to another (for example, from savings to checking) or if you have a non-sufficient funds(NSF) check.
- **Loan Billing Notices** let you receive your loan payment notices and late notices (instant cash, home equity loan, etc.) via e-mail. When you select an E-notice, you are also able to choose how many days before your due date you would like to receive it.

Sign Up Today!

Sincerely,

Good Federal Credit Union

Registration Procedures

Login to Computer Line from the GoodFCU home page

- Make sure your e-mail address is current.
- Choose the "E-Services" menu.
- Choose "E-Correspondence Sign Up" from the drop-down menu.

Select "Electronic" as your delivery method for the appropriate statements and/or notices. (You may choose to receive all your statements and notices electronically by checking the box at the top of the list.)

- Enter and confirm your e-mail address.
- Agree to the online disclosure.

Thank you for your cooperation.

To: goodfcu@gfcu.net
From: Hush322@kodak.net
Subject: Hi, this is Wayne Hush

Dear Good Federal Credit Union,

I signed up for the E-statement, transaction, and loan billing notices a few days ago, but I still haven't gotten my $100 mobile gas card. I am going on a trip to Las Vegas in two days, so it would be very useful for me to have the gas card. Therefore, please check if you have made a mistake in not sending me the gas card. Or see if it got lost on the way to my mailbox. I just want my gas card as soon as possible. Thank you.

Sincerely,

Wayne Hush

11 What is mentioned about GoodFCU?

(A) It is explaining a new mortgage loan.
(B) It is showing how much Mr. Hush borrowed from the bank.
(C) It is introducing a way to enjoy a special promotion.
(D) It is advertising their new deals.

12 What is one of the new services of GoodFCU?

(A) Loan payment notices
(B) A new Web site
(C) Customer service
(D) Electronic vouchers

13 What is the correct procedure to sign up for the service?

(A) Choose E-Customer service
(B) Choose E-Correspondence Sign Up
(C) Enter and change your password
(D) Enter your personal identification number

14 Why does Mr. Hush say he needs a gas card?

(A) He doesn't have any money for gas.
(B) His car uses up lots of gas.
(C) He will need lots of gas soon.
(D) He wants to sell it to another person.

15 What is Mr. Hush most likely not aware of?

(A) That the E-statement must have an online payment
(B) That not everyone receives $100 mobile cards
(C) That he is not eligible for the drawing
(D) That he does not have enough points to participate

PART 7

토익
빈출
어휘

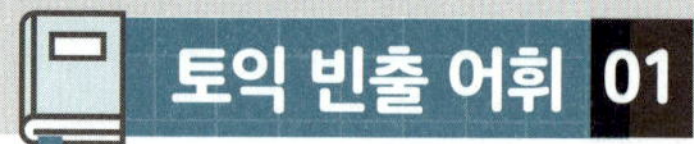

토익 빈출 어휘 01

1 Staff members are invited to Hugo Fine College's annual awards ceremony at the Lime Restaurant next Thursday.
직원들은 다음 주 목요일 Lime 레스토랑에서 있을 Hugo Fine College의 연례 시상식에 초대된다.

staff [stæf]	명 직원(=employee) 동 직원을 배치하다 staffing 명 직원채용 specialize in offering customized staffing solutions 맞춤형 직원채용 해결책 제공을 전문으로 하다
invite [inváit]	동 초대하다 invitation 명 초대, 초대장 invite all residents to attend the seminar 모든 주민들이 세미나에 참석하도록 초대하다
annual [ǽnjuəl]	형 매년의, 연례의(=yearly) complete the annual budget report 연간 예산 보고서를 작성하다
award [əwɔ́:rd]	명 상 동 수여하다 awards ceremony 시상식 awards banquet 시상식 연회 He was awarded a contract of 2 million dollars. 그는 2백만 달러의 계약을 따냈다.
ceremony [sérəmòuni]	명 의식, 행사 deliver a speech at an opening ceremony 개회식에서 연설하다

2 Ms. Smith is awaiting the delivery of some paper from Tucson Office Supplies in order to finish drafting the documents needed for tomorrow's meeting.
Smith 씨는 내일 회의에 필요한 서류 작성을 끝내기 위해 Tucson 사무용품점으로부터 종이 배달을 기다리고 있다.

await [əwéit]	동 기다리다(=wait for) They eagerly awaited the opening of the new hospital. 그들은 신설 병원의 개원식을 간절히 기다렸다.
delivery [dilívəri]	명 배달 deliver 동 배달하다, 전달하다 deliver the mail to the wrong address 편지를 잘못된 주소로 배달하다 deliver an address / deliver a speech 연설하다
supplies [səpláiz]	명 비품, 저장품 supply 동 공급하다, 주다 명 공급 office supplies 사무용품 an interruption in the electrical supply 전력 공급의 중단
draft [dræft]	동 초안을 작성하다 명 원고, 초안 type a draft of the report 보고서 초안을 작성하다
document [dákjumənt]	명 서류, 문서 동 기록하다 documentation 명 증빙서류 document the evidence 증거를 기록하다 submit the proper documentation 적합한 증빙서류를 제출하다

3 Vov Bike accepted assistance from Line Laboratories in creating the design of the new prototype model. Vov Bike는 새로운 시제품의 디자인을 만드는 데 Line 연구소의 지원을 받아들였다.

accept [əksépt]	동 받아들이다, 인정하다 acceptance 명 수락, 승인 accept responsibility for losses 손실에 대한 책임을 인정하다
assistance [əsístəns]	명 도움, 지원 assist 동 돕다 assistant 명 조수, 보조원 a replacement for a medical assistant 의료 보조원의 후임자
create [kriéit]	동 창출하다, 만들다 creation 명 창출, 창조 create a list of frequently asked questions 자주 묻는 질문들의 목록을 만들다 job creation 고용 창출
design [dizáin]	명 디자인, 설계 동 설계하다, 고안하다 design an advertising campaign 광고 캠페인을 고안하다
prototype [próutətàip]	명 원형, 견본, 시제품 The prototype vehicle met international standards. 차량 시제품이 국제 기준을 충족시켰다.

4 Mega Finance is a relatively new consulting firm that specializes in training financial advisors. Mega Finance는 금융 상담사 교육을 전문으로 하는 비교적 새로운 컨설팅 회사이다.

relatively [rélətivli]	부 상대적으로, 비교적 relatively inexperienced interns 상대적으로 경험이 적은 인턴들
consulting [kənsʌ́ltiŋ]	명 자문, 조언 consultant 명 고문(=advisor) consult (with) 동 상의하다 financial consultant 재정 고문 consult with his partners 그의 동료들과 상의하다
specialize in [spéʃəlàiz in]	동 ~을 전문으로 하다, 전공하다 specialized 형 전문의 specialized knowledge and expertise 전문 지식과 기술
train [trein]	동 ~을 훈련하다, 교육하다 training 명 교육, 훈련, 연수 provide year-round training to technical support staff 기술 지원 직원들에게 연중 교육을 제공하다
financial [fainǽnʃəl]	형 재정의, 금융의 finance 명 재정, 자금 동 ~에 자금을 조달하다 accountants and other finance professionals 회계사와 다른 재정 전문가

토익 빈출 어휘 02

1 Prior to becoming an analyst at Rising Holdings, Mr. Lee served as a consultant for its chief competitor. Rising Holdings에서 분석가가 되기 전에, Lee 씨는 그 회사의 주요 경쟁업체에서 상담직으로 일했다.

prior to [práiər tu]	전 ~에 앞서, ~전에(= before) It happened prior to the presentation. 그 일은 발표 전에 일어났다.
analyst [ǽnəlist]	명 분석가 analyze 동 분석하다 analysis 명 분석 analyze a sample 견본을 분석하다
serve [səːrv]	동 봉사하다, 시중들다 serve as ~로 근무하다, 일하다 serve as mayor 시장으로 일하다
chief [tʃiːf]	형 주된, (직급상) 최고위의 명 장, 우두머리 take over as the chief librarian 도서관장을 맡다
competitor [kəmpétitər]	명 경쟁자, 경쟁 업체 compete 동 경쟁하다 competition 명 경쟁 fierce competition 치열한 경쟁

2 Holden, Inc. is proud to offer our associates competitive compensation and outstanding opportunities.
Holden 사는 우리의 동료들에게 경쟁력 있는 보상금과 뛰어난 기회를 제공하게 된 것을 기쁘게 생각합니다.

proud [praud]	형 자랑스러운 pride 명 자존심, 자긍심 He looked with pride at his garden. 남자는 그의 정원을 자랑스럽게 바라보았다.
associate [əsəuʃiət]	명 동료; 연상되는 것 동 연상하다; 교제하다 형 동료의, 준- a close associate 친한 동료 an associate member 준회원 Don't associate me with that problem. 그 문제와 저를 결부시키지 마세요.
competitive [kəmpétətiv]	형 경쟁적인, 경쟁력 있는 compete (against/with) 동 ~와 경쟁하다 compete for first place 1등을 차지하기 위해 경쟁하다 compete with one's colleagues 동료들과 경쟁하다
compensation [kάmpənséiʃn]	명 배상, 보상(금) compensate 동 보상하다, 보충하다 compensate for the inconvenience 피해를 보상하다
outstanding [àutstǽndiŋ]	명 뛰어난, 두드러진; 미지불된, 아직 처리되지 않은 outstanding service 탁월한 서비스 outstanding debts of over $1,000 천 달러 이상의 미지급 채무

3 Legatin House Specialties' products are generally available at local retail stores.
Legatin House Specialties의 제품은 일반적으로 현지 소매점들에서 구매할 수 있다.

specialty [spéʃəlti]	명 전문, 전공; 특산품, 특제품 specialize 동 ~를 전문으로 하다; 전공하다 specialize in biochemistry 생화학을 전공하다
generally [dʒénərəli]	부 일반적으로 general 형 일반적인 generalize 동 일반화하다 the general public 일반 대중
available [əvéiləbl]	형 이용 가능한; 입수 가능한; 시간이 있는 availability 명 유효성(=validity), 유용성 Are you available on the weekend? 당신은 주말에 시간이 되나요?
local [lóukl]	형 지방의, 지역의 locals 명 지역 사람들 local community 지역 사회
retail [rí:teil]	명 소매, 소매상 형 소매의 retail (at/for) 동 ~에 소매되다 It retails for thirty dollars. 그것은 소매가로 30달러이다.

4 The weather forecast for tomorrow is partly cloudy with a chance of rain or even snow.
내일은 부분적으로 흐리며, 비나 심지어는 눈이 올 가능성이 있습니다.

forecast [fɔ:rkæst]	명 예측, 예상 동 예보하다, 예상하다(=predict) forecast economic growth 경제 성장을 예상하다
partly [pá:rtli]	부 부분적으로, 일부분 part 명 부분 take part in a vote 투표에 참여하다
cloudy [kláudi]	형 구름이 낀, 흐린 ↔ cloudless 형 구름 없는, 맑게 갠 cloudless skies 구름 없는 하늘
chance [ʧæns]	명 기회(=opportunity), 가능성(=possibility) the chance of a lifetime 일생일대의 기회
even [í:vn]	부 한층, 더욱; 심지어, ~조차도 형 평평한, 규칙적인 an even surface 평평한 표면

1 The Planning Department was pleased with the enthusiastic response to the post for volunteers to prepare for the anniversary events.
기획부는 기념 행사 준비를 위한 자원봉사자 공고에 대한 열광적인 반응에 매우 기뻐했다.

please [pli:z]	동 기쁘게 하다 pleased 형 기뻐하는 be pleased with the results 결과에 기뻐하다
enthusiastic [inθù:ziǽstik]	형 열광적인, 열렬한 enthusiasm 명 열광, 열정(=passion) enthusiastic audience members 열정적인 청중들
response [rispáns]	명 응답, 반응 respond 동 응답하다, 반응하다 respond to a question 질문에 응답하다
volunteer [vɑləntíər]	명 자원봉사자 동 자원하다 voluntary 형 자발적인 a voluntary worker = volunteer 자원봉사자
prepare [pripeər]	동 준비하다, 대비하다 preparation 명 준비(과정), 대비 wedding preparations 결혼 준비

2 The recent unusual weather accounts for the increase in the price of coffee.
커피 값의 인상은 최근 이상한 날씨에 기인한다.

recent [rí:snt]	형 최근의 recently 부 최근에(=lately, nowadays) He received a package from New York recently. 그는 최근에 뉴욕에서 온 소포를 받았다.
unusual [ʌnjú:ʒuəl]	형 흔치 않은, 이상한 ↔ usual 형 평소의, 보통의 later than usual 평소보다 늦은 unusual behavior 이상한(평소와 다른) 행동
account for [əkáunt fɔ́:r]	동 ~의 이유가 되다, ~을 해명하다; (비율) ~을 차지하다 account 명 계좌; 계정 account for 15% of the U.S. population 미국 인구의 15%를 차지하다 an e-mail account 이메일 계정
increase [ínkri:s]	명 증가, 인상 동 증가하다; 늘리다 pay increase 임금 인상
price [prais]	명 값, 가격; 대가; 물가 동 값을 매기다 at any price 어떤 대가를 치르더라도 price an item 제품에 값을 매기다

3 Mr. Nakamura is a highly regarded economist and has been recognized by his peers for his contributions to the field.
Nakamura 씨는 매우 명망 높은 경제학자이며, 경제학 분야에 대한 기여로 그의 동료들에게 인정 받고 있다.

highly [háili]	부 매우, 대단히(=greatly) high 형 높은 부 높게 height 명 높이 a highly experienced developer 매우 경험이 많은 개발자 a high standard 높은 기준
regard [rigá:rd]	동 ~을 …으로 여기다(=consider) 명 관심, 고려; 높은 평가 in regard of[to] = with regard to ~에 관해서
economist [ikánəmist]	명 경제학자 economize 동 절약하다 economy 명 경제 a market economy 시장 경제 economize on electrical appliance usage 전자 가전제품의 사용을 절약하다
recognize [rékəgnàiz]	동 알아보다; 인정하다, 승인하다 recognition 명 인식; 인정 promotion in recognition of achievement 공적의 인정으로 인한 승진
contribution [kántrəbjú:ʃn]	명 기여; 기부(금) contribute (to) 동 기여하다, 기부하다 a voluntary contribution 자발적인 기부

4 As the newly elected head of the business development committee, Sarah Chung will have to attend meetings frequently. 새로 임명된 기업 개발 위원회 회장으로서, Sarah Chung은 회의에 자주 참석해야 할 것이다.

newly [njú:li]	부 최근에, 새로 renew 동 재개하다; 갱신하다 newly redecorated 새롭게 재단장한 renew a license 면허를 갱신하다
elect [ilékt]	동 선출하다(=vote); 선택하다 election 명 선거; 당선 elect by ballot 투표로 선출하다 win an election 선거에서 이기다
development [divéləpmənt]	명 성장, 발달; 개발 develop 동 성장하다; 개발하다; 영향을 주다 develop special skills 특별한 기술을 개발하다
committee [kəmíti]	명 위원회(=board, council) audit committee 감사 위원회
frequently [frí:kwəntli]	부 자주, 흔히 ↔ infrequently 부 드물게 frequency 명 빈도 frequency of use 사용 빈도수

토익 빈출 어휘 04

1 Rather than having retirement celebrations separately, Holmark Publishing decided to hold an annual event every January.
Holmark 출판사는 은퇴 기념식을 별도로 갖는 대신 연례 행사를 매년 1월에 개최하기로 결정했다.

rather [rǽðər]	부 상당히(=somewhat, quite); 오히려, 차라리 rather than ~라기 보다, ~대신에 a rather complicated situation 상당히 복잡한 상황
retirement [ritáiərmənt]	명 은퇴 retire 동 은퇴하다 retired 형 은퇴한 retire from business 사업에서 은퇴하다
celebration [sèləbréiʃn]	명 기념, 축하행사 celebrate 동 기념하다, 축하하다 celebratory 형 기념하는 celebrate a holiday 명절을 기념하다
separately [sépərətli]	부 따로, 개별적으로(=individually) separate 동 분리하다 형 별개의, 분리된 a separate compartment 개별 칸
decide [disáid]	동 결정하다 decision 명 결정 decisive 형 결정적인, 결단력 있는 decisive proof 결정적인 단서

2 Because it covers every aspect of French cooking, the *Bleu School Guide* is considered the definitive resource for preparing authentic French cuisine. 프랑스 요리의 모든 측면을 다루고 있기 때문에, <Bleu School Guide>는 프랑스 정통요리를 준비할 수 있는 최고의 자료로 간주된다.

cover [kʌvər]	동 다루다; 덮다; 바르다 명 덮개, 커버; 표지 cover a mistake 실수를 숨기다 Don't judge a book by its cover. 겉을 보고 속을 판단하지 말아라.
aspect [ǽspekt]	명 측면, 양상 in every aspect 모든 면에서
definitive [difínətiv]	형 최종적인, 확정적인; 최고의, 완벽한 a definitive answer 확답
resource [ríːsɔːrs]	명 재료; 정보, 원천 resources 명 자원 Human Resources Department 인적 자원 부서
authentic [ɔːθéntik]	형 진짜인, 진품인 authenticate 동 진짜임을 증명하다, 법적으로 인정하다 authenticate a warranty 품질보증서의 진위를 확인하다

3 Next to the Staten Resort is a luxurious recreational area, complete with a swimming pool and a tennis court. Staten Resort 옆에는 수영장과 테니스 코트가 갖춰진 호화로운 휴양지가 있다.

next to [nekst tu]	전 바로 옆에(=adjacent to, beside) It's next to the file cabinet. 그것은 파일 캐비닛 옆에 있다.
luxurious [lʌgʒúəriəs]	형 아주 편안한; 호화로운 luxury 명 호화로움, 사치(품) luxury item 사치품
recreational [rèkriéiʃənl]	형 오락의, 레크리에이션의 recreation 명 오락 recreation center 레크리에이션 센터
area [ɛ́əriə]	명 지역, 구역(=region, district); (사물의 특정) 부분; 분야; 면적 gross area 총면적
complete [kəmplíːt]	형 완벽한, 완전한; 완료된 동 완료하다 completely 부 완전히, 전적으로 complete with ~이 완벽히 구비된 completely satisfied 아주 만족해하는

4 Eclectic John Electronics guarantees that any defective photocopy machine will be replaced with a new one. Eclectic John 전자 회사는 결함이 있는 그 어떠한 복사기도 새것으로 교환해 줄 것을 보장한다.

electronics [ilektrániks]	명 전자공학; 전자기술 electrical 형 전기의; 전기를 이용하는 electrical appliance 전자제품
guarantee [gærəntíː]	동 보증하다; 약속하다 명 보증, 담보물; 보증인 a written guarantee 보증서
defective [diféktiv]	형 결함이 있는 defect 명 결함 defect in a device 장치의 결함
machine [məʃíːn]	명 기계 동 기계로 만들다 machinery 명 기계류 machined to be used with ease 쉽게 이용하도록 기계화된
replace [ripléis]	동 대신하다; 교체하다 replacement 명 교환, 교체; 후임자; 교체품 request a refund or replacement 환불이나 교환을 요청하다

1 Chiado's Vegetarian Cuisine can accommodate parties of up to 50 people in its private dining room. Chiado 채식전문 식당은 개별 식사 공간에 50명의 인원까지 수용할 수 있다.

cuisine [kwɪzi:n]	명 요리법(=recipe); 요리 perfection in accommodations service, and cuisine 숙박 서비스와 요리의 완벽함
accommodate [əkɑ́mədèit]	동 숙박시키다, 수용하다 accommodation 명 숙박시설; 편의, 도움 to accommodate overseas clients 해외 고객들을 수용하다
party [pɑ́:rti]	명 파티, 모임; 일행; 정당, 당파; 당사자 a third-party intervention 제3자의 개입
up to [ʌp tu]	전 (최대) ~까지 The banquet room can seat up to 40 guests. 연회장은 최대 40명까지 손님을 앉힐 수 있다.
private [práivət]	형 사적인, 개인의; 민간의, 사립의 private talks with both parties 양당 간의 비공개 회담

2 At Schpielle Technologies, there are immediate job openings for highly experienced software developers. Schpielle Technologies에는 경력이 매우 많은 소프트웨어 개발자들을 찾는 급한 채용 건이 있다.

technology [teknɑ:lədʒi]	명 (과학) 기술; 기계, 장비 technological 형 (과학) 기술적인 technological problems with a computer monitor 컴퓨터 모니터의 기술적 문제
immediate [ɪmi:diət]	형 즉각적인 immediately 부 즉시, 즉각; 직접적으로 in the immediate future 가까운 미래에
opening [oupnɪŋ]	명 빈자리, 공석; 개막식; 첫 부분 open 형 열려 있는 동 문을 열다 the opening performance of the Royal Theater's new play Royal 극장의 새로운 첫 연극 공연
experienced [ɪkspɪriənst]	형 경험이 풍부한; 능숙한, 숙련된(=skillful) ↔ inexperienced 형 경험이 부족한, 미숙한 beginning and experienced golfers 초보자와 수준급의 골프선수
developer [divéləpər]	명 개발자 develop 동 개발하다, 발달시키다 development 명 개발, 발달 the regional development council 지역 개발 위원회

3 A definite schedule of events for the upcoming botanical garden show is available on the Regional Greenhouse Association's Web site. 다가오는 식물원 쇼의 확정된 일정은 지역 온실 협회 웹 사이트에서 확인할 수 있다.

schedule [skédʒuːl]	명 일정; 시간표 동 일정을 잡다 on schedule 일정에 맞추어 ahead of schedule 일정보다 앞서 behind schedule 일정보다 늦게 Office furniture is scheduled for delivery at 2:00 P.M. 사무용품이 오후 2시에 배달되기로 예정되어 있다.
upcoming [ʌpkʌmɪŋ]	형 다가오는, 곧 있을(=forthcoming) an upcoming highway project 곧 있을 고속도로 프로젝트
botanical [bətǽnikl]	형 식물(학)의 botanist 명 식물학자 a presentation by a renowned botanist 유명한 식물학자의 발표
regional [ríːdʒənl]	형 지역의, 지방의(=provincial) region(=district) 명 지역 a decrease in tourism in the region 지역 관광산업의 감소
association [əsòuʃiéiʃn]	명 협회; 연계, 제휴 associate 동 결부 짓다 명 (직장)동료 associated 형 관련된 construction associated with the replacement of the elevator 엘리베이터 교체와 관련된 공사

4 Customers can sign up to receive e-mails offering special savings, advance sale notices, and other benefits. 손님들은 특별가, 사전 할인 판매 공지, 그 외 각종 혜택을 제공하는 이메일을 수신하기 위해 등록할 수 있다.

sign up [saɪn ʌp]	동 가입하다, 등록하다(=enroll, register); 고용하다 sign up for a subscription 정기구독을 신청하다
special [spéʃl]	형 특별한, 특수한(=exceptional); 특정한(=specific) specialty 명 전문, 전공; 장기 specially 부 특별히, 특히 specially arranged snacks for diabetes 당뇨병 환자를 위해 특별히 준비된 간식
advance [ədvǽns]	형 사전의 명 진전, 발전; 선금 동 나아가다, 진행시키다 advanced 형 선진의, 상급의 advance payment 선금 advance forward 앞으로 나아가다 in advance 미리, 그전에
notice [nóutis]	명 공지 동 깨닫다, 알아차리다 notice an error in a document 서류의 오류를 알아보다 until further notice 추후 공지가 있을 때까지
benefit [benɪfɪt]	명 혜택, 이득 동 혜택을 주다; 혜택을 받다(=benefit from) benefits package 복리후생 제도 fringe benefit 부가 혜택

토익 빈출 어휘 06

1 On the Web page, subscribers have unlimited access to *Kinofilm Magazine*'s immense collection of movie reviews. 웹 페이지에서, 구독자들은 <Kinofilm> 잡지의 방대한 영화평을 무제한으로 이용하실 수 있습니다.

subscriber [səbskráibər]	명 구독자, 이용자 subscription 명 구독; 가입 a six-month subscription to a science journal 과학 학술지의 6개월분 구독
unlimited [ʌnlímitid]	형 무제한의, 무한정의 ↔ limited 형 한정된, 제한된(= restricted) limit 동 제한하다 명 한계, 제한 in a limited amount of time 제한된 시간 내에
access [ǽkses]	명 접근; 이용 동 접근하다, 이용하다 accessible 형 접근 가능한; 이용 가능한 online access to account information 계좌정보에 온라인 접속
immense [iméns]	형 거대한, 막대한, 방대한(= huge) an immense sum of money 막대한 돈
review [rivjúː]	명 평론, 보고서, 검토 동 검토하다, 논평하다 review safety precautions 안전조항을 점검하다

2 To ensure that the information center staff effectively respond to customer inquiries, all new hires must complete a rigorous training program. 정보센터 직원이 고객 문의에 효과적으로 응답하는 것을 보장하기 위해, 모든 신입 사원들은 엄격한 교육 프로그램을 마쳐야 한다.

ensure [inʃúər]	동 반드시 ~하게 하다, 보장하다(= make certain) ensure the accuracy of the data 데이터의 정확성을 보장하다
effectively [iféktivli]	부 효과적으로 effective 형 효과적인; 시행되는 effect 명 영향, 효과 effective next Tuesday 다음 주 화요일부터 시행되는
inquiry [inkwáiəri]	명 질문, 문의; 조사, 연구 inquire 동 질문하다, 조사하다 inquire about a default payment 체불 금액에 대해 문의하다
rigorous [rígərəs]	형 엄격한, 혹독한 rigorously 부 엄격히, 엄밀히 All contracts must be rigorously reviewed. 모든 계약서는 엄밀히 검토되어야 한다.
training [tréiniŋ]	명 교육, 훈련, 연수 train 동 훈련하다, 훈련시키다 job training 직업 훈련

3 Since Amanda Sevigny was hired as the marketing director, sales at Enboks Sportswear Company have increased dramatically.
Amanda Sevigny가 마케팅 부장으로 고용된 후부터, Enboks Sportswear 사의 매출은 극적으로 증가했다.

since [sins]	전 접 ~이후로; 접 ~때문에 부 이후로 ever since the economic crisis 경제공황 이후로
hire [haiər]	동 고용하다(=employ) hire a building manager 건물관리자를 고용하다
sale [seil]	동 판매하다 명 판매 sales 명 매출액, 판매량 record sales of mineral water 미네랄 워터의 기록적 매출
increase [inkríːs]	동 증가하다, 늘어나다 명 증가, 인상 ↔ decrease 동 감소하다 명 감소 increasingly 부 점점 더 increased participation 증가한 참여도
dramatically [drəmǽtikəli]	부 극적으로 dramatic 형 극적인, 급격한 dramatic rise in the cost 가격의 급격한 상승

4 As Mr. Rowdowski's secretary, you will be responsible for submitting his expense reports when he is out of the office in August.
Rowdowski 씨의 비서로서, 당신은 그가 8월에 사무실을 비울 때 비용 보고서를 제출할 책임이 있습니다.

secretary [sékrətèri]	명 비서(=assistant) secretarial 형 비서직의 the obligations of the secretary 비서의 의무
responsible [rispánsəbl]	형 책임지고 있는, 책임이 있는 responsibility 명 책임감; 의무 the responsibility of management 경영의 책임
submit [səbmít]	동 제출하다; 말하다, 진술하다 submit an order form 주문 양식을 제출하다
expense [ikspéns]	명 비용 expenditure 명 지출; 경비 travel expense 출장비
report [ripɔ́ːrt]	명 보고, 보고서 동 알리다, 발표하다; 보도하다 report the results 결과를 알리다

토익 빈출 어휘 07

1 The El Pedro City Limousine Service continually offers reliable and comfortable transportation to and from the airport. El Pedro 시 리무진 서비스는 믿을 만하고 편안한 공항의 왕복 운송수단을 지속적으로 제공한다.

continually [kəntínjuəli]	부 계속해서, 지속적으로 continuous 형 계속적인 continue 동 계속하다, 지속하다 ↔ discontinue 동 중단하다 The number of applicants has continually increased. 지원자들 수가 지속적으로 증가했다.
offer [ɔ:fər]	동 제의하다, 제공하다 명 제의, 제안; 제의한 액수 The discount offer is not valid. 할인 제안은 유효하지 않다.
reliable [riláiəbl]	형 믿을 만한, 믿을 수 있는(=dependable) reliability 명 신뢰성 reliant 형 의지하는 rely 동 의지하다 (on) rely on local publicity 지역 광고에 의존하다
comfortable [kʌmftəbl]	형 편안한, 안락한 comfort 명 편안; 위안 a comfortable work environment 편안한 작업 환경
transportation [trænspɔ:rtéiʃn]	명 운송수단 transport 명 운송, 수송 동 수송하다, 이동시키다 public transportation 대중교통

2 Although the clerk typed the item number carefully into the library's database, an error message was returned. 직원이 도서관의 데이터 베이스에 항목 번호를 주의 깊게 입력했음에도 불구하고, 오류 메시지가 나타났다.

although [ɔ:lðóu]	접 비록 ~이긴 하지만 despite 전 ~에도 불구하고 despite losses in other markets 다른 시장의 손실에도 불구하고
clerk [klɜ:rk]	명 직원, 점원 a sales clerk 점원, 판매원
item [áitəm]	명 항목; 물품 check the list item by item 항목마다 목록을 체크하다
carefully [kéərfəli]	부 조심스럽게, 주의 깊게 careful 형 신중한, 조심스러운 All data should be looked over carefully. 모든 정보는 주의 깊게 검토되어야 한다.
return [ritɜ́:rn]	동 돌려주다, 반납하다; 돌아오다 명 반납 Return defective product within sixty days of purchase. 결함이 있는 상품은 구매한 날로부터 60일 이내로 반납해주세요.

3 Trains were delayed briefly on Friday morning due to a minor electrical problem at the terminal.
기차는 금요일 아침 종착역에서 작은 전기 문제로 인해 잠시 지연되었다.

delay [diléi]	동 지연시키다, 연기하다 명 지연, 지체 frustration caused by flight delays 비행기 지연으로 인한 불만
briefly [bri:fli]	부 잠시, 짧게 brief 형 짧은, 간단한 a brief introduction 간략한 소개
due to [du:tu]	전 ~ 때문에(= because of, owing to) due 형 ~하기로 예정된 The presentation is due to start in 10 minutes. 발표는 10분 이내에 시작할 예정이다.
minor [máinər]	형 작은, 사소한 ↔ major 형 주요한, 중대한 a minor malfunction 사소한 오류
electrical [iléktrikl]	형 전기의; 전기를 이용하는 an electrical device 전기장치

4 Investors in Tripora Footwear Ltd. have wondered whether the company's impressive growth is sustainable. Tripora Footwear 사의 투자자들은 회사의 놀라운 성장이 지속 가능한 것인지 궁금해했다.

investor [invéstər]	명 투자자 invest 동 투자하다 investment 명 투자 investment transaction 투자 거래
whether [wéðər]	접 ~인지 아닌지(= if); ~는 아니는 He asked whether(= if) the applicant had any experience. 그는 지원자가 경력이 있는지 없는지 물었다.
impressive [imprésiv]	형 인상적인, 인상깊은 impression 명 인상; 감명 impress 동 ~에게 깊은 인상을 주다; 감동시키다 impress a supervisor 감독관에게 좋은 인상을 남기다
growth [grouθ]	명 성장 grow 동 성장하다, 증가하다 Income from advertising has been growing. 광고로 인한 이익은 증가했다.
sustainable [səstéinəbl]	형 지속 가능한 sustain 동 지속시키다 sustainable maintenance costs 지속 가능한 유지보수 비용

토익 빈출 어휘 08

1 A portion of the Legal Department's budget has been reserved for unexpected circumstances.
법무부 예산의 일부는 예기치 못한 상황을 위해 남겼다.

legal [lí:gl]	형 법적인, 합법적인 ↔ illegal 형 불법의 legalize 동 합법화하다 a fine for illegal parking 불법 주차에 대한 벌금
budget [bʌdʒɪt]	명 예산, 비용 동 예산을 세우다 budgetary 형 예산의 money budgeted for development programs 개발 프로그램을 위해 예산된 돈
reserve [rizɜ:rv]	동 비축하다; 예약하다 명 비축물 reservation 명 예약; 의구심 make a room reservation 방을 예약하다
unexpected [ʌnikspéktid]	형 예기치 못한, 뜻밖의(=unforeseen) expect 동 기대하다, 예상하다(=anticipate, predict) The weather conditions are expected to change. 날씨가 변할 전망이다.
circumstance [sɜ́:rkəmstæns]	명 환경, 상황(=situation, condition) under favorable circumstances 더 나은 상황에서

2 The fact that an advertisement appears on our Web site does not necessarily indicate our endorsement of the product or service.
우리 웹 사이트에 광고가 나타난다는 사실이 반드시 제품이나 서비스를 보증한다는 것을 명시하는 것은 아니다.

fact [fækt]	명 사실 as a matter of fact(=in fact) 부 사실은, 실제로는 a statement based on fact 사실을 토대로 한 진술
appear [əpíər]	동 ~처럼 보이다, 나타나다 appearance 명 (겉)모습, 외모; 출현 The novel appears brand new. 그 소설은 신작으로 보인다.
necessarily [nèsəsérəli]	부 어쩔 수 없이, 필연적으로 not necessarily 반드시 ~은 아닌 necessary 형 필요한, 필연적인 necessity 명 필수품 a necessary boarding document 탑승시 필요한 서류
indicate [índikèit]	동 ~를 나타내다(=demonstrate); 내비치다(=imply, suggest) indication 명 명시하는 말 indications of rapid growth in business 사업의 급격한 성장의 암시
endorsement [ɪndɔ:rsmənt]	명 보증, 지지; 배서 endorse 동 지지하다; 보증하다; (수표에) 배서하다 endorse a check 수표에 배서하다

3 The attached files may contain data that is confidential and should be accessed by the intended recipient only. 첨부된 파일은 기밀 자료가 들어 있을 수 있으며, 해당 수령인만 접근 가능합니다.

attach [ətǽtʃ]	동 붙이다, 첨부하다 attachment 명 부착물; 첨부파일 Attached is a list of the engineers' names. 기술자들의 명단이 첨부되어 있다.
contain [kəntein]	동 ~이 들어 있다, 담다 content 명 내용물 형 만족하는 the contents of the package 소포의 내용물 content with the result 결과에 만족한
confidential [kάnfidénʃl]	형 비밀의, 은밀한 confidentiality 명 비밀보장, 비밀 a confidentiality agreement 비밀유지 계약서
intended [inténdid]	형 (~을 위해) 만들어진, (~을) 대상으로 삼은 intentional 형 의도적인 intention 명 의향, 의도; 목적 have no intention of ~할 의도가 없다
recipient [risípiənt]	명 수신자, 수령인 receive 동 받다 receipt 명 영수증; 수령 receive prior approval 사전 승인을 받다

4 To reduce the amount of solid waste headed for landfills, the Sonian Company has recently implemented a recycling program.
매립지로 보내지는 고체성 폐기물의 양을 줄이기 위해 Sonian 사는 최근 재활용 프로그램을 시행했다.

reduce [ridjúːs]	동 줄이다, 감소하다; 할인하다 reduction 명 감소, 축소; 인하 a reduction in a music licensing fee 음원 저작료의 인하
amount [əmáunt]	명 양, 액수; 총액 amount to 동 (총액이) ~에 이르다; (상황이)~이 되다 amount to a total of 8 million dollars 총 800만달러에 이르다 amount to nothing 전혀 문제 되지 않다
waste [weist]	동 낭비하다 명 쓰레기, 낭비 wasted time and money 낭비된 시간과 돈
head [hed]	동 향하다, 가다; ~을 책임지다 명 책임자 the head of the Accounting Department 회계부서의 부장 appointed to head the committee 위원회를 책임지도록 임명된
implement [ímpləment]	동 시행하다(=carry out) implement a new dress code 새 복장 규정을 시행하다

토익 빈출 어휘 09

1 It is the Erudite Information Center's policy to respond to all customer inquiries as promptly and efficiently as possible. 모든 고객의 문의를 가능한 한 신속하고 효율적으로 응답하는 것은 Erudite 정보센터의 정책이다.

policy [páləsi]	명 정책, 방책 political 형 정치와 관련된, 정치적인 a changed political condition 변화된 정치적 상황
respond [rispá:nd]	동 응답하다; 반응하다(to) response (to) 명 응답; 반응 investor and consumer responses 투자자와 소비자의 반응
promptly [prɑ:mptli]	부 신속하게; 즉시(= immediately) Perishables must be delivered promptly. 상하기 쉬운 음식은 신속하게 배달되어야 한다.
efficiently [ifíʃəntli]	부 효율적으로 efficient 형 효율적인, 유능한 an efficient operating system 효율적인 운영 체제
possible [pásəbl]	형 가능한; 가능성 있는 as + 형용사/부사 + as possible 가능한 한 ~하게 as soon as possible 가능한 한 빨리 as much as possible 가능한 한 많이

2 Once all of the buyer's concerns have been addressed, an agent from Paulson Realty will present a revised contract for her to sign.
구매자들의 우려를 모두 처리하면, Paulson 부동산의 대리인이 서명할 수정된 계약서를 제시할 것이다.

concern [kənsə́:rn]	명 우려; 일, 관심사 동 걱정하다(over, about) concerning 전 ~에 관한 further information concerning the conference schedule 회의 일정에 관한 추가 정보
address [ədrés]	동 (문제 등을) 다루다; 말하다; (주소로) 보내다 명 주소; 연설 address customers' complaints 고객들의 불만사항들을 처리하다
present [prizént]	동 제시하다; 나타내다; 출석하다; 선물하다 명 선물; 현재 present an identification card 신분증명서를 제시하다
revise [riváiz]	동 수정하다, 개정하다 revision 명 수정; 변경 a major revision to the hiring procedure 채용 과정의 주요 변경사항
contract [kántrækt]	명 계약(서) 동 계약하다; 줄어들다, 수축하다 contracting an outside artist 외부 예술가와 계약하는 것

3 Prior to issuing an estimate, an Iris Painters representative will visit your home to measure the dimensions of the rooms you need painted. 견적서를 발행하기 전에 Iris Painters 대리인이 페인트칠이 필요한 방의 면적을 측정하기 위해 당신의 집을 방문할 것이다.

issue [íʃuː]	동 발표하다; 발행하다 명 주제; 문제; 발행호수 the July issue of *Sartorial* <Sartorial>의 7월호 잡지
estimate [estimət]	명 견적, 견적서 동 추정하다 estimation 명 평가, 평가치 The estimate is 85 dollars 견적가는 85달러입니다.
representative [rèprizéntətiv]	명 대리인, 대표자 형 대표하는; 전형적인, 대표적인 represent 동 대표하다 a customer service representative 고객 서비스 직원
measure [méʒər]	동 측정하다; 평가하다 명 조치, 정책 a preventative measure 예방 조치
dimension [diménʃn]	명 치수; 규모, 범위; 차원 the dimensions of the package 소포의 부피

4 A law firm specializing in negotiating property contracts was hired because of its reputation for honesty and integrity. 정직함과 진실성의 평판 덕에 부동산 계약 협상을 전문으로 하는 법률 회사가 고용되었다.

negotiate [nigóuʃièit]	동 협상하다; 성사시키다 negotiation 명 협상, 교섭 open to negotiation 절충이 가능한
property [prápərti]	명 재산, 소유물(=possession), 소유지; 부동산 a property consultant 자산 상담사
reputation [rèpjutéiʃn]	명 평판, 명성 reputable 형 평판이 좋은(=respected) a solid reputation for leadership 통솔력에 대한 확실한 평판
honesty [ánəsti]	명 정직, 솔직함 honest 형 솔직한, 정직한(=truthful) honest feedback 솔직한 피드백
integrity [intégrəti]	명 진실성(=sincerity) He is a man of integrity. 그는 진실한 사람이다.

토익 빈출 어휘 10

1 Construction on Rosette Avenue may affect attendance at conferences this summer since the road is the direct route to the convention center.
컨벤션 센터에 이르는 직접 경로이기 때문에 Rosette 거리의 공사는 이번 여름 회의 출석에 영향을 줄 수 있다.

construction [kənstrʌkʃn]	명 건설, 공사; 건축물 construct 동 건설하다; 구성하다 constructive 형 건설적인 ↔ destructive 형 파괴적인 constructive criticism 건설적인 비판
affect [əfékt]	동 영향을 미치다; (병이) 발생하다, 병이 나게 하다 effect 명 영향 a serious illness that can affect anybody 누구에게나 발생할 수 있는 심각한 질병
attendance [əténdəns]	명 참석, 출석; 참석자수 attendee 명 참석자 the number of conference attendees 회의 참석자의 수
conference [kánfərəns]	명 회의(= meeting); 회담, 협의(= convention) an international conference 국제 회의
direct [dirékt, dai-]	형 직접적인; 직행의; 정확한 동 ~로 향하다; 총괄하다; 지시하다 direction 명 지시사항; 방향 Improper transactions will be directed to the monitoring committee. 부적절한 거래는 감독위원회에 넘겨질 것이다.

2 A mechanical engineer inspects the manufacturing facilities at the Hobsontech factory to ensure that it is operating safely. 기계 기술자는 Hobsontech 공장의 제조 시설이 안전하게 작동하는지 확인하기 위해 점검한다.

inspect [inspékt]	동 살피다, 검토하다; 조사하다 inspection 명 조사, 검토 a safety inspection 안전 점검
manufacture [mænjufǽktʃər]	명 제조, 제품 동 제조하다 manufacturer 명 제조자, 제조업체 an automobile manufacturer 자동차 제조업체
facility [fəsíləti]	명 설비, 시설; 편의 facilitate 동 용이하게 하다; 쉽게 하다 facilitate a long-term lease 장기 임대를 가능하게 하다
ensure [inʃúər]	동 안전하게 하다; 확실하게 하다, 보증하다 ensure delivery within a week 일주일 내 배달을 보증하다
operate [ápərèit]	동 움직이다, 일하다; 작용하다; 수술하다 operation 명 작동; 수술; 기업, 사업체 Acacia Airlines has expanded its operations. Acacia 항공사는 사업을 확장했다.

3 Anticipating increased demand during the holiday season, Halcyion Photo accelerated the production of its most popular digital camera.
명절 기간 동안 증가할 수요를 예상하며 Halcyion Photo는 가장 인기 있는 디지털 카메라의 제작을 가속화했다.

anticipate [æntísipèit]	동 예상하다; 기대하다(=expect) anticipation 명 예상; 기대 in anticipation of growing demand 증가하는 수요를 예상하며
demand [dimǽnd]	명 수요; 요구 동 요구하다 meet increasing demand 증가하는 요구를 충족시키다
during [djúəriŋ]	전 ~동안; ~사이에, ~하는 중에 during a performance 공연 동안
accelerate [æksélərèit, ək-]	동 가속하다; 촉진하다 acceleration 명 가속; 촉진 accelerate implementation 실행을 가속화하다
popular [pápjələr]	형 인기 있는; 대중적인 popularity 명 대중성 a popular fallacy 흔히 있는 오류

4 The office renovation project has been postponed indefinitely due to a lack of funds.
사무실 보수 프로젝트는 자금 부족으로 인해 무기한으로 연장되었다.

renovation [renəvéiʃn]	명 수선, 수리 renovate 동 ~을 새롭게 하다 a newly renovated lobby 새로 단장된 로비
postpone [pouspóun]	동 연기하다, 지연하다(=delay) postpone a company picnic 회사 야유회를 연기하다
indefinitely [indéfənətli]	부 무기한으로 indefinite 형 무한정의; 분명히 규정되지 않은 for an indefinite period 무기한으로
lack [lǽk]	동 부족하다; ~이 없다(=short on) 명 결핍, 부족(=shortage); 부족한 것 a lack of effort 노력 부족
fund [fʌ́nd]	명 기금, 자금 동 자금을 제공하다 a heavily funded private university 기금을 많이 받는 사립대학

실전
모의고사

READING TEST

In the Reading test, you will read a variety of texts and answer several different types of reading comprehension questions. The entire Reading test will last 75 minutes. There are three parts, and directions are given for each part. You are encouraged to answer as many questions as possible within the time allowed.

You must mark your answers on the separate answer sheet. Do not write your answers in your test book.

PART 5

Directions: A word or phrase is missing in each of the sentences below. Four answer choices are given below each sentence. Select the best answer to complete the sentence. Then mark the letter (A), (B), (C), or (D) on your answer sheet.

101. In last week's strategy meeting, we discussed ways to increase ------- cooperation between departments.

(A) us
(B) our
(C) ours
(D) ourselves

102. Sun Cement must ------- find a way to sell most of the products it has in stock.

(A) quickness
(B) quicker
(C) quickest
(D) quickly

103. The company wants to hire applicants who either have experience ------- show particular interest in the field of industrial design.

(A) or
(B) of
(C) but
(D) so

104. Please make sure that the office supplies ------- before 5 P.M., when the office closes.

(A) delivered
(B) are delivered
(C) delivery
(D) are delivering

105. The personnel manager is ------- for training new employees and evaluating their performance.

(A) responsible
(B) responsibly
(C) responsibility
(D) responsibilities

106. If passengers board the train ------- a ticket, they have to pay a heavy penalty.

(A) outside
(B) without
(C) along
(D) between

107. Mr. Martin's ------- for improving the workflow will be reviewed by senior managers.

(A) recommend
(B) recommendation
(C) recommendable
(D) recommending

108. ------- direct flights from Edmonton to Nairobi are currently scheduled, so it is necessary to use connecting flights.

(A) No
(B) Not
(C) Never
(D) None

109. ------- David Garrett is the author of over 20 novels, the sixty-seven-year-old writer has never enjoyed much fame.

(A) Furthermore
(B) Nevertheless
(C) In spite of
(D) Although

110. Book Club members meet ------- a week to discuss books they have read and to share ideas on good books to read.

(A) one
(B) each
(C) every
(D) once

111. All the employees must be ------- in the use of fire extinguishers and basic fire drills.

(A) taken
(B) revealed
(C) trained
(D) understood

112. Pordice Express has the best prices for shipping goods via containers ------- any destination worldwide.

(A) to
(B) like
(C) with
(D) than

113. All personal information about our customers is strictly ------- and cannot be shared under any circumstances.

(A) confide
(B) confides
(C) confidential
(D) confidentially

114. Delly Catering Service, a catering company ------- the region for ten years, is currently offering a 30-percent discount for any events in the area.

(A) serves
(B) serving
(C) served
(D) server

115. Salary and wage increases at Arriba Delivery Service are based on the company's financial ------- and performance.

(A) condition
(B) conditional
(C) conditionally
(D) conditioned

116. The human-like robot for home use was ------- designed to wash dishes without breaking them.

(A) profoundly
(B) quite
(C) specially
(D) seldom

117. Beginning on September 1, the bank tellers at Zenith United Bank should report any unusual transactions ------- to headquarters.

(A) directs
(B) directly
(C) directing
(D) direction

118. The business consultant explains ------- you need to know about trading to become profitable in a free online video.

(A) what
(B) which
(C) where
(D) how

119. The quarterly newsletter from Estacana Laboratory provides information about ongoing studies and findings from previous studies.

(A) loyal
(B) approached
(C) detailed
(D) probable

120. The office should recruit several new employees ------- lessen the snowballing workload.

(A) so that
(B) for
(C) because
(D) in order to

Go on to the next page

121. ------- the meeting, Mr. Ashina volunteered to participate as a member of the factory safety committee, which organizes safety training.

(A) During
(B) When
(C) While
(D) Instead

122. By the time Ms. Quinn joined our firm as a Web designer, she ------- in the Web design field for many years already.

(A) works
(B) will work
(C) has worked
(D) had worked

123. ------- who wants to participate in the workshop on January 20 must contact Ms. Kameda by Friday.

(A) Anyone
(B) Others
(C) They
(D) Herself

124. Ms. Murata has been assigned to manage the acquisition process because she has a lot of experience in ------- contract negotiations.

(A) fluent
(B) noted
(C) delicate
(D) talented

125. As soon as Mr. Hartman has reviewed all the ideas for the marketing campaign, he will determine ------- proposal will be selected.

(A) whose
(B) who
(C) whom
(D) whoever

126. Aetna International's third quarter profits were 20 percent higher than previously -------.

(A) predict
(B) prediction
(C) predicted
(D) predicting

127. ------- Greenpoint Industries was founded, its goal was to develop cutting-edge technology in oil recycling.

(A) Despite
(B) In addition to
(C) On the other hand
(D) At the time

128. The company logo is so well designed that it is ------- recognizable and very memorable.

(A) universe
(B) universal
(C) universality
(D) universally

129. In the event that your V-12 motorcycle requires repairs, you should visit one of the ------- service centers.

(A) authorize
(B) authorized
(C) authorization
(D) authority

130. ------- three decades ago, the Kellen Corporation is now a leader in the field of building automated machinery.

(A) Arranged
(B) Produced
(C) Settled
(D) Established

PART 6

Directions: Read the texts that follow. A word, phrase, or sentence is missing in parts of each text. Four answer choices for each question are given below the text. Select the best answer to complete the text. Then mark the letter (A), (B), (C), or (D) on your answer sheet.

Questions 131-134 refer to the following e-mail.

To: Customer Services (customerservices@sierra.com)
From: Marc Bernard (marcone@saver.com)
Date: October 27
Subject: Broken watch

To Whom It May Concern,

I am hoping you will be able to give me some information on how to ------- (**131.**) a watch. I have had the model X27B for three years, and ------- (**132.**) last week it worked fine. Now, it doesn't work. I thought the battery was dead, so I changed the battery. ------- (**133.**), it still does not work. It is clear that the watch has malfunctioned due to a mechanical defect. As there are still two years remaining in the warranty period, I'd like to have my watch repaired free of charge.

------- (**134.**). Please let me know what I can do about it.

Thank you for your assistance.

Marc Bernard

131. (A) repair
(B) sell
(C) install
(D) purchase

132. (A) after
(B) unless
(C) by
(D) until

133. (A) Only
(B) However
(C) Also
(D) Even

134. (A) We advise you to call a repair center in your area.
(B) There is no authorized service center for Sierra Watch in my area.
(C) I look forward to meeting you on the day of the meeting.
(D) Fortunately, the technicians finally solved the problems.

Go on to the next page

Questions 135-138 refer to the following invitation.

Dear Mr. Montalban,

The Reinhardt Art Museum cordially invites you, ------- (135.) our generous donors, to a reception to celebrate our 20th anniversary. The reception will be held in the main hall of the museum on the evening of Friday, September 26, from 7:00 P.M. to 10:00 P.M. Please note that ------- (136.) is required for this reception.

If you plan to attend the reception, please check the ------- (137.) box at the bottom of the enclosed registration form. A return envelope has been provided for your convenience; we must receive your reply no later than September 20.

-------. (138.)

Sincerely,

Jennifer Petrocelli

Chief Public Relations Officer
Reinhardt Art Museum

135. (A) nevertheless
(B) as one of
(C) even if
(D) so as

136. (A) consolidation
(B) transition
(C) equation
(D) preregistration

137. (A) appropriate
(B) appropriately
(C) appropriation
(D) appropriateness

138. (A) We hope you will renew your subscription for the upcoming season.
(B) You will get up to 40% off the price of a single ticket.
(C) We will keep you posted once you have registered for the course.
(D) We look forward to seeing you at the reception.

Questions 139-142 refer to the following memo.

Thompson Tour

From: Personnel Department
To: Telephone Operators
Date: June 20, 2019
Subject: Summer Work Hours

In anticipation of increased phone traffic in the ------- (**139.**) season, we have decided to implement extended work hours during the months of July and August. As of July 1, work hours will be changed from 9 A.M. – 5 P.M. to 8 A.M. – 6 P.M. from Monday through Friday and from 9 A.M. – 2 P.M. on Saturdays. Telephone operators should ------- (**140.**) with their fellow workers to adjust the work schedule so that one person remains at work after regular work hours to respond to client calls.

Employees can receive additional ------- (**141.**) for extended work hours. ------- (**142.**).

Thanks in advance!

139. (A) open
(B) complete
(C) fast
(D) busy

140. (A) request
(B) confer
(C) occur
(D) reason

141. (A) compensation
(B) compensating
(C) compensates
(D) compensated

142. (A) Working overtime can cause an accumulation of stress.
(B) All overtime requests must be approved by a supervisor.
(C) The workers objected to working overtime without extra pay.
(D) They can choose to be paid for overtime, or they can take 48 hours off from work.

Go on to the next page →

Questions 143-146 refer to the following letter.

To Whom It May Concern,

On August 7th, I ------- High Sky Flight 747 from Edinburgh, Scotland, to Rio de Janeiro, Brazil. The
143.
flight itself was very pleasant. Upon arrival in Rio de Janeiro, I went through immigration and then went to collect my baggage.

However, I was extremely ------- to learn that my luggage was missing. I reported to your service desk
144.
that my baggage was missing. Then, I spent the entire week in Brazil without any luggage.

-------.
145.

Since my luggage seems to have disappeared, I am submitting a list of what was lost in the luggage for reimbursement.

I hope to hear from you ------- the next few days.
146.

Thank you for your attention to this matter.

Sincerely,

Justin Long

143. (A) took
(B) taking
(C) will take
(D) had taken

144. (A) satisfied
(B) informed
(C) disappointed
(D) relieved

145. (A) I still have not received my personal belongings.
(B) Please keep your personal belongings with you at all times.
(C) I am completely satisfied with your service.
(D) Claims for lost or damaged luggage are increasing.

146. (A) within
(B) until
(C) since
(D) from

PART 7

Directions: In this part you will read a selection of texts, such as magazine and newspaper articles, e-mails, and instant messages. Each text or set of texts is followed by several questions. Select the best answer for each question and mark the letter (A), (B), (C), or (D) on your answer sheet.

Questions 147-148 refer to the following text-message chain.

Weston 9:32 A.M.
Mr. Fielder, is your 10:30 A.M. appointment waiting in Conference Room One?

Fielder 9:37 A.M.
Right. That's Charlie Wilson. He runs a software company and is looking for venture capital because of a new product he developed.

Weston 9:40 A.M.
Would it be all right if I join the meeting? I'd like to see how you handle the interview and process his application.

Fielder 9:45 A.M.
I'm all for it. In fact, I was going to suggest that you attend the meeting.

147. Where most likely do Mr. Fielder and Ms. Weston work?

(A) At a bank
(B) At a software company
(C) At a job fair
(D) At an employment agency

148. At 9:45 A.M., what does Mr. Fielder mean when he writes, "I'm all for it"?

(A) He needs venture capital.
(B) He plans to meet Mr. Willson.
(C) He wants to develop some new products.
(D) He welcomes Ms. Weston to join the meeting.

Go on to the next page →

Questions 149-150 refer to the following form.

SUBSCRIBE TO *THE UTAH TIMES!*

Today! There is no time like the present!

• 1 year: 52 issues for 72 dollars

• 2 years: 104 issues for 130 dollars (save 14 dollars)

(   ) payment enclosed   (   ) bill me later

Name ____________ Phone ____________

Address ______________________________

City ____________ State ____________ Zip ____________

Please allow 2 to 3 weeks for delivery of your 1st issue.

149. How much is a one-year subscription per month?

(A) 5 dollars
(B) 6 dollars
(C) 8 dollars
(D) 10 dollars

150. What information is NOT asked for?

(A) Phone number
(B) Name
(C) Occupation
(D) Zip code

Questions 151-154 refer to the following online chat discussion.

Eleanor Tomlinson [10:29 A.M.]

Hello, Mr. Pugh. Do you have a second? I need to talk about the inventory issue.

Robert Pugh [10:30 A.M.]

Sure!

Eleanor Tomlinson [10:31 A.M.]

According to the database at our Salina warehouse, we have only one box of FSD seasonings. Lately, our deliveries have dramatically increased due to the opening of new establishments. Do you want me to order more?

Robert Pugh [10:32 A.M.]

No, you don't need to. We've switched to another manufacturer. We are planning to start carrying more affordable merchandise. While you were on vacation last week, I ordered a dozen of cases of the new product. They are not here yet.

Eleanor Tomlinson [10:33 A.M.]

Thanks for doing that instead of me!

Robert Pugh [10:35 A.M.]

Don't mention it. In addition, on Tuesday, I notified restaurants of our new product. They are already aware of it.

Eleanor Tomlinson [10:37 A.M.]

Thanks again!

151. What is mentioned about Ms. Tomlinson?

(A) She organized a new database.
(B) She recently took some time off.
(C) She placed an order last week.
(D) She shipped some merchandise today.

152. At 10:30 A.M., what does Mr. Pugh most likely mean when he writes, "Sure"?

(A) He is willing to answer Ms. Tomlinson's questions.
(B) He can do what Ms. Tomlinson requested.
(C) He is giving Ms. Tomlinson permission to work.
(D) He agrees to meet with Ms. Tomlinson.

153. What type of business do Mr. Pugh and Ms. Tomlinson probably work for?

(A) A courier service
(B) A food supplier
(C) A catering company
(D) A restaurant

154. What did Mr. Pugh do at the beginning of the week?

(A) He updated a menu.
(B) He trained a new clerk.
(C) He assisted Ms. Tomlinson with a clearance sale.
(D) He informed customers of a change.

Go on to the next page

Questions 155-156 refer to the following notice.

Attention: All recreation managers

This notice is a reminder about the necessity of maintaining proper pool safety at our facility. You are responsible for informing current staff as well as all new arrivals about our pool safety regulations. All regulations are important, and they must be followed at all times without exception.

(1) All lifeguards must keep a staff radio connected to their person in order to be in contact with other safety personnel.
(2) Lifeguards are required to be certified in first aid to be available at all times while on active duty, and to know emergency phone numbers and the location of the first-aid kit in case of an accident.
(3) Lifeguards are not to leave their posts unattended (except in the event of an emergency), and the use of earphones (mobile phones, MP3 players, etc.) is prohibited.
(4) Staff members are not allowed to smoke or drink because they need to set an example about safety.
(5) The facility must be kept clean and in order by the cleaning crew.

Because it has been difficult to keep our large facility clean, starting next month, we will have three cleaning shifts instead of two. Please let your staff know of this change.
That is all. We at the head office are confident in your ability to follow these guidelines.

Thank you.

155. Why was this notice written?
(A) To inform the staff about some new employees
(B) To stress the importance of following safety procedures
(C) To point out some flaws in a safety program
(D) To congratulate the staff on their performance

156. What are lifeguards NOT expected to be available while on duty?
(A) A staff radio
(B) Cleaning equipment
(C) An MP3 player
(D) Access to a first-aid kit

Questions 157-159 refer to the following e-mail.

To: Rosemary Howard (rosemaryh@Westwood.com)
From: Jordan Gelber (jgelber@Westwood.com)
Date: March 3
Subject: Language Feature

Dear Ms. Howard,

After viewing your Web page, I would like to ask you about the programming codes you used for the company's German Web site for your customers. —[1]—. I noticed that customers can view the Web page in a number of different languages, which is a feature that would be ideal for our customer base. —[2]—. Would it be possible to send me the codes and to tell me how to design this function? —[3]—. Then I can simply alter these language options for our targeted market to include Belgian, Norwegian, and Swedish consumers. —[4]—.

I hope to see you when I attend the managerial workshop in Berlin next week. It is my first visit to Germany, so I am looking forward to it. Perhaps we can meet up while I'm there in case I have any additional questions regarding the program.

Thank you for your time.

Jordan Gelber

157. Why was the e-mail written?
(A) To ask a person to check a written translation
(B) To request technical information
(C) To sign up for a workshop
(D) To correct some flaws in a program

158. Where might Mr. Gelber see Ms. Howard?
(A) In Germany
(B) In Belgium
(C) In Norway
(D) In Sweden

159. In which of the positions marked [1], [2], [3], and [4] does the following sentence best belong?

"I would like to employ this function and make it available for our Belgian customers."

(A) [1]
(B) [2]
(C) [3]
(D) [4]

Go on to the next page →

Questions 160-161 refer to the following advertisement.

Project Manager Needed

This is a wonderful opportunity for the right candidate. You could be part of a rapidly growing company that promotes from within while working from your own office anywhere in the world.

Qualifications Sought:

- Minimum 5 years' project management experience required
- On-line banking or high volume e-commerce applications preferred
- Proven ability to plan and manage finances/budgets and to report on progress
- Ability to adhere to established project methods and management guidelines
- Proven ability to communicate effectively in written English and Korean

Send résumé to: executiveplacement@projectmanager.com

160. What can the applicant expect as a work environment?

(A) Working on the Internet
(B) Working in product development
(C) Working at a retail store
(D) Working at a university

161. What must the applicant have to qualify for the job?

(A) At least five years' supervision experience
(B) On-line banking experience
(C) Fluency in 3 languages
(D) The ability to work well with people

Questions 162-164 refer to the following letter.

Dear Ms. Olivo,

This letter is confirmation that your contract has been renewed with Speed Access. Thank you once again for choosing us to be your home Internet provider for an additional 12 months. Within this package, you will find a personal information form, which you are required to complete and return to us by September 2. Please be aware that there is a penalty of $55 if you cancel the service prior to the termination of your contract.

As a valued customer, you will enjoy unlimited high-speed Internet and a personal e-mail address at no additional cost.

Feel free to contact our customer service center at 1-900-544-7878 if you experience any problems with your connection or if you would like to add any of our promotional packages. We are committed to providing you with great service, and Speed Access looks forward to developing a lasting relationship with you.

Sincerely,

Kai Chapman
Vice President, Customer Service Department

162. What was sent to Ms. Olivo with this letter?

(A) A warranty
(B) A brochure
(C) A form
(D) A discount coupon

163. Under what circumstances will Ms. Olivo be charged a $55 fee?

(A) If she adds an additional service
(B) If she cancels the service early
(C) If she deletes her personal e-mail address
(D) If she doesn't submit a form by September 2

164. What must Ms. Olivo do if she has a problem with the Internet?

(A) Call the customer service center
(B) Submit a written request
(C) Fill out a service complaint form
(D) Wait until her current contract expires

Go on to the next page

Questions 165-167 refer to the following article.

When seeking a job, people should keep in mind the idiosyncratic nature of the labor market. The market is pyramid shaped. —[1]—. Many available jobs are for entry-level positions while there are a smaller number of mid-level positions and considerably fewer top-level openings. —[2]—. Individuals who are interested in these top positions are often required to move to another city or region to find a job matching their skills and experience. —[3]—. Most candidates indicate that they do not desire to change their lives for a job, but when local jobs are seen as below their level of expertise, they are more likely to move. —[4]—. Studies show that employees who feel overqualified for their jobs burn out quickly and quit their jobs.

165. According to the article, what are job seekers reluctant to do?

(A) Apply for high-level positions
(B) Move to another area
(C) Burn out quickly
(D) Accept a mid-level job

166. According to the article, what will companies that hire overqualified employees face?

(A) High salary costs
(B) A large number of new applicants
(C) A high number of staff members who leave
(D) An increased number of applications for entry-level jobs

167. In which of the positions marked [1], [2], [3], and [4] does the following sentence best belong?

"This translates into tough competition for positions that are high ranking."

(A) [1]
(B) [2]
(C) [3]
(D) [4]

Go on to the next page

Questions 168-171 refer to the following advertisement.

SUNSET BEACH RESORT HOTEL

Think of an exotic destination, where the charm of the past is matched with modern conveniences and luxuries, a destination where visitors are pampered and treated royally. That destination is the refurbished Sunset Beach Resort Hotel. —[1]—.

Noted for its lush and famous tropical gardens, the hotel has added a modern fitness center and an open-air cafe near the pool. Within walking distance of the hotel are some of the island's more pristine beaches as well as numerous boutiques and souvenir shops. —[2]—.

Take advantage of the island's major sporting event. We are planning to have our grand reopening at the Vivace Iron Man Triathlon Competition in November. —[3]—. Customers who book rooms for two or more nights during the triathlon will receive room discounts and passes to the local zoo and aquarium as well as discounts on food at our new cafe.

This special promotion is available online at www.sunsetbeachresort.com as well as at travel agencies from now until the end of October. —[4]—. A down payment of $250, which is nonrefundable, is required for online reservations.

168. What is the purpose of this advertisement?

(A) To announce a sporting event
(B) To offer a hotel package
(C) To describe new facilities
(D) To persuade guests to make a deposit

169. What benefits will some guests get by staying at the hotel during the triathlon?

(A) Discounts at souvenir shops
(B) A free tour of the island
(C) Discounts at the poolside cafe
(D) A free pass to a local museum

170. What is NOT mentioned in this advertisement?

(A) Deposits cannot be returned.
(B) Online booking is available.
(C) Guests can stay for only two days.
(D) The special promotion is good through October.

171. In which of the positions marked [1], [2], [3], and [4] does the following sentence best belong?

"For other destinations on the island, the hotel offers free transportation."

(A) [1]
(B) [2]
(C) [3]
(D) [4]

Go on to the next page →

Questions 172-175 refer to the following e-mail.

To: Ivan Martin
From: Adelaide Cho (MK Distributors in Singapore)
Subject: A problem with the W1J-9HG air purifier

Dear Mr. Martin,

I'm e-mailing to inform you of a problem that has come to my attention regarding the W1J-9HG air purifier.

Several retail stores have been returning the air purifiers with complaints that the purifiers are emitting a strange smell. We tested ten of the purifiers in stock by running them for a few hours a day. After just five days, six of them began emitting a damp, pungent odor.

It would appear that the filters on these models are the cause of the problem. They are clogging up quickly and seem to be forcing dirt particles to recirculate along with the purified air. We tried replacing the filters, and a chrome filter seems to clear up the problem completely. Of course, we are not sure if this is a problem across the board, but we would like your authorization to replace the filters on the purifiers in our warehouse and request that you alter all the purifiers that are sent to Singapore in the future.

We look forward to your speedy reply.

Regards,

Adelaide Cho
MK Distributors in Singapore

172. What is the purpose of the e-mail?

(A) To notify a manufacturer of a problem
(B) To inquire about air purifiers
(C) To make a business appointment with a client in Singapore
(D) To discuss some research findings

173. What is reported about the W1J-9HG air purifier?

(A) It is very popular on the Singapore market.
(B) It would be suitable for release in Singapore.
(C) It is required to be tested again.
(D) It releases a bad smell after short-term use.

174. The word "authorization" in paragraph 3, line 4, is closest in meaning to

(A) power
(B) permission
(C) assistance
(D) arrangement

175. What does Ms. Adelaide Cho request?

(A) She requests that use of the patents be approved quickly.
(B) She requests that the purifiers be sent by air.
(C) She requests that later air purifiers be modified.
(D) She requests that Mr. Martin contact the distributor.

Go on to the next page →

Questions 176-180 refer to the memo and information.

To: All TechCom employees
From: Raymond Carter, Director of Human Resources

We understand that your productivity relies, in part, on how comfortable you are about your child's welfare while you are at work. TechCom is pleased to announce an on-site daycare center opening July. Although we will be subsidizing the operating costs of the center, parents must still pay a small fee.
TechCom's childcare will be managed by Sylvia Johnston, who is a certified teacher and has a Ph.D. in early childhood development. Ms. Johnston has taught third grade for 6 years, after which she successfully managed the Play House Daycare Center for 7 years. There is a large grassy area between TechCom's building and the south parking lot which will be fenced in and installed with playground equipment. Indoors, children will have an array of toys and games, including building blocks, books, board games, art supplies, and workbenches. In addition, we will be offering special activities. Refer to the attached schedule for times and costs. As well as full-day care, we will offer after-school care with certified teachers available to help with homework.
TechCom is very pleased to offer this special benefit to our employees and their families.

TECHCOM DAYCARE

Open: 8:00 A.M. – 9:00 P.M. Monday through Friday

Cost per Child
Full-day program 8:00 A.M. – 5:00 P.M. $80/wk.
After-school program 3:00 P.M. – 6:00 P.M. $30/wk.

Extended Hours for Full-Day or After-School Programs
6:00 P.M. – 9:00 P.M. $6/hr.
8:00 A.M. – 9:00 P.M. drop-ins $6/hr.

Additional Activities
Tumbling and Gymnastics
6 weeks 1 hr. / 2 times a week, on-site $120

Early Music or Intermediate Music
4 weeks 1 hr. / 2 times a week, on-site $80

Swimming Lessons
Children are walked 1 block to the YMCA pool
4 weeks 1 hr. / 2 times a week $100

Basketball Training
Children are walked 1 block to the YMCA gym
4 weeks 1 hr. / 2 times a week $100

Tuition is discounted for families enrolling multiple children. If you have suggestions or comments or require more information, e-mail raymondcarterdhr@techcom.com. Activity brochures are available on request.
A luncheon for interested parents will be catered on June 5 at the daycare site. This will be your opportunity to meet the daycare director, Sylvia Johnston.

176. What does the daycare director NOT have?

(A) A Ph.D. degree
(B) Experience as a teacher
(C) Experience teaching at TechCom Daycare
(D) Experience as a daycare manager

177. Why does TechCom offer on-site daycare?

(A) To improve staff convenience
(B) To make money
(C) To offer a good daycare service
(D) To test its products on children

178. What is the monthly cost of one child in daycare from 8:00 A.M. to 5:00 P.M.?

(A) $80
(B) $100
(C) $320
(D) $450

179. What activity is offered on-site?

(A) Gymnastics
(B) Swimming lessons
(C) Basketball training
(D) Band practice

180. How can parents get more information?

(A) By e-mailing Sylvia Johnston
(B) By e-mailing TechCom's chief executive officer
(C) By e-mailing the Human Resources director
(D) By talking to other parents

Go on to the next page

Questions 181-185 refer to the following article and announcement.

Bad News for the Economy

Experts Forecast a Rapid Recession during the Second Half of the Year

April 6th

Many experts have announced that they have determined a recession is in progress, with its peak estimated to be in October. The recession was caused by a decline in consumer purchasing since consumers are becoming more sensible about what they buy. A more likely cause would be the failure of economic growth. However, these causes are speculated by the public. Andrew Bushee, an expert at the Anderson Center at the University of California, outlined three main reasons for the recession. He listed the recent power crisis, inflation concerns, and significant global trade imbalances. At a press conference last week, he announced that a tight financial budget for the next year will be required to overcome the recession. At the top of the list of government priorities, according to the budget, should be allocating more time and effort to the sectors of the economy which will be the most effective at stimulating economic growth and development. According to the econometric model used by certain forecasters, the probability of more looming recession is as high as 90%. A dwindling GDP, increasing unemployment, reduced investments, and job cuts had already been predicted.

JOB CUT ANNOUNCEMENT

Due to the recent recession, we are announcing a cut of an additional 500 jobs over the next two years. The job cuts will be a part of our restructuring plan. Losing more than 10 percent of our workforce is one aspect of the plan that is essential in order to reduce costs and to become more efficient in our operating margin.

In addition to cutting a number of employees, we are asking remaining employees to take salary cuts and to trim expenses to the bone. Because the economy is in poor shape now and our company is suffering as a result, we need to be in decent financial shape.

Thank you.

181. When do experts predict the peak of the recession will be?

(A) This October
(B) In two years
(C) Next October
(D) At the beginning of the year

182. What is NOT a cause of the predicted recession?

(A) The energy crisis
(B) Major companies' restructuring
(C) A general increase in prices
(D) Trade imbalances

183. What is NOT a predicted outcome of the recession?

(A) Layoffs
(B) A decrease in investment
(C) Job cuts
(D) The bankruptcy of banks

184. Why is the company making job cuts?

(A) As a result of unsatisfactory work on the part of the employees
(B) To make sure the remaining employees receive adequate attention
(C) In order to employ new workers
(D) As a result of a decline in the economy

185. In the announcement, the word "aspect" in paragraph 1, line 3, is closest in meaning to

(A) part
(B) attempt
(C) grant
(D) extension

Go on to the next page →

Questions 186-190 refer to the following advertisement, table, and form.

AUS Business Commission

How to Build a Business from Scratch

Starting your own business isn't easy and poses unexpected challenges for most people. The AUS Business Commission provides new entrepreneurs with the tools required to make sound decisions about various issues regarding new business startups. In September, we're offering a series of seminars which you can see on our Web site at www.abc.org.au.

The cost of each session is Australian $95 with registration closing three working days before the scheduled seminar. All sessions will be held at the AUS Business Commission head office located at 512 Downsview in Melbourne. Registration forms can be faxed to 715-2387 or mailed to the address indicated on the form. Online registration is also available on our Web site at www.abc.org.au. Click on the "Registration" link.

SCHEDULE

Number	Title	Day	Date	Time
C805	Hiring Skilled Labor	Monday	September 8	12 P.M. - 4 P.M.
C806	Effective Managing Techniques	Tuesday	September 9	4 P.M. - 8 P.M.
C811	Preparing Company Policies and Protocols	Friday	September 19	9 A.M. - 1 P.M.
C825	Negotiating with Vendors and Suppliers	Tuesday	September 23	4 P.M. - 8 P.M.

AUS Business Commission

512 Downsview Boulevard Melbourne Australia 3831
Phone: 715-2323 / Fax: 715-2387 / www.abc.org.au. / e-mail: jhewitt@www.abc.org.au.

REGISTRATION FORM

Name: Jacqueline Williams
Address: 111 Elizabeth St, Sydney, NSW, 2000, Australia
Phone: (Phone) 545-2611 (Mobile Phone) 545-5667
E-mail: jwilliams@williamstextiles.au
Company name: Williams Textiles Limited
Seminar you wish to attend (indicate number): C825
Have you participated in a AUS Business Commission seminar before? No
Do you require accommodations to participate in the seminar? Yes
Payment: (Do not mail cash. Cash payments must be submitted in person.)
Credit card X **Check enclosed** ____
Credit card type AUSTEX ____ SUPR X BLUCARD ____
Credit card number 9876-5432-1234-5678
Comments / requests Please contact me by e-mail.

Note: We reserve the right to cancel a session due to a lack of interest. In that case, a full refund will be issued.

186. What kind of company is the AUS Business Commission?
(A) A job advertisement agent
(B) An asset management company
(C) A textile company
(D) A business training organization

187. In the advertisement, the word "poses" in paragraph 1, line 1, is closest in meaning to
(A) presents (B) positions
(C) models (D) affects

188. What is stated about the seminars?
(A) They can be paid for only by cash or check.
(B) They are offered at a discount under certain circumstances.
(C) They are directed at experienced businesspeople.
(D) They will be canceled if not enough people register for them.

189. On what date will Ms. Williams attend a seminar?
(A) September 8
(B) September 9
(C) September 19
(D) September 23

190. What is indicated about Ms. Williams?
(A) She works in the textile industry.
(B) She was a former client of the AUS Business Commission.
(C) She prefers to be contacted by phone.
(D) She doesn't need accommodations.

Go on to the next page →

Questions 191-195 refer to the following e-mail, information, and ticket.

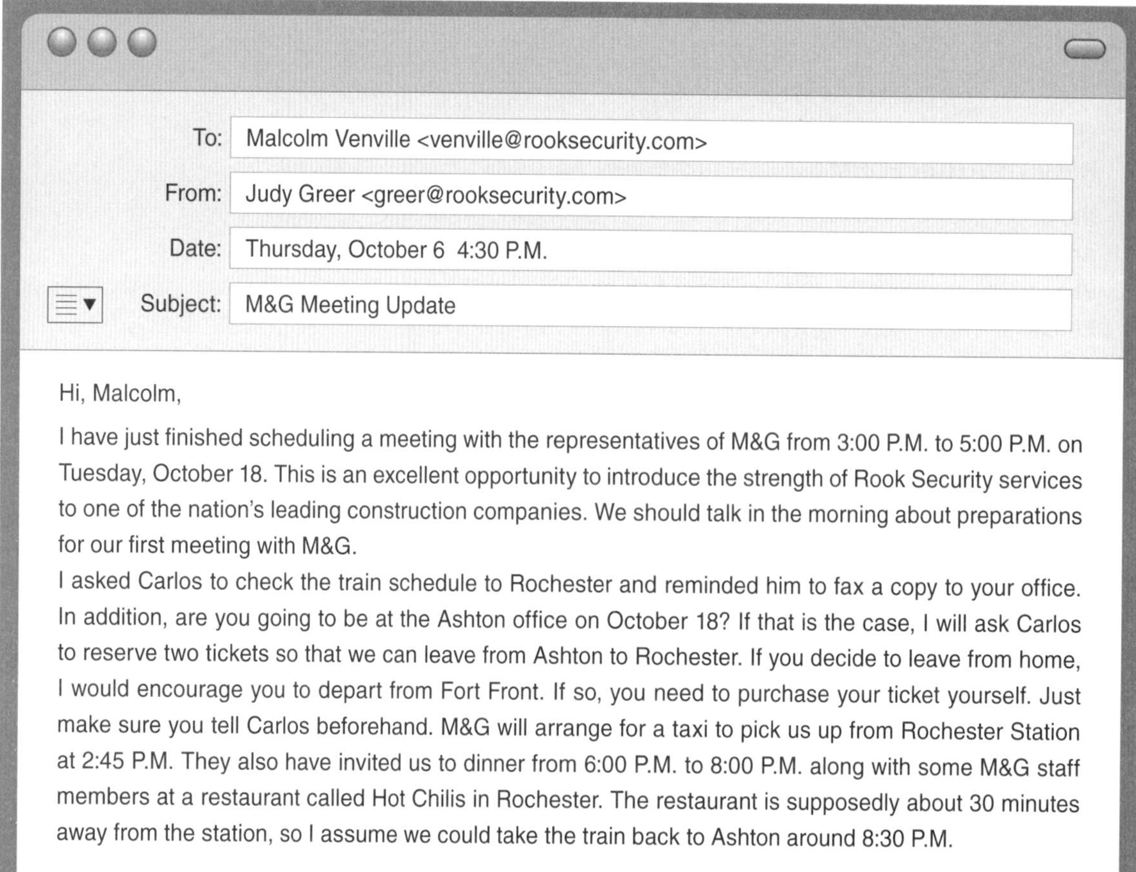

To: Malcolm Venville <venville@rooksecurity.com>

From: Judy Greer <greer@rooksecurity.com>

Date: Thursday, October 6 4:30 P.M.

Subject: M&G Meeting Update

Hi, Malcolm,

I have just finished scheduling a meeting with the representatives of M&G from 3:00 P.M. to 5:00 P.M. on Tuesday, October 18. This is an excellent opportunity to introduce the strength of Rook Security services to one of the nation's leading construction companies. We should talk in the morning about preparations for our first meeting with M&G.

I asked Carlos to check the train schedule to Rochester and reminded him to fax a copy to your office. In addition, are you going to be at the Ashton office on October 18? If that is the case, I will ask Carlos to reserve two tickets so that we can leave from Ashton to Rochester. If you decide to leave from home, I would encourage you to depart from Fort Front. If so, you need to purchase your ticket yourself. Just make sure you tell Carlos beforehand. M&G will arrange for a taxi to pick us up from Rochester Station at 2:45 P.M. They also have invited us to dinner from 6:00 P.M. to 8:00 P.M. along with some M&G staff members at a restaurant called Hot Chilis in Rochester. The restaurant is supposedly about 30 minutes away from the station, so I assume we could take the train back to Ashton around 8:30 P.M.

Judy

TRAIN LINK » **Operation Time, September-November**

Capetown-Lake Park LINE

Arrival	135(WE)	205(WD)	115(HD)	495(EX)
Ashton	12:03 P.M.	12:15 P.M.	12:03 P.M.	2:30 P.M.
Fort Front	12:38 P.M.	12:50 P.M.	–	–
Commontown	1:18 P.M.	1:30 P.M.	–	–
Kushana	1:55 P.M.	2:05 P.M.	1:45 P.M.	–
Rochester	2:25 P.M.	2:35 P.M.	–	–
Laurensville	2:40 P.M.	2:53 P.M.	2:20 P.M.	4:30 P.M.

EX – Express service; does not make all stops
WE – Operates on Saturdays and Sundays only
WD – Operates from Mondays to Fridays only
HD – Holiday schedule; does not make all stops, effective on September 18 and November 3

The railway's automated telephone service provides train information regarding the Service. Please call 020-1313.

Tickets

Purchasing with a credit card:

Tickets can be purchased and printed by visiting our Web site at www.trainlink.com/tickets, or by visiting the ticket booths at the station entrance.

Purchasing with cash:

Tickets can be purchased at El Plato newsstands in the stations, at ticket booths, or upon boarding a train.

Note: There is a $3 extra charge if you purchase a ticket on board a train.

* Please be informed that you can only purchase tickets with cash at the ticket booth at Fort Front until October 21 due to a temporary inspection of online system.

191. Where is Ms. Greer's office probably located?

(A) In Capetown
(B) In Ashton
(C) In Fort Front
(D) In Lake Park

192. What is indicated about M&G?

(A) Its office is located 30 minutes from the closest train station.
(B) It has been a partner of Rook Security for many years.
(C) Its latest project is to construct a new building for Hot Chilis.
(D) It is handling a part of Ms. Greer and Mr. Venville's travel arrangements.

193. Why might Ms. Greer and Mr. Venville start their return journey after 8:00 P.M.?

(A) They may attend dinner with prospective business clients.
(B) They want to wait until an express train is available.
(C) They have arranged to take a tour of Rochester after their meeting.
(D) They are vacationing and their choice of departure times is limited.

194. What train will Ms. Greer most likely take in order to attend the meeting?

(A) Train number 115
(B) Train number 135
(C) Train number 205
(D) Train number 495

195. If Mr. Venville departs from Fort Front for the meeting, how can he purchase his ticket?

(A) By using the railway's automated telephone system
(B) By going to an El Plato newsstand
(C) By visiting Train Link's Web site
(D) By paying cash at the ticket office

Go on to the next page →

Questions 196-200 refer to the following notice, schedule, and application.

MTT Medical Seminars, Inc.

1400 Westbury Avenue, Sarasota, Florida 60279

Join fellow doctors from across the country for education seminars in a variety of fields. MTT seminars are led by some of today's top physicians at our Rowland Campus. All courses are accredited by the American Council of Continuing Medical Education. Early registration is recommended as attendance is limited to 100 participants per seminar. Register online at www.mttmedseminars.com or call Valerie Bradshaw at 703-479-5500 for more information.

Please note that :

Tuition payments of the following amounts are due pending confirmation of registration.

$130 if registered by August 10
$140 if registered by August 17
$150 if registered by August 24
$175 at seminar (if seats are available)

Upcoming Seminars

September 3 1:00 P.M. – 4:00 P.M. *Emergency Medicine* Dr. Jason Isaacs, St. Mary's Hospital	September 9 3:00 P.M. – 5:00 P.M. *Primary Care and Women's Health* Dr. Lauren Graham, St. Joseph's Women's Hospital
September 18 12:00 P.M. – 3:00 P.M. *Infectious Diseases* Dr. Jason Kravits, Tampa General Hospital	September 22 6:30 P.M. – 9:00 P.M. *Pediatric Medicine* Dr. John Lee, University of Miami Medical Center

MTT ONLINE REGISTRATION FORM

Name : Robert Joy
E-mail : rjoy@stlukestexas.com
Address : 427 Oakmont Street, Houston, Texas 77030
Telephone : 832-640-2900
I am registering for : September 22
Registration submitted on : August 18

Thank you for your registration. You will receive confirmation by e-mail within 24 hours.

196. For whom is the advertisement intended?
(A) Medical students
(B) Nurses
(C) Facilities managers
(D) Doctors

197. What is NOT suggested about the seminars?
(A) They are expected to be full.
(B) They must be taken in order.
(C) They are led by some of the best physicians.
(D) They will all be held at the Rowland Campus.

198. When will emergency room care be discussed?
(A) On September 3
(B) On September 9
(C) On September 18
(D) On September 22

199. How much will Mr. Joy pay?
(A) $130
(B) $140
(C) $150
(D) $175

200. For what seminar is Mr. Joy registering?
(A) Pediatric Medicine
(B) Emergency Medicine
(C) Primary Care and Women's Health
(D) Infectious Diseases

| 정답 및 해설 p. 420

정답 및 해설

PART 5&6

UNIT 01 명사

SPARTA Check-UP! 1 p. 15

1 (C) **2** (C) **3** (B)

1 Henson 씨의 이력서에 있는 성과들은 그가 우리 팀의 귀중한 일원이 될 것임을 보여준다.

해설 빈칸은 문장의 주어 자리이고, 정관사 the의 한정을 받는 단어가 들어가야 될 자리이므로 명사 (C) accomplishments가 답이 된다.

어휘 résumé 이력서 valued 소중한

2 Lucy 씨는 자신이 월요일에 보낸 소포를 받았는지 확인하고자 오늘 오전에 전화했다.

해설 빈칸은 전치사의 목적어 자리로 명사가 필요하다. 따라서 (C) confirmation이 정답이다.

어휘 earlier 일찍 confirm 확인하다 confirmation 확인

3 주문을 할 때 주문 양식 아래에 반드시 당신의 서명을 포함해 주세요.

해설 빈칸 앞에 소유격 your가 있으므로 뒤에 명사 (B) signature를 써서 문장을 완성해야 한다. 이외에도 타동사의 목적어, 전치사의 목적어 자리나 관사(a, an, the) 그리고 지시대명사(this, that) 뒤에는 명사를 써야 한다는 것을 잊지 말아야 한다.

어휘 place an order 주문하다 include 포함하다 signature 서명

SPARTA Check-UP! 2 p. 16

1 (A) **2** (A) **3** (D)

1 Gabrawy 씨는 사무용품을 좀 더 주문하기 전에 보관함을 확인합니다.

해설 명사 뒤에 빈칸이 오면 형용사와 명사 모두 정답이 될 수 있으므로 해석을 해 봐야 한다. 의미상 more office supplies '보다 많은 사무용품'이라는 의미가 자연스러우므로 office와 함께 복합명사를 이루는 (A) supplies가 정답이 된다.

어휘 storage cabinet 물품 보관함 order 주문하다 office supplies 사무용품

2 JC 소프트는 그 분야에 높은 수준의 전문성을 갖춘 마케팅 과장을 찾고 있다.

해설 [a/an+형용사+단수 가산명사]의 구조이다. 부정관사 a 뒤에 빈칸이 있으므로 단수 가산명사 (A) level이 답이 된다.

어휘 look for ~을 찾다 expertise 전문성 field 분야

3 경영진 워크숍에 대한 초대장이 모든 부서장들에게 보내졌다.

해설 문장의 주어 자리로 명사가 와야 될 자리이다. 명사 (C) Invitation(초대장)이 들어갈 수 있는 자리인데, Invitation은 가산명사이고 그 앞에 a/an, the, 소유격 등과 같은 한정사가 보이지 않으므로 복수형 (D) Invitations를 써야 한다. 문장의 동사가 have been으로 복수로 쓰였다는 점도 복수명사를 써야 함을 말해 주고 있다.

어휘 management 경영(진)

SPARTA Check-UP! 3 p. 17

1 (D) **2** (D) **3** (C)

1 Holland & Barrett 사는 Tiaren Lakes 지역에서 유일한 최고의 낙농 제품을 다루는 유통회사다.

해설 형용사 only의 수식을 받는 명사 자리로, 의미상 주어와 동격 관계를 이루어 정답은 (D) distributor가 된다.

어휘 distribution 분배, 분포 distributor 유통업자

2 세미나 참석자들은 최소 2주 전에 미리 전화로 등록해야 합니다.

해설 문장의 주어 자리에 들어갈 사람명사와 사물명사를 구별하는 문제로 문맥상 '사람이 등록하다'가 적합하므로 보기 중 사람명사인 (D) attendees가 정답이다.

어휘 register 등록하다 by phone 전화로 at least 최소 in advance 미리 attendance 출석, 참석 attend 참석하다 attention 주의 (집중), 주목 attendee 참석자

3 일반적으로, 의사들은 환자의 의료 기록을 공개하기 위하여 서면 허가가 필요하다.

해설 빈칸은 분사 형태의 형용사 written(서면상의)의 수식을 받는 명사 자리. 타동사 need의 목적어로 위치할 수 있는 품사 역시 명사이므로 정답은 (C) authorization(인가, 허가)이다. written authorization은 '서면 허가'를 뜻하는 복합명사로 기억해 둔다.

어휘 generally speaking 일반적으로 말하면 release 공개하다 authorized 공인된 authorize 권한을 부여하다 authority 권한, 권위자

SPARTA Check-UP! 4 p. 18

1 (A) **2** (B) **3** (D)

1 Hyper 사는 디지털 오디오 제품 생산에 있어서 산업계의 선두주자가 되었다.

해설 has become 동사의 보어로 쓰일 수 있는 단어는 명사 또는 형용사이다. 주어진 명사 (A) leader와 (B) leadership 중 앞에 an이 있으므로 불가산 명사인 (B) leadership은 불가능하기 때문에 정답은 (A)이다.

어휘 industry 산업 production 생산 leader 지도자, 선두주자 leadership 지도력

2 Dmitri Glass 공장은 최근 안전 규정에 중요한 개정사항을 발표했다.

해설 빈칸은 명사 자리로 regulations와 함께 복합명사를 이루어 safety regulations은 '안전 규정'이라는 표현으로 사용된다. 따라서 정답은 (B) safety가 된다.

어휘 issue 발표하다 regulations 규정

3 Radisson 호텔은 등록 절차를 완료하기 위해서 손님들에게 주요 신용카드를 제출할 것을 요구한다.

해설 빈칸은 명사 자리로 process와 함께 복합명사를 이루어 registration process '등록 절차'라는 표현으로 사용한다. 따라서 정답은 (D) registration이 된다.

어휘 major 주요한 complete 완료하다 process 절차, 공정

SPARTA PRACTICE

p. 19

1	approval	**2**	inspectors	**3**	performance	**4**	safety
5	security	**6**	company	**7**	replacement	**8**	skills
9	lectures	**10**	Applicants	**11**	edition	**12**	director
13	assistance	**14**	Employees	**15**	safety		

1 이사회 구성원들은 시설 확장에 대한 승인을 표했다.

해설 타동사(indicated)의 목적어 자리이자 소유격 대명사 their 다음 명사 자리이므로 approval(승인)을 써야 한다.

어휘 indicate 나타내다 approval 승인 approve 승인하다 expansion 확장

2 한 팀의 검사 요원들이 정기적으로 모든 제품의 품질을 검사한다.

해설 전치사 of의 목적어 자리로 명사를 써야 하는데, 문맥상 검사의 주체인 사람명사 inspectors를 써야 한다.

어휘 inspector 검사자 inspection 검사 regularly 정기적으로 quality 품질

3 그 컨설턴트는 우리의 업무 성과에 대한 분석을 수행하였다.

해설 전치사 of의 목적어 자리로 명사 performance를 써야 한다.

어휘 conduct 수행하다 analysis 분석

4 모든 직원들은 금요일에 실시되는 안전 교육에 의무적으로 참석해야 한다.

해설 raining과 묶여 복합명사 '안전 교육'을 만드는 명사 safety를 써야 한다.

어휘 mandatory 의무적인 employee 직원 training 교육

5 방문객들은 중앙 출입구에 있는 접수원에게 보안 출입증을 받아야 합니다.

해설 복합명사를 구하는 문제로, 시험에 자주 나오는 security pass '보안 출입증'으로 암기해 두자.

어휘 visitor 방문객 pick up 얻다 secure 안전한 receptionist 접수원 main entrance 중앙 출입구

6 나는 금융 분야를 선도하는 회사에서 일하기를 원한다.

해설 부정관사 a/an 뒤에는 단수 가산명사만 쓸 수 있으므로 company가 답이 된다.

어휘 leading 선도하는, 이끄는 financial 금융의

7 Boniadi 씨는 그녀의 후임이 올 때까지 Maruti Holdings 사에서 계속 일할 것입니다.

해설 빈칸은 부사절에서 문장의 주어 자리이자 소유격 다음 명사 자리로 replacement를 써야 한다.

어휘 continue -ing 계속해서 ~하다 replace 교체하다 replacement 후임

8 홍보 과장직은 탁월한 의사소통 능력을 가진 후보를 요구하는 자리이다.

해설 skill은 가산명사이다. 단수 가산명사는 반드시 a/an, the 혹은 my, your와 같은 한정사와 함께 쓰여야 하며, 그렇지 않을 경우에는 복수형을 써야 한다. skill을 수식하는 한정사가 보이지 않으므로 복수형 skills를 써야 한다.

어휘 PR(=Public Relations) 홍보 candidate 후보자, 지원자 outstanding 뛰어난, 두드러진

9 Lowell Group은 시간 관리에 대한 강연을 제공함으로써 종업원들의 업무 생산성을 증가시켰다.

해설 lecture는 가산명사이다. 가산명사는 단수 앞에 부정관사 a/an, 정관사 the, 소유격 등과 같은 한정사의 수식을 받아야 하며, 그렇지 않을 경우에는 복수형을 써야 한다.

어휘 increase 증가시키다 productivity 생산성 time management 시간 관리 경영

10 지원자들은 이전 고용주들로부터 최소 2부의 추천서를 받아 제출해야 합니다.

해설 사람명사와 사물명사의 구별 문제로, 추천서를 제공해야 하는 주체는 사람이므로 사람명사 applicants를 써야 한다.

어휘 applicant 지원자 require 요구하다, 요청하다 reference 추천서 previous 이전의 employer 고용주

11 여행 안내서 다음 호에는 하이킹과 자전거 도로에 관한 정보가 포함될 것입니다.

해설 문장의 주어 자리이므로 명사인 edition을 써야 한다.

어휘 edit 편집하다 edition (간행물의) 판, 호 include ~을 포함시키다 trail 산길

12 SSI Group 사의 수석 매체 홍보이사는 모든 홍보 캠페인들의 기획을 조정합니다.

해설 문맥상 사람이 홍보 캠페인들의 기획을 조정하므로 사람 명사인 director를 써야 한다.

어휘 coordinate 조정하다 planning 기획 promotional campaign 홍보 캠페인

13 직원들은 기술적인 문제에 관한 도움이 필요하면 내선 번호 130으로 전화해 달라고 요청받았다.

해설 전치사 for의 목적어로 명사를 써야 하며, 기술적 문제에 대한 도움을 위해 전화하라는 문맥이므로 assistance를 써야 한다. assistant는 사람명사로 단수로 쓸 경우 관사 등의 한정사가 반드시 있어야 하므로 형태상으로도 답이 될 수 없다.

어휘 help desk 업무 지원 센터 extension 내선 번호 technical difficulty 기술적 문제

14 재택근무를 원하는 직원은 해당 문제에 대해 직속 상사와 상의해야 합니다.

해설 빈칸은 문장의 주어 자리이자 주격 관계대명사(who)절의 수식을 받는 사람 명사 employees를 써야 한다.

어휘 employee 직원 employment 고용 telecommute (컴퓨터 등의) 통신 시설을 이용하여 재택 근무하다 immediate supervisor 직속상관

15 컴퓨터 부품들을 제거할 때에는 기본적인 안전 예방 조치들이 준수되어야 한다.

해설 문맥상 '안전 예방 조치'라는 복합명사를 이루어야 하므로 명사 safety를 써야 한다.

어휘 safety precaution 안전 예방 조치 observe 준수하다 remove 제거하다 part 부품

SPARTA ACTUAL TEST

p. 20

1 (C)	2 (D)	3 (A)	4 (D)	5 (D)	6 (B)
7 (B)	8 (A)	9 (B)	10 (B)	11 (C)	12 (A)
13 (C)	14 (C)	15 (B)	16 (A)		

1 Horton 박사와 다음 약속을 잡기 위해, 오늘 영업시간 안에 그의 사무실로 전화해 주세요.

해설 보기가 appoint의 다양한 형태로 구성된 품사 문제. [To make+소유격(your)+형용사(next)+---+전명구(with Dr. Horton)]의 구조를 취하고 있으므로 빈칸은 소유격 및 형용사의 수식을 받는 명사 자리. 따라서 (C) appointment가 답이다.

어휘 make an appointment 약속하다 business hours 영업시간

2 화재 위험 상황에 대한 소방서장의 면밀한 평가 이후에, 25번째 연례 말리부 콘서트를 취소하기로 결정했다.

해설 보기가 evaluate의 다양한 형태로 구성된 품사 어형 문제. [After+형용사 (close)+---- of …]의 구조로 빈칸은 형용사의 수식을 받는 명사 자리이다. 따라서 (D) evaluation(평가)이 정답이다.

어휘 close 면밀한, 주의 깊은 current 현재의 conditions 상황 fire chief 소방서장 make a decision 결정하다

3 모든 구직자들은 중소기업에서 일하는 것에 대해 어떻게 생각하는지 설명하는 에세이를 가져올 것을 요구받는다.

해설 품사 어형 문제로, 빈칸은 동사(are asked) 앞 주어 자리이므로 명사 형태가 적절하다. 보기 중 명사는 (A) applicants(지원자), (B) applications(신청서)이며, 문맥상 에세이를 가져오라고 요구 받는 주체는 사람이므로 (A) applicants가 답으로 적절하다.

어휘 essay (논문 형태의) 과제물, 에세이 small business 중소기업

4 저희 유지보수 팀의 추가 지원이 필요하거나 문의 사항이 있다면 언제라도 저희에게 바로 연락 주십시오.

해설 품사의 알맞은 형태를 선택하는 문제. 빈칸은 형용사 further 뒤에 있으므로 형용사의 수식을 받을 수 있는 품사인 명사 (D) assistance가 답이 된다.

어휘 maintenance 유지, 보수 further 그 이상의, 추가의 feel free to 자유롭게 ~하다 contact 연락을 취하다 directly 바로

5 Landstar Electronics 사의 회장인 Robert Brown 씨는 기조연설에서 소프트웨어 기술, 재능 있는 인력 그리고 특허의 중요성을 강조했다.

해설 관사와 전치사 사이에 빈칸이 있으므로 들어갈 수 있는 형태는 명사형인 (D) importance가 답이 된다. (A) important와 (B) most important는 형용사이므로 뒤에 명사가 와야 하고, (C) importantly는 부사이므로 앞 또는 뒤에 수식 받는 동사가 와야 한다.

어휘 chairman 회장 emphasize 강조하다 talented 재능 있는, 솜씨 좋은 workforce 인력 patent 특허 keynote speech 기조연설

6 직원들은 공식적 업무상 법인 카드를 사용하는 권한이 주어지지만 사적인 비용에 사용하라는 것은 아니다.

해설 빈칸은 personal(개인의)이라는 형용사의 수식을 받을 수 있는 명사 자리이다. 보기 중 명사는 (B) expenses(비용) 밖에 없다. (A) expends는 현재시제 3인칭 단수 동사이고, (C) expended는 과거분사, (D) expensive는 형용사이다.

어휘 employee 직원 authorize 승인하다 credit card 신용 카드 official 공식적인 expense 비용

7 이번 시즌 Five Star 여행사의 특별 여행 패키지 상품은 고급 호텔의 독점적 할인율과 유럽식 아침식사 등의 멋진 혜택을 선보입니다.

해설 such as 다음에 두 가지 혜택을 언급하고 있으므로, (B) benefits라는 복수 명사가 와야 한다. (A) benefit은 관사(a)가 없기 때문에 답이 될 수 없다.

어휘 feature ~을 특징으로 하다 attractive 매력적인 such as ~와 같은 exclusive 독점적인 discount rate 할인율 continental breakfast 유럽식 아침식사

8 5월부터 고객 관리부 직원들은 여러 문제에 적절히 응대하기 위한 교육을 받게 될 것이다.

해설 빈칸 앞 customer service와 연결되는 명사 자리로 '고객 관리부 직원들'의 의미를 완성하는 (A) representatives가 정답이다.

어휘 respond to ~에 대답하다, 응대하다 properly 적절히 various 다양한 representative 대표, 직원 represent 대표하다

9 여행사는 소개할 새 관광명소에 대해 알아보기 위해 정기적으로 관광명소 잡지를 검토할 필요가 있습니다.

해설 품사 어형 문제로, 빈칸 앞의 부사 regularly를 보고 '새로운 장소를 발굴하기 위해, 정기적으로 관광명소의 ---를 알아보는 것이 필요하다'라는 문장에 적절히 들어갈 수 있는 품사를 찾으면 된다. review의 목적어로서, 그리고 of 이하의 수식을 받기에 적절한 명사는 (B) journals(잡지, 저널)이다.

어휘 travel agency 여행사 require 요구하다 regularly 규칙적으로, 정기적으로 review 검토하다 tourist attractions 관광명소 in order to ~하기 위해 site 장소

10 Thompson Virtual College는 원격 교육 강좌로 아프리카 역사와 언어를 가르칠 수 있는 강사들을 모집 중이다.

해설 recruit라는 동사를 받는 목적어로 가장 어울리며, 뒤의 capable of teaching(가르칠 수 있는)의 내용과도 어울리는 것은 '강사'를 뜻하는 명사 (B) instructors이다. (A) instruction은 '지시사항'을 나타내는 일반명사로 모집(recruit)의 대상이 될 수 없다. (C) instructed는 과거분사, (D) instructive는 '유익한'을 뜻하는 형용사이다.

어휘 recruit 모집하다 capable of ~을 할 수 있는 history 역사 language 언어 distance learning 원격 교육 course 강좌

11 신중한 기획 덕택에, Gastown에 새로운 기차역 공사가 지역사회에 불편을 거의 끼치지 않을 것이다.

해설 빈칸은 형용사(careful)의 수식을 받는 명사 자리로 과거분사인(planned)는 답에서 제외한다. (A) plan과 (B) planner는 가산명사로 단수로 쓰일 경우 관사 등의 한정사가 반드시 필요한데, 앞에 관사가 없으므로 형태상 답이 되기에 부적절하다. 따라서 '기획'의 의미를 갖는 불가산명사 (C) planning이 정답이다.

어휘 thanks to ~덕분에 careful 주의 깊은 cause ~을 초래하다 inconvenience 불편함

12 최신 생산 공장을 완성하기 위해 수정된 일정이 현재 일정의 대안으로 제안되었다.

해설 빈칸은 관사(an) 뒤 명사 자리이다. 따라서 보기 중 부사인 (B) alternatively는 제외시킨다. 이제 남은 "대안"이란 의미의 명사 (A) alternative와 (C) alternatives가 남게 되는데 빈칸 앞에 관사(an)으로 보아 단수 형태가 되어야 하므로 정답은 (A) alternative가 된다. alternativeness는 의미상 어색하다.

어휘 revised 개정된 complete 완성하다 state-of-the-art 최신의 propose 제안하다 currently 현재 alternative 대안 alternatively 양자택일로; 대안으로서

<13-16> 다음은 회람에 관한 문제이다.

발신: Elizabeth Manning
수신: Robert Jenkins
제목: 승진
날짜: 4월 21일

Jenkins 씨에게,

저는 인사부의 Elizabeth Manning입니다. 귀하의 승진이 우리 부서에 의해 수락됐음을 알리고자 합니다. 5월 1일 부로, 귀하의 새 직함은 영업 부장이며, Salt Lake 시에 있는 본사로 자리를 옮기게 됩니다. 5월 25일에 시작하여, 귀하의 봉급은 15퍼센트 임금 인상을 반영할 것입니다. 제가 당신께 영업 부장의 새로운 임무를 담은 공식 기술서를 포함하는 첨부 파일과 함께 이메일을 보내드리겠습니다.

당신이 알고 싶어 할 어떤 질문이든 기꺼이 답변해 드리겠으니, 주저하지 말고 제게 연락 바랍니다. 우리 회사를 위해 귀하가 할 더 많은 기여를 고대합니다.

진심으로,

Elizabeth Manning/인사부장

어휘 Human Resources Department 인적 자원부, 인사부 inform ~에게 알리다, 통보하다 promotion 진급, 승진 effective+시점 ~부터 시행되어 transfer 전근시키다 headquarters 본사 attached 첨부된 official 공식적인 description 기술, 묘사 hesitate 주저하다 look forward to ~하기를 고대하다 beginning+시점 ~부터 시작하여 paycheck 급료 reflect 반영하다 pay raise 임금 인상

13

해설 동사 어휘 문제로, 두 번째 단락에서 새로운 직함과 임금 인상 등의 내용이 담겨 있는 것으로 미루어 '귀하의 승진이 수락되었다(your promotion has been approved)'고 해야 자연스러우므로 (C) approved가 답이 된다. (A) notify ~에게 통보하다, (B) apply 지원하다, (D) cite 인용하다

14

(A) 그것은 에메랄드 컨트리클럽에서 오후 1시에 열리게 됩니다.
(B) 올해 저희는 Jenkins 홍보 부장님의 공로를 기념하고자 합니다.
(C) 5월 25일에 시작하여, 귀하의 봉급은 15% 급여 인상을 반영할 것입니다.
(D) 각 팀원은 작별 선물 구입을 위해 25달러씩 내주시기 바랍니다.

해설 빈칸 앞은 인사부의 Elizabeth Manning이 Robert의 승진을 알리며 새로운 직함과 장소를 안내하고, 빈칸 뒤는 이메일로 새로운 임무를 첨부해서 보내겠다는 내용이다. 보기 중 중간에 들어갈 가장 적절한 문장은 새로운 직함, 일하게 될 장소, 그 다음으로 급여 인상에 관한 내용이 들어간 (C)가 가장 적절하다.

15

해설 명사 어휘 문제로, 영업 부장으로서 새로운 '무엇에 관한' 공식 기술서인가를 고려했을 때, '책무, 임무'의 의미를 갖는 (B) responsibilities가 답으로 적절하다. (A) examples 예, 모범 (C) foundation 기초, 토대 (D) knowledge 지식

16

해설 품사 어형 문제로, the additional --- you will be making to our company과 같이 빈칸은 형용사 뒷자리이므로 형용사의 수식을 받는 명사가 필요하다. 보기 중 명사는 (A) contributions (기여, 공헌), (D) contributors (기여자, 공헌자)로, 문맥상 '당신이 할 더 많은 기여(contributions)'가 적절하므로 (A)가 답이 된다.

UNIT 02 대명사

SPARTA Check-UP! 1 p. 23

1 (C) **2** (B) **3** (D)

1 저희 여행사에 최소 24시간 전에 미리 전화하시면 할인된 가격에 항공편을 예약하실 수 있습니다.

해설 대명사의 격에 관한 문제로 주어 자리에 빈칸이 있으므로 주격 대명사 (C) You를 써야 한다.

어휘 reserve 예약하다 travel agency 여행사 in advance 미리

2 Felton 씨는 그의 직장 동료들에 의해 이달의 직원으로 선발되었다.

해설 빈칸 뒤의 co-workers라는 명사를 받는 대명사는 소유격이 알맞다. 따라서 정답은 (B) his가 된다.

어휘 select 선택하다, 선발하다 employee of the month 이달의 직원 co-worker 직장 동료

3 점원은 각 부서의 소포들을 하루에 두 번씩 수집하여 우편물실로 발송합니다.

해설 빈칸은 타동사 takes의 목적어 자리이다. 목적격과 소유대명사 둘 다 목적어 역할을 할 수 있으므로 문맥을 살펴봐야 한다. 빈칸에 들어갈 인칭대명사가 가리키는 것은 packages이므로 (D) them이 정답이다.

어휘 clerk 점원 collect 모으다, 수집하다 package 소포 mailroom 우편물실

SPARTA Check-UP! 2 p. 24

1 (D) **2** (D) **3** (D)

1 Lin 씨는 새로운 회계 소프트웨어에 대한 평을 하기 전에 본인이 직접 사용해 볼 것이다.

해설 [주어(Ms. Lin)+동사(will try)+목적어(the new accounting software)+재귀대명사] 구조의 문장이다. [주어+동사+목적어] 뒤에 주어를 강조하는 재귀대명사를 쓸 수 있는 자리로 강조 용법의 재귀대명사 (D) herself가 정답이다.

어휘 try (좋은지, 적당한지를 확인하기 위해) 써 보다, 해 보다 accounting 회계(학) comment 논평(하다)

2 회의 마지막에, 우리는 서류들을 계속 자세히 검토하고 있는 우리 자신을 발견하게 되었다.

해설 타동사의 목적어 자리로 목적격 대명사와 재귀대명사가 올 수 있다. 주어와 목적어가 같은 사람이므로 재귀대명사인 (D) ourselves가 정답이다.

어휘 look over 검토하다 in detail 상세하게, 자세히

3 팀워크가 강조됨에도 불구하고, PT 사의 많은 직원들은 여전히 혼자 일하는 것을 선호한다.

해설 'on one's own'은 'by oneself'와 마찬가지로 '혼자서'의 의미를 갖는 재귀대명사 관용 표현이다. 문맥상 '팀워크가 강조되지만, 많은 직원들이 여전히 혼자서 일하는 것을 선호한다'는 문맥이 성립되므로 (D) their own이 답이 된다.

어휘 emphasize 강조하다 prefer 선호하다

SPARTA Check-UP! 3

p. 25

1 (C) **2** (D) **3** (A)

1 Jim의 영업 경력과 그의 동료들의 경력이 그들이 국제 영업팀에 합류할 수 있도록 하였다.

해설 명사 어휘의 반복을 피하기 위해 지시대명사 that(단수), those(복수)를 쓴다. 문맥상 빈칸이 가리키는 명사 어휘가 experience로 단수이므로 (C) that이 정답이다.

어휘 experience 경험, 경력 colleague 동료 allow 허용하다

2 대부분의 회사는 자사의 제품과 타사의 제품을 구분하기 위해서 그들만의 브랜드를 사용한다.

해설 문맥상 앞에 쓰인 명사(products)의 반복을 피하기 위해 지시대명사를 써야 하는데 product가 복수로 쓰였으므로 (D) those가 정답이다.

어휘 distinguish 구별하다

3 3월 11일에 있을 워크숍에 참석하고자 하시는 분들은 월요일까지 Daiso 씨에게 연락해야 합니다.

해설 [-------+주격 관계대명사(who)+동사(want)]의 구조이다. 주격 관계대명사절의 동사 want가 복수이므로 빈칸에는 복수 명사가 선행사로 쓰여야 한다. 따라서 정답은 (A) Those이다.

어휘 participate 참가하다 contact 연락하다

SPARTA Check-UP! 4

p. 26

1 (A) **2** (A) **3** (D)

1 연락 모듈은 사람들 간 서로 연락하는 것을 도와준다.

해설 그 연락 모듈이 불특정 다수 간 연락하는 것을 돕는다는 것이므로 '서로'의 의미를 갖는 (A) one another가 정답이다.

어휘 contact 연락 get in touch with ~와 연락하다

2 세탁기가 제대로 작동하지 않으면 다른 것으로 교환하거나 전액 환불을 받을 수 있다.

해설 전치사의 목적어 자리로 적절한 대명사를 고르는 문제. '세탁기가 제대로 작동하지 않으니 다른 것으로 교환해 달라'가 문맥상 적절하므로 '정해지지 않은 다른 하나'를 의미하는 (A) another가 정답이다.

어휘 malfunction 제대로 작동하지 않다 full refund 전액 환불

3 에드먼튼에서 토론토까지의 일주일 탑승권은 통근하는 사람들에게 가장 경제적인 선택이지만 다른 대안도 존재한다.

해설 (A) one과 (C) another는 문장의 주어가 될 때 동사는 단수 취급을 하며 (B) other는 문장의 주어가 될 수 없다. 따라서 여기서 정해진 수가 아닌 상황에서 나머지들을 말하는 (D) others가 정답이 된다.

어휘 economic 경제적인 option 선택(권) commuter 통근자

SPARTA Check-UP! 5

p. 27

1 (D) **2** (D) **3** (A)

1 모든 기술직원들은 국제 컴퓨터 컨퍼런스에 참석하도록 권장 받는다.

해설 [부정대명사 of the 명사] 패턴 중에 of가 생략 될 수 있는 것은 유일하게 all뿐이다. 따라서 All (of) the technical staff members에서 답은 (D) All이 된다.

어휘 encourage 장려하다 international 국제적인

2 전국에 있는 우리 20개 지사 모두 각기 할당된 지역의 유통 센터 역할을 하는 자체 창고시설을 가지고 있다.

해설 [----+of+our twenty branch offices+around the country+has]의 구조로 동사가 단수이므로 일치되는 주어 자리에 (A) Most와 (B) All은 쓸 수 없다. 따라서 정답은 (D) Each이다. (C) Every는 대명사가 아닌 형용사이므로 주어 자리에 쓸 수 없다는 점에 주의한다.

어휘 branch 지사 warehouse 창고 distribution 유통 allocated 할당된

3 총 책임자는 헌신적이고 충직한 직원들에게 감사의 뜻을 표했다.

해설 빈칸은 부정대명사가 들어가야 할 자리로 (B) every는 대명사로 쓸 수 없고 (C) ones는 of 이하의 수식을 받을 수 없으며 (D) much는 대명사로 쓸 경우 <much of the 불가산명사>로 쓴다. 따라서 정답은 (A) all이 정답이다. all은 all (of) the 복수명사/불가산명사를 모두 쓸 수 있다.

어휘 express 표현하다 dedicated 헌신적인

SPARTA Check-UP! 6

p. 28

1 (A) **2** (C) **3** (B)

1 저는 귀사 영업 부서에 큰 기여를 할 수 있을 것이라 확신합니다.

해설 타동사의 목적어 자리로 목적격이 와야 한다. (C) yourself는 주어(I)와 같지 않으므로 답이 될 수 없고 (D) yours는 '소유격+명사'를 대신하는 역할을 하므로 답이 될 수 없다. 따라서 목적격인 (A) you가 정답이다.

어휘 assure 장담하다 contribution 기여, 공헌

2 Lee 씨는 자신의 탁월한 위기 관리 업무를 통해, 자신이 미래의 경영자임을 보여 주었다.

해설 [주어(Mr. Lee)+동사(has shown)+--+목적격 보어(to be a future executive)]의 구조이다. 목적어 자리에 쓰일 대명사가 주어 Mr. Lee와 동일하므로 재귀대명사 (C) himself가 정답이다.

어휘 excellent 뛰어난 risk-management 위기 관리 executive 간부, 중역

3 Hoffman 씨는 지사장 직을 맡아 달라고 초대하는 편지를 받았다.

해설 inviting의 목적어와 inviting의 의미상 주어 a letter가 동일하지 않다. [의미상 주어(a letter)+inviting(현재분사)+목적어(Mr. Hoffman)]에서 주어와 목적어가 동일하지 않으므로 재귀대명사가 아닌 대명사 목적격이 와야 한다. 따라서 (B) him이 정답이 된다.

어휘 receive 받다 invite 초대하다 branch manager 지사장, 지점장

SPARTA PRACTICE

p. 29

1 those	**2** Each	**3** None	**4** they
5 itself	**6** herself	**7** him	**8** her
9 Those	**10** their	**11** that	**12** ours
13 Some	**14** others	**15** its	

1 당신의 요구와 당신 파트너의 요구 사이에 타협점을 찾아야 한다.

해설 앞 명사의 수에 따라 that 또는 those를 쓴다. 문맥상 '당신의 요구와 당신 파트너의 요구'이며, needs를 대신해서 that 혹은 those로 써야 하는 문장이다. needs가 복수 형태이므로 those를 써야 한다.

어휘 make a compromise 타협하다 needs 요구

2 각 기사들이 월말까지 수정되었다.

해설 주어 자리로 of 이하의 한정을 받을 수 있는 대명사 Each를 써야 한다. Every는 형용사로 대명사 역할을 할 수 없다.

어휘 article 기사 correct 수정하다

3 자신의 일에 불만족스럽다고 말하는 직원들은 아무도 없었다.

해설 주어 자리로 of 이하의 한정을 받을 수 있는 대명사 None을 써야 한다. No는 형용사로 대명사 역할을 할 수 없다.

어휘 unsatisfied 불만족스러운

4 Bell 씨와 Corden 씨에게 연락하여 다음 주 월요일에 시간이 되는지 물어보십시오.

해설 빈칸은 주어 자리이나 재귀대명사는 주어 자리에 올 수 없으므로 they를 써야 한다.

어휘 contact 연락하다 ask if ~인지 아닌지 묻다 available (사람들을 만날) 시간[여유]이 있는

5 TJ International 사는 최고 품질의 제품을 생산함으로써 회사의 지위를 확고히 했다.

해설 [주어+타동사+목적어] 구조의 문장에서 주어와 목적어가 같을 경우에는 재귀대명사를 써야 한다. 문맥상 주어 TJ International과 목적어가 같으므로 itself를 써야 한다.

어휘 establish 설립하다; (지위, 명성을) 확고히 하다

6 Irvin 씨의 업무 기량은 매우 뛰어나서 그녀는 모든 업무를 혼자서 처리해 낼 수 있었다.

해설 [by+재귀대명사]는 '혼자서'를 의미한다. by 뒤에 Ms. Irvin을 받아 주는 재귀대명사 herself를 써야 한다.

어휘 skill 기량, 솜씨 efficient 효율적인, 유능한

7 Brian이 너무 설득력 있게 얘기했기 때문에 모든 부장들은 그에게 동의하였다.

해설 문맥상 전치사 with의 목적어는 Brian이고 동사 agreed의 주어는 all the directors이다. 주어와 전치사의 목적어가 같을 때는 재귀대명사를 쓰고, 다를 때는 일반 대명사를 쓴다. 이 문장에서는 주어(all the directors)와 목적어(Brian)가 같지 않으므로 him을 써야 한다.

어휘 persuasively 설득력 있게 director 관리자

8 병원에서 학생 자원봉사자로서의 일이 Paula로 하여금 간호사가 되는 데 관심을 갖게 했다.

해설 문장의 주어는 Paula's work이고 동사 made의 목적어는 Paula를 받아 주는 대명사를 써야 하므로 주어와 목적어가 동일하지 않다. 따라서 재귀대명사가 아니라 목적격 인칭대명사 her를 써야 한다.

어휘 volunteer 자원봉사자; 자원 봉사하다

9 광고에 관심 있는 사람들은 인사부의 Allen 씨에게 연락해야 한다.

해설 Those (who are) interested in ~은 '~에 관심 있는 사람들'이란 뜻으로 Those를 써야 한다.

어휘 interested in ~에 관심 있는 Personnel Department 인사부

10 일하는 사람들은 최소 그들의 월 소득의 20%를 저축함으로써 은퇴 준비를 해야 한다.

해설 [소유격+명사]의 구조이다. monthly income을 수식하는 소유격 their를 써야 한다.

어휘 retirement 은퇴 at least 최소한 monthly income 월 소득

11 미국의 생활 수준은 여전히 세계의 다른 모든 국가의 생활 수준보다 높다.

해설 문맥상 지시대명사가 가리키는 명사는 'standard of living'이며, 단수이므로 that을 써야 한다.

어휘 standard of living 생활 수준

12 AP 컴퓨터는 그들의 신모델을 조만간 출시할 것이나, 우리는 우리의 신모델에 대한 설계조차 마치지 못했다.

해설 문맥상 designing의 목적어는 our new model이다. [소유격+명사]를 받아 주는 소유대명사로 ours를 써야 한다.

어휘 release 출시하다 design 설계하다

13 지역 농부들 중 일부가 외국 농산물 생산업자들과의 경쟁에 맞서기 위해 그들의 힘을 모으기로 결정했다.

해설 [Some of the 복수명사+복수동사], [Each of the 복수명사+단수동사]의 구조이다. 동사가 have decided 복수이므로 Some을 써야 한다.

어휘 local 지역의 combine 결합하다 competition 경쟁 agricultural 농업의 producer 생산자

14 회사는 다른 회사들과 경쟁하기 위해 더 뛰어난 자질을 갖춘 시장 분석가들을 찾고 있다.

해설 전치사(against) 뒤에는 전치사의 목적어가 와야 하는데, other는 형용사의 기능뿐이다. 따라서 대명사 others(= other companies)를 써야 한다.

어휘 search for ~을 찾다 qualified 자격을 갖춘 analyst 분석가 compete against/with ~와 경쟁하다

15 회사의 10주년 기념식 때, Timeline 사는 향후 10년을 위한 야심 찬 프로젝트를 선보였다.

해설 [소유격+명사]의 구조이다. 문맥상 '회사의 10주년 기념식'이라는 의미가 되어야 하므로, Timeline을 받아 주는 소유격 its를 써야 한다.

어휘 anniversary celebration 기념 행사 unveil (새로운 계획, 상품 등을) 발표하다 ambitious 야심 찬

SPARTA ✔ ACTUAL TEST

p. 30

1 (C)	2 (C)	3 (C)	4 (A)	5 (A)	6 (A)
7 (C)	8 (A)	9 (A)	10 (A)	11 (A)	12 (D)
13 (A)	14 (D)	15 (B)	16 (D)		

1 Loudoun County는 거주민들이 지방 공무원들과 협력을 해서 그들 지역사회에서 자원 봉사할 것을 장려한다.

해설 대명사의 격을 묻는 문제. 빈칸의 위치는 명사(communities) 앞이므로 명사를 수식해 줄 수 있는 소유격 대명사 (C) their가 답이 된다.

어휘 encourage 장려하다, 용기를 주다 resident 주민, 거주자 volunteer 자원 봉사하다 community 지역사회, 공동체 cooperation 협력, 협동 civil servant 공무원, 관리

2 Charlotte이 다음 달에 교토에 가게 되면 그녀는 Lake View 호텔에 머무르게 될 것이다.

해설 [주어+will stay]의 구조이다. 문장의 주어 자리에는 주격 대명사를 써야 하므로 (C) she가 정답이다.

어휘 stay 머무르다 next month 다음 달

3 Andrew Harley는 다가오는 회사 워크숍을 위한 여러 활동을 자신이 직접 조정하는 일을 자원했다.

해설 알맞은 대명사의 격을 묻는 문제. [주어(Andrew Harley)+동사(volunteered)+목적어(to coordinate several activities)]의 형태로 완벽한 문장을 취하고 있기 때문에 주어(Andrew Harley)가 직접 여러 활동들을 챙기기 위해 자원했다는 의미로 재귀대명사(강조 용법)를 쓰는 것이 적절하다. 따라서 (C) himself가 정답.

어휘 volunteer 자원하다 coordinate 조직하다, 편성하다 upcoming 다가오는

4 모든 사무실의 배선을 다시 깔아서 전기 요금이 상당히 낮아졌다.

해설 [-------+of 복수 명사 + 복수 동사]의 구조로 보기 중 (C) every는 형용사로만 사용되므로 정답이 될 수 없고, 양을 나타낼 때 쓰는 (B) little은 of the(소유격) 다음 불가산명사를 써야 하므로 정답이 될 수 없다. 또한 (D) each는 부정대명사로 쓰일 때 동사를 단수 취급하므로 all of the(소유격)+복수 명사+복수 동사의 수 일치가 맞는 (A) all이 정답이다.

어휘 now that ~ 때문에 rewire 배선을 다시 하다 electric bill 전기 요금 considerably 상당히 lower 더 낮은

5 현대식 유조선의 평균 용량은 10년 전에 만들어진 가장 큰 화물선의 용량보다 더 크다.

해설 앞에 쓰인 단수명사(capacity)의 반복을 피하기 위해 지시대명사 (A) that으로 대신할 수 있는 자리이다.

어휘 capacity 용량, 수용력 cargo ship 화물선

6 등산 장비를 사용하는 사람은 누구나 개별적으로 사용법을 정확하게 배워야 할 책임이 있다.

해설 빈칸은 문장의 주어가 와야 할 자리로, 문맥상 사용하는 사람은 '누구든지'의 의미가 되어야 하므로 '~하는 사람은 누구나'를 뜻하는 대명사 (A) Anyone이 정답이다. 대명사(anyone)뒤에 [관계대명사+be동사](who is)가 생략되어 있는 문장 구조라고 보면 된다.

어휘 climbing equipment 등산 장비 personally 개인적으로 be responsible for ~의 책임이 있다 correctly 정확하게

7 Goldfields Logistics 사는 9월 17일에 주 경쟁업체인 Snyman Transport 사를 인수할 예정이다.

해설 빈칸은 타동사 purchase의 목적어인 명사 chief competitor 앞이므로 소유격이 와야 하므로 (C) its가 정답이다.

어휘 purchase 구매/매입하다 chief competitor 주 경쟁업체

8 Penna 씨의 비서인 Kravitz 씨는 그에게 최신 금융 뉴스에 대해 보고하는 것을 담당하고 있다.

해설 빈칸은 동명사의 목적어 자리이다. 보기 중 목적어 역할을 할 수 있는 것은 (A) him, (B) himself, (D) his이며 빈칸은 Mr. Penna를 가리키므로 (A) him이 정답이다.

어휘 assistant 비서 be in charge of ~를 책임지다 brief A(사람) on B(사물) ~에게 (~에 대해) 알려주다[보고하다] latest 최신의

9 Kim 씨는 예정보다 일찍 예산 보고서를 작성하고 Jessica가 그녀의 보고서를 끝마칠 수 있도록 도와줬다.

해설 finish는 '~을 끝내다, 완료하다'를 뜻하는 타동사이므로 빈칸은 finish의 목적어 자리이다. 주격인 (D) she는 오답이다. 문맥상 'Jessica 씨가 그녀를/그녀 자신을 끝마치다'는 어색하므로 (B) her와 (C) herself도 답이 될 수 없다. 'Jessica가 그녀의 보고서(her budget report = hers)를 끝낼 수 있도록 도와줬다'라는 내용이 자연스럽게 연결된다.

어휘 complete 완성하다, 끝내다 budget report 예산 보고서 ahead of ~보다 앞서, 미리

10 학부모 위원회 회원들은 다가오는 회의를 누가 조정할지 그들끼리 결정할 것이다.

해설 대명사 격을 묻는 문제. 문맥상 앞의 주어(Members)가 목적어와 같은 대상이므로 재귀대명사인 (A) themselves가 답이 된다. 참고로 among themselves라고 하면 '자기들끼리'라는 의미를 지닌다.

어휘 coordinate 조정하다 upcoming 곧 다가오는

11 회사가 고객에게 제공한 제품설명서가 너무 모호하여 고객들은 어떤 제품을 사야 할지 판단을 내리기가 어려웠다.

해설 문맥상 빈칸은 주어(customers)를 대신 받는 대명사 (A) they가 와야 한다.

어휘 product description 제품설명서 provide 제공하다 obscure 모호한 struggle 투쟁(고투)하다

12 침술치료사와 약초치료사들에 의해 사용된 것들을 포함해 질병에 대한 대체 치료법들이 우리의 웹사이트상에 논평되어 있다.

해설 빈칸에 어울리는 대명사를 찾는 문제이다. 빈칸 뒤가 과거분사(employed)이므로 빈칸과 employed 사이에 [who/which/that+be 동사]가 생략되었음을 미리 알아야 한다. 문장 앞의 복수 명사(treatments)를 받는 대명사 자리이므로 (D) those가 정답이다.

어휘 alternative 대안의 treatment 치료(법) employ 고용하다, 사용하다 acupuncturist 침술가 herbalist 약초 치료사 review 검토하다, 논평하다

⟨13-16⟩ 다음은 편지에 관한 문제이다.

Smith 부부
1534 Oxford가
필라델피아 PA 19121

Smith 부부께,

저희는 고객님께서 최근 해변가에 있는 Motawi Bungalow에서의 숙박에 관한 내용의 편지를 받았습니다. 지난달 고객님께서 예약하신 객실을 확인 전화한 시점에 이미 예약이 되어버린 것에 대해 진심으로 유감의 말씀을 드리고 두 분 고객님을 위한 대체 객실에 동의해 주신 데 대해 감사의 말씀을 드립니다.

다음 방문 시 50% 할인을 받을 수 있는 동봉된 쿠폰을 받아 주십시오. 불편함을 드린 데 대한 저희의 사과의 표시이며 고객님께서 주신 이해에 대한 감사의 표시입니다. 저희 웹 사이트에서 예약하실 때 Motawi의 지점 어떤 곳이

든 고르신 후 결제방법 선택 시에 쿠폰에 있는 코드번호를 입력하시면 됩니다. 다음에 고객님을 다시 뵙기를 고대합니다.

진심으로,

Felicity O'Dell
고객 서비스부

어휘 concerning 대한 recent 최근의 seashore 해변가 suite (호텔의) 스위트룸, 객실 confirmation 확인 accommodations 숙박 gratitude 감사 enclosed 동봉된 visiit 방문

13

해설 문맥상 예약 확인 전화를 했을 때 그 객실이 '다 찼다'가 자연스러우므로 '~를 차지하다, 사용하다'는 뜻의 보기 (A) occupied가 정답이다

어휘 continued 지속되는 misplaced 잘못된 intended 의도하는, 계획된

14 (A) 쿠폰을 떼어 내어 가능한 한 빨리 발송해 주세요.
(B) 편지 앞면에 쿠폰을 붙여 주세요.
(C) 유감스럽지만, 우리는 일어난 일에 대해서 어떤 책임도 질 수 없습니다.
(D) 다음 방문 시 동봉된 50% 할인 쿠폰을 받아 주십시오.

해설 빈칸 앞의 내용은 손님의 원했던 방이 이미 예약이 차서 대체 객실을 받아 준 것에 대해 감사하고 있고 빈칸 다음의 내용으로 보아 빈칸은 혜택을 제공한 것으로 볼 수 있다. 따라서 문맥상 적절하게 이어줄 문장은 (D)이다.

15

해설 편지를 작성한 사람(Felicity O'Dell)이 회사를 대표해서 이전 고객에게 부실한 서비스에 대해 사과하는 내용이므로 정답은 '저희'라는 의미인 (B) our이다.

16

해설 빈칸 앞에 주어가 없는 것으로 미루어 명령문 문장이라는 것을 알 수 있다. 동사원형 형태의 (D) select가 답이다. 참고로 앞의 'when booking ~'은 주어(you), 주어를 생략하고 동사를 -ing 형태로 만든 분사구문이라는 것도 알아 두자.

UNIT 03 형용사

SPARTA Check-UP! 1

p. 33

1 (B) **2** (A) **3** (B)

1 비행기 표를 출발 두 달 전에 예약한다면 상당한 할인 혜택을 받을 수 있다.

해설 [a+형용사+명사]의 구조이다. 명사(discount)를 수식하는 형용사가 필요한 자리로 (B) substantial(실질적인, 상당한)이 정답이다.

어휘 reserve 예약하다 depart 출발하다

2 Ana 씨는 보고서를 마감일 이내에 끝내는 것이 어렵다고 생각했지만, 어떻게든 제시간에 보고서를 제출했다.

해설 consider는 [consider+목적어+형용사] 형태로 쓰이는 5형식 동사이므로 빈칸은 형용사 자리이다. 따라서 (A) difficult가 정답이 된다.

어휘 though 비록 ~이지만 consider it A to V ~하는 것을 A라고 생각하다 manage 어떻게든 해내다 hand in 제출하다 on time 제시간에

3 회사 밖에서 기밀 정보에 대한 얘기를 나누는 것은 부적절하다.

해설 be동사(is)의 보어 자리이다. 따라서 빈칸에는 형용사인 (B) appropriate(적절한)가 오는 것이 적절하다. It은 가주어, to discuss는 진주어로 쓰였다.

어휘 discuss 상의(의논)하다 confidential information 기밀 정보

SPARTA Check-UP! 2

p. 34

1 (D) **2** (B) **3** (B)

1 모든 국제 여행자들은 출발하기 최소 2시간 전에 공항에 도착해야 한다.

해설 빈칸 뒤에 복수 가산명사(international passengers)가 연결되어 있으며, 복수 가산명사와 같이 쓸 수 있는 형용사는 보기 중 (D) All뿐이다. All은 복수 가산명사와 불가산명사를 모두 취한다.

어휘 at least 최소한 departure 출발

2 화물의 배송상태가 좋은지 확실히 하기 위해 각 소포의 내용물을 면밀히 살펴봐야 합니다.

해설 [each+단수 가산명사]는 '각각의, 각~'이라는 의미를 나타낸다. 문맥상 '각각의 소포'라는 의미가 되어야 하므로 (B) each가 정답이다.

어휘 inspect 점검하다 contents 내용물 ensure 확실히 하다 shipment 배송

3 Time Delivery 사의 요금 상승 때문에 우리는 다른 택배 회사를 찾고 있다.

해설 [another+단수 가산명사]의 구조에서 단수 가산명사(delivery company)를 수식할 수 있는 형용사는 보기 중 (B) another뿐이다. (A) some과 (D) other는 복수 가산명사와 불가산명사를 취한다.

어휘 rising 증가하는 rates 요금 look for ~을 찾다

SPARTA Check-UP! 3

p. 35

1 (D) **2** (B) **3** (A)

1 회의나 세미나와 같은 행사를 순조롭게 진행할 수 있도록 돕기 위해 최신의 시청각 설비가 이용 가능합니다.

해설 빈칸은 명사(audiovisual equipment)를 수식하는 형용사 자리이다. (D) latest는 '최신의'라는 의미의 형용사로 문맥상 audiovisual equipment의 장점을 설명하기 위한 수식어로 가장 적절하다. (A) late와 (C) later 역시 형용사이긴 하지만, late는 '늦은', later는 '~보다 나중의'를 뜻하여 의미상 어색하다.

어휘 audiovisual 시청각의 available 이용 가능한 run 운영하다 smoothly 순조롭게

2 모든 직원은 사무실에서 조용히 말함으로써 다른 동료들을 배려해야 한다.

해설 be동사 다음에는 형용사가 들어가는 자리이므로 (B) considerate와 (A) considerable이 나올 수 있으나 문맥상 '~에게 사려 깊은'의 의미의 (B)가 정답으로 가장 적절하다.

어휘 colleague 동료 softly 부드럽게, 조용히 considerable 상당한 considerate 사려 깊은, 신중한

3 좋은 조정자는 항상 냉정함을 유지하고, 다른 회사의 대표자들과 따지기 좋아하게 되는 것을 피해야 한다.

해설 빈칸은 동사(becoming)의 보어 자리이다. 형용사인 (A)와, (C) 중에서 주어가 사람이기 때문에 '논쟁을 즐기는'이 의미상 적절하다. arguable은 사람이 아니라 '사안'을 수식하는 어휘이다.

어휘 representative 대표자 firm 회사 argumentative 따지기 좋아하는, 시비를 거는 arguable 논쟁의 소지가 있는

SPARTA Check-UP! 4

p. 36

1 (C) **2** (B) **3** (D)

1 18세 이상이면, 국제평화 포스터 경연대회에 참석할 자격이 있습니다.

해설 be동사 다음 주어의 상태를 서술하는 형용사 자리다. 따라서 (C) eligible가 정답이 된다.

어휘 enter 참석하다 eligibility 적임, 적격

2 저희 퍼시픽 항공사는 어떠한 분실된 짐에 대해서도 책임을 지지 않는다는 점을 알려드리게 되어 죄송합니다.

해설 빈칸은 be동사의 보어 자리로 형용사가 들어가야 한다. 형용사인 (A) responsive(응답하는)와 (B) responsible(책임이 있는) 중에서, 문맥상 '항공사가 분실된 가방을 책임질 수 없어서 미안하다'는 내용이므로 (B)가 답이 된다. be responsible for(~에 대해 책임이 있다)라는 숙어와 be responsive to(~에 대응하다)라는 숙어 표현을 암기해 두자.

어휘 luggage 짐 respond 대답[응답]하다 response 대답, 응답

3 Jones 씨는 회의에 참석할 수 없지만 Park 씨가 거기서 회사를 대표할 것이다.

해설 [be able to부정사] '~할 수 있다'의 숙어 표현을 완성하는 (D) to represent가 정답이다.

어휘 represent (행사·회의 등에서 단체 등을) 대표하다

SPARTA PRACTICE

p. 37

1 complete	**2** ready	**3** optimistic	**4** evident
5 hopeful	**6** members	**7** a little	**8** interest
9 all	**10** every	**11** other	**12** other
13 beneficial	**14** responsible	**15** economic	

1 Evans Consulting 사는 철저한 분석을 통하여 고객의 완벽한 신뢰를 얻었다.

해설 [the+형용사+명사]의 구조로 명사 trust를 수식하는 형용사 complete를 써야 한다. complete는 '완성하다, 마치다'라는 의미를 갖는 동사이기도 하고, '완전한'이라는 의미를 갖는 형용사이기도 하다.

어휘 earn 얻다 trust 신뢰 client 고객 thorough 철저한 analysis 분석

2 의료 건물은 이번 달 말까지 사용을 위한 준비가 될 것이다.

해설 be동사 뒤에서 주어를 설명하는 형용사 보어가 필요한 자리이다. 따라서 정답은 형용사 ready이다.

어휘 medical 의료의

3 투자자들은 주식 시세에 대해 낙관적인 자세를 유지하고 있다.

해설 remain 동사는 be동사와 마찬가지로 불완전 자동사이다. 주어를 설명하는 형용사 보어가 뒤따르는 동사로, 형용사 optimistic(낙관적인)을 써야 한다.

어휘 investor 투자자 remain ~인 상태로 남아 있다 stock price 주식 시세

4 Anderson 씨는 이 자리에 가장 자격을 갖춘 인물임이 분명해 보인다.

해설 seem은 불완전 자동사로 주어를 설명하는 형용사 보어가 뒤따르는 동사이다. 따라서 형용사 evident(명백한)를 써야 한다.

어휘 evidently 명백하게 qualified 자격을 갖춘

5 출판사들은 새해가 오기 전에 책이 출간되기를 바라고 있다.

해설 be동사 다음 주어의 상태를 서술하는 형용사 자리이므로 hopeful을 써야 한다.

어휘 publisher 출판인, 출판사 hopeful 희망에 찬, 기대하는 hopefully 바라건대, 희망을 가지고 distribution 분배, 배급

6 많은 직원들이 마감 시한을 맞추기 위하여 주말에 일해야 한다.

해설 many 뒤에는 복수 가산명사를 써야 하므로 members가 답이 된다.

어휘 meet 충족시키다 deadline 마감일

7 Dalton 씨의 팀은 판매 실적을 올리기 위해 단지 약간의 격려가 필요했을 뿐이었다.

해설 encouragement는 여기에서 불가산명사로 이를 수식하는 a little을 써야 한다.

어휘 simply 단지 encouragement 격려 improve 향상시키다 sales results 판매 실적

8 이사회는 증가하는 투자에 대해 거의 관심을 보이지 않았다.

해설 little은 불가산명사를 수식한다. 따라서 불가산명사 interest(관심)를 써야 한다. interest는 어떤 일이나 분야에 대한 '관심, 흥미'를 나타낼 때 불가산명사이며, '취미활동, 관심분야'의 뜻으로 쓰일 때는 가산명사이다.

어휘 board of directors 이사회 increase 증가시키다 investment 투자

9 발표 중에 모든 휴대용 전자 장치가 꺼져 있는지 확인하십시오.

해설 every는 단수 가산명사와 함께 쓰고 all은 복수 가산명사 또는 불가산명사와 함께 쓰므로 복수 가산명사 mobile electronic devices 앞에는 all을 써야 한다.

어휘 ensure 확실하게 하다 turn off 끄다 presentation 발표

10 컴퓨터 사용자들은 30일마다 비밀번호를 바꾸기로 되어 있다.

해설 [every+시간]은 '그 시간마다'의 의미를 나타낸다. '매 30일마다 (every 30 days)'이라는 뜻을 만드는 every가 정답이다.

어휘 be supposed to ~하기로 되어 있다

11 S-Cable이 부도가 났을 때, 그 회사의 모든 고객들은 다른 케이블 공급업체를 이용할 수밖에 없었다.

해설 [other+복수 가산명사]의 구조이며 뒤따르는 명사가 cable providers로 복수 가산명사이므로 other를 써야 한다. another는 단수 가산명사를 수식한다.

어휘 go out of business 부도나다 be forced to do 어쩔 수 없이 ~하다 provider 공급자[업체]

12 웹 사이트는 뉴질랜드에 대한 관광, 여행, 그리고 다른 정보를 제공한다.

해설 [another+단수 가산명사]와 [other+복수 가산명사/불가산명사]의 구조에서 other는 복수 가산명사 혹은 불가산명사를 수식하고 another는 단수 가산명사만 수식하므로 불가산명사 information을 수식할 수 있는 단어는 other이다.

어휘 tourism 관광

13 매출액의 개선이 전체적으로 그 회사에 유익한 영향을 끼쳤다.

해설 매출액의 개선이 유익한 영향을 주었다는 문맥이므로 '유익한, 이로운'의 의미를 갖는 beneficial이 정답이다. benefitted는 동사 benefit(~에게 혜택을 주다)의 과거분사 형태로 '혜택을 받은'을 의미한다.

어휘 improvement 개선 sales figures 매출액 effect 영향, 효과 as a whole 전체적으로

14 Toronto 시는 스포츠 단지의 전체적인 유지보수 관리와 수리를 책임지고 있다.

해설 be responsible for는 '~을 책임지다'를 뜻하는 표현으로 '책임이 있는'의 responsible이 정답이다. responsive는 '반응하는, 응답하는'의 의미로 'be responsive to'와 같이 쓴다.

어휘 general 일반적인, 총체적인 maintenance 유지보수 sports complex 스포츠 단지

15 경제 지표가 지난 분기보다 조금 나아 보임에 따라 소비 심리가 어느 정도까지는 상승했다.

해설 economic은 '경제의', economical는 '절약하는'이라는 의미를 가지며, 문맥상 경제 지표의 의미를 나타내야 하므로 economic이 답이 된다.

어휘 indicator 지표 slightly 약간 consumer confidence 소비 심리 certain 어떤, 특정한 degree 정도

SPARTA ✔ ACTUAL TEST

p. 38

1 (C)	**2** (C)	**3** (C)	**4** (A)	**5** (D)	**6** (C)
7 (A)	**8** (A)	**9** (C)	**10** (A)	**11** (C)	**12** (A)
13 (D)	**14** (B)	**15** (C)	**16** (A)		

1 Sontag과 Washok이 운송 관련 문제를 해결하기 위해 공동 노력의 일환으로 최근 통합했다.

해설 품사 어형 문제로, 빈칸은 명사 effort 앞에 있으므로 명사를 수식할 수 있는 품사인 형용사가 필요하다. 따라서 (C) collaborative(공동의)가 정답이다.

어휘 recently 최근에 unite 결합하다, 합치다 in an effort to do ~하기 위한 노력의 일환으로 address 다루다, 해결하다 transportation-related 운송과 관련된 issue 이슈, 사안

2 획기적인 집은 다양한 종류의 자재와 구조적 해결방안을 활용한 실험적 대상이다.

해설 [관사+----+명사]의 자리에는 형용사가 와야 한다. (A) widen은 '넓히다'라는 동사, (B) width는 '넓이'라는 명사, (D) widely는 '넓게'라는 부사이다.

어휘 innovative 획기적인 experiment 실험, 실험물 variety 다양성 materials 자재 structural 구조적인 solution 해결방안

3 믿을 수 있는 서비스와 방식으로 Lynn 씨는 Walter 사의 수익을 지난해 천만 달러에서 천 5백만 달러로 올렸다.

해설 빈칸 뒤의 service와 formula는 명사이므로 앞에서 수식해 줄 수 있는 품사는 형용사인 (C) reliable이다. 보통 (D) rely라는 동사는 '~에 의존하다, ~을 필요로 하다'의 뜻으로 사용될 때에는 'rely on'과 같이 쓴다.

어휘 formula 공식, 방식 lift 들어올리다 revenue 수익 reliable 믿을 수 있는

4 MVI 본부장인 Don Magnuson은 새롭게 출시된 상품이 매우 수익성이 높을 것으로 믿는다고 회사 주주들에게 말했다.

해설 be동사 다음에 부사(very)의 수식을 받을 수 있는 품사는 형용사이다. 보기 중 형용사 (A) profitable이 정답이다. (B) profitably는 부사, (C) profited는 과거분사로 '수익을 본'을 뜻하며, (D) profits는 명사이다.

어휘 general manager 본부장 stockholder 주주 newly 새롭게 launch 시작하다, 출시하다 profitable 수익성이 높은

5 면접을 본 대부분의 지원자들은 공중 위생 분야에 10년 이상의 관리직 경력을 지니고 있었다.

해설 빈칸 뒤의 명사를 수식해주는 품사는 형용사이므로 (D) managerial이 정답이다.

어휘 applicant 지원자 interview 면접; 면접을 하다 field (업종의)분야 public health 공중 위생, 공중 위생학 manageably 다루기 쉽게, 온순하게 managerial 경영의

6 모든 과정이 올바른 순서로 진행되고 있는지 확실히 하기 위해 조립 설명서를 꼼꼼히 확인하세요.

해설 빈칸 뒤의 명사(steps)가 복수형이라는 사실에 주목한다. 가산명사이므로 (D) much는 제일 먼저 탈락. (B) most of는 most of the와 같이 of 뒤에 한정사가 붙어야 하므로 역시 답이 될 수 없다. (A) almost는 부사로 명사를 바로 수식할 수 없다. (C) all은 형용사로 쓰일 때 복수명사와 함께 사용되어 '모든'의 의미를 갖는다. 따라서 정답 (C).

어휘 review 검토하다 assembly manual 조립 설명서 carefully 주의 깊게 ensure 보장하다, 확실히 하다 carry out 수행하다 proper 적절한

7 Brown 씨는 저자들을 위해 계약과 저작권법에 대한 유익한 회의를 마련한 데 대해 칭찬 받았다.

해설 품사 어형 문제. [관사(an)+---+명사(meeting)]의 구조로 빈칸은 명사를 수식하는 형용사 자리이다. 보기 중 (A) informative, (B) informing, (C) informed가 모두 형용사 형태인데, (B), (C)와 같이 분사 형태의 형용사는 일반적으로 동사 의미를 그대로 가져와 현재분사는 능동의 의미, 과거분사는 수동의 의미를 갖게 된다. 즉, inform이 '~에게 알리다, 통지하다'의 뜻이기 때문에 informing은 '(~에게) 알리는, 통지하는'의 의미, informed는 '알림을 받은, 통지 받은' 또는 '(특정 상황에 대해) 많이 아는, 정보통인'이라는 고유 의미도 가지고 있다. 따라서 informing이나 informed는 명사 meeting을 수식하기에 의미상 부적절하며, '유익한, 유용한 정보를 주는'의 의미를 갖는 형용사 (A) informative가 답이 된다.

어휘 commend 칭찬하다 organize 조직하다 contract 계약(하다) copyright law 저작권법 author 저자

8 회전하는 집을 짓는 것은 기존 방식의 건물을 짓는 것과 비용에 있어 비슷하다.

해설 알맞은 품사를 선택하는 문제로 빈칸은 be동사 뒤에 있으므로 형용사 보어를 생각할 수 있다. 회전하는 건물 방식으로 짓는 것이 기존 방식으로 짓는 것과 비용 면에서 비슷하다고 해야 의미가 통하므로 '비슷한, 비교할 만한'의 의미를 갖는 (A) comparable이 정답이다. 분사 형태의 (D) comparing이 들어갈 경우 진행형 동사가 되는데, 사물주어가 비교하는 행위의 주체가 될 수 없기 때문에 정답이 될 수 없다.

어휘 build 짓다 revolving 회전하는 be comparable to ~에 필적하다, ~와 비슷하다 in cost 비용 면에서 conventional 기존의, 전통적인

9 기숙사 정책에는 감독관들이 적절한 시기에 학생들에게 숙소 요청을 받았음을 알려야 한다고 나와 있다.

해설 품사 어형 문제로, 빈칸 뒤 명사(manner)가 연결되어 있다는 점에서 명사 수식 형용사가 필요함을 알 수 있다. 따라서 '시기적절한'의 의미를 갖는 (C) timely가 답이 된다. in a timely manner[fashion]은 '적절한 시기에'를 의미하는 관용 표현이다.

어휘 dormitory 기숙사 policy 정책 state 진술하다 supervisor 감독자 acknowledge receipt of ~을 받았음을 알리다 accommodations 숙박 request 요청(하다)

10 고객들은 수속일 이전에 늦어도 48시간 안에 일정을 재조정하게 되면 추가 비용 없이 다른 날짜로 변경이 가능하다.

해설 extra cost(추가 비용)라는 명사를 수식할 수 있는 품사는 형용사이다. 보기 중 형용사는 (A) no이다. (B) not과 (D) never는 부사이고, (C) none은 대명사이다.

어휘 reschedule 일정을 재조정하다 at least 늦어도 check-in 수속의

11 주주 중의 한 명인 Christine Olson은 회사를 개편하는 계획에 대해 매우 비판적이다.

해설 Christine Olson을 보충 설명하는 보어가 나와야 하므로 '비판적인'의 의미를 지닌 형용사 (C) critical이 문맥상 그리고 구조상 가장 적절하다. '~에 관해 비판적이다'라는 의미의 숙어로 be critical of를 쓴다. (B) critic은 형용사처럼 보이지만 '비평가'를 뜻하는 사람 명사이다.

어휘 stockholder 주주 reorganize 개편하다 criticize 비판하다 critic 비평가

12 우리 안내데스크 직원 두세 명이 주말마다 오전 10시부터 오후 2시 30분까지 고객들의 전화를 받을 수 있다.

해설 해석하면 '주말마다'라는 개념이 필요하므로 정답은 every weekend가 된다. every Friday(매주 금요일), every Monday(매주 월요일) 등은 자주 나오는 시간을 나타내는 부사구이므로 알아두면 좋다. (B) much는 불가산명사를, (D) few는 복수 가산명사를 수식한다.

어휘 available 이용 가능한 take one's call ~의 전화를 받다 from A to B A부터 B까지

〈13-16〉 다음은 공지에 관한 문제이다.

서비스부에서 일하는 직원들에게, 20% 할인 쿠폰이 내일로 만료됨을 알려 드립니다.

어떤 상황에서도 예외는 없으며, 쿠폰이 만료되었고, 새로운 쿠폰이 2주 후에 발급됨을 정중히 알려주십시오.

또한 포켓 아울렛의 사장님인 밀로 샤르카브가 매장 확인차 다음 주 수요일 방문합니다. 그러니 부디 뒤쪽에 주차하신 분들은 사장님을 위한 자리를 하나 남겨 두십시오. 사장님께서는 매장을 둘러보신 후, 그분이 매장에 대해 원하시는 점들을 알려주실 겁니다. 현재 매장의 운영 상태에 대한 장단점에 대해서도 지적하실 겁니다.
단점이 많이 나올수록, 앞으로의 우리 근무가 힘들어질 것입니다. 그러니, 자신의 구역의 청결에 신경 쓰십시오. 그리고 언급할 필요도 없겠지만, 꼭 예의를 갖추십시오. 사장님 덕분에 저희가 근무하는 것입니다. 감사합니다.

어휘 aware ~을 알고 있는 Under no circumstances 어떤 상황에도 exception 예외 politely 정중하게 outlet 전문 매장 respectful 존경심을 보이는 pros and cons 장단점

13

해설 빈칸에는 주어인 those를 받는 관계사절의 본동사가 들어가야 한다. (A), (B)는 단수 주어를 받으므로 탈락이고, work은 완전자동사이므로 수동태가 될 수 없으므로 (C)도 오답이다. 따라서 (D) are working가 정답이 된다.

14

해설 문맥상 '쿠폰이 만료되는' 의미가 되어야 하므로 (B) expire 만기가 되다가 답이 된다. (A) return 돌아가다 (C) submit 제출하다 (D) violate 위반하다

15

해설 전후 문장을 보면, 사장님이 오시니 주차할 때 빈 자리를 남겨 놓으라는 내용이다. 따라서 빈칸에 적절한 어휘는 (C) vacant '비어 있는'이 가장 적절하다. (A) delicate 섬세한 (B) adequate 적당한 (D) block 막다

16 (A) 그는 현재 매장의 운영 상태에 대한 장단점에 대해서도 지적하실 겁니다.
(B) 전 우리가 모든 직원의 일정에 맞게 조정할 수 있기를 진심으로 바랍니다.
(C) 유감스럽지만, 그는 계획대로 발표를 할 수 없을 것입니다.
(D) 밀로 샤르카브가 새로운 직원들에게 업무에 대해 알려 줄 것이다.

해설 빈칸 앞 내용은 사장님이 매장에 방문할 계획을 알려주고 있다. 빈칸 뒤는 '단점이 많이 나올수록, 앞으로의 우리 근무가 힘들어질 것이다.'라는 내용으로 보아 사장님이 장단점을 지적할 것이라는 내용인 (A)가 적절하다.

UNIT 04 부사

SPARTA Check-UP! 1 p. 41

1 (C) **2** (B) **3** (C)

1 계약서에 서명하기 전에, Hopkins 씨는 그의 변호사에게 잠재적인 문제들에 대해 철저히 질문한다.

해설 [주어(Mr. Hopkins)+부사+동사(questions)] 구조이다. 문장의 주어와 동사 사이에는 부사를 써야 하므로 (C) thoroughly(철저하게)가 답이 된다.

어휘 sign a contract 계약서에 서명하다 question 질문하다, 의문을 제기하다 potential 잠재적인

2 기술적인 변화들은 본래 예상된 것보다 훨씬 더 천천히 일어난다.

해설 과거분사(predicted)를 수식하는 품사가 필요한 자리로, 부사를 써야 하므로 답은 (B) originally(본래)이다.

어휘 technological 기술적인 change 변화; 변화하다 predicted 예상되는

3 프로젝트 담당 과장은 사업 제안을 성공리에 완수한 것에 대해 그의 팀을 매우 자랑스럽게 생각했다.

해설 형용사(proud)를 수식해 줄 수 있는 품사는 부사이다. 따라서 (C) extremely(매우, 몹시)가 답이 된다.

어휘 be proud of ~을 자랑스러워하다 complete 완수하다 proposal 제안, 제의

SPARTA Check-UP! 2 p. 42

1 (B) **2** (A) **3** (D)

1 서명하기 전에 계약서의 모든 조항들을 신중히 검토하는 것이 매우 중요하다.

해설 빈칸은 '신중히 검토하는 것'이라는 뜻이 되어 to review를 수식하는 부사 자리이다. 따라서 (B) carefully가 정답이다.

어휘 important 중요한 review 검토하다 terms of the contract 계약 조항 sign 서명하다

2 자격이 뛰어난 지원자들을 주의 깊게 인터뷰한 후에, Nano Tech 사는 올해 10명 이상을 고용하기로 최종 결정했다.

해설 빈칸에는 동명사(interviewing)을 수식할 수 있는 품사가 들어가야 한다. 동명사를 수식하는 품사는 부사이므로 정답은 (A) carefully이다.

어휘 highly 매우 qualified 자격을 갖춘 applicant 지원자 carefully 주의 깊게

3 즉시 샘플을 받고자 하는 직원들은 생산 과장에게 바로 요청서를 제출할 수 있습니다.

해설 [동사(submit)+목적어(a request)+부사(----)+전명구(to the production manager)] 구조로 전명구의 의미를 강조해 주는 부사가 와야 할 자리이다. 따라서 (D) directly(직접, 바로)가 정답이다.

어휘 wish to ~하고자 하다 request 요청(서)

SPARTA Check-UP! 3 p. 43

1 (A) **2** (D) **3** (A)

1 연구부서는 다음 주에 있을 월간 회의 전까지 새로운 디자인에 대해 해야 할 일이 아직도 상당히 많다.

해설 의미상 적절한 부사를 고르는 문제. "연구부서는 다음 주에 있을 회의 전까지 새로운 디자인에 대해 할 일이 많다"는 문맥상, 보기 중 어울리는 것은 '여전히'를 뜻하는 (A) still이다. (B) always 항상 (D) shortly 곧, (C) yet은 주로 not~yet의 형태로 '아직 ~하지 않는'의 의미이다.

어휘 research 연구 considerable 상당한

2 최근 들어 대통령의 건강에 대한 안 좋은 소문이 돌고 있다.

해설 자동사(have been circulating)를 수식하는 품사는 부사이다. 따라서 형용사인 (C) latest(최신의)는 답에서 제외한다. (A) late는 (형) 늦은, (부) 늦게의 의미, (B) later는 (형) 나중의, (부) 나중에의 의미, (D) lately는 (부) 최근에의 의미로 문맥상 lately가 답이다.

어휘 rumor 소문, 풍문 circulate 유포하다, 순환하다

3 Simpson 씨는 땅 주인만이 부동산 개간을 인가할 수 있음을 분명히 했다.

해설 "땅 주인만이 개간을 인가할 수 있다"는 뜻이므로 명사구(the landowner)를 강조해 줄 수 있는 부사 (A) only가 정답이다. 나머지 부사는 의미상으로나 형태상으로 빈칸에 들어갈 수 없다.

어휘 make clear 분명히 하다 landowner 지주, 토지소유자 authorize 인가하다, 권한을 부여하다 improvement 개선 property 부동산

SPARTA Check-UP! 4 p. 44

1 (C) **2** (A) **3** (C)

1 영업사원들을 위한 금전적 인센티브 계획이 일부 직원들을 대상으로 매우 수익성 있음이 증명되었다.

해설 형용사 profitable를 수식할 수 있는 부사는 보기 중 (C) very(매우)이다. (D) well은 '잘, 훌륭하게'라는 의미로 보통 분사형태의 형용사나 동사를 수식하며, (A) enough는 수식할 형용사, 부사, 동사 뒤에 위치하는 부사이다.

어휘 financial 금융의, 재정상의 incentive 장려책, 인센티브 sales representative 영업사원 prove to ~임이 입증되다 profitable 수익성 있는

2 Swan 씨가 일요일에 싱가포르로 출발할 계획이었지만, 그 비행기는 이미 예약이 다 찼다.

해설 의미상 적절한 부사를 찾는 문제. "Swan 씨가 일요일에 싱가포르로 출발할 계획이었지만, 그 비행기는 이미 예약이 다 찼다"는 문맥이 자연스러우므로 답은 '이미, 벌써'를 뜻하는 (A) already이다. (C) soon(곧)은 의미상 주로 미래시제에 어울리는 부사이다.

어휘 leave for ~로 떠나다 fully 완전히 book 예약하다

3 Sun 사의 연간 수익은 더 많은 투자자들을 끌어들이기에 충분히 인상적이지 못했다.

해설 형용사나 부사 다음에 enough to do가 오면 '~하기에 충분히 ~한'이란 뜻이 된다. "좀 더 많은 투자자들을 끌어들이기엔 충분히 인상적이지 못했다"는 의미이므로 답은 (C) enough가 된다.

어휘 impressive 인상적인, 감동적인 attract 끌어들이다 fully 완전히, 전적으로, 충분히 quite 꽤, 상당히 rather 다소

SPARTA Check-UP! 5

p. 45

1 (B) **2** (C) **3** (A)

1 홍보 회사를 고용함으로써, Zuno Technologies는 매출액이 다음 두 분기에 걸쳐 급격히 증가할 것으로 기대한다.

해설 to rise를 수식할 수 있는 품사는 부사이므로 (B) dramatically(급격하게)가 답이 된다.

어휘 hire 고용하다 public relations 홍보 sales 매출액 dramatize 각색하다 dramatist 극작가 dramatic 극적인, 감격스러운

2 최근 보고에 따르면 대략 2만 명의 통근자들이 주 전역에 걸쳐 추가된 16개의 새로운 버스 노선의 혜택을 받게 될 것이라고 한다.

해설 숫자 20,000을 수식하여 '대략 2만 명의 통근자들'의 의미를 만들어 주는 부사 (C) approximately가 정답이다.

어휘 commuter 통근자 benefit from ~로부터 혜택을 받다 throughout (장소) ~도처에, (시간) ~내내 approximate 접근하다

3 큰 서점 체인은 새로이 개발된 지역에 편리하게 위치해 있는 오래된 서점을 수리할지 고려하고 있다.

해설 '편리하게 위치해 있는'이 문맥상 적당하므로 (A) conveniently가 정답이다.

어휘 consider 고려하다 renovate ~을 새롭게 하다, 수선[수리]하다 correctly 바르게, 정확하게 greatly 대단히 widely 널리; 매우

SPARTA Check-UP! 6

p. 46

1 (A) **2** (D) **3** (A)

1 Stellar Technical Institute의 모든 직원은 입사 직후 정보 공개를 하지 않겠다는 합의서에 서명해야 합니다.

해설 빈칸 뒤의 'after joining the company(입사한 후에)'와 의미상 자연스럽게 연결될 수 있는 부사는 '즉시'의 의미를 갖는 (A) immediately이다.

어휘 sign an agreement 계약하다 nondisclosure 비공개 immediately after ~한 직후

2 Brezel 사의 CEO가 된 직후, Mahat M. Ali는 마케팅 부서를 10% 확대했다.

해설 after becoming을 전치 수식하여 '직후'의 의미를 만드는 부사 (D) soon이 정답이다.

어휘 expand 확장하다

3 직원 회의는 월요일 10시 정각에 시작할 예정이어서 모든 직원은 예외 없이 참석해야 한다.

해설 start는 자동사로 [start at+시각]은 '~시에 시작하다'라는 표현이다. (B) soon은 가까운 미래의 불확실한 시간을 의미하는데, 뒤에 10시라는 정확한 시간이 나와 있으므로 어색하다. [promptly at+시각]은 '~시 정각에'라는 표현이므로 답은 (A) promptly이다.

어휘 scheduled to ~할 예정인 attend 참석하다 without exception 예외 없이

SPARTA PRACTICE

p. 47

1 originally	**2** adequately	**3** economically
4 increasingly	**5** hard	**6** hardly
7 late	**8** Regrettably	**9** only
10 yet	**11** substantially	**12** directly
13 conveniently	**14** approximately	**15** promptly

1 워크숍은 원래 오전 9시에 시작하기로 일정이 잡혀 있었다.

해설 [be동사(was)+부사+p.p.]의 구조이다. be동사와 p.p. 사이에 들어갈 수 있는 품사는 부사로 originally(원래)를 써야 한다.

어휘 schedule 일정을 잡다

2 우리의 새로운 직원 중 많은 사람이 아직 충분히 훈련을 받지 못했다.

해설 수동태 동사 have not yet been trained를 수식하는 자리이므로 부사 adequately(충분히)를 써야 한다.

어휘 train 교육하다

3 태양 에너지는 경제적으로 이로운 에너지 자원이다.

해설 형용사 beneficial을 수식하는 자리로 부사를 써야 한다. 따라서 economically(경제적으로)가 정답이다.

어휘 solar power 태양 에너지 source 원천, 자원 beneficial 유익한, 이로운

4 불충분한 인력 때문에 고객에게 서비스를 제공하는 것이 점점 더 어려워지고 있다.

해설 형용사 difficult를 수식하는 품사는 부사이므로 increasingly(점점 더)를 써야 한다.

어휘 insufficient 불충분한 staffing 직원 채용 serve ~에게 서비스를 제공하다 client 고객

5 전체 부서는 임무를 제시간에 완수하기 위해 매우 열심히 일했다.

해설 동사 worked를 수식하는 부사를 써야 할 자리이다. hard(열심히)와 hardly(거의 ~ 않다) 모두 부사이지만 문맥상 hard가 자연스럽다.

어휘 entire 전체의, 완전한 complete 완성하다 assignment 임무 on time 제시간에

6 복사기는 거의 사용되지 않았기 때문에 새것처럼 보인다.

해설 [has+부사+p.p.]의 구조로 부사를 써야 할 자리이다. hard와 hardly 모두 부사이지만 의미상 hardly(거의 ~않다)가 자연스럽다.

어휘 copy machine 복사기 look ~처럼 보이다

7 제안은 늦게 제출됐기 때문에 받아들여지지 못했다.

해설 late는 형용사로 '늦은', 부사로는 '늦게'의 의미이며, lately는 '최근에'란 의미의 부사이다. 문맥상 제안서가 늦게 제출되어 받아들여질 수 없는 것이므로 late가 정답이다.

어휘 proposal 제안 submit 제출하다

8 유감스럽게도, 올해는 자금 부족으로 학교 축제가 없을 것이다.

해설 문장 맨 앞에서 문장 전체를 수식해 줄 수 있는 부사가 필요하므로 Regrettably(유감스럽게도)가 정답이다.

어휘 festival 축제 lack of ~의 부족 fund 자금

9 Gonzales 씨는 상인으로 겨우 3개월 간 일해 왔지만, 고객들에게 높게 평가 받는다.

해설 종속절만의 의미상으로는 '이미(already)' 3개월 동안 일하다, '겨우(only)' 3개월 일하다 둘 다 자연스러우나, 주절의 내용상 '그가 고객들에게 높게 평가된다'로 only가 답으로 적절하다.

어휘 trader 상인, 거래자 highly 매우 regarded ~으로 평가되는 client 고객

10 아직 회사 보안 정책이 담긴 사본에 서명해서 돌려주지 않은 직원들은 즉시 그렇게 하도록 권고된다.

해설 still과 yet은 둘 다 '아직도'의 의미를 갖지만, still은 부정어(not) 앞에 써야 하므로 yet이 답이 된다. yet은 부정어 뒤, 또는 문장 끝에 올 수 있다.

어휘 sign 서명하다 return ~을 돌려주다 security policy 보안 정책 instruct 지시하다 immediately 즉시

11 Aron Airlines는 항공기를 추가로 인수함으로써 회사 운영을 크게 확대했다.

해설 의미상으로는 very(매우)와 substantially(상당히) 모두 가능해 보이지만 very는 형용사와 부사만을 수식할 수 있다. 이 문제에서는 동사 expand(확대하다)를 수식하는 부사 자리이므로 substantially를 써야 한다.

어휘 expand 확대하다, 확장하다 operation 사업, 운용 acquire 획득하다, 인수하다 additional 추가적인 aircraft 항공기

12 부서 관리자들은 비서가 아닌 Helen Mirren에게 경비 보고서를 직접 제출합니다.

해설 빈칸은 빈칸 뒤 전치사구(to Helen Mirren)를 수식하는 부사 자리로 'Helen Mirren 씨에게 직접 제출하다'의 의미가 되므로 directly를 써야 한다.

어휘 submit 제출하다 expense report 경비 보고서 rather than ~보다는 오히려

13 <Cosmopolitan News>에 따르면, Tower Records 사가 Piccadilly Avenue에 편리하게 위치한 상점을 곧 열 것이라고 한다.

해설 located를 수식하기에 적절한 부사를 골라야 한다. conveniently는 '편리하게'라는 의미이므로 의미상 located와 자연스럽게 연결될 수 있다. correctly(정확히)는 내용의 정확성을 의미하기 때문에 문맥상 어색하다.

어휘 according to ~에 따르면 soon 곧 open 열다 avenue 대로

14 본사에서 Missouri Conference Center까지 운전해서 가는 데 약 20분이 소요될 것이다.

해설 운전해서 가는 데 약 20분이 걸릴 거란 문맥이 자연스러우므로 '대략'의 의미를 갖는 approximately를 써야 한다. enough는 '(형) 충분한, (부) 충분히'의 의미로 문맥상 어색하다.

어휘 headquarters 본사

15 연회가 오후 7시 정각에 시작할 것이므로 모든 음식 공급 직원들은 오후 5시에 도착해야 한다.

해설 연회가 오후 7시 정각에 시작할 거란 문맥이 자연스러우므로 promptly를 써야 한다. '정각 ~시에'라는 표현은 'promptly/exactly/precisely+at 시각'으로 쓰므로 promptly가 정답이다.

어휘 banquet 연회 occasionally 가끔 catering 음식 공급

SPARTA ACTUAL TEST

p. 48

1 (A)	2 (A)	3 (A)	4 (C)	5 (D)	6 (D)
7 (D)	8 (D)	9 (C)	10 (B)	11 (B)	12 (A)
13 (A)	14 (C)	15 (A)	16 (D)		

1 Nova Vista Resort는 주요 관광 명소와 식당, 기념품 가게에 최적의 도보 접근을 제공하는 중심부에 위치해 있다.

해설 central의 다양한 형태가 제시된 있는 품사 어형 문제로, [be+p.p.(located)] 사이에 들어갈 수 있는 품사는 부사이다. 따라서 (A) centrally가 답이 된다.

어휘 walking access to ~에 걸어갈 수 있는 거리의 접근성 attractions 관광명소 souvenir shop 기념품 가게

2 새로 채용된 패션 편집자 Ashely Lee는, 올해의 유행을 반영한 새 의류 라인을 소개하는 Isaac Mizzoni의 런웨이쇼에 있게 된 것을 진심으로 기뻐하는 것처럼 보였다.

해설 [seem+----+형용사]의 빈칸 안에 들어가기에 알맞은 품사는 부사이다. 형용사를 수식해 줄 수 있는 것은 부사이므로 (A) truly가 정답이다.

어휘 newly 새롭게 featured ~을 특징으로 한 reflect 반영하다 trend 유행, 경향

3 Primex Electronics는 지난해 팔았던 제품들보다 더 경쟁력 있는 가격의 제품을 출시하기로 계획 중이다.

해설 [동사+비교급+---+형용사+명사]의 구조에서 빈칸은 뒤의 형용사(priced)를 수식해 주는 부사 자리이다. 따라서 (A) competitively가 정답이다.

어휘 launch 출시하다 product 제품 compared to ~와 비교하여

4 학위 프로그램에 지원한 지원자들은 최소한 세 개의 추천서가 행정 사무실로 직접 보내지도록 준비해야 합니다.

해설 품사-어형 문제로, 빈칸은 수동태 'be sent'를 수식하는 부사가 필요하다. 따라서 (C) directly가 정답이다.

어휘 applicant 지원자 degree 학위 letter of recommendation 추천서 administration 행정

5 서비스가 우리가 정한 높은 기준으로 수행되도록 하기 위해, Celebrity Cleaning 사의 관리자들은 그들이 담당한 모든 현장을 주기적으로 점검한다.

해설 품사의 알맞은 형태를 고르는 문제로, [주어(Celebrity Cleaning, Inc.'s supervisors)+----+동사(check)+목적어(every jobsite)]의 완전한 구조이므로 빈칸은 동사 수식 부사가 들어가야 할 자리이다. 따라서 (D) periodically(정기적으로, 주기적으로)가 답이 된다.

어휘 ensure 확실히 하다 perform 수행하다 standard 기준 supervisor 감독관, 관리자 jobsite 현장 in charge of ~을 담당하는, 책임지는

6 Jenkins 박사가 실험을 계속 진행할 자신의 권리를 강력하게 주장 했음에도 불구하고, Tess 의학 학회에서는 박사에 대한 재정 지원을 거절했다.

해설 Dr. Jenkins는 주어, asserted는 동사, his rights는 목적어로 문장에 필수적인 품사는 모두 갖추었다. 따라서 빈칸에는 목적어 앞이 동사를 수식해 주는 부사가 필요하므로 (D) forcefully가 답이 된다.

어휘 although ~함에도 불구하고 assert 주장하다 right 권리 retain 지속하다 refuse 거부하다, 거절하다 fund 재정 지원을 하다

7 Metropolitan 모텔은 전국 20개 이상 주요 고속도로의 편리한 곳에 위치해 있다.

해설 부사 어휘 문제로 문맥상 모텔(Motor Inns)이 어떻게 위치해 있는지를 고려해 볼 때 '편리한 곳에'의 의미를 갖는 (D) conveniently가 적절함을 알 수 있다. (A) consistently 일관되게, 지속적으로 (B) heavily 매우, 몹시 (C) frequently 자주

어휘 be located in/at ~에 위치해 있다 major 주요한 highway 고속도로 across the country 전국에 걸쳐

8 Cosa Vueno의 접수 담당자가 개업식 바로 전에 참가자들에게 명찰과 좌석표를 배부할 것이다.

해설 보통 부사는 동사, 형용사, 부사를 수식해 주지만, 전치사구(또는 접속사절)를 수식할 때도 사용된다. (D) shortly는 '곧, 바로'라는 의미로 이 문장에서 시간 전치사인 before 또는 after와 연결되어 '직전' 또는 '직후'를 나타낸다. 따라서 답은 (D) shortly이다.

어휘 receptionist 접수 담당자 distribute 배부하다 name tag 명찰 place card 좌석표 participant 참가자 shortly 곧 opening ceremony 개업식

9 새로운 검열법 때문에, 주류 광고는 거의 방송에 보일 수 없다.

해설 부사 자리 문제이다. [be동사+부사(---)+형용사(shown)]의 빈칸에 들어갈 품사는 부사 자리이다. (A) hard는 '열심히', (C) hardly는 '거의 ~하지 않는'의 의미로 문맥상 (C) hardly가 정답이다.

어휘 censorship 검열 alcoholic beverage 알코올 음료, 주류 advertisement 광고 media 방송 매체

10 최근 뒤바뀐 배달 사건 때문에 관리자의 훈계는 거의 한 시간이나 지속되었다.

해설 '시간이 지속되었다'라는 문장에서 보기의 부사 중, 시간과 같이 쓰일 수 있는 부사는 '거의'를 뜻하는 (B) nearly가 정답이 된다. (A) variously 다양하게 (C) finely 섬세하게 (D) openly 공개적으로

어휘 switched 뒤바뀐 incident 사건 admonition 훈계 last 지속하다

11 조사가 더 진행되기 전에, Kim 씨는 이미 공금 횡령으로 인해 유죄인 것이 밝혀졌다.

해설 'Before further investigation(조사가 더 진행되기 전에)'라는 전제에서 알 수 있듯이, 뒤의 문장은 이미 일어난 일을 설명하고 있다. 시기를 나타내는 부사 중 '이미'를 뜻하는 것은 (B) already이다. (A) later는 시간상 뒤를 의미하는 '나중에', (C) soon은 미래시제와 어울려 쓰이는 '곧'의 의미, (D) eventually는 '결과적으로'를 뜻한다.

어휘 further 그 이상의, 추가의 investigation 조사 carry out 수행하다 guilty 유죄 misappropriate 유용하다 public funds 공금

12 Icarus 항공에서는 당신이 적합한 비자를 소지하고 있지 않다면 탑승을 허가하지 않을 것인데, 이것은 결국 일부 승객들에게 많은 불편을 끼치고 말 것이다.

해설 which 뒤로 형용사절의 구조를 보면 which가 주격관계대명사, ends up이 동사, being이 동명사로 온 목적어이다. 빈칸 뒤에 inconvenient는 형용사로 부사의 수식을 받을 수 있다. 따라서 부사인 (A) extremely가 정답이다. (A) extremely 매우 (B) extreme 극한적인 (D) extremist 극단주의자

어휘 board 탑승하다 appropriate 적합한 end up (결과를) 초래하다 inconvenient 불편한 passenger 승객

〈13-16〉 다음은 편지에 관한 문제이다.

15471 South First가
Vanderbilt 테네시주 38358

Hagiwara 씨께,

12월 중국 출장에 관한 세부 사항을 완성하는 데 너무 오랜 시간이 걸려서 죄송합니다. 하지만 주말까지는 상세 일정표가 나올 것을 말씀드리게 되어 기쁩니다. 그동안 여기 임시 스케줄이 있습니다. (주: '최종 스케줄이 확정될 때까지 임시 스케줄을 참고하세요.'라는 의미)

- 12월 15일: 귀하는 저녁에 북경에 도착할 것입니다. Henry Hu 씨가 귀하를 만나서 귀하를 곧장 귀하의 호텔로 모실 것입니다.
- 12월 16일: 귀하는 오전 9시부터 오후 2시 사이에 세 곳의 서로 다른 공장을 방문할 것입니다.
- 12월 17일: Henry Hu 씨가 오전 7시에 귀하를 차로 마중 나갈 것이고, 귀하는 비행기 편으로 광저우로 가시게 됩니다. 귀하께 추후에 광저우 행사에 관한 세부사항을 발송 드리기 위해서 저희 지점장인 Richard Grant 씨는 광저우 행사를 계획하고 있습니다.
- 12월 18일: 귀하는 광저우에서 비행기 편으로 귀국하시게 됩니다.

진심으로,
Mary Molliconi

어휘 in the meantime 그 동안에 tentative 임시의, 잠정적인 pick up 데려오다, 데려가다 itinerary 일정

13

해설 빈칸을 중심으로 '중국 출장에 관한 세부 사항을 완성하는 것, 중국 출장에 관한 세부 사항을 결말짓는 것(to ---- the details of your trip)'의 뜻이 적절하므로 계획을 '완성하다, 결말짓다'라는 뜻을 갖는 (A) finalize가 정답이다. (B) terminate 해고하다, ~의 최후를 마무리하다, (행동을) 끝내다 (C) discontinue 그만두다, ~의 사용을 중단하다 (D) close (교섭을) 타결하다, (계약을) 체결하다, 폐쇄하다

14 (A) 한 주간의 여정을 간단히 알리러 즉시 지점으로 오십시오.
(B) 12월 말까지 남은 일정에 관한 세부 사항을 보내드리겠습니다.
(C) 하지만 주말까지는 상세 일정표가 나올 것임을 말씀드리게 되어 기쁩니다.
(D) 그러나 이 일정은 바뀔 수 있습니다.

해설 빈칸 앞은 12월 중국 출장에 관한 세부 사항을 완성하는 데 너무 오랜 시간이 걸려서 죄송함을 나타내고 있다. 빈칸 뒤는 임시 스케줄이 나오는 것으로 보아 문맥 상 가장 적절한 문장은 세부 일정표가 추후에 나오니 일단 임시 스케줄을 참고하라는 내용으로 이어진다고 볼 수 있다. 따라서 빈칸에 들어갈 가장 적절한 문장은 (C)가 된다.

15

해설 빈칸을 중심으로 'take A to B(A를 B로 데려가다)'의 어순이다. 'to B'는 전치사구이므로 이를 수식할 수 있는 품사인 부사 (A) directly가 적절하다. (B) direct 역시 부사로 쓰이긴 하지만 '(멈추거나 경로를 바꾸지 않고) 곧장'의 의미이므로 문맥상 어색하다.

16

해설 빈칸을 중심으로 '그는 귀하께 추후에 광저우 행사에 관한 세부 사항을 발송 드리기 위해서 광저우 행사를 계획하고 있다'는 내용이므로 '추후에, 나중에'라는 뜻을 가지는 at a later time이 적절하다. (A) latest (형) 최신의 (B) lately (부) 최근에 (C) lateness (명) 늦음, 지각

UNIT 05 전치사

SPARTA Check-UP! 1

p. 51

1 (D) **2** (B) **3** (B)

1 3D 음악 시스템을 11월 30일 전에 주문하는 고객들은 20% 할인 혜택을 받게 된다.

해설 '기준 시점 전에'라는 뜻을 표현하는 전치사(before)를 써야 할 자리이다. 기준 시점이 되는 '11월 30일 이전에'의 뜻으로 before November 30가 되어야 하므로 (D) before가 답이 된다.

어휘 order 주문하다 discount 할인

2 Jane Novak은 Sierra 대학에 있는 동안 인문과학 교수들에게 좋은 인상을 남겼다.

해설 빈칸 뒤에 기간을 나타내는 명사구 'her time at Sierra University'가 쓰였으므로 기간 명사를 받는 전치사 (B) During이 정답이다.

어휘 make an impression 인상을 남기다 humanities 인문과학

3 영업직원들은 5일 기간 중 넷째 날까지 그들의 주간 업무 할당량을 완수해야 한다.

해설 마감 시한(5일 중 네 번째 날)'까지'의 의미를 갖는 전치사가 필요한데, (A) until과 (B) by가 모두 '(특정 시점)까지'의 의미를 갖는다. 그러나 until은 언제까지 상태가 계속됨을 의미하며, by는 언제까지 완료가 되어야 함을 의미하므로 이 문제에서는 (B) by가 적절하다. 넷째 날까지 업무 할당량을 완수해야 한다는 문맥이다.

어휘 personnel 직원 quota 할당량

SPARTA Check-UP! 2

p. 52

1 (C) **2** (B) **3** (C)

1 Word Soft의 검색 기능은 사용자가 파일 안에 있는 단어들을 매우 쉽게 검색할 수 있도록 한다.

해설 빈칸 앞뒤로 명사 words와 a file이 나란히 있으므로 이 둘을 연결해 줄 의미상 적절한 전치사가 필요하다. '파일 안에 있는 단어들'이라는 의미를 나타내기 위해서 (C) within이 필요하다.

어휘 search function 검색 기능 allow 허용하다 search 검색하다

2 금융계 전체에 일고 있는 변화는 금융 시장의 급격한 변동을 통제하기 위한 노력을 보여주고 있다.

해설 문맥상 '금융 산업 전체에 일고 있는 변화'라고 해야 자연스럽게 연결될 수 있으므로 '~전체에'의 의미를 갖는 (B) throughout이 정답이다.

어휘 change 변화 occur 발생하다 financial industry 금융업계 effort 노력 control 통제하다 fluctuation 변동

3 Coogie 사는 직원들 간의 더 나은 의사소통을 촉진시키기 위하여 정기적으로 세미나를 개최한다.

해설 문맥상 '직원들 사이에서 더 나은 의사소통을 촉진시키다'라고 해야 자연스럽게 연결된다. 따라서 '(셋 이상) 사이에'를 뜻하는 (C) among이 정답이다.

어휘 hold 열다, 개최하다 regularly 정기적으로 promote 촉진시키다

SPARTA Check-UP! 3

p. 53

1 (C) **2** (C) **3** (B)

1 기술적인 문제에도 불구하고, 새로운 사무용 소프트웨어의 출시가 미루어지지 않을 것이다.

해설 despite는 양보의 개념을 나타내는 전치사구를 이끈다. (C) despite[in spite of] technical problems는 '기술적 문제에도 불구하고'라는 의미로 문맥상 가장 자연스럽다.

어휘 technical 기술적인 launch 출시 delay 지연시키다

2 보고서를 기다리는 대신에 부장 본인이 지점장 개개인에게 직접 전화했다.

해설 instead of는 '~대신에'라는 뜻을 갖는 전치사이다. 문맥상 '보고서를 기다리는 대신에(Instead of waiting for reports), 자신이 직접 전화를 했다'고 하여 자연스럽게 연결되므로 (C) Instead of가 정답이다.

어휘 branch manager 지점장 director 임원, 책임자

3 인사부장으로서 Philippe 씨는 새로운 직원들을 고용할 책임이 있다.

해설 '인사부의 부장으로서'란 문맥으로 '~의'라는 소유의 의미를 갖는 전치사 of가 정답이다.

어휘 director 부장 Personnel Department 인사부 be in charge of ~을 책임지다 hire 고용하다

SPARTA Check-UP! 4

p. 54

1 (B) **2** (A) **3** (D)

1 Baker 씨는 2백 명의 새로운 조립 라인 노동자를 고용하자는 제안에 동의했다.

해설 agree는 '누구의 의견과 일치하다, 누구의 의견에 동의하다'는 의미의 자동사로 전치사 (B) with를 동반한다.

어휘 hire 고용하다 assembly line 조립 라인

2 지역 주민들이 4번가에 주차장을 건설하자는 제안에 대한 우려를 나타냈다.

해설 빈칸은 '~에 대한 우려, 걱정'을 뜻하는 명사 concern과 어울리는 전치사를 묻는 문제로, concern은 전치사 over나 about을 동반한다. 정답은 (A) over이다.

어휘 local resident 지역 주민 voice 나타내다, 표하다 proposal 세안 parking lot 주차장

3 접객업소에서 손님들의 요구에 응하는 것이 특히 중요하다.

해설 형용사 responsive는 '~에 응하는, 응답하는'의 의미로서 전치사 (D) to를 동반하는 형용사이다.

어휘 hospitality business 접객업소 especially 특히 needs 요구

SPARTA Check-UP! 5

p. 55

1 (B) **2** (C) **3** (C)

1 Grand 호텔은 모든 손님이 도착하자마자 프런트 데스크에서 체크인할 것을 요구한다.

해설 빈칸 앞, 뒤에 명사가 있으므로 명사와 명사를 연결해 줄 수 있는 전치사가 필요하다. 'on/upon arrival'은 '도착하자마자, 도착 시에'라는 의미의 전치사 관용 표현이다. 정답은 (B) upon이다.

어휘 require 요구하다 check in (호텔 등) 수속을 밟다

2 새로운 식당은 전 세계의 이국적인 음식을 합리적인 가격에 제공한다.

해설 'at the price[cost/expense/charge] of ~'와 같이 비용 소요를 나타내는 표현들에 전치사 (C) at이 쓰인다.

어휘 exotic 이국적인 reasonable 합리적인

3 새로운 경영체제 하에서, 회사의 수익은 지난해 이래로 두 배가 되었다.

해설 'under the management[policy/direction/regulations]'와 같이 통제, 감독, 조건을 나타내는 표현들에 전치사 (C) under가 쓰인다.

어휘 management 경영(체제) double 두 배가 되다

SPARTA Check-UP! 6

p. 56

1 (D) **2** (D) **3** (A)

1 서비스 비용과 다른 서비스 정책들에 관하여, 고객들은 그들이 선호하는 어떤 방법으로든, 우리에게 전화 혹은 이메일로 연락할 수 있다.

해설 the service cost라는 명사 앞 빈칸에 (A) Regard, (B) Regards는 동사이므로 답이 될 수 없다. 목적어를 수반하는 분사형 전치사 (D) Regarding(~에 관하여)이 정답이다.

어휘 cost 비용 whichever 어떤 것이든

2 Hugo Cosmetics 사의 10주년을 기념하여 다음 주에 모든 모발 보호 제품이 20% 할인될 것이다.

해설 빈칸 뒤에 있는 celebration of와 어울려 쓰는 전치사를 고르는 문제로, 'in celebration of'는 '~을 기념하여, 축하하여'를 의미하는 전치사 관용 표현이다.

어휘 haircare 헤어 케어, 모발 보호 anniversary 기념일

3 뉴스 보도에 따르면, Nelson 은행이 1억 달러의 순이익을 보았다고 발표했다.

해설 전치사 according to(~에 따르면) 뒤에 정보의 원천(a news report)이 따라붙어, 'according to a news report'는 '뉴스 보도에 따르면'이라는 의미가 되므로 문맥상 가장 자연스럽다.

어휘 post 발표하다, 게재하다 net profit 순이익 million 백만

SPARTA PRACTICE

p. 57

1 before	**2** with	**3** from	**4** Despite
5 below	**6** as	**7** throughout	**8** for
9 over	**10** Because of	**11** by	**12** comply
13 concerning	**14** accordance	**15** manner	

1 Ogawa 씨는 10월 1일 전에는 출장에서 돌아올 수 없을 것이다.

해설 '기준 시간 전'을 표현하는 전치사 before가 문맥상 자연스럽다. 'before October 1'은 '10월 1일 전에'를 의미한다. within(~이내에) 뒤에는 기간을 나타내는 명사가 온다.

어휘 be able to ~할 수 있다 return from ~에서 돌아오다 business trip 출장

2 Barnett 씨는 나머지 마케팅 팀원들과 함께 바르셀로나로 출장 가기를 원한다.

해설 전치사 with는 '~와 함께'의 의미를 나타낸다. 문맥상 with를 써야 한다. '팀의 나머지 사람들과 함께(with the rest of the marketing team)'라는 의미가 되어야 하므로 문맥상 with를 써야 한다.

어휘 wish 희망하다 rest 나머지

3 최근 출시된 모델은 전국에 있는 저희 대리점 어디에서나 구입할 수 있습니다.

해설 문맥상 '출처'를 뜻하는 전치사 from이 필요한 자리이다. 구매의 출처가 전국에 있는 모든 대리점이라는 문맥이다.

어휘 recently 최근에 introduce 소개하다, 도입하다 purchase 구매하다 dealer 중개인, 대리점 nationwide 전국적인

4 가격 인하에도 불구하고 Pattice 사는 세전 수익을 30%까지 개선했다.

해설 가격 인하에도 불구하고 수익이 증가했다는 문맥으로 Despite을 써야 한다. Regardless가 단독으로 쓰이면 '개의치 않고'라는 의미의 부사이므로 뒤의 명사를 연결해 줄 수 없다. Regardless of로 쓰이며 '~와는 상관없이'를 의미하는 전치사의 기능을 갖는다.

어휘 cut 대폭 인하, 삭감 pre-tax profit 세전 수익(세금을 포함한 수익)

5 우리의 영업 성장이 이번 분기에 2%를 기록하였는데, 이것은 작년의 5%에 못 미치는 기록이다.

해설 '작년의 5%에 못 미친다'는 의미를 나타내기 위해서는 괄호 안에 '기준선 밑'을 나타내는 전치사 below를 써야 맞다. less는 little의 비교급으로 '양이 더 적음'을 의미한다.

어휘 sales growth 영업 성장 quarter 분기 rate 비율

6 고객들은 구매의 증거로 상점 영수증을 보관해 두어야 한다.

해설 '~로서'의 자격을 나타내는 전치사 as가 와서 '구매의 증거로서(as proof of purchase)'라는 의미를 형성하는 것이 적절하다.

어휘 be supposed to ~하기로 되어 있다, ~해야 한다 keep 보관하다, 유지하다 receipt 영수증 proof 증거

7 높은 이자율이 지역 전체의 주택 산업에 부정적으로 영향을 미쳤다.

해설 괄호 안에 전치사 throughout이 와서 '지역 전체에(throughout the region)'의 의미를 나타내는 것이적절하다.

어휘 interest rate 이자율 adversely 불리하게, 부정적으로 affect ~에 영향을 미치다 housing industry 주택 산업

8 콘서트의 수익금은 St. Mary Music School의 개조 공사를 위해 사용될 것이다.

해설 전치사 for는 '~을 위한'의 의미로 목적을 나타낸다. 문맥상 '개조 공사를 위하여(for the renovation)'가 자연스러우므로 for를 써야 한다.

어휘 proceeds 수익금 renovation 개조

9 지난 3개월 동안 모든 신입 사원들을 교육했지만, 모두가 열정을 보이지 못했다.

해설 뒤에 기간을 나타내는 표현이 나와 있으므로 '지난 세 달 동안'이라는 의미를 만드는 over를 써야 한다. 참고로 'over the past[last]+기간'은 현재완료를 동반하는 시간 부사구임을 기억한다.

어휘 recruit 신참, 신입 사원 enthusiasm 열정

10 홍보 캠페인 때문에 Ocean 시의 주민들은 관광객의 증가를 기대하고 있다.

해설 문맥상 '홍보 캠페인 때문에(Because of the publicity campaign)'라는 의미가 되는 것이 적절하므로 괄호 안에는 Because of를 써야 한다. in case of는 '~의 경우에(=in the event of)'를 뜻한다.

어휘 publicity campaign 홍보 캠페인 resident 주민 tourism 관광업; 관광객

11 세탁물이 내일 아침까지 배달되기를 원하신다면 20%의 추가 요금을 부담하셔야 합니다.

해설 내일 아침까지 세탁물 배달이 완료되어야 한다는 문맥이므로 '완료'의 의미를 갖는 전치사 by를 써야 한다. until은 언제까지 지속된다는 의미를 나타낸다.

어휘 laundry 세탁물 extra charge 추가 요금 bill 계산서, 청구서

12 현지 교통 규정을 준수하지 않으면 벌금을 부과 받거나 최대 한 달까지 수감될 수 있다.

해설 comply with는 '(명령, 규칙 등에) 따르다, 준수하다'는 의미를 갖는 동사로 전치사 with와 함께 쓸 수 있는 comply가 정답이다. observe도 의미상으로는 '준수하다'를 뜻하지만 타동사이므로 뒤에 전치사가 올 수 없다.

어휘 local 지역의 traffic regulation 교통 규정 fine 벌금을 부과하다 jail 투옥하다 up to 최대 ~까지

13 회의 일정에 관한 추가적인 정보 요청은 일정이 마무리되는 대로 이루어질 수 있을 것이다.

해설 문맥상 '회의 일정에 관한 정보'이므로 '~에 관하여'라는 의미의 전치사 concerning을 써야 한다. relating은 in relation to(~에 관하여)나 related to(~와 관련된) 등의 형태로 써야 괄호 안에 들어갈 수 있다.

어휘 request 요청 further 그 이상의, 추가적인 fulfill 이행하다 as soon as ~하자마자

14 모든 국제 영업 사원들은 지역 관습에 맞추어 행동해야 한다.

해설 in accordance with는 '~에 맞추어, ~에 따라서'라는 의미를 나타낸다. 문맥상 '지역 관습에 맞추어(in accordance with local customs)'가 자연스러우므로 accordance가 정답이다.

어휘 International 국제적인 sales representative 영업 사원 behave 행동하다 custom 관습

15 이 업계에서의 성공 여부는 신상품을 적시에 시판하는 능력에 달려 있다.

해설 괄호 앞의 in a timely와 연결될 수 있는 명사 manner가 정답이다. in a timely manner[fashion]은 '시기적절하게'를 뜻하는 관용 표현이다. basis를 써서 '시기적절하게'의 의미를 나타낼 수도 있는데, 이때는 'on a timely basis'와 같이 전치사 on을 써야 함에 주의할 것.

어휘 depend on ~에 의존하다 ability to ~하는 능력 introduce 소개하다, 도입하다

SPARTA ACTUAL TEST

p. 58

1 (A)	**2** (D)	**3** (B)	**4** (C)	**5** (D)	**6** (D)
7 (D)	**8** (B)	**9** (D)	**10** (C)	**11** (D)	**12** (B)
13 (B)	**14** (C)	**15** (D)	**16** (A)		

1 Antivirus 3.7 소프트웨어의 매출액이 지난 6개월 동안 세 배 증가했다.

해설 알맞은 전치사를 고르는 문제. '지난 6개월 동안 매출액이 세 배 증가했다'는 의미로 빈칸 뒤에는 '6개월(six months)'이라는 '기간'이 언급되어 있다. 기간명사와 어울리는 전치사는 in, within, for, through, throughout, during 등이 있다. (B) on은 '날짜, 요일', (C) at은 '시각', (D) of는 소유, 소속의 관계를 나타낸다.

어휘 sales 매출액 triple 세 배가 되다

2 Minsk의 심한 강설로 인해 지연된 기차가 다음 3시간 이내에 출발하도록 일정이 변경되었다.

해설 특정한 기간이나 거리 '~이내에'의 뜻을 가진 전치사는 (D) within이다.

어휘 delay 지연시키다 snowfall 강설 reschedule 재조정하다, 일정을 변경하다 depart 출발하다

3 Thompson 경영 대학원의 현장 회의 전반부는 오늘 늦게 Irene McDonell 씨가 진행할 예정이다.

해설 [be led+----+사람 이름]의 문장 형식에서 수동태의 행위 주체는 보통 문장의 마지막 부분에 'by+목적격'의 형태가 따라붙는다. '회의가 Irene McDonell 씨에 의해 진행된다'는 의미에서도 가장 어울리는 (B) by가 정답이다.

어휘 first half 전반 business school 경영 대학

4 면밀한 검사를 통해, 기술자는 전자레인지 기능 불량의 원인을 밝혀낼 수 있었다.

해설 주절의 의미를 파악하여 전치사구를 이끄는 알맞은 전치사를 고른다. 기술자가 문제의 원인을 알아냈다는 주절의 의미상 전치사구는 '면밀한 검사를 통해'라는 수단의 전치사 through를 쓰는 것이 적절하므로 (C)가 정답이다.

어휘 close 면밀한, 자세한 inspection 검사 technician 기술자 figure out 알아내다 malfunction 오작동, 기능 불량 microwave oven 전자레인지

5 <Town & Around> 출판물의 놀라운 성공으로 인해, 우리는 독자들에게 잡지의 온라인 버전을 제공하도록 요구 받았다.

해설 보기 중 전치사, 접속사가 모두 등장한 문제로 이러한 유형의 문제는 먼저 빈칸 뒤의 구조를 파악하는 것이 관건이다. (A) According to, (D) Due to는 전치사, (B) Similarly는 부사, (C) Unless는 접속사로, 빈칸 뒤에는 명사구(the extraordinary success of ~)가 연결되어 있으므로, (B), (C)는 답에서 제외시킨다. 출판물의 놀라운 성공으로 인해 온라인 버전 요구를 받은 것이므로 이유를 나타내는 전치사 (D)가 정답이다.

어휘 extraordinary 놀라운 publication 출판(물) prompt 촉구하다, 강하게 요구하다

6 배심원들은 재판 기간에 걸쳐 설문 작성을 완료해야 한다.

해설 duration은 '지속 기간'을 의미하므로, '재판이 지속되는 내내'의 의미를 완성시키는 (D) throughout이 정답이다. '~사이에'라는 의미의 (A) between이 혼동될 수 있으나 between은 '두 대상 사이'를 의미하므로 답과 거리가 멀다.

어휘 member of the jury 배심원 complete 완성하다, 작성하다 questionnaire 설문지 duration (지속되는) 기간 trial 재판

7 65세 이상의 사람들과 연령 면제의 자격이 있는 사람들은 추가 지시사항을 위해 시 재무부에 연락해야 한다.

해설 빈칸 앞뒤의 문맥을 파악하여 적절한 전치사를 선택한다. 보통 전치사 문제는 전치사 고유 의미를 파악하여 문맥상 어울리는 전치사를 선택하도록 하거나, 특정 단어(동사, 명사, 형용사, etc.)와 어울리는 전치사를 고르는 관용 표현 문제로 출제되고 있다. 이 문제에서는 '추가 지시사항을 알기 위해 재무과에 연락해야 한다'는 의미이므로 '목적(~을 위해)'의 전치사 (D) for가 답이 된다.

어휘 eligible for ~에 대해 자격이 있는 exemption 면제 treasury 재무부 further 추가적인 instructions 명령, 지시

8 우리 Great Little Trading 사에서는 공동노력에 가치를 두고 가능한 최고의 근무환경을 제공하려고 힘씁니다.

해설 알맞은 전치사를 선택하는 문제로 빈칸 뒤에 'Great Little Trading Company'라는 회사명이 언급되어 있는데, 장소, 위치, 지점을 나타내는 전치사는 at이므로 (B) At이 답이 된다.

어휘 joint effort 협력 strive 애쓰다, 분투하다 working conditions 근무환경

9 Ford 씨는 우리의 발표 기술 교육 중 하나를 무료로 등록할 것을 요청하는 이메일을 모든 직원에게 발송했다.

해설 알맞은 전치사를 선택하는 문제. 전치사 문제는 문맥상 어울리는 전치사 고유 의미를 묻는 문제와 특정 품사와 어울려 쓰이는 전치사 문제가 출제되고 있다. 빈칸 앞에 위치한 동사 register는 자/타동사가 모두 가능하며, 자동사로 쓰일 경우에는 전치사 for를 동반하므로 (D) for가 정답이다.

어휘 send 발송하다 request 요청하다, 요구하다 register 등록하다 presentation skill 발표 기술 session 회기, (교육)기간 for free 무료로

10 더 좋아진 기상청 경보 시스템에도 불구하고 올해의 토네이도 시즌은 수십 년 만에 최악이었다.

해설 빈칸 뒤에 문장이 아닌 명사구로 끝나는 것으로 보아 전치사가 답이 됨을 알 수 있다. (A) Even if(설령 ~라 하더라도)와 (D) Although(비록 ~이지만)는 양보 접속사, (B) While(~하는 동안)은 기간을 나타내는 접속사로 보기 중 전치사는 (C) Despite(~에도 불구하고)뿐이다.

어휘 warning system 경보 시스템 weather forecast station 기상청 tornado 토네이도, 회오리 바람 decade 10년

11 <Deccan Herald>의 기사는 Blue Rush 유람선이 국제 해상 안전 규정을 온전히 준수하지 않고 있다는 것을 명백히 밝혔다.

해설 [be동사(was not)+부사(fully)+----+명사구(international maritime safety regulations)] 구조로 빈칸은 be동사 뒤 형용사 자리인데, 뒤에 명사구가 왔으므로 이를 연결해 줄 수 있는 전치사도 필요하다. 문맥상으로 '~을 준수하는'이란 의미를 완성시켜야 하므로 (D) compliant with가 답이 된다.

어휘 article 기사 clearly 명백히 state 언급하다 fully 온전히, 완벽히 maritime safety regulations 해상 안전 규정

12 웹 프로그래머 직책은 관련 분야에 대한 넓은 지식 외에도 광범위한 컴퓨터 경험을 요구한다.

해설 '웹 프로그래머 일은 넓은 지식 ---- 광범위한 컴퓨터 경험을 요구한다'는 문맥으로 지식과 경험을 둘 다 필요로 한다는 의미이므로 빈칸에는 이 두 요소를 연결해 줄 수 있는 (B) in addition to(~이외에도)가 필요하다.

어휘 position 지위 require 요구하다 extensive 넓은 vast 광범위한 knowledge 지식 related 관련된 field 분야 otherwise 그렇지 않으면 in addition to ~외에도 meanwhile 한편 even though 비록 ~일지라도

〈13-16〉 다음은 이메일에 관한 문제이다.

수신: 고란카 라조빅 <lazovic@nus.edu>
발신: 트레이시 로페즈 <lopez@limebooks.com>
날짜: 7월 24일
제목: 귀하께서 찾으시는 희귀본

어제 고객님의 이메일에 대한 응답으로 서신을 보냅니다. 고객님이 구매에 관심 있는 도서는 현재 재고가 없다는 것을 알려드리게 되어 유감입니다.

그러나 저희는 고객님을 위해 다음 주 내에 출판사로부터 도서를 주문할 수 있을 것입니다.

만약 이 선택 사항에 관심 있으시면 이메일에 답신을 주시고, 고객님의 전화번호도 알려 주시기 바랍니다.

저희는 이 품목이 언제 배달 가능한지 연락드리겠습니다.

고객님의 답장을 고대합니다.

진심으로,

트레이시 로페즈
고객 서비스
라임 북스

어휘 in response to ~에 답하여, 응하여 be able to 동사원형 ~할 수 있다 order 주문하다 publisher 출판사, 발행자 reply to ~에 답하다 delivery 인도, 배달 look forward to+(동)명사 ~을 고대하다 response 응답, 대답 be sorry to inform A that 주어+동사 A에게 ~을 알리는 것이 유감이다 be interested in ~하는 데 관심이 있다 purchase 구입(하다) in stock 재고가 있는

13 (A) 손상된 상태에서 반환된 각 물품에 대해 교체 비용이 청구될 것입니다.
(B) 고객님이 구매에 관심 있는 도서는 현재 재고가 없다는 것을 알려드리게 되어 유감입니다.
(C) 고객님이 주문품들을 받지 못했다는 소식에 매우 유감입니다.
(D) 고객님이 주문한 책들은 배송비가 공짜입니다.

해설 빈칸 앞의 내용으로 보아 이 글은 고객의 응답 서신이고 빈칸 뒤의 시작 However(그러나)에서 단서를 찾을 수 있다. 빈칸 뒤는 고객들을 위해 출판사에 도서를 주문할 수 있으나 시간이 좀 걸린다는 글이므로 빈칸에 들어갈 적절한 문장은 보기 중 현재 재고가 없다고 알리는 (B)가 적절하다.

14

해설 보기에 제시된 전치사 중 빈칸을 중심으로 문맥을 완성할 수 있는 전치사의 의미를 묻는 문제이다. '다음 주 내에 출판사로부터(from the publisher within the next week) 책을 주문할 수 있을 것이다'가 문맥상 자연스러우므로 '~이내에'의 의미를 갖는 (C) within이 정답이다. (A) when(~할 때)은 시간 접속사이므로 뒤에 '주어+동사'를 수반한다.

15

해설 빈칸 앞에 제시된 문장의 내용과 연결될 수 있는 명사를 고르는 문제이다. '만약 이 선택 사항(=귀하를 위한 도서 주문)이 고객님의 관심을 끈다면'의 문맥이므로 빈칸에는 (D) option(선택권)이 적절하다. (A) moment 순간, 기회 (B) author 저자, 작가 (C) advantage 이점

16

해설 빈칸은 동사 자리로, 조동사 뒤이므로 동사원형 형태가 와야 한다. 사람(통지 대상)을 목적어로 취해서 '~에게 알리다, 통지하다'라는 의미의 notify가 정답이다.

UNIT 06 동사의 종류

SPARTA Check-UP! 1 p. 61

1 (B) **2** (D) **3** (C)

1 Albert 씨가 사무실에 정시에 도착한다면 매일 끝 무렵이면 하루 업무를 완료할 수 있을 것이다.

해설 빈칸 뒤에 목적어가 없으므로 자동사 자리이다. 사무실에 '도착하다'는 의미로 자동사인 (B)가 정답. 나머지는 모두 타동사로 빈칸에 올 수 없다.

어휘 on time 정시에 daily task 하루 업무

2 관리자는 모든 직원이 수요일 회의에 참석할 것을 요구하는 공지를 게시했다.

해설 문맥상 빈칸에는 '회의에 참석하다'라는 의미가 적절하다. 전치사 in과 함께 쓰이는 자동사 (D) participate가 정답이다. (B) attend는 '참석하다'의 의미일 때는 타동사이므로 오답이다.

어휘 demand 요구하다 participate 참석하다

3 모든 신입사원은 다음 5일 동안 컴퓨터 프로그램 수업에 등록할 수 있습니다.

해설 어휘 문제로 문맥상 '등록하다'라는 의미가 되어야 하므로 정답은 (C) enroll이다.

어휘 enroll in ~에 등록하다

SPARTA Check-UP! 2 p. 62

1 (B) **2** (C) **3** (D)

1 관리자는 영업 사원이 단골 고객과 언쟁을 벌이자 결국 그를 해고하기로 결심했다.

해설 동사 become 뒤에 주어 상태를 설명할 때 형용사 (B) argumentative가 와야 한다.

어휘 fire 해고하다 argumentative 언쟁을 벌이는

2 Blue Sky Restaurant의 주인은 지역 신문에 부정적인 평이 난 것에 대해 실망했다.

해설 that절 이하의 사실에 대해 식당 주인이 실망했다는 의미이므로 수동형인 be p.p. 형태의 (C) disappointed가 정답이다.

어휘 negative 부정적인 review 평 disappoint 실망시키다

3 고객의 편의를 위해 호텔 매니저가 오전 7시부터 자정까지 일주일 내내 안내 데스크에 상주한다.

해설 문맥상 '호텔 매니저가 오전 7시부터 자정까지 일주일 내내 안내 데스크에 상주한다.'는 의미로 쓰였으므로 빈칸에 (D) available(만날 수 있는)를 써야 한다.

어휘 convenience 편의, 편리함 probable 있음직한, 있을 법한 eligible ~에 적임의, 적당한 considerable 상당한, 적지 않은

SPARTA Check-UP! 3 p. 63

1 (C) **2** (D) **3** (C)

1 수업 후에, 중간고사 시험을 위해 함께 공부하는 계획을 논의해 보자.

해설 뒤에 목적어(our plan)이 바로 있으므로 타동사이거나 전치사를 동반한 자동사가 들어간다. (A) talk, (B) speak, (D) remark는 자동사이기 때문에 성립되지 않으므로 오답이다. (C) discuss는 '~을 논하다'라는 타동사이고 뒤에 그에 합당한 목적어(our plan)이 있으므로 정답이다.

어휘 midterm 중간의

2 Harrison Corporate 사는 귀하의 승진이 승인되었음을 알리게 되어 기쁩니다.

해설 빈칸 뒤에 [to 사람+that+주어+동사]가 온 것으로 보아 보기 중 3형식 동사인 (D) announce가 정답임을 알 수 있다. (A) tell, (B) inform, (C) convince는 모두 4형식 동사로 [사람+명사절]이 나와야 한다.

3 SpeedMax Shipping 사는 모든 고객들에게 규격을 초과하거나 무거운 품목들은 추가적인 배달 시간이 필요하다는 것을 알린다.

해설 that절 이하의 사실을 all clients에게 알릴 때 전치사 to 없이 목적어를 가져올 수 있는 동사는 advises이므로 정답은 (C)이다.

어휘 oversized 규격을 초과한 additional 추가적인

SPARTA Check-UP! 4 p. 64

1 (D) **2** (C) **3** (D)

1 Donald 박물관의 방문객들은 관람 시 사진을 찍거나 비디오 촬영하는 것이 금지된다.

해설 숙어로 prohibit A from B를 알아 두자. 문장은 수동태로 [A(Visitors to the Donald Museum)+동사(are prohibited)+from+B(taking photographs or making video recordings)]의 구조로 쓰인 문장이다. 그러므로 정답은 (D) from이다.

어휘 prohibit A from B A가 B하는 것을 금지하다 take photographs 사진을 찍다

2 우리는 어떻게 그들이 매출을 잃지 않고 오래된 시스템을 새것으로 교체할 수 있었는지 이해해야 한다.

해설 replace A with B의 구조에서 명사 A(old system)을 명사 B(new one(system))으로 바꾸었다는 구조이므로 (C) with가 적당하다.

어휘 replace 교체하다 sales 매출(액)

3 파키스탄 국립은행은 은행 영역의 유동성 문제를 해결하기 위해 몇 가지 조치를 취해 왔다.

해설 '조치를 취하다'라는 숙어로 take measures라는 표현을 알아 두자. 같은 뜻으로 take actions = take steps도 있다.

어휘 take measures 조치를 취하다 liquidity problem 유동성 문제

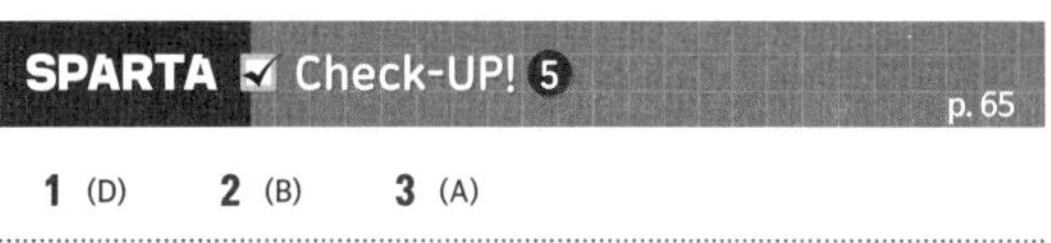

SPARTA Check-UP! 5 p. 65

1 (D) **2** (B) **3** (A)

1 회계부서의 Johnson 씨는 부서원 모두에게 회사 부사장님으로부터 수신한 이메일을 보냈다.

해설 뒤에 간접 목적어(everyone), 직접 목적어(the e-mail)를 취할 수 있는 4형식 동사인 (D) forwarded가 정답이다.

어휘 accounting 회계 department 부서

2 몇 차례의 요청 후, Luxar 사는 인사부장에게 회사 카드를 승인해 줄 것이나 분실하게 되면 그에게 책임을 물을 것이다.

해설 뒤에 간접 목적어(HR manager), 직접 목적어(company card)를 취할 수 있는 4형식 동사인 (B) grant가 정답이다.

어휘 request 요청 hold someone responsible ~에게 책임을 묻다

3 오늘 오후 제가 귀하께 주문 청구서를 첨부하여 이메일을 보냈습니다.

해설 동사(send)의 목적어(an e-mail) 뒤에 받는 사람(you)가 오려면 전치사 (A) to가 필요하다.

어휘 attach 첨부하다 invoice 청구서

SPARTA Check-UP! 6

p. 66

1 (A) **2** (D) **3** (B)

1 Chang 씨의 보고서는 내년을 위해 매니저들이 고용의 필요성을 인식하게 했다.

해설 5형식 동사인 (A) made가 적절하다. 'make+목적어+형용사'

어휘 aware of ~을 알다 hiring 채용 coming 다가오는

2 HDC Financial 사는 직원들이 고객들과 대화할 때 스스로가 전문가다운 태도를 기대한다.

해설 빈칸 앞에는 동사(expects)가 있고 when 절이 이끄는 분사구문이 뒤에 나와 있다. 즉, 빈칸은 동사가 쓰일 자리가 아니다. (A) conduct는 오답이며, 빈칸 앞에는 명사이자 expect의 목적어가 있으므로 명사가 쓰이게 되면 목적어가 2개가 되기 때문에 (B) conductor 역시 정답이 될 수 없다. expect는 바로 뒤에 목적어나 목적어+목적 보어의 형태를 취할 수 있으며, 여기서는 expect의 목적격 보어로 to부정사가 사용된 것이다.

어휘 in a professional manner 전문가다운 태도로 speak with ~와 말하다 customer 고객

3 우리의 온라인 서비스는 당신에게 당신의 계좌를 보고 청구서를 지불하며 심지어는 다른 계좌로 자금을 이체할 수 있도록 합니다.

해설 빈칸은 본동사 자리로, to부정사를 목적격 보어로 취하는 5형식 동사 (B) allows가 정답이다.

어휘 view 보다 transfer 이체하다, 전송하다

SPARTA PRACTICE

p. 67

1 rose	**2** offered	**3** angry	**4** got
5 discussed	**6** clean	**7** took	**8** notify
9 given	**10** choose	**11** made	**12** arrived
13 proceed	**14** affordable	**15** allows	

1 작년에 작황이 나빴기 때문에 식품 가격이 올랐다.

해설 빈칸 뒤 'because of'는 뒤에 명사(혹은 명사구)를 가져오며 전체는 부사구가 된다. 따라서 핵심문장은 'Food prices ----' 까지이며, 결국 빈칸 안에는 동사가 와야 하고, 그 자체로서 완전한 문장을 형성해야 하므로 자동사만 올 수 있다. 따라서 rise의 과거형인 rose가 정답이다. raise는 주로 타동사로 쓰이며 뜻은 '~를 올리다, 들어올리다'이다. rise는 자동사로서 '오르다'라는 의미이다.

어휘 harvest 수확

2 내 친구가 회사에서 가장 중요한 자리를 내게 제안했다.

해설 문맥상 내 친구가 제안했다는 능동의 의미이므로 offered가 정답이다.

어휘 position 자리

3 그가 약속에 늦을 때마다, 나를 화나게 만든다.

해설 'It makes me angry'는 5형식 문장 구조를 취하고 'make'가 사역동사이기 때문에 목적격 보어로는 원형 부정사가 오든지 아니면 형용사가 와야 한다. 'angrily'는 부사이므로 목적격 보어가 될 수 없다. 목적격 보어 자리에 부사를 자주 함정으로 넣는다는 것을 알아둘 것.

어휘 whenever ~할 때마다 appointment 약속

4 새 임원은 행정 보좌관이 서류작업을 모두 처리하도록 했다.

해설 동사 다음에 목적어 'the administrative assistant'가 나온 후 to부정사가 나왔다. 사역동사 let은 뒤에 '목적어+동사원형'의 형태가 나와야 하므로, 이 문장에서는 5형식 사역동사인 got이 정답이 된다.

어휘 director 임원 administrative assistant 행정 보좌관 take care of ~를 처리하다 돌보다 paperwork 서류 작업

5 조직 효율성에 관한 회의 동안 기조연설자는 신입 직원들을 위한 관리 프로그램의 장점을 얘기했다.

해설 괄호 뒤에 바로 목적어(the merits)가 연결되어 있으므로 타동사가 들어가야 한다. 의미상으로는 talk와 discuss 모두 가능하지만 talk는 전치사 to/with/about 등을 동반하는 자동사이므로 답이 될 수 없다.

어휘 during ~하는 동안에 keynote speaker 기조연설자 merit 장점

6 SW 47 진공 청소기는 고급 필터 기술을 사용하여 카펫을 깨끗하게 유지하고 새것처럼 보이게 합니다.

해설 빈칸 앞 to부정사(to keep)에서 keep은 'keep + 목적어 + 목적 보어(형용사)'의 패턴으로 쓰이므로 형용사 clean이 정답이다.

어휘 vacuum cleaner 진공 청소기

7 재무이사는 월요일 이사 회의를 위해서 새로 생긴 고속열차를 탔다.

해설 '(교통수단 따위를) 타다'라는 의미를 가지고 있는 타동사 take를 선택하는 문제이다.

어휘 board meeting 이사 회의

8 Lee 씨에게 그녀의 사무실에 금요일까지 그녀의 소포가 배달될 것이라고 통보해 주세요.

해설 뒤에 목적어가 하나 오고 that절이 오는 4형식 동사는 정해져 있다. 그 중 자주 출제되는 4가지 동사 inform, notify, tell, advise를 반드시 외워 둘 것.

어휘 deliver 배송하다

9 이 이야기들은 그들에게 수년 간 큰 즐거움을 주었다.

해설 them이라는 사람 목적어와 enormous pleasure라는 사물 목적어를 취할 수 있는 4형식 동사 give의 능동완료형인 have given이 정답이다.

어휘 enormous 엄청나게 많은 pleasure 기쁨

10 우리 가족에게 가장 좋은 집을 선택하는 데 도움이 되도록 우리는 상당한 부동산 시장조사를 끝냈다.

해설 빈칸은 준사역동사인 help의 목적격 보어 자리. help는 목적격 보어를 'to부정사' 또는 '동사원형'을 취하므로 정답은 동사원형인 choose이다.

어휘 significant 상당한 real estate 부동산

11 부동산 관리 프로그램은 직원들이 우리의 환경을 더 잘 인식하게 만들어 주었다.

해설 make(사역동사)+목적어+목적 보어의 5형식 구문이다. 따라서 정답은 made가 된다. 프로그램이 직원들로 하여금 환경을 더 잘 인식하게 만들

어 주었다는 의미이다.

어휘 aware of ~알다 surroundings 환경

12 가구가 어제 도착했고 우리 사무실에 잘 어울려서 매우 만족했다.

해설 문장에 알맞은 동사를 구하는 문제로, yesterday의 쓰임으로 보아 과거 시제이어야 하며 arrive는 자동사이므로 수동태가 될 수 없기 때문에 답은 arrived가 된다.

어휘 pleased with ~에 만족하는

13 경찰서장은 그 형사에게 증거가 수집된 후 조사를 계속하라고 지시했다.

해설 뒤의 전치사 with와 어울리는 동사는 proceed이다.

어휘 detective 형사 investigation 조사 evidence 증거 gather 모으다

14 줄어든 연료값 때문에, 자동차 장기 여행은 다시 한번 대부분의 사람들에게 가능하게 되었다.

해설 2형식 동사 become 다음 보어로 형용사 어휘를 묻는 문제로 '~할 여유가 되다'는 뜻으로 affordable이 적절하다.

어휘 due to ~ 때문에 decreased 줄어든

15 GUID 시스템은 우리 고객들이 개발 비용을 절감하고 여러 곳에서 온 데이터를 통합하게 해 준다.

해설 본동사로, to부정사를 목적격 보어로 취하는 5형식 동사 allows가 정답이다. allowing은 현재 분사형태로 동사가 될 수 없다.

어휘 unify 통합하다

SPARTA ✔ ACTUAL TEST

p. 68

1 (A)	**2** (C)	**3** (B)	**4** (C)	**5** (A)	**6** (C)
7 (C)	**8** (A)	**9** (D)	**10** (A)	**11** (B)	**12** (A)
13 (D)	**14** (A)	**15** (C)	**16** (B)		

1 Titan Chemicals의 임원들은 연구 및 개발 지출비를 늘릴 것을 약속했다.

해설 빈칸 앞 have동사와 함께 현재완료 have p.p.형을 완성하는 동사 어휘 문제로 make a commitment '전념하다, 노력하다, 약속하다'의 의미를 알면 쉽게 해결할 수 있다. 따라서 (A) made가 정답이다.

어휘 executive 임원 research 연구 development 개발 spending 지출 face 직면하다 show 보여주다 comply 따르다, 준수하다

2 서버와 관련된 어떤 문제가 발생하면 고객들의 문의에 즉각 답변해 주시기 바랍니다.

해설 동사 어휘 문제를 풀 때는 해석하기 이전에 동사 다음을 살펴보고 답의 단서를 찾아 본다. 뒤에 전치사(to)가 나와 있으므로 빈칸에는 자동사 (C) respond가 들어가야 한다. 나머지 보기는 타동사이다.

어휘 occur 일어나다 promptly 즉시 inquiry 문의

3 뛰어난 투구와 시기적절한 안타로 어제 야구경기는 대단히 재미있었다.

해설 make 동사 문형을 묻는 문제로 목적어를 설명해 주는 목적격 보어로 형용사 (B) exciting가 빈칸에 들어가야 한다. (D) excitable는 형용사지만 의미상 맞지가 않다.

어휘 pitching 투구 timely 시기적절한 excitedly 흥분하여 excitable 흥분을 잘하는

4 회사가 유럽 시장에서의 성공을 발표했을 때 회사는 포상으로 모든 직원들이 일주일의 휴가를 갖도록 허락했다.

해설 목적격 보어로 to부정사를 취하는 불완전 타동사가 들어가야 하므로 (C) allowed가 답이 된다. let, have, make는 목적격 보어로 동사원형을 취하는 사역동사이다.

어휘 announce 발표하다

5 사무실 임대기간이 만료되면 EK Investment 사는 도심지로 이전할 것입니다.

해설 빈칸은 동사 자리로 동사가 아닌 (B) expiring, (C) expiration는 오답이다. 동사인 (A) expires와 (D) is expired 중 expire는 자동사로 수동태가 될 수 없으므로 (A) expires가 정답이다.

어휘 lease 임대, 임대차 계약 expire 만료되다, 만기가 되다 relocate 이전하다 downtown area 도심지

6 몇 가지 핵심적인 변화를 도입한 뒤에 우리 회사는 고객들에게 좋은 가격과 서비스를 제공할 수 있을 것이다.

해설 문맥상 '제공한다'는 의미의 (C) offer가 정답이다. offer A B 또는 offer B to A (A에게 B를 제공하다)의 문형으로 사용된다.

어휘 implementation 도입 improved 좋아진, 개선된

7 판매 책임자와 그의 팀은 프로젝트를 일정대로 가까스로 마무리 지었다.

해설 'have/get+사물+형용사/과거분사'는 '사물을 형용사/과거분사 상태로 되게 하다.'란 뜻의 구문이다. project가 수동적으로 마무리되는 것이기 때문에 complete의 과거분사 형태 (C) completed가 정답이다.

어휘 manage to 가까스로 ~ 하다 on schedule 일정대로

8 의약과 석유 산업을 제외한 대부분의 산업에 대한 일반인들의 생각이 1년 전과 거의 같은 상태에 있다.

해설 2형식 remain 동사의 보어로 형용사를 물어보는 문제. 'remain close to ~에 가까운 상태로 있다' 로 묶어서 암기해 두면 좋다.

어휘 except for ~을 제외하고 drug 약품

9 해외로 배송되는 섬유 제품들은 국제 라벨 부착 요건을 준수해야 한다.

해설 빈칸은 [자동사 + 전치사] 표현인 conform to'(규칙, 명령, 지시 등을) 따르다, 준수하다'를 알면 쉽게 해결할 수 있다. 따라서 (D) conform이 정답이다. 동의어인 comply는 전치사 with와 어울려 comply with의 형태로 쓰인다.

어휘 textile product 섬유 제품, 직물 ship 배송하다 overseas 해외로 labeling requirements 라벨 부착 요건 update 갱신하다 confront (문제나 곤란한 상황에) 맞서다

10 회사 계약서를 이메일에 첨부할 때 암호로 보호하여 문서들을 안전하게 보관하십시오.

해설 빈칸은 5형식 동사로 쓰이는 keep 동사의 목적격 보어 자리로 목적어인 these documents를 보충 설명하는 형용사 자리이다. 따라서 (A) secure가 정답이다.

어휘 attach 첨부하다 contract 계약서 protect 보호하다 secure 안전한 security 안전 securely 안전하게

11 모든 사무용품의 신청은 처리 권한이 있는 적절한 부서 관리자에게 서면으로 신청해야 한다.

해설 'make a request'라는 표현을 알아야 All requests를 받는 동사를 찾을 수 있다.

어휘 make a request 요청하다 in writing 서면으로 appropriate 적절한

12 컴퓨터 실력을 향상시키려면 Baton Career Center에 연락하여 저비용 코스에 대해 알아보십시오.

해설 빈칸은 동사 자리로 문맥상 (A) contact와 (B) speak가 혼동될 수 있는데 speak는 자동사이므로 빈칸 뒤에 전치사가 와야 한다. 단 speak가

타동사로 쓰이는 경우는 뒤에 언어가 나오는 경우에만 가능하다. 따라서 타동사인 (A) contact가 정답이다. 참고로 (C) touch가 '연락하다'의 의미로 쓰이는 경우에는 'get in touch with ~'의 형태로 사용한다는 것도 알아 두자.

어휘 improve 향상시키다 low-cost 저비용의 contact 연락하다 speak 말하다 touch (둘 이상의 사물표면 등이) 닿다, 접촉하다 connect 연결하다

〈13-16〉 다음은 이메일에 관한 문제이다.

수신: subscriptions@gardener.com
발신: Hboyd@naoro.co.kr
제목: 정기구독 #364954

관계자분에게,

저는 <가드너스 시크릿> 정기구독을 취소하고자 합니다. 귀사의 기사와 사진 에세이는 언제나 유익하고 흥미롭긴 하지만, 저는 더 이상 그것들을 즐길 시간이 없습니다.

사실 지난 6개월분 대부분이 여전히 읽지 못한 상태로 놓여 있습니다. 제 정기구독이 다음 5월까지 효력이 있는 것으로 알고 있습니다. 만약 귀사의 기록에 이것이 사실인 것으로 확인된다면, 제가 구독료로 지불한 금액의 절반인 75달러를 환불해 주시기 바랍니다.

이 문제에 대한 귀사의 신속한 처리에 미리 감사드립니다.

진심으로,
해롤드 보이드

어휘 subscription 정기구독 informative 유익한 interesting 흥미로운 no longer 더 이상 ~ 않다 in fact 사실 issue (잡지, 신문 등의) 호 put aside 치워놓다 unread 읽지 않은 record 기록 refund 환불 in advance 미리 prompt 신속한 attention 주의 matter 문제 confirm 확인하다 renew 갱신하다 active 유효한

13

해설 문맥에 맞는 동사 어휘 선택 문제이다. 뒤따르는 문장을 보면 '즐길 시간이 없다(I no longer have the time to enjoy them)'라고 되어 있으므로 '정기 구독을 취소하겠다(cancel my subscription)'고 하는 것이 의미가 통한다. 따라서 정답은 (D) cancel이다.

14

해설 문맥에 맞는 부사 어휘 선택 문제이다. '여전히 읽지 않은 상태(still unread)'가 문맥에 맞으므로 정답은 (A) still이다.

15 (A) 독자 여러분들은 저희의 특별 기념호를 받으시게 됩니다.
(B) 제 생각에 귀사의 주문 과정에 심각한 문제가 있다고 생각되는군요.
(C) 제 정기 구독이 다음 5월까지 효력이 있는 것으로 알고 있습니다.
(D) 귀사의 고객 서비스에 상당히 실망했습니다.

해설 빈칸 앞의 내용은 글쓴이가 잡지 구독을 취소하고자 하는 이유를 제시하고 있다. 빈칸 바로 뒤 내용과 문맥상 자연스럽게 연결할 수 있는 문장은 보기 중 구독이 언제까지 효력이 있다는 내용인 (C)가 가장 적절하다.

16

해설 [접속사(if)+주어(your records)+----+명사절(that this is correct)]의 구조이므로 빈칸에는 if절의 동사를 써야 한다. 따라서 정답은 (B) indicate이다.

UNIT 07 수 일치

SPARTA Check-UP! 1

p. 71

1 (A) **2** (D) **3** (A)

1 교육 세미나의 많은 지원서 양식은 다음 달 말까지 인사부서에 제출되어야 한다.

해설 문장의 주어는 지원서들(Application forms)이다. 따라서 정답은 (A) need가 되어야 한다.

어휘 application 지원 Personnel Department 인사부서

2 분석가들은 회사들에게 고객 안전을 위해 비용을 할당하고 온라인 프라이버시를 최고로 중요하게 다루어야 한다고 충고한다.

해설 문장 구조상 빈칸에는 주어 역할을 하는 명사가 들어가야 한다. 문맥상 충고하는 주체로서 사람을 나타내는 명사가 필요하므로 사물명사인 (A) Analysis와 동사 (B) Analyze는 오답이다. 동사(advise)의 형태로 보아 주어가 복수가 되어야 하므로 정답은 (D) Analysts이다.

어휘 advise 충고하다 allocate 할당하다 consumer 소비자 security 안전 analysis 분석 analyze 분석하다 analyst 분석가

3 고객서비스센터에서는 불만 접수일로부터 15일 이내에 서면으로 통지 내용을 고객에게 보내야 한다.

해설 빈칸은 주어 자리이므로 일단 보기 중 동사인 (B) complain과 (C) complains는 먼저 탈락하며, 남은 보기는 명사 (A) complaint와 동명사 (D) complaining인데 빈칸 뒤 be동사 형태를 보면 단수 형태인 is라는 것을 알 수 있다. 따라서 주어는 단수가 되어야 하므로 (A)가 정답이다.

어휘 written notice 서면 통지

SPARTA Check-UP! 2

p. 72

1 (A) **2** (C) **3** (C)

1 내 동료들 각각은 5년 이상의 컴퓨터 시스템과 건축 설계 경력이 있다.

해설 each는 단수동사를 받는다. 따라서 정답은 (A) has이다.

어휘 colleague 동료

2 7월 1일 전까지 우리 자전거를 구매한 사람은 모두 자전거 잠금 장치를 무료로 받을 수 있다.

해설 선행사가 anyone인 관계대명사에 적합한 동사의 형태를 찾아야 한다. anyone은 단수동사로 받기 때문에 정답은 (C) purchases이다.

어휘 available 이용 가능한

3 회사에 있는 모든 사람들은 이런 기회는 자주 생기지 않는다는 것을 깨닫는다.

해설 주어인 Everyone은 항상 단수동사로 받는다. 따라서 (C) realizes가 답이 된다.

어휘 opportunity 기회 come along 생기다

SPARTA Check-UP! ③ p. 73

1 (C) **2** (B) **3** (B)

1 나라에 있는 아주 소수의 의료 전문가들만 진정으로 자폐증을 진단하고 치료하는 법을 안다.

해설 주어인 'a group of+복수명사' 구조는 복수동사로 받으므로 정답은 (C) know이다.

어휘 diagnose 진단하다 autism 자폐증

2 지역은 규모 면에서는 작을지 몰라도 다양한 사업체들이 지역 전체에 걸쳐 산재해 있다.

해설 'a variety of+복수명사' 구조로 동사를 복수인 (B) are로 받아야 한다.

어휘 a variety of 다양한 intersperse 흩뿌리다

3 Solomon Brothers 사는 양질의 자동차 관련 서비스를 제공하는 업체라고 정평이 나 있다.

해설 빈칸은 문장의 동사 자리로 문장의 주어인 고유명사 Solomon Brothers는 복수 형태라 하더라도 단수 취급하므로 보기 중 단수동사인 (B) enjoys가 정답이다.

어휘 reputation 평판 provider 공급업체

SPARTA Check-UP! ④ p. 74

1 (D) **2** (D) **3** (D)

1 매니저는 20명의 직원과 함께 해외에서 이메일로 들어오는 모든 주문을 처리한다.

해설 이 문장의 주어는 the manager이고 together with는 주어를 수식하는 수식어구이다. 따라서 주어는 단수이므로 단수동사인 (D) takes가 정답이 된다.

어휘 incoming 들어오는 overseas 해외의

2 도시의 소아병원에서 의사 혹은 간호사들은 일주일에 적어도 3회는 철야 작업을 한다.

해설 either A or B 문형은 동사를 B에 수 일치시킨다. 따라서 정답은 (D) work이다.

어휘 overnight 밤새도록 at least 적어도

3 사고 취약 지역이었던 고속도로에 몇 대의 새 전등이 설치되었나.

해설 there is(are) ~로 시작하는 구문의 전체 동사의 수는 be동사 다음에 나오는 명사에 따라 결정된다. 이 문장에서는 복수명사인 'several new lamp posts'가 이에 해당되므로 복수 동사가 따라오게 된다. 따라서 정답은 (D) were이다.

어휘 several 몇몇의 lamp post 전등, 가로등 install 설치하다 freeway 고속도로 accident-prone area 사고 취약 지역

SPARTA PRACTICE p. 75

1 does	**2** are	**3** is	**4** banks
5 specializes	**6** require	**7** have	**8** is
9 are	**10** is	**11** works	**12** will be sent
13 competitors	**14** predict	**15** benefits	

1 Powell Electronics 사는 원본 영수증 없이 반환된 제품은 환불해 주지 않는다.

해설 회사명은 고유명사로 복수형이라 할지라도 단수 취급하므로 does를 써야 한다.

어휘 refund 환불 without ~없이 original receipt 영수증 원본

2 Morgan Stanley 사에서 완성한 회계 수치를 곧 볼 수 있을 것으로 예상한다.

해설 주어인 figures가 복수이므로 적절한 be동사는 are이다.

어휘 figure 수치 be expected to 기대되다

3 주문한 가구는 5월 11일 배송될 예정이다.

해설 가구(furniture)는 불가산명사로 단수 취급하므로 is가 정답이다.

어휘 deliver 배송하다

4 온 나라의 저축은행이 경제침체에서 회복하기 시작했다.

해설 동사가 복수(have begun)이므로 주어인 저축은행(savings bank)도 복수로 써야 한다.

어휘 recover from 회복하다

5 그는 기업분쟁을 전문으로 하는 법률 회사에 채용되었다.

해설 선행사는 law firm이므로 단수동사인 specializes가 정답이다.

어휘 specialize in ~을 전문으로 하다 dispute 분쟁

6 광범위한 훈련이 필요한 신입 직원의 수가 감소했다.

해설 선행사 employees가 복수이므로 정답은 require이다.

어휘 extensive 광범위한, 대규모의

7 예산 관리를 포함한 다양한 책무가 관리자에게 위임되었다.

해설 문장의 주어는 A variety of responsibilities이므로 <A variety of 복수명사+복수동사>로 수 일치를 하려면 have를 써야 한다.

어휘 responsibility 책임, 책무 including ~를 포함하는 manage 관리하다 budget 예산

8 Central 병원에 채용된 의사의 수는 상대적으로 적다.

해설 The number of(··의 수)는 단수 취급하므로 적절한 동사는 is이다

어휘 relatively 상대적으로

9 많은 직원들이 증권거래 세미나 참석에 관심이 있다.

해설 '많은'이란 의미를 가진 'a number of'는 복수 취급하므로 are가 정답이다.

어휘 attend 참석하다 securities trading 증권거래

10 다른 에너지 공급업체들과 함께 전기 회사는 요금을 내린다.

해설 전기회사(The electric company)가 주어이므로 동사는 단수인 is이다.

어휘 along with ~와 함께 lower 낮추다

11 팀의 매니저는 동료와 같이 매일 추가 근무를 한다.

해설 주어는 the team manager이므로 정답은 단수동사인 works이다.

어휘 together with ~와 같이 coworker 동료 work overtime 추가 근무하다

12 연례 여름 행사에 대한 일정표를 포함한 편지가 새 관리자에게 보내질 것이다.

해설 주어는 A letter이고, containing ~ events까지가 앞의 letter를 수식하

므로 동사는 단수형이어야 한다. 조동사는 단/복수의 형태가 같으므로 will be sent를 써야 한다.

어휘 contain 포함하다 annual 매년의 supervisor 관리자

13 확장 계획을 준비하기 위해, 전자 회사는 몇몇 경쟁사에서 직원을 채용했다.

해설 several of ~ 뒤에는 복수명사가 온다.

어휘 prepare for ~을 준비하다 recruit 채용하다

14 Highlander 자산 관리를 맡은 Temple 씨와 함께 많은 이들은 회사가 사업부채 측면에 초점을 맞출 거라 예측한다.

해설 주어가 복수 의미인 many (people)이므로 동사는 복수 형태인 predict이다.

어휘 in charge of ~를 맡은, 책임진 focus on ~에 집중하다 debt 부채

15 DK 클럽의 회원권에는 스포츠 시설 및 상을 받은 클럽 레스토랑의 식사 할인과 같은 다양한 혜택이 포함되어 있다.

해설 '다양한'이란 뜻의 a range of 뒤에는 복수명사가 나온다.

어휘 include 포함하다 sports facility 스포츠 시설

SPARTA ✔ ACTUAL TEST

p. 76

1 (B)	2 (A)	3 (B)	4 (B)	5 (B)	6 (A)
7 (A)	8 (A)	9 (A)	10 (A)	11 (A)	12 (A)
13 (D)	14 (B)	15 (B)	16 (A)		

1 목요일 저녁 재즈 콘서트 할인 티켓은 Klein 씨의 사무실에서 구할 수 있다.

해설 문장의 동사는 are이다. 동사가 복수이므로 주어도 당연히 복수 형태가 돼야 한다. 따라서 답은 (B) tickets이다.

어휘 available 구할 수 있는

2 일기예보에서 오늘 오후에 비가 올 것으로 예상해, 암 건강 재단은 모금행사를 연기하기로 결정했다.

해설 빈칸은 주어 자리이므로 보기에서 (A) forecast와 (B) forecasts가 가능한데, 동사의 형태가 expects로 단수이므로 단수명사인 (A) forecast가 답임을 알 수 있다. a weather forecast(일기 예보)를 덩어리째 알아두자. forecast는 '예보, 예측'이라는 명사적 의미도 있지만 '예측하다'는 동사의 뜻도 있다.

어휘 weather forecast 일기예보 cancer 암 foundation 재단 창설, 설립 decide to ~하기로 결정하다 postpone 연기하다 (=put off) fundraiser 모금행사

3 다음 달 마케팅 제안서의 적시 완성은 마케팅 직원과 영업직원들 간의 명료한 의사소통이 필요하다.

해설 문장의 동사가 없으므로 빈칸에는 동사가 필요하다. 주어가 completion으로 단수이므로, 정답은 (B) requires이다.

어휘 timely 시기에 맞춘, 적시의 completion 완성, 완료 clear 명백한, 이해하기 쉬운 require 요구하다, ~을 필요로 하다

4 환경을 위해서 종이 봉투나 기저귀 같은 일회용품의 사용을 줄여야 한다.

해설 주어가 명사이므로 단수동사가 나와야 한다. 따라서 (B) has가 정답이 된다.

어휘 disposable item 일회용품 paper bag 종이 봉투 diaper 기저귀 reduce 줄이다 environment 환경

5 운전자들은 방문객을 위한 주차 공간이 녹색지역으로 제한되어 있다는 것을 기억해야 한다.

해설 that 절에 동사는 are이므로 주어도 복수형 (B) spaces가 와야 한다.

어휘 remind 상기시키다 parking space 주차 공간

6 약속을 변경하고 싶은 사람들은 우리 접수 담당자에게 오늘 오후 6시까지 연락해야 합니다.

해설 빈칸은 관계대명사 who 이하의 수식을 받는 자리이다. 인칭대명사와 재귀대명사는 수식을 받을 수 없으므로 (C) Yourself와 (D) They는 오답이며, who 이하의 동사가 복수(wish)이므로 동사와 수 일치되는 (A) Those가 정답이다.

어휘 reschedule 일정을 변경하다, 조정하다 appointment 약속 receptionist 접수 담당자

7 회사의 새로운 인사정책은 직원들이 현재 직무에서 일을 잘 수행하지 못한다면 다른 직무로 이동하는 것을 금지한다.

해설 restrict(금지하다)의 알맞은 형태를 묻는 문제로, 빈칸은 주어(The firm's new human resources policy)와 목적어(employees) 사이에 위치에 있으므로 동사가 필요하다. 따라서 동사의 기능을 할 수 없는 (B) restricting은 답에서 제외되며, 목적어가 있다는 점에서 수동의 (D) was restricted도 답이 될 수 없다. 단수인 (A) restricts와 복수인 (C) restrict 중 주어가 policy로 단수이므로 (A)가 답이다.

어휘 firm 회사 human resources 인적 자원 policy 정책 transfer to ~로 전근하다 perform 수행하다 current 현재의 role 역할

8 원자력 발전소의 관리자는 의심스러운 징후가 탐지될 경우 발전소의 안전 감독원으로부터 사전 통보를 받는 것으로 예상한다.

해설 빈칸 앞에는 Managers of the nuclear power plant가 주어로, 빈칸 뒤에는 to부정사가 왔다. 빠진 품사는 동사가 되고 to부정사를 받으므로 원형 그대로 온다. 또한 주어가 복수이므로 복수형인 (A) expect가 정답이다.

어휘 manager 관리자 nuclear power plant 핵 발전소 notify 알리다, 통보하다 ahead of ~을 앞서 safety inspector 안전 감독원 in case ~할 경우 suspicious 의심스러운 sign 징후 detect 감지하다

9 Luxor 호텔에서 도보거리 내에 있는 휴양 시설들에는 수영장과 야외 식사용 테이블을 갖춘 넓은 공원이 있다.

해설 빈칸에 들어갈 알맞은 동사의 형태를 묻고 있다. 주어는 Recreational facilities로 복수이고, 문장에 동사가 없으므로 빈칸에는 복수동사가 들어가야 한다. (C) including은 문장의 본동사가 될 수 없으므로 탈락. (B) is including, (D) includes는 동사의 수 일치에서 오답이 된다.

어휘 recreational facilities 휴양 시설 within walking distance of 도보로 갈 수 있는 거리에 spacious 넓은

10 우리의 직원 모두는 각자 우리의 고객을 위해 최고 수준의 서비스를 제공하기 위해 헌신한다.

해설 빈칸은 문장의 동사 자리. 따라서 문장에서 동사가 될 수 없는 (C) to dedicate와 (D) dedicating은 탈락이다. Each of the employees에서 동사는 단수 취급하므로 (B) dedicate 또한 답이 될 수 없다. 따라서 답은 (A) is dedicated가 된다.

어휘 employee 직원, 피고용인 provide 제공하다 level 수준 be dedicated to ~에 헌신하다

11 개인적인 정보 서류는 사전 허가가 없으면 직원들에게 배포되지 않는다.

해설 전체 주어는 copies로 복수이고, 빈칸은 본동사 자리이므로, (A)가 정답이다.

어휘 personal information 개인 정보 distribute 배포하다 prior authorization 사전 허가

12 전국적으로 저축은행들이 장기적 경기 침체로부터 회복하고 있다는 소식 때문에 기업들은 투자를 늘리고 있다.

해설 빈칸 본동사의 주어 The news는 복수 형태처럼 보이지만 단수 취급하므로 단수동사 (A) encourages가 와야 한다. 주어 The news를 수식하는 that 이하 긴 관계대명사절에 헷갈리지 않도록 한다.

어휘 savings bank 저축은행 recover 회복하다 recession 경기침체 investment 투자

<13-16> 다음은 편지에 관한 문제이다.

고객 서비스
코레이아 전자제품
주앙 가 32
페어필드, 호주

고객 서비스센터에게;

저는 최근 귀사의 온라인 상점에서 디지털카메라를 주문했습니다. 하지만 어제 그것을 받았을 때, 렌즈에 작은 금들과 화면 스크린에 긁힌 자국들이 있는 것을 발견했습니다. 웹 사이트에 따르면 귀사는 가능한 한 최상의 상태로 물품들을 배달해 줍니다. 만약 어떠한 결함이라도 있다면 새것으로 교체 받을 수 있다고 했습니다. 따라서 저는 이 카메라를 새것으로 당장 교환해 주실 것을 요청합니다.

제조사는 MacCom이고 모델 번호는 I-3935입니다. 청구서를 첨부했습니다. 거기에 쓰여 있는 주소로 새 제품을 보내주십시오. 결함이 있는 제품을 반송하는 것이기에, 배송비는 귀사에서 부담하시기 바랍니다. 가능한 한 빨리 새 제품을 받길 원합니다.

제 요청을 즉시 처리해 주십시오.

감사합니다.

진심으로,

케턴 차우한

어휘 appliance 설비, 전기제품 crack 금 immediate 즉각적인 invoice 청구서 defective 결함이 있는 shipping charge 배송료

13

해설 주어인 단수 your company와 목적어 items, 그 사이에 들어갈 동사를 찾는 문제이다. 따라서 단수동사 (D) delivers가 정답이다. (A) deliver는 복수동사, (B) delivery는 명사, (C) deliverable은 형용사이다.

14

해설 새로운 절 앞에 쓰여서 앞 문장과의 의미를 자연스럽게 연결해 주는 것을 골라야 한다. 앞에서 이 회사의 규칙을 설명한 후, 뒤에서 자신이 요구하는 내용을 말하고 있으므로 이 관계에서 가장 자연스러운 말은 (B) Therefore(따라서, 그러므로)이다.

15

해설 여기서 it은 앞 문장에 나온 invoice의 대명사이다. 따라서 address와 invoice의 관계로 '그 위에 적힌'이라는 수동의 뜻을 이루는 과거분사 (B) written이 정답이다.

16 (A) 가능한 한 빨리 새 제품을 받길 희망합니다.
(B) 저는 이번 일에 매우 만족했습니다.
(C) 보다 많은 정보를 얻으시려면 고객서비스부서 Mirah Rahman에게 전화 주십시오.
(D) 고객 카드를 신청하시려면 고객서비스 직통전화 1-800-555-3266로 전화하시면 됩니다.

해설 빈칸 앞으로는 카메라 주문을 한 후 문제가 생겨서 교환 요청을 하고 있다는 것을 알 수 있고, 빈칸 뒤로는 그 요청이 즉시 처리되길 바라고 있으므로 빈칸에 들어갈 적절한 문장은 보기 중 새 제품을 빨리 받기 희망한다는 (A)가 가장 적절하다.

UNIT 08 태

SPARTA Check-UP! 1

p. 79

1 (D) **2** (B) **3** (C)

1 인사부장은 신입 사원들에게 사규에 관해 설명했다.

해설 본동사가 필요하므로 (A) explaining는 제외한다. 주어(personnel manager)가 단수이므로 복수동사 (B) are being explained도 답이 될 수 없다. 주어와 동사 explain은 능동 관계이다. 따라서 정답은 (D) explained이다.

어휘 company policy 사규

2 직원들은 사용하지 않는 설비들을 수거하여 처분하거나 자선단체에 기부할 것이다.

해설 빈칸은 조동사 다음 동사원형 자리로 보기 중 동사원형인 (B) collect, (D) be collected 중 빈칸 다음 목적어가 있는 능동태이므로 (B) collect가 정답이 된다.

어휘 unused 사용하지 않는 equipment 장비 dispose of 처분하다 donate 기부하다

3 Charlotte Foods 사는 내년에 많은 새로운 아이템을 출시할 것이라고 어제 발표했습니다.

해설 빈칸은 동사 자리로 목적어 that 절을 취하는 능동태 (C) announced와 (D) have announced 중 선택하면 된다. 주어는 고유명사(회사명)이므로 복수형이라도 단수 취급하므로 (C) announced가 정답이다.

어휘 announce 발표하다 release 출시하다

SPARTA Check-UP! 2

p. 80

1 (B) **2** (A) **3** (D)

1 제품을 다음 날 받을 수 있으려면 모든 사무용품 주문들은 오후 6시 전에 Weaton 씨에게 제출되어야 한다.

해설 선택지에서 be동사 다음에 쓰일 수 있는 것은 분사나 명사. 문장의 주어인 'All orders'가 사물이므로 수동태의 문장으로 완성을 해야 한다. 따라서 'must be submitted'의 형태로 써야 한다. 답은 (B).

어휘 following day 다음 날

2 현재 우리는 시간도, 돈도, 인력도 부족하기 때문에 계획의 변수는 완전히 수정되어야만 한다.

해설 be동사 뒤에는 현재분사나 과거분사가 오고, 주어(parameters)와 동사(revise)의 의미 관계는 수동이므로 (A) revised가 정답이다.

어휘 parameter 매개 변수 personnel 인력, 인사 revise 수정하다

3 가장 최근의 선적에 대한 지불이 마감이라서 일주일 이내에 지불이 되어야 한다.

해설 빈칸 앞의 and는 절을 연결해 주는 등위접속사이다. 따라서 접속사 and 다음에 주어인 The payment가 생략된 것임을 알 수 있다. payment가 주어로 오게 되면 수동형이 되어야 하므로 빈칸에는 수동태를 사용한 (D) be received가 와야 한다.

어휘 receive payment 대금을 받다 due 지불기일이된, 마감의

SPARTA Check-UP! 3

p. 81

1 (C) **2** (D) **3** (C)

1 저희 고객은 가능한 최선의 결정을 내리는 데 필요한 모든 정보를 입수할 수 있습니다.

해설 본동사가 필요하므로 일단 (D) being은 제외. 주어(clients)가 복수이므로 (A) is도 오답이다. 문맥상 주어와 동사(give)는 수동이 되어야 한다. give가 목적어를 두 개 취하는 4형식 동사라는 점에 주의한다. 정답은 (C)이다.

어휘 access 접근, (자료들의) 이용 appropriate 적절한

2 모든 방문객들은 새로운 빨간 벽돌의 Millennium 건물에 있는 대학의 메인 안내데스크에 보고하도록 요청 받는다.

해설 시제와 태를 묻는 문제이다. 빈칸 앞의 복수 주어인 visitors와 맞게 복수동사가 쓰여야 하고, 방문객들이 보고하도록 부탁받는 것이므로 수동태가 쓰여야 한다. 이 두 가지 요건을 충족하는 답은 (D) are asked이다. (A) asks는 수 일치가 맞지 않고 (B) asking은 문장의 동사 역할을 할 수 없으며, (C) is asking은 수 일치와 태, 둘 다 틀렸다.

어휘 report 보고하다 red-brick 빨간 벽돌의

3 직원들은 회사에 전화로 병결을 알리려고 한다면 하루 전에 미리 인사부의 Tomson 씨에게 연락해야 한다.

해설 빈칸 앞에 동사가 있으므로 (D) requires는 탈락이다. require는 '~을 요구하다, 요청하다'라는 타동사로 목적어가 있어야 하는데 빈칸 뒤에 목적어가 없으므로 정답이 될 수 없다. be동사 뒤에 명사가 오게 되면 명사 보어가 되고 주어와 동격이 되어야 하므로 (B) requirement 역시 답이 될 수 없다. be required to V를 '~하는 것이 요구되다, ~해야 한다'는 뜻으로 알아 두자. 답은 (C)이다.

어휘 Personnel Department 인사부 in advance 미리 call in sick 전화로 병결을 알리다

SPARTA Check-UP! 4

p. 82

1 (A) **2** (D) **3** (B)

1 미국의 산업 심리학자들은 비행 안전에 관한 문제에 점점 열중하고 있다.

해설 숙어로써 'be(become) involved in ~에 열중하다, 연관되다'라는 의미이다.

어휘 industrial 산업의 psychologist 심리학자 increasingly 점점 더, 더욱 더 issue 문제

2 HR Mortgage 사는 조사를 받고 있는 은행과 밀접하게 관련되어 있다고 보도되었다.

해설 숙어로 'be associated with ~와 연관이 있다'라는 의미이다.

어휘 be associated with ~과 관련되다 under investigation 조사 중인

3 비즈니스 워크숍에 참석하는 데 관심 있는 어떤 직원들이라도 인사 부장인 Besson 씨에게 연락해야 한다.

해설 숙어로 'be interested in ~에 관심이 있다'라는 의미이다.

어휘 be interested in ~에 관심 있다 enclosed 동봉된 hopeful 희망적인 listed 표에 나와 있는, 상장된

SPARTA PRACTICE

p. 83

1 be recommended	**2** has	**3** are pleased
4 encouraged	**5** was sent	**6** planning
7 take	**8** has been reserved	**9** has been enhanced
10 be delayed	**11** was hired	**12** saw
13 was	**14** has been concentrating	
15 applies		

1 회원이 되려면 현 클럽 회원으로부터의 추천이 있어야 합니다.

해설 '현 클럽 회원으로부터 추천을 받는다'라는 의미의 수동태이므로 be recommended가 정답이다.

어휘 recommend 추천하다 current 현재의

2 우리의 예측과는 반대로 실업률이 3분기 연속해서 올랐다.

해설 rise는 자동사이기 때문에 수동태가 될 수 없으므로 was는 답이 될 수 없다.

어휘 contrary to ~과 반대로 in a row 연속해서

3 저희 회사의 전기 난방기 광고에 관한 귀하의 편지를 받게 되어 기쁘며, 이 편지와 함께 최근에 나온 저희 회사의 카탈로그 한 부를 동봉합니다.

해설 우리(We)라는 주어가 편지를 받아 기쁜 것이므로 수동형 표현이 되어야 한다. 정답은 are pleased이다. '~로 인해 기뻐하다'란 표현으로 be pleased with도 함께 알아 두자.

어휘 receive 받다 enclose 동봉하다 latest 최근의

4 모든 직원들은 가급적 빨리 새로운 업무 절차 편람을 숙지하도록 강력히 권장되고 있다.

해설 직원들이 새로운 절차를 숙지하도록 '권장 받는다'는 수동의 의미이므로 encouraged가 정답이다.

어휘 familiarize oneself with ~를 숙지하다 procedures manual 절차 지침

5 다행히도 가격 목록을 보내기 전에 틀린 곳을 고치기에는 아직 너무 늦지 않았다.

해설 수동형 문장으로 목록이 '보내지는' 것이므로 was sent가 맞다.

어휘 correct the mistake 잘못을 고치다

6 모든 지원자들은 오리엔테이션에 참석할 예정인데, 오리엔테이션은 월요일 오전 8시에 유럽식 아침 식사와 함께 시작될 것이다.

해설 지원자들이 참석을 계획 중이라는 능동의 의미가 되어야 하므로 정답은 planning이다.

어휘 catered 출장 주문 요리된 continental breakfast 유럽식 아침식사

7 금요일 오후에 지역 거주민을 위한 사교 행사가 우리의 넓은 모임실에서 열릴 것이다.

해설 '열리다'라는 의미의 take place는 자동사로, 수동형으로 표현될 수 없다.

어휘 resident 주민 take place 일어나다 spacious 넓은

8 Hannel 연회장은 9월 12일 직원 감사 만찬을 위해 예약되었다.

해설 연회장이 예약되는 것이므로 수동형인 has been reserved가 정답이다.

어휘 reserve 예약하다 appreciation 감사

9 우리 회사 컴퓨터의 주 기억용량이 늘어나 15%의 판매 증가가 기대된다.

해설 주어(capacity)와 동사(enhance)는 수동 관계로, has been enhanced가 정답이다.

어휘 capacity 용량, 수용량 enhance (질 또는 능력을) 높이다, 강화하다

10 비행기 출발이 몇 시간 지연될 것이라는 소식을 듣게 되자, 우리는 짐 찾는 곳 주변을 운동 겸 걸었다.

해설 비행기가 지체되는 것이기 때문에 수동형인 be delayed가 정답이다.

어휘 departing 떠나는 delay 지연시키다

11 그는 Advance Data Technology 사에 채용되었으나 회사가 12월 초에 파산하면서 직업을 잃었다.

해설 주어와 동사 hire는 의미상 수동이 되어야 한다. 'by+행위자'가 단서가 될 수 있다.

어휘 hire 고용하다 go bankrupt 파산하다

12 부장은 조립 라인의 생산량 증가를 보고 깊은 인상을 받았다.

해설 부장이 생산량을 보고 깊은 인상을 받은 것이므로 주어와 능동 관계인 saw가 되어야 한다.

어휘 impress 인상을 주다 improve 개선하다 production 생산량

13 우리가 설문조사를 통해 받았던 가장 큰 불만 중의 하나는 고객들이 물품 배송을 기다리기를 좋아하지 않는다는 것이었다.

해설 one of the 뒤에는 복수명사가 오지만 동사는 단수 형태로 와야 하며, 뒤의 that 절과 함께 쓸 수 있어야 한다. has는 that 절을 받을 수 없다.

어휘 survey 설문조사 complaint 불만, 불평 delivery 배달

14 제품 경쟁력은 영업부서에서 최근 몇 달 동안 관심을 가지고 지켜본 사항 중에서 가장 중요한 측면이다.

해설 목적어인 attention을 받을 수 있는 능동형이 되어야 하고 문장 뒤에 in recent months란 표현을 봐서 현재 완료시제가 되어야 한다.

어휘 competitiveness 경쟁력 aspect 측면 attention 주목, 관심 recent 최근의

15 Lee 씨가 회계법인 회사에 지원한다면 그는 자격을 충분히 갖추었기 때문에 아마 그 자리를 얻게 될 것이다.

해설 apply for는 사람을 주어로 할 때 능동태가 되어야 하므로 is applied가 아니라 applies가 되어야 한다.

어휘 accounting 회계의 firm 회사 be likely to ~할 것 같다 qualified 자격을 갖춘

SPARTA ACTUAL TEST

p. 84

1 (B)	2 (C)	3 (D)	4 (C)	5 (D)	6 (C)
7 (C)	8 (D)	9 (A)	10 (B)	11 (A)	12 (D)
13 (A)	14 (C)	15 (B)	16 (A)		

1 모든 사용자 지침서는 고객들에게 그 장치 사용법을 확실히 이해시키기 위해 규격화되어야 한다.

해설 사용자 지침서(user's manual)는 규격화되어야 한다는 수동의 의미이므로 답은 (B) formatted이다.

어휘 in order to ~하기 위해 device 장치

2 모든 신입 직원들은 시민권이 있음을 증명하기 위해 그들의 운전 면허증과 사회 보장 카드를 인사 부장에게 보여 줄 준비가 되어 있어야 한다.

해설 빈칸은 be동사 뒤이므로 현재분사(-ing)나 과거분사(-ed) 또는 일반 형용사가 적절하다. 보기 중 (C) prepared가 이에 해당되며, 직원들이 준비되어야 하는 대상이므로 문맥상으로도 적절하다.

어휘 driver's license 운전면허증 social security card 사회 보장 카드 Human Resources 인사부 proof 증명 citizenship 시민권

3 새로운 계획하에 총 3백 5십만 제곱미터의 땅이 대학 건축 용도로 남겨지게 되었다.

해설 동사의 올바른 형태를 묻는 문제. 능동태 문장은 목적어가 있어야 하는데 이 문장에서는 빈칸 다음에 전치사가 나오므로 (A) reserves는 오답이다. (D) has been reserved가 수동태이므로 정답이다.

어휘 construction 공사 university 대학 reserve 예약하다, 남겨두다

4 가구 제작에 필요한 견목은 시간 내에 공장에 도착하기 위해서 두 달 전에 미리 주문해야 한다.

해설 동사 형태 문제. 조동사 must 뒤에 be동사로 미루어보아 보기 중 정답으로 가능한 것은 (B) ordering과 (C) ordered로 좁힐 수 있다. 가구제작용 견목이 주문되어야 하므로 정답은 수동형인 ordered가 된다.

어휘 in advance 사전에

5 당신이 신입 사원이라면 귀하의 이름과 사진, 확인번호가 들어간 신분증용 사진을 찍게 될 것입니다.

해설 빈칸 앞에 be동사가 나온 것으로 미루어 일단 수동태 문장임을 의심해 본다. 다른 세 보기의 품사는 모두 명사로 사진, 사진술인데 빈칸에 넣게 되면 문맥이 이상해진다. 따라서 정답은 'photograph(~의 사진을 찍다)'의 수동형을 이루는 (D) photographed가 정답이다.

어휘 include 포함하다

6 놀랍게도 환자는 아무런 치료도 받지 않고 단지 두 시간 만에 병원에서 퇴원했다.

해설 release와 patient의 관계를 점검하자. release의 대상이 없으므로 주어인 patient와 동사인 release의 의미 관계는 수동이어야 하므로 (C) was relesed가 정답.

어휘 surprisingly 놀랍게도 patient 환자 release 퇴원시키다 proper 적합한 treatment 치료

7 연간 보고서는 내일 아침에 이메일로 영업부 과장에게 보내져야 한다.

해설 문맥상 연간 보고서는 send의 대상이 되므로 수동태의 형식을 취해야 한다. 정답은 (C) be sent이다.

어휘 annual report 연간 보고서 manager of the Sales Department 영업부 과장

8 전기 자동차에 새로운 충전용 배터리가 설치될 때까지 최저 제한 속도 내에서 운전하세요.

해설 [접속사(Until)+주어(the new rechargeable battery)+동사(---)+전명구(in the electric car)]구조로, 빈칸은 동사가 필요한 자리. 보기에 제시된 동사 install은 '~을 설치하다'를 뜻하는 타동사로서 빈칸 뒤 목적어가 없다는 점에서 수동태가 들어가야 한다는 점을 알 수 있다. 따라서 능동의 (A) were installing, (B) would be installing은 탈락되며, (C) to be installed는 동사의 기능을 할 수 없으므로 (D) has been installed가 답이 됨을 알 수 있다.

어휘 rechargeable battery 충전용 배터리 electric car 전기 자동차 keep -ing ~하는 것을 유지하다, 계속해서 ~하다 within ~이내에 minimum speed limit 최저 제한 속도

9 인터넷법과 규정이 승인되고 나면, 사이버 범죄는 현저히 감소하고 인터넷 사용자들은 네티켓을 더 인식하게 될 것이다.

해설 문장의 주어인 the Internet laws and regulations는 승인되는 대상이므로 수동태 (A) are approved가 정답이 된다. 'be approved (by+승인하는 주체) ~에 의해 승인되다'로 사용되어 'by+승인하는 주체'는 보통 생략된다.

어휘 regulation 규제 noticeable 뚜렷한, 현저한 decrease 감소 cyber crime 사이버 범죄 aware of ~을 알고 있는, 인식하고 있는

10 시카고에 있는 Face to Face Holdings의 재무 분석가들은 회사가 자산 중 일부를 매각할 때 주주 가치에 대한 영향을 연구해 왔다.

해설 동사의 알맞은 형태를 묻는 문제로, [주어(Financial analysts ~)+동사(--)+목적어(the effects)] 구조로 빈칸은 동사 자리이다. 따라서 (C)는 답에서 제외하며, 문장의 주어가 analysts로 복수이므로 단수동사인 (A) researches 역시 답이 될 수 없다. 빈칸 뒤 목적어(the effects)가 있다는 점에서도 수동형인 (D) will be researched도 오답이다. 따라서 (B) have researched가 답이 된다.

어휘 financial analyst 재무 분석가 effect 영향 shareholder 주주 asset 자산

11 Orenstein 박사는 새로이 설립된 경제 기획 위원회에 가입을 권유 받고 주저 없이 그 제안을 수락하였다.

해설 동사의 적절한 형태를 묻는 문제. 문장의 동사는 accepted이고, 접속사 and가 있으므로, 빈칸은 동사 자리가 되어야 한다. 동사 invite는 '~을 초대하다, ~을 권하다'의 의미로서 문장에서는 Orenstein 박사가 초대나 권고를 받는 대상이 되어야 하므로 능동이 아닌 수동태의 형태가 필요하다.

어휘 invite A to A가 ~하도록 초대하다, 권유하다 established 설립된, 제정된 economic 경제의 planning 기획 without hesitation 주저 없이

12 수천 명의 통근자들은 터널이 수리되는 동안 도시에 드나들 수 있는 대체 도로를 이용해야만 한다.

해설 동사의 적절한 형태를 묻는 문제. 우선 동사(repair)는 '수리하다'의 타동사이므로, 빈칸 다음에 목적어가 없는 문제와 같은 상황에서는 능동형이 아닌 수동형이 쓰여야 함을 주의하자. 따라서 보기 중 능동태인 (A) repairs, (B) is repairing, (C) has repaired는 탈락이다. 정답은 (D) is being repaired이다.

어휘 commuter 통근자 alternative 대안의, 대체의 route 노선, 도로

〈13-16〉 다음은 공지에 관한 문제이다.

수신: 전 직원들
제목: 보안 업그레이드

Edmonton-Hewitt 사는 현재 전체 보안 시스템을 개선하는 작업을 하고 있습니다.
우리 시스템을 개선하기 위한 조치의 하나로, 우리는 모든 직원들을 위한 새 사원증을 만들 것입니다. 10월 4일부로 현재의 사원증 카드는 더 이상 건물 어디에서도 사용하지 못합니다.
다음 주 월요일, 모든 직원들은 보안 부장인 Ted Hargraves로부터 새 사원증을 받아야 합니다. 이 시스템은 카드가 배부된 다음 날부터 시행될 예정입니다.
그러나 우리 시스템이 점차 새로운 시스템으로 전환함에 따라, 약간의 문제가 발생할 수도 있음을 염두해 두십시오. 이런 문제를 보시거나 이 전환 과정과 관련된 우려사항이 있으시면 3층의 보안 사무실로 연락을 주십시오.

어휘 security 안전 entire 전체의 step 조치, 단계 identification card 신분증, 사원증 employee 직원 following day 다음 날 distribution 배부 gradually 점차적으로 aware ~을 인지하고 있는 arise 생기다, 발생하다 notice 알아차리다, 깨닫다; 공지 issue 문제점; 발행하다 concern 우려 transition 변화 security office 보안 사무실 likewise 마찬가지로 indeed 실제로 (강조의 의미로 사용)

13

해설 빈칸은 부사 자리로 보기 중 현재진행 시제와 어울리는 부사인 (A) currently가 정답이다. (B) recently(최근에)와 (C) previously(이전에)는 과거시제와 어울리고 (D) shortly(곧)는 미래 시제와 어울리는 부사이다.

14 (A) 그러나 이 기계들은 낡고 구식이어서 가끔 제대로 작동하지 않았습니다.
(B) 모든 직원들은 출근 첫날에 직원등록 번호를 배정받습니다.
(C) 10월 4일부로 현재의 사원증 카드는 더 이상 건물 어디에서도 사용하지 못합니다.
(D) 지금부터 건물 안에 있는 동안은 반드시 사원증을 착용하셔야 합니다.

해설 빈칸 앞 내용은 현재 시스템 보완 작업을 하고 있으며 모든 직원들을 위한 새로운 사원증 카드가 만들어질 것이라고 알리고 있고 빈칸 다음 문장은 새로운 사원증을 받는 날을 제시하고 있다. 따라서 문맥상 자연스럽게 이어줄 수 있는 문장은 기존의 사원증이 더 이상 사용 불가하다는 내용인 (C)이다.

15

해설 빈칸 앞에 동사 is가 있는 것으로 보아 (C) will service는 일단 제외한다. 전후 문맥을 보면 시스템이 '서비스된다'는 의미가 되어야 하고 뒤에 목적어도 없으므로 수동태 (B) to be serviced가 답이다. 'is to' 부분은 예정, 계획의 의미를 함축한 be to 용법이다.

16

해설 빈칸 앞의 내용은 '새 시스템으로 바뀌고 있다'고, 뒤는 '문제가 다소 발생할 수 있으므로 주의하라'는 내용이다. 추론해 볼 때 전후 반대되는 내용을 말하는 것이므로 보기 중 가장 적합한 단어는 '그렇지만'의 의미를 가진 접속부사 (A) However이다. 참고로 however는 문두, 문미에도 모두 위치할 수 있다는 점을 알아 두자.

UNIT 09 시제

SPARTA Check-UP! 1 p. 87

1 (C) **2** (A) **3** (C)

1 대량 해고가 회사에 심각한 영향을 주기까지 단지 몇 달밖에 걸리지 않는다.

해설 사실을 이야기하는 것이므로 현재시제 (C) takes가 정답.

어휘 large-scale 대규모의 layoff 해고 impact 영향을 주다

2 이사회와 경영진들이 IMK 건물의 재건을 이야기하기 위해서 다음 주 중에 회동할 것이다.

해설 우선, 문장에 접속사가 없으므로 동사는 1개가 와야 한다. 문장에 동사가 없으므로 빈칸은 동사가 들어가야 할 자리. 동명사와 to부정사는 준동사이므로 답이 될 수 없고, 뒤에 next week라는 미래시제와 어울리는 부사가 나와 있으므로 미래시제 (A) will convene이 되어야 한다.

어휘 management 관리, 경영, 경영진 restoration 재건, 복구 convene 모으다, (모임·회의를) 소집하다 소환하다

3 최고 경영자와 많은 다른 회사의 중역들이 최근에 한 달간 유럽에 있는 새로운 지사를 둘러봤다.

해설 부사 recently와 어울리려면 과거시제 또는 현재완료를 써야 하므로, 보기 중 적절한 것은 (C) conducted이다.

어휘 executive 중역 satellite office 지사 conduct 이행하다

SPARTA Check-UP! 2 p. 88

1 (C) **2** (B) **3** (D)

1 제품 개발팀은 현재 새로운 아이디어들의 실현 가능성에 대해 논의하고 있다.

해설 빈칸은 동사 자리이며 현재진행시제의 단서 at the moment(지금)으로 인해 (C) is discussing이 정답이다.

어휘 feasibility 가능성 at the moment 지금

2 저희는 새로운 부사장 Kate 씨께서 11월 1일부터는 직무를 수행하게 된 것을 발표하게 되어 기쁩니다.

해설 현재완료 진행시제인 (A) has been starting이 정답이 되려면 시간의 기간이 문장에 있어야 하므로 오답이다. 문장의 주어 Kate 씨가 사람이므로 수동태인 (C) is started와 (D) is being started 역시 오답이다. 내용상 능동태가 와야 하고, 'November 1'이라는 시간이 왔으므로 미래진행형인 (B)가 적절하다.

어휘 be pleased to ~하게 되어 기쁘다 announce 발표하다 vice president 부사장

3 Yoon 씨는 금요일 돌아왔을 때 시차 적응으로 고생하고 있어서 회의는 다음 주까지 연기되었다.

해설 문맥상 Yoon 씨가 금요일에 귀국한 후 시차 적응 때문에 고생하고 있었다는 것이므로 과거진행형인 (D) was suffering가 정답이다.

어휘 jet lag 시차증(시차로 인한 피로) postpone 연기하다

SPARTA Check-UP! 3 p. 89

1 (D) **2** (D) **3** (A)

1 Central Waste Removal의 많은 직원들은 지난 10년 동안 이 지역 사회에서 서비스 산업의 중요한 역할을 해왔다.

해설 'for the last ten years(지난 10년간)'의 시간 부사구는 현재완료와 어울린다. 현재완료시제인 (D) have been이 가장 적절하다.

어휘 community 지역 사회

2 노동자들이 건설 현장에 도착하기 전에, 재료들은 사라졌다.

해설 comma 뒤의 내용인 '재료가 사라지다'의 시제는 '건설 현장에 노동자들이 도착한 것'보다 전이다. 그런데 건설 현장에 노동자들이 도착한 것이 과거시제이기 때문에 그것보다 이전이 되려면 대과거 시제(과거완료)를 사용해야 한다. 따라서 답은 (D) had disappeared이다.

어휘 construction 건설 site 현장, 장소 material 재료

3 Town Village 매장이 오픈할 때까지 수백 명의 고객들이 매장 회원 카드 신청을 하게 될 것이다.

해설 문두의 'by the time+주어+현재시제(by the time store opens)~'의 형태로 보아 미래완료 동사 (A) will have signed up이 적절하다.

어휘 store 매장 hundreds of 수백 명의

SPARTA Check-UP! 4 p. 90

1 (B) **2** (C) **3** (D)

1 Raymond 씨는 연례 직원 회의에 참석할 수가 없어서, 그의 사무실로 회의록을 보내 달라고 요구했다.

해설 주절의 동사로 주장, 명령, 제안, 요구 등의 단어가 쓰였을 때 that절 동사는 주절의 동사와 수 일치를 시키지 않고 <(should)+동사원형> 형태로 나타낸다.

어휘 annual 연례의 request 요청하다

2 모든 지원자는 인사부서에 그들의 이력서를 즉각 제출할 필요가 있다.

해설 that 절의 주어가 every applicant로 단수인데 동사가 submits가 아니라 submit로 원형이 나올 수 있는 경우는 that 앞에 이성적 판단의 형용사(necessary)가 있는 경우이다.

어휘 applicant 지원자 promptly 즉시, 즉각 necessary 필요한

3 마케팅 책임자는 컨설팅 회사에 가장 유망한 시장에 대한 데이터를 분석하고 보고하도록 요청했다.

해설 <제안, 요구 동사+that+주어+(should)+동사원형>에서 should가 생략된 형태로 원형인 (D) analyze가 정답이다.

어휘 report 분석하다, 보고하다 analyze 분석하다

SPARTA PRACTICE

p. 91

1 works	2 started	3 have finished
4 will be made	5 will relocate	6 will have to be
7 has served	8 attend	9 have increased
10 signed	11 had hired	12 wrote
13 arrive	14 be submitted	15 will discontinue

1 Pat Louis는 보통 시간이 있을 때마다 헬스클럽에서 그의 아내와 운동을 한다.

해설 현재시제와 어울리는 부사 usually가 있으므로 현재시제를 써야 한다.

어휘 usually 보통, 대개

2 고품질 레이저 프린터들이 1년 전부터 인기를 얻기 시작했다.

해설 1년 전(a year ago)이란 확정된 과거시점이 나왔으므로 과거시제 started가 정답이다.

어휘 gain popularity 인기를 얻다

3 그들은 짐을 다 꾸리자마자 집으로 이사해 들어갈 것이다.

해설 시간과 조건의 부사절에서는 현재[완료]시제가 미래[완료]시제를 대신한다.

어휘 packing 짐 꾸리기 move 이사하다

4 최근 발생한 네트워크상의 문제 때문에, 내일 오후 2시와 4시 사이에 우리 서버 컴퓨터들에 대한 수리 작업이 있을 것이다.

해설 수리가 일어나는 것은 내일(tomorrow)이라는 미래의 일이기 때문에, 시제는 미래시제가 맞다.

어휘 due to ~ 때문에

5 다음 달에 우리 회사의 마케팅부서는 넓은 사무실로 이전하게 될 것이다.

해설 다음 달(Next month)이란 미래의 일이므로 will relocate가 정답.

어휘 ample 충분한

6 최근에 사고가 증가하고 있으므로 향후 2주 동안 안전 검사가 강화되어야 한다.

해설 'the next two weeks'라고 하는 미래 표시어가 있으므로 미래시제이며, 문맥상 '최근 사고가 증가하므로 안전 검사가 강화되어야 한다'는 수동의 의미를 가지므로 미래시제 수동태가 정답이 된다.

어휘 recent 최근의 safety inspection 안전 검사

7 Phoenix 씨는 지난 10년 동안 Grobal Network 사의 최고 재무 관리사로 근무했다.

해설 served는 과거 시제, has served는 현재완료 시제이다. 단서는 for the last 10 years(지난 10년 동안)로, 과거부터 현재까지 계속 되는 시점을 나타낸다. 따라서 현재완료 시제인 has served를 써야 한다.

어휘 serve 일하다 chief financial officer(= CFO) 최고 재무 관리사

8 판매팀의 모든 직원들은 오늘 회의에 참석하는 것이 중요하다.

해설 important는 이성적 판단의 형용사이므로 뒤에 나오는 that 절에는 동사원형이 와야 한다.

어휘 attend a meeting 회의에 참석하다

9 Keen Rock 제품의 매출이 지난해 상당히 상승했다.

해설 문장 끝의 기간을 나타내는 'in the past year' 표현에서 시제는 완료 형태가 와야 한다는 것을 알 수 있다.

어휘 substantially 상당히

10 Jane은 지난주 그녀의 일을 도울 직원으로 Bork 씨를 채용하는 정식 계약서에 서명했다.

해설 과거 시간부사구 'last week'이 나왔으므로 동사의 시제도 과거가 되어야 한다. 정답은 과거시제인 signed이다.

어휘 sign 서명하다 contract 계약(서) hire 고용하다 assistant 보조원

11 Letscher 씨는 회사를 떠나기 전에 자신의 자리를 채울 적합한 후임자를 고용했다.

해설 문맥상 before 절에 있는 과거 시제 left 보다 앞선 시제가 들어가야 하므로 대과거 had hired를 써야 한다.

어휘 hire 고용하다 suitable 적합한, 적당한 replacement 후임 fill 채우다

12 Edward Duran은 그가 작년에 퇴직할 때까지 여러 잡지와 신문에 스포츠 기사를 썼다.

해설 'last year'와 함께 'until his retirement'로 미뤄 보아 과거시제 wrote가 적절하다.

어휘 until ~까지 retirement 퇴직, 은퇴

13 고객들이 오늘 오후에 도착했을 때 사장은 회의 석상에서 그것에 관해 말씀하실 것입니다.

해설 시간 및 조건의 부사절은 주절이 미래시제라도 현재시제로 표현한다는 것을 꼭 알아 두자.

어휘 conference 회의 client 고객

14 Wilson 씨는 이번 달 판매 보고서를 월말까지 제출할 것을 요구했다.

해설 that 이하에서 주체가 sales report이므로 보고서가 '제출된다는' 의미로 수동태가 와야 하고, 요구 동사 'request+that+S+동사원형'이므로 be submitted가 답이다.

어휘 request 요구하다 sales report 판매 보고서 submit 제출하다

15 올해가 지난 후 자동차 제조업자는 모든 4 도어 세단 생산을 중단하고 새로운 스포츠카를 소개할 것이다.

해설 미래의 시간의 부사구 'After the current year'가 있으므로, 미래시제 will discontinue를 써서 문장을 완성해야 한다.

어휘 discontinue 중단하다 introduce 소개하다, 도입하다

SPARTA ACTUAL TEST

p. 92

1 (D)	2 (C)	3 (A)	4 (B)	5 (D)	6 (C)
7 (B)	8 (A)	9 (B)	10 (D)	11 (D)	12 (B)
13 (B)	14 (B)	15 (D)	16 (A)		

1 최고 마케팅 책임자가 지난주 승인을 위해 기획안을 제출하기 전에 수정했다.

해설 동사(revise)의 다양한 시제가 제시되어 있는 것으로 미루어 문맥상 알맞은 시제를 선택하는 문제이다. before절이 it was submitted ~ last week로 과거시제이므로 주절의 시제는 과거시제(revised) 또는 과거완료시제(had revised)가 와야 적절하다. 따라서 (D) revised가 정답이다.

어휘 chief marketing officer(CMO) 최고 마케팅 책임자 proposal 기획안 approval 승인

2 White 씨는 Hampshire 대학교에서 3년 전에 가르쳤고 다음 학기에 다시 돌아올 수도 있다.

해설 동사의 형태로 보아 적절한 시제를 선택해야 한다. 시제 문제는 특정 시제와 어울리는 시간부사가 제시되기 마련인데, 과거시제임을 알 수 있는 'three years ago(3년 전에)'가 제시되었으므로 (C) taught가 정답이다.

어휘 teach 가르치다 return 돌아오다, 반품하다 semester 학기

3 지난주, 더블린의 캐나다 대사관에서 새로운 비자 신청 절차를 시행했다.

해설 보기의 동사 형태로 보아 적절한 시제를 선택해야 한다. 보통 시제를 물을 경우, 특정 시제와 어울리는 시간부사가 제시되기 마련인데, 'Last week(지난주에)'가 제시되었으므로 (A) implemented가 정답이다.

어휘 embassy 대사관 visa application 비자 신청 procedure 절차 implement 시행하다

4 인사부서는 Vieri 씨가 7월 14일 금요일부터 보조 책임자로 새 일을 시작한다고 알렸다.

해설 빈칸은 문장의 동사 자리이고, 뒤에 목적어인 her new job이 있으므로 능동형이다. 수동태인 (C) is started와 (D) is being started는 제외하고, 7월 14일 금요일이라는 특정 날짜가 언급되었기 때문에 완료시제도 쓰일 수 없다. 의미상 앞으로 일을 하는 것이기 때문에 미래진행형 (B) will be starting이 정답이다.

어휘 announce 발표하다 as of ~일자로,~현재

5 McKay 씨는 내년 이맘때 쯤까지 우리의 총 수출이 40퍼센트 이상 증가할 것이라고 말한다.

해설 뒤에 by this time next year(내년 이맘때까지)라는 미래의 한 시점이 언급되고 있으므로 단순과거인 (A) increased와 과거완료인 (B) had increased는 답이 될 수 없다. 단순미래 (C) will increase와 미래완료 (D) will have increased 중에서 by this time next year(by+미래의 시간 부사구)가 '~까지'라는 의미로 완료의 의미를 내포하기 때문에 정답은 (D) will have increased이다. '미래의 어느 시점까지 ~할 것이다'의 의미를 가지는 미래완료 시제는 'by+전치사구' 형태와 자주 쓰이는 것을 알아 두자.

어휘 total 전체, 총 export 수출

6 그가 시장으로 선출된 이후로 매년 시의 쇼핑 구역을 재건축할 것을 제시했지만, 대중은 거의 관심을 보이지 않았다.

해설 since는 완료시제와 함께 쓰이는데 since가 접속사로 쓰이면 since로 시작한 절은 과거 또는 완료시제를 취하고 주절은 현재완료(has recommended)를 취한다. 보기의 elect를 보면 since절은 '그는 시장으로 당선된 이래로'라고 해석되는 문장임을 알 수 있는데, 수동의 의미를 지니고 있으므로 수동태이면서 과거시제를 쓰고 있는 (C) was elected가 정답이다.

어휘 mayor 시장 rebuild 재건축하다 district 구역, 지역

7 수 년전 Hyde 씨가 산악인이었을 때, 그는 물이 높은 고도에서는 더 낮은 온도에서 끓는다는 것을 알았다.

해설 올바른 시제를 고르는 문제이다. 변하지 않는 사실(불변의 진리)은 항상 현재시제를 쓴다. 따라서 (B) boils가 정답이다.

어휘 mountain climber 산악인 boil (물이나 액체가)끓다, 끓이다 temperature 온도, 기온 altitude 높이, 고도, 해발

8 집의 화재 위험 검사가 끝나자마자 당신은 다른 특별한 제한 없이 일상적인 활동을 재개하셔도 좋습니다.

해설 집은 검사되는 것이므로 수동태가 쓰여야 하고 시간 부사절 when, while, as soon as에서는 미래 대신에 현재를, 미래완료 대신에 현재완료를 사용한다. 그러므로 빈칸에는 현재동사가 쓰여야 한다. 따라서 정답은 (A) is이다.

어휘 fire risk 화재 위험 resume 재개하다 restriction 제한

9 많은 공급자들이 최근 이 프로그램에 참여하고 있고, 이것이 믿을 만하다고 생각한다.

해설 부사 recently를 보면 문맥상 완료시제가 와야 한다는 것을 알 수 있다. 과거부터 지금까지 프로그램에 참여하고 있다는 의미이다. 보기 중 적합한 것은 (B) have been participating이다.

어휘 participate 참여하다 recently 최근에 reliable 믿을 만한

10 Jeff Rouse는 San Diego Art School을 졸업하기도 전에 영화 감독으로서의 경력을 시작했다.

해설 'even before he graduated(졸업도 하기 전에)'에서 종속절의 시제가 과거 graduated로 되어 있으므로, 그전에 있었던 '영화감독으로서의 경력을 시작하다'는 과거완료시제로 쓰여 있어야 한다. 따라서 정답은 (D) had begun이다.

어휘 career 경력 graduate 졸업하다

11 Quinn 씨가 우리 회사에 웹 디자이너로 입사했을 무렵, 그녀는 이미 수년 동안 웹디자인 분야에서 일한 경력이 있었다.

해설 빈칸에 들어갈 시제는 과거시제인 joined보다 전의 일이므로 과거 완료시제(had+과거분사)를 써야 한다. 따라서 정답은 (D) had worked이다.

어휘 join 가입하다, 입사하다 firm 회사 field 분야 already 이미 work 일하다

12 Ace Electronics 사가 신제품을 출시한 이래로, 총 판매 수치가 눈에 띄게 증가했다.

해설 since가 '~이후 지금까지'라는 의미의 접속사로 쓰일 때, 주절에는 현재완료시제를 쓰고 since가 이끄는 종속절에서는 과거시제를 쓰므로 빈칸에는 과거시제의 동사가 와야 한다. 그리고 목적어 its new product를 동반해야 하므로 수동태는 쓸 수 없다. 따라서 정답은 (B) released이다.

어휘 product 제품 total 전체의, 총계의 sales figures 판매 수치 increase 늘어나다 noticeably 눈에 띄게, 현저하게 release 출시하다, 발표하다

〈13-16〉 다음은 편지에 관한 문제이다.

Juno 전기의 Charring Cross 역의 환풍 장치 점검

6월 10일에 Juno 전기는 런던 Charring Cross 역의 환풍 장치를 점검했습니다.

이 점검을 기반으로, Juno 전기는 건물의 환풍 장치가 몇몇 부품 교체를 포함하여 광범위한 수리작업이 필요하다는 것을 발견했습니다.

이 작업을 완성하기 위한 견적액은 1,700파운드입니다. 이 액수는 부품과 인건비를 포함합니다.

우리가 추천한 변화들이 여러분께 더욱 안락하고 쾌적한 업무 환경을 보장해 드릴 것입니다.

웹 사이트에서 볼 수 있듯이, Juno는 불필요한 비용을 없애고 고객의 요구를 충족시키기 위한 방법을 활발히 찾고 있습니다.

감사합니다.

어휘 inspection 조사, 점검 ventilation system 환풍 장치 based on ~을 기반으로 하여 extensive 광범위한 replacement 교체 part 부품 labor cost 인건비 recommend 추천하다 guarantee 보증하다 comfortable 안락한 pleasant 쾌적한, 기쁜 working conditions 업무 환경 seek out ~을 찾아내다 eliminate 제거하다 unnecessary 불필요한 meet 충족시키다 needs 수요, 요구 estimated cost 견적 비용 figure 수치

13

해설 보기의 구성으로 보아 시제를 결정하는 문제로 파악할 수 있다. 시제 문제는 보통 특정 시제와 어울리는 시간부사구를 제시하기 마련이지만, Part 6에서는 지문의 맥락을 파악하여 시제 일치를 시키는 문제로 출제되는 경우도 있다. 이 문제도 On June 10만으로는 미래시제인지, 과거시제인지 판단하기 힘들지만 아래 문장 (Based on this inspection, Juno Electrical Service discovered that ~)에서 알 수 있듯이 이미 Juno 전기가 점검을 완료했으므로 과거시제 (B) inspected를 쓰는 것이 적절하다.

14 (A) 건설비용에 대한 견적서 없이는 입찰이 되지 않을 것입니다.
(B) 이 작업을 완성하기 위한 견적액은 1,700 파운드입니다.
(C) 그 집의 마지막 보수 작업이 곧 마무리될 것으로 예상됩니다.
(D) 저희 수리 직원들이 가전제품을 무료로 수리해 줄 수 있습니다.

해설 빈칸 앞 내용은 환풍 장치에 수리작업이 필요하다 했으며 빈칸 뒤의 내용은 바로 액수가 부품과 인건비를 포함한다고 했으므로 정확한 견적액을 제시하고 있는 (B)가 정답이 된다.

15

해설 명사 어휘 문제로, 무엇이 부품과 인건비를 포함하는지 (This ---- covers both parts and labor costs.)를 파악하는 것이 관건인데, 앞 문장에서 견적액이 1,700 파운드라고 했으므로 이 금액을 가리키는 것으로 볼 수 있다. 따라서, '수치, 숫자'의 의미를 갖는 (D) figure가 정답이다.
(A) connection 연결 (B) procedure 절차 (C) problem 문제

16

해설 부사 어휘 문제로, Juno 전기가 불필요한 비용을 없애고 고객의 요구를 충족시키기 위한 방법을 어떻게 찾고 있는지를 고려해 볼 때, '활발히'의 의미를 갖는 (A) actively가 문맥상 적절하다. (B) lately(최근에)는 일반적으로 완료시제와 어울려 쓰인다는 점도 참고로 알아 두자. (C) decreasingly 점점 줄어 (D) apparently 듣자 하니, 보아 하니

UNIT 10 to부정사

SPARTA Check-UP! 1

p. 95

1 (A) **2** (B) **3** (A)

1 Howell Consulting 사는 생산성을 향상시키기 위해 운영체제를 변경하기로 결정했다.

해설 문장의 본동사인 decide는 to부정사를 목적어로 취하는 동사 중 하나이므로 정답은 to부정사인 (A) to change이다.

어휘 decide 결정하다 operating system 운영체제 in order to V ~하기 위하여 increase ~을 향상시키다 productivity 생산성

2 등산객들은 가시로부터 다리를 보호하기 위해 일 년 내내 긴 바지를 입는 것이 권장된다.

해설 [be+encouraged+to부정사]의 수동태 구조로 빈칸에는 동사원형인 (B) wear가 들어가야 한다.

어휘 mountain hiker 등산객 throughout the year 일 년 내내 thorn 가시(나무)

3 관리자들은 직원들의 부상 가능성을 최소화할 수 있도록 직원들이 안전 예방조치를 알고 지킬 수 있도록 확실히 하는 것이 중요하다.

해설 [가주어(it) + be동사(is) + 형용사(important) 전치사(for) + 주어+----+동사]의 구조이다. 따라서 내용상 '관리자들이 직원이 ~하도록 시키다'를 완성하려면 빈칸의 자리에 to부정사가 와야 한다. 따라서 (A) to가 정답이다.

어휘 make sure 확실히 하다 follow 따르다 safety precautions 안전 예방 조치 minimize 최소화하다 risk of injuries 부상의 위험

SPARTA Check-UP! 2

p. 96

1 (A) **2** (C) **3** (A)

1 Knightley 씨가 혼자서 통계 분석을 끝마치는 것은 불가능하다.

해설 가주어(it)과 진주어(to ~)가 쓰인 강조구문이다. 진주어로 to부정사가 필요하므로 finish 앞에 (A) to가 필요하다.

어휘 possible 가능한 finish 끝내다, 마치다 statistical 통계적인

2 우리는 고객들이 식료품을 인터넷으로 구매하는 것이 가능하게 만드는 온라인 판매 사이트를 개설했다.

해설 consumers 뒤에 진목적어 to purchase가 있으므로 빈칸에는 가목적어 it이 필요하다. 따라서 정답은 (C) it이다.

어휘 launch 개설하다 purchase 구매하다

3 새로운 마감일을 맞추기 위해 우리의 전략을 완성하는 것이 중요하다.

해설 진목적어 to meet 이하를 받는 가주어 it을 세우고 be동사 뒤에 형용사가 필요한 자리이다. 따라서 정답은 형용사형인 (A) important(중요한)이다.

어휘 finalize 완료하다 strategy 전략 deadline 마감일

SPARTA Check-UP! 3

p. 97

1 (D) **2** (B) **3** (A)

1 정기 점검을 하기 위해 오늘 구내에서 이 자판기를 치웠습니다.

해설 문맥상 목적을 뜻하는 to부정사가 필요하다. 빈칸 뒤에 동사가 있으므로 전치사인 (C) despite는 답이 될 수 없고, 뒤에 주어가 없으므로 접속사인 (B) as if도 답이 될 수 없다. (A) so as는 so as to로 써야 한다. 따라서 답은 (D) in order to이다.

어휘 remove 제거하다, 치우다 vending machine 자판기 regular maintenance 정기 점검

2 소매업체는 회사 카탈로그에 실린 모든 제품의 가격을 임의로 바꿀 수 있는 권리를 가지고 있다.

해설 문장의 동사는 reserves이고 접속사가 없으므로 동사원형인 (A) alter는 나올 수 없다. to부정사가 형용사로 쓰일 때 부정사는 명사를 수식하는 기능을 하며 명사 뒤에 위치한다. 'reserve the right to V(~할 권리를 가지다)'라는 표현은 자주 나오는 표현으로 묶어서 암기해 두면 좋다. 정답은 (B) to alter이다.

어휘 retailer 소매업체 alter 변경하다 without notice 통보 없이, 임의로

3 나노 기술 연구를 촉진하기 위하여, 정부는 나노 기술 연구소 건립에 드는 비용을 50%까지 지불할 것을 제안했다.

해설 [----+명사(research)+전치사(in)+명사(nanotechnology)]의 구조이다. '나노 기술 연구를 촉진하기 위해 (To promote research in nanotechnology)'가 문맥에 맞으므로 to부정사를 써야 한다. 따라서 (A) To promote가 정답이다.

어휘 research 연구 government 정부 offer 제안하다 up to ~까지 cost 비용 institute 연구소 promote 홍보하다, 촉진하다, 승진시키다 promotion 홍보, 촉진, 승진

SPARTA Check-UP! 4

p. 98

1 (B) **2** (C) **3** (D)

1 경영진은 직원들과 그들의 가족들을 다음 주 금요일에 있을 회사 연례 피크닉에 참석하도록 초대하고자 한다.

해설 [would like+----]의 구조이다. would like는 to부정사와 함께 쓰는 동사이므로 would like to invite가 되어야 한다. 따라서 정답은 (B) to invite이다.

어휘 management 경영진 attend 참가하다 annual 연례의

2 많은 외국 기업들이 일단 규제 완화가 시행되면 일본에서 그들의 사업을 확장하기를 희망한다.

해설 빈칸은 to부정사를 목적어로 갖는 동사 hope와 같이 쓰였으므로 to부정사 자리이다. 따라서 정답은 (C) expand이다.

어휘 deregulation 규제 완화 carry out 실행하다, 집행하다 expansion 확장 expand 확장하다 expansive 광범위한

3 비록 수상자의 자격에 관한 논쟁이 있었지만 심판들은 그들의 결정을 고수했다.

해설 동사 allow는 3형식에서는 목적어로 동명사를 취하지만 5형식에서는 목적격 보어로 to부정사를 사용한다. 5형식 구조이므로 to부정사인 (D) to stand가 정답이다.

어휘 controversy 논쟁, 논의 qualification 자격, 권한 winning contestant 수상자 stand 고수하다

SPARTA PRACTICE

p. 99

1 to postpone **2** to receive **3** to change **4** to adhere
5 to work **6** to criticize **7** attend **8** establish
9 to transmit **10** take **11** announce **12** to work
13 to wrap **14** to **15** to enter

1 경기가 불황일 때에는 기업들이 소프트웨어 업그레이드를 미루는 경향이 있다.

해설 동사 tend는 to부정사를 취하는 동사로 자주 사용되며 tend to V는 '~하는 경향이 있다, ~하기 쉽다'라는 의미를 가리킨다.

어휘 economy 경제 poorly 저조하게, 형편없이 tend to ~하는 경향이 있다 postpone 연기하다

2 개인 재정 관련 조언을 제공하기 위해 고객들로부터 지시를 직접 받을 필요가 있다.

해설 '~할 필요가 있다'는 의미로 need 뒤에 to부정사가 와야 한다.

어휘 instructions 지시, 교훈, 교육 client 고객 personal 사적인, 개인적인 financial advice 재정 관련 조언

3 당신이 연회 메뉴를 변경하기로 결정한 경우에는 행사 최소 10일 전까지 환영행사 위원회와 상담하셔야 합니다.

해설 decide는 to부정사와 같이 사용되어 '~하기로 결정하다'의 의미를 완성시킨다.

어휘 in the event that ~할 경우에 decide to ~하기로 결정하다 banquet 연회 consult 상담하다 reception committee 환영 위원회

4 모든 직원들은 작업 현장에서 일하는 동안에 안전 지침에 명시되어 있는 규정들을 준수해야 한다.

해설 require A to V(A에게~하도록 요구하다)와 A be required to V(A는~하도록 요구 받다, 요구되다)는 같은 표현이므로 빈칸에는 to부정사가 들어가야 한다.

어휘 be required to V ~하는 것이 요구되다, ~하도록 요구받다 adhere to 고수하다 regulation 규정, 규칙 stated in ~에 명시되어 있는 safety manual 안전 지침

5 Cramer 씨의 징짐 중 하나는 몇 가지 복잡한 문제를 동시에 처리하는 능력이다.

해설 앞에 ability라는 명사가 왔으므로, 뒤에는 '~할 수 있는 능력'이라는 뜻을 완성시켜줄 to work가 오는 것이 적합하다.

어휘 quality 자질 ability 능력 several 여러 complex 복잡한

6 Tom은 당신이 그의 프로젝트에 관련된 문헌을 읽지도 않고서 그것을 비난할 권리는 없다고 생각한다고 내게 말했다.

해설 뒤의 his project를 목적어로 받을 동사가 필요하고 앞뒤로 명사가 나와 있으므로, criticism이라는 명사가 아닌 to criticize가 정답이 된다.

어휘 express 표현하다 have the right to ~할 권리가 있다 literature 문학, 문헌 pertain to ~와 관련되다

7 그 시기에 다른 약속이 있어서 참석할 수 없게 된 것을 유감스럽게 생각합니다.

해설 be able to V(~을 할 수 있다)라는 관용적 표현에서 동사는 원형 그대로 와야 한다.

어휘 regret 후회하다, 안타깝게 생각하다 engagement 약속, 업무 attend 참석하다 attendance 참석

8 투자자들은 이 나라 최대의 도시인 Mumbai에 지사 설립을 열망하고 있다.

해설 [be+형용사+to부정사]의 구조로, 'be eager to V'는 '간절히 ~하기를 열망하다'라는 의미의 관용적 표현이다.

어휘 investor 투자자　be eager to 간절히 ~하고 싶어 하다　establish 설립하다　large 큰, 거대한

9 우리 제품은 디지털 장비 사용자들이 컴퓨터 데이터를 아날로그 전산망에 전송할 수 있도록 한다.

해설 앞에 to부정사 용법의 to가 온 것으로 보아 동사는 원형 그대로 와야 정답이 된다.

어휘 product 제품　allow 허용하다　user 사용자　equipment 장비　transmit 전송하다

10 고속도로 안전청에서는 이번 연휴 철에 다음과 같은 예방 조치를 취할 것을 당부하고 있습니다.

해설 to부정사의 동사는 원형을 쓰므로 take가 정답이다.

어휘 highway 고속도로　safety board 안전위원회　remind 상기시키다　following 그다음의, 다음과 같은　precaution 예방조치

11 George Frankman은 내일 회의에서 은퇴를 발표할 것으로 예상된다.

해설 expect(기대하다)라는 동사는 '목적어가 ~하기를 예상하다, 기대하다'라는 의미로 'expect+목적어+to부정사'의 구조를 띤다. 여기서는 수동태로 쓰여 목적어가 주어 자리로 가고, be expected to V로 사용되었다.

어휘 be expected to ~이 기대되다, ~이 예상되다　announce 발표하다　retirement 은퇴

12 Thomson & Thomson 사는 마감일까지 그 프로젝트를 마무리하기 위해 전 직원이 협동하여 일하기를 바란다.

해설 'would like+목적어+to부정사' 구문으로, '목적어'로 하여금 'to 부정사 하기를 원하다(= want+목적어+to부정사)'라는 의미를 가리킨다.

어휘 corporation (대)기업　complete 완성하다; 완전한　due date 만기일

13 깨지기 쉬운 제품이 파손되지 않도록 티슈페이퍼를 사용하여 포장할 필요가 있다.

해설 '~하기 위하여 사용된다'라는 목적 표시 용법은 to부정사가 사용되어야 한다.

어휘 necessary 필요한　wrap 포장하다　fragile 부서지기 쉬운 연약한　item 물건, 제품　keep A from -ing A가 ~하는 것을 방지하다

14 여행객들은 적어도 출발 이틀 전에 항공사에 전화해서 예약을 확인해야 한다.

해설 Travelers are advised to V 형태로 주어(Travelers)와 동사(are advised)가 있으므로 빈칸 뒤의 confirm이 동사원형이 되려면 to부정사 형태로 쓰여야 한다.

어휘 traveler 여행자　be advised to V ~하도록 조언을 받다　confirm 확인하다　flight 항공편　at least 최소한　prior to ~에 앞서　departure 출발

15 "직원 전용" 표시가 있는 사무실에는 회사 직원들만 출입할 수 있다.

해설 동사 allow는 목적격 보어로 to부정사를 취한다. 수동태로 사용될 경우에도 be allowed 뒤에 to부정사는 그대로 있어야 한다.

어휘 staff 직원　be allowed to ~하도록 허용되다　enter 들어가다

SPARTA ACTUAL TEST p. 100

1 (B)	**2** (B)	**3** (B)	**4** (A)	**5** (A)	**6** (C)
7 (D)	**8** (D)	**9** (C)	**10** (B)	**11** (A)	**12** (B)
13 (A)	**14** (A)	**15** (D)	**16** (C)		

1 예산 변경 사항이 이사회에 의해 통과될 것 같지 않다.

해설 'be unlikely to 동사원형'은 '~일 것 같지는 않다'라는 의미로 쓰인다. pass는 타동사인데 빈칸 뒤에 목적어 역할을 하는 명사가 없으므로 수동형인 be passed가 되어야 한다. 따라서 답은 (B) to be passed이다.

어휘 budget 예산　be unlikely to V ~일 것 같지 않다　the board of directors 이사회　pass 통과시키다

2 판매 관리자는 50% 이상 매출액을 증가시킬 것을 약속했다.

해설 동사의 개별 어법을 묻는 문제이다. promise는 'to+동사원형'의 부정사를 목적어로 취하는 동사이기 때문에 정답은 (B) to increase이다.

어휘 promise to ~할 것을 약속하다　sales volume 판매량, 매출액　more than ~ 이상의

3 LCD 모니터의 저렴한 가격은 소비자들이 우리의 제품을 구입하도록 만든다.

해설 동사의 구조를 물어보는 문제이다. encourage는 'encourage+목적어+to부정사'의 구조를 취한다. 따라서 (B) to buy가 정답이 된다.

어휘 reasonable 적당한, 합리적인　encourage 장려하다

4 회사가 어떻게 운영되는지를 이해하려면 직원들은 경영 조직에 대한 지식을 지니고 있어야 한다.

해설 [In order to+동사원형]의 구조이므로 (A) understand가 정답이다.

어휘 in order to+동사원형 ~하기 위해　operate 운영하다　management structure 경영 조직

5 Hanson Motors의 부사장인 Chris Cunningham은 중동에 있는 새로운 지사들을 방문할 기회를 곧 가질 것이다.

해설 형용사적 용법의 to부정사는 명사 뒤에서 형용사처럼 앞의 명사를 수식해 준다. 이 경우에서는 뒤에 나오는 명사구(the new branch offices~)를 이끌고 앞에 나오는 명사(a chance)를 뒤에서 수식할 수 있는 (A) to visit이 들어가는 것이 가장 적절하다. a chance to(~할 기회)를 한 덩어리로 기억해 두자.

어휘 vice president 부사장　branch office 지사

6 사장은 혁신적인 전략을 개발하기 위해 모든 직원들이 함께 작업하길 원한다.

해설 적절한 단어 형태 선택 문제이다. 'would like+목적어+to V'의 형태를 숙지하고 있으면 쉽게 정답을 구할 수 있다. 정답은 (C) to work이다.

어휘 president 사장　develop 개발하다, 발달하다　innovative 혁신적인　strategy 전략

7 우리 회사의 정책은 직원들에게 항상 연방 안전 규정에 따라 행동할 것을 요구한다.

해설 'require+목적어+to 동사원형' 구문은 '~에게 ~하도록 요청하다'라는 의미로 쓰인다. 문맥상 회사의 정책이 직원들에게 연방 안전 규정에 따라 '행동할 것'을 요구한다는 의미가 되어야 하므로 빈칸에 적절한 형태는 to부정사인 (D) to act이다.

어휘 in accordance with ~에 따라　federal 연방의　safety regulation 안전 수칙　at all times 항상

8 직무 기술서는 채용 후보자와 현재의 직원들이 그들로부터 무엇을 기대하는가를 알게 한다.

해설 문제의 핵심은 동사 enable이다. 동사 enable은 'enable+목적어+to 동사원형'의 형태를 취한다. 따라서 정답은 (D) to know가 된다.

어휘 job description 직무 기술서 enable A to A가 ~하는 것을 가능하게 하다 prospective employee 채용 후보자 current 현재의 expect 기대하다

9 항공편의 출발 시각을 알아보기 위해 항공사에 전화하실 때 항공편 번호를 꼭 가지고 계세요.

해설 'call an airline ---- find out that ~'에서 빈칸 뒤에 동사 원형 find가 왔다. 또한 call과 함께 쓰여 '~하기 위해 전화하다'라는 뜻이 자연스러우므로 to부정사의 부사적 용법이 사용된 문장임을 알 수 있다. 답은 (C) to이다.

어휘 airline 항공사 find out ~을 알아내다 departure 출발 make sure to 꼭 ~하다

10 보석을 거부할 권리는 법원의 합법적인 권한인데, 이는 특히 판사가 피고인이 이성적인 결정을 하는 데에 있어 부적당하다고 생각하는 경우이다.

해설 to부정사가 명사를 수식해 주는 것을 알면 쉽게 (B) to refuse를 선택할 수 있다. right to be educated(교육을 받을 권리), right to speak(말할 권리), opportunity to see(~를 볼 기회), plan to have a vacation(휴가 보낼 계획) 등은 to부정사가 명사를 꾸며주는 경우이니 알아 두면 좋다.

어휘 constitutional 헌법적인, 합법적인 right 권리 the accused 피고인 unfit 맞지 않는 rational decision 이성적인 결정

11 우리의 해외 고객들을 충분히 수용하기 위해서 그린 호텔은 모든 손님들에게 유럽과 아시아로 거는 무료 국제전화를 제공한다.

해설 동사원형 accommodate가 빈칸에 들어가 to부정사를 이루는데, 빈칸 앞에 fully라는 부사가 들어가 혼동을 주고 있다. 부사와 관계없이 동사원형으로 to부정사를 이룬다는 점을 기억하자.

어휘 fully 충분히, 넉넉히 accommodate 수용하다, 숙박시키다 overseas 해외의, 외국의 accommodation 숙박시설

12 영업사원들은 브레인스토밍 회의 도중 긴 휴식시간을 원치 않아서, 종종 점심이 배달되도록 지시한다.

해설 '지시하다'라는 의미의 동사 order는 [5형식 동사+목적어+to 동사원형]의 구조로 쓰인다. 목적어인 lunch는 배달되는(delivered) 대상이 되므로 수동형의 to부정사 to be delivered가 되어야 한다. 따라서 정답은 (B) to be이다.

어휘 brainstorming session 아이디어 회의 order A to 동사원형 A가 ~하도록 지시하다 deliver 배달하다

〈13-16〉 다음은 공지에 관한 문제이다.

수신: 새로 승진한 모든 과장님들

신임 과장들을 위한 오리엔테이션이 9월 8일 화요일에 있을 예정이라는 것을 알리는 글입니다.

새로 승진한 과장들은 다른 일정이 없는 한 모두 참석해 주셔야 합니다. 이 오리엔테이션에서는 복지 혜택, 업무수행 능력 평가 과정, 보안 정책 등에 대한 주제를 다루게 됩니다.

새 직원 신분증과 주차권이 제공될 것입니다. 오전 10시까지 제퍼슨 빌딩 12층 5번 회의실로 와주시기 바랍니다. 이 시간은 과장직에 대한 이해를 높여 줄 것입니다.

어떤 질문이라도 있으시면 제게 연락 바랍니다.

진심으로,
에밀리 베리스
인사부

어휘 promoted 승진된 attend 참가하다 arrangement 일정 address 다루다 benefit 복지 혜택 process 절차, 과정 confidential 기밀의 provide 제공하다 managerial 관리의

13

해설 주어진 4개의 동사 형태 중 어법에 맞는 동사 형태를 고르는 문제이다. let 5형식 동사는 목적어 뒤에 목적어와의 관계가 능동이면 동사원형이 뒤따르는 동사로 정답은 (A) know이다. 그 외에 make, have 동사도 [make/have+목적어+동사원형] 구조를 갖는다는 사실을 알아 두자.

14

해설 동사 어휘 문제로, 새로 승진한 모든 과장들의 참석을 요구하는 문맥이 자연스러우므로 (A) required가 정답이다. compare (비교하다) include (포함하다) report (보고하다)

15

해설 '~와 같은'의 뜻을 갖는 such as는 뒤에 구체적인 예를 들 때 사용하는 표현이다. '오리엔테이션은 복지 혜택, 근무 수행 평가 과정, 그리고 보안 정책과 같은 주제를 다룬다'라고 해야 의미가 통하므로 (D) such as가 정답이 된다. (A) so that ~할 수 있도록(접속사), (B) besides 그 외에(접속부사)/~외에(전치사), (C) likewise 이와 마찬가지로(접속부사)

16 (A) 오리엔테이션 일정은 다음과 같습니다:
(B) 그 매니저는 심장마비를 일으켜 현재 머시 병원에서 회복 중입니다.
(C) 이 시간은 과장직에 대한 이해를 높여 줄 것입니다.
(D) 정수기 옆 휴게실에 신청서가 있습니다.

해설 앞뒤 문맥상 빈칸 앞의 내용은 새로 승진한 과장들을 위한 오리엔테이션이 있을 것을 알리고 있고 빈칸 다음 뒤로는 새로 승진한 과장님들에게 질문이 있으면 연락 바란다는 마무리를 하고 있으므로 이 오리엔테이션이 무엇에 도움이 된다는 글인 (C)가 가장 적절하다.

UNIT 11 동명사

SPARTA Check-UP! 1

p. 103

1 (D) **2** (D) **3** (B)

1 새 S20 배터리에 대한 가장 큰 불평은 그것들을 충전하는 것이 다른 브랜드의 것보다 더 많은 시간이 걸린다는 것이다.

해설 be동사의 보어인 that절(명사절)의 주어 자리로 빈칸 뒤 또 다른 목적어 them을 취할 수 있는 것은 동명사이다. 따라서 (D) recharging이 정답이다.

어휘 complaint 불평 recharge 충전하다 take time 시간이 걸리다

2 회계부는 추가적인 자금 지원을 보류함으로써 프로젝트를 지연시켰다.

해설 by -ing는 '~함으로써'라는 의미이며, 이때 by는 전치사이므로 빈칸 뒤 명사구(형용사+명사)를 목적어로 취하는 동명사 (D) withholding이 정답이다.

어휘 delay 지연시키다 by -ing ~함으로써 funding 자금 조달 withhold 보류시키다

3 Carey 씨는 그들의 보험 증권이 승인되면 바로 신청자에게 이메일을 발송할 것을 제안합니다.

해설 빈칸은 타동사 suggest의 목적어 자리이다. [타동사+--------+명사] 형태이므로 뒤에 명사구를 목적어로 취하는 동명사인 (B) sending이 정답이다.

어휘 suggest 제안하다 applicant 신청자 immediately 즉각 insurance policy 보험 증권 approve 승인하다

SPARTA Check-UP! 2

p. 104

1 (B) **2** (C) **3** (C)

1 품질 관리에 있어서 보다 향상된 방법을 개발하는 것은 장기적으로 더 큰 이익을 가져다줄 것이다.

해설 문법 구조상 빈칸은 주어 자리이므로 (A) Develop, (C) Developed는 부적절하다. 명사 (D) Development와 동명사인 (B) Developing은 둘 다 주어가 될 수 있으나 빈칸 뒤에 나오는 an improved method를 목적어로 취하기 위해서는 동명사인 (B) Developing이 답이 되어야 한다. lead to는 '~로 인도하다'는 뜻 또는 '~한 결과가 되다'라는 뜻으로 많이 사용되며, 여기서 to는 전치사 to이다.

어휘 quality control 품질 관리 profitability 유익, 이익 in the long run 결국, 장기적으로

2 많은 회사들은 세계적인 경쟁의 기준을 충족시키기 위해 직원들을 재훈련시키는 과정을 경험하고 있다.

해설 빈칸 앞에 전치사를 보면 명사 역할을 할 수 있어야 하고, 빈칸 뒤의 명사(their employees)를 보면 목적어와 같이 사용될 수 있어야 함을 알 수 있다. 정답은 동명사인 (C) retraining이다.

어휘 go through 겪다, 경험하다 process 과정 retrain 재교육하다

3 신중한 기획과 일관된 품질 덕분에, 새로 설립된 Kolof Bakery 사는 빠르게 시장을 주도하는 회사가 되었다.

해설 [전치사(Thanks to)+형용사(careful)+----] 구조이다. 빈칸에는 불가산 명사를 써야 한다. 단수 가산명사 앞에는 한정사(a/an, the)가 있어야 하는데 빈칸 앞에 한정사가 없기 때문이다. (A) planner와 (B) plan은 단수 가산명사이므로 빈칸에 들어갈 수 없다. 따라서 정답은 (C) planning이다.

어휘 careful 주의 깊은, 신중한 consistent 일관된 product 제품 quality 품질 newly 새로 established 설립된 quickly 빠르게 leader 지도자 plan 계획, 설계도 planning 계획

SPARTA Check-UP! 3

p. 105

1 (B) **2** (B) **3** (B)

1 인터넷에서의 몇몇 서비스들은 찾기 어렵거나 절판된 책들을 찾는 데 도움이 된다.

해설 빈칸 앞 at은 전치사 이므로 [전치사+형용사+명사]의 형태와 [전치사+동명사+명사]의 형태가 모두 가능하다. 따라서 문맥에 적절한 것을 선택해야 한다. '책들을 찾는 데 도움이 된다'가 문맥상 적절하므로 동명사인 (B) locating이 정답이다.

어휘 locate 찾다, 위치하다 helpful 도움이 되는

2 Able 잡지사에 많은 글을 기고한 Canet 씨는 청중들에게 자기소개를 한 후에, 그의 이야기를 시작했다.

해설 after라는 전치사 뒤에, 동사는 동명사 (B) introducing이 와야 한다.

어휘 audience 청중 deliver 전달하다

3 이력서를 철저히 검토한 결과 유감스럽게도 귀하의 신청서를 거절하기로 결정했습니다.

해설 after는 전치사이고 reviewing은 동명사이다. 동명사를 수식하는 것은 부사이며, 문맥상 '귀하의 이력서를 검토한 후에'가 적절하므로 (B) thoroughly가 정답이다.

어휘 thorough 철저한 thoroughly 철저히 unfortunately 유감스럽게 reject 거절하다

SPARTA Check-UP! 4

p. 106

1 (B) **2** (D) **3** (B)

1 Amplipiers의 생산 부서는 새로운 오디오 장비 개발에 예산의 절반을 썼다.

해설 spend+시간/돈+(in) V-ing는 '~하는 데 시간(돈)을 쓰다'라는 의미의 숙어 표현이다. 문장의 동사가 spent, 목적어가 half its budget이므로 빈칸에는 V-ing 형태가 적절하다. 따라서 (B) developing이 정답이다.

어휘 Production Department 생산 부서 budget 예산 audio equipment 오디오 장비

2 측량 기술자는 지난 수요일에 5501 Marcus Avenue에 대지 경계선들의 측량을 완료했습니다.

해설 finish는 동명사를 목적어로 취하는 동사로 (D) mapping이 정답이다.

어휘 survey 측량 technician 기술자 map (지도 작성을 위해) 측량하다 property line 대지 경계선

3 새로운 급여 시스템이 완전히 구현될 때까지 기존의 보고 방식을 계속 이용하세요.

해설 continue는 to부정사와 동명사를 모두 취할 수 있는 타동사이다. 빈칸 뒤 명사구(the old reporting method)가 이어지고 있으므로 보기 중 동명사인 (B) using이 정답이다.

어휘 payroll system 급여 시스템 fully 완전히 implement 실행하다 method 방법, 방식 usage 사용법 useful 유용한

SPARTA PRACTICE

p. 107

1 Maintaining	2 scheduling	3 placing
4 carefully	5 instead of	6 postponing
7 modifying	8 working	9 helping
10 developing	11 providing	12 enhancing
13 writing	14 committed	15 finding

1 Dudley Holdings 사에서는 고객들에게 최상의 서비스를 유지하는 것이 최우선 과제이다.

해설 명사 Maintenance가 빈칸에 들어가면 빈칸 뒤의 명사구와 연결되지 않으므로 빈칸 뒤의 명사구를 목적어로 취하면서 문장의 주어를 이루는 Maintaining을 써야 한다.

어휘 maintain 유지하다 exceptional 예외적인, 특별한 priority 우선사항

2 최근 소프트웨어의 오류로 인해 추가 공지가 있을 때까지 온라인 일정표에 새로운 행사를 기입하는 것을 삼가십시오.

해설 schedule과 scheduling은 모두 명사 역할이 가능하므로 from 뒤에 와 전치사의 목적어로 사용될 수 있지만 뒤에 목적어에 해당하는 명사구가 오고 있으므로 scheduling이 정답이다.

어휘 error 오류 refrain from 자제하다, 삼가다 schedule ~을 표에 기입하다 calendar 행사 예정표, 일정표 notice 공지

3 온라인 상에서 귀하가 주문한 컴퓨터를 일주일 이내에 받게 될 것입니다.

해설 빈칸에는 목적어(your order)를 취하면서 전치사 of의 목적어가 될 수 있는 동명사가 필요하다.

어휘 place an order 주문하다 online 온라인상에서

4 관리자를 뽑기 위해 10명의 지원자를 신중하게 면접한 후에 사장이 직접 Koepp 씨를 선택했다.

해설 동명사(interviewing)를 수식할 수 있는 것은 형용사가 아닌 부사이다. 그러므로 (A) carefully (신중하게)가 정답이다. 이 문제는 [전치사(after) + 부사(carefully) + 동명사(interviewing) + 목적어(ten candidates)] 형태의 문장 어순으로도 쉽게 문제를 해결할 수 있다.

어휘 candidate 후보자 position 직책

5 직원들은 이제 출장 요청서를 서류 양식으로 제출하지 않고 온라인으로 보냅니다.

해설 뒤에 동명사를 잇는 전치사 자리로 because of(~ 때문에)와 instead of(~대신에) 둘 다 전치사이다. 문맥상 '서류 양식을 제출하는 것 대신에 온라인으로 보낸다'가 되므로 instead of를 써야 한다. instead of V-ing '~하는 것 대신에는'와 같이 자주 쓰이는 [전치사+V-ing] 패턴으로 알아 두자.

어휘 send in 보내다 electronically 전자적으로, 컴퓨터로 submit 제출하다

6 가격이 더 떨어질 것으로 예상되기 때문에 구입을 몇 주 더 미룰 것을 권유합니다.

해설 recommend는 동명사를 목적어로 취하는 동사이다. 따라서 정답은 postponing이다.

어휘 price 가격 expect to ~을 예상하다 fall 떨어지다 further 더, 더 나아가 recommend 추천하다 postpone 연기하다 purchase 구매, 구매한 것; 구매하다

7 Gold Post의 새로운 최고경영자인 Spike Jonze는 회사의 투자 전략들을 수정할 것을 제안했다.

해설 suggest는 동명사를 목적어로 취하며 문맥상 '수정하는 것'이므로 능동태인 modifying를 써야 한다.

어휘 suggest 제안하다 modify 수정하다 investment 투자 strategy 전략

8 Steil 씨는 5월에 Wilton Shop에서 일하기 시작했지만, 벌써 7월에 보조 관리자로 임명되었습니다.

해설 begin은 타동사로 쓰일 때 to부정사와 동명사를 모두 목적어로 취하는 동사 중 하나다. 따라서 working을 써야 한다.

어휘 already 벌써, 이미 name (일자리직책에) 지명[임명]하다

9 Malcolm 사는 우리 회사가 모든 프로젝트의 목표를 달성하는 데 대단히 중요한 역할을 합니다.

해설 in은 전치사이므로 뒤에는 명사 형태(명사/동명사/명사절)가 와야 한다. 따라서 동사인 help는 오답이다. [전치사+-------+명사구] 형태이므로 뒤의 명사구를 목적어로 취하는 동명사인 helping을 써야 한다.

어휘 play a role in V-ing ~하는 데 역할을 하다 critical 대단히 중요한 achieve 달성하다

10 Queens의 주민들은 수년간 사용되지 않았던 부지를 개발할 것을 제안했다.

해설 propose(제안하다)의 목적어 역할을 하면서 뒤의 'the lot'이라는 목적어를 가져야 하므로 동명사 developing이 정답이 된다.

어휘 resident 거주지 lot 부지 unused 이용되지 않은

11 Andrew Jackson이 이끄는 기상팀은 지역에 정확한 일기 예보를 제공하는 데 헌신하고 있다.

해설 동사 (is dedicated)와 명사이자 목적어인(weather forecasts)를 취하는 동사의 성질을 가지고 있는 동명사 providing이 정답이다.

어휘 meteorologist 기상학자 lead 이끌다 dedicate 헌신하다, 바치다 provide 제공하다 accurate 정확한 weather forecast 일기 예보 local 지역의

12 Dreamworks는 회사의 경쟁력 우위를 향상시켜야 하는 사명감을 가지고 사업 운영의 해결책을 제공하는 데 중점을 두고 있다.

해설 commitment to(~에 대한 헌신, 기여)의 to는 전치사이므로 뒤에는 명사나 명사 상당 어구가 연결되어야 한다. 따라서 동명사 enhancing이 정답이다.

어휘 focus 초점을 맞추다; 초점 solution 해결책 commitment 헌신, 전념 enhance 향상시키다 competitive 치열한 advantage 이점, 혜택

13 적어도 30일 전에 서면으로 알리면 계약자는 언제든지 보험을 중단할 수 있다.

해설 빈칸 앞 in과 어울려 [전치사+명사] 숙어 표현으로 in writing은 '서면으로'라는 의미를 지닌다. 따라서 writing이 정답이다.

어휘 notification 알림, 통지 in writing 서면으로 at least 최소한 in advance 미리 policyholder 보험 계약자 discontinue 중단하다 policy 증권 at any time 언제라도

14 Forbes 경영진은 재활용 비용을 줄이기 위해 주변 지역 사회와 협력하여 노력하고 있습니다.

해설 보기는 각각 be scheduled to V(~하도록 예정되어 있다)와 be committed to 명사/V-ing(~에 헌신하다)의 형태로 쓰인다. 빈칸 뒤에 to V-ing의 형태가 있으므로 committed가 정답이다.

어휘 management 경영진 be committed to work cooperatively 협력하여 일하다 surrounding community 주변 지역[사회] recycling cost 재활용 비용

15 우리는 다음 주주 회의 동안 회사에 대해 더 많은 내용을 알게 되길 기대한다.

해설 가장 혼동하기 쉬운 것 중 하나가 look forward to 다음의 동사 형태를 묻는 문제이다. to부정사 다음이 원형이라는 것과 혼동해 동사원형을 쓴다고 착각하기 쉽지만, 'look forward to'의 to는 전치사이다. 따라서 뒤에 오는 것은 명사 역할을 할 수 있는 동명사 형태 finding이 와야 적절하다.

어휘 look forward to -ing ~하기를 기대하다 find out 알아내다 during ~동안에 shareholder's meeting 주주 회의

SPARTA ✔ ACTUAL TEST

p. 108

1 (B)	2 (A)	3 (D)	4 (C)	5 (D)	6 (C)
7 (C)	8 (A)	9 (D)	10 (D)	11 (D)	12 (D)
13 (A)	14 (A)	15 (B)	16 (D)		

1 Ziatech은 화학제품들을 합성하는 새로운 방법의 개발에 꾸준히 매달려오고 있다.

해설 빈칸 앞 전치사(on)와 빈칸 뒤의 명사구(new ways)를 연결해 주어야 하므로 명사와 동사의 역할을 모두 할 수 있는 품사를 찾아야 한다. (A) development는 명사지만, 뒤의 new ways(새로운 방식)를 매끄럽게 이어줄 수 없고, (C) develop은 동사원형이며, 과거분사일 경우((D) developed) 형용사 역할을 하는데, 이미 앞에 있는 형용사(new)앞에 오기엔 문맥이 부자연스럽다. '새로운 방법을 개발하는 것에 꾸준히 매달린다'라고 완성시켜 주는 것은 동명사 (B) developing이다.

어휘 continuously 계속적으로 synthesize 합성하다 chemical product 화학제품

2 Turner 씨는 마감 기일까지 프로젝트를 끝내기 위해서 자정까지 작업할 것을 제안했다.

해설 suggest는 동명사를 목적어로 취하는 동사이다. 따라서 (A) working이 정답이 된다.

어휘 midnight 자정 get A done A를 끝내다

3 호텔 방침은 음식점에서 일하는 모든 직원들이 주방과 음식 저장실에 들어가기 전에 그들의 손을 씻고 모자를 착용할 것을 요구한다.

해설 '전치사 + 동명사'의 형태로 전치사(before) 다음에는 동명사 (D) entering이 와서 뒤의 명사(kitchen)를 목적어로 가진다.

어휘 policy 정책 require 요구하다 put on ~을 쓰다 storage room 저장실

4 주 일반기금 할당량과 학비와의 균형을 유지하는 것은 현재의 난제이고 가장 중요한 책무 중의 하나이다.

해설 뒤의 be동사(is)가 나온 것을 보아 be동사 앞의 구(balance between state general fund allocations and student tuition)가 주어 역할을 하는 것을 알 수 있다. 빈칸 뒤의 구를 목적어로 받으면서 주어로서 명사 역할을 할 수 있는 동명사 (C) Maintaining이 적합하다.

어휘 balance 균형 state 주 general fund 일반기금 allocation 할당 student tuition 학비 ongoing 진행되고 있는 challenge 도전, 난제

5 Greensboro 국립 박물관은 웹 사이트를 정기적으로 업데이트함으로써 박물관의 방문객 수를 늘렸다.

해설 동명사(updating) 앞에서 동명사를 수식하는 것은 형용사가 아니라 부사이므로 (D) regularly가 정답이다.

어휘 increase 늘리다 visitor traffic 방문객 수 regular 정기적인 regularity 규칙적인 패턴 regularize 합법화[규칙화]하다 regularly 정기적으로

6 Roberts 씨는 소설을 쓰면서 자유시간을 즐기는 아마추어 작가이다.

해설 이 문제를 해결하기 위해 두 가지를 알아야 한다. '~하는 데 시간을 소비하다'라는 의미일 때는 'spend+시간 -ing'의 형식을 사용한다. 또 빈칸 뒤에 목적어가 되는 명사(novels)가 있으므로, 동명사가 와서 목적어를 취해야 하므로 정답은 (C) composing이다.

어휘 writer 작가 compose 작곡하다, 작문하다

7 통신사들은 고객들에게 먼저 통보하지 않고 계약 내용을 변경할 수 없다.

해설 '동명사+목적어'의 구조로, 명사(customers)를 목적어로 갖는 타동사이면서 전치사(without)의 목적어가 될 수 있도록 동명사 (C) notifying을 써야 한다.

어휘 contract 계약(서) without ~없이 notify 통보하다, 알리다 customer 손님

8 Vector 발전소의 안전 규정들이 지난달 새로운 기준을 따르기 위해 수정되었다.

해설 빈칸 앞 in order to(~하기 위하여)의 to는 전치사 to가 아니라 to부정사의 to이므로 빈칸은 동사원형이 와야 한다. 따라서 (B) comply가 정답이다. 전치사 to 뒤에는 명사나 동명사가 와야 한다.

어휘 safety 안전 protocol 규정 power plant 발전소 modify 수정하다 comply with ~을 준수하다, 따르다 standard 기준

9 최신형의 기구와 기술의 도입을 통해, GoodFuels 사는 그들의 모든 원자력 발전소의 방사능 누출 위험성을 낮추기 위한 기여를 보여주었다.

해설 commitment to의 to는 전치사이다. 따라서 명사 및 명사 상당어구가 연결되어야 하는데 빈칸 뒤에 명사구(the risk of radiation leaks)가 연결된 점에서 이를 목적어로 취할 수 있는 동사의 기능도 필요하므로 동명사 (D) lowering이 답이 된다.

어휘 introduce 소개하다 up-to-date 최신형의 equipment 기구 technology 기술 commitment 헌신 lower 낮추다 risk 위험 radiation leak 방사능 누출 nuclear power plant 원자력 발전소

10 Washock 씨는 회사 예산을 관리하는 것뿐만 아니라 지역 하청업자들과의 많은 회의를 준비한다.

해설 In addition to의 to는 전치사이므로 뒤에 명사(the company's budget)인 목적어를 취할 수 있는 동명사가 와야 한다. 따라서 답은 (D) managing이다.

어휘 in addition to ~뿐만 아니라 manage 해내다 budget 예산 organize 준비하다 정리하다 a number of 많은 local 지역의 subcontractor 하청업자

11 Power Electronics 사의 CEO인 Tony Goldwyn은 모든 부서의 수익 보고서를 간절히 기다리고 있는 중이다.

해설 빈칸은 타동사 await의 목적어 자리로 빈칸 뒤 reports와 복합명사(earnings reports)를 이루는 (D) earnings가 정답이다. 참고로 earnings는 '수익'이라는 의미로 -ing형 명사이며 항상 복수형태로 쓰인다.

어휘 eagerly 열망하여, 간절히 await 기다리다 division 부서 earn (돈을) 벌다 earnings (기업의) 수익

12 회사의 새로운 부서를 편성하는 데 거둔 Mike Waters의 성공 때문에 경영진은 그를 정규 컨설턴트로 고용하기로 결정했다.

해설 동사의 알맞은 형태를 묻는 문제로, 전치사 다음에는 동명사가 와야 한다. 따라서 (D) organizing이 정답이 된다.

어휘 division 부, 과 management 경영진

<13-16> 다음은 편지에 관한 문제이다.

베이언 플라자 아파트
애틀랜틱 가 C-205 번지, 넵튠 시
뉴저지 95124

새로 입주하시는 분들께,

최근 베이언 플라자 아파트를 임대하기로 한 당신의 결정에 축하를 드립니다. 이 편지는 당신의 임대 계약이 검토되었고, 체결되었음을 확인해 드리기 위함입니다. 저희는 여러분께서 도시의 대서양 방면에 위치해 있는 새롭게 단장된 저희 건물로 이사 오신 것을 즐기시게 될 것이라 확신합니다. 여러분께서는 멋진 대서양의 풍경은 물론이고 걸어서 갈 수 있는 거리 내에 위치한 몇몇 최고급 레스토랑과 이 도시의 유적지 등의 편의시설을 만끽하게 될 것입니다.

세입자로서 여러분은 입주일까지 전기와 통신 시설이 사용 가능하도록 할 책임이 있습니다. 만약 유지 관리상의 문제가 발생한다면, 24시간 대기 중인 현장 시설 관리 기술자에게 요청하시면 됩니다.

우리는 여러분을 위해 일하기를 고대합니다. 베이언 플라자 임대에 감사드립니다.

행운을 기원하며,

마크 스미스

어휘 rent 임대하다; 임대 renovate 개조하다 walking distance 걸어서 갈 수 있는 거리 tenant 입주자 be responsible for ~할 책임이 있다 activation 활성화 move-in date 입주일 look forward to -ing ~하기를 고대하다 rental contract 임대 계약서 review 검토하다

13

해설 알맞은 품사를 고르는 문제. [소유격(your)+형용사(recent)+---] 구조로 빈칸은 소유격과 형용사의 수식을 받는 명사 자리이다. 따라서 (A) decision이 답이 된다.

14 (A) 이 편지는 당신의 임대 계약이 검토되었고, 체결되었음을 확인해 드리기 위함입니다.
(B) 귀하는 임차 비용을 지불하지 않았기 때문에 귀하의 임대 계약이 만료됨을 통보받게 됩니다.
(C) 귀하는 만료일까지 거주지의 임차 계약을 포기할 것을 명령 받습니다.
(D) 귀하는 건물의 열쇠를 집주인에게 전달하고 거주지를 떠날 것을 요구 받게 됩니다.

해설 글의 첫 시작에 고객이 아파트를 임대하기로 한 결정을 알 수 있고, 빈칸 다음 문장에는 아파트의 장점들을 나열한 것으로 보아 문맥상 들어갈 적절한 문장은 임대차 계약이 체결되었다고 알리는 (A)가 가장 적절하다.

15

해설 전치사 선택 문제. 내용상 '~를 걸어서 갈 수 있는 거리 이내에(walking distance of)'라고 연결되어야 의미가 통하므로 '(범위나 거리, 장소, 기간) 안에, 이내에'를 뜻하는 전치사 (B) within이 답이 된다.

16

해설 동명사 어휘 선택 문제로, 지문 전체의 맥락상 임대에 대한 감사를 표시하는 문장으로 파악해 볼 수 있으므로 '임대하다'를 뜻하는 (D) renting이 정답이다. visiting은 타동사이므로 뒤에 전치사가 바로 연결될 수 없으며, going은 보통 전치사 to를 동반한다.

UNIT 12 분사

SPARTA Check-UP! 1

p. 111

1 (D) **2** (C) **3** (D)

1 간소화된 세금 프로젝트는 나라가 인터넷으로 구매한 제품에 대해서 세금을 부과하게 할 것이다.

해설 보기 중에서 명사인 tax project(세금 프로젝트)를 수식할 수 있는 것은 분사이다. 현재분사는 수식을 받는 명사와 능동적 관계, 과거분사는 수동적 관계인데, 문제에서 'tax project'는 간소화하는 주체가 아니라 수동적으로 간소화되는 것이므로, 과거분사인 (D) streamlined가 수식하는 것이 자연스럽다.

어휘 tax 세금 state 주 impose 강요하다, 부과하다 purchase 구매하다 streamline 간소화하다

2 NK 빌딩 뒤편의 주차구역은 주차장 서쪽이 모두 찰 때까지 닫혀 있을 것이다.

해설 2형식 동사 remain의 보어 자리로 형용사가 와야 한다. 보기 중 형용사인 현재분사 (A) closing와 과거분사 (C) closed 중 주어와 보어와의 관계가 수동의 관계이므로 (C) closed가 정답이 된다.

어휘 parking area 주차 지역 parking lot 주차장

3 호텔과 컨퍼런스 센터를 연결하는 중앙 홀은 저희 고객들은 사용할 수 있습니다.

해설 A concourse 주어, is가 동사이므로 빈칸은 동사 자리가 아니다. 따라서 동사인 (A) connects와 (C) is connecting은 오답이며 '연결하는'이라는 의미로 앞의 명사 A concourse를 수식하는 (D) connecting이 정답이 된다.

어휘 concourse 중앙 홀 connect 연결하다 available 이용 가능한

SPARTA Check-UP! 2

p. 112

1 (A) **2** (A) **3** (D)

1 비록 전시회에서 비평가들은 Crew 씨의 예술 작품을 매혹적이라고 생각했지만, 그 작품은 많은 방문객들을 끌어들이지는 못했다.

해설 전체 문장이 5형식으로, [주어(critics)+동사 (found)+목적어(artwork)+목적격 보어(---)]구조이다. 이 목적격 보어는 목적어의 상태를 설명, '작품들은 사람들을 매료시키는 주체'이므로 -ing를 사용해야 된다. 따라서 정답은 (A) fascinating이다.

어휘 critic 비평가들 artwork 예술 작품 exhibition 전시회 fascinate 반하게 하다, 매료하다 attract 매혹하다

2 Biogen Science는 3분기 연속되는 손실 이후, 믿기지 않는 수익을 공시하며 놀라운 회복을 보였다.

해설 빈칸 앞에 관사(an)이 있고 뒤에 명사(recovery)가 있으므로 형용사 (A) amazing을 써서 문장을 완성해야 한다.

어휘 post 게시하다, 고시하다, 공표하다 consecutive 연속적인 amazing 놀랄 만한, 굉장한 amazement 놀라움 amaze 몹시 놀라게 하다 amazingly 놀랍게도, 굉장하게

3 경기 불황 때문에 주거용 부동산에 관심을 갖는 투자자들의 수가 전혀 증가하지 않고 있다.

해설 빈칸에는 뒤에 오는 전치사구와 주어(in residential real estate)를 연결

해 줄 수 있는 어형이 나와야 하는데, 투자자들이 투자하는 것에 대한 관심을 갖게 되는 것이므로, 과거분사형인 (D) interested가 나와야 한다.

어휘 investor 투자자 real estate 부동산, 물적 재산 depression 불황

SPARTA Check-UP! 3

p. 113

1 (B) 2 (B) 3 (C)

1 우리는 당신이 게시판에 게시할 공고문을 준비할 때 이 견본에 나와 있는 형식을 따를 것을 권고합니다.

해설 접속사 when 뒤에 주어와 동사가 오지 않고, 보기들이 동사의 형태를 지니고 있기 때문에 분사구문이 되어야 한다는 것을 알 수 있다. 빈칸 다음에 목적어 역할을 하는 명사(announcements)가 왔기 때문에 능동형 분사구문이 되어야 하므로, (B) preparing이 정답이 된다.

어휘 announcement 공고, 발표 bulletin board 게시판 recommend 권고하다 follow 따르다

2 성공적으로 그 프로젝트를 마친 후에 모든 팀원들은 예상하지 못한 보너스를 받았다.

해설 빈칸에는 Having p.p.와 Having been p.p.가 모두 들어갈 수 있으므로 능동/수동을 확인해야 한다. 목적어 the project와 주절의 주어 all team members는 능동의 관계이므로 (B) Having이 정답이다.

어휘 successfully 성공적으로 unexpected 예상하지 못한

3 A&C와 계약을 체결하는 데 실패했기 때문에 영업부장이 어제 해고되었다.

해설 분사구문으로 종속절의 주어가 주절의 주어(the manager)와 같고, 시제의 경우 '계약을 체결하지 못한 것'이 '해고된 것'보다 먼저 일어난 일이므로, 완료 분사구문이 나와야 한다. 따라서 (C) Having failed가 정답이 된다.

어휘 fail to ~하지 못하다 sign the contract 계약을 체결하다 dismiss 해고하다

SPARTA Check-UP! 4

p. 114

1 (D) 2 (B) 3 (B)

1 진공청소기는 부품들이 파손된 상태로 배달되었기 때문에 제조업체로 다시 보내졌다.

해설 빈칸 뒤에 있는 명사(condition)을 꾸며주는 형용사 자리로 '파손된 상태'라는 뜻이 적합하므로 과거분사인 (D) damaged가 정답이다.

어휘 vacuum cleaner 진공청소기 manufacturer 제조업체

2 반송용 봉투에 지불금액을 넣어 12월 15일까지 Deron Electronics 사로 보내 주세요.

해설 준동사 문제(분사) 전치 수식. postage-paid envelope(반송용 봉투)이라는 명사를 꾸며주는 형용사 자리다. '동봉되어지는 봉투'이므로 과거분사인 (B) enclosed가 정답이다.

어휘 postage-paid 우편요금이 지불된 payment 지불, 지급

3 예상한 대로, 월말에 공장 운영비가 20퍼센트까지 증가할 것이다.

해설 '예상한 대로, 월말에 공장 운영비용이 20퍼센트까지 증가할 것이다'라는 의미가 되어야 하므로 (B) projected(예상하다)가 정답이다. as projected는 '예상한 대로'라는 의미로 묶어서 암기해 두는 것이 좋다.

어휘 project 예상하다 operating cost 운영비용, 경영비용

SPARTA PRACTICE

p. 115

1 required	2 limited	3 celebrated
4 repeated	5 enclosed	6 provided
7 opposing	8 allowing	9 revised
10 expected	11 seeking	12 reconfirming
13 using	14 accompanied	15 experienced

1 회사는 부품 조립에 필요한 시간을 단축함으로써 회사의 이윤을 증대시켰다.

해설 명사(time)를 수식하는 형용사가 필요하며, time과 require와의 관계가 수동이므로 과거분사 required가 정답이다.

어휘 profit 이익 assemble 조립하다 part 부품

2 한정된 기간 동안 30달러 이상의 모든 구매에 대하여 무료 샘플이 제공됩니다.

해설 명사(period)를 수식하는 형용사가 필요하고 limit과 period와의 관계가 수동이므로, 과거분사 limited를 써야 옳다.

어휘 limit 제한하다, 한정하다

3 새로운 패키지 여행은 지역에서 가장 유명한 관광지들을 포함합니다.

해설 부사(most)의 수식을 받으며 빈칸 뒤에 오는 복합명사(tourist attractions)를 수식할 수 있는 품사인 형용사 celebrated(유명한)를 고르면 된다.

어휘 include 포함하다 tourist attraction 관광 명소

4 지역 주민들의 반복 요청 끝에, 시 위원회는 시 기념비를 세우는 것에 마침내 동의했다.

해설 문맥상 '반복되는 요청 끝에'라는 의미이므로 과거분사 형태인 repeated를 써서 문장을 완성해야 한다.

어휘 resident 거주민 erect 세우다 monument 기념비, 기념 건조물

5 다음 번 저희 가게 방문 시, 전체 구매에 대해 10% 할인을 보장하는 동봉된 쿠폰을 받아 가세요.

해설 빈칸 앞에 정관사(the)가 있고 뒤에 명사(coupon)이 있으므로, 문맥에 알맞은 과거분사 enclosed '동봉된'을 써야 한다.

어휘 guarantee 보장하다 purchase 구매하다; 구매

6 주문을 하시려면 첨부된 주문서를 작성해서 돈과 함께 소책자에 제공된 반송용 봉투에 넣어서 보내주시기만 하면 됩니다.

해설 형용사 절에서 관계대명사 'which'와 be동사가 생략된 문장(in the reply envelope (which is) provided)으로 봐도 답을 알 수 있고 앞에 있는 명사(the reply envelope)를 후치 수식해 주는 과거분사(provided)로 봐도 정답을 알 수 있다.

어휘 place an order 주문하다 booklet 소책자(= pamphlet)

7 공장장은 새로운 주차장 건설 계획에 대해, 반대의견을 표명해 달라는 요청을 받았다.

해설 명사(point of view)를 수식하는 형용사가 필요하다. point of view와 oppose는 능동관계가 성립되므로, 정답은 opposing이다. 참고로 'the opposing point of view(반대 관점, 반대 의견)'로 묶어서 익혀 두면 좋다.

어휘 plant manager 공장장　present 나타내다, 표현하다　parking lot 주차장

8 T&T 소프트웨어는 고객들이 새로운 e-비즈니스 시대의 혜택을 마음껏 누릴 수 있도록 광범위한 응용 프로그램과 운영체계를 제공합니다.

해설 앞의 명사(applications and operating systems)를 수식하면서, 목적어(customers)를 취하는 현재분사인 allowing이 정답이다.

어휘 application (컴퓨터) 응용 프로그램　operating system 운영체계　era 시대, 시기

9 수정된 월별 보고서를 제출하지 않은 사람들은 가능한 한 빨리 자신의 직속 상관과 면담을 해야 한다.

해설 명사 'monthly reports(월별 보고서)'를 수식하는 형용사가 필요하다. 'monthly reports(월별 보고서)'는 '수정되는' 것이므로 수동의 revised이 답이다.

어휘 immediate supervisor 직속 상관

10 수출 침체와 기업 설비 투자의 급격한 감소 때문에 올 하반부 경기가 예상보다 훨씬 느리게 성장했다.

해설 접속사 뒤의 '주어+동사'가 생략이 되고 분사가 온 형태. 생략된 의미상의 주어 it은 economy를 지칭하며, economy와 expect는 수동이 되어야 한다.

어휘 sagging 처진, 하락한　steep 가파른　corporate 법인의, 회사의

11 영업과 관련된 비용을 상환받고자 하는 직원들은 모든 영수증을 회계부서로 제출해야 합니다.

해설 문장에 이미 동사(should submit)가 있으므로 빈칸에는 명사(Employees)를 꾸며주는 현재분사 seeking이 와야 한다.

어휘 reimbursement 상환, 변상　submit(= hand in) 제출하다　receipt 영수증　Accounting Department 회계부서

12 Thomson Electronics는 지난해 수익을 5억불까지 올리면서 업계 선두로서 위상을 재확인했다.

해설 'reconfirming = and reconfirm'이라는 의미로 주어진 빈칸에는 현재분사를 써야 한다.

어휘 reconfirm 재확인하다　status 지위, 신분

13 Hopkins에 있는 지역 공항을 이용하는 손님들은 보안 검색대에서 너무 많은 시간이 소요된다고 불평한다.

해설 문장에 동사(complain)이 있으므로, 명사(Travelers) 뒤에 있는 빈칸은 분사 자리이다. 문맥상 '지역 공항을 이용하는' 여행객을 뜻하므로, 현재분사 using이 정답이다.

어휘 complain 불평하다　security checkpoint 보안 검색대

14 심한 바람이 동반된 뇌우가 전 지역에 영향을 미칠 것으로 예상된다.

해설 문장에 이미 동사(is expected to)가 있으므로 빈칸은 분사를 써야 하는데, 빈칸 뒤에 목적어가 없으므로 과거분사 accompanied를 써야 한다.

어휘 thunderstorm 뇌우　gusty 바람이 심한, 돌풍이 많은　be expected to ~할 것으로 예상되다

15 우리의 목표들을 더욱 효과적으로 충족시키기 위해 우리는 기업문화를 발달시켜 줄 경험 많고 에너지가 넘치는 부사장을 원하고 있다.

해설 형용사(energetic '에너지가 넘치는')과 함께 명사(senior executive)를 수식할 수 있는 형태를 골라야 한다. 문맥상 experienced '경험 있는, 숙련된'이 적절하다.

어휘 senior executive 부사장 전무[상무]　meet 충족시키다　goal 목표　effectively 효율적으로, 효과적으로

SPARTA ✔ ACTUAL TEST

p. 116

1 (A)	**2** (C)	**3** (A)	**4** (B)	**5** (C)	**6** (D)
7 (D)	**8** (B)	**9** (A)	**10** (D)	**11** (C)	**12** (A)
13 (D)	**14** (C)	**15** (D)	**16** (C)		

1 Advanced Data Technology는 공학 분야에 매우 숙련된 연구원들이 많습니다.

해설 '형용사+명사'의 형태를 완성해야 한다. 빈칸 앞의 부사가 수식할 수 있는 것은 형용사, 동사, 부사가 있는데, 빈칸 뒤에 researchers로 명사가 있으므로 뒤의 명사를 수식하고 빈칸 앞 부사의 수식을 받는 것은 형용사가 된다. 보기 중 '숙련된'을 뜻하는 (A) experienced가 답이다.

어휘 highly 매우, 아주　researcher 연구원　field 분야

2 CEO는 경영진 부장에 의해 발표된 재정보고서 분석이 만족스럽다고 여겼다.

해설 [find+목적어+목적격 보어] 구조에서 목적격 보어가 현재분사인지 과거분사인지 묻는 문제이다. 목적어인 analysis(분석)는 감정을 느끼는 대상이 아니므로 감정동사 satisfy는 능동형인 (C) satisfying가 되어야 한다.

어휘 analysis 분석　financial report 재정 보고서　present 제출하다, 제시하다

3 리포터 Harold Gilliam과 함께한 멋진 인터뷰에서 세계적인 여배우 Michelle Beasley는 연예 산업에 있어 명성의 공허함에 관해 솔직하게 말했다.

해설 사물명사(interview)를 수식하는 감정동사(fascinate'매혹시키다')의 적절한 분사 형태는 -ing의 (A) fascinating이다.

어휘 reporter 기자　world-famous 세계적으로 유명한　actress 여배우　candidly 솔직하게　emptiness 공허함　fame 명성　industry 산업

4 지역 사회에 의해 기부된 기금은 박물관 내 다수의 전시품들을 새 단장하는 데 사용될 것이다.

해설 문장의 주어인 'The funds' 뒤에 빈칸이 오고 그 다음에 문장의 동사 'will be used to'가 나오고 있으므로 --- by the community는 주어인 'the funds'를 수식하는 분사구에 해당한다. 따라서 과거분사 (B) donated와 현재분사 (C) donating이 정답 후보들이다. the funds가 동사 donate의 대상이며 행동의 주체인 the community가 by 다음에 왔으므로 '지역사회에 의해 기부된 기금'을 나타내는 과거분사 (B) donated가 정답이다.

어휘 fund 기금　donate 기부하다　community 지역 사회　refurbish 개장하다, 새단장하다　exhibit 전시품, 진열품

5 저희는 수업에 참여하시는 개인이나 전문가 단체들의 요구에 맞도록 융통성 있는 프로그램 구성을 제공해 드립니다.

해설 빈칸은 앞에 올 명사구(individuals or groups of professionals)를 뒤에서 수식해 주는 형용사의 기능을 하는 분사가 와야 하는 자리이다. 문맥상 수업에 '참여하는' 개인이나 전문가 단체들의 요구에 맞도록 융통성 있는 프로그램 구성을 제공해 준다는 내용이 되어야 하므로 능동의 의미를 표현하는 현재분사 형태 (C) attending이 와야 한다.

어휘 offer 제공하다　flexible 융통성 있는, 유연한　format 전체 구성　fit 맞다, 일치시키다　need 요구, 필요　individual 개인　professional 전문가　attend 참여하다　attendance 참가, 출석

6 수하물을 맡기었든 맡기지 않았든 항공사 측은 그 안에 든 보석류, 현금에 대해 책임지지 않는다.

해설 빈칸은 명사구 'jewelry or cash'와 전치사 'in' 사이에 위치하고 있으므

로 앞에 있는 명사구를 후치 수식해 줄 수 있는 분사 형용사의 형태가 와야 하는 자리이다. 의미상 '보석류 등의 물건이 수하물에 담겨 있는' 표현이 맞으므로 수동의 의미를 표현하는 과거분사 형태가 오는 것이 적절하다. 따라서 정답은 (D) contained이다. 빈칸 뒤에 목적어가 나오지 않고 전치사 'in'이 오는 것도 과거분사형이 와야 하는 또 다른 근거가 된다.

어휘 be responsible for ~에 책임이 있다 check (짐 등을) 맡기다, 보관하다 container (화물 수송용) 컨테이너, 그릇, 용기 contain 담고 있다, 포함하다 contained in ~에 포함된

7 새로운 계약을 목요일 날 다시 교섭할 때, 우리는 계약 조건을 명심해야 하고 만약의 경우에 대비해서 옛날 계약서를 복사해야 한다.

해설 이 문제를 위해서는 분사구문 구조를 알고 있어야 한다. 여기서는 주절의 주어인 we가 '계약을 하는 주체'이므로 (D) renegotiating이 정답이다.

어휘 keep something in mind ~을 명심하다 contract 계약서

8 국제통화기금은 다른 나라에 재정적 부채가 있어 일시적인 어려움을 겪고 있는 나라들에 대부를 해주기 위해 설립되었다.

해설 언뜻 보면 복잡해 보이는 문장이지만 질문의 요지는 'have difficulties -ing(~하는 데 어려움을 겪고 있다)' 구문을 묻고 있다. 따라서 빈칸에는 -ing형이 와야 한다.

어휘 establish 설립하다 provide 제공하다 loan 대출(금); 빌려주다 temporary 일시적인 difficulty 어려움, 문제 financial 재정적인 obligation 의무

9 1971년 건립된 Bluewave 사는 6개국의 나라에 3만천 명이 넘는 직원들을 고용하고 있다.

해설 문장의 주어인 The Bluewave Company를 수식하는 분사구문의 시제와 태에 관한 문제로 동사 found(설립하다) 뒤에 목적어가 없으므로 수동태가 와야 한다. 따라서 능동인 (B) Founding과 완료형 (D) Having founded는 제외시킨다. (C) Been founded가 올바른 분사구문이 되려면 being founded가 되어야 한다. 여기서는 설립된 것이 시간상 앞선 상황이므로 완료형 having been founded에서 having been이 생략되고 남은 (A) Founded가 정답이다.

어휘 found 설립하다 employ 고용하다 employee 직원

10 오늘 오후 회의에서 논의된 대로, 우리는 새로운 제품을 늦어도 5월 8일까지 출시할 것이다.

해설 접속사 As 다음에 나올 적절한 단어의 형태를 찾아야 한다. 분사구문의 형태로 'as + 과거분사(~된 대로)'를 알면 쉽게 풀리는 문제이다. as discussed(논의된 대로)는 자주 쓰이므로 알아 두도록 한다.

어휘 launch 출시하다, 착수하다 no later than 늦어도

11 경영진은 새 프로젝트에 대한 좋은 아이디어를 내도록 마케팅 부서의 직원들을 격려해 왔다.

해설 빈칸 앞에 be동사의 과거분사형인 been이 있으므로 빈칸에는 동사의 현재분사나 과거분사형이 와야 한다. 문장의 주어인 Management가 행위의 주체가 되고, 빈칸 뒤에 동사의 목적어인 employees도 등장하므로 빈칸에는 능동의 의미를 형성하는 현재분사 (C) encouraging이 오는 것이 가장 적절하다.

어휘 management 경영진 encourage A to A가 ~하도록 격려하다 come up with 제시하다, 제안하다

12 새로 출시한 냉장고의 첫해 판매 실적이 아주 실망스러워서 회사는 시장에서 그 제품을 철수시키는결정을 내렸다.

해설 so ~ that 구문에서 so의 품사는 부사이기 때문에 so 바로 다음에 나올 수 있는 품사는 형용사나 부사이다. 문장 구조를 보면 주어가 sales이고 동사는 be동사인 were이므로, 빈칸에는 보어가 와야 한다. 따라서 주어인 'sales(판매)'와 호응하는 형용사 역할을 하는 분사 (A) discouraging(낙담시키는)이 정답으로 적절하다. discourage와 같은 감정분사는 주어가 사물일 때는 -ing, 주어가 사람일 때는 -ed를 쓴다.

어휘 make a decision 결정하다 withdraw 철수하다, 철회하다 discouraging 실망스러운 discourage 낙담시키다

〈13-16〉 다음은 광고에 관한 문제이다.

구인

직위 : 소프트웨어 엔지니어
회사 : M2M 솔루션
위치 : 산호세
급여 : 60,000달러 이상

M2M 솔루션 사는 고객들의 컴퓨터에 대한 다양한 요구에 창의적인 상상력과 효과적인 해결책을 제공함으로써 이미 명성을 쌓아 놓은 성장해 가고 있는 회사입니다.

우리는 현재 우리의 팀에 합류할 재능 있는 컴퓨터 전문가를 찾고 있습니다. 후보자는 엔지니어링이나 프로그래밍 분야에서 3 ~ 6년의 경험이 있어야 하며 C++과 유닉스의 업무 지식을 가지고 있어야만 합니다. 저희는 팀과 같이 일을 할 수 있을 뿐만 아니라 자신이 솔선수범해 행동할 자신감도 있는 상상력을 지닌 사람을 찾고 있습니다.

혜택은 다음의 것들을 포함합니다: 12일의 유급 휴가, 회사 차와 이사 비용. 게다가 모든 직원들은 회사에서 1년간 일한 뒤에는 연간 이익을 공유하는 보너스를 받을 자격이 있습니다.

인사 담당자인 밍카 젠킨스에게 minkaj@m2msolutions.net으로 당신의 이력서를 이메일로 보내주세요. 그녀는 면접 일정을 잡기 위해 당신에게 연락할 것입니다.

어휘 imaginative 상상력이 풍부한 effective 효율적인 a variety of 다양한 candidate 후보자 imagination 창의력 self-confidence 자신감, 자기 확신 on one's own initiative 자발적으로 benefit 혜택, 이익 relocation 이전 expense 비용 contact 연락하다 arrange 약속하다, 정렬하다

13

해설 빈칸은 부정관사 a 뒤에 위치하고 있으므로 의미상 적절한 명사가 와야 하는 자리이다. 문맥상 '이미 명성을 쌓아 놓은 성장하는 회사입니다'라는 의미가 되어야 하므로 빈칸에 적절한 명사는 '명성, 평판'이라는 의미의 (D) reputation이다.

어휘 excellence 뛰어남, 우수, 탁월 character 성격, 특징 value 가치 reputation 명성, 평판

14

해설 빈칸은 'on their own ---'라는 전치사 구에서 own과 결합하여 복합명사를 형성하는 적절한 의미의 명사가 와야 하는 자리이다. 문맥상 자신이 '솔선수범하여' 행동하는 자신감을 지닌다는 의미가 돼야 하기 때문에 빈칸에 적절한 표현은 '솔선수범'이라는 의미의 명사 (C) initiative이다.

어휘 initial 처음의, 초기의, 머리글자, 첫 글자; 머리글자를 쓰다 initiation 착수, 창시, 가입 initiative 솔선, 주도권 initially 처음에는

15

해설 빈칸은 be동사와 전치사 to 사이에 위치하고 있으므로 의미상 적절한 과거분사가 와야 하는 자리이다. 문맥상 '모든 직원들이 연간 이익을 공유하는 보너스를 받을 자격이 있다'는 의미가 되어야 하기 때문에 be entitled to N(~할 자격이 있다) 숙어 표현을 갖출 수 있다. 따라서 정답은 (D)이다.

어휘 enable 할 수 있게 하다, 시키다 encourage 격려하다 설득하다 enlarge 확대하다, 늘리다 entitle 자격(권리)을 주다

16 (A) 서비스업에 폭넓은 경험이 있는 분들의 지원을 환영합니다.
(B) 자격을 갖춘 지원자들은 영어와 불어 둘 다에 능숙해야 합니다.
(C) 그녀는 면접 일정을 잡기 위해 당신에게 연락할 것입니다.
(D) 이 정보에 대한 접근은 권한을 받은 직원에게만 한정됩니다.

해설 이 글은 구인 광고다. 빈칸 앞으로 이미 자격요건과 혜택들을 나열했고 지원 방법 이후에 어울리는 문장을 선택하는 문제다. 보기 중 이메일을 보내면 면접 일정을 잡기 위해 연락할 것이라는 (C)가 적절하다.

UNIT 13 등위접속사와 상관접속사

SPARTA Check-UP! 1

p. 119

1 (B) **2** (C) **3** (C)

1 사장은 직원들이 일에 대한 헌신, 그리고 관련 분야에서 전문성을 갖기를 원합니다.

해설 [want+목적어+to부정사] 구조가 앞에 나와 있고 have는 '~을 가지다, 소유하다'라는 뜻의 타동사이다. 타동사 뒤에는 목적어가 필요하고 'communication skills, commitment, expertise' 등 명사가 위치하고 있다. 등위접속사 and는 명사, 형용사, 부사, 절 등을 모두 연결시켜 줄 수 있고 A, B, and C 의 형태로 나열시킬 수 있으므로 정답은 (B) and가 된다.

어휘 commitment to ~에 대한 헌신, 노력, 봉사 expertise 전문(성), 능통(함)

2 다음 주에 Hart 씨는 출장을 가지만, 부재 시에도 이메일로 연락하실 수 있습니다.

해설 빈칸은 두 개의 동사구 will be away와 can be reached를 연결할 수 있는 등위접속사 자리이다. 등위접속사 (A) so는 완전한 문장과 문장을 연결하므로 오답이며 (B) nor 뒤에는 주어와 동사가 도치된 형태가 와야 하므로 역시 오답이다. (D) then은 부사이므로 연결 기능이 없다. 따라서 (C) but이 정답이다.

어휘 on a business trip 출장 중인 reach 연락하다, 도달하다 in one's absence 부재 시

3 회사 주차장이 다음주에 재포장되므로, 모든 직원들은 그 주 동안 대중교통을 이용할 것을 권고 받았다.

해설 접속사 문제이다. 문장의 동사는 will be repaved/are advised의 2개이고, 접속사는 없으므로 빈칸의 자리는 접속사 자리이다. 따라서 전치사인 (A) except(제외하고)는 탈락. 다음 주에 회사 주차장을 재포장할 것이므로, 직원들은 대중교통을 이용하기 바란다는 내용이 되어야 하므로 정답은 '그래서, 그러므로'의 결과를 나타내는 (C) so이다.

어휘 repave 도로를 재포장하다 be advised to ~하도록 권고 받다

SPARTA Check-UP! 2

p. 120

1 (A) **2** (B) **3** (B)

1 판매 담당자는 고객을 잃게 되는 요인이 높은 가격도, 노력의 부족도 아니라고 말했다.

해설 빈칸 앞뒤로 각각 high prices와 a lack of effort라는 명사구가 나열되어 있고 그 앞에는 neither가 있으므로 빈칸에는 이와 함께 상관접속사를 이루는 (A) nor가 오는 것이 적절하다. 'neither A nor B'는 'A도 B도 아니다'라는 의미의 상관접속사이다.

어휘 a lack of ~의 부족 factor 요소

2 주지사는 자신의 계획이 환경을 정화시킬뿐만 아니라 가치 있고 보수가 높은 일자리를 많이 창출해 낼 것이라고 믿고 있다.

해설 빈칸에는 not only와 상관적으로 쓰이는 단어가 필요하므로 (B) but이 정답이다.

어휘 governor 주지사 clean up 깨끗하게 하다 environment 환경 create 창출하다 meaningful 의미 있는 well-paid 보수가 좋은

3 Suto 씨와 그녀의 동료 둘 다 고객들을 대하는 데 유능하고 정직하다는 것이 증명되었다.

해설 문장의 적절한 동사 형태를 찾아야 한다. 주어의 both A and B, 즉 Suto 씨와 동료 둘 다 주어이므로 동사는 복수 형태가 와야 한다. 따라서 (B) have proved가 정답이다.

어휘 associate 동료 able 유능한 deal with 다루다 client 고객

SPARTA PRACTICE

p. 121

1 or	**2** and	**3** but	**4** and
5 license	**6** or	**7** yet	**8** nor
9 either	**10** or	**11** or	**12** but
13 not only	**14** Both	**15** but	

1 저희는 환불수표를 발행하거나 당신의 계좌로 입금해 드리겠습니다.

해설 A 혹은 B라는 선택의 내용이다. 문맥적으로 수표를 발행해 주거나 또는 계좌로 입금하겠다는 의미이므로 정답은 or가 된다.

어휘 issue 발행하다 refund 환불 credit 입금하다 account 계좌

2 유람선은 500명 승객을 위한 장소와 여가 공간을 포함한다.

해설 문장은 '배에 500명의 승객을 위한 장소와 그리고 여가 공간이 있다'는 의미가 되어야 하므로 접속사로 and가 들어가야 한다.

어휘 cruise ship 유람선 passenger 승객

3 우리는 지난 이사회 결과를 기다리고 있지만, 그들이 아직 도착하지 않았다.

해설 but과 or는 문법적인 기능은 같으므로 보기에 but과 or이 동시에 나오면 문맥을 파악하여 문제를 풀어야 한다. 빈칸 앞 문장은 '결과를 기다리다'이고 뒤 문장은 '아직 도착하지 않았다'이므로 문맥상 but을 써야 한다.

어휘 wait 기다리다 result 결과 board meeting 이사회

4 이 설문에 대한 직원 응답이 저희 파일에 필요하며, 이것은 저희가 회사를 일하기 더 좋은 공간으로 만드는 데 도움이 될 것입니다.

해설 문맥상 두 문장을 연결해 주는 적절한 접속사는 and이다. 문장의 주어는 직원 응답(Employees' responses)으로 우리는 직원 설문 응답이 필요하고 이는 회사에 도움이 될 것이라는 의미이다.

어휘 responses to ~에 대한 응답, 반응 questionnaire 설문지

5 면허나 공사 허가증을 신청하기 전에 개발업자들은 특정 환경 영향 평가를 시행해야 한다.

해설 관사(a) 다음에 위치하는 품사는 명사이고, 등위접속사 or가 연결하고 있는 명사(permit 허가증)와 함께 어울리는 것은 license '면허'이다.

어휘 conduct 수행하다 impact 영향 assessment 평가

6 다음 달부터 이메일 또는 전화로 콘서트 입장권을 구매할 수 있다.

해설 이메일이나 혹은 전화로 구매할 수 있다는 선택의 의미이므로 or가 정답이다.

어휘 as of ~를 시점으로 purchase 구입하다

7 Worthington Motors에서 최근에 생산된 모든 자동차 모델들은 더 무거운 자재로 만들어졌지만 상대 모델보다 더 좋은 연비를 제공한다.

해설 문맥상 앞 문장과 뒤 문장이 상반되는 내용이므로 등위접속사 yet이 정답이다.

어휘 be made of ~로 만들어지다 typically 전형적으로 counterpart 상대되는 것[사람]

8 조합원이나 경영진 양측 모두 정부의 중재를 요청하지 않았기 때문에 조합 간부들은 이번 달에 항의 계획을 세울 것으로 예측된다.

해설 neither A nor B의 구문이다. 앞에 neither이 있으므로 정답은 nor이다.

어휘 mediation 중재 map out 계획을 세우다 protest 항의

9 입장권들은 온라인 또는 입구 옆에 있는 매표소에서 구입할 수 있다.

해설 빈칸 뒤에 or이 있으므로 either를 써야 한다.

어휘 admission ticket 입장권 purchase 구매하다 ticket office 매표소 entrance 입구, 문

10 고객이 파손된 불량 제품을 받을 경우, 저희는 대체상품을 발송하거나 고객님에게 전액 환불해 줄 것이다.

해설 문맥상 '~이거나 또는'의 의미를 갖는 선택의 or가 정답이다.

어휘 replacement 교체품 refund 환불

11 단체에 등록하기 위해서 자동차 면허증이나 출생증명서를 보여 주어야 한다는 것을 알았다.

해설 either A or B의 구문이다. 앞에 either이 있으므로 정답은 or이다.

어휘 register 등록하다 birth certificate 출생 증명서

12 운수업체는 적절한 선적, 배, 창고 그리고 짐을 내리는 절차에 책임은 있지만 제품의 포장에 대해서는 책임이 없다.

해설 not A but B의 (A가 아니라 B이다)의 변형으로 'A, but not B (A이지만 B는 아니다)'라는 구문이다.

어휘 carrier 운수업체 loading 선적, 하역 vessel 배, 항공기 discharge ~에서 짐을 내리다 packaging 포장

13 회사의 이사들은 높은 급여뿐만 아니라 회사가 세우게 될 기준 때문에 보상 급여에 반대했다.

해설 not only (because of) A but also (because of) B의 구문이다. 뒤에 but also가 있으므로 정답은 not only이다.

어휘 oppose 반대하다 compensation package 보상 급여

14 McDonnel 씨와 Douglas 씨 두 사람 모두 그들의 상사가 준비하는 중요한 발표에 도움이 되고자 추가 근무를 할 것이다.

해설 both A and B 구문이다. 접속사 Whether은 보통 or과 같이 사용된다. and 앞뒤로 병렬 구조이므로 Both가 답이다.

어휘 work overtime 추가 근무하다 supervisor 상사

15 이 상품이 잘 팔리지 않는 이유는 값이 비싸서가 아니라 품질이 나빠서이다.

해설 상관 접속사의 짝을 이루는 문제로 not A but B 구문을 알면 쉽게 풀 수 있다.

어휘 reason 이유 merchandise 상품 well 잘 quality 품질

SPARTA ACTUAL TEST

p. 122

1 (A)	**2** (D)	**3** (B)	**4** (C)	**5** (A)	**6** (D)
7 (A)	**8** (C)	**9** (A)	**10** (B)	**11** (B)	**12** (C)
13 (A)	**14** (D)	**15** (D)	**16** (C)		

1 Lee 씨는 회의에 거의 항상 늦게 가는데도 그 점에 대하여 별로 신경 쓰지 않는 것 같다.

해설 뒤 문장이 완전하므로 관계대명사인 (C) which는 쓸 수 없고, (B) or와 (D) although는 의미가 통하지 않는다. 정답은 (A).

어휘 care about 신경 쓰다

2 언론과 지역사회 둘 다 노인들을 부양하는 데 주지사의 새로운 정책에 열렬하게 갈채를 보냈다.

해설 상관접속사의 짝을 이루는 문제로, both A and B 구문으로 문두에 both를 보고 정답이 (D) and가 됨을 알 수 있다.

어휘 press 언론 local community 지역사회 enthusiastically 열렬히 applaud 박수치다 governor 주지사 support 부양하다, 지원하다

3 귀하께서 자사 월간지의 구독 갱신을 아직 하지 않으셨다면, 오늘 온라인으로 등록하시거나 가장 가까운 곳의 물류센터를 직접 방문해 주십시오.

해설 보기로 either, neither, both, not only 또는 or, nor, and, but (also) 등이 제시되었다면 상관접속사 문제를 먼저 떠올릴 수 있어야 한다. 빈칸 뒤에 [A(sign up online today), or B(visit the nearest distribution center~)] 의 구조로 연결되어 있으므로 'either A or B'의 형태를 취해야 문장이 완성된다. 따라서 (B) either가 정답이다.

어휘 renew 갱신하다 monthly 매월의, 한 달에 한 번의 sign up 등록하다 distribution center 유통[물류]센터 in person 몸소, 직접

4 일기 예보는 오늘 비가 올 가능성이 60%였다고 말했지만, 사실 화창한 날씨와 함께 하루 종일 높은 기온을 유지했다.

해설 조건절을 이끄는 접속사 (D) if를 제외하고, (A) and, (B) or, (C) but는 모두 등위접속사이므로 빈칸 앞뒤의 문맥을 파악하여 자연스럽게 연결해 줄 수 있는 답을 고른다. 빈칸 앞은 비올 확률이 60%라고 했으며, 빈칸 뒤에는 화창한 날씨와 높은 기온을 유지했다는 내용이므로 상반된 내용을 연결해 주는 접속사 (C) but이 답이 된다.

어휘 weather forecaster 일기예보 chance of ~할 가능성 in fact 사실상 temperature 기온 remain (~인 상태로) 남아 있다

5 하루에 1,000달러를 초과하는 인출은 계좌주와 공인인증기관 모두에게서 서명을 받아야 한다.

해설 빈칸 앞뒤 문장을 연결해 줄 수 있는 알맞은 단어를 선택하는 문제. 보기와 같이 both나 whether, either, not only 등이 제시되어 있다면 먼저 이와 짝을 이루는 어구가 있는지 확인한다. (A) both는 'both A and B: A, B 둘 다', (B) whether는 'whether A or B: A인지 B인지', (C) either는 'either A or B: A, B 둘 중 하나', (D) not only는 'not only A but (also) B: A뿐만 아니라 B 역시'의 구조를 갖는 상관 어구로 빈칸 뒤 and가 있다는 점에서 (A) both를 바로 선택할 수 있다.

어휘 withdrawal 인출, 철회 sign 서명하다 account holder 계좌주 authorized 인가된 signatory (공식 합의서의) 서명인, 조인국

6 Juno 아파트 단지의 경비원들은 주민들의 주차공간을 자주 감시할 뿐만 아니라, 그 영역의 미확인된 차량에 딱지도 붙인다.

해설 상관접속사 구문을 묻는 문제다. not only A but also B 'A뿐만 아니라 B도' 구문이다. 문장 앞에서 not only는 (D) but also와 함께 쓰이므로 정답은 (D)이다.

어휘 complex 복합적인, 복합건물 security officer 경비원 frequently 자주 monitor 감시하다 resident 주민 ticket 딱지를 붙이다 unidentified 미확인된

7 신규 직원들은 건강 보험과 치과 보험 또는 건강 보험과 안과 보험을 제공하는 복지 혜택을 받는다.

해설 health and dental insurance와 health and vision insurance를 or가 연결하고 있으므로 or와 함께 사용될 수 있는 상관접속사는 (A) either이다.

어휘 benefit package 복지제도 dental insurance 치과 보험 vision insurance 안과 보험

8 Maria는 신발 가게의 일을 정말로 좋아하지만 그 일이 좀 더 신나기를 바란다.

해설 알맞은 접속사를 고르는 문제이다. 문맥상 '그녀의 일을 좋아하다'와 '일이 좀 더 신나기를 바라다'는 역접의 관계를 이루므로 (C) but이 정답이다.

어휘 exciting 흥분시키는, 자극적인

9 아시아 전반의 주식시장은 지난달에 비교해 안정적으로 보이지만, 보이는 대로가 전부는 아니다.

해설 절과 절을 잇는 것은 접속사이고 문맥상의 의미로는 대치 상태가 되어야 적절하다. 보기 중 접속사는 (A) but과 (C) nor가 있다. (B) also는 추가의 의미를 지닌 '또한'이므로 내용이 자연스럽지 않다. '그러나'를 의미하는 (A)가 정답이다. also는 앞에 부정을 나타내는 내용이 와야 하며, (D) despite는 '~함에도 불구하고'를 뜻하는 전치사이다.

어휘 stock market 주식시장 stable 안정적인 compared to ~와 비교해

10 Coachella Valley 음악 축제 티켓과 공연자의 음반은 Columbus Civic Center 매표소에서 구입할 수 있습니다.

해설 빈칸 앞은 Coachella Valley Music Festival tickets라는 명사구가 오고 빈칸 뒤에서 the performers' albums라는 명사가 나온 뒤 be동사 are가 이어진다. 두 가지가 같이 판매되고 있다는 내용으로 적절히 연결하는 것은 등위접속사 and가 된다. (A) either는 '둘 중 하나'라는 뜻을 의미하고, (C) that은 관계대명사, (D) so는 절과 절을 연결하는 접속사이다.

어휘 festival 축제 performer 공연자 album 음반 on sale 판매 중 box office 매표소

11 Diane Nicholls는 지난주에 국제 마케팅지 자리를 제안 받았지만 아직 응답을 하지 않았다.

해설 알맞은 접속사를 찾는 문제. has still not responded의 주어는 앞 문장의 주어 Diane Nicholls와 일치하므로 생략된 채 연결된 문장이다. 앞의 내용상 지난주에 국제 마케팅 직업을 제의 받은 내용과 응답하지 않은 내용이 매끄럽게 연결되려면 등위접속사로 동사를 역접관계로 이어주는 (B) but이 정답이 된다.

어휘 offer 제안하다 international 국제적인 respond 응답하다 although ~함에도 불구하고 unless ~하지 않는 한 nor ~도 아니다

12 봉투에 보통 혹은 고급 인화를 원하는지 표시해 주시고 또한 각각의 사진 크기도 표시해 주세요.

해설 빈칸의 앞, 뒤에 '보통' 혹은 '고급'을 뜻하는 형용사가 등위 구조를 이루고 있으므로 선택의 등위접속사 or를 써야 한다. (A) nor는 이중 부정의 등위접속사로 쓰일 수 있고, (B) so는 원인과 결과의 문장 연결 등위접속사이고, (D) and는 부가의 등위접속사이다.

어휘 indicate 가리키다, 지시하다, 나타내다 regular 통상의, 보통의 deluxe 호화로운, 사치스러운, 고급의 photograph 사진

〈13-16〉 다음은 회람에 관한 문제이다.

메모

날짜: 7월 5일
발신: 제프리 페퍼, 이사, 데이터 매니지먼트 리서치
수신: 애론 브랜스타인, 이사, 리서치 프로그램스
제목: 추천-찰스 페로우-고객 데이터 바이러스 프로젝트

찰스는 고객 데이터 바이러스 프로젝트에서 특수 임무를 맡아 지난 5개월 동안 일해 왔습니다. 이 시간을 빌려 그가 CVP 임무를 맡으면서 보여 준 헌신적인 기여에 대해서 추천하려 합니다.

곧 자신의 위치로 복직할 것이기에 그의 프로젝트에 대한 기여와 그의 노력에 대해서 알아주셨으면 합니다. 프로젝트 담당자로서 그가 보여준 엄청난 의욕은 이번 프로젝트에서 프로그래머로서뿐만 아니라 동료이자 프로젝트팀 구성원으로서 매우 중요한 역할을 해 주었습니다. 또한 그는 내가 일했던 사람들 중에 가장 생산적인 프로그래머입니다.

저는 이 기업이 프로젝트에서 보여준 그의 보기 드문 기여에 대해 인정해 주어야 한다고 생각합니다.

어휘 commendation 추천 assignment 임무 exceptional 드문 contribution 기여 recognition 인정 enthusiasm 의욕 colleague 동료

13

해설 '(시간, 노력 등을) 필요로 하다, 걸리다, 필요로 하다'는 뜻으로 'take+목적어+to부정사'를 써야 한다. 따라서 답은 (A)이다.

14

해설 'as a programmer' 뒤에 'but also as a colleague ~'가 쓰인 것으로 보아 not only A but also B의 병렬구문임을 알 수 있다. but also에서 also는 자주 생략된다. '프로그래머로서뿐만 아니라 동료와 프로젝트 팀 구성원으로서'로 해석된다. 따라서 (D)가 정답이다.

15 (A) 이 문제에 관해 가능한 한 빨리 저에게 연락 주십시오.
(B) 또한, 작년에 저희는 Charles Perrow의 공로를 기념했습니다.
(C) 연례 직원 오찬은 에메랄드 클럽에서 오후 1시에 열리게 됩니다.
(D) 또한 그는 내가 일했던 사람들 중에 가장 생산적인 프로그래머입니다.

해설 빈칸 앞부분에서는 프로젝트에서 뛰어난 공을 세운 찰스를 칭찬했고, 뒷부분에서는 회사가 그의 기여를 인정해 줘야 한다고 했다. 이 내용에서는 어떠한 시상식이나 기념 파티 같은 이벤트도 나와 있지 않으므로 (A)와 (C)는 어색하고, 이미 작년에 치하했다고 하는 (B)도 이상하다. 정답은 찰스의 뛰어남을 한 마디로 평가한 (D)이다.

16

해설 보기가 같은 단어의 변형들로 제시되었으므로 문법 문제이다. 빈칸 다음에 명사 performance가 나오므로, 이를 수식할 수 있는 형용사가 쓰여야 한다. 따라서 형용사인 (C) exceptional(예외적인, 뛰어난)이 답이다.

UNIT 14 관계대명사

SPARTA Check-UP! 1

p. 125

1 (A) **2** (B) **3** (A)

1 데이터를 공유할 수 있는 전자 장치를 사용하는 의료 서비스 제공자들의 수가 증가하고 있습니다.

해설 주어는 The number, 동사는 is increasing이며, 빈칸부터 data까지는 문장 형태로 healthcare providers를 수식하므로 빈칸은 관계대명사 자리이다. 선행사인 healthcare providers(의료 서비스 제공자들)가 사람을 가리키며 빈칸 뒤에 주어가 없으므로 사람을 수식하는 주격 관계대명사 (A) who가 정답이다.

어휘 the number of ~의 수 healthcare provider 의료 서비스 제공자 electronic device 전자 장치 capable of ~를 할 수 있는 share 공유하다

2 귀하는 회의 동안에 논의될 모든 안건들을 상세히 설명하는 문서를 받게 될 것이다.

해설 문장의 주어는 You, 동사는 will receive이며, 빈칸부터 the meeting까지가 앞의 issues를 수식하므로 빈칸은 관계대명사 자리이다. 선행사인 issues(안건들)는 사물이며 빈칸 뒤에 주어가 없으므로 사물을 수식하는 주격 관계대명사 (B) that이 가능하다.

어휘 document 문서 detail 상세히 설명하다 discuss 논의하다

3 Car Life Insurance 사는 대부분의 자동차 수리 비용에 대해 전액 보상하는 보험을 제공하고 있습니다.

해설 빈칸 앞 which는 관계대명사로 policies를 수식한다. 관계대명사절에는 반드시 동사가 있어야 하므로 빈칸은 동사 자리이다. 관계대명사절의 동사는 수식을 받는 선행사와 수 일치를 해야 한다. 선행사가 복수(policies)이므로 선행사와 수 일치되는 (A) provide가 정답이다.

어휘 policy 증권, 보험 vehicle 탈것, 자동차 coverage (보험) 보상, 보상 범위 repair bill 수리 비용

SPARTA Check-UP! 2

p. 126

1 (D) **2** (D) **3** (C)

1 관공서는 여러 사무실과 그 사무실을 운영하는 직원들로 구성되어 있다.

해설 선행사 employees(고용인)를 받는 관계대명사는 (D) who만이 가능하다. employees who run them에서 them은 various offices를 받는다.

어휘 civil service 시민 봉사, 공공 업무 organization 조직, 단체 be composed of ~으로 구성되다 various 여러 가지의 employee 직원 run 운영하다

2 Fine Arts는 Lena Rivers 지역의 공공 예술 프로젝트를 지원하는 것이 임무인 단체이다.

해설 빈칸 이하는 주절의 동사(is)의 주격 보어인 사물 명사 an organization을 수식하는 자리로 소유격 관계대명사 (D) whose가 정답이다. 앞의 명사 an organization과 뒤의 명사 mission은 '조직의 임무'라는 소유의 의미를 나타낸다.

어휘 mission 임무, 사명 support 지원하다

3 죄송하게도, 귀하께서 주문하신 품목이 현재 재고가 없습니다.

해설 선행사 다음에 목적어 없이 주어와 타동사가 왔으면 목적격 관계대명사

자리임을 알아야 한다. (D) what은 선행사를 받지 않음을 주의한다. 답은 (C) that이다.

어휘 order 주문하다 currently 현재 out of stock 재고가 없는

SPARTA Check-UP! 3

p. 127

1 (B) **2** (B) **3** (A)

1 주택 대출을 받는 것과 관련된 여러 종류의 비용이 있다.

해설 문장의 본동사 are가 있기 때문에 빈칸에는 동사가 들어갈 수 없으므로 (A) associate는 제거한다. 빈칸 앞의 명사 charges와 연결되지 못하는 명사 (C) association도 제거한다. 수식 받는 명사 charges와 associated는 '관련된 비용'이란 뜻의 수동 관계이므로 정답은 (B)이다.

어휘 a variety of 여러 가지의 charge 비용 associate 관련시키다

2 저희가 채용을 위해 인터뷰한 3명의 후보 중 Pere 씨가 에너지 캠페인에 대해 가장 잘 알고 있는 것으로 보입니다.

해설 candidates와 we 사이에 목적격 관계대명사 whom이 생략된 문장이다. 빈칸은 관계대명사절에서 동사 자리이며, 목적격 관계대명사절은 목적어가 없는 불안전한 문장으로 이루어져야 한다. 따라서 정답은 능동태인 (B) interviewed이다.

어휘 candidate 후보자 interview 인터뷰하다 appear ~인 것 같다, ~처럼 보이다

3 Kolache 공장에서 일하는 직원들은 연말에 한 달간의 유급휴가를 받게 될 것이다.

해설 문장의 주어는 Workers, 동사는 will receive이다. 따라서 빈칸은 동사 자리가 아니므로 (C) will work와 (D) are worked는 오답이다. 빈칸 앞 workers를 수식하는 현재분사와 과거분사를 구별하는 문제로 빈칸 뒤 목적어가 없으나 work는 명사를 수식하는 과거분사(p.p.)로 쓸 수 없는 자동사이므로 현재분사형인 (A) working가 정답이다.

어휘 work 일하다 receive 받다 paid vacation 유급휴가

SPARTA Check-UP! 4

p. 128

1 (A) **2** (B) **3** (A)

1 경영 컨설턴트는 사업에서 이익을 내기 위해 당신이 알아야 할 것들에 대해 설명해 준다.

해설 품사 문제로 [동사(explains)+----+주어(you)+동사(need to know)]의 구조이다. 타동사 know의 목적어 역할을 할 수 있는 명사 상당 어구가 빈칸에 들어가야 한다. 따라서 정답은 (A) what이다.

어휘 trading 상거래, 무역 profitable 이익이 남는

2 주주들에게 가장 감명을 준 것은 올해 Melcam 사가 기업브랜드의 국제적인 인지도를 높였다는 것이다.

해설 [----+타동사+목적어+동사] 구조로 주어가 없는 불완전한 문장을 이끄는 관계대명사 (B) What이 정답이다.

어휘 impress 감명을 주다 stockholder 주주 boost 올리다, 신장시키다 recognition 인지도, 인식

3 식당의 경영진은 보수 공사를 위해 식당이 3주 동안 폐쇄될 것임을 발표했다.

해설 타동사인 announced의 목적절로 뒤에 절(수동 문장)이 완전 구조이므로 정답은 (A) that이 된다.

어휘 management 경영진 renovation 보수 공사

SPARTA PRACTICE

p. 129

1 who **2** that **3** which
4 that **5** you **6** who
7 who **8** whose **9** for
10 whom **11** verifying **12** distributed
13 will be holding **14** incurred **15** written

1 회사는 석사 학위나 박사 학위가 있는 인테리어 디자이너를 찾고 있다.

해설 빈칸 앞에 선행사로 나온 디자이너(designer)는 사람이므로 이를 수식하는 관계대명사 who가 정답이다.

어휘 seek ~찾다

2 Diaz 씨는 Kodic 사의 최신 카메라가 소매 시장에서 큰 성공을 거둘 것이라고 예측합니다.

해설 빈칸부터 marketplace까지의 문장 형태가 동사 predicts의 목적어이다. 따라서 빈칸은 명사절 접속사 자리이다. 명사절 접속사 that 뒤에는 완전 문장이, what 뒤에는 불완전 문장이 오는데 빈칸 뒤에는 완전 문장이 이어지므로 (A) that이 정답이다.

어휘 predict 예측하다 success 성공 retail marketplace 소매 시장

3 죄송합니다만 손상되거나 15일 이상 전에 구입한 제품은 환불해 드릴 수 없습니다.

해설 선행사인 상품은 사물이므로 관계대명사 which가 정답이다.

어휘 reimburse 환급하다 damaged 손상된

4 창고에는 인쇄 용지가 있다면, 그것을 Park 씨에게 갖다 주세요.

해설 선행사가 인쇄용지(copy paper)이므로 that이 정답이다.

어휘 bring A to B A를 B로 가져다주다

5 저희 상품 구매 시 귀하께서 받으신 무료 식사 쿠폰을 제시해 주시기 바랍니다.

해설 coupon 다음 목적격 관계대명사 which가 생략된 형태로 '귀하가 받은 쿠폰'이 되어야 하므로 주어 자리에 쓰는 인칭대명사 주격 you를 써야 한다.

어휘 present 제시하다 complimentary 무료의 purchase 구매

6 저는 오는 토요일 10차 연례회의에서 연설을 하는 데 동의한 Nelson 박사께 감사하고 싶습니다.

해설 사람(Nelson 박사)을 받을 수 있는 관계대명사는 who이다.

어휘 deliver an address 연설하다 annual conference 연례회의 coming 다가오는

7 인터뷰 진행자는 대학을 졸업한 직후 바로 회사를 창업한 Sandra에게 가장 감명받았다.

해설 Sandra라는 사람을 받을 수 있는 것은 who이다.

어휘 impressed by ~에 감명을 받다 establish 세우다 graduate from ~를 졸업하다

8 신규 지원서를 처리하는 일을 하는 사람은 인사 부장인 Peter Kim이다.

해설 관계대명사 뒤에 완전한 문장이 있으므로 소유격 관계대명사 whose가 정답이다.

어휘 process 처리하다 application 지원서

9 인사과는 환급을 요청한 모든 경비를 기록하고 있습니다.

해설 관계대명사 앞에 오는 전치사는 의미상 관계대명사절의 동사나 선행사에 연결되어야 한다. request reimbursement for는 '~에 대한 상환[환급]을 요청하다'라는 의미의 숙어이며 for는 '~에 대해'라는 뜻으로 선행사 expenses(비용)와 연결되어 '비용에 대해 당신이 환급을 요청했다'는 의미를 나타내는 for를 써야 한다.

어휘 HR Department 인사과 record 기록하다 expense 지출, 비용 request 요청하다 reimbursement 상환, 환급, 배상

10 월간 계좌 명세서가 보내져야 할 부장들의 이름들은 메뉴얼에 나와 있다.

해설 전치사와 목적격 관계대명사의 구조로 whom이 필요하다.

어휘 account 계좌 statement 명세서 manual 설명서

11 지원자들은 직위에 대한 자격 여부를 입증하는 서류를 제출해야 합니다.

해설 '지원자들의 자격 여부를 입증하는 서류'라는 의미로 [주격 관계대명사+be동사]가 생략된 형태로 보면 된다. 따라서 verifying을 써야 한다.

어휘 submit 제출하다 verify 입증하다 eligibility 적임, 적격

12 나는 American Medical Society에서 매월 배포하는 <Times Journal>을 구독한다.

해설 '매월 저널이 배포된다'는 의미이므로 정답은 distributed이다. 바로 앞에 관계대명사 which is가 생략되었다고 보면 된다.

어휘 subscribe to ~을 구독하다 distribute 배포하다

13 모든 신입 직원들은 회사가 다음 달에 개최할 오리엔테이션에 참석해야 한다.

해설 the company 앞에 목적격 관계대명사 which가 생략된 형태로 문맥상 '회사가 개최될 오리엔테이션'이 아니라 '회사가 개최할 오리엔테이션'이 적절하므로 능동태인 will be holding을 써야 한다.

어휘 employee 직원 attend 참석하다 orientation session 오리엔테이션 hold 개최하다

14 수년 동안 출장 목적으로 발생한 항공 마일리지는 세금 공제가 되는 비용입니다.

해설 '수년 동안 출장 목적으로 발생한 항공 마일리지'라는 의미로 앞에 [주격 관계대명사+be동사]가 생략된 형태로 보면 된다. 따라서 incurred를 써야 한다.

어휘 in many years 수년 동안 incur (비용을) 발생시키다 tax-deductible 소득 공제가 되는 expense 비용

15 관심 있는 지원자들은 지원서 양식에 있는 날짜까지 이력서와 자기소개서를 제출해야 한다.

해설 지원서에 써진 날짜란 의미이므로 written이 정답이다. 앞에 which was가 생략된 형태다.

어휘 submit 제출하다 application from 지원서

SPARTA ✔ ACTUAL TEST

p. 130

1 (A)	2 (B)	3 (B)	4 (A)	5 (B)	6 (B)
7 (B)	8 (D)	9 (A)	10 (D)	11 (B)	12 (D)
13 (D)	14 (C)	15 (D)	16 (C)		

1 지난주부터 운영되어 온 버스 노선은 7분마다 각 정류소에 정차한다.

해설 관계대명사 문제로 사물인 주어 The bus line의 수식구가 되는 부분을 연결하는 관계대명사는 (A) which이다. (B) whom은 목적격 관계대명사, (C) who는 사람을 선행사로 받는 주격 관계대명사, (D) what은 선행사를 포함하므로(=the thing that) 앞에 선행사가 없을 때 올 수 있다.

어휘 operate 운영하다, 작동하다 since ~이후로

2 IPTV 연결 문제를 겪는 계약자들께서는 24시간 내내 이용이 가능한 헬프 데스크에 연락하셔야 합니다.

해설 관계대명사 문제. 문장의 동사는 are experiencing, should call, is의 3개이므로, 빈칸의 자리는 관계대명사 자리가 되어야 한다. 빈칸 앞에 명사를 받고 있으므로 선행사를 수식하는 형용사절을 이끄는 관계사의 자리임을 알 수 있다. 따라서 명사절만 이끄는 (C) what은 답이 될 수 없다. 빈칸은 are experiencing의 주어 자리이므로, 완전한 문장을 이끄는 소유격 관계대명사인 (D) whose 역시 탈락. 선행사가 사람이므로 정답은 (B) who가 된다.

어휘 subscriber 정기구독자, 회원 experience 경험하다 connection 연결 available 이용이 가능한 around the clock 24시간 내내

3 Trevor Satchell의 주주들이 재정 위기에 대해 우려를 표명해서, 그가 주주자본에 대한 분기별 회의를 다음 주까지 연기했다.

해설 보기의 구성으로 보아 관계사 문제로 볼 수 있으므로 빈칸 앞뒤의 구조를 먼저 확인한다. 빈칸 앞에는 주어(선행사)로서 사람명사인 Trevor Satchell이 위치해 있고, 빈칸 뒤에는 [---+명사(shareholders)+동사(have expressed)+목적어(concern)] 구조를 취하고 있으므로 빈칸은 뒤의 명사를 한정해 주는 소유격 관계대명사가 들어가야 옳다. 따라서 (B) whose가 답이 된다.

어휘 shareholder 주주 express concern 우려를 표명하다 financial 재정상의 crisis 위기 postpone 연기하다 quarterly meeting 분기별 회의 stockholder equity 주주 자본

4 세미나는 자동차 산업에서 원자재 가격에 영향을 미치는 많은 요인들에 대해 살펴볼 것이다.

해설 앞에 the many factors가 오고 있고 빈칸 이하 절(affect ~ industry)에 주어가 없으므로 사물을 선행사로 취하는 주격 관계대명사인 which나 that이 빈칸에 올 수 있다. 따라서 (A) that이 정답이다.

어휘 examine 조사하다, 검토하다 factor 요인 affect 영향을 미치다 cost of a raw material 원자재 가격 automotive industry 자동차 산업

5 모든 광고물은 출판물이 진열되기를 바라는 배포일보다 최소 15일 전에 도착해야 한다.

해설 빈칸 앞의 in 이하는 선행사인 the release date of the issue를 수식해 주는 관계명사절이다. 빈칸에 올 관계대명사는 선행사 the release date를 받고 전치사 in과 함께 쓰일 수 있는 (B) which가 되어야 한다. '전치사+관계대명사'의 형태는 앞 문장과의 공통 명사가 뒤 문장에서 전치사의 목적어일 때 쓰인다.

어휘 prior to ~에 앞서 release 발표, 출시, 공개 display 진열하다

6 Delly Catering Service 사는 지난 10년 동안 이 지역에서 서비스 한 외식업체이며, 현재 이 지역의 모든 행사에 대해 30% 할인된 가격을 제공하고 있습니다.

해설 분사 선택 문제이다. [명사 (a catering company) + ---- + 명사 (the region)]의 구조이다. 빈칸에는 능동의 의미를 갖도록 현재분사 형태를 써야 한다. 따라서 (B) serving이 정답이다. 빈칸 앞에 which is가 생략되었다.

어휘 catering 음식 제공 서비스 region 지역 currently 현재 discount 할인하다; 할인

7 직원들은 오전 7시 30분까지 회의실로 와야 하며, 그 후에 신입 사원들을 소개하고 회사 정책을 검토하는 간단한 설명회가 있을 예정이다.

해설 빈칸 앞에 전치사 after가 있고 때를 나타내는 선행사 7:30 A.M.이 있으므로 빈칸에는 전치사와 함께 쓰일 수 있는 사물에 쓰는 관계대명사 (B) which가 와야 한다. after which는 관계부사 when으로 바꿔 쓸 수 있다. (A) while은 '~동안'을 뜻을 지닌 접속사이며 (C) where은 장소를 나타내는 선행사 다음에 오는 관계부사이고 (D) what은 선행사를 포함하는 관계대명사이다.

어휘 report 출두하다 boardroom 회의실 information session 설명회 review 검토하다 policy 정책, 방침

8 인사 변동 양식에는 개인정보가 바뀐 직원들을 위한 칸을 포함하고 있다.

해설 빈칸 앞에 오는 선행사 'those employees'를 수식하는 관계절을 이끄는 관계대명사가 와야 하는 자리이다. 빈칸에 들어갈 관계대명사는 뒤에 오는 명사절 'personal status'를 꾸며주어 '~의 개인 사정'이라는 의미가 되도록 해야 하므로 빈칸에 가장 적절한 관계대명사는 소유격 (D) whose이다.

어휘 personnel change form 인사 변동 양식 status 상황, 상태

9 유감스럽게도, 토론이 끝난 후 회계사의 결정을 존중하지 않을 사람들이 있을 것으로 보인다.

해설 보기에서 of which나 of whom의 경우 수식을 받는 선행사가 없기 때문에 부적절하며, <전치사+관계대명사> 뒤에는 주어, 동사의 완벽한 문장이 와야 하는데, 여기서는 빈칸 뒤에 주어가 없으므로 오답이다. 복합관계대명사 (B) whatever(= anything which)는 의미상 회계사의 결정을 존중하는 주체가 되기에는 어색하다. 대명사 those는 관계대명사 who의 수식을 받아 '~하는 사람들'이라는 의미로 쓰인다. 따라서 정답은 (A) those who이다.

어휘 unfortunately 유감스럽게도, 공교롭게도 discussion 토론 respect ~을 존중하다, 존경하다 accountant 회계사 decision 결정

10 Nutty 사는 2층 공사할 때 생기는 소음이 발생시킨 모든 문제에 대해서 사과한다.

해설 problems를 후치 수식하는 형용사를 선택하는 문제이다. 분사를 형용사처럼 사용할 때에는 분사와 피수식어와의 관계가 가장 중요하다. 피수식어가 분사가 나타내는 행동을 직접 행할 수 있는 경우(능동)라면 현재분사(-ing)가 적당하고 행동을 당하는 경우(수동)라면 과거분사(p.p.)가 어울린다. 이 문제는 문제가 발생하는 것이기 때문에 정답은 (D) caused이다.

어휘 apologize 사과하다

11 환불을 원하신다면 원래 주문에 제공된 배송 라벨을 붙여 주십시오.

해설 빈칸의 단어가 없어도 문장은 완벽하게 쓰일 수 있다. 따라서 문장의 필수 구성요소인 주어, 동사, 목적어 등은 아닐 것이다. 그렇다면 앞의 명사를 수식해 주는 수식어구를 찾는다. the shipping label은 제공되는 것이므로 수동형의 과거분사인 (B) provided가 정답이다. (which is) provided에서 '관계대명사+be동사'가 생략된 문장이다.

어휘 attach 첨부하다, 붙이다 refund 환불

12 마이애미에 있는 한 호텔이 일주일 이상 머무르는 고객들에게 무료 영화 티켓을 제공하기로 결정했다.

해설 적절한 분사 형태를 고르는 문제이며, customers는 머무르는 주체가 되므로 (D) staying이 정답이다.

어휘 offer 제공하다 free 무료의 stay 머무르다

〈13-16〉 다음은 광고에 관한 문제이다.

하급 회계 보조원 구함

메이드스톤 에듀케이션 서비스는 금융시장과 생명과학, 컴퓨터 교육 그리고 공공부문에 집중하는 전문 교육회사입니다.

우리는 현재 하급 회계 보조직으로 일할 유능한 사람을 찾고 있습니다. 재무부장에게 보고하는 하급 회계 보조원은 채무자와 채권자, 은행, 비용 관리를 제1의 책무로 두면서 재무부 내에서 중요한 역할을 할 것입니다.

합격자는 엄격한 마감일을 맞출 수 있는 융통성 있는 팀 플레이어가 될 것입니다. 비슷한 분야에서 최소 1~2년의 경력을 우대합니다. 회계 소프트웨어의 지식을 요구합니다. 광범위하고 국제적인 고객기반을 두고서 즐겁고 아주 혁신적인 환경에서 일하는 데 관심이 있는 분은 메이드스톤 에듀케이션에 연락해 주시기 바랍니다.

이 직책에 지원하기 위해, 여러분의 이력서를 뉴욕 매이드스톤 에듀케이션 서비스 인사부 사서함 4059로 보내 주시기 바랍니다.

어휘 professional 전문적인 focus on ~에 초점을 맞추다 literacy 읽고 쓰는 능력 significant 상당한 strict 엄격한 advantage 이점, 이득 required 필수적인, 요구된 enjoyable 즐거운, 유쾌한 innovative 혁신적인 extensive 광범위한 talented 재능 있는

13

해설 'as Maidstone Education Services focuses on financial markets, ~'의 문장에서 주어(Maidstone Education Services)가 주절의 주어와 동일하므로 접속사와 함께 생략하고 목적어(financial markets, ~)를 취한 동사 focuses on을 현재분사로 바꾼 분사구문 문장이므로 (D) focusing이 정답이 된다.

14 (A) 회사 확장에 대비하여 회계 보조직 두 명이 고용되었습니다.
(B) 재무부장으로 당신이 승진되었음을 알리게 돼서 기쁩니다.
(C) 우리는 현재 하급 회계 보조직으로 일할 유능한 사람을 찾고 있습니다.
(D) 당신은 재무부장으로의 진급 대상으로 고려되고 있습니다.

해설 빈칸 앞은 회사설명이 나와 있고 빈칸 바로 뒤는 해야 하는 일들과 자격 요건들이 나열되고 있는 것으로 보아 보기 중 구인을 알리는 (C)가 정답이다.

15

해설 play a role은 '역할을 하다'를 뜻하는 관용 표현. 따라서 (D) role이 정답이 된다. (A) lead 선도, 지휘 (B) job 일, 직업 (C) post 기둥, 푯말

16

해설 선택지의 구성으로 보아 알맞은 관계대명사를 찾는 문제이다. 'team player(선행사-사람) ---- can meet(동사) strict deadlines(목적어)' 구조이므로 빈칸은 주격 관계대명사 (C) who가 들어갈 자리이다. (A) which는 사물명사를 선행사로 취하며, (B) what은 선행사를 포함한 관계대명사(the thing that), (D) whom은 목적격 관계대명사로 '선행사+목적격 관계대명사+주어+동사' 구조를 갖는다.

UNIT 15 명사절과 명사절 접속사

SPARTA Check-UP! 1 p. 133

1 (B) **2** (B) **3** (D)

1 어느 누구도 우리 부서에 대해 접수된 불만 사항이 있었다고 말해주지 않았기 때문에, 이 문제를 살펴볼 시간이 필요하다.

해설 told의 목적어로서 명사절 연결어가 필요한데, 빈칸 뒤의 절이 완전한 문장이므로 (B) that이 적절하다.

어휘 complaint 불평, 불만 file (신청·항의 등을) 제출[제기]하다

2 이 새로운 기계의 좋은 점들 중 하나는 그것은 분명히 에너지를 절약하기 위해서 만들어졌다는 것이다.

해설 be동사의 보어 자리에 문장을 이끄는 명사절 접속사를 구하는 문제로, 뒤에 완전한 문장이 있으므로 (B) that이 정답이다.

어휘 aspect 양상, 측면 conserve 보존하다, 절약하다

3 내년에 은퇴할 것인지 질문받았을 때 Frederic 씨는 절대 일을 그만두지 않을 거라고 했다.

해설 whether는 'if ~ or not(~인지 아닌지)' 의 의미로 'whether+절'의 패턴을 취하거나 "whether A or B/whether A or not"으로도 쓰인다. 이 문장은 원래 'When (Mr. Frederic was) asked whether he will retire next year, he said ~'이었으나, 종속절과 주절의 주어가 같으므로 생략하고 be동사도 함께 생략해 준 분사구문이 적용되었다.

어휘 retire 은퇴하다 quit 그만두다

SPARTA Check-UP! 2 p. 134

1 (A) **2** (A) **3** (D)

1 보고서 조사결과는 손님들이 실제 매장을 방문하는 것보다 온라인으로 주문하는 것을 선호한다는 것을 보여 준다.

해설 빈칸은 indicate의 목적어 역할을 할 수 있는 명사절 접속사 자리이다. 뒤에 완전한 문장이 왔으므로 (A) that이 정답이다. 참고로 indicate는 명사절 접속사 that을 자주 취하는 동사 중 하나이다.

어휘 finding 조사결과 prefer A to B B보다 A를 더 선호하다

2 마케팅 부장은 하계 관광 캠페인에 관한 모든 것이 완벽하다는 것을 확인했다.

해설 형용사 뒤의 명사절 연결어는 (A) that이다. made sure의 목적어로 뒤의 문장을 연결하는 명사절 접속사가 답이 되므로 that이 정답이다.

어휘 make sure that ~임을 확신(확인)하다

3 Pannel 사의 평면 TV는 이미 할인된 상태이기 때문에, 이번 주말 세일에 해당하지 않을 것이다.

해설 the fact that S+V (완전한 절) '주어가 동사라는 사실'의 문장이다. the fact와 that 이하의 내용이 동격이므로 정답은 (D) that이다.

어휘 flat-screen television 평면 텔레비전 qualify for ~의 자격을 얻다

SPARTA Check-UP! 3 p. 135

1 (D) **2** (B) **3** (A)

1 올여름 사람들 사이에 떠도는 의문은 과연 사람들이 Anna Lopez의 새 CD를 들을 것인지 여부이다.

해설 be동사 다음 보어 자리로 명사절 접속사가 들어가야 할 자리로 의미상 '사람들이 새로운 CD를 들을지 말지가 의문이다.'라는 표현이 되므로 정답은 (D) whether이다.

어휘 in the air (소문 등이) 퍼져서

2 Arizona Microtek 사가 MSL 모델을 계속 만들 것인지 아닌지 결정하고 나면, 우리는 다음에 해야 할 업무가 무엇인지 알게 될 것이다.

해설 타동사 decide의 목적어 자리이며 절을 이끄는 명사절 접속사가 필요하다. 의미상 '모델을 계속 만들 것인지 아닌지 결정하다'라는 뜻이므로 (B) whether가 정답이다.

어휘 once 일단 ~하면, ~하자마자 manufacture 제조[생산]하다 assignment 연구 과제, 할당된 임무

3 Ace Electronics의 Brian Cox 사장은 Max Express 사와 계약을 연장할지 말지를 놓고 숙고하고 있다.

해설 whether는 '~인지 아닌지'를 의미하면서 'whether+주어+동사 또는 'whether+to부정사'의 구조를 취할 수 있으므로 정답은 (A) whether이다.

어휘 consider 고려하다, 숙고하다 renew 갱신하다 contract 계약

SPARTA Check-UP! 4 p. 136

1 (C) **2** (A) **3** (C)

1 관리자들은 어떻게 회사가 비용을 계속해서 최소화할 수 있는지 아이디어를 내놓도록 요구 받을 것이다.

해설 회사가 비용을 줄이는 방법을 이야기하고 있고, 빈칸 이하가 완전한 절의 구조를 갖추고 있다. 방법을 이야기하는 명사절 접속사 (C) how가 적합하다.

어휘 contribute 기부하다 기여하다 minimize 최소화하다

2 어떤 모델을 선택하든, 에어컨과 오디오 시스템은 차량에 무료로 설치될 것이다.

해설 선택하는 모델에 상관없이 설치해 준다는 의미이므로 (A) Whichever (=anything which)가 적절하다.

어휘 install 설치하다 free of charge 무료로

3 귀하가 어떤 것을 선택하시든 이번 주말까지 배송될 수 있음을 보증합니다.

해설 복합관계대명사는 '선행사+관계대명사'의 형태의 선행사를 포함한 관계대명사로 명사절과 양보 부사절의 기능을 하며, 불완전한 문장을 이끈다. 빈칸은 명사절 접속사 that 다음, 빈칸을 포함한 주어 (---you choose will be ~)자리이므로 복합관계대명사 (A) whoever와 (C) whichever 중 해석을 통해 적절한 복합관계대명사를 선택해야 한다. 의미상 'whichever = anything which'로 '~하는 어떤 것이든지'가 가장 어울리므로 정답은 (C) whichever가 된다. (B) whenever와 (D) however는 복합관계부사이므로 문장에서 주어 역할을 할 수 없다.

어휘 assure 보증하다 choose 선택하다 deliver 배달하다

SPARTA PRACTICE
p. 137

1 that	**2** that	**3** that	**4** That
5 that	**6** what	**7** what	**8** that
9 that	**10** that	**11** that	**12** whether
13 whether	**14** Whoever	**15** whichever	

1 그는 아파트를 나서기 전에 문이 모두 잠겼는지 확인했다.

해설 동사 ensure의 목적어절로 완전한 문장 all the doors 이하를 연결할 수 있는 접속사 that이 필요하다.

어휘 ensure 확인하다　lock 잠그다

2 인사부장은 회사 고용 정책이 3월부터 변경될 것이라고 밝혔습니다.

해설 [동사+-----+문장] 형태이다. indicated 뒤에 완전한 문장 형태이므로 문장을 명사 성질로 만드는 명사절 접속사 that을 써야 한다.

어휘 indicate 나타내다, 보여주다　hiring policy 고용 정책　starting ~부로

3 그들은 주문한 카탈로그가 영업일 3일 이내에 도착할 것임을 보장했다.

해설 목적절이 완전한 문장이므로 that이 정답이다.

어휘 guarantee 보장하다　business day 영업일

4 좌석이 좁다는 것이 항공 여행객들이 자주 하는 불만이었다.

해설 완전한 문장인 seats are small을 이끌 수 있는 것은 접속사 that이다.

어휘 frequent 잦은　complaint 불만

5 분석가는 그 회사가 파산하지 않을 것이고 오히려 이익을 낼 거라고 예측했다.

해설 접속사 that으로 완전한 형태의 목적어 절을 이끌고 있다. what은 뒤에 불완전한 절이 와야 한다.

어휘 predict 예측하다　go bankrupt 파산하다　profit 이익

6 주지사가 예산을 줄이기 위해 무엇을 했는지는 잘 알려져 있다.

해설 뒤 문장 the governor did의 목적어가 없이 불완전하다. 불완전한 절을 이끌 수 있는 what이 정답이다.

어휘 reduce 줄이다

7 성취도 평가는 개선이 필요한 부분을 직원들이 알게 하는 방법의 하나로 사용된다.

해설 동사 need to be 이하 절의 주어가 보이지 않는다. 관계사 what(= the thing which)이 정답이다.

어휘 performance evaluation 성취도 평가　improve 개선하다

8 Northlake Holdings 사 사장인 Sean Bean 씨는 올가을 공사 마감일을 맞출 수 있을 것으로 기대한다.

해설 '~을 기대하다'라는 뜻의 [be hopeful that 완전한 문장] 구조로 that을 써야 한다.

어휘 construction 공사　deadline 마감일　meet 충족시키다

9 지난 분기 보고서는 Global Electronics의 실적이 예상보다 낮았음을 보여 주었습니다.

해설 [동사+-----+완전한 문장] 형태이다. 뒤에 완전한 문장이 이어지므로 that을 써야 한다.

어휘 quarterly report 분기 보고서　earnings 수익　lower 더 낮은

10 내일부터 새로운 복장 규정이 시행될 거라는 것을 모든 사람이 알고 있다.

해설 형용사 aware 다음 the new dress 이하 절을 이끌 수 있는 것은 접속사 that이다.

어휘 dress code 복장규정　take effect 효력이 발생하다

11 접수원의 책무 중 하나는 나가는 소포 발송이 올바르게 처리되었는지 확인하는 것입니다.

해설 [make sure that 완전한 문장]은 '~을 확실하게 하다'의 숙어 표현으로 that을 써야 한다.

어휘 desk clerk 접수원　responsibility 책무　outgoing 나가는 package 소포　address 처리하다　correctly 올바르게

12 프로젝트는 대규모 사업이라, 나는 그가 혼자서 모든 일을 할 수 있을 것인지 의문이다.

해설 명사절을 이끄는 접속사 whether이 정답이다. 뒤 문장이 완전하므로 what은 들어갈 수 없다.

어휘 huge 큰　undertaking 사업, 프로젝트　by oneself 혼자서

13 나는 Nick에게 정부가 자금을 댄 연구프로젝트를 끝마쳤는지 아닌지 물었다.

해설 뒤에 or not이 나왔고 '~인지 아닌지'란 의미인 접속사 whether이 정답이다.

어휘 research 연구　fund 자금을 대다

14 어느 누가 샘플을 주문했더라도 하루가 가기 전에 배송부서에서 가져가는 것이 좋다.

해설 선행사+관계대명사가 합해진 Whoever가 정답. 문제에서는 명사절을 이끌면서 'anyone who(~하는 사람은 누구라도)'의 의미이다.

어휘 order 주문하다　department 부서

15 그런 경우라면 전화나 이메일로 연락해 주시면 귀하가 원하시는 대로 교환이나 환불해 드리겠습니다.

해설 정답은 anything that의 뜻을 가진 복합관계대명사 whichever가 정답이다. 뒤에 (주어)+동사가 오고 '선호하는 것은 어느 쪽이라도'의 의미이다.

어휘 replacement 교환　refund 환불

SPARTA ACTUAL TEST
p. 138

1 (A)	**2** (C)	**3** (B)	**4** (A)	**5** (D)	**6** (A)
7 (B)	**8** (C)	**9** (C)	**10** (D)	**11** (D)	**12** (D)
13 (D)	**14** (D)	**15** (D)	**16** (A)		

1 저희는 회의실에서 음식을 먹고 음료 마시는 것을 삼갈 것을 요청 드립니다.

해설 동사 ask와 you please ~ 절을 연결해 주는 접속사 (A) that이 정답이다.

어휘 refrain from ~을 삼가다

2 당신이 우리의 점포나 사무실, 유통센터 등 어디에서 일하든지 우리 IMP 그룹에서 당신이 성취할 수 있는 것에는 한계가 없습니다.

해설 빈칸에는 전치사 on의 목적어로서 명사절을 이끌 수 있는 연결어가 필요하고, 전치사 on의 명사절로 동사 achieve의 목적어가 빠진 불완전한 문장이 왔으므로 (C) what이 와야 한다.

어휘 corporate 회사　distribution center 유통센터　achieve 성취하다

3 고객들이 회사의 서비스를 계속 이용하는지 여부는 서비스 요금보다는 회사가 제공하는 서비스의 질에 달려 있을 것이다.

해설 문장에서 주어가 될 수 있는 명사절 접속사를 묻는 문제로, (B) Whether (~인지 아닌지)가 정답이 된다.

어휘 client 고객 retain 보유하다, 유지하다 depend on ~에 달려 있다 quality 품질 fee 요금, 수수료

4 저희는 회사에서 사용할 5색 프린터를 귀사에 주문하고 싶다는 것을 알려드립니다.

해설 4형식으로 쓰인 'advise+목적어+that+S+V'의 형태가 수동이 된 표현이다. 답은 (A) that이다.

어휘 please be advised that (공식 편지 등에서) ~라는 사실을 알려 드립니다

5 Comfort 항공사는 예정된 수리로 인해 현재 시간부터 1월 1일까지 항공편을 제한 운항하게 되었음을 고객들께 알려 드립니다.

해설 inform+목적어+that S+V (4형식 표현) '목적어에게 S가 V하다고 알리다'라는 뜻의 표현이다. 명사절 접속사 that 다음에는 완전한 문장이 나와야 한다.

어휘 inform ~에게 알리다 scheduled 예정된

6 정부 관리들은 그 법안을 통과시킬지 말지를 두고 논쟁을 벌였다.

해설 전치사의 목적어 자리로 명사절 접속사 자리이다. whether or not to 부정사(to V 할지 말지) 표현을 숙지하면 좋다.

어휘 government officer 정부 관리, 공무원 pass the bill 법안을 가결하다, 통과시키다 quarrel 싸우다, 다투다

7 개봉이 되었든 그렇지 않든 간에 컴퓨터 소프트웨어 제품은 환불되지 않기 때문에 고객들은 주의해야 한다.

해설 [--- A or B]의 구조이다. 'A이든 B든 간에'가 문맥에 맞으므로 빈칸에는 (B) whether를 써야 한다.

어휘 careful 주의 깊은 refundable 환불 가능한 whether ~인지 어떤지 besides 그 외에

8 효과적으로 경쟁하기 위해, 회사는 그 분야 경쟁업체들이 무엇을 성취하고자 하는지를 알고 있어야 한다.

해설 전치사 of의 목적어로 명사절이 오는 경우이다. '~을 이룩하다, 성취하다'의 의미를 지니고 있는 타동사 accomplish 다음에 목적어 역할을 하는 단어가 없다. what은 주어나 목적어가 없는 문장에서 주어나 목적어의 역할을 하면서 동시에 문장과 문장을 이어주는 접속사의 역할을 한다. 따라서 문제에서 문장과 문장을 이어주는 역할을 하면서 accomplish의 목적어 역할도 하는 (C) what이 정답이 된다. 접속사인 (A) that, (B) whether, (D) how는 뒤의 문장이 완벽해야 한다.

어휘 compete 경쟁하다 effectively 효과적으로 be aware of ~을 알다, 인식하다 competitor 경쟁자, 경쟁상대 try to ~하려고 하다 accomplish 성취하다, 이룩하다 whether ~이든지 아니든지

9 전국적인 조사는 정부가 이라크 사람들의 마음을 얻는 싸움에서 졌다는 것을 보여 준다.

해설 빈칸 앞에 주어, 동사가 있고 빈칸 뒤도 주어 동사가 갖추어진 문장이므로 문장을 이끄는 접속사가 쓰여야 한다. suggest는 '~라는 것을 암시하다, 시사하다'의 뜻이므로 목적절로 쓰이기 위해서는 that이 필요하다. 따라서 정답은 (C) that이다. (B) on, (D) for는 전치사이기 때문에 바로 제거하고, (A) if는 의미상 맞지 않는다.

어휘 nationwide 전국적인 battle 싸움, 전쟁

10 당신이 신입사원이든 현재 직원이든 간에, 시장점유율을 확장하기 위한 다음 주 연수회에 등록할 수 있다.

해설 부사절을 이끌며 뒤의 or와 어울려야 하므로 (D) whether가 정답이다.

어휘 enroll in 등록하다 expand 확장하다, 늘리다

11 고객들은 우리 사무용 가구들이 어떻게 만들어지는지 볼 수 있도록 Birmingham 공장 견학에 초대되었다.

해설 동사 see 다음에 절이 왔다. how는 to부정사나 절을 이끌어 '~하는 방법, 어떻게 ~하는가'의 뜻을 지닌다. [주어+동사] 구조가 '우리 가구가 만들어진다'로 부사 수식이 덧붙을 수 있으므로 (D) how '어떻게'가 답이다.

어휘 tour 둘러보다 factory 공장 office furniture 사무 가구

12 Harper 씨의 발표가 Walton Motor 사의 임원들에게 얼마나 설득력 있었는지 아직 확실하지 않습니다.

해설 품사 어형 문제로 how 절의 문장 구조를 파악하는 것이 관건이다. [how+----+주어(Ms. Harper)+동사(was)] 구조에서 빈칸은 형용사, 부사가 가능한데 뒤에 연결되는 주어, 동사에서 동사가 be동사이면 보어로서 형용사가, 일반 동사이면 동사 수식 부사가 와야 한다. 따라서 형용사 (D) persuasive가 답이 된다.

어휘 presentation 발표(회) executive 임원 persuade 설득하다 persuasive 설득력 있는

〈13-16〉 다음은 설명서에 관한 문제이다.

내일 열릴 바비큐 모임에 70명 정도의 인원이 참석할 것으로 예상됩니다. 4시간 동안 우리가 무엇을 할 수 있을지 봅시다. 우리는 빵을 많이 만들어야 할 것 같은데 당장 시작해볼까요.

여기 좋은 빵을 만드는 단계가 있습니다. <u>작은 실수로도 빵이 잘못 만들어질 수 있으니 잘 읽으시기 바랍니다.</u>

첫 번째, 그릇에 밀가루와 물을 섞습니다. 여기 이미 밀가루를 섞어 놨기 때문에 우리가 할 일은 물과 섞기만 하면 됩니다. 반죽 위에 소금을 살짝 뿌려 주시고 375도로 8분 동안, 혹은 빵이 부풀어 오를 때까지 반죽을 구워 냅니다.

자, 빵이 만들어졌습니다. 아시다시피, 다른 조에서 고기와 파스타를 담당하고 있고, 우리는 꽤 쉬운 편입니다.

어휘 bread 빵 step 단계 flour 밀가루 bowl 그릇 rise 오르다 be in charge of ~을 담당하다 recipe 조리법 substitute 대체하다 slightly 조금

13

해설 문장의 주어는 Around 70 people 복수이고 대략 '70명 정도가 참석할 것이라고 예상되는 것'이므로 수동태인 (D) are expected가 정답이다.

14

해설 본동사 see의 목적절을 만드는 문제이다. see 뒤에 목적어가 와야 하는데, 뒤에 문장이 이어지므로 we can do 이하를 목적절로 바꿔줘야 한다. 목적절을 만들 수 있는 것은 that과 what이 있는데 do의 목적어가 빠져 있으므로 불완전한 문장을 이끄는 (D) what이 정답.

15 (A) 간단한 저녁 식사와 파티 음식들의 요리법들을 쉽게 찾을 수 있습니다.
(B) 성함과 전화번호를 저희 호출기 555-1272번에 남겨 주십시오.
(C) 그 조리법에서는 마가린을 버터 대신으로 쓸 수 있습니다.
(D) 작은 실수로도 빵이 잘못 만들어질 수 있으니 잘 듣고 배우시기 바랍니다.

해설 빈칸 앞 내용은 다음의 내용으로는 좋은 빵을 만드는 단계를 나열할 것이라는 것을 예상할 수 있고 빈칸 다음은 그 단계를 나열하고 있으므로 보기 중 적절하게 이어줄 문장은 주의해서 보라는 (D)이다.

16

해설 'Sprinkle salt ---- on top of the dough,'이 문장은 주어가 없이 명령형의 문장으로 완전한 문장이다. 괄호 안에 올 수 있는 것은 부사밖에 없으므로 (A) slightly가 정답이다.

UNIT 16 부사절과 부사절 접속사

SPARTA Check-UP! 1 p. 141

1 (A) 2 (D) 3 (A)

1 회의가 늦게 시작했음에도 불구하고 회의가 끝나기 전에 우리는 합의에 도달할 수 있었다.

해설 빈칸은 문장과 문장을 연결하는 접속사 자리로, '비록 ~임에도 불구하고'를 뜻하는 (A) Although가 문맥상 적절하다.

어휘 come to an agreement 합의에 이르다

2 정비가 끝날 때까지 컴퓨터 사용이 일시 정지될 것이다.

해설 문맥상 '~까지'를 뜻하는 접속사 (D) until이 필요하다. 뒤에 <주어+동사>가 있으므로 (C) up to는 '~까지'라는 의미는 맞으나 전치사이므로 답이 될 수 없다.

어휘 access 접근 suspend 정지하다

3 글리슨 씨는 새로운 영업팀에 배정된 이후로 계약을 하나도 따내지 못하고 있다.

해설 「접속사+주어+동사」 형태가 되어야 할 부사절에는 팀 배정을 받은 과거 사실이, 주절에는 '계약을 따내지 못하고 있다'는 현재까지의 진행 사항에 대한 내용이 제시되어 있다. 두 절을 연결할 수 있는 접속사로는 '~한 이래로'의 뜻을 가진 (A) Since가 가장 적절하다.

어휘 assign (사람을) 배치하다 win a contract 계약을 성사시키다, 계약을 따내다

SPARTA Check-UP! 2 p. 142

1 (A) 2 (B) 3 (A)

1 우리의 현재 공급업체가 할인을 제공하는 데 동의하지 않는다면, 더 나은 거래를 제공할 수 있는 다른 업체를 찾아봐야 할 것이다.

해설 적절한 접속사 어휘를 묻는 문제. 주절은 '새 업체를 찾아야 할 것이다'이고, 종속절은 '현재의 업체'에 대해 얘기하고 있으므로, 앞뒤의 내용이 상반되는 의미가 적절하다. '현재의 업체가 할인을 제공하는 데 동의하지 않는다면, 다른 업체를 찾을 수밖에 없다'는 의미가 자연스러우므로 정답은 '만약 ~하지 않는다면'의 (A) Unless이다.

어휘 deal 거래 because 왜냐하면 as if 마치 ~처럼

2 시스템 관리자가 너무 중요한 기록을 조작했기 때문에 그것은 회사의 연간 재무 보고서에 중대한 영향을 미쳤다.

해설 so ~ that과 such ~ that 용법을 구별하는 문제. so ~ that과 such ~ that은 둘 다 '너무 ~해서 …하다'를 의미하는 구문이지만 so는 부사, such는 한정사라는 점에서 일반적으로 so ~ that 사이에는 형용사나 부사, such ~ that 사이에는 명사가 위치한다. 빈칸 다음에 important records라는 명사가 위치해 있다는 점에서 (B) such를 선택해야 하는 문제다.

어휘 administrator 관리자, 행정인 manipulate 조작하다 significant 중요한 influence 영향, 영향력 annual financial report 연간 재무 보고서

3 까다로운 감독관은 우리가 다음 날 아침까지 보고서를 제출할 수 있도록 우리들을 늦게까지 남아 있도록 했다.

해설 두 문장을 한 문장으로 적절히 이어줄 수 있는 접속사가 필요하다. 두 절의 의미를 파악해 보면 뒷부분의 절이 '목적'의 의미를 가지고 있음을 알 수 있다. 목적의 의미를 담고 있으며, 종속절을 주절과 연결하는 접속사는 (A) so that '~하기 위해'이다. (B) however(그러나)와 (C) moreover(더욱이)는 접속부사로 혼자서는 두 개의 절을 연결할 수 없다.

어휘 demanding 까다로운 supervisor 감독자 submit 제출하다

SPARTA Check-UP! 3 p. 143

1 (D) 2 (B) 3 (B)

1 새 컴퓨터가 그들 회사에 좋은 투자로 여겨졌는데도 불구하고, 그들은 그것을 사지 않기로 결정했다.

해설 빈칸 다음에 <주어+동사>이므로 접속사가 필요하다. 접속사는 (D) Although뿐이며 나머지 보기는 모두 전치사이다.

어휘 investment 투자

2 제품의 매출 증대를 위해 우리에게 필요한 것은 보다 적극적인 판촉 활동이다.

해설 문장 구조를 살펴보면 전체 문장의 동사가 is이고, 그 앞까지가 문장의 주어 역할을 하는 절이므로, 빈칸에는 접속사 역할을 하는 명사절 접속사 (B) What이 알맞다. 관계부사인 (C) Why와 부사절 접속사인 (A) Although, (D) Because는 뒤에 완전한 문장이 와야 한다.

어휘 boost 경기를 부양하다, 끌어올리다 active 적극적인 promotional activity 판촉 활동

3 날씨가 점점 추워지고 있기 때문에 업무 시간에는 사무실 문을 닫고 히터를 켜 놓아야 한다.

해설 빈칸 뒤에는 '주어 동사, 주어 동사~' 구조가 나와 있으므로 빈칸은 절과 절을 연결해 줄 수 있는 접속사가 들어갈 자리이다. (D) Because of는 전치사이므로 탈락. '날씨가 추워지고 있기 때문에 문을 잘 닫고 히터를 켜라'는 문맥이 자연스러우므로 (B) Now that '~하기 때문에'를 고르면 된다.

어휘 necessary 필요한 turn on ~을 켜다 during the work 업무 시간에

SPARTA Check-UP! 4 p. 144

1 (B) 2 (B) 3 (C)

1 계약서에 서명할 때 Angela Winkler는 그녀의 비서를 동반할 것이다.

해설 부사절 접속사 When 다음에는 문장이 와야 한다. 콤마 전에 동사가 없으므로, 분사구문으로 봐야 한다. 빈칸 뒤 목적어 the agreement가 있으므로 능동태인 (B) signing가 정답이다.

어휘 sign 서명하다 agreement 계약, 협정 accompany (사람과) 동반하다, 동행하다 secretary 비서

2 일단 이사회에 의해서 승인이 되면, 새로운 프로젝트는 11월 21일부터 실행될 것이다.

해설 '일단 승인이 되면'이라는 뜻의 분사구문이 되어야 한다. 분사구문의 주어가 생략되어 있으므로 주절의 주어와 같은 the new project가 부사구문의 주어이다. the new project가 승인되는 것이므로 과거분사인 (B) approved가 정답이다. 동사 approve는 '~을 승인하다'는 뜻의 타동사이므로 (C) approving이 오려면 뒤에 목적어가 와야 한다.

어휘 approve 승인하다 board of directors 이사회 implement 실행하다, 실시하다 as of ~부터

3 Elton이 은퇴하겠다는 공지를 받은 이래, Craig 씨는 후임자를 찾고 있는 중이다.

해설 has been -ing로 주절이 현재완료진행 시제이므로 '그 시점 이후로 계속'되어 왔다는 의미를 가지기 위해 접속사 (C) Since가 적절하다.

어휘 retire 은퇴하다 replacement 후임자

SPARTA Check-UP! 5

p. 145

1 (B) **2** (A) **3** (A)

1 몇몇 지방대학에서 많은 학생들이 채용담당자들을 만날 기회를 가질 수 있는 취업 박람회를 열었다.

해설 관계사로 연결된 문장을 독립절로 만들어 보면 'many students will have chances to meet recruiters in a job fair'가 된다. a job fair가 중복되기 때문에 그 부분을 관계사로 바꾸어야 하는데, a job fair가 장소 개념으로 사용되고 있으므로 장소를 표현하는 관계부사 (B) where가 가장 알맞다.

어휘 job fair 채용 박람회 recruiter 채용담당자

2 휴가를 어디로 가시려고 계획하시건, Top World Travel이 가장 저렴한 항공요금을 제공해 드린다는 것을 믿어 주세요.

해설 완전한 절을 이끌면서 부사절 역할을 할 수 있는 복합관계부사를 선택하는 문제이다. 복합관계부사 (A) Wherever와 (C) However 중, 의미상 (A) Wherever가 적절하다.

어휘 plan 계획하다 lowest 가장 낮은 airfare 항공료

3 복장 규정이 얼마나 엄격하든지 간에, 각자의 개성을 표현할 수 있는 방법은 있다.

해설 'no matter how+형용사/부사 (얼마나 ~할지라도)'는 'however+형용사/부사'와 같은 뜻이다. 정답은 (A) how이다.

어휘 no matter what = whatever 무엇이든지 간에
no matter who = whoever 누구든지 간에
no matter where = wherever 어디든지 간에
no matter when = whenever 언제든지 간에

SPARTA Check-UP! 6

p. 146

1 (B) **2** (B) **3** (D)

1 회사는 우리에게 기숙사를 제공해 준다. 하지만, 전적으로 무상은 아니다.

해설 적절한 의미의 접속부사를 선택하는 문제로 문맥상 빈칸 앞 문장 '회사가 기숙사를 제공한다'와 빈칸 뒤 문장 '무상은 아니다'의 관계가 역접 관계이므로 '그러나'의 의미를 가지고 있는 (B) however가 답이다.

어휘 dormitory 기숙사 free of charge 무료로

2 나는 다음 주 화요일까지 출장이니, 친구들이 전화하거든 내가 가능한 한 빨리 그들에게 회신하겠다고 말해 주세요.

해설 빈칸 앞뒤 문장들이 '~이니까(이유) ~해 달라'는 맥락으로 이어져야 한다. 의미상 적합한 접속부사는 (B) so뿐이다.

어휘 otherwise 그렇지 않다면 furthermore 더욱이

3 우리 회사는 도심에 위치하고 있는데다가, 몇 개의 지하철역과도 아주 가깝다.

해설 접속부사 어휘 문제로, 앞뒤 문장을 연결하는 적합한 단어를 선택하면 된다. 빈칸 앞 내용은 '회사가 도심에 위치하고 있다'이며, 빈칸 뒤 내용은 '몇 개의 지하철역과 아주 가깝다'라는 내용으로 도심에 위치해서 지하철역과 가깝다는 또 다른 장점을 이야기하므로 보기 중 (D) besides(게다가)가 가장 알맞다.

어휘 locate 위치하다 quite 꽤

SPARTA PRACTICE

p. 147

1 If	**2** Although	**3** While	**4** After
5 if	**6** so	**7** Although	**8** before
9 Although	**10** Unless	**11** Although	**12** if
13 finishing	**14** submitted	**15** reviewing	

1 만일 당신이 고속도로를 이용해서 회의장에 갈 계획이라면, 교통 상황에 문제가 없는지 반드시 미리 확인하도록 하십시오.

해설 문맥상 '~한다면'의 뜻을 가진 접속사 If가 정답이다.

어휘 conference 회의 via ~을 통해 ahead of time 시간에 앞서서, 미리

2 비록 제가 당신을 추천하신 분들 중 한 분께는 연락을 취하지 못했지만, 다른 모든 분들이 당신에 대해서 좋게 말하므로 당신을 팀에 합류시키기로 결정했습니다.

해설 빈칸 이하에 절이 나오므로 접속사인 Although가 정답이 된다.

어휘 references 추천(인) warmly 따뜻이 add 추가하다

3 Pierce 씨가 회의에 참석하는 동안 모든 전화를 그의 비서에게로 연결하세요.

해설 빈칸 다음에 완전 구조의 절이 나오므로 앞에는 접속사 While이 와야 한다.

어휘 direct a call 전화상으로 연결하다 administrative assistant 비서

4 Victoria는 휴가에서 돌아와 보니 아주 중요한 고객으로부터 온 전화 몇 통을 받지 못했다는 것을 알게 되었다.

해설 문맥상 '휴가에서 돌아온 후 ~한 사실을 알았다'가 되어야 하므로 접속사 After가 정답이다.

어휘 notice 알다, 인지하다 miss 놓치다

5 직원들은 그들이 직장에 늦게 도착하게 될 경우에 그들의 직속 상관에게 연락해야 한다.

해설 문맥상 조건(~인 경우에)의 의미를 갖는 접속사 if가 답이 된다.

어휘 contact 연락하다 immediate supervisor 직속 상관 anticipate 고대하다

6 내일 외국에서 온 손님들이 참여할 수 있도록 연례 총회의 일정이 다시 조정되었다.

해설 that과 어울릴 수 있는 접속사 찾기 문제로 so가 적절하다. so that '~할 수 있도록' (= in order that S+V)

어휘 reschedule 일정을 재조정하다

7 회계사들은 회사 내에서 일해야 하지만, 회사는 그들에게 특별한 경우에는 재택근무를 하도록 허락할 수도 있다.

해설 빈칸 뒤에는 'S+V, S+V~' 구조가 나와 있으므로 빈칸은 2개의 절을 연

결해 주는 접속사가 들어갈 자리이다.

어휘 work on ~에서 일하다 allow 허락하다 work at home 재택근무하다

8 Benjamin 씨가 고객과의 중요한 미팅을 위해서 CA 호텔에 일찍 도착할 것이니, 그가 체크인하기 전에 모든 게 완전히 준비되어야 합니다.

해설 문장 앞부분에 will be가 쓰였으므로 시간의 부사절을 이끄는 접속사가 아닌지 확인해 볼 필요가 있다. since는 주절에 have+p.p.가 와야 한다.

어휘 meeting with ~와의 회의 be sure that ~를 주의하다, 확실히 하다 fully 완전히, 충분히

9 새로운 기계의 부품들이 즉시 보내져야 한다는 우리의 요구에도 불구하고 그것들이 월말 전까지 도착할 수 없다고 통보 받았다.

해설 빈칸 뒤의 절을 이끌 수 있어야 하고, 문맥상으로도 '양보' 의미의 부사절 접속사 Although가 알맞다.

어휘 request 요청하다 inform 통지하다

10 건설 구역에 관한 어떠한 조치가 취해지지 않는다면 교통체증은 계속해서 악화할 것이다.

해설 뒤에 <S+V>가 쓰였으므로 절을 이끌고 의미상 적절한 접속사 Unless를 써야 한다.

어휘 construction zone 건설 현장 traffic congestion 교통체증

11 비록 생산 수치가 지난해보다 좋지만 여전히 개선해야 할 여지가 있다.

해설 빈칸 뒤에 주어(production figures)와 동사(are)가 있으므로 절을 이끄는 접속사 Although를 써서 문장을 완성해야 한다.

어휘 figure 수치 room for ~을 할 여지

12 만약 제품에 관한 문제가 도매업자와 해결될 수 없을 경우, 제조업자에게 전화하도록 고객들에게 상기시켜야 한다.

해설 뒤에 <S+V>가 쓰였고 문맥상 '~하면' 이라는 조건 부사절 접속사를 써야 하므로 if가 정답이다.

어휘 remind 상기시키다 manufacturer 제조업자 resolve 해결하다 wholesaler 도매업자

13 점심 식사를 마친 후에 Smith 씨는 Sam's Club으로 쇼핑가기로 결정했다.

해설 '접속사 + 주어'가 생략된 분사구문으로 뒤에 목적어가 있으므로 'finishing'을 써서 문장을 완성해야 한다.

어휘 decide to ~을 하기로 결정하다 go shopping 쇼핑가다

14 만약 이번 달 10일까지 지원서가 제출된다면, 그 지원서는 검토될 것이다.

해설 If절 이하 S+V가 생략된 분사형 구문이다. 생략된 주어는 지원서(application)이기 때문에 수동의 의미인 submitted '제출된'이 정답이 된다.

어휘 application 지원서 review 검토하다

15 불만사항을 철저히 검토하고 난 뒤, 회사는 직원 한 사람을 조립 라인에 더 배치하기로 결정했다.

해설 S+V를 생략한 분사형 구문으로 주어인 company가 생략되어 있다. 회사(company)가 검토하는 것이므로 정답은 능동형인 reviewing이다.

어휘 complaint 불만 thoroughly 완전히

SPARTA ✔ ACTUAL TEST

p. 148

1 (A)	**2** (B)	**3** (C)	**4** (D)	**5** (A)	**6** (C)
7 (B)	**8** (B)	**9** (A)	**10** (B)	**11** (B)	**12** (A)
13 (C)	**14** (B)	**15** (D)	**16** (A)		

1 우리가 최종 승인을 하고 재고가 확인될 때까지는 어떠한 종류의 주문도 처리되지 않습니다.

해설 주어 앞에 부정의 No가 들어가 있으므로 내용은 부정문이다. 빈칸 앞의 '어떠한 종류의 주문도 처리되지 않는다'는 문장과 빈칸 뒤의 '우리가 최종 승인을 하고 재고가 확인되다'를 매끄럽게 연결하는 접속사는 (A) until(~까지)이 된다.

어휘 process 처리하다, 진행하다 until ~까지(기간) even 심지어, ~마저도

2 Ben Gardiner가 이전 영업사원의 후임자로 고용되었는데, 그가 그 일에 가장 적합했기 때문이었다.

해설 보기 (A) until, (B) because, (D) so that은 부사절 접속사. (C) not only는 'not only A but also B (A뿐만 아니라 B 역시)'의 상관구문을 이루는 부사로 구성되어 있으므로 빈칸 앞뒤의 문맥을 살펴 답을 고른다. 빈칸 뒤에는 주어, 동사를 갖춘 절이 연결되어 있으므로 (C)는 탈락이다. 빈칸 앞은 '이전 영업사원의 후임으로 고용되었다'는 내용이, 빈칸 뒤에는 '그가 가장 자격이 있다'는 내용이 연결되어 있으므로 고용된 이유가 자격을 갖추었기 때문이라는 이유 접속사가 들어가야 옳다. 따라서 (B) because가 답이 된다.

어휘 employ(= hire) 고용하다 replacement 후임자 former 이전의 sales representative 영업사원 qualified 자격을 갖춘

3 고객들이 여러 서비스 제공업체들의 연락을 받을 수 있지만, 그들이 받은 어떠한 요청에 대해서도 응답할 의무는 없다.

해설 [----+주어(customers)+동사(may be contacted) ~, there is no requirement ~]의 구조를 파악해 볼 때 빈칸은 절을 연결시켜 줄 수 있는 접속사가 필요하다. '고객들이 비록 여러 서비스 업체들의 연락을 받을 수 있지만, 응답의 의무는 없다'는 문맥으로 양보절을 이끄는 접속사 (C) Although가 답이 된다. 복합관계부사인 (D) Whenever(~할 때마다) 역시 절을 이끌 수 있으나 문맥상 주절과 연결이 되지 않는다.

어휘 contact 연락을 취하다 service provider 서비스 제공업체 requirement 필요조건, 요건 respond to ~에 응답하다 solicitation 요청, 간청

4 Julie가 자신에 대해 거의 말을 하지 않았기 때문에, 나는 Julie가 결혼한 줄 몰랐다.

해설 빈칸 앞뒤를 보면 두 개의 완전한 문장이라는 것을 알 수 있다. 따라서 빈칸은 문장을 연결해 주는 접속사가 들어가야 한다는 것을 먼저 짐작해 볼 수 있다. 보기 중 (A) between과 (B) unlike는 품사가 전치사이므로 우선 제외한다. 남은 보기를 넣어 문맥에 맞춰 보면 '~ 때문에'라는 이유의 접속사인 (D) since가 자연스럽다는 것을 알 수 있다.

어휘 seldom 거의 ~않다

5 제조 주문이 보통 겨울 동안 밀려들기 때문에 Shock Snow Boarding 직원들은 이 시기에 초과 근무를 하도록 요구 받는다.

해설 빈칸의 앞 문장과 뒤 문장의 내용은 인과관계에 어울리므로, 접속사 중 인과관계를 나타낼 수 있는 (A) as가 정답이 된다. as는 전치사, 접속사, 부사가 모두 가능하며 각 품사별로 의미가 매우 다양하므로 여러 의미를 잘 알아 두어야 한다. (B) if는 '~ 한다면'을 뜻하는 조건 접속사, (C) once는 '~하자마자'라는 뜻의 부사절 접속사이다. (D) whether는 '~이든, 아니든'을 의미하며 whether A or B의 형태로 사용된다.

어휘 ask 묻다, 부탁하다 overtime 초과 근무 manufacturing order 제조 명령, 제조 주문 surge 밀려오다

6 개개인이 Tunnel 박물관을 아무리 자주 방문하더라도, 그곳에는 항상 관람객들의 흥미를 끄는 새로운 전시품이 있다.

해설 부사 often과 함께 어울리며, 양보의 부사절을 이끌 수 있는 복합관계부사는 보기 중 (C) However이다.

어휘 exhibit 전시품, 진열품 interest 관심, 흥미

7 Office Max가 그들의 웹상에서 온라인 결제 옵션을 제공하기 시작한 이후에는 당신이 구매하고자 하는 사무용품을 주문하는 것이 더 쉬워질 것입니다.

해설 빈칸 뒤에는 [주어(Office Max)+동사(starts)+목적어(offering an online payment option)]의 구조로 구성되어 있으므로 빈칸 앞의 문장과 연결되기 위해 접속사가 필요하다. 따라서 접속사로 쓰일 수 있는 (B) after가 답이 된다. 문맥상으로도 '온라인 결제 옵션이 제공된 이후에 주문이 더욱 더 쉬워진다는 의미로 자연스럽게 연결된다. 보기 (A) instead는 '그 대신에'라는 부사, (B) after '~이후에'는 전치사 혹은 접속사, (C) during '~동안에'라는 전치사, (D) beyond '~을 넘어'라는 전치사이다.

어휘 place an order 주문하다 office supplies 사무용품 online payment option 온라인 결제 방식

8 Harley 씨는 발표 준비를 아직 마치지 못했지만 월례 영업 회의를 이끌어 가기 위해 제시간에 그것을 완성할 것이다.

해설 문맥상 알맞은 접속사를 선택하는 문제로, 빈칸이 포함된 종속절과 주절의 의미를 먼저 파악한다. 종속절은 Harley 씨가 아직 발표 준비를 끝내지 못했다는 것이고, 주절은 회의를 이끌기 위해 제시간에 그것(발표 준비)을 준비할 것이란 내용이므로 상반된 내용을 연결해 주는 양보 접속사 (B) Even though가 적절하다.

어휘 finish -ing ~하는 것을 끝내다 presentation 발표 complete 완성하다, 완수하다 in time 제시간에 lead 이끌어가다 monthly 월례의 sales meeting 영업 회의

9 귀하가 등록하신 어학 강좌가 전자기록부에 바르게 등록되어 있지 않다면, 저희가 실수를 바로 잡을 수 있도록 가급적 빨리 연락해 주시기 바랍니다.

해설 알맞은 접속사를 찾는 문제. 빈칸 앞뒤를 보면 연락해 달라는 앞의 내용(please contact us)과 실수를 바로잡는다는 뒤의 내용(we may rectify the error)이 매끄럽게 연결되기 위해서 '~하기 위해'라는 뜻의 '목적'을 나타내는 접속사 (A) so that이 정답임을 알 수 있다. (B) if는 조건 접속사면서 이미 앞에 조건부 문장이 나와 있으므로 오답이 되고, (C) which는 관계대명사, (D) due to는 원인을 나타내는 전치사이므로 답이 될 수 없다.

어휘 sign up for (~을) 등록하다 record 기록하다, 녹음하다 correctly 정확하게, 올바르게 electronic 전자의 register 등록하다; 기록부 contact 연락하다 rectify 바로잡다 error 실수

10 고객들이 매일의 소비 패턴을 알려 주는 월간 명세서를 받기 시작한 이후로 가장 사용량이 많은 시간대의 전기 사용이 6개월 동안 4% 감소했다.

해설 보기 중에 전치사, 접속사가 모두 등장한 문제로, 먼저 빈칸 뒤에 절이 연결되어 있는지, 명사구가 연결되어 있는지 확인한다. 빈칸 뒤 [주어(customers)+동사(began receiving)~] 형태의 절이 연결되어 있으므로 전치사 (A) despite는 일단 답에서 제외한다. 빈칸 앞, 뒤의 문맥을 살펴볼 때, 고객들이 매일의 소비 패턴을 알려 주는 월간 명세서를 받기 시작한 이후로 전기 사용량이 감소했다는 것이므로 '~이래로'의 의미를 갖는 접속사 (B) since가 답이 된다.

어휘 electricity 전기 peak hour 최대치를 나타내는 시간, 가장 혼잡한 시간 decline 감소하다 monthly statement 월간 명세서 illustrate (설명을 위해 실례나 삽화 등을) 이용하다, 분명히 보여 주다 consumption 소비

11 지역 책임 이사가 인도로 출장 간 동안에 Marissa에게 타이페이에 있는 대만 본사 운영을 감독하는 일이 맡겨졌다.

해설 빈칸 앞의 문장과 뒤 문장의 내용 관계를 보면, 어떤 접속사가 필요한지 알 수 있다. '지역 담당 이사가 출장 나가 있는 동안에 Marissa가 운영 감독하는 일을 맡았다' 라는 의미가 되어야 하므로 (B) while이 정답이다. (A) due to는 '~때문에', (C) once는 '하자마자', (D) except for '~을 제외하고'라는 뜻이다.

어휘 assign 맡기다 monitor 감독하다 operation 운영 headquarters 본사 regional director 지역 담당 이사 business trip 출장

12 직원은 아무리 바쁠지라도 매 3시간마다 15분씩의 휴식을 취하는 것이 의무 사항입니다.

해설 빈칸 뒤의 busy라는 형용사를 받는 접속사로 적절한 것은 how 계통의 접속사이므로 정답은 (A) no matter how가 된다.

어휘 mandatory 의무적인 break (짧은) 휴식 no matter how 아무리 ~하더라도 so far as ~하는 한 nevertheless ~함에도 불구하고 in order that ~하기 위해

⟨13-16⟩ 다음은 편지에 관한 문제이다.

Tracy Jakes
3100 Timmons 가
텍사스 휴스턴 77027

Jakes 씨께,

최근 Williams 배관 난방 주식회사에서 귀하의 구매에 대해 감사의 말씀 드립니다. 난방 기구를 고객님 사무실용으로 선택해 주셔서 기쁩니다.

저희 회사 정비부서 직원인 Sam Dumiak이 고객님께 전화를 드려서 장비 설치 과정에 관해 의논 드릴 것입니다. 이 기계는 난방 효율을 극대화하기 위해 설계되어 있습니다. 적절한 곳에 설치가 성공적으로 이루어지면 다른 추가 난방기기는 필요 없을 것입니다.

Dumiak 씨가 전화를 드려서 고객님께 세부 내용에 관해 말씀을 드리고 궁금한 점은 어떤 것이든 질문해 주시면 답변 드릴 것입니다.

진심으로,
Karen Chitty, 매니저
Williams 배관 난방 주식회사

어휘 appreciate 감사하다 recent 최근의 heating equipment 난방 기구 installation process 설치 과정 detailed 상세한 donation 기부 properly 적절하게 solar panel 태양 집열판 sharply 급격히 apparatus 기구

13

해설 빈칸에 자연스러운 명사를 고르는 문제이다. 문맥상 'Williams 배관 난방 주식회사에서 --- 해 주신 것에 대해 고맙다'라는 의미가 되어야 하므로 '구입, 구매'의 의미인 (C) purchase가 정답이다.

14

해설 문맥에 맞는 동사 형태를 찾는 문제. 문장을 보면 'Sam Dumiak from our Maintenance Department will call you tomorrow --- the installation process ~' 인데, 이 중 주어는 Sam Dumiak, 동사는 will call, 목적어는 you이다. 따라서 일단 문법적으로 본다면 보기 (A) will discuss와 (D) discusses가 들어가면 동사가 중복되므로 답이 될 수 없다. 따라서 빈칸 앞뒤를 연결해 줄 수 있는 to부정사(~에 관해 논의하기 위해)인 (B) to discuss가 답이 된다.

15 (A) 사무실 난방시스템이 제대로 작동하지 않고 있습니다.
(B) 거주자들은 태양 집열판을 효과적으로 사용하기 때문에 전기료를

아주 조금 지불합니다.
(C) 머지않아, 난방용 석유에 대한 수요가 급격히 떨어질 것입니다.
(D) 이 기계는 난방 효율을 극대화하기 위해 설계되어 있습니다.

해설 배관 난방 회사가 사무실용의 난방기 교체에 대해서 자사를 선택해 준 것을 감사해하고 있는 빈칸 앞 문장과 빈칸 뒤는 추가 난방기가 설치되면 다른 추가 난방기기가 필요 없음을 알리는 글의 문장을 적절하게 이어주는 문장은 난방기의 장점을 설명하는 (D)가 가장 적절하다.

16

해설 빈칸 사이의 문장을 잘 살펴보면 주어와 동사가 갖추어진 완전한 문장이라는 것을 알 수 있다. 따라서 빈칸은 두 문장을 연결해 주는 접속사 (A) once가 답이 된다. (B) afterward는 부사이고 (C) following이나 (D) upon은 전치사이다.

UNIT 17 원급, 비교급, 최상급

SPARTA Check-UP! 1

p. 151

1 (B) **2** (D) **3** (A)

1 성능이 향상된 데스크톱 유닛들은 최대한 능률적으로 업무를 수행할 수 있게 할 것입니다.

해설 as ~ as 사이에는 원급 형용사나 부사가 오므로 명사인 (C) efficiency, 비교급인 (D) more efficient는 답이 될 수 없다. 비교 구문 as ~ as를 지워 보면 빈칸은 동사(perform)를 수식하는 부사 자리임을 알 수 있다. 따라서 정답은 (B).

어휘 upgraded 개량된, 향상된 efficiently 능률적으로

2 그들은 다른 연구원들만큼 능률적이지만, 자세히 분석해 본 결과 그들은 나머지 사람들보다 더 많이 생산하여 더 나은 성과를 얻을 수도 있었다는 점이 밝혀졌다.

해설 뒤에 as가 있는 것으로 볼 때 동등비교 구문 'as ~ as … (…만큼 ~한)'이 되어야 한다. 따라서 정답은 (D).

어휘 efficient 능률적인 researcher 연구원 analysis 분석 indicate 나타내다

3 연료비가 계속 오르고 있는 요즘에는 우리 모두 가능한 한 많은 에너지를 보존하는 것이 중요하다.

해설 원급 비교를 완성하는 as much as possible 구문을 기억해 놓고 풀면 쉽게 고를 수 있다. (B) more와 (C) than은 비교급에 사용되고 (D) very는 정도를 나타내는 부사이다.

어휘 rising 오르고 있는 fuel 연료 important 중요한 conserve 보존하다

SPARTA Check-UP! 2

p. 152

1 (A) **2** (B) **3** (A)

1 주택 시장의 문제들은 경제학자들이 예상했던 것보다 더 강하고 더 오래 지속될 것이다.

해설 빈칸 앞 비교급(stronger and more persistent)의 쓰임으로 미루어 [비교급+than]의 형태를 떠올릴 수 있어야 한다. 따라서 (A) than이 정답이다.

어휘 housing market 주택 시장 persistent 끈질긴, 집요한, 지속되는 foresee 예상하다

2 기업인수 분권화에 대한 우리의 정책은 각 지점에 대한 더 큰 유연성을 부여한다.

해설 비교급을 강조하는 부사(even)이 앞에 보이므로, 뒤에는 비교급 (B) greater가 온다.

어휘 decentralize (중앙 정부의 권력을) 분권화하다 acquisition 습득 (기업)인수, 매입 allow 허용하다 flexibility 유연성

3 이 두 명의 지원자들 중, Park 씨가 급여 업데이트 프로젝트에 임하기에 더 적격이다.

해설 Of these two applicants를 보아 둘 중 한 명을 가리키는 것이므로 비교급이 와야 한다. 나머지 보기는 부사이며 비교급인 (A) better가 정답이다.

어휘 applicant 지원자 qualified 자격이 있는 payroll 급여

SPARTA Check-UP! 3

p. 153

1 (B) **2** (A) **3** (C)

1 우리 K-Dex Express는 국내에서 가장 빠른 배송을 하도록 온 힘을 쏟지만, 당일 배송은 보장할 수 없다.

해설 최상급 문제. [정관사+---+명사]에 들어갈 형용사의 형태로는 최상급인 (B) speediest가 알맞다. (A) more speed와 (D) most speed는 형용사 형태가 아니고, (C) speedily는 부사이므로 오답이다.

어휘 although ~함에도 불구하고 make an effort to ~하려고 노력하다 delivery 배달 guarantee 보장하다 shipping 운송

2 위암 협회는 위암 연구계에서 가장 높이 평가 받는 과학자들 중 몇 명을 과학 프레젠테이션을 위해 모을 것이다.

해설 빈칸은 정관사(the)와 형용사 regarded를 수식해 주는 부사 highly 사이에 위치해 있으므로 뒤에 오는 highly를 수식하여 최상급 표현을 할 수 있는 (A) most가 빈칸에 오는 것이 가장 적절하다. 또한, '~에서 가장 ~한'을 나타낼 때 범위가 되는 'in stomach cancer research'가 나와 있으므로 최상급 표현이 와야 한다. 답은 (A).

어휘 stomach cancer 위암 gather 모으다 regarded 존경 받는 scientific 과학의, 과학상의

3 광범위한 직장 내 훈련은 높은 수준의 생산성을 보장하는 단연 최고의 방법이다.

해설 최상급을 강조해서 '단연 가장 ~한'이란 의미를 만드는 부사를 구하는 문제로 (C) by far가 정답이 된다.

어휘 on-the-job training 직장 내 훈련 method 방법

SPARTA Check-UP! 4

p. 154

1 (B) **2** (C) **3** (C)

1 비행이 5시간 이상 연착된 승객들은 30% 할인된 티켓을 받을 자격이 있다.

해설 관용표현 'more than(~이상)'을 이용하여 '5시간 이상 연착'이라는 의미가 되어야 문맥이 자연스럽다. 정답은 (B).

어휘 delay 지연시키다 qualify 자격이 되다 discounted 할인된

2 광고는 판매 중인 모든 사무용 가구에 실제 할인율 15% 대신, 35% 할인이 적용된다고 명시했다.

해설 관용표현 'rather than(~대신에)'을 이용하여, 적용되는 할인율이 15%가 아니라 35%라고 하는 것이 문맥상 가장 적절하다.

어휘 state 명시하다, 밝히다 discount 할인 actual 실제의

3 우리 회사는 더 이상 당신에게 판매 책임자로서의 서비스를 요구하지 않음을 알려드리게 되어 유감스럽게 생각합니다.

해설 관용표현 'no longer(더 이상~ 않다)'을 이용하여, 회사가 서비스를 더 이상 요구하지 않음을 나타내는 것이 문맥상 알맞다.

어휘 require 요구하다 sales representative 판매 책임자

SPARTA PRACTICE

p. 155

1	most	**2**	lighter	**3**	The greater	**4**	easily
5	stronger	**6**	better	**7**	better	**8**	closer
9	easiest	**10**	most	**11**	a lot	**12**	largest
13	greater	**14**	more quickly	**15**	most		

1 우리 전체 직원 중에서 Paul Nicholls가 가장 책임감 있는 직원이다.

해설 대상이 'Of all of our employees'이므로, 비교급이 아닌 최상급인 most가 적절하다.

어휘 responsible 책임감 있는

2 알루미늄 제품들이 유리보다 더 가볍고 재활용이 가능하다.

해설 뒤에 than이 있는 것으로 미루어 비교급을 써야 함을 알 수 있다.

어휘 light 가벼운, 밝은 recyclable 재활용 가능한

3 제의가 클수록 더 많은 부담을 감수해야 할 것이다.

해설 뒤의 문장이 'the+비교급'으로 시작하므로, 앞 문장도 'the+비교급'으로 일치시킨다.

어휘 pressure 압력, 부담

4 주택 대출은 지금보다 과거에 더 쉽게 받을 수 있었다.

해설 more 앞에 동사를 수식하는 것으로 형용사가 나올 수 없으므로 비교급은 부사를 수식해 줘야 알맞다. 따라서 easily가 비교급을 받아 동사를 수식해 준다.

어휘 housing loan 주택 대출 obtain 취득하다 easily 쉽게

5 SDI 사의 주요 목표는 국내와 국제 부서 간에 훨씬 더 강한 유대를 만드는 것이다.

해설 even이나 much 같은 부사는 비교급을 강조해 주는 부사로 사용된다. 앞의 even을 보면 비교급이 와야 함을 알 수 있다.

어휘 major 주요 objective 목표 establish 설립하다 tie 유대관계 domestic 국내의 international 국제적인

6 두 명의 지원자 중에 Sampson 씨가 그 직책에 더 적합하다.

해설 비교하는 대상이 둘이면 비교급, 셋 이상이면 최상급이다. 'Between the two applicants'라고 했으므로 비교급이 와야 한다.

어휘 applicant 지원자 qualified 자격 있는 position 직책

7 두 컨설턴트 가운데 Wilkinson 씨가 현재 경력 면에서는 더 낫다고 말할 수 있다.

해설 of the two가 있으므로, 'the+비교급'을 써야 한다.

어휘 consultant 상담가, 자문위원 stage 단계 career 경력, 이력

8 내가 정말 인상 깊었던 것은 그 회사의 영업팀이 다른 팀들보다 세부적인 사항에 훨씬 더 세심한 관심을 기울였다는 점이다.

해설 문장에 비교급의 대상 앞에 사용되는 than이 있는 것으로 보아 비교급 형태의 closer가 정답이다.

어휘 impress 인상을 심어주다 pay attention to ~에 집중하다, ~에 관심을 기울이다

9 여러 길 중에서 녹색 라인이 Cicada 빌딩까지 걸어가기에 가장 쉽다.

해설 빈칸 앞에 최상급에 쓰이는 정관사(the)가 있으므로 최상급을 써야 하고 앞에 be동사(is)가 있으므로 형용사의 최상급을 써야 한다.

어휘 different 다른, 다양한 path 길, 작은 길, 통로

10 우리는 지난밤에 환경에 대한 세미나에 갔는데, 몇 년 동안 참석했던 것들 중 가장 흥미로웠던 토론회였다.

해설 빈칸 앞의 정관사 the와 in years라는 범주로 보아, 비교급이 아닌 최상급이 필요하다.

어휘 environment 환경 discussion 논의, 토론

11 보고서에 의하면, 연구개발부서는 지난달에 평소보다 더 많은 비용을 택배 서비스에 소비했다.

해설 very는 원급을 강조하는 부사이고, 비교급을 강조하는 부사는 much, even, far, a lot, still 등이 있다.

어휘 report 보고서 Research and Development Department 연구개발부서 courier 배달 택배(회사)

12 중국 경제는 반세기 이내에 세계 최대 규모가 될 것으로 예상된다.

해설 빈칸 앞의 정관사 the와 뒤의 in the world라는 범주로 보아 최상급이 필요하다.

어휘 economy 경제 is expected to ~이 예상되다 within ~ 이내로 half-century 반세기

13 올해 말에 우리의 효율성에 대한 평가가 높으면 높을수록 우리가 받을 보너스도 커질 것이다.

해설 '~하면 할수록 더욱 더 ~하다'라는 'the+비교급, the+비교급'의 구문이므로 비교급으로 일치시킨다.

어휘 efficiency 효율성 rating 평가 at the end of this year 이번 해 말에

14 편지를 정시에 배달하기를 원한다면, 우리가 했던 것보다 일을 빨리 진행해야 한다.

해설 before라는 비교 대상과 뒤에 than이 있으므로 동사(proceed)를 수식해 주는 부사(quickly)를 써서 more quickly가 정답이다.

어휘 proceed 진행하다, 계속하다 deliver 배달하다

15 이 일자리를 얻기 위해 가장 중요하게 꼽는 자격조건 중의 하나는 지원자가 외국어로서 영어를 말할 수 있어야 한다는 점이다.

해설 'one of the many ~'는 '수많은 ~중 하나'라는 뜻으로 문맥상 어색하다. 뒤의 형용사를 최상급(most)으로 수식해 '가장 중요한 자격조건 중 하나'로 완성시키는 것이 문맥상 더 자연스럽다.

어휘 qualification 자격조건 applicant 지원자 foreign language 외국어

SPARTA ✔ ACTUAL TEST p. 156

1 (A)	2 (D)	3 (D)	4 (D)	5 (A)	6 (C)
7 (C)	8 (A)	9 (D)	10 (B)	11 (D)	12 (B)
13 (C)	14 (C)	15 (A)	16 (A)		

1 저희는 고객의 민감한 재무 데이터가 과거 어느 때보다 안전하다는 것을 확신합니다.

해설 more ~ than 사이에 빈칸이 있으므로 형용사나 부사의 원급 중 하나가 정답이다. 빈칸 앞의 more를 없애면 동사 is와 빈칸이 연결되며, is는 2형식 동사로 형용사를 보어로 취하므로 형용사인 (A) secure가 정답이다.

어휘 ensure 보장하다, 확신하다 sensitive 민감한 secure 안전한 security 안전 securely 안전하게

2 3분기 회계연도에서 Franklin 사는 평균 이상의 매출액에 도달하는 것에 성공했다.

해설 빈칸 뒤의 than은 비교급의 대상 앞에 나오는 전치사/접속사이므로, 비교급으로 표현된 (D) higher가 정답이 된다.

어휘 quarter 분기 fiscal year 회계연도 reach 도달하다

3 건강보험료는 지난 5년간 수입보다 오르는 속도가 훨씬 더 빨랐다.

해설 비교급을 수식할 수 있는 부사를 찾는 문제. 비교급 수식이 가능한 부사는 정답인 (D) much 외에 even, still 등이 있다.

어휘 health insurance 건강 보험 premium 보험료 할증료 earnings 소득, 수입

4 새롭고 혁신적인 디젤 엔진은 다른 회사의 엔진들보다 조용하게 작동한다.

해설 [----+than]의 구조로 빈칸에는 비교급을 써야 한다. 또한 빈칸에 쓰이는 품사는 동사(work)를 수식해야 하므로 부사여야 한다. 따라서 부사의 비교급 (D) more quietly가 정답이다.

어휘 innovative 혁신적인 quiet 조용한

5 회사의 내부자들에 의하면, Manutek 주식회사의 재정 상태는 최근의 뉴스 보도가 명시한 것보다 더 약하다.

해설 빈칸 뒤의 than을 보면 비교급이 와야 하는 것을 알 수 있다.

어휘 insider (조직·단체의) 내부자 financial 재정적인 weak 약한 indicate 나타내다, 내비치다

6 Peach Health 센터는 나라에서 가장 포괄적인 암 연구 시설들을 제공한다.

해설 빈칸 앞에 most가 있고, 뒤에 cancer research 복합 명사가 있으므로 2음절 이상의 형용사가 필요하다. 따라서 정답은 (C) comprehensive 이다.

어휘 cancer 암 facility 시설 comprehensive 포괄적인

7 Montaz Motorcycles 사는 생산팀과 연구팀 사이에 협력관계를 더 강화하길 원한다.

해설 품사 판정 문제와 비교급 문제가 복합된 문제이다. [동사(make)+목적어(the partnership between the Product and Research departments)+----] 구조이므로 빈칸에는 5형식 동사 'make'의 목적보어가 쓰여야 한다. 형용사를 써야 할 자리로 형용사(strong)의 비교급 (C) stronger가 문맥상 적절하다.

어휘 partnership 협력관계 strength 힘 strengthen 강화하다

8 소비자들에게 있어서 인터넷 전화의 주된 이점은 일반 휴대전화 서비스보다 훨씬 저렴하다는 것이다.

해설 비교급(cheaper)을 수식하는 부사는 (A) even이다.

어휘 prime 주요한 advantage 이점, 이익 cheap 값싼, 저렴한

9 당신의 서비스가 경쟁사들의 서비스만큼 신뢰할 수 없다면, 다수의 소중한 고객들을 잃게 될 것이다.

해설 as ~ as 사이에 빈칸이 있으므로 형용사나 부사의 원급 중 하나가 정답이다. 빈칸 앞의 as를 없애면 is 동사와 빈칸이 연결되며, is는 2형식 동사로 형용사를 보어로 취하므로 형용사인 (B) reliant와 (D) reliable 중, 문맥상 '당신의 서비스가 경쟁사들의 서비스만큼 신뢰할 수 없다면'이 되어야 하므로 정답은 (D) reliable가 된다.

어휘 competitor 경쟁사 valued customer 소중한 고객 reliably 확실하게 reliant 의존하는 reliability 신뢰 reliable 신뢰할 만한

10 건물이 빨리 완공되면 될수록, 회사들은 그들의 새 사무실을 더 빨리 열 수 있을 것이다.

해설 '~하면 할수록 더욱 더 ~하다'라는 'the+비교급, the+비교급' 구문. the better는 문맥상 어울리지 않으므로 탈락한다. 따라서 정답은 (B).

어휘 finish 완결하다, 끝내다　quickly 빠르게

11 부서 관리자들은 그들의 비서가 아닌 Marc Platt에게 직접 경비 보고서를 제출합니다.

해설 빈칸 뒤 than과 짝을 이루어 '~보다는 오히려'라는 의미를 가지는 (D) rather가 정답이다.

어휘 submit 제출하다　expense report 비용 보고서　directly 직접　assistant 비서

12 우리 Allegro 사무실이 최근 기업 조사에서 고객 만족에 대하여 최고의 등급을 받았다.

해설 빈칸 앞에 최상급 앞에 쓰이는 정관사(the)가 있고 뒤에는 명사(rating)이 있으므로, 형용사의 최상급 (B) highest를 써야 한다.

어휘 rating 평가, 평점　customer satisfaction 고객 만족

〈13-16〉 다음은 편지에 관한 문제이다.

Eldridge 씨,

우리의 단골 탑승 VIP고객으로서, 우리는 Platinum Club에 당신을 초대하고자 합니다.

이 회원 자격이 생기면 귀하는 전 세계 Falcon 항공의 스위트룸과 휴게실에 대한 배타적인 이용권한을 갖게 됩니다. 또한 2시간 이상 소요되는 비행편의 좌석을 우선적으로 업그레이드할 수 있을 뿐만 아니라 항공여행 전후에 무료식사와 음료를 제공 받게 될 것입니다.

저희와 여행하는 동안 귀하에게 항상 최상의 케어와 서비스를 제공할 것입니다.

Falcon 항공은 우리의 Platinum Club members를 위해 하루 24시간 대기하는 전담 고객서비스부서를 갖추고 있습니다.

귀하의 성원에 저희가 얼마나 감사하고 있는지 보여드릴 수 있기를 희망합니다.

진심으로,
Gail Pembridge
인적 관리 및 VIP 부서
Falcon Airlines International

어휘 flier 탑승자　membership 회원 자격　exclusive 배타적인　access 접근　suite 스위트룸　across ~ 전역에서　preferential 우선권이 있는　complimentary meal 무료 식사　at all times 항상　special branch 특별부서　customer service representative 고객서비스 직원　on call 대기 중인　appreciate 감사하다　patronage 애용

13

해설 알맞은 전치사를 넣어 문장 전체를 수식하는 전명구(부사구)를 찾는 문제. (A) For는 준비와 목적의 전치사, (C) As는 자격 표시 전치사이다. 'VIP고객으로서'와 같이 해석되어야 하므로 자격을 부여하는 전치사 (C) As가 정답이다.

14

해설 care나 service를 수식해 '최고급 관리와 서비스'라는 의미가 와야 한다. 명사 care를 수식하는 최상급 형용사, 의미상으로 가장 잘 어울리는 (C) finest가 정답이다. 원급 형용사 fine은 '좋은'이라는 뜻과 함께 '양질의, 완벽한, 최고급의'와 같은 뜻을 가진 형용사다. (B)의 luxurious는 '고급의'라는 긍정적 의미와 함께 '호화스러운, 사치스러운'이라는 다소 부정적인 뉘앙스가 있기 때문에 본문의 의미와 어울리지 않는다고 봐야 한다.

15

해설 주격 관계대명사 who 이후 be동사의 보어까지 찾는 문제로, 관용어구 be on call이 들어간 (A)가 정답이다. on call 24/7 for ~는 '~를 위해 하루 24시간 내내 대기 중인'이라는 의미의 비즈니스 전문 용어이다.

16 (A) 귀하의 성원에 저희가 얼마나 감사하고 있는지 보여드릴 수 있기를 희망합니다.
(B) 고장은 발권 웹 사이트 업그레이드 작업에 의해 야기되었습니다.
(C) 우리는 승객들에게 불편을 끼친 점을 사과드립니다.
(D) 어떠한 수하물도 24kg의 무게 제한을 초과할 수 없습니다.

해설 빈칸 앞 내용은 항공사가 고객들에게 Platinum Club members에 초대하는 글이다. 회원 혜택과 방법을 나열한 후 마지막에 글의 마무리로 적절한 문장을 찾아야 한다. 보기 중 항공사가 고객의 성원에 얼마나 감사하고 있는지 보여드릴 수 있기를 희망한다는 (A)가 정답이다.

UNIT 18 가정법과 도치

SPARTA Check-UP! 1

p. 159

1 (D) **2** (A) **3** (C)

1 Kim 씨가 조기 퇴직을 결심한다면, 경영진은 그녀가 속한 부서의 아래 직원을 승진시켜 공석을 채울 것이다.

해설 가정법 현재 구조 'If+주어+현재형 동사 ~, 주어+will+동사원형'를 묻는 문제이다. 답은 (D).

어휘 retire 퇴직하다 void 공백 상태

2 만약 그녀가 어제 보고서를 끝냈더라면, 그녀는 지금 새 프로젝트를 시작할 수 있을 텐데.

해설 if절의 시제가 과거완료(had completed)이므로 주절의 시제는 [would/could/might+have+p.p.]형태의 가정법 과거완료 구문이나 문장 끝에 today가 있는 것으로 보아 '현재 사실에 반대되는 시점'을 나타내는 혼합 가정법 [would/could/might+동사원형]이 적절하다. 따라서 (A) could start가 정답이 된다.

어휘 complete 완료하다, 끝마치다

3 프로젝트가 우리의 국제적인 사업파트너들과 함께 시작되었더라면, 이러한 비용의 초과들은 확실히 없었을 것이다.

해설 과거의 사실과 다른 내용을 가정하는 가정법 과거완료 구문이다. if절이 가정법 과거완료 시제(had started)이므로 주절의 시제는 'would/should/could/might+have+p.p.'가 되어야 한다. 문맥상 '~했더라면 이러한 비용의 초과는 확실히 없었을 것이다'라는 의미가 되어야 하기 때문에 빈칸에 적절한 표현은 (C) have been eliminated이다.

어휘 partner 동료, 협력자 overrun 초과 certainly 확실히 eliminate 제거하다

SPARTA Check-UP! 2

p. 160

1 (D) **2** (D) **3** (C)

1 Peters 씨가 공장을 방문하는 동안 필요한 것이 있다면, 본사의 Jane Kim에게 연락하시기 바랍니다.

해설 가정법 미래 도치 구문을 묻고 있다. 가정법 미래 도치 구문은 Should로 시작하며 if가 빠지므로, 빈칸에는 (D) Should가 들어가야 한다.

어휘 visit 방문 contact 연락하다

2 재무 고문이 조사 결과를 더 일찍 발표했었더라면, 우리는 시장의 변화에 대응할 수 있었을 것이다.

해설 가정법 과거완료 도치구문 'Had+주어+p.p. ~, 주어+조동사의 과거형+have+p.p.'을 묻고 있다. 빈칸에는 (D) could have reacted가 들어가야 한다.

어휘 financial 재정의, 재무의 release 발표하다 finding 조사 결과

3 Roy 씨가 오전 7시 기차를 탔더라면, 시간에 맞춰 수산 부서 회의에 참석할 수 있었을 것이다.

해설 주절의 동사는 [조동사 과거형 (might)+have+been(과거분사)]의 형태이고 부사절에서 조동사 Had가 문두에 나온 것으로 보아, 가정법 과거완료 시제의 조건절에서 if가 생략되고 주어-조동사가 도치된 문장임을 알 수 있다. 그러므로 빈칸에는 catch의 과거분사형인 (C) caught가 들어가야 한다.

어휘 on time 시간에 맞게, 정시에 weekly 주간의

SPARTA Check-UP! 3

p. 161

1 (D) **2** (B) **3** (D)

1 문제가 발생했을 때 Freeman 씨가 수리 회사에 연락했더라면, 지금쯤 그는 곤경을 겪지 않을 것이다.

해설 'Had he contacted ~'는 가정법 과거완료의 'If he had contacted ~'에서 If가 생략되며 동사와 주어가 도치된 것이고, 주절 마지막에 now가 있어 이 문장이 혼합가정법이라는 것을 알 수 있다. 과거에 전화하지 않은 사실을 한 것으로 가정했으므로, 현재에 곤경을 겪지 않는다는 가정 상황은 (D) wouldn't be로 표현한다.

어휘 repair company 수리 회사 predicament 곤경, 궁지

2 나는 결코 모회사와 자회사가 동시에 파산했다는 발표를 Paramount 사가 할 것이라고는 생각하지 않았다.

해설 부정어를 강조하기 위해 부정어(Never)가 문장 맨 앞에 나오면 문장의 주어와 동사가 도치되는데, 여기서는 본동사가 일반 동사(think)이므로 대신에 조동사가 주어 앞에 들어간다. 주어와 시제를 고려하면 (B) did가 정답이다.

어휘 bankruptcy 파산 parent company 모회사 subsidiary company 자회사 at the same time 동시에

3 유럽으로의 출장이 국경일에 있을 뿐만 아니라 내 아내의 휴가 계획과도 상충한다.

해설 Not only가 문장 맨 앞에 나와서 도치가 일어난 문장이다. 문맥을 자세히 들여다보면 not only, (but) also 구문임을 알 수 있다.

어휘 business trip 출장 national holiday 국경일 conflict with ~와 상충되다

SPARTA Check-UP! 4

p. 162

1 (A) **2** (C) **3** (B)

1 경영 컨설턴트의 조언을 따랐더라면, 지금 이러한 재정 위기에 처하지 않을 텐데.

해설 if절에는 had followed라는 가정법 과거완료의 형식을 취하고 있고 주절 문장 끝에는 now가 있어 혼합 가정법임을 알 수기 있다. 따라서 주절은 would not be라는 가정법 과거의 형식을 취해야 하므로 정답은 (A)가 된다.

어휘 follow 따르다 consultant 상담사 advice 충고, 조언 crisis 위기

2 우리 회사가 복지혜택에 돈을 투자했었더라면, 지금 이직률이 그렇게 높지는 않을 텐데.

해설 Had our company invested라는 가정법 과거완료의 도치 형식을 취하고 있고 문장 끝에는 now라는 말이 있어서 혼합 가정법임을 알 수 있다. 따라서 주절은 would not have라는 가정법 과거의 형식을 취해야 하므로 정답은 (C) would not have가 된다.

어휘 invest 투자 turnover 이직률

3 제안서 마감일이 촉박했지만, Benshaw 씨는 아직 시간이 많이 남은 것처럼 행동했다.

해설 as if 뒤로, 사실과는 반대인 '아직 시간이 많이 남은 것처럼'이라고 해야

적절하다. 이 때, 동사가 과거형이 되어야 하므로 정답은 (B) had이다.

어휘 due date 마감일 proposal 제안서 tight 촉박한

SPARTA PRACTICE

p. 163

1 would	**2** would	**3** reduced
4 have left	**5** Had	**6** taken
7 had	**8** known	**9** should
10 arrive	**11** Should	**12** had spent
13 would have been	**14** have	**15** could have left

1 내가 지금 바쁘지 않으면, 네가 과제를 끝낼 수 있도록 도와줄 것이다.

해설 가정법 과거로, 현재 사실과 반대되는 내용을 가정으로 하는 문장이다. 실제로는 I가 바쁘지만, 바쁘지 않다면 해 주겠다는 것을 가리키며, 가정하는 상황을 나타내는 문장의 동사가 과거형(were), 뒤의 문장은 조동사의 과거형(would)이 와야 적합한 형태가 된다. 따라서 정답은 would이다. 참고로, 가정법 과거에서 be동사는 주어와 관계없이 were를 쓰는 것을 기억해 둔다.

어휘 help out 돕다 assignment 과제

2 금리가 더 낮아진다면, 판매 목표를 달성할 것이다.

해설 가정법 과거형의 주절은 '조동사의 과거형+동사원형'이 연결되면 if절은 과거 동사(were)가 된다. 답은 would.

어휘 interest rate 금리 lower 낮추다 achieve 성취하다

3 만약 우리 회사가 적자를 반으로 줄이면, 우리 경쟁력이 전보다 더 강해질 것이다.

해설 가정법 과거 문제이다. 가정법 과거형 문장의 가정하는 앞 문장에는 과거형 동사가 와야 한다. 따라서 정답은 reduced가 된다.

어휘 reduce 줄이다, 축소하다 deficit 적자 by half 반으로 competitiveness 경쟁력

4 그 소문이 퍼지지 않았다면, 그녀는 떠나지 않았을 수도 있었을 것이다.

해설 가정법 과거완료의 도치를 묻는 문제. 뒤 문장의 동사를 묻는데, 가정법 과거완료는 도치가 if절에서만 이루어지고 뒤는 똑같이 '조동사의 과거형+have+p.p.~'를 유지한다. 따라서 정답은 have left이다.

어휘 rumor 소문 spread 퍼지다

5 경영진이 좀 더 일찍 조치를 취하였다면, 파업은 일어나지 않았을 것이다.

해설 주절의 wouldn't have happened를 보아, 가정법 과거완료임을 알 수 있다. Should로 문장이 시작되려면, 가정법 미래의 도치구문에서 나올 수 있다.

어휘 management 경영진 strike 파업

6 그가 좀 더 많은 시간을 들였다면, 결과가 더 나았을 것이다.

해설 가정법 과거완료의 문장에서 had+p.p.형태의 동사가 와야 하므로 능동태 과거형인 took는 오답이 되고 taken이 정답이다.

어휘 result 결과

7 만약 공장이 화재로 손상되지 않았더라면, 연말까지 주문량을 달성했을 것이다.

해설 뒤의 would have been을 보아 가정법 과거완료 문장이다. were가 오려면 가정법 과거 문장이어야 한다.

어휘 plant 공장 damage 손상시키다; 피해 complete 끝마치다 end of the year 연말

8 만약 회사가 재정적 어려움을 겪고 있다는 것을 알았더라면, 우리는 그 회사와 계약하지 않았을 것이다.

해설 가정법 과거 완료의 도치 구문에서 동사 형태를 묻는 문제. knew는 일반 과거, known은 과거분사이므로 정답은 known이 된다.

어휘 suffer 고통을 겪다 financial 재정적인 difficulty 어려움 contract 계약

9 만약 도움이 필요하다면, 언제든지 전화 주세요.

해설 가정법 미래에서는 'If+주어+should+동사원형, ~'으로 시작하므로 빈칸에 들어갈 알맞은 조동사는 should가 된다.

어휘 feel free to 사양하지 말고 ~하세요.

10 만약 사무실 문이 열리기 전에 도착한다면, 보안 요원이 들여보내 주지 않을 것이다.

해설 가정법 미래의 도치 구문이다. 조동사(should)의 영향을 받아 동사는 동사원형이 정답이다.

어휘 arrive 도착하다 security guard 보안 요원, 경비원

11 혹시 당신의 연구에 도움이 필요하다면, 저에게 언제든지 전화하세요.

해설 가정법 미래 도치 구문이다. If you should need any help ~ '혹시라도 도움이 필요하다면 ~'이 되어야 하므로 If를 생략하고 도치로 should를 앞에 써야 한다.

어휘 research 연구 any time 언제든지

12 근본적으로 만약 디자인 팀이 온라인 게임에 보다 많은 시간은 할애했다면, 거의 완벽한 게임이 될 수 있었을 것이다.

해설 가정법 과거완료 문장은 if절 동사가 'had+p.p.'형으로 와야 하므로 정답은 had spent가 된다.

어휘 basically 근본적으로 almost 거의 perfect 완벽한

13 만약 생산량이 10% 이상 올라갔더라면, 1990년 이래 최고의 평균 생산량이 되었을 것이다.

해설 가정법 과거완료의 주절 문장은 [주어+조동사의 과거형+have+p.p.~]의 구조를 갖는다. would have been이 정답이다.

어휘 average 평균 yield 생산량

14 만약 물건에 어떤 문제가 있다면, 당신의 지역 수리공에게 연락하세요.

해설 가정법 미래의 도치 구문이다. had는 가정법 미래에 나올 수 없다.

어휘 contact 연락하다 local 지역 repairman 수리공

15 만약 월례 회의가 취소된 걸 미리 알았더라면, 우린 어제 저녁에 일찍 퇴근할 수 있었을 것이다.

해설 가정법 과거완료의 도치구문이고 주절은 도치에 영향을 받지 않으므로, could have left가 정답이다. could leave라면 가정법 과거의 일을 나타낼 때에 사용 가능하다.

어휘 in advance 미리, 사전에 monthly meeting 월례 회의 cancel 취소하다 early 일찍

SPARTA ACTUAL TEST p. 164

1 (C)	2 (C)	3 (D)	4 (A)	5 (B)	6 (D)
7 (C)	8 (D)	9 (B)	10 (C)	11 (B)	12 (C)
13 (A)	14 (C)	15 (B)	16 (C)		

1 독점을 종식하기 위한 절차들이 취해졌더라면, 경쟁이 확실히 사라졌을 것이다.

해설 If절에 가정법 과거완료가 쓰였으므로 종속절에도 가정법 과거완료에 알맞은 짝을 찾아 문장을 완성해야 한다. 'If+주어+had+p.p., 주어+would/should/could/might+have+p.p.' 문장 구조이므로 정답은 (C) would have been eliminated이다.

어휘 monopoly 독점 eliminate 제거하다, 삭제하다

2 청구서 발부 부서에서 어려움이 있으시다면, 저에게 연락 주십시오.

해설 가정법 미래 구문에서 if가 생략된 형태. [If+S+should+동사원형, 명령문] 구조에서 if가 생략되면 조동사가 도치되어 문두에 위치하는 형태 [Should+S+동사원형, 명령문]가 된다. 그러므로 정답은 동사원형인 (C) experience이다. 주절이 명령문 형태로 될 수 있는 것은 if 조건문과 가정법 미래밖에 없다는 것도 참고하자.

어휘 difficulty 어려움

3 진공 청소기가 제대로 작동하지 않을 경우, 고객 서비스 센터에 연락하시면 교환 또는 환불해 드리겠습니다.

해설 가정법 미래의 도치로, 앞에 (D) Should가 와야 한다.

어휘 vacuum cleaner 진공 청소기 properly 제대로 exchange 교환하다 refund 환불하다

4 우리 제품의 특징이 광고에서 강조된다면, 손님들이 지금보다 훨씬 더 많이 제품을 구매할 것이다.

해설 가정법 과거형의 문장이다. 따라서 빈칸에 알맞은 형태는 '조동사의 과거형+동사원형'인 (A) would buy이다.

어휘 feature 특징 emphasize 강조하다 advertisement 광고

5 회사가 지난달에 면접을 진행했었다면, 그 직책이 충원되었을 수도 있다.

해설 가정법 과거 완료로, [If+주어+had+p.p. ~, 주어+have+p.p.+동사원형] 구조를 이룬다. 따라서 정답은 (B) had conducted이다.

어휘 certainly 확실히 position 위치 자리, 직위

6 식수가 법에 의한 품질기준이 충족한다면, 그 물은 안심하고 마실 수 있다는 것을 의미한다.

해설 if가 들어간 조건절 문장이다. 빈칸은 if절 내에서 주어(drinking water)와 목적어(the standards) 사이에 위치하고 있으므로 의미상 적절한 동사가 와야 하는 자리이다. 'meet the standard'은 '기준에 미치다, 기준을 충족시키다'라는 의미의 표현으로, '식수가 법의 기준을 충족한다면'이라고 해석되어야 한다. 따라서 정답은 3인칭 단수 주어의 맞는 현재 시제 동사 (D) meets이다.

어휘 standard 기준 law 법 considered ~으로 간주되다 drinkable 마실 수 있는

7 우리 회사가 지난 2년에 걸쳐 중대한 개혁을 이행하지 않았다면, 심각한 재정상의 압박과 파산 위기를 겪었을 것이다.

해설 Had we not implemented는 If we had not implemented의 가정법 구문에서 접속사 if가 생략되고 도치된 것이므로 종속절의 동사는 would have suffered 형태로 와야 한다. 따라서 (C)가 답이다.

어휘 severe 심각한, 심한 fiscal 재정상의, 회계의 pressure 압력 bankruptcy 파산

8 출판 전에 자료를 검토할 편집자를 회사에서 고용했더라면, 책자의 구성이 더 나았을 거라고 관리자가 말했다.

해설 that절에 가정법 과거 완료의 도치 문장(had the company hired an editor)이 왔으므로 앞에 동사로는 이와 짝을 이루는 would have p.p. 형태가 와야 한다. 빈칸 앞에 would 대신 쓸 수 있는 could가 있으므로 빈칸에는 have p.p.의 표현이 사용된 (C) have organized 또는 (D) have been organized가 올 수 있는데, 주어와 동사가 '매뉴얼이 구성되다'는 수동 관계이므로, 수동태 (D) have been organized가 정답이다.

어휘 comment 논평하다, 의견을 말하다 manual 안내서, 소책자 editor 편집자 go over 검토하다 material 자료 organize 구성하다

9 직원들의 전문적인 지식과 직업 윤리가 없었더라면, Powell 씨는 자신의 부서가 수익을 내는 데 결코 성공하지 못했을 것이다.

해설 'without+명사'가 의미상 '~이 없었더라면'으로 해석되면서 가정법 과거나 가정법 과거완료의 조건절을 이끈다. have+p.p.(have succeeded)가 보이므로 가정법 조동사 (B) would가 정답이다.

어휘 make a profit 이익을 내다 expertise 전문지식 ethic 윤리

10 그가 대학에 다닐 때 좀 더 열심히 공부했더라면, 의과 대학에 쉽게 입학할 수 있었을 것이다.

해설 형태상 If 절의 과거완료 had studied와 일치하고, 의미상 입학 허가를 받을 수 있는 가능성이나 능력을 나타내는 가정법 과거완료 형태가 들어가야 한다. (A) could는 뒤의 과거동사 won 때문에 올 수 없고, (B) must have는 가정법에서 사용하지 않고, (D) have는 문장 어법과 내용에 맞지 않는다. 정답은 (C) would have이다.

어휘 university 대학 admission 입학 medical school 의과 대학

11 직원들이 화학 공장을 들어서기 전에 보안 규정을 알고 있었더라면, 사고는 피할 수 있었을 것이다.

해설 주절의 동사 'could have been avoided'로 보아, 이미 일어난 일의 반대되는 가정을 나타내는 가정법 과거완료임을 알 수 있다. 정답은 (B) Had이다.

어휘 safety regulation 보안 규정 enter 출입하다 chemical factory 화학 공장 accident 사고 prevent 예방하다, 방지하다

12 직원들의 프로젝트에 대한 진심 어린 헌신이 없었다면, 이 놀라운 보고는 가능하지 않았을 것이다.

해설 without 가정법을 묻는 문제. 문맥상 '직원들의 프로젝트에 대한 진심 어린 헌신이 아니었다면'이라는 의미여야 되므로, (C) Without이 정답이 된다. (A) Provided (that)는 '~이라는 가정하에'라는 조건을 나타낸다. (B)는 'Only+부사구/부사절+조동사+주어+동사'라는 도치구문으로만 가정을 나타낸다.

어휘 sincere 진심 어린 devotion 헌신 remarkable 놀랄 만한, 주목할 만한 provided (that) (만약) ~라면

〈13-16〉 다음은 정보에 관한 문제이다.

고객님께,

Astica Sambo Furniture를 애용해 주셔서 감사합니다!

고객님이 구매하셨을 때 받으신 영수증은 저희의 무료 배송 서비스 세부 사항을 보여줍니다. 저희가 배송시간과 날짜를 영수증 상에 표시했습니다. 저희 배송부서는 이 일정을 지킬 수 있도록 최선을 다할 것입니다.

만약에 지연이 발생한다면 미리 저희가 연락을 드릴 것입니다. 18세 이상 되는 누군가가 물품에 대해 서명을 할 수 있도록 지정된 장소에 있으셔야 합니다.

기록상 영수증을 보관해 두십시오. 만약에 배송 일정을 다시 잡을 필요가 있거나 문의사항이 있으시면 우리 고객 서비스 부서 800-555-1096으로 전화해 주십시오.

13

해설 문장의 동사 자리로 수 일치를 통해 오답으로 제거할 수 있는 것은 없다. 따라서 그 다음 단계인 수동과 능동을 가려, 동사 indicate는 타동사이므로 빈칸 뒤 목적어가 있어 수동태인 (C) are indicated는 탈락. 나머지 보기를 보고 시제 문제라고 판단하고 문맥에 알맞은 시제를 고르면 된다. 앞의 내용에서 이미 편지를 받는 사람은 회사에 주문한 상태라는 것을 알 수 있다. 따라서 문맥상 과거부터 현재에 영향을 미치는 현재완료시제 (A) have indicated가 적합하다.

14

(A) 그 사이에 임시 일정표를 받아주십시오.
(B) 지역 정부는 저희가 제안한 마감일에 동의하지 않았습니다.
(C) 저희 배송부서는 이 일정을 지킬 수 있도록 최선을 다할 것입니다.
(D) 일정이 정해졌으므로, 배송부서는 회의를 위한 포스터를 디자인할 것입니다.

해설 빈칸 앞은 '구매 시 받은 영수증에 무료 배송 서비스의 날짜와 시간 등 세부 정보가 있다'는 것이고, 빈칸 뒤는 '지연되면 미리 연락 드릴 것이며 18세 이상의 성인이 물품을 받아야 한다'는 내용이 이어진다. 따라서 보기 중, (C)의 '배송 기일을 지키기 위해 노력하겠다'는 내용이 가장 적합하다.

15

해설 빈칸은 가정법 미래의 도치구문에서 if가 생략되어 주어와 동사가 도치된 형태이다. 따라서 정답은 보기 중 (B) Should가 된다. 도치 전의 문장은 'If there should be a delay, ~'였다.

16

해설 명령문으로, 알맞은 동사 어휘를 물어보는 문제이다. 문맥상 '기록을 위해 영수증을 보관해 달라'가 적절하므로 '(계속) 간직[보관]하다'의 의미를 가지고 있는 (C) retain이 정답이다.

PART 7

UNIT 19 주제/목적

패러프레이징 연습 p. 171

1 (A) **2** (B) **3** (A) **4** (B)

1

주차에 관한 변경된 정책은 11월 11일부터 시행될 예정입니다. 초과 근무하는 직원들은 지정된 구역에 주차하기 위해서 승인을 얻어야 합니다.

(A) 저녁 교대 근무자의 주차에 관한 새로운 정책은 11월 11일부터 시작될 것이다.
(B) 모든 직원들은 그들의 차량을 주차하는 것을 허락 받아야 한다.

2

만약 당신이 결함 있는 제품을 반품하길 원한다면, 물건을 구매한 달 이내에 구매 증빙으로 영수증을 제시하셔야 합니다.

(A) 어떠한 불량 제품도 새것으로 교환 가능하다.
(B) 환불을 받기 위해서, 서류가 제시되어야 한다.

3

업계의 급격한 경향 변화로 인하여 지속된 심각한 경제불황에도 불구하고, 올해의 판매 목표를 달성해 주신 여러분의 노고에 감사를 표하는 바입니다.

(A) 우리는 경제불황을 극복하기 위해 고군분투해 온 직원들에게 감사하고 싶다.
(B) 올해의 판매 수치는 어느 때보다도 높다.

4

3일 전에 귀사의 온라인 쇼핑몰에서 주문했고, 상품이 어제 도착했습니다. 그러나, 배송 물품 중 일부가 소포에 포함되지 않았음을 알려드립니다.

(A) 우리는 이 거래를 철회할 것이다.
(B) 배송품 중 일부가 누락되었다.

SPARTA PRACTICE p. 172

1 (A) **2** (D)

공지

인사부의 연례 인력 개발 세미나가 9월 21일 오전 10시에 1층 우편실 맞은편 회의실 22호에서 열릴 것입니다.

어휘 annual 연례의 seminar 세미나

1. 공지의 목적을 묻는 문제

이 공지의 목적은 무엇인가?

(A) 직원들에게 세미나에 참석하도록 격려하기 위해
(B) 직원들에게 세미나 일정 변경을 공지하기 위해
(C) 직원들에게 보고서를 제출하도록 독려하기 위해
(D) 직원들에게 세미나의 새로운 주제를 공지하기 위해

해설 'The annual human resources seminar ~ will take place on September 21 at 10 A.M. in Meeting Room 22'에서 세미나 관련 사항 안내 및 참석할 것을 당부하는 공지임을 알 수 있다. 그러므로 정답은 (A)이다.

친애하는 피터슨 씨께,

최근에 귀하께서 주문한 릴리 컬렉션 중 두 접시를 귀하가 받았을 때, 깨져 있었다는 소식에 매우 유감을 전합니다. 저희 플라워 파인 차이나 앤 글래스 주식회사는 고객 서비스를 자랑하고 있으며, 기꺼이 귀하께 교환품을 보내드립니다. 귀하의 파손된 제품을 반환하실 반품 키트를 동봉합니다. 그러므로 귀하께서는 물건을 포장만 하시고, 배달 운송 서비스인 0232-512-2446으로 전화만 주시면 됩니다. 반환되는 물건을 받자마자, 저희가 무료로 교환품을 보내드릴 것입니다.
다시 한번 불편을 드려 죄송합니다. 귀하의 거래에 감사드립니다.

진심으로,

데니스 클레인,
고객서비스 부장
플라워 파인 차이나 앤 글래스 주식회사

어휘 plate 접시 cracked 깨진 take pride in ~을 자랑하다 replacement 교환품 enclosed 동봉된 return kit 반품 키트 damaged 손상된 pack 포장하다 free of charge 무료로 apologize 사과하다

2. 편지의 주제를 찾는 문제

편지에서 주로 논의되는 것은 무엇인가?

(A) 잘못 배송된 주문품
(B) 빠진 상품
(C) 품절된 상품
(D) 문제의 해결책

해설 편지 상단에 언급한 제품의 문제점에 대한 해결책을 제시하기 위한 편지이므로 'we are pleased to send you replacements' 정답은 (D)이다.

SPARTA ACTUAL TEST p. 173

1 (A) **2** (A) **3** (D) **4** (B) **5** (B) **6** (C)
7 (D) **8** (B)

<1-2> 다음은 이메일에 관한 문제이다.

발신: 카일 챈들러
수신: 제니퍼 코넬리
제목: 감사합니다.

당사의 제품에 관심을 기울여 주셔서 감사합니다. 저희는 어떤 종류의 올리브 오일(엑스트라 버진, 버진, 정제)이라도 귀사에게 기쁜 마음으로 공급할 것입니다. 저희는 이런 종류의 오일을 유리병(250ML, 500ML, 750ML, 1000ML), 캔(3L, 5L, 10L, 18L), 190kg 드럼통과 대량의 형태로 제공합니다. 그리고 주문 받는 즉시 유리 단지, 페트병, 캔과 같이 다양한 포장 형태를 이용하여 블랙 올리브와 그린 올리브를 제공할 수 있습니다.

또 저희는 고급 품질의 올리브 오일 비누를 만들어 수출합니다. 당사의 비누는 수제품으로 100% 자연산입니다. 저희는 귀사가 원하시는 즉시, 등록 상표인 'Olive Land'로 제품을 공급할 것입니다.

당사 제품의 정가표, 카탈로그, 주문서를 동봉해 드립니다. 기입해서 보내 주시면 됩니다. 추가적인 상세한 정보를 원하면 저희에게 연락주세요. 귀사와의 거래를 기대합니다.

카일 챈들러
수출입 매니저, Chandler's Olive Land

어휘 appreciate 감사하다 product 제품 supply 공급하다 olive oil 올리브 오일 refined 정제된 in bulk 대량으로 glass bottle 유리 단지 tin 캔 various types 다양한 형태 packaging 포장 export 수출하다 high-quality 고급 품질 handmade 수제의 natural 자연의 brand name 상표명 price list 정가표 order form 주문서 detail 세부 사항 look forward to ~를 기다리다

1. 이메일의 목적을 찾는 문제

이 이메일은 왜 쓰였는가?

(A) 잠재 고객에게 제품을 판촉하기 위해
(B) 화물 인수를 통지하기 위해
(C) 견적을 요청하기 위해
(D) Jennifer Connelly 씨에게 감사를 표하기 위해

해설 'We would be happy to supply you with any types of olive oil.'에서 자사의 제품을 홍보하면서 이메일 수신자 측과 거래를 시작하고 싶다는 의사를 밝히고 있으므로 정답은 (A)이다.

2. 이메일의 주제를 찾는 문제

무엇에 관한 이메일인가?

(A) 판매할 물건의 묘사
(B) 올리브 오일의 종류
(C) 제조 기술
(D) 용기의 용량

해설 'We would be happy to supply you with any types of olive oil'의 주제문을 보면 판매상품의 소개가 주제인 것을 알 수 있다. 그러므로 정답은 (A)이다.

〈3-5〉 다음은 공지에 관한 문제이다.

저희는 세계 최고의 요리사들이 브리티시 컬럼비아에서 가장 좋아하는 생선인 연어를 어떻게 요리하는지 알고자 합니다. 또한 저희는 가정에서 요리하시는 분들과 직업 요리사의 작품을 모두 인정합니다. 따라서 이번 요리 콘테스트는 비전문가와 전문가로 나뉘는 두 가지의 참가 종류가 있습니다.

참가 자격 : 비전문가와 전문가들. 전문가는 요리로 소득의 일부를 버는 사람으로 규정됩니다. 모든 참가자는 최소 18세 이상이어야만 합니다.

참가 시 동봉해야 할 것 : 각각의 조리 비법이 읽기 쉽도록 손으로 쓰거나 타이핑된 참가 양식에 동봉되어야 합니다(아래 참조). 참가 양식은 복사본도 됩니다. 조리법은 연어를 주재료로 사용해야 합니다(최소 1/4킬로그램). 조리법 당 조리 분량은 10인분 또는 그 이하여야 합니다. 경쟁자들은 조리법이 독창적인 것임을 보증해야 합니다. 각각의 조리법 제출물들은 귀하가 어떻게 그런 조리법을 만들어냈는지 50단어 이하로 설명해야 합니다.

상품 : 50명의 준 결승자들은 우수 인증서를 받게 됩니다. 8명의 최종 결승자들(각 종목마다 4명씩)은 밴쿠버에 있는 <ABC 매거진> 본사행 1박의 숙박과 항공요금을 포함한 여행권을 얻게 됩니다. 최종 결승자들의 조리법은 곧 출간되는 요리책 <브리티시 콜럼비아의 맛>에 출판될 것입니다.

어휘 prepare 준비하다 salmon 연어 recognize 승인하다, 인정하다 chef 주방장 cook-off 요리 콘테스트 category 종류, 종목 define 규정하다 entrant 참가자 recipe 조리법 submission 제출물 legible 읽기 쉬운, 알아볼 수 있는 hand-printed 손으로 작성된 photocopy 복사하다 feature 특색으로 하다 in a prominent manner 현저한 방식으로, 여기서는 '주재료로 쓰이는'의 의미 contestant 경쟁자 warrant 보증하다, 보장하다 original 독창적인 merit 우수함 certificate 증명서, 임명서 airfare 항공 요금 lodging 숙박 headquarters 본사 forthcoming 다가오는, 곧 나오려고 하는

3. 공지의 주제를 찾는 문제

공지는 무엇에 관한 것인가?

(A) 출판물의 홍보
(B) 식당에 대한 평가
(C) 새 조리법을 배우는 방법
(D) 대회 묘사

해설 이 공지 글에는 뚜렷한 주제문이 보이지 않는다. 그러므로 세부적인 사항을 조합하여 주제를 찾을 수밖에 없다. 첫 단락의 'this cook-off has two entry categories'와 'WHO CAN ENTER', 'WHAT THE ENTRY MUST INCLUDE', 'THE PRIZES' 등의 항목을 조합하여, 주제가 대회 묘사라는 것을 알 수 있다. 그러므로 정답은 (D)이다.

4. 전반적인 내용 관련 인물을 추론하는 문제

누가 이 공지를 작성했을 것 같은가?

(A) 원양 어업 협회
(B) 정기 간행물 출판사
(C) 수석 요리사
(D) 출장요리업체

해설 마지막 단락에서 'including airfare and one night's lodging, to *ABC Magazine* headquarters in Vancouver'와 'The finalists' recipes will be published in the forthcoming cookbook *A Taste of British Columbia*.'을 봤을 때 한 잡지사에서 개최한 대회이므로 이 공지는 잡지사에서 작성했음을 알 수 있다. 그러므로 정답은 (B)이다.

5. 전반적인 내용 관련 인물을 추론하는 문제

누가 이 공지에 관심이 있을 것 같은가?

(A) 식당 사장들
(B) 전문가와 비전문가 요리사
(C) 칼럼니스트
(D) 요식업계 연구자들

해설 'WHO CAN ENTER : Amateurs and professionals.'에서 참가자들을 전문가와 비전문가로 지정했으므로 이 사람들이 본 공지에 관심을 가질 수 있다. 그러므로 정답은 (B)이다.

〈6-8〉 다음은 기사에 관한 문제이다.

주식거래소는 어제 소수의 서비스에 집중하기 위해서 뷰티 & 트렌드 무역 회사를 팔기로 합의했다고 발표했습니다. 이번 주에 발행되는 "재무 보고서" 발간 이전에 발표가 있을 것입니다.

반지, 귀걸이, 팔찌 같은 작은 물건들을 생산하는 뷰티 & 트렌드는 스테디 앤 이라고 불리는 확인 시스템을 가진 경쟁회사인 파티 앤 크래프트에게 매각되었다. 파티 앤 크래프트의 사장은 아직 뷰티 & 트렌드와 합병하지 않겠다고 약속했지만, 결국 두 회사는 하나의 큰 회사로 합병할 것입니다.

인수 조건은 아직 알려지지 않았지만 뷰티 & 트렌드가 계속해서 적자를 보고 있다고 말했으며, 파티 앤 크래프트사의 CEO이자 회장인 릴레이 씨는 그 합병이 주주들의 불확실함을 감소시킬 것이라고 말했습니다.

어휘 stock exchange 주식거래소 reach an agreement 동의하다 merge 합병하다 acquisition 인수 disclose 폭로하다, 밝히다

6. 주제를 찾는 문제

이 기사는 무엇에 관해 주요로 논의하고 있는가?

(A) 확인 시스템의 거대한 손실
(B) 새로운 책의 출판
(C) 회사 매각 확정
(D) 주식 거래의 전자식 확인

해설 맨 첫 문장에 "The stock exchange announced yesterday that it has reached an agreement to sell the Beauty & Trend trade corporation ~"라고 나와 있듯이 어제 뷰티 & 트렌드 회사를 팔기로 했으므로 (C)가 답이 된다.

7. 세부 사항을 묻는 문제

파티 앤 크래프트에서 팔지 않는 것은?

(A) 다이아몬드 반지
(B) 귀걸이
(C) 팔찌
(D) 시계

해설 두 번째 문단에서 파티 앤 크래프트는 뷰티 & 트렌드의 경쟁 회사라고 나와 있으므로 뷰티 & 트렌드의 생산 품목인 장신구류에서 언급되지 않은 (D)가 정답이다.

8. 세부 사항을 묻는 문제

뷰티 & 트렌드는 무엇인가?

(A) 보석점
(B) 장신구 회사
(C) 재무 프로그램
(D) 플라스틱 칼

해설 "Beauty & Trend, a company that produces small items such as rings, earrings, and bracelets ~"에 나와 있듯이 장신구를 생산한다고 했으므로 정답은 (B)가 된다.

UNIT 20 세부 내용

패러프레이징 연습

p. 179

1 (B) **2** (B) **3** (A) **4** (A)

1

> 이 서류를 작성할 때, 많은 역사적인 자료를 보유한 밴쿠버 공립 도서관의 자료들을 참고하는 것이 좋습니다.

(A) 역사적인 도서관에 관한 보고서를 제출하는 것이 중요하다.
(B) 업무를 위해 몇몇 역사적인 도서들을 참고하는 것이 좋다.

2

> 만약 당신이 이 수업을 듣기 원한다면, 당신이 해야 할 일은 바로 접수처에 직접 방문하여 등록 신청서를 작성하는 것입니다. 수업의 수용 인원이 제한적이어서 우리는 당신이 망설이지 말 것을 제안합니다.

(A) 계획을 미리 꼼꼼히 세우는 것이 더 좋다.
(B) 자리를 확보하기 위해 접수처에 직접 방문하여 수업에 등록해야 한다.

3

> 개정된 규정에 따라서, 우리는 이 건물 외관의 디자인을 바꿀 계획입니다.

(A) 우리는 수정된 건축법을 준수하기 위해 건물의 일부를 변경할 것이다.
(B) 이 건물의 외관이 도시의 다른 곳들과 조화를 이루지 못한다.

4

> 저는 데이비스 씨와 원자재의 대량 구매를 위해 상담 일정을 정하고 싶습니다. 제가 무엇을 해야 할까요?

(A) 저는 데이비스 씨와 사업상 대화를 나눌 약속을 정하고 싶습니다.
(B) 저는 상품을 해외로 유통하는 것에 관한 질문을 하고 싶습니다.

SPARTA PRACTICE

p. 180

1 (C) **2** (C) **3** (C)

우승자 이름은 유명 광고업자와 크래머 음료의 사장, 유명 스포츠 인사인 John Hawkes, 그리고 골드슨 앤 하퍼의 창조 부서장인 Mike McGlone으로 구성된 심사위원단에 의해 선택될 것입니다. 대회는 적절한 이름을 찾지 못한다면 취소될 것입니다. 우승자는 천 달러를 현금으로 받을 것입니다.

어휘 judge 심사원 figure 인물, 거물 suitable 적절한

1. 공지의 세부 내용을 묻는 문제

몇 명의 심사위원이 당선자를 결정할 것인가?

(A) 2명
(B) 3명
(C) 4명
(D) 5명

해설 The winning name ~ at Goldson and Harper.에서 총 4명으로 구성된 심사위원단이 당선 이름을 선택할 거라고 했으므로 (C)가 정답이다.

아파트 관리

정규직 관리인을 급하게 구함.
디트로이트 도시의 중간지구에 위치한 600가구 복합단지. 매력적이고 안전한 동네.

직무 : 전화 받기, 세입자가 될 사람들에게 아파트 보여 주기, 정비 직원들의 일정을 짜고 관리하기, 온라인 문의사항들에 응답하기, 신문 광고 유지하기, 행정 보조들을 고용하고 훈련시키기.

어휘 full-time 정규직의 immediately 즉시 unit 편성 단위 (구성), 가구 complex (건물 등의)집합체, 단지 midtown 중간지구 desirable 바람직한, 탐나도록 매력적인 duty 임무, 직무 prospective 장래의 tenant 세입자 maintenance 보수, 정비 respond 응답하다 inquiry 문의사항 administrative 행정의, 경영상의 assistant 보조

2. 틀린 정보를 묻는 문제

아파트 복합단지에 대해 언급되지 않은 것은 무엇인가?

(A) 600개의 가구가 있다.
(B) 안전한 동네이다.
(C) 임대 가격은 그 도시의 평균 이하이다.
(D) 복합 단지는 내도시에 위치해 있다.

해설 지문 첫 부분에 '600 unit complex in midtown Detroit. Desirable, safe neighborhood.'에서 (A), (B), (D)의 내용이 모두 언급되어 있다. 아파트 관리인을 구하려는 광고이므로, 임대 가격에 대한 내용은 나와 있지 않다. 그러므로 정답은 (C)이다.

이 회의는 앞으로의 지사와 회의 운영 방식에 관한 상당히 중요한 토론이기 때문에 나는 모든 회의 참가자들이 회의에 앞서 타 지점의 직원들과 연락해서 특별한 요구나 아이디어에 관해 논의할 것을 권하는 바입니다.

어휘 branch 지사 attend 참가하다, 참석하다 meeting 회의 contact 연락하다, 만나다 prior to ~이전에, ~에 앞서

3. 추후 당부 사항을 묻는 문제

회의 이전에 회의 참가자들은 누구와 연락해야 하는가?

(A) 사내 직원
(B) 동료 관리자들
(C) 다른 지점의 직원들
(D) 회의하고자 하는 고객

해설 "I want all who are attending the meeting to contact the employees at other branches to discuss any special needs or ideas they may have prior to the meeting."에서 회의에 참석하기 전에 먼저 특별한 요구사항이나 아이디어를 가지고 있을지 모를 다른 지점의 직원들과 연락을 취해 볼 것을 권하고 있으므로 정답은 (C)가 된다.

SPARTA ACTUAL TEST

p. 181

1 (A) **2** (C) **3** (D) **4** (C) **5** (B) **6** (A)
7 (A) **8** (B) **9** (A)

〈1-3〉 다음은 광고에 관한 문제이다.

직장까지 운전해서 출근하는 데 너무 많은 시간이 걸리나요?
매일 교통체증에 갇혀 있는 데 지치셨나요?

Adventure 자전거 매장이 완벽한 해결책을 가지고 있습니다: 바로 자전거입니다.

지금부터 7월 15일까지, 저희의 전 모델을 정가에서 20% 할인하여 제공합니다. 자전거 장비와 도구들도 40% 할인된 가격에 드립니다. 마지막으로, 명품 브랜드의 자전거 의류를 50% 저렴하게 구입하시고 타이어와 자전거 안장은 표시 가격에서 60% 할인된 가격에 구입하세요.

Adventure는 30년 이상 자전거 판매업을 해 왔습니다. 저희 창립자의 신념은 "그곳에 가는 데 자전거보다 더 좋은 방법은 없다"였습니다.

Adventure는 가장 박식한 직원들만을 채용한다고 확신합니다. 저희 직원들은 여러분이 필요로 하는 것을 제공하기 위해 여기에 있습니다. 단골 고객님들 덕분에, 저희는 주에서 가장 인기 있는 자전거 매장입니다. 버나드 가 140번지로 오셔서 매장을 살펴보세요. 즉시 여러분에게 딱 맞는 자전거를 찾아드리겠습니다.

Adventure에서 여러분은 좋은 자전거를 보장받을 수 있습니다!

어휘 drive to work 운전해서 출근하다 be tired of ~에 지치다
be held up in traffic 교통체증에 갇히다 solution 해결
regular price 정가 equipment 장비 apparel 의복, 의류
purchase 구매하다, 사다 sticker price 표시 가격, 소비자 가격
founder 창립자 knowledgeable 지식이 있는; 박식한
loyal 충성스러운; 성실한 in no time 즉시, 지체 없이
guarantee 보증하다 set of wheels 차, 자동차

1. 세부 내용을 묻는 문제

이 광고에서 언급된 자전거 타기의 좋은 점은 무엇인가?

(A) 짧아지는 통근 시간이 짧아지는 것
(B) 건강해지는 것
(C) 자연을 즐길 수 있는 것
(D) 운전하지 않아서 돈을 아낄 수 있는 것

해설 여기서는 제목에 답이 있다. 제목에 'Do you spend too much of your day driving to work?'라는 질문이 있고 'Adventure Bicycle Shop has the perfect solution: a bicycle.'이라고 해결책을 제시하고 있다. 그러므로 정답은 (A)이다.

2. 세부 내용을 묻는 문제

의류에 대한 할인은 얼마나 제공되나?

(A) 20%
(B) 40%
(C) 50%
(D) 60%

해설 의류를 나타내는 단어를 먼저 찾아야 한다. 지문에 있는 apparel(의복)이라는 어휘의 뜻을 알아야 풀 수 있는 문제이다. 두 번째 단락에서 'get the finest brand names in biking apparel for 50% off'라고 언급했으므로 정답은 (C)이다.

3. 사실 정보를 찾는 문제

Adventure 자전거 매장에 대해 언급된 것은 무엇인가?

(A) 시내 중심가의 편리한 위치에 있다.
(B) 새로운 장소에 매장 하나를 막 개장했다.
(C) 항상 할인된 가격에 제품을 판매한다.
(D) 직원들은 제품에 대해 많은 것을 안다.

해설 지문을 읽고 세부적인 내용을 찾는 문제. 네 번째 단락 첫째 문장 'Adventure makes sure to hire only the most knowledgeable staff members.'로 보아 직원들은 제품에 대해서 많은 것을 알고 있다고 할 수 있다. 그러므로 정답은 (D)이다.

〈4-6〉 다음은 이메일에 관한 문제이다.

수신: 전 직원 <employees@glanahotel.com>
발신: 경영진 <management@glanahotel.com>
날짜: 11월 2일
제목: '이달의 직원' 프로그램

최고 경영자 Graham Beckel은 지난달 말, 여러분 모두에게 새로운 '이달의 직원' 프로그램을 발표했습니다. 이 프로그램은 호텔의 예산을 아끼고, 어려운 기한을 맞추고, 손님들을 친절하게 모시며, 열정으로 업무를 수행하는 데 탁월한 기여를 보여 준 정규직 직원들을 선발할 것으로 예상됩니다.

글라나 호텔 손님과 직원들은 누구든지 추천안을 제출할 수 있습니다. 양식은 업무 지원 센터에서 이용 가능하며, 우리의 웹 사이트에서도 다운로드 받을 수 있습니다. 이달의 추천은 11월 20일까지입니다. 응모함이 정문 바로 옆에 설치되었습니다. 관리자들은 추천된 사람들을 검토하여 이달 말 웹 사이트를 통해 당선자들의 이름을 발표할 것입니다.

선발된 직원들은 상금과 최고 경영자가 서명한 감사증을 받게 되며, 또한 그들은 매월 직원들의 공로를 인정하는 저녁 만찬에도 초대됩니다.
우리는 이러한 방법으로 훌륭한 직원들을 많이 얻으리라 믿습니다.

진심으로,

경영진

어휘 exceptional 탁월한, 보통 이상의 commitment 기여, 헌신
meet 충족시키다 duty 의무, 임무 nomination 지명, 추천; 추천된 사람 due ~까지로 예정된 entry box 응모함 set up 설치하다
monetary prize 상금 recognition (공로 등에 대한) 인정
main entrance 정문 reception desk (호텔의) 접수처, 프런트

4. 세부 내용을 묻는 문제

추천 양식을 어디에 제출할 수 있는가?

(A) 매니저 사무실에서
(B) 호텔 웹 사이트에서
(C) 정문 옆에서
(D) 접수처에서

해설 추천 양식을 제출하는 곳을 묻는 문제로, 두 번째 단락 세 번째 줄의 'An

entry box has been set up just next to the front door.'에서 응모함이 정문 바로 옆에 설치되었다고 했으므로 next to the front door를 By the main entrance로 바꿔 표현한 (C)가 정답이다.

5. 사실 정보를 찾는 문제

선택된 직원에 관하여 언급된 것은?

(A) 그들은 월간 저녁 식사에 그들의 가족을 데려올 수 있다.
(B) 그들은 상으로 돈을 받을 것이다.
(C) 그들은 호텔에서 적어도 6개월 이상 일했다.
(D) 그들은 11월 20일에 선발될 것이다.

해설 '이달의 직원' 프로그램에 관하여 맞는 진술을 고르는 문제로, 세 번째 단락의 'The selected employees will receive a monetary prize ~'에서 선발된 직원들이 상금(monetary prize)을 받을 것이라고 했으므로 monetary prize를 money로 바꿔 표현한 (B)가 정답이다.

6. 사실 정보를 찾는 문제

Beckel 씨에 관하여 진술된 것은?

(A) 그는 감사증에 서명할 것이다.
(B) 그는 자기 직원들의 이름을 모두 알고 있다.
(C) 그는 경영진에게 이메일을 보냈다.
(D) 그는 매월 매니저들과 만난다.

해설 먼저 Beckel이 누구인지를 확인하면 맨 첫 줄에 'CEO Graham Beckel ~'이라고 했으므로 이 사람이 호텔의 최고 경영자임을 알 수 있으며, 세 번째 단락의 'The selected employees will receive a monetary prize and a certificate of appreciation signed by the CEO'에서 선발된 직원들이 상금과 함께 Graham Beckel이 서명한 감사증을 받을 거란 사실을 알 수 있으므로 (A)가 정답이다.

〈7-9〉 다음은 공지에 관한 문제이다.

안전 규칙

모든 직원은 이 작업실을 이용할 때 몇 가지 특별한 규정을 준수해야 합니다.

- 이 작업실에서는 언제나 신체와 손, 얼굴, 안경까지 보호하는 안전복을 착용해야 하며, 출입구 쪽의 대기실에서 벗어야 합니다.
- 작업실을 나가기 전에 대기실에서 안전복을 벗어 '안전복'이라고 적혀 있는 함에 넣습니다.
- 실린더나 접시, 깡통을 차가운 저장소나 벽장에 넣기 전에 알맞은 표시를 붙입니다.
- 튀는 길 막기 위해 모든 용기는 인진 박스가 있는 기트로 옮겨야 합니다. 이때 누출을 피하기 위해 뚜껑이 올바로 봉인되어 있는지 확인합니다.
- 만약 누출이 발생했다면 각 작업 장소에 붙어 있는 오염 물질 제거 규약을 따릅니다. 만약 서비스 직원의 도움이 필요하다면 내선 번호 320번의 앨런 씨와 통화를 합니다.

위에 언급한 규정들은 여러분의 안전을 위해 실행하고 있습니다. 이 규정을 무시한 직원에게는 직속상관이 주의 통지서를 보낼 것입니다.

어휘 be obliged to ~해야 한다 apparel 의복 eye wear 안경류 be disposed of ~을 버리다 antechamber 대기실 doorway 현관, 출입구 deposit 두다 stow 넣다 avert 피하다 splatter 튀기기 receptacle 용기, 그릇 hamper 바구니, 박스 ensure 확실하게 하다 seal 봉인 seepage 누출 decontamination 오염 물질 제거 foregoing 앞서 언급한 in place (법, 규칙 등이) 실행 중인 ignore 무시하다 grievance 불만

7. 글의 목적을 묻는 문제

이 공지를 한 이유는?

(A) 직원들에게 안전 규칙을 알리기 위해
(B) 직원들에게 유니폼이 바뀐다고 알리기 위해
(C) 어느 직원의 불만사항을 받아들이기 위해
(D) 새 장치 사용을 위한 가이드라인을 제공하기 위해

해설 제목(Security Rules)과 더불어 첫 문장에서 모든 직원은 이 작업실을 이용할 때 몇 가지 구체적인 사항을 준수해야 한다고 했으므로 (A)가 정답이다.

8. 세부 내용을 묻는 문제

작업실을 이용하는 직원은 안전복을 어디에 두어야 하는가?

(A) 수레 위에
(B) 함 안에
(C) 벽장 속에
(D) 작업 공간에

해설 두 번째 세부사항, 'Before exiting the workroom, remove safety attire in the antechamber and deposit it in the containers labeled "safety garments"'에서 작업실을 나가기 전에 대기실에서 안전복을 벗어 '안전복'이라고 적혀 있는 함에 넣으라고 언급하고 있다. 그러므로 정답은 (B)이다.

9. 추후 당부 사항을 묻는 문제

이 공지문에서 직원들에게 앨런 씨와 연락을 취하라고 제안한 이유는 무엇인가?

(A) 엎질러진 것을 치울 때 도움이 필요한 경우를 대비하여
(B) 여분의 실린더와 접시를 사야 할 때를 대비하여
(C) 관리자에게 기구가 없어졌다고 알려야 할 경우를 대비하여
(D) 실험실 테스트를 위한 허가를 얻어야 할 때를 대비하여

해설 마지막 세부사항 If a leak occurs, carry out ~ Mr. Allen at extension 320에서 만약 누출이 발생하면 각 작업장에 붙어 있는 오염 물질 제거 규약을 따른다고 되어 있고, 만약 서비스 직원이 필요하면 앨런 씨와 통화해야 한다고 언급되어 있다. 그러므로 정답은 (A)이다.

UNIT 21 동의어 / 추론

SPARTA PRACTICE

p. 188

1 (A) **2** (C) **3** (A) **4** (A) **5** (B) **6** (A)
7 (B)

12월 1일부터 1월 30일까지 운영할 전시회에서는 기원전 5세기부터 2세기 말까지의 가장 매력적인 고대 건축물 중 몇몇을 선보입니다. 전시뿐만 아니라 학술 전문가의 강의를 포함한 많은 특별 행사가 있을 예정입니다.

어휘 exhibition 전시회 feature 특징으로 다루다 fascinating 매혹적인 architectural 건축의 complement 보충하다 scholarly 학문적인

1. 동의어 찾는 문제

세 번째 줄의 단어 "complement"와 의미상 가장 가까운 것은

(A) 향상시키다
(B) 획득하다
(C) 고르다
(D) 설명하다

해설 동의어를 묻는 질문은 단어 자체의 뜻보다는 문장 안에서의 의미로 파악한다. "There will be a number of special events to complement the exhibit" 부분으로 전시를 보완하고, 더 좋게 만든다는 뜻으로 enhance와 같은 의미로 쓰였다. 그러므로 정답은 (A)이다.

구독자분들께 전하는 정보

구독 연장 요청은 귀하의 현 구독이 만료되는 날의 일주일 전에 자동으로 발송되며, 다음의 조건들을 대상으로 합니다.

어휘 subscriber 구독자 renewal 갱신 automatically 자동으로 expiration date 만료일 subject to ~을 대상으로 하는

2. 동의어 찾는 문제

세 번째 줄의 단어 "conditions"와 의미상 가장 가까운 것은

(A) 목표
(B) 제안
(C) 조항
(D) 이름

해설 해당 문장에서 현재의 구독이 만료되기 일주일 전에 구독 갱신 요청서가 자동 발송된다고 하면서, 다음의 조건들을 대상으로 한다고 했으며, 아래에는 갱신 관련 항목들이 언급되어 있다. 그러므로 '조건'의 의미로 쓰인 conditions와 의미가 유사한 (C) terms가 답이 된다.

레저부의 책임자인 조 리드는 올해 이 시기에 열리는 다양한 행사들로부터 버는 돈이 일 년 내내 오락시설과 레저시설을 유지하는 데 중요한 역할을 한다고 말했다.

어휘 a variety of 다양한 maintain 유지하다 amenities 오락시설

3. 동의어 찾는 문제

두 번째 줄의 단어, "maintaining"과 의미상 가장 가까운 것은

(A) 유지하기
(B) 방어하기
(C) 선언하기
(D) 찾아보기

해설 해당 문장에서 maintain은 '(건물이나 기계 등을 점검 보수해가며) 유지하다'란 뜻으로 쓰였으므로 이와 유사한 의미의 (A)가 답이 된다. keep up은 '(수준 등이) 내려가지 않게 하다, 유지하다'를 의미한다.

작년 우리 회사의 연휴 파티를 준비할 때, 귀하가 제공한 서비스와 품질은 우수했습니다. 저는 귀하께서 이 상황을 바로잡고 제가 받지 못한 꽃들과 색깔이 잘못 배달된 꽃들에 대한 환불을 제공해 주실 것이라 믿습니다. 그렇지 않다면, 저는 이번 12월 5일에 있을 회사의 연휴 파티에 거래처를 바꿀 것입니다.

어휘 rectify 교정하다, 바로잡다 elsewhere 다른 곳으로

4. 동의어 찾는 문제

두 번째 줄의 "rectify"와 의미상 가장 가까운 것은

(A) 고치다
(B) 제거하다
(C) 단순화하다
(D) 통합되다

해설 "you will rectify this situation ~"의 내용에 대해 그렇게 하지 않으면, 거래처를 바꾸겠다고(If not, I may take my business elsewhere ~) 말하는 것으로 미뤄 '고치다, 변경하다'의 뜻임을 알 수 있다. 그러므로 정답은 (A)이다.

마지막으로, 저는 오늘 직장에 있는 동안 사람들이 당신이 이곳 체육관에 부착해 놓은 광고지에 대해서 얘기하는 것을 들었다는 것을 알려드리고 싶군요. 사람들은 당신의 레스토랑을 얼마나 좋아하는지 그리고 그들이 얼마나 개업 기념 파티를 놓치고 싶지 않은지에 대해 얘기하고 있었습니다. 저는 당신이 상당히 많은 참석자를 갖게 될 것으로 생각합니다.

어휘 overhear 어쩌다 듣다 flyer 광고 전단 turnout 참석자 수

5. 추론 문제

글쓴이에 대해서 암시되고 있는 내용은 무엇인가?

(A) 그는 레스토랑에서 근무한다.
(B) 그는 체육관에서 일한다.
(C) 그는 파티의 기획자이다.
(D) 그는 파티에서 바텐더를 할 것이다.

해설 'Finally, I want ~ the flyer you posted here at the gym.(마지막으로, 저는 오늘 직장에 있는 동안 사람들이 당신이 이곳 체육관에 부착해 놓은 광고지에 관해서 얘기하는 것을 들었다는 것을 알려드리고 싶군요.)' 라고 하므로 근무지가 체육관임을 알 수 있다. 그러므로 정답은 (B)이다.

개조를 마친 오클랜드 예술관이 이번 주 목요일에 축하 정찬과 함께 첫 전시를 할 것이다. 초청 받은 하객들은 호평을 받고 있는 화가 스테판 슈와츠의 신작 약 30점이 선보일 전시회에 참석할 것이다. 이 행사는 3월 2일부터 약 3주간 화요일에서 일요일 오전 10시부터 오후 7시까지 대중에게 선보일 예정이다.

어휘 renovated 개조된 debut 처음 나가다 feature 특징으로 다루다, 특별히 포함하다 acclaimed 호평을 받은 open to the public 대중에게 공개하다

6. 추론 문제

오클랜드 예술관은 아마도 주중 어떤 날에 휴관할 것 같은가?

(A) 월요일
(B) 목요일
(C) 토요일
(D) 일요일

해설 본문 마지막에 언급된 'This event will then be open ~ Tuesday through Sunday'에서 화요일부터 일요일까지 대중에게 공개된다는 것은 월요일에 전시하지 않는 것을 암시하므로 휴관하는 날은 월요일이라 볼 수 있다. 그러므로 정답은 (A)이다.

Constable Bistro의 소유주이자 수석 요리사인 존 콘스태블 씨는 이 역사적인 건물을 복원하는 데 1년이 걸렸다. 이 장소는 오라클 공원 맞은편, 킹 가와 2번가의 교차로에 위치해 있으며 아름다운 경관을 자랑한다. "이곳은 아치형 문들과 큰 고전적인 벽화가 있는 굉장히 멋진 공간입니다."라고 콘스태블 씨가 말했다.

어휘 head chef 수석 요리사 restore 복원하다 boast 자랑하다 mural 벽화

7. 추론 문제

Constable Bistro의 장소에 관해 무엇이 암시되어 있는가?

(A) 고대 유적들 옆에 있다.
(B) 길 모퉁이에 위치해 있다.
(C) 여러 개의 공원에 둘러싸여 있다.
(D) 다른 식당들과 한 구역 내에 있다.

해설 본문에서 "The location boasts ~ at the intersection of King Street and 2nd Street across from Oracle park."로 언급된 바와 같이 2개의 도로가 교차하고 맞은편에 공원이 있다는 것은 구도상 길모퉁이를 암시한다. 그러므로 정답은 (B)이다.

SPARTA ACTUAL TEST p. 190

1 (D)	2 (B)	3 (A)	4 (C)	5 (B)	6 (D)
7 (A)	8 (D)	9 (D)			

⟨1-2⟩ 다음은 이메일에 관한 문제이다.

수신: P&M 경영진
발신: 사업 경영 위원회
날짜: 7월 21일
제목: 사업 전략 보고서

업계의 수년간 경험 덕분에 P&M 사는 고품질의 건설 장비 제조에 대해 받아 마땅한 우수한 평가를 받고 있습니다. 그러나 우리는 기로에 서 있습니다. 여러분 모두 아시다시피, 지난 2년간 제조 비용이 9% 증가하였습니다. 우리는 이러한 인상된 비용을 감당할 방법에 대해 수많은 선택안을 살펴보았습니다. 일부 사람들은 우리 제품의 가격 인상을 제안하였으나, 대다수 사람들은 그렇게 하면 소비자들이 낙담해서 떠날 것이라고 생각합니다.

최근의 인상에도 불구하고, 우리는 여전히 수익률을 유지하고 있습니다. 그러므로 우리의 현재 사업 전략이 효과적이라는 것을 명심하십시오. 예를 들어, 우리의 텔레비전과 라디오 광고는 광범위하게 방송되고 있고, 광고들에 대한 소비자들의 반응도 좋습니다. 이러한 이유로 우리는 마케팅 예산을 같은 수준으로 유지할 것을 권합니다. 그러나 우리는 새롭고 혁신적인 제품들의 연구와 개발을 위해 더 많은 자금을 마련할 것을 권고합니다. 이 제품들은 우리가 업계에서 리더로 남아 있도록 도우며, 또한 계속해서 총수입과 수익 모두를 증가시켜 줄 것입니다.

이는 상승하는 가격으로 인한 추가 비용을 감당하는 데 도움이 될 것입니다.

어휘 executive 경영진 operation 운영, 경영 committee 위원회 strategy 전략 corporation 법인; 주식회사 stellar 우수한, 주요한 well-deserved 당연히 받아 마땅한 have a reputation for ~으로 유명하다[평판이 좋다] manufacture 제조하다 construction 건설; 공사 machinery 기계류 crossroad 교차 도로 option 선택(권) cover 손실을 메우다; (비용 등을) 감당하다 increase 증가; 늘리다 suggest 제안하다 majority 대다수 discourage 낙담시키다 drive away 몰아내다, 쫓아내다 recent 최근의 profitability 수익성 keep in mind 명심하다 effective 효과적인 air 방송하다 respond 응답하다; 반응하다 recommend 추천하다, 권하다 budget 예산 remain 남다 fund 자금 set aside 마련하다, 챙겨두다, 떼어 놓다 innovative 혁신적인 field 분야 revenue 총수입 profit 수익 extra 여분의 expenditure 지출; 비용

1. 추론 문제

P&M사에 관해서 무엇이 암시되어 있는가?

(A) 이 회사의 광고는 인기가 좋지 못하다.
(B) 이 회사의 경영 전략은 거의 효율적이지 못하다.
(C) 이 회사 제품의 질은 감소하였다.
(D) 이 회사는 상반기에 추가 지출을 효과적으로 충당하였다.

해설 이 이메일은 상단에 작성 날짜가 'July 21' 7월 21일인 상반기 직후로 언급되어 있고, 지문 중반에서 'Despite the recent increases, we have still maintained our profitability.' 작성 시기까지는 최근의 제조 비용의 상승에도 여전히 수익성이 유지된다고 밝히고 있으므로 정답은 (D)이다.

2. 동의어 찾는 문제

첫 번째 단락, 세 번째 줄의 단어 "cover"와 의미상 가장 가까운 것은

(A) 줄이다
(B) 지불하다
(C) 숨기다
(D) 손을 뻗다

해설 지문에서 cover의 의미는 '(비용을) 감당하다'로 해석이 되므로 '비용을 지불하다'란 뜻이라고 볼 수 있다. 그러므로 정답은 (B)이다.

⟨3-5⟩ 다음은 평론에 관한 문제이다.

6월 5일

인도의 맛

토요일 저녁에 카쉬미르라는 브라이트웰의 새로운 인도 음식점에서 식사를 했다. 브라이트웰의 거의 모든 음식점을 평가했지만, 카쉬미르는 내가 가 봤던 최고의 식당들 중 하나라고 솔직하게 말할 수 있다. 음식은 환상적이었고, 분위기는 인도식으로 장식되었으며 서비스는 인상적이었고, 효율적이었다. 지난 토요일 식당의 화려한 개업을 축하하기 위해 시디퀴 씨는 모든 고객들에게 주요리 구매 시 무료 음료 한 잔씩을 제공했다.

여느 인도 음식점에서 기대할 수 있듯이, 메뉴는 매우 다양한 기호를 만족시킬 것들이 포함되어 있었다.

주요리들은 맛있는 비리야니, 탄두리와 티카 요리들이 포함되어 있다. 모든 메뉴는 매일 신선하게 준비되고 적당한 가격이다.

카쉬미르는 6월 6일부터 6월 10일까지 할인된 가격에 다양한 메뉴를 제공하고 있다. 모든 주요리는 밥과, 달콤하고 매운 소스, 그리고 난과 함께 제공된다. 카쉬미르는 브라이트웰의 하이 스트리트에 있다. 매일 오전 11시부터 오후 10시까지 영업을 하고 있다. 식당은 또한 보는 규모의 행사를 위한 출장요리를 겸하고 있다.

라자 슐먼
<브라이트웰 데일리 리포트>

어휘 taste 맛　honestly 진심으로　dining 식당　ambience 분위기　complimentary 무료의　naan 난, 인도에서 먹는 납작한 빵　locate 위치해 있다　critic 비평가　chef 주방장　moderately 적당히

3. 전반적인 내용의 문제

라자 슐먼은 누구일 것 같은가?

(A) 음식 비평가
(B) 기자
(C) 요리사
(D) 음식점 소유주

해설 글을 쓴 사람이므로, 글의 전반적인 목적을 확인해 봐야 한다. 식당에 대한 평가를 하고 있으므로 보기 중 어울리는 것은 비평가의 (A)이다.

4. 세부 내용을 묻는 문제

카쉬미르에 관해 언급된 것은 무엇인가?

(A) 카쉬미르 애비뉴에 있다.
(B) 아침식사가 가능하다.
(C) 가격이 적절하다.
(D) 월요일에는 문을 닫는다.

해설 세부 사항에 관해 묻는 문제는 보기를 정확하게 확인 지문에서 찾아봐야 한다. 세 번째 문단에서, 'All menu items are freshly prepared daily and reasonably priced.'에서 정답은 (C)임을 알 수 있다.

5. 동의어 찾는 문제

첫 단락 세 번째 줄의 "ambience"와 의미상 가장 가까운것은

(A) 준비
(B) 분위기
(C) 조명
(D) 선택

해설 ambience의 뜻은 '분위기'이고 지문에서도 식당의 분위기에 대해 설명하고 있는 부분이므로 정답은 (B)이다.

〈6-9〉 다음은 편지에 관한 문제이다.

포겔 씨에게,

저희 이곳 Geneva 전자회사는 지난 5년 동안 케이트 맥키넌 씨와 함께 일할 수 있어서 기뻤습니다. 그녀는 신참의 영업 직원으로 일을 시작했고, 뛰어난 일 처리로 단지 2년 후에 상급 영업 직원으로 승진했습니다. 두 직책 모두에서 그녀는 끊임없이 연간 판매 목표를 초과 달성하였습니다.

저는 Geneva 전자회사에 지난해 하반기에 영업 부장으로 합류하였고, 바로 그 당시부터 그녀가 저의 팀에서 함께한다는 것은 행운이었습니다. 그녀는 고객을 이해하는 능력은 출중하고, 항상 긍정적인 태도를 가지고 있습니다. 그녀는 매우 바쁜 업무 환경에서도 팀워크가 좋으며, 그것을 그녀의 타고난 리더십 기술을 보여 줍니다.

Geneva 전자회사에 입사하기 앞서서 맥키넌 씨는 고객서비스 직원의 역할을 수행한 적이 있어, 고객의 불만을 처리하는 능력 또한 매우 우수합니다. 팀에서의 그녀의 특출한 성과는 그녀에게 더 많은 업무를 할당하게 하였습니다.

따라서, 저는 진심으로 맥키넌 씨가 지원한 직책에 그녀를 추천하며, 그녀가 귀사에 엄청난 자산이 될 것임을 믿어 의심치 않는다.

진심으로,

저스틴 써록스
판매부장
Geneva 전자회사

어휘 junior 신참의　sales representative 영업 직원　outstanding 뛰어난　promote 승진시키다　associate 동료　consistently 끊임없이　exceed 초과하다　yearly 1년에 한 번　fortunate 행운의　that very moment 바로 그 당시　distinguished 훌륭한, 출중한　reflect 반영하다　hold a position 직책을 차지하다　superior 상급의　handle 다루다, 처리하다　customer complaint 고객 불만　exceptional 뛰어난　accordingly 따라서

6. 글을 쓴 목적을 묻는 문제

써록스 씨는 이 편지를 왜 썼는가?

(A) 맥키넌 씨를 승진하게 하기 위해서
(B) 맥키넌 씨에 관해 정보를 요청하기 위해서
(C) 수상자로 맥키넌 씨를 지명하기 위해서
(D) 맥키넌 씨가 새로운 직장을 찾는 것을 돕기 위해서

해설 마지막 문장에서 'Accordingly, I heartily recommend Ms. McKinnon ~ to your company.'에 언급된 바와 같이 맥키넌 씨를 다른 회사에 추천하기 위해서 쓴 글이므로 정답은 (D)이다.

7. 추론 문제

맥키넌 씨에 관해서 무엇이 암시되었는가?

(A) 그녀는 항상 판매 분야에서 일한 것은 아니다.
(B) 그녀는 결코 관리자였던 적이 없다.
(C) 그녀는 Geneva 전자회사에 대해 써록스 씨에게서 알게 되었다.
(D) Geneva 전자회사에 재직할 동안 3개의 다른 직책을 맡았다.

해설 세 번째 문단에서 'Having held a position as a customer service representative before joining Geneva Electronics, ~ to handle customer complaints.'에서 언급된 바와 같이 맥키넌 씨는 Geneva 전자회사에 입사하기 전에 고객 서비스 직원으로 일한 이력이 있으므로 항상 판매직에만 종사한 것은 아님을 알 수 있다. 그러므로 정답은 (A)이다.

8. 틀린 정보를 찾는 문제

맥키넌 씨의 자질들 중 하나로 언급되지 않은 것은 무엇인가?

(A) 리더쉽
(B) 긍정적인 태도
(C) 문제 해결 능력
(D) 자발적인 출장

해설 두 번째 문단에서 'She works ~ reflects her natural leadership skills.'에서 (A), 'Her ability ~ has a positive attitude.'에서 (B), 'Ms. McKinnon ~ handle customer complaints.'에서 (C)가 언급되었으므로 언급되지 않은 것은 (D)이다.

9. 동의어 찾는 문제

두 번째 단락 네 번째 줄의 "reflects"와 의미상 가장 가까운 것은

(A) 영향을 미치다
(B) 고려하다
(C) 실현하다
(D) 보여주다

해설 지문에서 그녀의 자연스러운 리더쉽이 발휘된다는 의미가 적합하므로 이와 가장 유사한 '보여주다'의 의미를 가진 (D)가 정답이다.

UNIT 22 맥락 완성

맥락 완성 연습

p. 197

1 (B) **2** (A) **3** (B) **4** (C)

저희는 이제 반섬-홀든 인슈어런스의 새 이름 하에서 일하고 있습니다. 고객님의 청구 계좌는 변경되지 않을 것입니다. 하지만 저희가 제공할 수 있는 서비스의 다양성이 향상될 것임을 기대하실 수 있습니다.

어휘 insurance 보험 claims account (보험료 청구용) 청구 계좌 alter 변경하다

1. 알맞은 접속부사 찾기 문제

(A) 예를 들면
(B) 그러나
(C) 요컨대
(D) 그러므로

해설 빈칸 앞은 보험 청구 계좌가 바뀌지 않을 거라는 내용(Your claims account will not be altered.)이며, 빈칸 뒤에 제공되는 서비스의 증가를 기대할 수 있다고 했으므로(you can expect the variety of services that we can provide you to improve.) 역접의 의미인 (B)가 정답이다.

올해 전시회는 3월 1일부터 8월 31일까지 관심 있는 사람들이라면 누구에게나 개방될 것입니다. 더불어 2월 20일 수요일 저녁때쯤에 아트 센터의 직원들만을 포함할 예행연습이 있을 것입니다.

어휘 night 저녁 rehearsal 리허설, 예행연습

2. 알맞은 접속부사 찾기 문제

(A) 게다가
(B) 대신에
(C) 구체적으로 말하면
(D) 결과적으로

해설 빈칸 앞뒤의 문장을 논리적으로 연결해 주는 접속부사를 묻는 문제이다. 빈칸 앞에는 올해 전시회가 언제 열릴 거라는 정보를 제공하고 있으며(The exhibition will be open to anyone interested from March 1 to August 31 this year.), 뒤에는 그 전에 예행연습이 있을 거라 내용이 연결되어 있으므로(on the night of Wednesday February 20, there will be a rehearsal which will include the staff members of the art center.) 이 두 문장을 자연스럽게 연결해 줄 수 있는 것은 부연, 첨가의 기능을 하는 In addition으로 정답은 (A)이다.

저는 Heughan 스튜디오라고 불리는 회사에서 근무하고 있으며, 현재 신인 영화 배우들과의 인터뷰를 위한 장소를 물색하고 있습니다. 저희는 당신의 업장이 방송을 촬영하기에 적합하다고 생각하였습니다. 저희 촬영 기사들 중 한 명이 오늘 당신의 업장에 방문할 것입니다. 만날 수 있는 시간을 알려 주십시오.

어휘 currently 현재 shoot a broadcast 방송 촬영을 하다 cinematographer 촬영기사 establishment 시설 availability 이용 누, 유효성

3. 알맞은 지시어 찾기 문제

(A) 나의
(B) 너의
(C) 그것의
(D) 그의

해설 맥락상 발신인의 회사인 방송국에서 글을 읽는 수신인의 업장에 찾아가는 상황이므로 이를 2인칭으로 언급한 정답은 (B)이다.

직원 복지 프로그램 실행에 관해 제안해 주셔서 감사합니다. 당신이 계획한 목적은 재정적으로나 논리상의 관점 모두에서 매우 합리적으로 보입니다. 또한, 왜 그 프로그램이 우리 회사를 위해 유리할 것인지에 관해 당신이 제공한 조사도 설득력이 있었습니다. 저는 그것을 추진하기로 결정했습니다.

어휘 implementation 수행 lay out 계획하다 reasonable 합리적인 logistically 논리상의 관점으로 persuasive 설득력이 있는 go ahead 추진하다

4. 알맞은 지시어 찾기 문제

(A) 나
(B) 너
(C) 그것
(D) 그들

해설 본문에서 추진하기로 결정될 수 있는 대상은 수신인이 앞서 했던 제안인 것을 알 수 있으므로 이것을 지시하는 정답은 (C)이다.

SPARTA PRACTICE

p. 198

1 (C) **2** (A)

귀하의 커피 테이블 주문에 빠진 동봉물에 대해 사과 드립니다. 그 조립 도구 세트는 오늘 빠른 우편으로 발송되어, 내일 도착할 것입니다. 저희는 세트와 함께, 귀하께서 다음 크로그 가구 구매 시 사용할 수 있는 20% 할인 카드 또한 포함했습니다. 귀하의 커피테이블을 위한 조립 도구 모음을 받지 못하여 생긴 불편에 대해 사과드립니다. 크로그는 귀하의 지속적인 단골 거래를 기대하고 있습니다.

어휘 apologize 사과하다 missing 잃어버린 enclosure 동봉(물) order 주문 assembly 조립 toolkit 도구 모음 inconvenience 불편 continued 지속적인, 계속되는 patronage 단골(로 거래해줌), 후원 include 포함하다 discount 할인

1. 맥락을 완성시키는 문제

지문에 표시된 [1], [2], [3], 그리고 [4] 중에서 다음의 문장이 들어가기에 가장 좋은 위치가 어디인가?

"저희는 세트와 함께, 귀하께서 다음 크로그 가구 구매 시 사용할 수 있는 20% 할인 카드 또한 포함했습니다."

(A) [1] (B) [2] (C) [3] (D) [4]

해설 'The assembly toolkit is being mailed to you today by overnight express mail for arrival by tomorrow.'에서 빠른 우편으로 빠진 누락된 조립 도구 세트를 보낸다고 하면서 'We have also included, along with the kit, a 20% discount card for your next Krog Furniture purchase.'에서 보면 할인 카드를 또한(also) 포함했다고 볼 수 있으므로 정답은 (C)이다.

수신: 기술지원 직원들
발신: Willem Dafoe
날짜: 9월 7일
제목: 새로운 구내전화

내부의 의사소통을 더 쉽게 하기 위하여, 새로운 구내 전화 번호 시스템이 고

안되었습니다. 여러분의 새로운 구내 전화번호가 첨부된 것을 찾을 수 있을 겁니다. 번호 "1"은 여러분이 기술 지원팀에 있음을 나타냅니다. "0"은 구내 전화번호가 적어도 세 자리여야 하기 때문에 사용되었습니다. 마지막 번호는 여러분의 자리 번호입니다. 자리들은 사무실에서 연속으로 번호가 붙여졌습니다. 직원이 어디에 앉는지를 안다면, 구내 전화번호 검색표를 갖고 있지 않더라도 그 또는 그녀의 내선 번호를 알 수 있을 것입니다.

어휘 tech(technology) 기술 support 지원, 지지 extension 구내전화 internal 내부의 communication 의사소통 devise 궁리하다, 고안하다 identify (신분을)증명하다, 확인하다 digit 전화번호 cubicle 자리, 열람실, 사무실 consecutively 연속적으로 determine 결정하다, 확정하다

2. 맥락을 완성시키는 문제

지문에 표시된 [1], [2], [3], 그리고 [4] 중에서 다음의 문장이 들어가기에 가장 좋은 위치가 어디인가?

"여러분의 새로운 구내 전화번호가 첨부된 것을 찾을 수 있을 겁니다."

(A) [1] (B) [2] (C) [3] (D) [4]

해설 'Attached, you will find your new extensions.' 문장에서 보면 '새로운 구내번호가 첨부되어 있다'고 하면서, 바로 그 다음 맥락에 바로 구체적인 구내번호(The number "1" identifies)가 언급되는 것이 자연스럽다. 그러므로 정답은 (A)이다.

SPARTA ACTUAL TEST p. 199

1 (A)	2 (B)	3 (B)	4 (D)	5 (D)	6 (A)
7 (B)	8 (A)	9 (A)	10 (C)		

〈1-3〉 다음은 편지에 관한 문제이다.

2월 17일

Reddick 씨 귀하,

FC 은행에 관심을 가져 주셔서 감사 드립니다. 저희는 하이델부르그의 지점장 자리를 위한 당신의 온라인 신청서와 이력서를 받았습니다. 안타깝게도, 저희는 그 직책에 과거 2년간의 관리 경험을 요구하고 있습니다. 그러나, 저는 당신의 이력서가 인상적이어서 당신이 부지점장 자리에 좋은 후보가 될 수 있을 거라고 생각합니다. 저희는 현재 디어 파크 지사에서 채용을 진행하고 있습니다. 저는 당신의 이력서를 그 지점의 지역 부장에게 전달하였지만, 새로운 지원서를 온라인상에서 제출하셔야 합니다. 당신은 이번 주 안에 그 부장으로부터 연락을 받으실 겁니다. 지원해 주셔서 감사합니다. 저는 이것이 당신에게 흥미로운 기회가 되기를 희망합니다.

진심으로,

Bridget Regan

FC 은행
인사부 담당자

어휘 interest 흥미 application 신청서 résumé 이력서 unfortunately 불행히도 previous 이전의 currently 현재 forward 전달하다 submit 제출하다 opportunity 기회 of interest 흥미로운 impressed 감명받은 candidate 후보

1. 편지의 목적을 묻는 문제

이 편지의 주된 목적은 무엇인가?

(A) 지원자에게 그가 자격요건을 충족시키지 못했다는 것을 알리기 위해
(B) 지원자에게 그가 지원한 자리는 더 이상 공석이 아니라는 것을 알리기 위해
(C) 지원자와 인터뷰 일정을 잡기 위해
(D) 지원자에게 추가 정보 제공을 요청하기 위해

해설 지문 초반을 보면 'Unfortunately, we require 2 years of previous managerial experience for that position.(안타깝게도, 저희는 그 직책에 과거 2년간의 관리 경험을 요구하고 있습니다.)'라고 하므로 정답은 (A)이다.

2. 추후 당부 사항을 묻는 문제

Regan 씨는 Reddick 씨에게 무엇을 하도록 제안하는가?

(A) 디어 파크 지점에 직접 신청할 것
(B) 새로운 신청서를 작성할 것
(C) 디어 파크 지사의 고용 담당 과장에게 이메일을 보낼 것
(D) FC 뱅크의 관리직 훈련 프로그램에 등록할 것

해설 지문 후반에 보면 'I forwarded your résumé to the district manager of that branch, but you will also need to submit a new application online.(저는 당신의 이력서를 그 지점의 지역 관리 담당 부장에게 전달했지만, 새로운 신청서를 온라인상에서 제출하셔야 합니다.)'라고 하므로 신청서 작성을 제안하고 있다는 것을 알 수 있다. 그러므로 정답은 (B)이다.

3. 맥락을 완성시키는 문제

지문에 표시된 [1], [2], [3], 그리고 [4] 중에서 다음의 문장이 들어가기에 가장 좋은 위치가 어디인가?

"그러나, 저는 당신의 이력서가 인상적이어서 당신이 부지점장 자리에 좋은 후보가 될 수 있을 거라고 생각합니다."

(A) [1] (B) [2] (C) [3] (D) [4]

해설 'Unfortunately, we require 2 years of previous managerial experience for that position.'에서는 앞서 나왔던 지점장 직책이 경력 때문에 거부당했음을 알려준다. 하지만 제시된 문장의 내용을 보면 부지점장 자리는 가능하다고 말하고 있다. [2] 뒤에 관련 내용이 이어지므로 정답은 (B)이다.

〈4-7〉 다음은 기사에 관한 문제이다.

오클라호마 (10월 29일) — 간식과 다양한 음료를 제공하는 지역 소재의 카페인 Joe's Addiction의 영업이 호황을 이루고 있다. 이 업체가 주로 지역 주민들을 상대로 영업을 함과 동시에, 다른 도시로부터 유입된 회사원들의 업장 방문을 더욱더 많이 보게 된다고 매장주인 조 맨데스가 말하였다. 주요 원인은 최근에 상가 주변으로 새로운 사무 복합 단지가 들어섰기 때문이라고 그녀는 생각한다.

"이 지역의 모든 변화는 특히 우리 사업의 급성장을 불러일으켰습니다."라고 멘데스 씨가 언급하였다. "저희는 항상 합리적인 가격으로 서비스를 제공하고 있으며, 요즘은 바쁜 점심시간을 이용해 저희를 방문하는 사업가들을 많이 볼 수 있습니다. 몇몇 분들은 심지어 일주일에도 여러 번 들르십니다."

다음 달부터, 이 음식점은 건강식을 위한 특별한 샐러드 바를 추가할 예정이다. "저희는 이 지역에서 나고 자란 과일과 채소와 제철 식자재를 이용한 다양한 메뉴를 제공하기 위해 노력하고 있으며, 10년 동안 우리를 꾸준히 찾아주신 고객님들께도 진심으로 감사하고 있습니다."고 멘데스 씨는 말했다. 또한, 멘데스 씨는 주말과 휴일 점심에 카페를 여는 것도 고려 중이다. 관심이 있다면, 사우 이스턴 가에 있는 Joe's Addiction을 확인해 보세요.

어휘 boom 호황을 이루다 serve 제공하다, 봉사하다 complex 복합단지 lead to (결과적으로) ~에 이르다 surge 급상승 strive 노력하다, 애쓰다 various 다양한 seasonal 제철의 sincerely 진심으로

4. 세부사항을 묻는 문제

기사에 따르면, Joe's Addiction은 왜 매출 성장을 보이는가?

(A) 식당을 개조하였다.
(B) 서비스 가격을 내렸다.
(C) 좋은 평판을 받고 있다.
(D) 많이 늘어난 사무실과 가깝다.

해설 첫 문단에서 'While the establishment ~ some new office complexes were recently built nearby.'에서 알 수 있듯이 매장 주변에 새로운 복합 단지가 들어서면서 외부 지역 손님들이 많이 찾아오고 있다고 언급하고 있으므로 정답은 (D)이다.

5. 세부사항을 묻는 문제

멘데스 씨는 곧 무엇을 할 계획인가?

(A) 새로운 지역에 개업하기
(B) 추가 자금 확보하기
(C) 더 많은 요리사 구인하기
(D) 제공할 메뉴 늘리기

해설 세 번째 문단에서, Starting next month, the restaurant is adding a special salad bar to provide healthy food.'에서 보면 다음 달부터 건강식을 위한 새로운 메뉴가 추가될 것임을 알 수 있다. 그러므로 정답은 (D)이다.

6. 틀린 정보를 찾는 문제

Joe's Addiction에 관해 언급되지 않은 것은 무엇인가?

(A) 토요일마다 점심식사가 제공된다.
(B) 10년 이상 영업해 왔다.
(C) 한 개인이 소유하고 있다.
(D) 저렴한 식사를 제공한다.

해설 지문 후반에서 'Ms. Mendes is also considering opening the cafe for lunch on weekends and holidays.'에서 알 수 있듯, 주말에 점심식사를 제공할 것을 고려 중에 있다는 것은 지금은 현재 토요일에 점심식사를 제공하지 않는다는 것을 의미한다. 그러므로 본문에 언급되지 않은 (A)가 정답이다.

7. 문장 삽입 문제

지문에 표시된 [1], [2], [3], 그리고 [4] 중에서 아래 문장이 들어가기에 가장 좋은 위치는 어디인가?

"몇몇 분들은 심지어 일주일에도 여러 번 들르십니다."

(A) [1]
(B) [2]
(C) [3]
(D) [4]

해설 [2] 앞에서 'we're now seeing a ~ during busy lunchtime.' 내용에서 알 수 있듯이 최근 들어 바쁜 점심시간에 더욱 많은 사람들이 방문하고 있음을 언급하고 있다. 그래서 'a lot of businesspeople'을 Some of them으로 연결한 정답은 (B)이다.

〈8-10〉 다음은 추천서에 관한 문제이다.

관계자분께:

저희는 마케팅 고문인 강유정 씨의 채용으로 엄청난 이익을 얻었습니다. 내부분의 의뢰인들이 지역 소규모 기업을 위한 저희의 혁신적이고 유익한 교육에 항상 만족했습니다. 그러나 여러 경쟁사들이 더욱 저렴한 가격으로 제공되는 온라인 교육 상품 때문에 저희의 매출이 급격하게 감소하던 중이었습니다. 저희 업체가 다른 업체들과 경쟁하기 위해 서비스 비용을 더 낮추는 것을 심각하게 걱정하였기 때문에 기존고객을 유지하고 새로운 고객을 끌어들일 전략을 제안함으로써 강 고문은 문제 해결을 위해 노력했습니다.

우선, 저는 우리 업체 서비스만의 독보적인 측면을 강조하기 위한 홍보물을 제작하자는 그녀의 제안을 실행에 옮겼습니다. 또한, 각각의 업체들에게 우리의 깊이 있는 재정 분석과 전문적인 컨설팅 서비스를 강조했습니다. 차이를 만드는 것은 우리 마케팅의 가장 중요한 부분이 되었고, 실제로 결실을 보았습니다. 지금은 상황이 꾸준히 좋아지고 있고, 이것이 강 고문의 노력 때문에 가능했다는 것을 알고 있습니다. 그녀를 강력히 추천합니다!

진심으로,

조던 필
조던 필 소유자
필 센터

어휘 employment 채용 advisor 고문 informative 유익한 competitor 경쟁자 affordable 값이 알맞은, 저렴한 dramatically 극적으로 lower 낮추다 compete with 경쟁하다 retain 보유하다 attract 끌어모으다 promotional 홍보의 in-depth 심오한

8. 세부사항을 묻는 문제

필 씨는 강 씨가 무엇을 하도록 고용하였는가?

(A) 사업에 조언 제공하기
(B) 재정 전략 분석하기
(C) 고객 반응 수집하기
(D) 마케팅 자료 제작하기

해설 첫 문장에서 '마케팅 고문'으로 채용했다고 언급되었고 'Because I was seriously ~ for attracting new ones.'에서 언급된 바와 같이 강 씨는 업체 문제 해결을 위해 제안을 하는 역할로 고용되었음을 알 수 있다. 그러므로 정답은 (A)이다.

9. 추론 문제

필 센터에 관해 무엇이 암시되어 있는가?

(A) 온라인 서비스를 제공하지 않는다.
(B) 다수의 지사를 보유하고 있다.
(C) 지역에서 가장 낮은 가격으로 상담을 하고 있다.
(D) 정기적으로 과목명을 바꾼다.

해설 'However, due to the online training services ~ sales dropped dramatically.'에서 알 수 있듯 현재 필 센터는 가격이 저렴한 온라인 서비스를 제공하지 못하고 있어 매출이 급격히 하락했음을 짐작할 수 있다. 그러므로 정답은 (A)이다.

10. 문장 삽입 문제

지문에 표시된 [1], [2], [3], 그리고 [4] 중에서 아래 문장이 들어가기에 가장 좋은 위치는 어디인가?

"차이를 만드는 것은 우리 마케팅의 가장 중요한 부분이 되었고, 실제로 결실을 맺었습니다."

(A) [1]
(B) [2]
(C) [3]
(D) [4]

해설 앞 문장 'First of all, ~ our in-depth financial analysis of each business.'에서 이 업체만의 독창적인 부분을 강조하며 홍보를 했다고 언급하고 있으며, 이 뒤 문장에서 'We are now steadily improving, due to Ms. Kang's efforts.' 이 노력의 결과로 꾸준히 상황이 개선되고 있음을 나타내고 있다. 그러므로 시간의 흐름과 인과관계를 따져 보았을 때 이 사이에 위치하는 게 논리적이다. 그러므로 정답은 (C)이다.

UNIT 23 편지/이메일

SPARTA PRACTICE

p. 206

1 (C) 2 (D) 3 (A)

발신: Jake McLaughlin, 매니저
수신: Shaine Jones

Shaine께,

당신은 어제 이메일에서 우리의 최신 상품에 대한 보고서를 어떻게 써야 하는지를 물었지요. 보고서의 목적은 그 상품의 판매 잠재력에 대해 우리의 주주들의 정확한 예측을 하기 위함이에요.

어휘 procedure 절차, 순서 accurate 정확한 prediction 예측, 예언 shareholder 주주 potential 잠재력, 잠재력 있는

1. 이메일의 목적을 찾는 문제

이 이메일의 목적은 무엇인가?

(A) 판매 예측을 하기 위한 것
(B) 질문하기 위한 것
(C) 설명을 주기 위한 것
(D) 신제품을 시연하기 위한 것

해설 첫 문장 'You asked in yesterday's e-mail what the procedure for writing a report on our newest products is'에서 어제 자신이 질문 받은 내용을 언급한 후, 뒤에 보고서 쓰는 방법이 이어지고 있으므로 보고서를 쓰는 방법을 알려 주기 위해 편지를 썼음을 알 수 있다. 그러므로 정답은 (C)이다.

미노키 여행사
4-7-1 마토가오카, 메구로 구
도쿄, 152-8799
전화: (03) 5487-5561
팩스: (03) 5487-5562

에드워드 올슨
9월 10일
2-1-3 노미즈, 초푸 시
도쿄, 182-8799

올슨 씨 귀하,

미노키 여행사를 선택해 주셔서 감사합니다. 곧 있을 여행에 대한 귀하의 예약이 모두 확인되었습니다. 왕복 모두 직항임을 유의하시기 바랍니다. 다음의 여행일정을 검토해 주시기 바랍니다. 변경사항이 있으시다면 10월 15일까지 제게 알려 주시기 바랍니다.

어휘 choose 선택하다 reservation 예약 confirm 확인하다 upcoming 다가오는 obtain 획득하다 direct flight 직항 direction 약도, 방향 itinerary 여행 일정

2. 편지의 목적을 찾는 문제

편지의 목적은 무엇인가?

(A) 여행 패키지 광고하기 위해
(B) 여행일정의 변경사항 공지하기 위해
(C) 티켓 지불 요청하기 위해
(D) 다가오는 여행 계획 확인하기 위해

해설 'Thank you for choosing the Minoki Travel Agency. Your reservations for your upcoming trip have been confirmed.'이므로 정답은 (D)이다.

3. 사실 정보를 찾는 문제

올슨 씨에 관해 알 수 있는 것은 무엇인가?

(A) 도쿄행 직항편을 이용할 것이다.
(B) 일등석 비행기를 이용할 것이다.
(C) 단골 고객이다.
(D) 사업차 여행할 것이다.

해설 'Note that we were able to obtain direct flights in both directions.'에서 도쿄로 직항편을 이용할 것임을 알 수 있다. 그러므로 정답은 (A)이다.

SPARTA ACTUAL TEST

p. 207

1 (B) 2 (A) 3 (B) 4 (D) 5 (A) 6 (C)
7 (D) 8 (D) 9 (B) 10 (A)

⟨1-3⟩ 다음은 편지에 관한 문제이다.

12월 11일

시진 서플라이즈 귀하:

제가 새로운 공급업체를 찾고 있을 때, 맥퀸 메디컬 그룹의 동료 중 한 명에게서 귀사를 추천 받았습니다. 그는 지난 10년 동안 귀사의 지원을 잘 받아오고 있던 터라 귀사를 추천해 주었습니다. 제가 현재의 업체와 겪어왔던 몇 가지 문제들을 언급했을 때, 그는 귀사의 직원들이 매우 정중하고 고객들을 배려한다는 점을 강조했습니다.

저는 그가 말했던 것이 사실임을 이미 알게 되었습니다. 제가 온라인으로 주문하려고 했을 때, 몇 가지 기술적인 오류가 생겨서 귀사의 고객 관리 부서에 전화를 했고, 저는 담당자 중 한 명인 이샤 씨로부터 즉각적인 응답을 받았습니다. 그녀는 웹 사이트 복구를 기다리는 대신 팩스로 주문할 것을 제안했습니다. 주문하는 마지막 단계까지 그녀가 너무 효율적으로, 그리고 침착하게 알려 주어서 놀랐습니다. 이제 저는 주문을 완료했고, 요청 받은 대로 간단한 피드백을 제출합니다.

처음에 있었던 기술적인 문제에도 불구하고, 저는 고객 관리 서비스에 매우 기쁘며, 앞으로 귀사로부터 받을 서비스를 고대하고 있습니다.

귀사의 친절하고 전문적인 지원에 감사 드립니다.

진심으로,

서지 하우드
KPC 전문가 협회

어휘 be referred to ~을 추천 받다 vendor 행상, 판매 업체 courteous 정중한, 공손한 attentive 배려하는, 사려 깊은 place an order 주문하다 immediate 즉시의, 즉각적인 instead of ~ 대신에 calmly 침착하게 direct 안내하다, 알려주다 brief 간단한; 주요한 initial 최초의 look forward to ~하기를 고대하다 specialize in ~을 전문으로 하다 decade 10년

1. 추론 문제

시진 서플라이즈에 관하여 알 수 있는 것은?

(A) 사무용품 판매를 전문으로 한다.
(B) 10년 이상 운영해 왔다.
(C) 고객 서비스 직원들이 피드백을 제공한다.
(D) 온라인 서비스를 약 일주일 간 이용할 수 없었다.

해설 동료로부터 Seegene Supplies를 소개 받은 Serge Houde 씨가 이 업체에 보내는 편지임을 알 수 있고, 동료가 10년 간 이 업체와 거래를 잘 해와서 추천했다는 내용 (He recommended your company as he has been enjoying your services for the last 10 years.)을 통해, Seegene Supplies는 최소 10년 이상 운영해 왔음을 알 수 있다. 따라서 for the last 10 years를 for more than a decade로 바꿔 표현한 (B)가 정답이다.

2. 추론 문제

하우드 씨의 이전 공급업체에 관하여 알 수 있는 것은?

(A) 고객 서비스가 좋지 않았다.
(B) 웹 사이트가 사용하기 어려웠다.
(C) 배달 시간대가 합리적이지 못했다.
(D) 가격이 너무 비쌌다.

해설 첫 번째 단락, 마지막 줄의 "When I mentioned some problems I had been experiencing with my current vendor, he emphasized that your staff is very courteous and attentive to customers."에서 Houde 씨가 현재의 업체와의 문제를 동료에게 얘기했을 때, Seegene Supplies의 직원들은 매우 공손하고 고객들을 배려한다고 했으므로 Houde 씨는 이전 회사에서 고객 서비스와 관련된 문제를 겪었음을 유추할 수 있다. 그러므로 (A)가 정답이다.

3. 세부 사항을 묻는 문제

하우드 씨가 시진 서플라이즈에 그의 주문서를 보낸 방법은?

(A) 이메일로
(B) 팩스로
(C) 전화로
(D) 우편으로

해설 Houde 씨가 온라인으로 주문을 하려고 했을 때, 문제가 발생해서 고객 서비스에 연락을 했고, 상담원이 온라인 대신 팩스로 주문하라고 했다 (She also suggested placing my order by fax instead of waiting for the Web site to go back online.)는 말을 통해 Houde씨가 팩스로 주문서를 보냈음을 알 수 있다. 따라서 (B)가 정답이다.

〈4-7〉 다음은 이메일에 관한 문제이다.

받는 사람: tdament@gantengineering.com
보내는 사람: rrcross@GPSwebdesign.com
날짜: 8월 29일
제목: 귀하의 문의

Dament 씨께,

온라인으로 GPS Web Design에 연락해 주셔서 감사합니다. 귀하의 회사, Gant Engineering에 대한 당신의 질문에 답변을 드리고, 귀사의 제품들을 위한 매스컴의 보도량을 늘리는 데 도움을 드릴 수 있는 방법에 대해 이메일을 드립니다.

GPS Web Design은 15년 전에 설립되었습니다. 저희는 국내외 많은 유명한 기관들을 위한 디자인 상담가로서 도움을 드리고 있습니다. 저희 고객들은 마닐라의 CFC Manufacturing, 뉴욕의 Freezer corporation, 그리고 런던의 UK Automation을 포함합니다. 저희와 함께 작업을 하면서, 인터넷상에서 국제 보도 증가와 온라인 미디어 인지도에 더 효율적인 선점 혜택을 받을 수 있습니다.

만약 GPS 웹 디자인과 함께 일을 하길 결정하신다면, 저희는 당신이 실망하는 일은 없을 것이라고 확신합니다. 우리 회사는 기한 내 그리고 예산에 맞게 작업을 완성하는 데 선망의 대상이 되는 좋은 평판을 가지고 있습니다. 저는 당신이 매우 긍정적 결과를 볼 수 있을 것이라고 자신 있게 말씀 드릴 수 있습니다.

저희가 당신의 요구사항들을 더 깊이 있게 이야기할 수 있는 회의를 잡기 위해 864-555-5142로 직접 전화해 주십시오. 소식을 들을 수 있기를 기대하겠습니다.

진심을 담아,

Roger R. Cross
홍보 담당자, GPS Web Design

어휘 inquiry 질문 contact 연락하다, 접촉하다 enhance 향상시키다 media coverage 매스컴의 보도(량), 언론 보도 범위 product line 제품군 establish 설립하다 serve 서비스를 제공하다 consultant 상담사 domestically 국내에서 internationally 해외에, 해외로 manufacturing 제조업 automation 자동화 benefit 유익하다, ~에서 득을 보다 efficient 능률적인, 효율적인 lead 선두, 선점 presence 존재, 인지도 assure 장담하다, 확언하다 disappoint 실망하다 enviable 부러운, 선망의 대상이 되는 reputation 평판, 명성 budget 예산 confident 자신 있는 encouraging 격려의, 힘을 북돋아 주는 arrange 처리하다, 주선하다 requirement 필요, 필요조건 depth 깊이 representative 대표

4. 이메일의 목적을 찾는 문제

Cross씨는 왜 이메일을 보냈는가?

(A) Gant Engineering과 사전 예약된 미팅을 확인하기 위해
(B) 기업 제안서를 작성하는 방법을 설명하기 위해
(C) 새로운 프로젝트의 시작 정보를 제공하기 위해
(D) Dament 씨의 질문에 응답하기 위해

해설 이메일을 보낸 목적을 묻는 전체지문 관련 문제로, 이메일 시작 부분인 'I am writing in response to your inquiry about your company ~'에 단서가 있다. 이 부분에서 이메일을 쓴 사람은 GPS Web Design 소속의 직원이며, 회사의 정보에 대한 물음에 답하고 있으므로 정답은 (D)이다.

5. 추론 문제

Gant Engineering이 무엇을 하길 가장 원할 것 같은가?

(A) 언론 보도 증가시키기
(B) 새로운 공장 시설 건축하기
(C) 서비스 가격 상승시키기
(D) 새로운 제품 생산성 향상시키기

해설 Gant Engineering이 하고 싶어 하는 것을 묻고 있는 세부사항 문제이다. 그들이 무엇을 요청하고 있는지 파악하면 쉽게 정답을 찾아 낼 수 있다. 이메일의 초반에 Gant Engineering을 소개하는 부분에서 그는 'how we can help enhance media coverage for your product lines' 라며 고객사의 제품군들을 위한 매스컴의 보도량을 늘리는 데 도움을 줄 수 있는 방법을 찾기를 원한다고 언급하고 있으므로 정답은 (A)이다.

6. 사실 정보를 찾는 문제

GPS Web Design에 대해 언급된 것은 무엇인가?

(A) 그것은 최근에 몇몇 신입 직원들을 고용했다.
(B) 수수료가 다른 컨설팅 회사보다 더 경쟁력 있다.
(C) 그것은 한 개 이상의 국가에서 운영되고 있다.
(D) 본부가 Kuala Lumpur에 있다.

해설 GPS Web Design이라는 특정 회사에 대해 언급된 것이 무엇인지 묻는 세부사항 관련 문제이다. "GPS Web Design"이라는 특정 회사가 소개되는 두 번째 단락을 살펴보면, 회사는 15년 전에 설립되었고 (established 15 years ago), 한 개 이상의 국가(in New York and London)에서 운영되고 있다고 언급하고 있으므로 정답은 (C) 이다. (A) 새로운 직원 채용, (B) 수수료, 그리고 (D) 본부의 위치에 관련된 정보는 언급되어 있지 않으므로 오답이다.

7. 동의어 문제

세 번째 단락, 첫 번째 줄의 "assure"과 가장 비슷한 의미의 단어는?

(A) 주장하다
(B) 진정시키다
(C) 홍보하다
(D) 약속하다

해설 지문에 등장한 "assure"과 유사한 의미의 어휘를 묻고 있는 문제로 문맥에 따라 가장 적절한 의미를 파악하도록 한다. 'we can assure you that you will not be disappointed.'는 고객이 실망하게 하지 않는다는 것을 자신있게 이야기할 수 있다라는 의미로 이 문장에서의 "assure"의 의미는 "약속하다"와 바꾸어 쓰일 수 있으므로 정답은 (D)이다.

〈8-10〉 다음은 편지에 관한 문제이다.

2월 11일
카밀르 에트비 씨
드라이버스 플레이스 562
프리토리아, 남아프리카 1294

에트비 씨께,

저희 남아프리카 마이닝 인더스트리는 채굴 보조원을 대상을 한 지난주 <케이프타운 타임즈>에 광고를 낸 직책에 관해 귀하의 신청서를 받았습니다. 귀하께 이 자리는 이미 채워졌음을 알리게 되어 유감스럽게 생각합니다. 그럼에도 불구하고 저희는 7월에 다른 지역에서 채굴을 시작할 계획이며, 저희는 귀하께서 이 직책에 적합할 거라고 생각합니다. 괜찮으시다면, 귀하의 정보를 파일로 유지하려고 합니다. 그 지역은 요하네스버그에 있는 저희 주요 생산 시설에서 멀리 떨어져 있지 않지만, 케이프타운, 보츠와나, 그리고 다른 아프리카 국가들로 출장이 필요할 것입니다. 우리 회사에 자리가 날 경우를 위해 지속적으로 저희 웹 사이트를 확인해 주세요. 귀하의 구직에 행운이 있기를 바랍니다.

안부 전하며,

다리엔 프로보스트, 인사부 관리자

어휘 application 지원(서), 신청(서) mining 채굴, 채광 regarding ~에 관해 suitable for ~에 적합한 keep A on file A를 파일로 보관하다 facility 시설 vacancy 빈자리 job search 구직 fail to ~하지 못하다 qualification 자격 요건

8. 편지의 목적을 찾는 문제

편지의 주된 목적은 무엇인가?

(A) 지원자에게 직위에 대한 자격요건을 충족시키지 못했음을 알리기 위해
(B) 지원자에게 그의 경력에 대한 추가 정보를 요청하기 위해
(C) 지원자와의 인터뷰 일정을 잡기 위해
(D) 지원자에게 그가 지원한 직위가 더 이상 유효하지 않음을 알리기 위해

해설 인사 관리자인 프로보스트 씨가 에트비 씨에게 보내는 편지로, 서두에서 프로보스트 씨가 에트비 씨의 입사 지원서를 받았다고 했고(We at the Mining Industry of South Africa received your application regarding the position), 이미 해당 직이 채워졌음을 알리게 되어 유감이라고 했으므로(We are sorry to inform you that this position has already been filled.) 해당 직책이 이미 채워져 더 이상 유효하지 않다는 것을 알리기 위해 쓰였음을 알 수 있다. 따라서 (D)가 정답이다.

9. 세부 사항을 묻는 문제

남아프리카 마이닝 인더스트리의 주요 시설은 어디에 위치해 있는가?

(A) 케이프타운
(B) 요하네스버그
(C) 프리토리아
(D) 보츠와나

해설 지문 중반부에서 주요 생산 시설이 요하네스버그에 있다는 것을 밝히고 있으므로(The location is not far from our main production facilities in Johannesburg) 정답은 (B)이다. (A)는 구인 광고가 나간 지역이고(the position that was advertised last week in the *Cape Town Times*), (A), (D)는 7월에 시작할 채굴 장소에 뽑히게 될 사람이 출장을 가게 될 지역(it will require some travel to Cape Town, Botswana, and other African countries.)이며, (C)는 에트비 씨가 살고 있는 지역(Mr. Camille Atebe, 562 Drivers Place, Pretoria, South Africa 1294)이다.

10. 추후 당부 사항을 묻는 문제

프로보스트 씨는 에트비 씨에게 무엇을 하라고 제안하는가?

(A) 다른 공석을 위해 웹 사이트를 확인하라고
(B) 그의 자격요건에 대한 더 많은 정보를 보내라고
(C) 고용에 대해 주요 시설에 연락하라고
(D) 신문에 실린 구인 광고를 읽으라고

해설 지문 하단부에서 프로보스트 씨는 앞으로 이 회사에 자리가 생길 경우를 위해 지속해서 웹 사이트를 확인해 달라고 했으므로(Please keep checking our Web site for any future vacancies that may arise in our organization.) future vacancies를 additional job openings로 바꿔 표현한 (A)가 정답이다.

SPARTA PRACTICE

p. 214

1 (B) **2** (D)

회계 관리자 구인

블랜드 사는 북동지부 회계 관리직에 지원할 능숙하고 성실한 전문가를 찾고 있습니다. 지원자는 경영대학원 석사 학위 및 공인회계사 자격증 소지자로 회계 분야에서 최소 10년 이상의 경력과 5년 이상의 관리 경력이 있어야 합니다. 대략 1년에 20일 정도 국내외 지사로 출장을 가며, 매우 근면한 자세가 필요한 직무입니다. 직원 혜택으로 종합 의료 보험 및 가족 치과 보험 혜택을 받을 수 있으며, 급여는 십만 달러 이상이며, 근무 연수에 따라 상당한 퇴직 연금뿐만 아니라 계약 종료 시 보너스가 추가로 지급됩니다. 이력서와 자기소개서를 루스 주시니아 씨의 메일 ruthjuice@bland.com으로 보내주세요.

어휘 certify 증명하다 domestic 국내의 hardworking attitude 근면한 자세 a six-figure salary 여섯 자릿 수의 봉급 (십만 달러가 넘는 액수 의미) substantial 상당한 pension 연금

1. 구인 광고의 자격요건을 묻는 문제

다음 중 지원자에게 요구되는 것은 무엇인가?

(A) 최소 5년 이상의 회계 분야 경력
(B) 출장 의사
(C) 유머 감각
(D) 고소득 이력

해설 지문 중반에서 'The job will include 20 days of travel a year to domestic and international locations. A very hardworking attitude is a requirement' 부분에서 1년에 20일 이상의 출장과 근면한 자세가 언급되었으나 (D)의 고소득 이력은 명시된 바 없고, (A)는 10년 이상의 경력이므로 틀렸다. 그러므로 정답은 (B)이다.

심장이나 혈압에 문제가 있으십니까? 건강식을 하는 데 관심은 있지만 직접 요리할 시간이 없으십니까? 매주 초에 우편으로 7일 분량의 건강식을 받는 '건강한 식품' 프로그램을 시도해 보십시오. 식사는 당신의 집 문 앞으로 냉동되어 배달되오니 전자레인지에 데우기만 하면 몇 분 안에 맛있고 건강에 좋은 저녁식사가 요리됩니다! 500명의 관계자가 참여한 한 연구에서 저지방, 저염도 식사 계획을 실시한 지 10주가 지난 후에 73%는 콜레스테롤 수치가 떨어졌고, 75%는 혈압이 떨어진 것을 발견했습니다. 거의 모두가 건강해진 것을 느끼며 심지어 몸무게도 어느 정도 줄었다고 말했습니다. 그렇다면 당신은 무엇을 기다리고 계십니까? 우리 '건강한 식품'에서는 이 프로그램이 건강상의 문제에 대한 확실한 치료법이 아니라는 것은 알지만 우리의 식사가 건강상의 문제점들을 다루는 법을 배우는 출발점을 제공할 것이라고 생각합니다. 이외에도 이것은 단순히 요리할 시간이 없는 사람들을 위한 해결책이기도 합니다. 저희는 아침 식사, 점심 식사, 저녁 식사를 제공합니다. 오늘 전화하셔서 상세한 정보를 얻으세요.

어휘 blood pressure 혈압 worth ~의 값만큼의 분량, ~어치 deliver 배달하다, 전하다 microwave 전자레인지 participant 관계자, 참여자 low-fat, low-sodium 지방과 소금기가 적은 drop 하락 cholesterol 콜레스테롤 report 말하다, (연구, 조사 등을) 보고하다 cure 치료법, 치료제 maintain 주장하다, 단언하다 manage 다루다, 관리하다

2. 상품 광고의 틀린 정보를 찾는 문제

이 식사를 해야 하는 대상에 들지 않는 사람은 누구인가?

(A) 혈압이 높은 사람
(B) 요리할 시간이 별로 없는 사람
(C) 콜레스테롤 수치가 높은 사람
(D) 55세가 넘은 사람

해설 초반에서, '~ blood pressure problem?' (A)가 해당되고, '~ don't have time to cook it yourself?' (B)가 해당된다. 지문 중반에, '~ 73% of people recorded a drop in their cholesterol levels, ~'에서 (C)가 해당되므로, 내용에서 언급되지 않은 (D)가 정답이다.

SPARTA ACTUAL TEST

p. 215

1 (C) **2** (A) **3** (C) **4** (D) **5** (D) **6** (C)
7 (C) **8** (C) **9** (A)

<1-3> 다음은 광고와 관련된 문제이다.

- 매물: 대지 4분의 3 에이커에 건평 4,460평방피트. 침실 5개, 욕실 3개
- 장소: 보스톤 메사추세츠, 로간 국제공항으로부터 16마일 거리
- 문화시설: Desert Ranch 사유지의 주택을 구매하시면 헬스강좌와 테니스 코트, 수영장이 있는 Desert Ranch Health 리조트 회원권을 얻으실 수 있습니다. 매달 내셔야 하는 회비는 450달러인데 차량 출입통제 관문으로 관리되는 이 지역 월 수수료는 185달러입니다.
- 메모: 1994년 스타일의 이 주택은 안뜰을 중심으로 지어졌으며 분수대와 모퉁이 벽난로도 하나씩 갖추고 있습니다.

Desert Ranch 사유지에는 25개의 집이 들어서 있으며 7가구가 더 공사 중입니다. 이 지역이 1989년에 세워진 이후로 8차례의 부동산 재거래가 있었습니다. 가장 고가로는, 150만 달러에 매물로 내놓았던 4,750 평방피트짜리 가구 딸린 주택이 145만 달러에 팔린 적이 있었습니다. 매물가격은 185만 달러였는데 160만 달러에 팔린 1에이커 대지에 건평 5,600평방피트 가옥을 포함, 메사추세츠의 전 지역에서 올 상반기에 4가구가 백만 달러 이상에 팔렸습니다.

어휘 amenity 문화시설 home ownership 주택소유권 membership 회원자격 fitness class 헬스 강좌 monthly due 매월 회비 resale 재판매 furnished 가구가 딸린 list ~ at+가격 (그 가격)으로 ~을 매물로 내놓다 be sold for+가격 ~에 팔리다

1. 세부 정보를 묻는 문제

메사추세츠는 공항으로부터 얼마나 떨어져 있는가?

(A) 3마일
(B) 5마일
(C) 16마일
(D) 25마일

해설 광고의 장소 부분에 'Where: Boston, Massachusetts, 16 miles from Logan International Airport.'라고 언급되어 있는 부분에서 메사추세츠 공항으로부터 16마일 떨어져 있음을 알 수 있다. 그러므로 정답은 (C)이다.

2. 상품의 특징을 묻는 문제

다음 중 어느 것이 이 주택의 특징으로 광고된 것인가?

(A) 벽난로
(B) 온수 욕조
(C) 고급 부엌
(D) 4개의 침실

해설 광고의 메모 부분에 'This 1994-style home is built around a courtyard with a fountain and a corner fireplace.'라고 언급된 부분에서 주택의 코너에 벽난로가 설치되어 있다는 것을 광고하고 있으므로 정답은 (A) A fireplace이다.

3. 틀린 정보를 찾는 묻는 문제

이 광고에 따르면, 사실이 아닌 것은 무엇인가?

(A) 이 침실 5개짜리 주택은 보스톤의 메사추세츠에 있다.
(B) 이 1994년 스타일의 주택은 안뜰을 중심으로 지어졌다.
(C) Desert Ranch 사유지에는 진행되고 있는 주택 공사가 없다.
(D) 이 공동체는 1989년에 세워졌다.

해설 광고의 메모 부분에 'Desert Ranch Estates has 25 homes with seven more under construction.'이라고 언급된 부분에서 현재 Desert Ranch 사유지에는 25개의 집이 있고 7가구가 공사 중에 있음을 알 수 있다. 따라서 이곳에 진행되고 있는 주택 공사가 없다고 한 (C)는 사실이 아니다. 그러므로 정답은 (C)이다.

〈4-6〉 다음은 광고에 관한 문제이다.

플랫아이언 건축자재 회사

표시된 업무에 대해 주말 교대근무가 요구될 수 있음.

손실 예방 관리자
학사 학위, 탁월한 의사소통 능력, 지도력 및 인력관리 능력을 갖추고 있어야 함. 2년 이상의 손실 예방 경력을 우대함. 소매업 정책 및 절차에 대한 기본적인 업무 지식이 요망됨. 어느 정도의 주말 근무가 요구되는 직책임.

납품 트럭 운전기사
영업용 운전 면허증이 있어야 하며, 지도를 볼 줄 알아야 하며, 구체적인 지시사항과 및 납품 지시를 준수해야 함. 다른 사람의 도움 없이 최대 30kg의 무게를 다루고 옮길 수 있어야 함. 주 7일 근무가 가능해야 함.

고객 서비스부 직원
최소 1년 이상 콜센터나 고객 서비스부 근무 경력이 있어야 함. 전문대학 졸업 학위를 우대함. 컴퓨터 관련 지식과 능숙함이 요구됨. 주말 근무가 요구됨.

행정 비서
탁월한 문서 및 구두 의사전달 능력과 조직력, 다양한 업무를 소화할 수 있는 능력이 요구됨. 컴퓨터 관련 지식과 능숙함이 요구됨.

다음의 주소로 이력서를 보내 주십시오 : 인사부
플랫아이언 건축자재 회사
655 브레모 로드 655번지
마리에타시, 조지아 주 78240

전화나 이메일은 사양합니다.

어휘 shift 교대 근무 require 요구하다 indicate 가리키다 loss 손실 prevention 방지 communication 의사소통 leadership 지도력 skill 솜씨 prefer 우대하다 at least 최소한 experience 경력 basic 기본적인 knowledge 지식 retail 소매 policy 정책 procedure 절차 position 근무처, 직장, 직책 delivery 배달 follow 따르다 specific 구체적인 instructions 지시 handle 다루다 move 옮기다 weigh 무게가 나가다 assistance 도움 availability 유용성 knowledge 지식 proficiency 능숙함 administrative 행정적인 organizational skill 조직력 résumé 이력서

4. 구인 광고의 자격요건을 묻는 문제

손실 예방 관리자의 자격 요건은 무엇인가?

(A) 탁월한 회계 관리 능력
(B) 야간 근무에 대한 의향
(C) 통신학 학위
(D) 소매업 절차에 대한 지식

해설 구직 광고 상단의 손실 예방 관리자(Loss-prevention manager)의 자격 요건을 보면 '소매업 정책 및 절차에 대한 기본적인 지식이 요망됨. (Basic working knowledge of retail policies and procedures required.)'라고 밝히고 있다. 소매업 절차에 대한 기본적인 지식이 있어야 하므로 정답은 (D)이다.

5. 틀린 정보를 찾는 문제

주말 근무와 관련이 없는 직책은 무엇인가?

(A) 손실 예방 관리자
(B) 납품 트럭 운전기사
(C) 고객 서비스 부 직원
(D) 행정 비서

해설 구인광고의 초반부에 '표시된 업무에 대해 주말 교대 근무가 요구될 수 있음. (Weekend shifts required where indicated.)'라고 밝히고 있다. 손실 예방 관리자(Loss-prevention Manager), 납품 트럭 운전기사(Delivery Driver), 고객 서비스부 직원(Customer Service Coordinator)의 경우 각각 하단에 '어느 정도의 주말 근무가 요구되는 직책임. (Some weekend work is required for this position.)', '주 7일 근무가 가능해야 함.(Requires availability 7 days a week.)', '주말 근무가 요구됨.(Weekend work is required.)'라고 쓰여 있는 반면에 행정 비서(Administrative Assistants)직에는 주말 근무에 대한 아무런 언급이 없다. 그러므로 정답은 (D)이다.

6. 지원 요령을 묻는 문제

후보들은 각 직책에 어떻게 지원하게 되는가?

(A) 온라인을 통해
(B) 전화로
(C) 우편으로
(D) 직접

해설 구인광고 하반부에 주소와 함께 이력서를 보내라는 내용이 나와 있으며, 제일 마지막 문장에 '전화나 이메일은 사양합니다.(No phone calls or e-mails, please)'라고 나와 있으므로 우편으로만 지원 가능하다는 것을 알 수 있다. 그러므로 정답은 (C)이다.

〈7-9〉 다음은 광고에 관한 문제이다.

최고의 기회 매니저 구함

세계에서 가장 빠르게 성장하는 시장에 안착하십시오. 오리츠 텔레콤은 국제 할인 통신의 선두주자이며 기술 지원팀 직원과 경험 많은 매니저를 구하고 있습니다. 오리츠의 고객은 국제 통화를 할 때 40% 이상의 할인을 받을 수 있습니다. 게다가 고객들은 인터넷과 팩스 서비스에서도 상당한 할인을 즐길 수 있습니다. 더 나아가 재발신 전화와 같은 혁신적인 기술들로 인해 고객들은 다른 회사에는 없는 서비스를 이용할 수 있습니다.

하지만 우리 서비스에 대한 수요가 늘어나면서 시장에 대한 적극적이고 효과적인 대응의 필요성 또한 늘어나고 있습니다. 오리츠 텔레콤은 매주 토요일, 일요일은 쉬며 일 년에 삼 주의 휴가와 효과적인 업무 스케줄을 제시하고 있습니다. 이 제안은 사교성 있고 좋은 연봉으로 일하기 원하는 기술자에게 있어서는 굉장한 기회입니다.

정보가 더 필요하시다면 901-222-1111로 전화를 걸거나 웹 사이트 www.ortiz.org에 방문해 주시기 바랍니다.

어휘 get in on the ground floor (프로젝트 등에) 처음부터 관여하다 fastest-growing 급속도로 성장하는 international 국제의 experienced 경험이 많은 call 통화 substantial 상당한 savings 절약된 금액 innovative 혁신적인 feature 특징, 기술 return call 재발신 전화 utilize 이용하다 carrier (전화 서비스를 제공하는) 회사 aggressive 적극적인, 호전적인 lucrative 수익성이 있는, 효과적인 outstanding 굉장한, 두드러진 cheap 값이 싼

7. 구인광고의 회사 소개를 묻는 문제

오리츠 통신회사가 제공하는 기술들에는 어떤 것이 있는가?

(A) 문자 메시지
(B) 빠른 인터넷
(C) 싼 국제 통화
(D) 음성 메시지

해설 첫 번째 문단에 'Ortiz customers can save 40% or more on their international calls.'가 언급되었듯이 오리츠 고객은 해외통화에서 40%를 할인받을 수 있으므로 정답은 (C)이다.

8. 세부 사항을 묻는 문제

고객들이 할인 받지 못하는 부분은 무엇인가?

(A) 인터넷
(B) 팩스
(C) 케이블 TV
(D) 국제통화

해설 첫 번째 문단 'Ortiz customers can save 40% or more on their international calls ~ fax and Internet services.'에 언급되었듯이 오리츠 고객은 인터넷, 팩스, 국제 통화에서 할인을 받을 수 있으나 (C)에 대한 언급은 없다. 그러므로 정답은 (C)이다.

9. 직책의 임무에 관한 세부 사항을 묻는 문제

근무시간의 스케줄은 어떻게 되는가?

(A) 직원들은 매주 주말은 쉰다.
(B) 직원들은 매년 2주의 휴가를 갈 수 있다.
(C) 직원들은 6개월마다 3주의 휴가를 갈 수 있다.
(D) 직원들은 매주 2일은 아무 날이나 쉴 수 있다.

해설 두 번째 문단에 '~ a lucrative commission schedule and 3 weeks of vacation per year with every Saturday and Sunday off.'와 같이 나왔듯이 1년에 3주, 그리고 매주 주말은 휴식을 취할 수 있다고 나오므로 정답은 (A)이다.

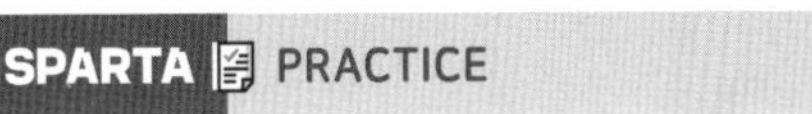

UNIT 25 공지/회람

SPARTA PRACTICE p. 222

1 (C) **2** (A)

공지

2020년 5월 20일

회사는 Kevin Brennan 씨가 다른 일을 하기 위해 2020년 5월 31일 회사의 재무이사로서 사임할 것임을 알립니다. 임원들은 지난 3년 반 동안 회사의 사업에 그가 공헌한 것에 감사하고 미래에도 그가 잘 되기를 바라는 바입니다.
저희는 Joy Kocay 씨가 2020년 6월 2일부터 새로운 재무이사로 우리 회사로 오실 것임을 기쁘게 알리는 바입니다. Joy Kocay 씨는 유능한 회계사로 Business School of New York City College를 졸업했습니다. 그는 14년 동안 은행 자원 업무를 맡았으며, 현재는 뉴욕에 있는 ING Capital Group에 재직하고 계십니다.

Kimberly Jones
인사부장

어휘 resign 사임하다 finance director 재무이사 pursue 쫓다, 추구하다 contribution to ~에 대한 공헌 future 미래 pleased 기쁜 join 참여하다 qualified 적격의, 자격이 있는 accountant 회계사 graduate from ~를 졸업하다 currently 현재 personnel department 인사부 manager 관리자

1. 공지의 주제를 묻는 문제

이 공지의 주제는 무엇인가?

(A) 고용 제의
(B) 전략 제안
(C) 인사 변경
(D) 회사 합병

해설 'We are pleased to announce that Joy Kocay will join the company as the new finance director on June 2, 2020.'에서 finance director가 새로 온다는 것을 알 수 있으므로 정답은 (C)이다.

회람

제목 : 새 진화 시스딈
수신 : 전 직원
발신 : Dylan Walsh
날짜 : 9월 30일, 2019

우리의 새 전화시스템은 원래 3주의 기간 동안에 걸쳐 설치되는 것으로 계획되었으나 이번 주말에 설치될 예정입니다. 월요일 아침부터 새로운 시스템이 작동될 것입니다. 각 부서원들은 전화를 받지 못할 경우에 상대방이 여러분에게 음성 메시지를 남길 수 있도록 하는 개인용 음성 메일을 계속해서 사용하게 될 것입니다.
월요일 오전 10시, 11시, 그리고 오후 1시 30분에 회의실 3호에서 제안된 시스템에 대한 20분간의 소개가 있을 것입니다. 우리의 새로운 전화 시스템의 특징을 충분히 이용하기 위해서 이 중에 한 번은 꼭 참석을 해 주시기 바랍니다.

어휘 staff 직원 install 설치하다 A rather than B B 대신 A period 기간 originally 원래 planned 계획된, 예정대로의 operational 작동하는 continue to 계속 ~하다 individual 개인적인 voice mail 음성 메일 conference room 회의실 make full use of 충분히 활용하다 feature 특징

2. 추후 당부 내용을 묻는 문제

직원들은 무엇을 하도록 요구되는가?

(A) 시스템 소개 시간에 참석한다.
(B) 내선 번호를 선택한다.
(C) Dylan Walsh에게 전화한다.
(D) 새로운 전화 시스템에 관하여 안내서를 읽는다.

해설 맨 마지막 문장 'Please plan to attend one of these sessions so that you will be able to make full use of the features of our new phone system.'에서 'Attend one of the introductory sessions'을 알 수 있으므로 정답은 (A)이다.

SPARTA ACTUAL TEST

p. 223

1 (B)	2 (C)	3 (D)	4 (C)	5 (C)	6 (B)
7 (A)	8 (A)	9 (C)	10 (B)	11 (A)	

⟨1-3⟩ 다음은 회람에 대한 문제이다.

수신: 전 직원
발신: 자재부 부장
주제: 카트리지 재활용 프로그램

1억 개 이상의 다 쓴 카트리지가 올해 우리 매립지들을 오염시킬 것으로 추정됩니다. 이것은 미래에 심각한 환경 문제를 가져올 수 있습니다. 지금 우리 모두는 다 쓴 카트리지들을 팔아서 그 수를 줄이는 것을 도울 수 있습니다!

우리의 중요한 천연자원들을 보존하고 보호하기 위한 노력으로 우리 회사는 TRC과 함께 카트리지 재활용 프로그램을 시작했습니다. TRC은 우리가 있는 곳으로부터 그들이 있는 곳으로 다 쓴 카트리지들을 운반하는 데 드는 비용을 부담합니다. 더불어 그 회사는 우리 회사가 절약하여 그들에게 보내는 재사용할 수 있는 모든 카트리지에 대해 상당한 액수를 지불합니다. 이 돈은 회사 사교 클럽이나 지역 자선단체 혹은 어린이 병원에 기부될 것입니다. 어떤 다 쓴 카트리지도 버리지 마십시오. 저에게 궁금한 것들에 대해서 문의하세요. 모든 이들이 협력해서 이 프로그램이 성공하길 바랍니다. 우리가 깨끗하고 푸른 미래를 준비하는 데 도움이 되는 여러분의 역할을 기대합니다.

어휘 estimate 견적하다, 추정하다 landfill 매립지 in conjunction with ~와 함께 cover 덮다, (비용, 손실 등을) 보상하다 charity 자선(행위), 자선단체 address (항의 등을) 제출하다, (문제 등을) 처리하다

1. 세부 사항을 묻는 문제

카트리지 재활용 프로그램의 주요 목적은 무엇인가?

(A) 이익을 남기기 위해
(B) 자연 자원을 보호하기 위해
(C) 자선단체에 생필품을 기부하기 위해
(D) 사무실을 깨끗하게 유지하기 위해

해설 두 번째 문단에서 'In an effort to conserve and protect our vital natural resources ~'에서 정답을 확인할 수 있다. 그러므로 정답은 (B)이다.

2. 세부 사항을 묻는 문제

회람에 따르면, 돈이 기부될 곳은 어디인가?

(A) 지역 사회 내에 있는 많은 사교클럽들에
(B) 전국적인 자선단체들에
(C) 사내 사교 클럽들에
(D) 여성 전문 병원에

해설 두 번째 문단, 넷째 줄에서 'This money will be donated to company social clubs, local charities, or the children's hospital.'에서 정답이 (C) To social Clubs in the company라는 것을 확인할 수 있다.

3. 추후 당부 사항을 묻는 문제

직원들은 무엇을 하도록 요청되는가?

(A) 다 쓴 카트리지들을 버린다
(B) 어린이 병원에 기부한다
(C) 다 쓴 카트리지를 개인적으로 판다
(D) 이 프로그램에 참여한다

해설 지문 후반에서 'I hope that everybody cooperates and helps make this successful.'에서 언급되어 있다. 그러므로 정답은 (D)이다.

⟨4-7⟩ 다음은 공지에 관한 문제이다.

방문객 여러분 귀하,

최근 들어, 이스트레이크 도시가 성장을 지속하고 있어 이스트레이크 병원이 엄청난 수의 환자들을 받고 있습니다. 그러므로 이스트레이크 병원은 시설에 대해 몇 가지의 개선을 제공하기로 결정했습니다. 이러한 계획 중 하나는 응급실 환자를 위한 새로운 주차장뿐만 아니라, 응급실로 통하는 새 정문을 만드는 것도 포함됩니다. 목표는 우리의 환자와 직원들을 위해 응급실의 정문을 더 안전하고 편리하게 만드는 것입니다. 공사 기간 동안 응급실 정문은 구급차만 사용할 수 있습니다. 응급실의 모든 다른 방문객들은 소아과와 구내식당 사이에 위치한 동문을 사용하셔야 합니다. 공사 기간 동안 주차는 동문 근처로 제한될 것이므로, 응급실을 이용하시는 방문객들만 동쪽 주차장에 주차하시기 바랍니다. 불편을 드려 죄송합니다만 저희는 이러한 개선들이 우리의 응급실 서비스를 매우 향상시킬 수 있을 거라 믿습니다. 다가오는 공사 계획에 관한 더 자세한 정보를 보려면 저희 웹 사이트 www.westlakehospital.org.를 방문해 주시기 바랍니다.
협조에 감사드립니다.

어휘 tremendous 엄청나게 큰 facility 시설 consist of ~으로 구성하다 emergency room 응급실 convenient 편리한 pedoatric 소아과의 cooperation 협조

4. 공지의 목적을 찾는 문제

이 공지의 목적은 무엇인가?

(A) 병원 수리를 위한 기부를 요청하려고
(B) 새 병원의 건설을 알리려고
(C) 병원의 다가오는 공사를 대중에게 알리려고
(D) 병원 공사 일정의 지연을 보고하려고

해설 공지의 목적은 대부분 지문의 초반부에 있음을 주의하자. 공지를 받는 대상이 'Dear Visitors'이고, 'Eastlake Hospital has decided to make some upgrades to our facilities.'라고 하므로 정답은 (C)이다.

5. 세부 사항을 묻는 문제

이스트레이크 병원이 공사를 계획하게 된 이유는 무엇인가?

(A) 시설의 노후화
(B) 경영진 내의 변경
(C) 환자 수의 증가
(D) 제공되는 서비스의 증가

해설 지문 초반에 Eastlake Hospital has experienced tremendous growth in patient volume.라고 하고 있으므로 공사를 계획하게 된 이유는 (C)임을 알 수 있다.

6. 동의어, 유의어를 묻는 문제

두 번째 줄의 단어 "volume"과 의미가 가장 가까운 것은

(A) 소리
(B) 수량
(C) 손상
(D) 정보

해설 'tremendous growth in patient volume'은 환자 수 급증이라는 표현이므로 정답은 (B)이다.

7. 추후 당부 사항을 묻는 문제

공사가 진행 중인 동안 대중들은 무엇을 할 수 없는가?

(A) 응급실 정문으로 입장
(B) 소아과에 있는 환자 방문
(C) 구내식당에서 식음료 구입
(D) 응급실 주차장의 주차

해설 'During construction, the ER entrance will be for ambulances only.'라고 하므로 정답은 (A)이다. (D)의 경우 'Throughout the construction period, parking will be limited near the east entrance, so we ask that only visitors to the ER park in the east lot.'라고 하여 동쪽 주차장은 이용이 가능하므로 정답이 될 수 없다.

〈8-11〉 다음은 회람에 관한 문제이다.

직원들에게,

여러분들 대다수가 알고 있는 것처럼 의료 비용이 지난 몇 년간 폭등했습니다. 우리 회사의 계속된 흑자 경영에도 불구하고 점점 늘어나는 의료 보험료 지급 비용이 더 이상 무시할 수 없는 문제가 되었습니다. 이러한 상황에 대응하기 위한 노력으로 우리가 제공하는 의료 혜택 범위를 변경하기로 결정하였습니다. 또한 병가 제도도 변경하였습니다. 우리는 공평하고, 동시에 재정적으로 지불 능력도 갖출 수 있도록 많은 노력을 했습니다.

우리는 이러한 제도 변경이 모든 사람에게 영향을 미치는 중요한 문제라는 것을 인식하고 있습니다. 따라서 세부조건들을 검토해 보고, 생길 수 있는 모든 의문사항들에 대한 답을 하기 위한 특별회의를 마련했습니다.

아래 명시된 여러분들의 회의시간에 주의를 기울여 주십시오.
5월 셋째 주
판매부 - 월요일 오전 9시
회계부 - 월요일 오후 2시
제작부 - 화요일 오전 9시
고객 서비스부 - 수요일 오후 2시
총무부 - 목요일 오후 4시

어휘 aware 알고 있는, 인식하는 skyrocket 급격히 상승하다
despite ~에도 불구하고 insurance 보험 situation 상황
coverage 혜택 범위 alter 변경하다 fair 공정한 fiscally 재정적으로
recognize 인지하다, 알다 serious 심각한 matter 문제, 사실
affect 영향을 주다 arrange 준비하다, 정리하다 arise 발생하다
note 주목하다, 써놓다 sick leave 병가

8. 공지의 목적을 묻는 문제

이 메모의 목적은 무엇인가?

(A) 의료 혜택의 변경을 알리기 위해
(B) 부서를 재편성을 알리기 위해
(C) 삭감된 건강관리 비용을 알리기 위해
(D) 판매가 급상승되었다는 것을 알리기 위해

해설 세 번째 줄에서 'we have decided to make certain changes in the medical coverage that we offer'에서 공지의 목적이 (A)에 해당한다는 것을 알 수 있다.

9. 세부 사항을 묻는 문제

회의는 왜 마련되었는가?

(A) 직원들에게 새 업무를 할당하기 위해
(B) 의료보험에 대한 의견을 얻기 위해
(C) 직원들의 의문 사항에 답하기 위해
(D) 병가제도에 대한 계획을 수립하기 위해

해설 두 번째 문단, 마지막 줄에서 '~ special meetings to go over the details and to answer any questions that may arise.'에 모임의 목적이 나와 있다. 그러므로 정답은 (C)이다.

10. 세부사항을 묻는 문제

월요일 오후 회의에 참석해야 할 사람은 누구인가?

(A) 판매원
(B) 부기계원
(C) 접수계원
(D) 고객서비스 직원

해설 'Accounting - Monday 2:00 P.M.'이라고 지문에 명시되어 있다. 따라서 보기 중 회계 관련 업무자는 부기계원을 나타내는 Bookkeeping staff이다. 그러므로 정답은 (B)이다.

11. 사실 정보를 찾는 문제

메모에서 언급된 것은 무엇인가?

(A) 회사 사업이 계속해서 성공하였다.
(B) 의료비용이 작년 이래로 급격하게 상승하였다.
(C) 회의는 이번 달 초에 열릴 것이다.
(D) 병가제도는 변경되지 않는다.

해설 지문 초반에서 'Despite the continued success of our business ~'에서 회사의 사업이 계속 성공하였다는 것이 언급되었다. 그러므로 정답은 (A)이다.

UNIT 26 기사

SPARTA PRACTICE

p. 230

1 (B) **2** (A) **3** (D)

Claude Forbes House of Fashion의 수석 디자이너인 Jacob D. Dumelle는 청년 디자이너 단체에서 시상하는 '올해의 디자이너'에 선정되었습니다. Dumelle 씨는 자신의 2019년 가을 컬렉션에서 최첨단의 디자인과 다양한 소재의 창의적인 사용으로 이름이 나 있었습니다. 그는 지난 9월에 있었던 단체의 10주년 기념행사에서 가졌던 비밀 투표를 통해 동료들로부터 상을 받게 되었습니다. "그의 디자인은 매우 발전 가능성이 있고, 앞으로 그가 보여줄 가능성에 대해 기대하는 바가 크다"고 지난해에 올해의 디자이너로 뽑힌 Lynn Collins 씨가 말했습니다.

어휘 chief 우두머리, 최고의 name 거명되다 guild 단체 recognize 인정하다 cutting-edge 최첨단의 innovative 창의적인, 혁신적인 material 소재 select 선택하다 award 상 peer 동료 secret ballot 비밀 투표 anniversary 기념일 show 보여주다 potential 잠재력 expect 기대하다

1. 세부 사항을 묻는 문제

Collins 씨는 누구인가?

(A) 2018년 Claude Forbes의 수석 디자이너이다.
(B) 2018년 '올해의 디자이너' 상의 수상자이다.
(C) 청년 디자이너 단체의 우두머리이다.
(D) Dumelle 씨의 스승이다.

해설 본문의 하단에서, "~ said last year's designer of the year, Lynn Collin에서, Collins가 작년도의 '올해의 디자이너' 수상자임을 알 수 있다. 그러므로 정답은 (B)이다.

어반 운송은 어제, 연례 주주 총회에서 화물 관리 본부들을 싱가포르에 있는 본사 근처로 한 곳에 모을 것이라고 발표했다. 어반 운송은 이전까지 화물 관리 본부들을 아시아 전역에 국지적으로 두고 운영했다. 그러나 통신기술 향상과 시장의 경쟁이 점차 심해지면서 어반 운송은 운영 본부들을 중앙 통제하기에 이르렀다. 새로운 관리 본부들은 큰 타워에 입점할 예정으로, 첨단 기술을 이용하여 화물 위치를 추적하고 많은 선적 일정을 관리하게 될 것이다. 관리 본부의 직원들은 또한 새로운 과학 기술을 이용하여 기상 상태를 관찰하고 대체 수송로를 찾아낼 것이다.

어휘 shareholders' meeting 주주총회 centralize 중앙으로 집중하다 freight 화물 운송 control operation 관리 본부 headquarters 본사 operate 운영하다 localized 현지화된, 국지화된 improvement in ~의 향상 increasingly 점차 competitive 경쟁이 심한 marketplace 시장 combine 결합하다 motivate A to 동사원형 A가 ~하도록 자극하다 house 입주하다 utilize 이용하다 state-of-the-art 첨단의 track 추적하다 shipment 선적, 화물 numerous 수 많은 chart (지도 등에) 표시하다 alternate 대체의 route 노선

2. 세부 사항을 묻는 문제

이 기사에 따르면 관리 본부 직원들의 임무는 무엇인가?

(A) 기상 상태 관찰하기
(B) 직원 근무 일정 순환하기
(C) 청구 내역 발부하기
(D) 업무 능률 지수 주시하기

해설 마지막 문장, "The operations ~ weather conditions"를 보면 직원들이 기상 변화를 관찰할 것이라고 되어 있다. 그러므로 정답은 (A)이다.

3. 세부 사항을 묻는 문제

이 기사에 따르면 왜 회사가 관리 본부를 집결하는가?

(A) 싱가포르에 있는 직원을 줄이기로 결심했다.
(B) 어반 운송은 새로운 유형의 통신기술을 발명했다.
(C) 본부들 중 하나를 매각하기로 했다.
(D) 어반 운송은 좀 더 효율적으로 운영을 하고자 했다.

해설 지문 중반에 "However, ~ to centralize its operations."를 보면 통신 기술의 발전과 과열된 경쟁적인 시장으로 인해 어반 운송이 회사의 운영을 집중시키도록 만들었다고 되어 있다. 이것은 경쟁적인 시장에서 살아남고 발전된 과학 기술을 회사 운영에 이용하고자 한다는 것이므로 관리 본부를 집중시키기로 결심한 것은 선택 문항 중 회사 운영을 효과적으로 하길 원했기 때문이라고 볼 수 있다. 나머지 선택 문항들에 관한 내용은 기사 어디에도 언급되지 않았다. 그러므로 정답은 (D)이다.

SPARTA ACTUAL TEST

p. 231

1 (A) **2** (A) **3** (B) **4** (A) **5** (B) **6** (A)
7 (A) **8** (A) **9** (D) **10** (C)

<1-3> 다음은 기사에 관한 문제이다.

피터스버그

브로드 가의 아트리엄 쇼핑센터에 위치한 'A Taste of Italy'이 5년 전에 개업한 이래, 남쪽 지역의 인기 있는 식당이 되었습니다. 그 이름이 의미하듯이 전통적인 홈메이드 이태리 요리를 제공합니다. 'A Taste of Italy'은 경영진의 변화를 겪으며 최근 두 달 동안 문을 닫았고, 지난주 다시 문을 열었습니다. 새로운 주방장인 케빈 브래넌은 영양가가 풍부한 샐러드와 화덕 피자와 입맛을 당기는 전채요리를 포함하는 광범위한 메뉴를 선보이고 있습니다. 그의 전문 요리 중 몇 가지는 살짝 튀긴 왕새우를 곁들인 매운 레드 소스의 링귀니와 청고추와 버섯, 소시지, 토마토를 곁들인 스파게티 캇차토레와 같은 뛰어난 파스타 요리를 포함합니다. 집에서 만든 뛰어난 후식 티라미수를 위해 배를 남겨 두시기 바랍니다. 'A Taste of Italy'은 맛있는 많은 요리들과 함께 피터스버그 주민들 사이에서 인기를 다시 얻을 수 있을 것입니다.

어휘 located 위치해 있는 imply 암시하다, 의미하다 feature 특색으로 삼다 homemade 집에서 만든 management 경영진 extensive 광범위한 include 포함하다 hearty 영양가가 풍부한 brick-oven 화덕 enticing 마음을 끄는, 유혹하는 entrée 전채요리 specialty 전문, 전공 such as ~와 같은 linguini 링귀니(국수류) sauteed 살짝 튀긴, 소테로 한 served 제공된 spicy 매운 cacciatore 캇차토레(통닭 등을 토마토·향초(香草)·조미료 등으로 조리한 것) save 남기다 room 여지, 공간 signature 테마, 기호 dessert 후식 reclaim 되찾다

1. 기사의 목적을 찾는 문제

기사의 목적은 무엇인가?

(A) 식당을 평가하려고
(B) 요리 강습을 광고하려고
(C) 2개의 식당을 비교하려고
(D) 위치의 변경을 공고하려고

해설 기사에서 목적은 글의 상단부나 하단부에 위치함을 주의하자. 후반에서 With so many delicious items to choose from, A Taste of Italy is sure to reclaim its popularity with Petersburg residents.에서 식당

을 평가하는 내용임을 알 수 있다. 그러므로 정답은 (A)이다.

2. 사실 정보를 찾는 문제

브래넌 씨에 관해 언급된 것은 무엇인가?

(A) 파스타 요리에 숙련된 사람이다.
(B) 유기농 원료만 사용한다.
(C) 식당을 개조했다.
(D) 두 달 전에 A Taste of Italy에서 일하기 시작했다.

해설 중반에 'The new chef, Kevin Brennan 이후의 글 중 'Some of his specialties include excellent pasta dishes'에서 브래넌 씨는 파스타 요리에 숙련된 사람임을 알 수 있다. 그러므로 정답은 (A)이다.

3. 추론 문제

이 식당에 관해 암시된 바는 무엇인가?

(A) 경영진이 직원의 대부분을 교체했다.
(B) 뛰어난 후식을 제공하고 있다.
(C) 가장 인기 있는 요리는 링귀니이다.
(D) 새 장소로 옮겼다.

해설 지문 후반에서 'Be sure to save room for his signature dessert, homemade tiramisu'이므로 정답은 (B)이다.

〈4-7〉 다음은 기사에 관한 문제이다.

퍼스 - 지난 몇 년 동안에 걸쳐서, 퍼스는 국내에서 관광지로 가장 빠르게 성장하는 도시 중 하나로 지명되었다. 이 추세는 지속될 것으로 보인다.

비록 다른 도시들이 이 지역에서 관광의 중추로 여전히 인식되고 있음에도 불구하고, 퍼스 지역의 스완강과 협곡은 특히 관광과 관련 산업 분야의 국내외 기업들의 이목을 사로잡고 있다. 벌써 몇몇 기업들은 시장을 선점하기 위해 퍼스로 그들의 회사를 이전했다. 그 결과로, 이 도시의 고용 기회는 매우 치솟았다.

주민 헬렌 리더스 씨는 이전에 건축가였는데, 관광 및 숙박업 행정 분야에서 대학원 학위를 취득하기 위해 3년 전에 퍼스로 돌아왔다. 그녀가 건축업계에서 취업하기에 어려움을 겪었던 반면에, 현재의 분야에서는 그런 문제가 없었다. "졸업하자마자 여러 고용 제안을 받았고 제가 원했던 회사를 선택할 수 있었습니다."라고 리더스 씨가 말했다.

지난 18개월 동안에는 관련 분야의 기회가 꾸준히 성장했다. 퍼스로 이전했던 회사 중에 하나인 세이토 여행사가 이 성장의 한 예시이다. 세이토 여행사의 채용담당자인 존 객비노 씨는 "우리 회사는 처음 시작할 당시 5명의 정직원으로 시작했는데 5명 전체가 빠르게 충원되었습니다. 그리고 올해 말까지 적어도 5명의 새로운 직원을 채용할 계획입니다."라고 말했다.

더 많은 사업체들이 퍼스로의 이전 가능성을 고려할수록, 이 분야 고용의 대한 수요가 더욱 증가하고 있다.

이 수요를 맞추기 위해서, 웨스턴 오스트레일리아 대학교는 최근에 특별히 관광과 그 관련 분야의 신입생 입학 정원을 늘렸다. 웨스턴 오스트레일리아 대학교의 교육과정 책임자인 사라 암스트롱 씨는 고등학교 졸업생들이 관광업에서 진로를 고려해 볼 것을 권유하고 있다. "전문적인 지식뿐만 아니라 성공적인 사업가는 어려운 상황을 분석하고 다룰 능력을 가져야 합니다. 그 난관에 관한 창의적인 해결책을 찾을 수 있어야 합니다. 그것을 잘 할 수 있다면, 이 분야가 적합할 것입니다."라고 헬렌 씨는 덧붙였다.

어휘 name 지명하다　tourist attraction 관광명소　hub 중추　operation 운영, 기업　soar 치솟다　advanced degree 대학원 학위　recruitment 채용　meet a demand 수요를 맞추다　admit 입학 허가를 하다　tourism 관광업　related 관련된　coordinator 책임자　consider a career 진로를 고민하다　possess 가지다　suitable 적합한

4. 세부사항을 묻는 문제

기사에 따르면, 왜 몇몇 기업들이 퍼스로 이전했는가?

(A) 발전 가능성이 있다.
(B) 자질을 갖춘 인력들이 많다.
(C) 산업의 중추이다.
(D) 대중교통에 접근성이 좋다.

해설 첫 문장 'Perth has been named ~ for tourist attractions in the country.'와 'Perth's Swan River ~ related fields.'에서 언급된 바와 같이 퍼스는 유리한 자연조건으로 관광명소로 가장 빠르게 성장하고 있음을 나타내고 있다. 그러므로 정답은 (A)이다.

5. 추론 문제

리더스 씨는 왜 그녀의 직업을 바꾸었을 것 같은가?

(A) 그녀가 학교로 돌아오고 싶어 했기 때문에
(B) 건축 분야의 일자리 수가 제한적이었기 때문에
(C) 암스트롱 씨가 그녀를 고용했기 때문에
(D) 그녀가 최근에 퍼스로 이사했기 때문에

해설 세 번째 문단 중반에서 'While she had difficulty ~ no such problems in her current field.'를 보면 예전 직업 관련 분야인 건축에 비해 관광 관련 산업이 고용 기회가 많아 퍼스 지역으로 돌아왔음을 언급하고 있다. 그러므로 정답은 (B)이다.

6. 추론 문제

세이토 여행사에 관해서 무엇이 함축되어 있는가?

(A) 인력을 늘리고 있다.
(B) 전국에 사무실이 있다.
(C) 주로 임시직을 제공한다.
(D) 퍼스의 신생 기업 중 하나이다.

해설 네 번째 문단 하단에서 'And I'm planning to fill at least another 5 positions by the end of the year.'에서 연말까지 5명을 더 충원할 계획을 언급하고 있어 정답은 (A)이다.

7. 진위 여부 확인 및 추론 문제

암스트롱 씨에 관해 무엇이 진실인 것 같은가?

(A) 그녀는 대학에 고용된 상태다.
(B) 그녀는 채용회사를 운영한다.
(C) 그녀는 세이토 여행사에서 일했다.
(D) 그녀는 지역 고등학교에서 가르치고 있다.

해설 마지막 문단 네 번째 줄에서 "Sarah Armstrong the a program coordinator in Western Australia University, ~ developing a career in tourism.'에서 언급된 바와 같이 한 대학에서 교육프로그램 조정을 맡고 있으므로 교직원인 걸 알 수 있다. 그러므로 정답은 (A)이다.

〈8-10〉 다음은 기사에 관한 문제이다.

거리의 경찰관들은 특히나 심리적 스트레스와 불안감을 많이 느낀다. 통계를 살펴보면 그 이유를 알 수 있다. 2018년에 총 201명의 경찰관이 거리에서 죽었다. 그 중 절반 이상은 체포하던 중에 죽었고, 25%는 도움 요청에 응하다가 죽었으며 14%는 일상적으로 차량을 정지시키던 중에 죽었다.

경찰관의 불안감을 증대시키는 한 가지 요소는 경찰 살해범일 것 같은 사람과 법을 준수하는 일반 시민들을 구별할 방법이 없다는 것이다. 미 연방 수사국의 전문가들은 연쇄 살인범과 킬러범을 포함한 많은 흉악범들에 대해서 상세하게 설명해 왔다. 그러나 경찰 살해범의 특징을 밝혀주지는 못하고 있다. 전문가들이 말할 수 있는 것은, 그들은 경찰관이 위험인물로 인지하지 못하는 사람일 수 있다는 것이다.

경찰관이 스트레스를 받는 중요한 원인 한 가지는 사건은 점점 늘어나는데 그것들을 처리할 인력이나 시간은 부족하다는 점이다. 2018년에는 범죄로 인한

희생자가 2천 9백만 명이었다. 이듬해에는 그 수치가 12% 늘었고, 그 이후로 계속 늘고 있다. 반면 경찰 인원은 늘지 않아 경찰관과 시민의 비율은 여전히 2명 대 1천 명이다. 증가하는 범죄 사건과 점점 더 흉악해지는 범행에 맞서 경찰관은 적극적인 범죄 예방이라는 이상적인 역할을 수행할 수 없다. 단지 수동적으로 그것도 간신히 범죄에 대처할 뿐이다.

어휘 typically 전형적으로 psychological 심리적인 insecurity 불안정, 불안감 statistics 통계수치 make arrest 체포하다 respond to ~에 대응하다 routine 일상적인 element 요소 intensify 강화하다 tell A from B A와 B를 구별하다 cop killer 경찰 살해범 law-abiding 법을 준수하는 expert 전문가 come up with ~을 생각해내다 detailed 상세한 felon 흉악범 serial killer 연쇄 살인범 rapist 강간범 fail to ~ 하지 못하다 characteristic 특징 the last 가장 ~ 하지 않을 듯한 perceive 알아채다 case 사건 manpower 인력 handle 다루다 victim 희생자 figure 수치 policeman-to-citizen ratio 경찰관 대 시민의 비율 face with ~에 직면한 escalated 증가하는 degree 정도 fulfill 수행하다 prevention 방지

8. 주제를 묻는 문제

이 기사는 주로 무엇에 관한 것인가?

(A) 경찰관들의 스트레스와 불안감의 원인
(B) 2018년의 범죄 통계와 단속
(C) 미국의 거리 보안의 악화
(D) 경찰관들의 심각한 부족

해설 첫 문장 'A police officer on the streets typically feels a high degree of psychological stress and insecurity. 경찰관의 스트레스와 불안감을 말하므로 정답은 (A)이다.

9. 거짓 정보를 찾는 문제

2018년 경찰 사망 통계와 관련해서 옳지 않은 것은?

(A) 201명의 경찰이 거리에서 죽었다.
(B) 100명 이상의 경찰관이 범인을 체포하던 중에 죽었다.
(C) 40명 이상이 도움 요청에 응하다가 죽었다.
(D) 대부분 차량을 정지시키던 중에 죽었다.

해설 첫 문단 넷째 줄에서, (A) 201명의 경찰이 길에서 죽었고 'a total of 201 police officers were killed on the streets.' (B) 201명의 반 이상이 범인 체포 중에 죽었으며 'Over half of them died while making arrests' (C) 200명 중 25%인 약 50명 정도가 도움에 응답하다고 죽었으므로 '25% while responding to calls for help' 정답은 (D)이다. 차량 통제하다가 죽은 경찰관의 수는 가장 적은 비율이다.

10. 세부 사항을 묻는 문제

경찰관의 이상적인 역할로 제시되고 있는 것은?

(A) 범죄에 대한 즉각적인 반응
(B) 정치적인 자유를 보호하는 것
(C) 적극적인 범죄 예방
(D) 처벌의 시행

해설 지문 하단에서 '~ police officer simply cannot fullfil the ideal role of active prevention of crime.'에서 적극적인 범죄 예방이 이상적인 역할이라고 언급하고 있다. 그러므로 정답은 (C)이다.

UNIT 27 온라인 대화문

SPARTA PRACTICE

p. 238

1 (B) **2** (B) **3** (D)

케시 베이츠
안녕하세요, 스미스 씨. 네퍼 씨 보셨나요? 오늘 아침 내내 그를 찾고 있는데요.

제이든 스미스
네, 그가 리드 씨와 고객과 함께 회의실로 가는 것을 보았어요. 그를 찾는 이유가 무엇인가요?

케시 베이츠
구내식당에 있는 테이블 위에 자신의 휴대폰을 두고 갔어요. 그래서 그에게 돌려주려고요.

제이든 스미스
음, 제 생각엔 그들이 일을 끝낼 때까지 기다리는 게 좋겠어요. 매우 중요한 회의인 것 같아서 방해 받고 싶어 하지 않을 것 같아요.

어휘 look for ~을 찾다 conference room 회의실 client 고객 return 돌려주다 suggest 제안하다 seem ~인 것 같다 important 중요한 interrupt 방해하다

1. 추후 당부 사항을 묻는 문제

베이츠 씨가 다음에 할 일은 무엇인가?

(A) 회의실로 간다
(B) 회의가 끝난 뒤 휴대폰을 돌려준다
(C) 계속 네퍼 씨를 찾는다
(D) 구내식당에 있는 테이블에 휴대폰을 두고 온다

해설 스미스의 마지막 말에서 "Well, I suggest you just wait until they're done"이라고 기다리라고 제안하고 있다. 따라서 케시가 앞으로 할 행동으로 알맞은 것은 (B)가 됨을 유추할 수 있다.

조셉
우리 모든 유럽지사에서의 비용 추적을 할 수 있는 소프트웨어가 있나요? 물론 안전과 보안이 최우선 고려사항입니다.

패스마크 소프트웨어 직원
걱정할 필요가 없습니다. 어떤 프로그램들은 오류가 조금 있지만 속도가 아주 빠르고, 어떤 것들은 조금 느리지만 100% 정확도를 보장합니다. 당신에게 이메일로 정보를 보내 드릴까요?

조셉
좋아요. 감사합니다.

어휘 keep track of ~을 추적하다 expense 비용 boast 자랑하다 a bit 약간 guarantee 보장하다

2. 글의 목적을 묻는 문제

이 문자 메시지 대화문은 무엇에 관한 것인가?

(A) 유럽지사의 지출에 관한 문의
(B) 재무관련 소프트웨어에 관한 문의
(C) 소프트웨어 보증에 관한 문의
(D) 온라인 서비스에 관한 문의

해설 첫 문장 "Do you have any software that will let me keep track of our expenses in all our Europe an divisions?"에서 알 수 있듯이 조셉

은 재무관련 소프트웨어를 구입하고자 하는 것을 알 수 있다. 그러므로 정답은 (B)이다.

3. 숨은 의도 찾기 문제

직원이 쓴 "걱정할 필요가 없습니다"는 무엇을 의미하는가?

(A) 상품을 고를 때 보안이 가장 중요하다.
(B) 상품의 어떤 정보도 이메일로 제공될 수 있다.
(C) 소프트웨어 프로그램 중 하나는 아주 정확성이 높다.
(D) 그의 회사는 다양한 프로그램을 취급하고 있다.

해설 강조의 표현으로써, 해당 문구는 앞에 '특정 소프트웨어'를 가지고 있는지 묻는 질문에 '대부분의 제품을 가지고 있다'는 의도로 말한 것이다. 그러므로 정답은 (D)이다.

SPARTA ✔ ACTUAL TEST

p. 239

1 (A)	2 (C)	3 (B)	4 (C)	5 (A)	6 (D)
7 (B)	8 (C)	9 (C)	10 (C)		

〈1-2〉 다음은 문자 메시지에 관한 문제이다.

대니 드비토 (오전 9:10)
안녕하세요, 샤론 씨. 지난밤에 뉴스룸 24에서 연락을 받았어요. 우리 연구팀 중에서 한 명과 오늘 인터뷰하고 싶어 하더라고요.

샤론 루니 (오전 9:11)
무엇에 관한 거죠?

대니 드비토 (오전 9:13)
우리가 한창 작업 중인 현재 시 프로젝트에 대한 대중의 반응에 관해서요. 오늘 저녁 뉴스거리로 보도하고 싶어 해요. 제가 세스를 추천했는데, 그는 현재 외근 중이에요. 그래서 말인데 당신이 그들을 만나볼래요?

샤론 루니 (오전 9:14)
물론이죠. 당신이 요청한 것에 관한 투표 결과 분석이 거의 다 끝났어요. 인터뷰를 하기에 정말 좋은 시간이 되겠어요.

대니 드비토 (오전 9:21)
좋습니다. 방금 뉴스룸 24의 이안 첸과 통화했거든요. 그가 약 한 시간 후에 도착한대요. 그는 당신이 그 보고서를 보여달라고 제안했어요.

샤론 루니 (오전 9:23)
좋아요. 그럼 인터뷰가 끝나면 당신께 제출하고 보고할게요.

어휘 public reaction 대중 반응 segment 한 프로 vote 투표

1. 추론 문제

드비토 씨에 관해 무엇이 암시되어 있는가?

(A) 루니의 상관이다.
(B) 그는 오늘 누군가를 인터뷰할 예정이다.
(C) 그는 오늘 업무 일정을 바꿀 예정이다.
(D) 그는 2층에서 루니 씨와 만날 예정이다.

해설 오전 9시 14분에 드비토가 요청한 일을 했다는 'I'm almost done ~ you asked me to.' 샤론의 메시지를 미루어 볼 때, 드비토가 샤론에게 지시하고 보고 받는 상관임을 알 수 있다. 그러므로 정답은 (A)이다.

2. 숨은 의도 찾기 문제

오전 9시 21분에 드비토 씨가 쓴 "그는 당신이 보고서를 보여달라고 제안했어요."는 무엇을 의미할 것 같은가?

(A) 자료 분석을 함으로써 결과가 마무리될 것이다.
(B) 세스는 피드백의 사용이 필요할지도 모른다.
(C) 조사 결과를 오늘밤 뉴스로 방송될지도 모른다.
(D) 서류는 도난당하지 않을 것이다.

해설 앞서 나온 'It would be a good time for the interview.' 샤론의 메시지와, 후에 언급된 'That sounds good.'에서 샤론이 거의 끝내가고 있는 투표의 결과를 담은 그 보고서가 방송될 가능성을 짐작할 수 있다. 그러므로 정답은 (C)이다.

〈3-6〉 다음은 문자메시지에 관한 문제이다.

루피타 농요 [오후 7:30]
모두들 안녕하세요. 제가 30분 전에 출근했을 때, 7층에 모든 에어컨이 다 켜져 있었어요. 어떻게 그렇게 된 건지 아시는 분 있으십니까?

윈스턴 듀크 [오후 7:33]
제가 오늘 저녁에 사무실을 떠나기 직전 6시에는 전부 꺼져 있었는데요.

엘리자베스 모스 [오후 7:35]
맞아요. 저도 6시 30분쯤에 서류가방 가지러 다시 올라갔을 때도 에어컨은 꺼져 있었어요.

루피타 농요 [오후 7:37]
좋아요. 지난 목요일에도 이런 일이 있었던 것을 고려해 볼 때, 제 생각에는 분명 문제가 있는 것 같습니다.

윈스턴 듀크 [오후 7:42]
동감입니다. 출근 전에 또 에어컨이 켜져 있었던 게 분명해요. 제가 교대 근무로 출근할 때 건물 관리인인 최 씨에게 수리해 달라고 말해 볼게요.

루피타 농요 [오후 7:48]
설치했던 회사에 연락해 보면 어떨까요? 제 생각엔 그게 더 나을 것 같군요.

윈스턴 듀크 [오후 7:51]
그럴게요.

어휘 go to work 출근하다 definitely 확실하게 building supervisor 건물 관리인 shift 교대근무 installation 설치

3. 추론 문제

농요 씨에 관해 맞는 것은 무엇인가?

(A) 그녀는 유지관리부서에서 일한다.
(B) 그녀는 야간교대 근무를 한다.
(C) 그녀는 직장 부근에 산다.
(D) 그녀는 임시직이다.

해설 첫 문장 'When I went to work 30 minutes ago, all the air conditioners on the 7th floor were on.'의 농요의 메시지에서 그녀의 출근 시간이 이 메시지를 보낸 30분 전인 오후 7시인 것을 미루어 짐작할 수 있다. 그러므로 정답은 (B)이다.

4. 세부사항을 묻는 문제

에어컨이 꺼져 있는 것을 마지막으로 본 사람은 누구인가?

(A) 농요 씨
(B) 듀크 씨
(C) 모스 씨
(D) 최 씨

해설 오후 7시 35분에 'When I went up there again to take my briefcase around 6:30 P.M., the air conditioners were off.'라고 언급된 모스의 메시지 이후로 더 이상 확인한 사람이 없으므로 정답은 (C)이다.

5. 숨은 의도 찾기 문제

오후 7시 42분에 듀크가 쓴 "동감입니다."는 무엇을 의미할 것 같은가?

(A) 그는 에어컨이 수리가 필요하다고 여긴다.

(B) 그는 농요의 요청을 따를 계획이다.
(C) 그는 보수 서비스가 즉각 제공될 것이라고 생각한다.
(D) 그는 최 씨가 그가 에어컨을 끄는 것을 봤다고 알고 있다.

해설 이 메시지를 전후에서 에어컨이 비정상적으로 작동했음을 언급하고 있다. 그러므로 정답은 (A)이다.

6. 추후 당부 사항을 묻는 문제

듀크 씨는 앞으로 무엇을 할 것 같은가?

(A) 부장에게 문제를 보고한다
(B) 에어컨을 켠다
(C) 서류를 작성한다
(D) 다른 회사에 전화한다

해설 바로 직전 메시지에서 농요가 'Why don't we contact the company that did the installation'이라고 언급하고 있으므로 설치 회사에 전화할 것을 알 수 있다. 그러므로 정답은 (D)이다.

⟨7-10⟩ 다음은 온라인 대화문에 관한 문제이다.

파커 세박 오전 9:45
여러분, 반가운 소식입니다! 최고로 효율성이 높은 자동화 검사 시스템을 위한 새로운 장비가 우리 공장에 도착했습니다. 이미 사용해 봤는데 대량 작업을 마무리하는 데 걸리는 시간이 상당히 줄어들 것이라 예상합니다. 또한 생산성이 대폭 증가하는 것을 분명 보게 될 것입니다.

마이클 체너스 오전 9:48
네, 맞습니다. 이번 주에 몇몇 상품들을 검사할 때, 기계들이 매우 매끄럽고 빠르게 작동하여서 제가 직접 큰 차이를 몸소 깨달았어요. 이 장비들은 예전 것보다 거의 2배 빨라요. 당신들도 아시다시피, 고장도 거의 나지 않습니다.

사마트 샤크라바티 오전 9:51
마이클, 좋은 소식이네요. 저도 곧 사용해 보길 간절히 희망합니다!

사라 콜란젤로 오전 9:51
당신의 공장에만 있나요? 제가 5년 전에 입사한 이래 여기는 기계를 전혀 교체하지 않고 있어요.

파커 세박 오전 9:53
제가 듣기론 본사가 모든 공장에 들여놓을 장비 구입을 결정했다고 해요, 사라 씨. 플리마우스와 브리스톨에 9월 1일과 10월 14일에 각각 설치할 예정이고요.

메기 질렌할 오전 9:55
사실 그렇지 않습니다. 일정이 변경되어서 본래의 일정 대신에 이번 주 금요일 오전 11시 경에 장비가 배송될 거예요. 설치하는 데 아마도 하루가 걸릴 것이어서 장비를 들여놓을 공간이 필요하다는 것을 직원들에게 사전에 공지해야 할 겁니다.

어휘 effective 효율적인 inspection 검사 facility 시설, 공장 considerably 상당하게 complete 완료하다 notice 알아차리다 productivity 생산성 advance 앞당기다 notify 알리다 in advance 사전에

7. 주제를 묻는 문제

주로 무엇을 논의하고 있는가?

(A) 새로운 공장을 열 계획
(B) 장비 개선
(C) 장비의 효율성
(D) 곧 있을 회의

해설 오전 9시 45분에 'The new machines for the highly effective automatical inspection system have arrived at our facility.'에서 공장에 장비가 더욱 효율적인 기계로 바뀌었음을 알리고 있으므로 정답은 (B)이다.

8. 숨은 의도 찾기 문제

오전 9시 48분에, 체너스 씨가 "네, 맞습니다."라고 썼을 때, 무엇을 의도한 것 같은가?

(A) 그는 시간 내에 작업을 끝냈다.
(B) 그는 설치 제안을 받아들였다.
(C) 새로운 장비는 직원들이 더욱 생산적이게 할 것이다.
(D) 갱신된 사보는 예전 것보다 더 좋다.

해설 앞선 메시지에서 장비의 교체로 생산성이 높아졌음이 언급되어 있고, 이후에도 체너스 씨가 이용했을 때 작업속도가 2배나 향상되었음을 언급하고 있으므로 정답은 (C)가 적절하다.

9. 추론 문제

콜란젤로 씨에 관해 무엇이 암시되어 있는가?

(A) 그녀는 새로운 감독관이다.
(B) 그녀는 곧 본사에 방문할 것을 희망한다.
(C) 그녀는 세박 씨와 같은 곳에서 일하지 않는다.
(D) 그녀는 예전 장비를 수리해야 할 필요가 있다.

해설 9시 51분에 'Are they only for your factory?'의 메시지에서 콜란젤로 씨가 자기네 공장에는 지난 5년간 기계를 교체 안 해서 세박 씨에게 되묻는 것임을 알 수 있다. 이로 미루어 짐작해 봤을 때, 이 두 사람은 같은 공장에서 일을 하지 않고 있음을 알 수 있다. 그러므로 정답은 (C)이다.

10. 세부사항을 묻는 문제

질렌할 씨가 온라인 채팅 대화문에 왜 메시지를 보냈나?

(A) 배송 일정을 바꾸기 위해
(B) 추천을 하기 위해
(C) 동료들에게 변경사항을 알리기 위해
(D) 도움을 요청하기 위해

해설 마지막 메시지에 'Actually, no. Now that the plan was rescheduled, they will be delivered this Friday around 11:00 A.M. instead of the time listed on the original schedule.'에서 언급된 바와 같이 장비 설치 일정이 최종으로 변경되었음을 알 수 있다. 그러므로 동료들에게 변경사항을 알리는 정답은 (C)이다.

UNIT 28 이중 지문

SPARTA PRACTICE

p. 246

1 (B) **2** (B) **3** (D) **4** (A) **5** (C)

〈1-5〉 공지와 이메일에 관한 문제이다.

Ana de Armas 씨가 고객 서비스의 부장이 됩니다.

부사장실에서는 Ana de Armas 씨가 고객 서비스 부장직을 받아들였다는 소식과 함께 8월 14일부로 업무를 공식적으로 시작할 것임을 알리게 되어 기쁜 바입니다.

de Armas 씨는 12년 전 프레시디움에서 마케팅 직원으로 그녀의 업무를 시작했습니다. 그녀의 지식과 기술, 능력은 뛰어났고 5년 뒤 고객 서비스부의 차장으로 함께할 것을 요청 받았습니다. 지난 7년 동안 그녀는 그 업무를 탁월하게 수행했고, 이제 로베르타 파게트의 은퇴로 인해 비어 있는 고객서비스의 부장직을 받아들이는 데 충분한 준비가 되었습니다.

de Armas 씨는 수석 부사장인 피터 맥카티에게 바로 보고할 것이며, 이 수석 부사장은 "마케팅과 광범위한 산업 관계에 있어 Ana의 전문지식은 프레시디움과 우리 고객 모두에게 막대한 자산이 될 것입니다. 그녀는 우리 고객 서비스가 확장되고 강화되는 데 있어 도움이 될 것입니다"라고 말했습니다.

de Armas 씨에게 축하를 보냅니다. 새로운 직책에 대해 최선을 다해 줄 것을 바랍니다.

수신: Ana de Armas
발신: Barry Allen
날짜: 8월 2일 화요일
제목: 축하합니다!

de Armas 씨께,

우리는 귀하께서 저희와 함께 있어 주셔서 기쁘며 계속된 지도력을 보여줄 것에 대해 기대하는 바입니다.

고객 서비스 부서가 우량 고객 중 몇몇을 위해 주최하는 공식 오찬에 귀하를 초대하는 바입니다. 행사는 레이놀즈 건물의 210호에서 내일 오전 11시 30분부터 오후 1시 30분까지 있을 예정입니다.

귀하께서 새 직책을 공식적으로 시작하기 전에 있는 행사이지만, 귀하를 아직 만나보시 못한 우리 고객들 중 몇 분에게 소개할 수 있는 좋은 기회가 될 것입니다. 또한, 귀하의 새로운 상사가 연설할 예정이랍니다!
참석 여부에 대해 알려주시기 바랍니다.

Barry Allen

어휘 accept 받아들이다 officially 공식적으로 career 업무, 직책 apparent 분명한, 명백한 excel 능가하다, 뛰어넘다 ready to do ~할 준비가 된 take over 받아들이다 vacant 비어있는 directly 즉시, 바로 far-reaching 널리 미치는, 원대한 tremendous 막대한 asset 자산 instrumental 도움이 되는 strengthen 강화하다 delighted 기쁜 look forward to ~하기를 고대하다 host 주최하다 take place 일어나다, 발생하다 introduce 소개하다

1. 전반적인 내용을 묻는 문제

이 공지는 어디에서 볼 수 있을 것인가?

(A) 경제 전문지에서
(B) 회사 소식지에서
(C) 시 신문에서
(D) 회사 재정 보고서에서

해설 글이 게시되는 장소는 글의 주제와 긴밀한 연관이 있으므로 전반적인 내용을 묻는 문제로 분류된다. 첫 지문, 첫 문장에서 부사장실의 입장을 전달하고 있으므로 'The Vice President's office is pleased to announce that ~' 사내에서 볼 수 있는 소식지 등에 나올 만한 얘기임을 알 수 있다. 그러므로 정답은 (B)이다.

2. 추론 문제

공지가 de Armas 씨에 관해 암시하고 있는 것은 무엇인가?

(A) 다른 회사에서 채용되었다.
(B) 여러 번 승진을 했다.
(C) 파게트 씨와 일할 것이다.
(D) 새로운 역할을 임시적으로 맡을 것이다.

해설 첫 지문, 두 번째 문단, 'Ms. de Armas began her career ~ which was made vacant because of Roberta Paquette's retirement.'의 내용에서 알 수 있는 것은 승진을 여러 번 했다는 것이다. 그러므로 정답은 (B)이다.

3. 동의어 찾는 문제

공지에서, 두 번째 단락, 두 번째 줄의 "apparent"와 가장 의미가 가까운 어휘는

(A) 일시의, 임시의
(B) 진심의
(C) 애매한
(D) 분명한

해설 글의 맥락을 고려해 보면 apparent의 뜻은 '명백한, 분명한'의 의미이다. 그러므로 정답은 (D)이다.

4. 통합 지문 문제

오찬에서 누가 연설할 것인가?

(A) 피터 맥카티
(B) 로베르타 파게트
(C) 베리 앨런
(D) 아나 드 아르마스

해설 이메일 마지막 줄에서 오찬에 관한 내용이 나오는데, "Plus, your new boss will be making a speech!"라고 하고 있으므로, Ana de Armas 씨의 상사를 찾아봐야 한다. 이 부분은 공지 마지막 문단, 'Ms. de Armas will be reporting directly to Senior Vice President Peter McCarthy'에서 정답이 (A)임을 알 수 있다.

5. 세부사항을 묻는 문제

오찬에 관해 알 수 있는 것은 무엇인가?

(A) 직원들을 위한 것이다.
(B) 참석을 위한 표가 필요하다.
(C) 8월 14일 이전에 열릴 것이다.
(D) 식당에서 열릴 것이다.

해설 오찬에 관한 얘기는 이메일에서 하고 있다. 이메일을 보낸 날짜가 8월 2일이고, 첫 문단 마지막 문장에서 내일이라고 'It will be tomorrow' 하고 있으므로 정답은 (C)이다.

SPARTA ✓ ACTUAL TEST

p. 248

1 (A)	2 (B)	3 (D)	4 (A)	5 (D)	6 (C)
7 (D)	8 (D)	9 (B)	10 (A)	11 (A)	12 (B)
13 (A)	14 (A)	15 (C)			

〈1-5〉 다음은 기사와 이메일에 관한 문제이다.

Blackberry Hill 지역 재개발

5월 7일

하워드 시―시 의회에서는 시립 박물관이 Bainford가에 위치한 종전보다 넓은 건물로의 이전을 결정한 이후, Blackberry Hill의 박물관 부지를 활용하기 위한 입찰을 모집하고 있습니다. 지역 및 전국 개발업체들로부터 많은 제안서가 제출되었습니다. 그 중 특히 두 제안서가 강력한 경쟁자로 떠오르고 있습니다.

한 가지 유력한 입찰안은 Lean 건설의 것으로서, 부지에 사무용 단지 건설을 제안했습니다. 이 사업은 새로운 기업들을 유인할 수 있고 향후 5년간 지역 주민들에게 일자리를 제공할 수 있을 것입니다. 그러나 이런 야심찬 사업을 완수하는 데 거의 3년이 소요됩니다. 게다가 건물을 임차하게 될 기업들이 그들의 직원에 대한 전일 주차 혜택을 요구하게 되면, 지역 내 주차 문제는 현재의 어려운 실정보다 더욱더 현저해질 것입니다. 3년 이력의 이 회사는 현재 런던과 파리에서 유사한 건설 프로젝트를 진행 중입니다.

경합을 벌이는 또 하나의 입찰안은 시에서 경력을 쌓아온 민간 개발업체인 Maverick 산업이 제안한 것입니다. 이 업체는 멋지고 새로운 쇼핑 지구를 구상하고 있습니다. 이 사업은 주민들에게 백화점, 식당 그리고 영화관을 제공해 줄 것입니다. 이는 주민들에게 부족한 쇼핑과 오락 지구를 제공하기 때문에 시 입장에서는 매력적인 제안입니다. 기억하시는 바와 같이, Maverick 산업은 Waterfront 지구의 재개발을 맡아 추진했습니다.

<하워드시 헤럴드>가 실시한 한 여론 조사에서 주민들에게 어느 계획을 선호하는지 질문했습니다. 결과는 Maverick의 개발 계획을 조금 더 지지하는 것으로 나타났습니다. 비록 주민들이 두 가지 계획 각각 시 경제에 좋은 효과를 가져다 줄 것이라는 데 대체로 의견을 같이하고 있으나, 노골적인 한 이익 단체는 기존에 공공서비스를 제공해 왔던 지역의 상업적인 개발에 강력히 반발하며 현 부지를 지역 공원으로 남겨둘 것을 시에 청원하고자 서명을 모으는 중입니다.

Brent Ackerly
<일간 Eagle Eye>

발신: Christopher Plummer <cplummer@lean.com>
수신: Brent Ackerly <backerly@eed.com>
날짜: 5월 8일
제목: 시 프로젝트

Ackerly 씨에게,

저는 5월 7일자 당신 기사에 실린 몇몇 주장을 받아들일 수 없습니다. 제가 생각하기에 독자들을 위해 반드시 고쳐져야 할 몇 가지 잘못된 점을 발견했습니다.
Lean 건설의 사업은 기사에서 주장하는 3년이 아닌 2년 이내에 완공이 가능합니다. 그리고 만약 우리가 서두른다면, Lean 건설이 구상 중인 건물의 1층 공간은 착공일로부터 1년 이내에 개장할 수 있습니다.
저자가 기술한 대로, 시의 주차 여건은 실로 큰 문제가 되고 있습니다. 그러나 Lean 건설의 부사장인 Kannan Pradesh 씨가 이미 시 집행부와 몇 차례 만남을 가져 가능한 해결책을 논의했습니다.

진심으로,

Christopher Plummer
Lean 건설 사장

어휘 renovation 재개발 region 지역 since ~이후에 relocate 이전하다 across 건너, 가로질러 spacious (공간이) 넓은 city council 시 의회 accept 받아들이다, 수락하다, 용인하다 bid 입찰 proposal 제안(서) submit 제출하다 developer 개발(업)자 in particular 특별히 emerge 떠오르다 contender 경쟁자 promising 유망한 construction 건설 suggest 제안하다 office complex 사무실 단지 serve to ~하는 데 도움이 되다 attract (사람 등을) 매료시키다, 끌다 provide 제공하다 resident 거주자, 주민 ambitious 야심적인, 대규모의 complete 완수하다 additionally 게다가 business tenant 입주 사업자 full-day parking 전일 주차 privilege 특권, 특전 employee 직원 pronounced 명백한 firm 기업 currently 현재 undertake 진행하다 similar 유사한 competing 경쟁하는 commercial developer 민간개발업체 elaborate 정교한, 정밀한 attractive 매력적인 lack ~이 부족하다 recall ~을 기억하다 be in charge of ~을 맡다 renovate 재개발하다 district 지역, 지구 poll 여론 조사 conduct 진행하다, 수행하다 indicate 나타내다, 가리키다 slightly 약간 scheme 계획 generally 일반적으로, 대체로 have an effect on ~에 효과를 가져다주다 outspoken 거리낌 없는, 솔직한 interest group 이익 단체 oppose ~에 반대하다 commercial 상업적인 public service 공공서비스 collect signatures 서명 운동을 하다 petition A to V A에게 ~할 것을 청원하다 set aside 따로 남겨두다 have a problem with ~을 받아들이지 못하다 claim 주장, 논거 correct 수정하다 benefit 혜택, 이익 reader 독자 complete 완수하다 state 언급하다, 말하다 rush 서두르다 plan to ~할 계획이다 construct 건설하다 starting date 착공일, 시작일 author 저자 situation 여건 pose (위험성을) 내포하다, 지니다 council executives 시 집행부 occasion 기회, 경우 discuss ~에 대해 논의하다 possible solution 가능한 해결책

1. 기사의 목적을 묻는 문제

기사의 주된 목적은?

(A) 대중들에게 재개발 가능성에 대해 알리려고
(B) 두 개발업체의 이력을 소개하려고
(C) 건설 계획안에 대한 독자의 의견을 구하려고
(D) 시립 박물관의 새로운 소재지를 알리려고

해설 기사 첫 문장에서 'the city council has been accepting bids for the use of the museum's space on Blackberry Hill'에서 박물관 부지를 새롭게 활용하기 위한 입찰을 모집 중이라고 언급하고 있다. 그러므로 재개발을 알린다는 내용의 (A)가 정답이다.

2. 가치 판단을 묻는 문제

주민 대다수가 두 계획안에 대해 생각하는 바는?

(A) 수많은 주차 문제를 유발할 것이다.
(B) 경제에 이로울 것이다.
(C) 상업적 개발이 해롭다고 본다.
(D) 수준 낮은 박물관 대체 계획이다.

해설 기사에 보도되는 주제에 대한 사람들의 찬반의 가치 판단을 묻는 문제이다. 문제 해결에 중요한 단서를 주는 역접의 접속사 although로 시작되는 부분 지문 하단에 'Although residents generally agree that either plan will have a positive effect on the city's economy'에서 두 개의 계획이 시 경제에 긍정적인 영향을 줄 것이라는 데 동의하고 있다고 언급되어 있다. 그러므로 정답은 (B)이다.

3. 추론 문제

하워드 시에 대해 암시된 바는?

(A) 지역 개발이 필요하다.
(B) 과거에 Lean 건설사를 고용한 적이 있다.
(C) 너무 많은 오락 시설이 있다.
(D) 주차가 큰 문제가 된다.

해설 기사의 두 번째 문단 하단에서 "~ and the parking problem in the area could be even more pronounced than its already high level. (지역 내 주차 문제는 현재도 어려움)"을 통해 정답을 알 수 있다. 그러므로 정답은 (D)이다.

4. 이메일의 주제를 묻는 문제

이메일에 따르면, 기사에 대한 Plummer 씨의 주된 불만은 무엇인가?

(A) 기자가 공사 기간을 부정확하게 예측하고 있다.
(B) Kannan Pradesh의 진술을 잘못 해석하고 있다.
(C) 여론 조사의 통계를 왜곡하고 있다.
(D) 설명이 한쪽에 치우쳤다.

해설 이메일은 Plummer 씨가 불만을 전하기 위한 목적의 서신이므로 불만 사항이 곧 이 글의 주제가 된다. 그러므로 이 문제는 전반 내용을 묻는 문제이다. 두 번째 문단에서 'Lean Construction's project can be completed in two years, not the three years that the article states.'에서 기사에서는 완공 기간이 3년이라고 했으나 실제로는 2년 이내에 가능하다고 나와 있다. 결국 공사 기간의 부정확한 예측이 주된 불만이다. 그러므로 정답은 (A)이다. 참고로, 년수를 이용한 구체적인 숫자보다 일반적인 표현으로 정답을 나타낸 것에 주목하자. 패러프레이징 중에서도, 일반화시켜 표현한 것이 정답이 되는 경우가 많다.

5. 통합 지문 문제

Plummer 씨에 대해 암시된 바는?

(A) 하워드 시에 거주한다.
(B) 최근 분양 아파트를 건설했다.
(C) 예전에 하워드 시와 일한 적이 있다.
(D) 유럽에서 일했다.

해설 공지의 두 번째 지문에서, '~ undertaking similar building projects in London and Paris.' Lean 건설사가 런던과 파리에서 일하고 있음을 알려주고 있다. 이메일에서 Plummer 씨가 Lean 건설사 직원임을 하단 발신인 정보에서 확인이 가능하므로, 정답은 (D)이다.

〈6-10〉 다음은 이메일과 설문 조사에 관한 문제이다.

수신 조 코르티즈 <jcortese@gletter.com>
발신 고객 서비스 <cservice@amazonsupplies.com>
날짜 12월 11일
제목 귀하의 최근 주문 건

코르티즈 씨에게

저희 아마존 서플라이즈 사의 목적은 탁월한 상품과 고객서비스를 제공하는 것입니다. 그래서, 저희는 정기적으로 고객들에게 저희가 어떻게 행동했는지 알려 달라고 요청 드리고 있습니다. 판매 기록에 따르면, 귀하는 12월 7일에 구매하셨습니다. amazonsupplies.com에서의 당신의 구매 경험에 대해서 알려주신다면, 감사 드릴 것이고, 그러면 저희는 지속적으로 높은 수준의 고객 만족을 유지할 수 있을 것입니다. 단지 약 10분 이내에 작성이 가능합니다. 그러니 이번 달 말까지 응답해 주시고, 다음 달에 20퍼센트 할인 쿠폰을 받으세요. 설문 조사를 시작하시려면 amazonsupplies.com/survey 링크를 클릭하세요.

감사합니다.

---

www.amazonsupplies.com/survey

설문 조사에 응해 주셔서 감사합니다. www.amazonsupplies.com에서 당신의 최근 온라인 구매 경험과 가장 일치하다고 생각하는 대답을 선택해 주세요.

1. 최근 구매 날짜 : 12월 7일
2. www.amazonsupplies.com 웹 사이트를 얼마나 자주 방문하는가?
   ___ 하루에 한 번 ___ 일주일에 한 번 ___ 한 달에 한 번
   _X_ 분기별로 ___ 매년
3. 웹 사이트에서 다양한 종류의 구매 가능한 상품들을 보았다.
   _X_ 매우 그렇다 ___ 그렇다 ___ 그렇지 않다 ___ 매우 그렇지 않다
4. 웹 사이트가 둘러보기에 편하다는 것을 알았다.
   ___ 매우 그렇다 _X_ 그렇다 ___ 그렇지 않다 ___ 매우 그렇지 않다
5. 최근에 무엇을 구매하였나?
   _X_ 복사기 ___ 문구류 ___ 사무용품
   ___ 사무용 가구 ___ 컴퓨터 ___ 컴퓨터 주변기기

논평 :
저는 이번 달 초에 구매한 것에 매우 만족했습니다. 몇 달에 한 번씩 사무용지를 정기적으로 주문하고 있습니다. 불행히도 우리 사무실 복사기가 갑자기 고장나는 바람에 즉시 새것으로 교체해야 했습니다. 저는 당신 회사의 판매직원과 이야기를 나누었는데 저희 사무실 작업량을 고려해서 기존에 사용했던 것과 다른 모델을 추천해 주었습니다. 지금까지 바쁜 저희 사무실에서 잘 쓰고 있습니다. 추천과 다음 날 빠른 배송에 매우 감사드립니다.

어휘 superior 우월한 routinely 일상적으로 complete 작성하다 experience 경험 appreciate 감사하다 customer satisfaction 고객 만족 respond 응답하다 match 부합하다, 맞추다 replace 교체하다 volume 양 expedited 빠른

6. 세부사항을 묻는 문제

아마존 서플라이즈 사에 관해 무엇이 나타나 있는가?

(A) 저렴한 가격으로 상품을 제공한다.
(B) 여러 해외 지사를 보유하고 있다.
(C) 고객으로부터 정기적으로 피드백을 요청한다.
(D) 최근에 제품군을 늘렸다.

해설 첫 지문 첫 번째 줄에 언급된 'So we routinely ask our customers to find out how we are doing.'에 따르면 정기적으로 고객에게 피드백을 요청하는 것을 알 수 있다. 그러므로 정답은 (C)이다.

7. 동의어를 찾는 문제

이메일에 따르면, 첫 번재 단락 첫 번째 줄의 단어 "aim"의 의미와 가장 가까운 것은

(A) 요청사항
(B) 지시
(C) 결과
(D) 의도

해설 본문 속에 'aim'은 회사를 운영하는 방침이기 때문에 이에 가상 가까운 것은 '의도'의 뜻을 가진 (D)이다.

8. 통합지문 문제

코르티즈 씨에 관해 무엇이 함축되어 있는가?

(A) 그는 아마존 서플라이즈에서 처음으로 물품을 구매했다.
(B) 그는 배달에 문제를 겪었다.
(C) 그는 개인 정보를 변경했다.
(D) 그는 아마도 내년에 할인을 받을 것이다.

해설 첫 지문에 마지막에 'So please respond by the end of this month and receive a 20-percent discount coupon next month.' 조사에 응하면 다음 달에 할인 쿠폰을 받을 수 있음을 언급하고 있다. 이에 두 번째 조사 지문이 작성되었으므로 할인을 받을 조건이 된다. 첫 지문 작성 날짜가 12월 11일임을 감안해 본다면 다음 달은 다음 해가 되는 것을 알 수 있다. 그러므로 정답은 (D)가 적절하다.

9. 추론 문제

코르티즈 씨는 그의 가장 최근의 구매에 관해 무엇을 암시하는가?

(A) 배송이 예상보다 오래 걸렸다.
(B) 그는 조언에 만족했다.

(C) 결함이 있는 상품이 보내졌다.
(D) 무료 배송이었다.

해설 두 번째 지문 논평 하단에서 'I really appreciated the recommendation ~'로 언급된 바와 같이 구매가 판매 직원의 훌륭한 조언이 있어 만족스러웠다고 평가하고 있다. 그러므로 정답은 (B)이다.

10. 세부사항을 묻는 문제

코르티지 씨는 보통 무엇을 구매하는가?

(A) 문구류
(B) 복사기
(C) 책상 부속품
(D) 컴퓨터

해설 두 번째 지문 논평 상단에, 'I regularly place orders for paper supplies to make copies every few months.'라고 언급된 바와 같이 용지 구입을 정기적으로 하고 있는 것을 알 수 있다. 그러므로 정답은 (A)이다.

〈11-15〉 다음은 기사와 이메일에 관한 문제이다.

필라델피아 (10월 1일) - 가장 사랑 받은 미국 스토리 연합(ABSS)은 5만 달러의 상금이 걸려 있는 경연의 최종 진출자로 7명의 촉망 받는 신인 작가들을 선출하였다. 지난 3년에 걸쳐 해마다 수여된 이 상금은 신인 작가들의 작품에 관련된 비용을 원조하기 위한 것이다.

이전에는, 실존 인물과 사건을 그린 논픽션만 수상 자격이 되었다. 하지만 경연이 4번째 해를 맞고 있는 올해부터 ABSS가 역사적인 허구 인물들까지 범위를 넓힐 것을 결정하였다.

"다양한 소설의 컨셉과 스타일은 상당히 인상 깊었고 올해는 최고조에 달했습니다. 모든 출품작들이 주제도 매우 다양하고 다양한 시대에 초점을 맞추고 있기 때문에 역사적 사실에 대해 더욱 독특하고 다양한 관점을 제공하였습니다. 그러므로 7명으로 최종 진출자들을 좁히는 데 매우 애를 먹었습니다."라고 ABSS의 이사인 애나 보든이 밝혔다.

7명의 출품자들은 ABSS의 이사진들을 한 달 전에 만나서, 집필 목적과 동기에 대한 질문에 답을 했다. 심사위원단에 의해 엄중히 결정된 최종 우승자는 다음 달에 발표된다. 그들에 대해 알고 싶다면, www.abssmoviefestival.com 웹 사이트에 방문하라.

수신: fleck@gp.com
발신: m.boden@abss.com
날짜: 11월 12일
제목: 축하합니다!

플렉 씨에게,

사랑 받는 미국 스토리 연합을 대신하여, 올해 경연에 우승하신 것을 진심으로 축하 드리고 싶습니다. 관련된 보도 자료와 우승에 관한 더욱 자세한 사항은 별도의 이메일로 발송하여 드리겠습니다. 그러고 나서 올해 말에 간단한 시상식을 통하여 상금을 전달해 드리겠습니다. 당신의 일정과 맞출 수 있게 그때 다른 계획과 겹치는지 알려주시겠어요? 시상식 일정과 장소가 결정되자마자 즉시 연락드리겠습니다.

안부를 전하며,

애나 보든
ABSS 이사

어휘 promising 촉망받는, 유망한 budding writer 신인작가 competition 경연 award 수여하다 yearly 해마다 intend ~할 작정이다 detail 자세히 설명하다 nonfiction (소설 같은 허구 이야기가 아닌) 산문 작품 be eligible for ~의 자격이 있다 considerably 상당히 various 다양한 perspective 관점 event 사건 narrow down 좁히다 board of directors 이사진 motivation 동기 determine 결정하다 panel 심사위원단 press release 보도자료 separately 별도로 schedule conflicts 일정 중복 calendar 일정(표) accordingly 따라서 immediately 즉시

11. 세부사항을 묻는 문제

올해 경연은 지난해 경연과 어떻게 다른가?

(A) 다른 형식의 소설을 허용한다.
(B) 여러 우승자를 선출할 것이다.
(C) 더 많은 상금이 수여될 것이다.
(D) 국제적으로 홍보된다.

해설 기사의 두 번째 문단에서, '~ starting this year, when the competition is in its fourth year, the ABSS has decided to expand eligibility to historical fiction novels.' 올해부터 논픽션 소설까지 영역을 확대했다고 한다. 그러므로 정답은 (A)이다.

12. 동의어를 찾는 문제

기사에서, 세 번째 단락 첫 번째 줄에 "considerably"와 가장 의미가 가까운 것은?

(A) 예술적으로
(B) 상당히
(C) 감성적으로
(D) 역사적으로

해설 본문 속의 'considerably'는 다양한 소설의 콘셉트와 스타일이 인상 깊었다는 것을 강조하고 있으므로 정답은 (B)가 적절하다.

13. 추후 당부 사항을 묻는 문제

기사에 따르면, 독자들은 온라인에서 무엇을 배울 수 있는가?

(A) 심사위원에 대해 읽기
(B) 신청 지침 확인하기
(C) 참가자들에게 투표하기
(D) 예고 비디오 보기

해설 첫 지문 마지막에 언급된 'If you want to ~ www.abssmoviefestival.com.'에서 인칭대명사 'them'은 앞선 언급된 심사위원단(a panel)을 의미하므로 정답은 (A)이다.

14. 통합지문 문제

플렉 씨에 관해 무엇이 암시되어 있는가?

(A) 그는 9월에 인터뷰에 응했다.
(B) 그는 보든 씨와 일한다.
(C) 그는 영화를 만들었다.
(D) 그는 3년 전에 상금을 받았다.

해설 두 번째 지문에서 플렉 씨는 이 경연의 우승자라는 통보를 받고 있다. 이에 우승자인 플렉 씨는 우승 통보 전에 7인의 결승 진출자로서 첫 지문에 언급된 것(The seven entries ~ answer questions concerning their production goals and writing motivation.)처럼 첫 지문이 작성된 10월보다 한 달 전인 9월에 ABSS 이사진과의 인터뷰에 응했음을 짐작할 수 있다. 그러므로 정답은 (A)이다.

15. 추후 당부 사항을 묻는 문제

이메일에서, 플렉 씨는 무엇을 하라고 요청 받는가?

(A) 시상식을 예약할 것
(B) 기자회견에서 발표하는 것
(C) 그가 참여 가능한 시간을 확인하는 것
(D) 심사위원으로 참여하는 것

해설 두 번째 지문 마지막에 언급된 'Would you ~ schedule conflicts on your calendar at that time so that we can plan accordingly?'에서 시상식이 있을 시기에 일정 중복이 있을 경우 알려 달라고 당부 받고 있다. 그러므로 정답은 (C)이다.

SPARTA PRACTICE

p. 258

1 (B) **2** (D) **3** (A) **4** (C) **5** (D)

〈1-5〉 다음은 전단지, 웹 페이지 그리고 표에 관한 문제이다.

할인: EXcopy 2000 컬러 프린터

저는 최근 일일 보고서와 다른 회사 문서들을 출력하기 위해 EXcopy T-2000을 구매했습니다. 당시에 저는 오직 적은 페이지 수만을 출력할 수 있다는 것을 알지 못했고 그것은 제 용도 목적을 만족시키지 못합니다. 저는 현재 분당 100페이지를 출력할 수 있는 EXcopy 프린터기를 구매할 계획입니다.
EXcopy T-2000은 분당 50페이지를 출력하거나 30페이지를 양면으로 출력해야 하는 작은 업무에 적합합니다. 프린터기는 사용되지 않았으며 여전히 공장에서 나온 포장 상태 그대로 있습니다. EXcopy는 그들의 모든 기계의 수명 동안 대체 부품을 제공하기로 약속했습니다. 그러므로 비록 이 모델이 지난주부터 생산이 중단되었다고 하더라도 앞으로 대체 부품을 구하는 데 아무런 문제가 없을 것입니다. 이러한 진행상황으로 비록 제가 본래 75달러를 지불했지만 기계에 대해 단지 50달러만을 요구합니다. 관심 있다면, 아래의 휴대폰 연락처로 저에게 연락해 주세요. 저는 매일 사무실에 있지 않지만 당신에게 기계를 보여 드리기 위해 잠시 들를 수 있는 시간을 낼 수 있습니다.

Jason Wells
023-453-4032

EXcopy 프린터기들

EXcopy 기계들은 많은 다른 프로젝트 수요에 적합한 것은 물론 제안서, 팸플렛과 다른 전문적인 서류들을 곧바로 출력할 수 있게 해 줍니다. 모든 기계들은 레터, 리갈, A4를 포함한 대부분의 표준적인 종이 양식들과 호환 가능합니다. 이 빠르게 볼 수 있는 비교 차트는 당신의 수요에 적합한 제품을 선택하는 데 도움을 줄 것입니다. 완전한 제품 사양은 excopy.com/printer_specs에서 찾을 수 있습니다.

모델번호	최대 출력 용량(단면)	최대 출력 용량(양면)	가격
T-1500	30	15	$65
T-2000	50	30	$75
M-1500	80	50	$120
M-2000	100	80	$165

어휘 recently 최근의 daily 매일의 realize 깨닫다 insufficient 불충분한 capacity 용량, 수용 original 원래의 replacement 교체, 대체 discontinue 중단하다 demand 수요 enable 가능하게 하다 proposal 제안서 compatible 호환 가능한 comparison 비교 specification 설명서, 사양

1. 전단지의 목적을 묻는 문제

Wells 씨가 EXcopy T-2000을 판매하길 원하는 이유는 무엇인가?

(A) 그것은 그의 사무실에 너무 크다.
(B) 그것은 큰 프로젝트를 처리할 수 없다.
(C) 그는 더 이상 프린터기를 필요하지 않는다.
(D) 그는 더 쉽게 작동할 수 있는 기계를 원한다.

해설 Wells 씨가 EXcopy T-2000을 판매하길 원하는 이유가 무엇인지 묻는 질문으로, 첫 번째 지문인 전단지를 이용하여 문제를 해결해야 한다. 글의 목적은 주로 지문의 상단부에 위치한다. 첫 번째 단락에 당시에는 적은 양의 페이지만을 출력할 수 있는지 몰랐으며 나의 목적에 부합하지 않는다고 나와 있으므로 (At the time, I did not realize that it can only print a small number of pages and is insufficient for my purposes.) 정답은 (B)가 된다.

2. 전단지의 세부 내용을 묻는 문제

전단지에 따르면, 왜 기계의 가격이 상대적으로 낮은가?

(A) 중고 기계이다.
(B) 대체 부품이 필요하다.
(C) 공장 정리 세일의 일부이다.
(D) 더 이상 제작되지 않는 모델이다.

해설 왜 기계의 가격이 상대적으로 낮은지 묻는 질문으로, 첫 번째 지문 전단지를 이용해 문제를 해결해야 한다. 지난주 부로 해당 모델 생산이 중단되어서 해당 내용을 반영하여 50달러를 받겠다는 내용이 나와 있으므로(even though this model has been discontinued as of last week. In light of this recent development I am only asking $50 for the machine ~) 정답은 (D)가 된다.

3. 추후 당부 사항을 묻는 문제

관심 있는 구매자들은 어디에서 기계를 볼 수 있는가?

(A) Wells 씨의 사무실에서
(B) 공장 전시실에서
(C) 사무 용품 가게에서
(D) EXcopy 판매 대리점에서

해설 관심 있는 구매자들이 어디에서 기계를 볼 수 있는지 묻는 질문이다. 첫 번째 지문 마지막 문단에 관심 있는 경우 기계를 보기 위해서 사무실에서 만날 약속을 잡자는 내용이 나와 있으므로(I am not in the office every day, but I can arrange a time for you to come by to look at the machine.) 정답은 (A)가 된다.

4. 웹 페이지의 세부 내용을 묻는 문제

웹 페이지에 따르면, 모든 EXcopy 기계들이 일반적으로 무엇을 가지고 있는가?

(A) 초경량이다.
(B) 다양한 색깔로 나온다.
(C) 다양한 종이 크기들을 수용한다.
(D) 견본 프로젝트 설명서를 포함한다.

해설 웹 페이지를 이용해 문제를 해결해야 한다. 두 번째 문장에 모든 기계들은 레터, 리갈, A4를 포함한 대부분의 표준 종이 양식과 호환 가능하다고 나와 있으므로(All machines are compatible with most standard paper formats including letter, legal, and A4.) 따라서 답은 (C)이다.

5. 통합 지문 문제

Wells 씨는 T-2000을 대신하기 위해 어떤 EXcopy 모델을 구매할 것인가?

(A) T-1500
(B) T-2000
(C) M-1500
(D) M-2000

해설 첫 번째 지문의 상단부에 분당 100페이지를 출력할 수 있는 프린터기를 구매할 거라는 내용과(I am now planning to purchase a EXcopy printer with a printing capacity of 100 pages per minute), 세 번째 지문에 있는 표에 나타난 최대 출력 용량을 통해 정답이 (D)가 됨을 알 수 있다.

SPARTA ACTUAL TEST p. 260

1 (C)	2 (A)	3 (B)	4 (B)	5 (B)	6 (D)
7 (B)	8 (D)	9 (D)	10 (C)	11 (C)	12 (A)
13 (B)	14 (C)	15 (B)			

〈1-5〉 다음은 편지들과 설명서에 관한 문제이다.

로더 씨 귀하,

귀사의 업소용 주방용품 신제품 라인에 대해 문의하기 위해 편지를 씁니다. 저는 벨기에 브뤼셀에 새로 생긴 메자닌 레스토랑에서 근무하고 있습니다. 저희는 약 90일 후에 개업을 할 것이기 때문에 조만간 주방 기기를 구입하려고 합니다. 저희는 아카시아 비스트로의 매니저에게서 귀사를 추천 받았습니다. 그는 귀사가 고품질 업소용 제품 라인을 갖추고 있고, 현재 국제 배송에 대한 할인요금을 제공하고 있다고 말했습니다.

저희는 6개의 버너를 갖춘 업소용 가스레인지와 최소 15 평방피트의 저장 용량을 갖춘 냉동고도 찾고 있습니다. 저에게 제품 설명이 있는 제품 목록과 국제 배송 요금 및 가격 정보를 보내주시기 바랍니다.

안녕히 계십시오,

로이 리

리 씨에게,

우리 제품에 대한 관심에 감사합니다. 이 편지에 당신이 요청하신 정보를 함께 보내드립니다.

저희 팰콘 설비의 업소용 주방기기 회사는 모든 종류의 식당 업계가 필요로 하는 제품들을 취급합니다. 당신도 알다시피, 저희 회사는 현재 10주년을 축하하기 위해 고객님들께 특별한 기회를 제공하고 있습니다. 이 행사 기간동안 2개 제품 이상을 구매하시면 배송료의 10퍼센트를 할인 받을 자격이 되십니다. 이 기회를 놓치지 마세요.

로더
팰콘 설비

팰콘 설비의 업소용 주방 기기	
스테인레스 스틸 업소용 냉장고 19.5 평방피트 용량 고성능 냉각 시스템 다이내믹 콘덴서가 고온에서의 성능을 개선함 밀폐 실내 캐비닛이 청소를 용이하게 함	1,595 파운드
오븐이 장착된 48인치 업소용 이중 연료 레인지 이중 연료 레인지가 전자 오븐과 함께 외부 장착 가스 화구의 정밀함을 제공 20k BTU 화력을 갖춘 6개의 가스버너 고른 열전달 시스템	2,470 파운드
싱크대 하단 장착 제빙기 24시간 안에 50파운드에 달하는 얼음 제조 한번에 25파운드까지 얼음 저장	945 파운드
13.8 평방피트의 용량을 갖춘 서리 제거 냉동기 약 483파운드의 냉동 음식을 보관 5개의 도어를 갖춘 선반	685 파운드

배송비: 국내 100파운드, 국제 130파운드
(10일 동안만 배송비 특별 할인)

어휘 commercial 상업의 appliance 기구, 장비 establishment 시설 shipping rate 배송비 freezer 냉동 장치 cubic feet 평방피트 storage 저장 merchandise 상품 celebrate 경축하다 be entitled to ~하는 데 자격이 있다 condenser 냉각기 sealed 봉인한 range 요리용 레인지

1. 첫 번째 편지의 세부 내용을 묻는 문제

첫 번째 편지에 따르면, 로이 씨가 팰콘 설비의 장비에 관심을 갖게 된 이유는 무엇인가?

(A) 지역 상점에서 구할 수 있다.
(B) 가격이 적당하다.
(C) 동료에게 추천 받았다.
(D) 잡지에 제품 평이 실려 있었다.

해설 첫 번째 편지를 보면 '저희는 아카시아 비스트로의 매니저에게서 귀사를 추천 받았습니다. 그는 귀사가 고품질 업소용 제품 라인을 갖추고 있고, 현재 국제 배송에 대한 할인요금을 제공하고 있다고 말했습니다. (We were referred to your company by the manager of Acacia Bistro. He mentioned that you have a new line of high-end commercial appliances and that you are currently offering discounted international shipping rates.)'라고 하므로 같은 업종에 종사하는 동료에게서 추천 받았음을 알 수 있다. 그러므로 정답은 (C)이다. 또한 국제 배송비의 할인 혜택이 제품이 싸다는 뜻은 아니므로 (B)는 정답이 되지 못한다는 점에 주의해야 한다.

2. 첫 번째 편지의 세부 내용을 묻는 문제

메자닌 레스토랑이 주방기기를 필요로 하는 이유는 무엇인가?

(A) 식당 개업을 준비하고 있다.
(B) 사업을 막 확장했다.
(C) 현재의 장비를 교체할 필요가 있다.
(D) 장비가 너무 오래된 것이다.

해설 편지의 첫 번째 문단을 보면 '저희는 약 90일 후에 문을 열 생각을 하고 있기 때문에 조만간 주방 기기를 구입하려고 합니다.(We are looking to purchase some kitchen equipment soon as we expect to be open in about 90 days.)'라고 하므로 정답은 (A)이다.

3. 통합 지문 및 추론 문제

로이 씨는 어떤 제품을 주문할 가능성이 큰가?

(A) 냉장고
(B) 가스레인지
(C) 제빙기
(D) 냉동고

해설 첫 번째 편지에서 보면 '저희는 6개의 버너를 갖춘 업소용 가스레인지와 최소 15 평방피트의 저장 용량을 갖춘 냉동고를 찾고 있습니다. (We are looking to purchase a commercial grade gas range with six burners and a freezer with at least 15 cubic feet of storage capacity.)'라고 하므로 가스레인지, 냉동고를 필요로 한다는 사실을 알 수 있다. 세 번째 지문에서 팰콘 설비의 장비 설명을 보면 가스레인지는 6개의 버너를 갖추고 있으므로 로이 씨가 원하는 제품이지만 냉동고는 용량이 13.8 평방피트로 용량이 부족하다. 따라서 로이 씨가 주문할 가능성이 큰 제품은 가스레인지이다. 그러므로 정답은 (B)이다.

4. 세 번째 설명서의 거짓 정보를 묻는 문제

업소용 냉장고에 대해 광고되고 있는 기능이 아닌 것은 무엇인가?

(A) 청소하기 쉽다.
(B) 에너지 효율적이다.
(C) 스테인레스 스틸 제품이다.
(D) 강력한 콘덴서가 달려 있다.

해설 제품 설명서의 첫 칸의 냉장고의 기능을 보면 '스테인레스 스틸(Stainless Steel)', 다이내믹 콘덴서가 고온 환경에서의 성능을 개선합니다. (Dynamic condenser improves performance in high-temperature environments)', '밀폐 실내 캐비닛이 청소를 용이하게 함.(Sealed cabinet interior for easy cleaning)'이라고 되어 있다. 따라서 (A), (C), (D)는 언급되어 있지만 에너지 효율에 대한 언급은 없으므로 정답은 (B)이다.

5. 세 개 지문의 통합 문제

만약에 로이가 할인을 받게 된다면, 얼마를 배송비로 지불할 것 같은가?

(A) 130 파운드
(B) 117 파운드
(C) 100 파운드
(D) 90 파운드

해설 우선 첫 지문인 편지의 마지막에 '저에게 제품 설명이 있는 제품 목록과 국제 배송 요금 및 가격 정보를 보내주시기 바랍니다. (Please send me a product list with descriptions and pricing information as well as your international shipping rates.)'로 미뤄 로이 씨는 국제배송 요금에 해당함을 알 수 있다. 세 번째 지문인 제품 설명서의 제일 하단에 배송비 항목을 보면 국제배송 요금은 130파운드이며 두 번째 편지를 보면 특별 판촉 기간 동안 조건에 맞춰 구매하면 이 배송비의 10퍼센트를 할인 받을 수 있다고 하고 있다. 그러므로 로이가 국제 배송비의 할인을 받게 된다면 배송비로 지불하게 될 비용은 117 파운드이다. 그러므로 정답은 (B)이다.

〈6-10〉 지침, 서식, 그리고 이메일에 관한 문제이다.

장비 이용에 관한 지침

의료 기술 협회는 고급 의료 장비를 운용 및 유지하고 의료업계의 연구 개발을 지원하기 위해 전문적인 조언을 제공하고 있습니다. 우리는 많은 병원과 의료장비회사에 장비를 대여해 주고 있습니다. 장비 예약 신청서는 사전에 모든 장비의 요청을 위해 작성되어야만 합니다. 협회의 숙련된 전문가들이 시범을 보이고 전문적이고 특별한 프로젝트를 위한 장비 사용에 대해 신청자들을 도울 수 있습니다.

장비 예약을 위한 지침은 다음과 같습니다;

A. 장비 대여가 24시간을 초과하거나 대여 비용이 130달러를 초과할 경우, 신청자 부서의 담당자가 반드시 승인을 해야만 합니다.
B. 요청하신 장비가 "고감도"라고 지정되어 있다면, 아래와 같은 경우에만 이용 가능합니다,
 (1) 협회의 전문가가 장비 사용에 함께할 시간이 될 때,
 (2) 장비 사용자가 협회에서 정기적으로 개최하는 작동 및 안전 교육을 이수했고 훈련증서를 제출한 후

장비 예약 신청서

장비 예약 신청서	
신청번호	#8232
날짜	1월 29일
신청직원 성명	제시카 디나게
부서	해부학
부장	요한 올젠
구내번호	6819
장비코드/모델명	GFP-775 4F/광학 현미경
비용 (1일 당)	$178
고감도 장비 여부	■ 예 □ 아니요
고감도 장비 교육 여부	□ 예 ■ 아니요
대여 요청 일시/시간	2월 5일, 오전 9시 - 오후 3시
목적 용도	생물학적 샘플의 수분 표면 관찰
교육 수료증 첨부	없음

신청직원 서명
Jessica Dinnage
부장 승인
(필요 시)
Johan Olsen

수신: 제시카 디나게
발신: 구스타브 몰러
날짜: 1월 30일
제목: 장비 요청 #8232

디나게 씨께;

오늘 아침에 당신의 요청서를 받았습니다. 안타깝게도, 귀하가 예약하신 장비는 다른 업체에서 대여 중이고 2월 7일까지는 이용이 불가능할 것 같습니다. 게다가, 귀사가 요청하신 고감도 장비에 지정된 전문가인 메리 로만 박사가 다음 주에 세미나에 참석할 예정이어서 2월 10일까지 자리를 비웁니다. 로만 씨가 돌아오는 이후 날짜로 예약을 다시 해 드리고 싶습니다. 날짜를 정하기 위해 저에게 이메일이나 전화를 주세요. 번거롭게 해 드려 죄송합니다.

친애하는,

구스타브 몰러
의료 기술 협회

어휘 association 협회 advanced 고급의 specialist 전문가 hold 개최하다 tutorial (개별) 지도 apply 적용하다 charge 부과하다 exceed 초과하다 assist 돕다 sensitivity 민감도 regularly 정기적으로 anatomy 해부학 observe 관찰하다 hydrated 수화한 surface 표면 biological 생물학적인 attachment 첨부 certificate 수료증 signature 서명 instrument 장비 moreover 더욱이 apologize 사과하다

6. 추론 문제

누가 지침에 관심이 있을 것 같은가?

(A) 장비 제조업체
(B) 영업 부장
(C) 기술 업체
(D) 연구진

해설 이 글을 읽을 만한 독자를 찾는 문제로 첫 지문에 언급된 'The medical Technology Association ~ to support research and development activities in the medical industry.'를 보면 연구개발 활동을 지원한다고 하기 때문에 정답은 (D)이다.

7. 동의어를 찾는 문제

지침서에서, 첫 번째 단락 두 번째 줄의 "support"와 가장 의미가 가까운 것은

(A) 들어올리다
(B) 돕다
(C) 개최하다
(D) 자금을 마련하다

해설 단어 앞뒤에 언급된 내용을 살펴보면, 연구 개발을 지원하기 위해 장비와 전문적 조언을 제공한다는 맥락을 확인할 수 있다. 그러므로 가장 유사한 의미의 정답은 (B)이다.

8. 통합지문 문제

예약 신청서에 왜 올젠 씨의 서명이 요구되는가?

(A) 디나게 씨가 24시간 이상 장비를 사용할 것이기 때문에
(B) 요청한 장비가 고감도로 분류되었기 때문에
(C) 디나게 씨가 회의를 참석해야 하기 때문에
(D) 대여료가 매우 비쌌기 때문에

해설 첫 지문 중반에 언급된 'If it takes ~ approved by the applicant's department supervisor.'에서 알 수 있듯이 대여 시간이나 대여료가 일정 기준 이상이면 장비를 신청한 사람이 속한 부서 책임자의 승인이 필요하게 된다. 두 번째 지문의 예약 신청서 하단에 요청 여부에 따라 부서의 책임자의 승인을 확인하는 서명란이 있는데 여기서 '올젠'의 성명을 확인할 수 있고 또한 대여 비용이 첫 지문에서 언급한 130달러를 초과

한 178달러인 것을 확인할 수 있다. 그러므로 정답은 이를 통합한 (D)이다.

9. 통합지문 문제

로만 박사에 관해 무엇이 암시되어 있는가?

(A) 그녀는 디나게 씨의 상관이다.
(B) 그녀는 2월 내내 부재중이다.
(C) 그녀는 회의에서 발표할 예정이다.
(D) 그녀는 장비 작동 중에 반드시 동참해야한다.

해설 세 번째 지문, 세 번째 줄에서, 로만 박사가 고감도 장비에 지정된 전문가임을 'the specialist for your requested high-sensitivity instrument, Dr. Mary Lohmann' 알려 주고 있다. 첫 번째 지문 하단 B의 (1)에서, 협회 전문가가 장비 사용에 가능한 경우에 'When a specialist of our association is available to operate the equipment, or' 장비를 예약할 수 있다고 나온다. 따라서 정답은 (D)이다.

10. 추후 당부 사항을 묻는 문제

디나게 씨는 몰러 씨에게 어떤 정보를 언급할 것인가?

(A) 그녀가 이용해야 하는 장비의 유형
(B) 그녀가 협회로 반납할 날짜
(C) 그녀가 장비를 빌리고자 하는 다른 날짜
(D) 통화 가능한 연락처

해설 세 번째 지문에 언급된 전반적인 내용과 'Please call or e-mail me to decide on a date.'에서 이 편지를 수신한 디나게 씨는 장비를 대여할 추후 새로운 일정을 몰러 씨에게 알릴 것을 알 수 있다. 그러므로 정답은 (C)이다.

<11-15> 다음은 편지, 이메일과 지시사항에 관한 문제이다.

GoodFCU 전자명세서 또는 전자알림 등록하고
$100 주유 카드에 당첨되세요!

허쉬 고객님께,

고객님은 현재 Good FCU 계좌의 전자명세서를 받아보고 계시기 때문에, 빠르고 간편한 방법으로 월별, 분기별 명세서를 컴퓨터 라인으로 받아보는 방법을 제공하는 것에 대해 잘 아실 것입니다. 또 다른 전자 알림으로 좋은 것이 거래와 대출 지불을 알려주는 비자 전자명세서입니다.

지금부터 7월 31일 전까지 전자명세서나 전자알림에 등록하셔서 100달러 상당의 주유 카드 3장 중 1장에 당첨될 기회를 놓치지 마세요. 여름 여행에 안성맞춤입니다!

- **VISA 전자명세서는** 사용하시는 GoodFCU 계좌의 전자명세서와 동일합니다. 컴퓨터라인으로 VISA 전자명세서를 볼 수 있을 때 이메일로 알려드립니다. 또, 온라인 결제를 위한 링크도 함께 제공될 것입니다.
- **거래 공지는** 이메일로 보내지며, 잔액을 초과해서 거래를 하거나 잔고 부족 수표가 있을 경우에 알려드립니다.
- **대출 지불 공지는** 대출금 납입 알림과 대출금 연체 알림(즉석 대출, 주택 담보 대출 등)을 이메일로 받을 수 있습니다. 전자 알림을 선택할 때 지급 만기일 며칠 전까지 받고 싶은지 설정할 수 있습니다.

오늘 등록하세요!

친애하는,

좋은 연방 신용 조합

등록 절차

GoodFCU 홈페이지에서 컴퓨터라인에 로그인하세요.
- 이메일 주소가 현재 사용하는 것인지 확인하세요.
- "전자 서비스 메뉴"를 선택하세요.
- 드롭 다운 메뉴에서 "전자 메일 등록"을 선택하세요.

명세서 또는 알람을 받는 방법으로 "온라인"을 선택하세요. (모든 명세서와 알림을 전자 상으로 받아보시기 위해서 목록 맨 위에 있는 체크박스를 선택하시면 됩니다.)
- 이메일 주소를 입력하시고 다시 한번 확인해 주세요.
- 온라인 정보 공개에 동의해 주세요.

협조해 주셔서 감사합니다.

수신: goodfcu@gfcu.net
발신: Hush322@kodak.net
제목 : 안녕하세요, 웨인 허쉬입니다.

Good FCU 귀하,

며칠 전에 전자명세서, 처리 알람, 대출 알람에 등록했으나, 100달러 상당의 주유 카드는 아직 받지 못했습니다. 이틀 후에 라스베가스로 여행을 갈 예정이므로 그 카드가 있다면 굉장히 유용할 것 같습니다. 그러므로 주유 카드를 실수로 안 보내셨거나, 오는 데 문제가 있었는지 확인해 주시기 바랍니다. 저는 주유 카드를 최대한 빨리 받고 싶을 뿐입니다. 감사합니다.

친애하는,

웨인 허쉬

어휘 currently 최근의　statement 명세서　quarterly 분기의
transaction 거래　via ~을 통해서　overdraft 과다인출
transfer 전송　loan 대출　method 방법　appropriate 적절한

11. 세부사항을 묻는 문제

GoodFCU 사에 대해 무엇이 언급되어 있는가?

(A) 새로운 담보 대출을 설명하고 있다.
(B) 허쉬 씨가 은행에서 얼마나 빌렸는지 보여 주고 있다.
(C) 특별한 행사를 누릴 수 있는 방법을 소개한다.
(D) 새로운 거래에 대해 광고하고 있다.

해설 첫 번째 지문에서, GoodFCU 사가 메일을 보내는 것을 확인할 수 있다. 지문 중반에 'Sign Up for E-statements or E-notices ~ be entered to win one of three $100 mobile gas card'에 언급된 바와 같이 전자명세서로 새로 등록하는 고객들에게 100달러짜리 주유 카드에 당첨될 기회가 있다고 참여를 유도하고 있으므로 정답은 (C)이다.

12. 세부사항을 묻는 문제

GoodFCU 사가 제공하는 새로운 서비스 중에 하나는 무엇인가?

(A) 대출금 납입 공지
(B) 새로운 웹 사이트
(C) 고객 서비스
(D) 전자 쿠폰

해설 첫 지문에서 전자 계산서를 신청하면, monthly/quarterly account statement(월별/분기별 명세서)와 transaction notices and the loan billing notice(거래 공지와 대출 지불 공지)를 살펴볼 수 있으니 신청함으로써 새로운 서비스를 이용해 볼 것을 추천하고 있다. 그러므로 정답은 (A)이다.

13. 세부사항을 묻는 문제

서비스에 등록하기 위해서 거쳐야 할 올바른 과정은 무엇인가?

(A) 전자 고객서비스 선택
(B) 전자 서비스 등록
(C) 비밀번호 입력 및 변경
(D) 식별 번호 입력

해설 두 번째 지문에 따르면, 'Choose "E-Correspondence Sign Up" from the drop-down menu'와 'Select "Electronic" as your delivery method for the appropriate statements and/or notices'에서 언급된 바와 같이 메뉴에서 "전자 메일 등록"을 선택하고 명세서 또는 알람을 받는 방법으로 "온라인"을 선택해야 한다. 이로써 전자 서비스를 등록해야 함을 알 수 있다. 그러므로 정답은 (B)이다.

14. 세부사항을 묻는 문제

허쉬 씨는 왜 주유 카드가 필요하다고 하는가?

(A) 주유할 돈이 없다.
(B) 차가 휘발유를 많이 소모한다.
(C) 곧 휘발유가 많이 필요하다.
(D) 다른 사람에게 팔고 싶어 한다.

해설 세 번째 지문, 두 번째 줄에서 'a trip to Las Vegas in two days, so it would be very useful'에서 알 수 있듯이 허쉬 씨는 이틀 후에 라스베가스로 여행을 가는데, 주유 카드가 있다면 유용하게 쓸 수 있을 것이라고 이야기하고 있다. 그러므로 정답은 (C)이다.

15. 통합지문 문제

허쉬 씨가 알지 못할 것 같은 사실은?

(A) 전자명세서는 온라인으로 지불을 해야 한다
(B) 모두가 100달러 주유 카드를 받는 건 아니다
(C) 허쉬 씨는 추첨할 자격이 안 된다
(D) 허쉬 씨는 포인트가 부족해서 참여할 수 없다

해설 세 번째 지문, 두 번째 문장에서, 허쉬 씨가 'I still haven't gotten get my $100 mobile gas card'라며 전자계산서를 신청했는데 주유 카드를 받지 못하고 있다고 언급하고 있다. 그러나 첫 지문 중반에, 'be entered to win one of three $100 gas card'에서 알 수 있듯이 당첨이 되어야만 카드를 받을 수 있다. 그러므로 첫 지문과 세 번째 지문을 통합해 봤을 때, 정답은 (B)이다.

실전 모의고사

p. 290

101 (B)	102 (D)	103 (A)	104 (B)	105 (A)	106 (B)
107 (B)	108 (A)	109 (D)	110 (D)	111 (C)	112 (A)
113 (C)	114 (B)	115 (A)	116 (C)	117 (B)	118 (A)
119 (C)	120 (D)	121 (A)	122 (D)	123 (A)	124 (C)
125 (A)	126 (C)	127 (D)	128 (D)	129 (B)	130 (D)
131 (A)	132 (D)	133 (B)	134 (B)	135 (B)	136 (D)
137 (A)	138 (D)	139 (D)	140 (B)	141 (A)	142 (D)
143 (A)	144 (C)	145 (A)	146 (A)	147 (A)	148 (D)
149 (B)	150 (C)	151 (B)	152 (A)	153 (B)	154 (D)
155 (B)	156 (C)	157 (B)	158 (A)	159 (B)	160 (A)
161 (A)	162 (C)	163 (B)	164 (A)	165 (B)	166 (C)
167 (B)	168 (C)	169 (C)	170 (C)	171 (B)	172 (A)
173 (D)	174 (B)	175 (C)	176 (C)	177 (A)	178 (C)
179 (A)	180 (C)	181 (A)	182 (B)	183 (D)	184 (D)
185 (A)	186 (D)	187 (A)	188 (D)	189 (D)	190 (A)
191 (B)	192 (D)	193 (A)	194 (C)	195 (D)	196 (D)
197 (B)	198 (A)	199 (C)	200 (A)		

[PART 5]

101 지난주에 있었던 전략 회의에서, 우리는 부서 간의 협조를 증진할 수 있는 방안에 대해 논의했다.

해설 [타동사(increase)+---+명사(cooperation)] 구조로 되어 있으므로 빈칸에는 명사 앞에서 형용사 역할을 하는 소유격 대명사가 쓰여야 한다. 따라서 (B) our이 정답이다.

어휘 strategy 전략 discuss 논의하다 way 방법 increase 증가시키다 cooperation 협조 department 부서

정답 (B)

102 Sun 시멘트 사는 현재 재고로 있는 제품의 대부분을 팔 수 있는 방법을 빨리 찾아내야 한다.

해설 [조동사(must)+---+본동사(find)] 구조로 되어 있다. 조동사와 본동사 사이에 들어갈 수 있는 품사는 부사로 (D) quickly가 정답이다.

어휘 way 방법 sell 팔다 product 제품 in stock 재고가 있는

정답 (D)

103 회사는 산업 디자인 분야에 경험이 있거나 특별한 관심을 보이는 지원자를 고용하고 싶어 한다.

해설 [either+동사+---+동사]의 구조이다. 등위접속사 문제로 either A or B의 구조가 되어야 하므로 (A) or이 정답이다.

어휘 hire 고용하다 applicant 지원자 either A or B A 아니면 B experience 경험 particular 특별한 field 분야 industrial design 산업 디자인

정답 (A)

104 사무실이 문을 닫는 오후 5시 전까지 반드시 사무 용품을 배달해 주시기 바랍니다.

해설 that절 이하의 주어가 사무용품(office supplies)이므로 동사 deliver(배달하다)는 수동태로 쓰여야 한다. 따라서 (B) are delivered가 정답이다.

어휘 make sure 확실히 하다 office supplies 사무용품 deliver 배달하다 delivery 배달

정답 (B)

105 인사 과장은 신입 사원을 훈련하고 그들의 업무 수행 능력을 평가할 책임이 있다.

해설 [be동사+---+전치사]의 구조로 형용사가 필요한 자리이다. be responsible for '~의 책임을 지다'라는 뜻으로 문맥상 적절하다. 따라서 정답은 (A) responsible이다.

어휘 personnel 인사의 employee 종업원 evaluate 평가하다 performance 업무수행 responsible 책임이 있는 responsibility 책임

정답 (A)

106 승객이 승차권 없이 기차에 탑승한다면, 무거운 벌금을 내야 할 것이다.

해설 문맥에 맞는 전치사 선택 문제이다. 의미상 '승차권 없이'가 자연스러우므로 정답은 (B) without이다.

어휘 passenger 승객 board 탑승하다 penalty 벌금 outside 바깥에 without 없이 along 따라서 between 사이에

정답 (B)

107 업무 흐름 개선을 위한 마틴 씨의 제안이 선임 과장들에 의해 검토될 것이다.

해설 [소유격('s)+---]의 구조이다. 소유격은 명사를 수식하므로, 빈칸에는 명사가 들어가야 한다. 따라서 정답은 (B) recommendation이다.

어휘 improve 개선하다 workflow 업무 흐름 review 검토하다 senior 선임의 recommend 추천하다 recommendation 추천

정답 (B)

108 에드몬튼에서 나이로비로 가는 어떤 직항편도 현재로서는 일정 잡힌 것이 없기 때문에 비행기를 환승해서 이용하는 것이 필요하다.

해설 품사 판정 문제이다. [---+명사(direct flights)] 구조이다. 명사를 수식하는 품사는 형용사이므로 no를 써야 한다. 따라서 정답은 (A)이다. (B) Not과 (C) Never는 부사이고 (D) None은 대명사이다.

어휘 direct flight 직행 항공편 currently 현재 schedule 일정을 잡다 connecting flight 환승할 비행기

정답 (A)

109 데이빗 가렛은 20권이 넘는 소설을 집필한 작가이지만, 67세가 된 지금까지 많은 명성을 누려보지는 못했다.

해설 접속사/전치사 선택 문제이다. [----+주어+동사, 주어+동사] 구조로 되어 있으므로 빈칸에는 접속사가 쓰여야 한다. 의미상 적절한 접속사는 Although이므로 정답은 (D)이다. (C) In spite of는 전치사이기 때문에 주어, 동사가 뒤따르지 못하므로 오답이다.

어휘 author 저자, 작가 enjoy 누리다 fame 명성 furthermore 더구나 nevertheless 그럼에도 불구하고 in spite of ~에도 불구하고

정답 (D)

110 독서 클럽 회원들은 주에 한 번 모여서 자신들이 읽은 책에 대해 토론하고, 읽으면 좋을 만한 책에 대해 의견을 교환한다.

해설 [---+a week]의 구조로 빈칸에는 빈도를 나타내는 부사가 필요하다. '일주일에 한 번'의 뜻을 나타내는 once가 사용되어야 한다. 따라서 (D) once가 정답이다.

어휘 discuss 토론하다 share 나누다

정답 (D)

111 모든 종업원들은 소화기 사용 및 기본적인 소방훈련에 대해 교육 받아야 한다.

해설 동사 어휘 문제이다. 의미상 '교육을 받아야 한다'가 자연스러우므로 정답은 (C) trained이다.

어휘 employee 종업원 fire extinguisher 소화기 fire drill 소방훈련 reveal 누설하다 train 훈련하다

정답 (C)

112 포디스 익스프레스 사는 세계 어느 곳이든지 컨테이너를 이용해 물건을 배송하는 데 있어 최고의 가격조건을 갖추고 있다.

해설 전치사 선택 문제. [shipping+goods+---+any destination] 구조로, 동사 ship과 어울려 '~로 보내다'의 뜻이 되어야 하므로 정답은 (A) to이다.

어휘 ship 배송하다 via ~를 이용하여 destination 목적지 worldwide 전 세계의

정답 (A)

113 저희 고객님들의 모든 개인 정보는 극비 사항이며 어떤 상황에서도 공유될 수 없습니다.

해설 품사 판정 문제. [be동사(is)+부사(strictly)+---] 구조로 빈칸은 be동사 뒤 보어가 들어가야 할 자리이며 동시에 부사(strictly)의 수식을 받는 자리이므로 형용사를 써야 한다. 따라서 정답은 (C)이다.

어휘 personal information 개인 정보 customer 고객 strictly 엄격히 share 공유하다 under any circumstances 어떤 상황에서건 confide (비밀을) 털어놓다 confidential 기밀의

정답 (C)

114 델리 케이터링 서비스 사는 지난 10년 동안 이 지역에서 봉사해 온 외식업체로, 현재 이 지역의 모든 행사에 대해 30% 할인된 가격을 제시하고 있습니다.

해설 분사 선택 문제이다. [명사(a catering company)+--+명사(the region)]의 구조이다. 빈칸에는 능동, 진행의 뜻을 갖도록 현재분사 형태의 형용사를 써야 한다. 따라서 정답은 (B) serving이다.

어휘 catering 음식 제공 서비스 region 지역 currently 현재 discount 할인하다 serve 봉사하다

정답 (B)

115 Arriba 택배 사의 봉급 및 급여 인상은 회사의 재정 상태 및 운영 실적에 근거한다.

해설 [소유격(the company's)+형용사(financial)+---+접속사(and)+명사(performance)] 구조이다. 소유격과 형용사는 모두 명사를 수식하는 품사이므로 빈칸에는 명사가 와야 한다. 또한 접속사 and 다음에 온 명사(performance)와 병렬을 이루기 위해 빈칸에 명사가 필요하다. 따라서 정답은 (A)이다.

어휘 salary 봉급 wage 급여 increase 증가 delivery 배달 based on ~에 근거한 financial 재정의, 금융의 performance 성과 condition 조건 conditional 조건의

정답 (A)

116 인간 형태의 가정용 로봇은 접시를 깨지 않고 설거지할 수 있도록 특별히 설계되었다.

해설 부사 어휘 선택 문제이다. 의미상 '특별히 설계되다'가 자연스러우므로 정답은 (C) specially이다.

어휘 human-like 인간 같은, 인간 형태의 design 설계하다 wash dishes 설거지하다 profoundly 심오하게 quite 꽤 specially 특별히 seldom 거의 ~ 않다

정답 (C)

117 9월 1일부터 제니스 유나이티드 은행의 직원들은 발생하는 모든 비정상적인 거래를 바로 본사에 보고해야 한다.

해설 품사 판정 문제이다. [----+전치사(to)+명사(the headquarters)]의 구조이다. '전치사+명사'는 부사구를 만들기 때문에 그 앞에는 부사구를 수식하는 품사인 부사를 써야 하므로 (B) directly가 정답이다.

어휘 beginning ~부터 bank teller 은행원 report 보고하다 unusual 비정상적인 transaction 거래 headquarters 본사 directly 직접 direction 방향

정답 (B)

118 경영 컨설턴트는 무료 온라인 동영상에서 거래 이익을 내기 위해 당신이 알아야 할 것들에 관해 설명해 준다.

해설 품사 판정 문제로, [동사(explains)+---+주어(you)+동사(need to know)] 구조이다. 타동사 know의 목적어 역할을 할 수 있는 명사 상당 어구가 빈칸에 들어가야 한다. 따라서 답은 (A) what이다.

어휘 consultant 컨설턴트 explain 설명하다 trading 상거래, 무역 profitable 수익성이 있는 free 무료의

정답 (A)

119 에스타카나 연구소에서 분기별로 발행하는 소식지는 현재 진행 중인 연구 과제와 이전 연구로부터 얻은 결과에 대해 자세한 정보를 제공한다.

해설 형용사 어휘 선택 문제이다. 명사 information을 수식하는 형용사로, 의미가 통하는 형용사는 (C) detailed(자세한)이다.

어휘 quarterly 분기의 newsletter 소식지 laboratory 연구소 provide 제공하다 information 정보 ongoing 현재 진행 중인 finding 조사[연구] 결과 previous 이전의 study 연구 loyal 충성스러운 approach 접근하다 detailed 자세한 probable 있을 법한

정답 (C)

120 눈덩이처럼 늘어나는 업무량을 완화하기 위해 사무실에서는 몇 명의 신입사원을 고용해야 할 것이다.

해설 [---+동사원형(lessen)+목적어(the snowballing workload)] 구조이다. 빈칸은 [to부정사+동사원형] 구조가 되어야 하므로 보기 중 답이 될 수 있는 것은 (D) in order to이다. (A) so that과 (C) because는 접속사로 뒤에 절이 와야 하고, (B) for는 전치사로 동명사를 써야 한다.

어휘 recruit 고용하다 several 대여섯의 employee 종업원 lessen 줄이다 snowball 눈덩이; (눈덩이처럼) 점점 커지다 workload 작업량 in order to ~하기 위해

정답 (D)

121 회의 중에, 아쉬나 씨는 안전교육을 기획하는 공장 안전위원회의 일원으로 참여할 것을 자원했다.

해설 전치사/접속사 선택 문제이다. [---+명사(the meeting)] 구조이다. 빈칸에는 뒤에 명사를 취하는 전치사를 써야 하므로 답은 (A) During이다. 나머지 선택지들은 뒤에 절이 와야 하므로 답이 될 수 없다.

어휘 volunteer 자원하다 participate 참가하다 safety 안전 organize 기획하다

정답 (A)

122 퀸 씨가 우리 회사에 웹 디자이너로 입사했을 무렵, 그녀는 이미 수년 동안 웹 디자인 분야에서 일한 경력이 있었다.

해설 시제 문제로, 빈칸에 들어갈 과거시제인 joined보다 전의 일이므로 과거완료 시제(had+p.p.)를 써야 한다. 따라서 정답은 (D) had worked이다.

어휘 join 입사하다, 가입하다 firm 회사 field 분야 already 이미

정답 (D)

123 1월 20일에 있을 워크숍에 참석하고자 하는 사람은 누구든지 금요일까지 카메다 씨에게 연락해야 한다.

해설 [---+주격 관계대명사(who)+동사(wants)] 구조이다. 주격 관계대명사절의 동사 wants가 단수 현재를 나타내므로 빈칸에는 단수 명사가 선행사로 쓰여야 한다. 따라서 정답은 (A) Anyone이다.

어휘 contact 연락하다 others 다른 사람들

정답 (A)

124 무라타 씨는 까다로운 계약 협상과 관련해 많은 경험을 가지고 있기 때문에 회사 인수 절차를 관리하는 업무를 담당하게 되었다.

해설 형용사 어휘 선택 문제이다. [---+명사(contract)+명사(negotiation)] 구조이다. 의미상 '까다로운 계약 협상'이 자연스러우므로 정답은 (C) delicate이다.

어휘 assign 임무를 할당하다 manage 관리하다 acquisition 인수 process 과정 experience 경험 contract 계약 negotiation 협상 fluent 유창한 noted 저명한 delicate 까다로운 talented 재능 있는

정답 (C)

125 하트만 씨는 새로운 광고 캠페인에 대한 모든 아이디어를 검토하자마자 누구의 사업 제안서가 선택될 것인지 결정할 것이다.

해설 품사 판정 문제로, [----+명사(proposal)] 구조이다. 명사 앞에는 형용사를 써야 하므로 의문형용사 whose를 써야 한다. 따라서 (A)가 정답이다.

어휘 review 검토하다 determine 결정하다 proposal 제안서 select 선택하다

정답 (A)

126 애트나 인터내셔널사의 3분기 수익이 이전에 예상된 것보다 20% 이상 높게 나왔다.

해설 [부사(previously)+----] 구조이다. 보기 중 부사의 수식을 받을 수 있는 것은 분사 형태인 (C)와 (D)인데, 내용상 '과거에 예상되었던 것보다'의 뜻이 되도록 수동의 의미를 갖는 과거분사를 써야 한다. 따라서 정답은 (C) predicted이다.

어휘 quarter 분기 previously 과거에 predict 예상하다 prediction 예상

정답 (C)

127 그린포인트 인더스트리스 사가 설립될 당시, 그들의 목표는 유류 재활용 분야에 첨단 기술을 보유하는 것이었다.

해설 [----+주어+동사, 주어+동사] 구조이다. 빈칸에는 뒤에 절이 따를 수 있는 접속사적 역할을 하는 표현을 선택해야 한다. at the time은 접속사적 역할을 하여 뒤에 주어, 동사가 뒤따를 수 있다. 따라서 정답은 (D)이다. (A) Despite와 (B) In addition to는 전치사로 뒤에 명사가 나오며 (C) On the other hand는 부사적 표현이다.

어휘 found 설립하다 cutting-edge 첨단의 technology 기술 recycling 재활용 despite ~에도 불구하고 in addition to ~외에도 on the other hand 반면에 at the time 당시에

정답 (D)

128 회사 로고는 매우 잘 디자인되어 있어서 일반적으로 잘 인지되고 기억에 매우 잘 남는다.

해설 품사 판정 문제이다. [---+형용사(recognizable)] 구조로 형용사를 수식하는 자리이므로 부사를 써야 한다. 따라서 (D) universally가 답이다.

어휘 recognizable 인지 가능한 memorable 기억에 남는 universe 우주 universal 우주의, 전 세계의 universality 보편성 universally 보편적으로

정답 (D)

129 고객님의 V-12 오토바이를 수리해야 할 경우, 고객님께서는 공인 서비스 센터 중 한 곳을 방문하셔야 합니다.

해설 품사 판정 문제이다. [the+----+명사(service centers)] 구조이다. 빈칸은 명사를 수식하는 형용사를 써야 할 자리로, 분사 형태의 형용사인 (B) authorized(인가된, 공식적인)가 정답이다.

어휘 require 요구하다 repair 수리 authorized 인가된 authorization 위임 authority 권한

정답 (B)

130 30년 전에 설립된 켈렌 사는 현재 건물 자동화기기 제조분야의 선두 회사이다.

해설 동사 어휘 선택 문제이다. 의미가 통하는 단어는 '설립된(Established)'으로 정답은 (D)이다.

어휘 decade 10년 corporation 회사 leader 지도자 field 분야 automated 자동화된 machinery 기계류 arrange 배열하다 produce 생산하다 settle 정하다 establish 설립하다

정답 (D)

[PART 6]

⟨131-134⟩ 다음은 이메일에 관한 문제이다.

수신: 고객 서비스부 (customerservices@sierra.com)
발신: 마크 버나드(marcone@saver.com)
날짜: 10월 27일
제목: 시계 고장

관계자분께,

저는 귀사가 시계를 수리할 수 있는 방법에 대한 정보를 주실 수 있기를 바랍니다. 저는 3년 동안 X27B 모델을 사용해 왔고 지난주까지만 하더라도 시계가 잘 작동했습니다. 지금은 시계가 작동하지 않습니다. 저는 배터리가 수명이 다 되었다고 생각해서 배터리를 교환했습니다. 그러나 시계는 여전히 작동되지 않고 있습니다. 기계적 결함으로 시계가 작동되지 않는 것이 분명합니다. 보증기간이 아직 2년이 남아 있기 때문에, 저는 시계를 무상으로 수리하고자 합니다.
제가 사는 지역에는 시에라 시계의 공식 서비스 센터가 없습니다. 제가 어떻게 해야 하는지 알려 주시기 바랍니다.
귀사의 도움에 감사드립니다.

마크 버나드

어휘 broken 고장 난 information 정보 dead (배터리) 수명이 다 된 work 작동하다 malfunction 오작동하다 mechanical 기계적인 defect 결함 warranty period 보증 기간 free of charge 무료로 assistance 원조, 보조 authorized 인가된 area 지역 repair 수리하다 sell 팔다 install 설치하다 purchase 구입하다

131

해설 문맥에 맞는 동사 어휘 선택 문제이다. 빈칸 뒤에 a watch를 목적어로 쓸 수 있는 동사는 선택지 모두 가능하다. 그러나 문제 뒤를 보면 지난주까지 작동되다가 그 뒤부터 작동되지 않는다는 내용이 나오므로, 시계가 고장났다는 사실을 알 수 있다. 따라서 '고치다'는 의미의 (A) repair가 정답이다.

정답 (A)

132

해설 문맥에 맞는 전치사 선택 문제이다. [등위 접속사(and)+---+명사(last week)] 구조에는 접속사를 쓸 수 없으므로 unless를 제외하면 3개의 전치사(after, by, until)가 남는다. '3년 동안 X27B 모델을 써왔고, 지난주까지는 작동이 잘 됐다'가 문맥상 의미가 통하기 때문에 (D) until이 정답이다.

정답 (D)

133

해설 문맥에 맞는 부사 어휘 선택 문제이다. [----, 주어(it)+동사(does still not work)] 구조로 되어 있다. however는 접속사가 아니라 부사로, 앞 문장과 뒤 문장을 의미상 연결해 준다는 의미에서 접속 부사이다. 주어진 4개의 부사 중에 이전 문장과 어울려 문맥이 통하는 부사는 '그러나(however)'이다. 따라서 (B)가 정답이다.

정답 (B)

134 (A) 지역 내 수리 센터에 전화해 보실 것을 권합니다.
(B) 제가 사는 지역에는 시에라 시계의 공식 서비스 센터가 없습니다.
(C) 그럼 회의 때 뵙기를 고대하고 있겠습니다.
(D) 다행히, 기술자들이 마침내 문제들을 해결했습니다.

해설 문맥상 적절하게 이어줄 문장을 고르는 문제. 빈칸 위 본문 내용은 시계를 구입한 고객이 문제가 생겨 시계를 무상으로 수리하고자 하는 내용이다. 빈칸에 들어갈 보기 중 적절한 문장은 '본인의 지역에는 서비스 센터가 없다'라고 하는 (B)가 적절하며, 빈칸 바로 뒤 문장에서 '어떻게 해야 하는지를 알려 달라'는 글에서도 유추할 수 있다. (A)는 회사가 고객에게 할 수 있는 말, (C)는 회의에서 만나는 경우는 아니고, (D)는 빈칸 다음 내용을 비추어 볼 때 아직 해결되지 않았음을 알 수 있기 때문에 답이 될 수 없다.

〈135-138〉 다음은 초대장에 관한 문제이다.

몬탈반 씨께,

라인하르트 미술관은 저희의 관대한 기부자 중 한 분이신 귀하를 박물관 개관 20주년 환영 행사에 정중히 초대합니다. 환영행사는 9월 26일 금요일 저녁 7시부터 10시까지 주 전시장에서 개최될 예정입니다. 이 환영행사 참석을 위해서는 사전 등록이 필요하다는 점을 유념하시기 바랍니다.

만약 이 환영행사에 참석하실 예정이시라면 동봉된 등록 양식 하단에 있는 해당 칸에 표시해 주시기 바랍니다. 이 회신 봉투는 귀하의 편의를 위해 제공된 것입니다. 저희는 9월 20일까지는 회신을 받아야 합니다.

저희는 환영 행사장에서 귀하를 뵙게 되기를 고대하고 있습니다.

감사 드리며,

제니퍼 페트로첼리 / 선임 홍보관
라인하르트 미술관

어휘 cordially 정중하게, 진심으로 invite 초대하다 generous 관대한, 후한 donor 기부자 reception 환영 행사 celebrate 기념하다 anniversary 기념일 note 주목하다 bottom 바닥, 하단 enclosed 첨부된 registration 등록 form 양식 return envelope 회신용 봉투 convenience 편의 receive 받다 reply 응답 no later than ~까지 nevertheless 그럼에도 불구하고 even if ~라 할지라도 appropriate 적절한 appropriately 적절히 look forward to ~하기를 기다리다, 기대하다

135

해설 [대명사(you), ----+명사 복수(our generous donors),] 구조이다. 명사 뒤에 콤마 삽입구는 명사를 설명하는 동격어구이다. 문맥상 '박물관의 거액 기부자 중 하나'가 자연스러우므로 (B) as one of가 정답이다.

정답 (B)

136

해설 문맥에 맞는 명사 어휘 선택 문제이다. '리셉션 참석을 위해서는 사전 등록이 필요하다'가 문맥에 맞으므로 (D) preregistration이 정답이다. 다른 보기들은(consolidation 강화, 통합/transition 변천, 과도기/equation 균등화) 문맥에 어울리지 않는다.

정답 (D)

137

해설 품사 판정 문제로, [정관사(the)+---+명사(box)] 구조이다. 빈칸이 명사 앞에 있으므로 형용사를 써야 한다. 따라서 정답은 (A) appropriate 이다.

정답 (A)

138 (A) 우리는 귀하께서 다음 시즌을 위해 구독을 갱신해 주시기를 바랍니다.
(B) 당신은 표 한 장에 40% 할인을 받으실 겁니다.
(C) 일단 귀하께서 이 과정에 등록하시면 저희가 계속 소식을 알려 드리도록 하겠습니다.
(D) 저희는 리셉션 장에서 귀하를 뵙게 되기를 기대하고 있습니다.

해설 빈칸 앞 내용은 미술관의 기부자 중 한 분이신 몬탈반 씨를 개관 20주년 리셉션에 초대하는 내용이다. 리셉션 장소와 시간을 알렸으며 주의 사항도 알리고 있다. 빈칸 바로 앞에서는 참석을 원할 시 등록 양식을 작성해 9월 20일까지 회신해 달라고 요청했다. 따라서 빈칸에 들어갈 초대장의 적절한 마무리 문장은 보기 중 (D)이다.

〈139-142〉 다음은 회람에 관한 문제이다.

톰슨 투어

발신 : 인사부
수신 : 전화교환원
날짜 : 2019년 6월 20일
안건: 여름 근무 시간

성수기 중 통화량 증가가 예상됨에 따라, 저희는 7월과 8월 동안 연장 근무를 시행하기로 결정했습니다. 7월 1일부로, 업무 시간이 월요일에서 금요일은 종전 오전 9시-오후 5시에서 오전 8시-오후 6시로 변경될 것이며, 토요일은 오전 9시-오후 2시까지로 변경될 것입니다. 교환원 여러분들은 동료들과 상의해 최소 한 사람은 정규 근무시간 이후에도 사무실에서 고객의 전화를 받을 수 있도록 업무 시간을 조정하셔야 합니다.

직원들은 연장근무에 대해 추가 보상을 받을 수 있습니다. 초과근무에 대해 수당을 받거나 48시간 휴가를 취할 수 있을 것입니다.

미리 감사합니다!

어휘 personnel department 인사부 operator 조작자, 전화 교환원 anticipation 예상 traffic (전화의) 통화량 implement 시행하다 extend 연장하다 as of ~부로 fellow worker 직장동료 adjust 수정하다 regular 규칙적인 respond 응답하다 request 요청하다 confer 의논하다 occur 일어나다 compensation 보상 overtime 초과근무

139

해설 문맥에 맞는 형용사 어휘 선택 문제이다. '통화량 증가가 예상됨에 따라(In anticipation of increased phone traffic)'라는 내용과 문맥이 통하는 표현은 성수기(busy season)이므로 정답은 (D) busy이다.

정답 (D)

140

해설 동사 어휘 선택 문제이다. [--- + 전치사(with) + 명사(their fellow workers)] 구조이므로 전치사 with와 함께 쓸 수 있는 자동사를 선택해야 한다. '~와 상의하다(confer with)'로 전치사 with와 함께 쓰는 동사는 (B) confer이다.

정답 (B)

141

해설 [동사(receive) + 형용사(additional) + ----] 구조이므로 빈칸에는 동사(receive)의 목적어가 될 수 있으며, 동시에 형용사의 수식을 받는 명사를 써야 한다. 따라서 정답은 (A) compensation이다.

정답 (A)

142 (A) 초과 근무는 스트레스의 누적을 유발할 수 있습니다.
(B) 모든 초과근무 신청은 상사의 승인을 받아야 합니다.
(C) 근로자들은 특별 수당도 받지 못하는 초과 근무를 하는 것에 반대했습니다.
(D) 초과 근무에 대해 수당을 받거나 48시간 휴가를 취할 수 있을 것입니다.

해설 빈칸 앞은 회사가 전화 교환원 직원들에게 성수기 중 근무 시간 조정에 관한 내용을 전달하고 있다. 연장 근무로 인해 선택적 보상을 받을 수 있다고 빈칸 바로 앞에서 전달했으므로 빈칸 뒤는 선택적 보상에 관한 글을 예상할 수 있다. 따라서 보기 중 초과 근무 수당이나 휴가 중 하나를 선택할 수 있다는 (D)가 정답이다.

⟨143-146⟩ 다음은 편지에 관한 문제이다.

관계자 분께,

8월 7일 날, 스코틀랜드 에딘버러에서 브라질 리우데자네이루까지 가는 하이스카이 항공사 747편을 이용했습니다. 비행 자체는 즐거웠습니다. 리우데자네이루에 도착했을 때, 입국 사무소를 지나서 여행 가방을 찾기 위해 갔습니다.

그러나 가방이 없어졌다는 것을 알고 정말 실망했습니다. 저는 이 사실을 귀하의 서비스 데스크에 신고했습니다. 그런 후에 브라질에서 일주일 내내 제 가방도 없이 보냈습니다. 아직도 제 개인 소지품들을 받지 못했습니다.

제 가방이 없어진 걸로 보이기 때문에 보상을 위해 가방에서 분실된 물품의 목록을 첨부해 보냅니다.

며칠 내에 귀하로부터 소식이 있기를 바랍니다.
이 문제에 대한 당신의 관심에 감사 드립니다.

진심으로,

저스틴 롱

어휘 flight 비행　pleasant 즐거운　arrival 도착　immigration 이민, 입국 관리　collect 모으다　baggage 수화물　extremely 매우　missing 행방불명 된　report 신고하다　belongings 소지품　submit 제출하다　reimbursement 환급, 보상　matter 문제

143

해설 하나의 문장에는 하나의 주어와 동사가 필요하다는 문장의 기본 개념과 시제를 종합해 푸는 문제. 빈칸에는 동사가 필요한 자리로 일단 (B) taking은 답에서 제외. 뒤의 "The flight itself was very pleasant."의 시제가 과거라는 점에서 여행한 사실이 과거임을 알 수 있다. 따라서 (A) took가 답이다.

정답 (A)

144

해설 문맥에 어울리는 동사 어휘 문제. 가방이 없어졌다는 사실을 알고 (~ to learn that my luggage was missing)라는 내용이 연결되어 있으므로 실망했다(disappointed)는 의미가 들어가야 자연스럽다.

정답 (C)

145 (A) 하지만 아직도 제 개인 소지품들을 받지 못했습니다.
(B) 항상 개인 소지품을 잘 챙기고 다니시기 바랍니다.
(C) 저는 귀사의 서비스에 완전히 만족합니다.
(D) 분실 또는 파손된 짐에 대한 배상금 청구가 늘고 있습니다.

해설 빈칸 앞 내용은 항공기를 이용한 고객이 공항에서 짐을 잃어버린 내용을 전달하고 있고 빈칸 뒤 내용을 통해 아직 가방을 찾지 못한 상태라는 것을 알 수 있다. 따라서 보기 중 여전히 개인 소지품을 받지 못했다고 전하는 (A)가 정답이다.

146

해설 전치사 문제로, 문맥상 '앞으로 며칠 이내에'라는 의미가 연결되어야 한다는 점에서 (A) within(~이내에)이 답이 된다. 이처럼 within 뒤에는 특정 기간을 나타내는 명사(구)가 등장한다. 참고로 답으로 선택하기 쉬운 until(~까지)은 뒤에 다음 주 금요일(until next Friday)이라든가 9월 10일(until September 10th) 같은 구체적인 시점이 언급된다.

정답 (A)

[PART 7]

⟨147-148⟩ 다음은 문자 메시지에 관한 문제이다.

Weston [오전 9시 32분] Fielder 씨, 당신의 10시 30분 약속이 회의실 1호죠?
Fielder [오전 9시 37분] 맞아요. Charlie Wilson과 약속이에요. 그는 소프트웨어 회사를 운영하고 있고 그가 개발한 신제품 때문에 벤처 투자자금을 구하고 있어요.
Weston [오전 9시 40분] 제가 회의에 참석해도 괜찮을까요? 당신이 어떻게 인터뷰를 하는지 그리고 그들의 신청을 어떻게 처리하는지 알고 싶어요.
Fielder [오전 9시 45분] 저는 대찬성이에요. 사실 당신이 회의에 참석해야 한다고 제가 제안할 예정이었어요.

어휘 appointment 약속　run 운영하다　venture capital 벤처 자금　handle 처리하다　application 신청

147. 전반 내용을 묻는 문제

Fielder 씨와 Weston 씨는 어디에서 일할 것 같은가?

(A) 은행에서
(B) 소프트웨어 회사에서
(C) 취업 박람회에서
(D) 직업소개소에서

해설 Fielder의 말 '~ is looking for venture capital because of a new product development'에서 대화가 돈을 빌려주는 은행에서 일하고 있음을 파악할 수 있다. 그러므로 정답은 (A)이다.

148. 숨은 의도를 찾는 문제

오전 9시 45분에 Fielder가 쓴 "저는 대찬성이에요"는 무엇을 의미하는가?

(A) 그는 벤처 자금이 필요하다.
(B) 그는 Willson 씨를 만날 계획이다.
(C) 그는 신제품을 개발하고 싶어 한다.
(D) 그는 Weston 씨가 회의에 참석하는 것을 환영한다.

해설 Weston이 9시 40분에 회의 참석 의사를 밝혔더니 Fielder가 뒤이어 "In fact, I was going to suggest that you attend the meeting."이라

고 말하며 Weston이 회의에 참석할 것을 흔쾌히 허락하고 있다. 그러므로 정답은 (D)이다.

〈149-150〉 다음은 양식에 관한 문제이다.

<UTAH TIMES>의 구독 신청을 하십시오!

오늘! 바로 지금이 신청하실 기회입니다.

- 1년: 72달러에 52부
- 2년: 130달러에 104부 (14달러 절약)

( ) 현금 동봉 ( ) 추후 청구

이름 ____________ 전화번호 ____________

주소 ________________________________

시 ____________ 주 ____________ 우편번호 ____________

첫 호를 배송하는 데 2~3주의 여유 기간을 주십시오.

어휘 subscribe to ~을 구독하다 present 현재 issue 발행물 payment 지불 enclose 동봉하다 bill ~에게 계산서를 보내다 zip (code) 우편번호 allow 허락하다 delivery 배달

149. 세부 내용을 묻는 문제

일 년 구독을 한다면 한 달에 얼마의 비용이 드는가?

(A) 5달러
(B) 6달러
(C) 8달러
(D) 10달러

해설 '1 year: 52 issues for 72 dollars'에서 1년 구독료는 $72이며, 12개월로 나누면 1개월 당 $6가 되므로 정답은 (B) 6 dollars이다.

150. 틀린 정보를 찾는 문제

요청된 정보가 아닌 것은 무엇인가?

(A) 전화번호
(B) 이름
(C) 직업
(D) 우편번호

해설 중간의 'Name, Phone, Address, City, State, Zip'에서 언급되지 않은 것은 직업이므로 정답은 (C) Occupation이다.

〈151-154〉 다음은 온라인 대화문에 관한 문제이다.

일리나 탐린슨 [오전 10:29]
안녕하세요, 퓨 씨. 잠깐 시간 되세요? 재고에 관해 상의할 게 있어요.

로버트 퓨 [오전 10:30]
물론이죠!

일리나 탐린슨 [오전 10:31]
우리 사일라이나 창고의 자료에 따르면 FSD 사의 조미료가 딱 한 박스밖에 남지 않았어요. 최근에 새로운 업체들이 문을 열면서 배송이 급격하게 늘었거든요. 제가 더 주문할까요?

로버트 퓨 [오전 10:32]
아니요, 그럴 필요 없습니다. 다른 제조업체로 변경했어요. 더욱 저렴한 제품을 취급할 계획이에요. 당신이 지난주 휴가를 가 있는 동안 제가 새 제품으로 12 상자를 주문해 두었어요. 아직 도착하지는 않았고요.

일리나 탐린슨 [오전 10:33]
저 대신 해 주셔서 감사합니다!

로버트 퓨 [오전 10:35]
별말씀을요. 또한 화요일에는 우리의 새 제품에 대해 식당에도 통보해 두었어요. 이미 이 소식에 대해 알고 있습니다.

일리나 탐린슨 [오전 10:37]
다시 한번 감사드려요!

어휘 inventory 재고 seasoning 조미료 establishment 업체 manufacturer 제조업체 affordable 가격이 알맞은 dozen 12개의 aware 알고 있는

151. 세부사항을 묻는 문제

탐린슨 씨에 관하여 무엇이 언급되었는가?

(A) 새로운 자료를 준비했다.
(B) 최근에 휴가를 갔다.
(C) 지난주에 주문을 했다.
(D) 오늘 상품을 보냈다.

해설 10시 32분 퓨 씨의 메시지 'While you were on vacation last week, I ordered a dozen of cases of the new product.'에서 언급된 것 같이 탐린슨은 지난주에 휴가를 갔음을 알 수 있다. 그러므로 정답은 (B)이다.

152. 숨은 의도를 찾는 문제

오전 10시 30분에 퓨 씨가 "물론이죠!"라고 썼을 때, 무엇을 의미하는 것 같은가?

(A) 탐린슨 씨의 질문에 기꺼이 답할 것이다.
(B) 탐린슨 씨가 요청한 것을 할 수 있다.
(C) 탐린슨 씨에게 작업할 것을 허가하고 있다.
(D) 탐린슨 씨와 만날 것을 동의한다.

해설 앞서 나온 탐린슨의 메시지 'I need to talk about the inventory issue.'에서 알 수 있듯이 탐린슨 용건에 관한 이야기가 이어질 것을 알 수 있다. 그러므로 정답은 (A)이다.

153. 추론 문제

퓨 씨와 탐린슨 씨는 어떤 업종에서 일할 것 같은가?

(A) 식품 택배회사
(B) 식품 유통업체
(C) 출장 요리업체
(D) 식당

해설 10시 31분 탐린슨의 메시지 'Lately, our deliveries have dramatically increased due to the openings of new establishments.'에서 언급된 바와 같이 이 두 사람은 제품을 주문해서 배송해 주는 유통업체인 것을 미루어 짐작할 수 있다. 그러므로 정답은 (B)이다.

154. 세부사항을 묻는 문제

퓨 씨는 주 초반에 무엇을 했는가?

(A) 메뉴를 갱신했다.
(B) 신입 사원을 교육했다.
(C) 탐린슨 씨가 재고정리 판매하는 것을 도왔다.
(D) 고객들에게 변경 사항을 알렸다.

해설 퓨 씨의 메시지 '~ on Tuesday, I notified restaurants of our new product.'에서 화요일에 거래처인 식당에게 변경 사항을 알렸음을 알 수 있다. 그러므로 정답은 (D)이다.

〈155-156〉 다음은 공지에 관한 문제이다.

여가 프로그램 기획 관리자들께,

본 게시문은 우리 시설 내에서 올바른 수영장 안전을 유지하는 데 필요한 사항을 주지시키기 위한 것입니다. 여러분들은 새로운 직원들뿐만 아니라 기존의 직원들에게 우리 수영장의 안전 수칙을 지도할 의무가 있습니다. 모든 수칙은 중요성을 지니고 있으며 예외 없이 항상 따라야 합니다.

(1) 구조원 전원은 다른 안전 요원들과의 연락을 유지하기 위해 직원용 무전기를 휴대하여 각자 지정인과 교신할 수 있어야 한다.
(2) 구조원들은 응급 처치 과정을 수료한 자로, 근무 중 언제라도 출동이 가능하며, 사고 발생을 대비해서 비상 연락처와 구급상자의 위치를 숙지해야 한다.
(3) 구조원들은 (비상사태를 제외하고) 담당 구역을 방치해 두어서는 안 되며 이어폰 (휴대폰, MP3 플레이어 등의) 사용을 금지한다.
(4) 직원들은 안전에 대한 모범을 보여야 하므로 흡연과 음주를 금한다.
(5) 청소 담당반은 시설의 청결과 정돈을 유지해야 한다.

대규모 시설을 청결히 유지하는 데 무리가 있었으므로 다음 달부터 2교대가 아닌 3교대로 운영할 것입니다. 이러한 변동 사항을 직원들에게 알려 주시기 바랍니다.
이상으로 마칩니다. 본부에서는 여러분들이 상기 수칙들을 준수할 것임을 확신합니다. 감사합니다.

어휘 attention ~앞(일반 업무 서식에서 수신자를 의미함)
reminder 주지, 상기시키는 것 necessity 필요 maintain 유지하다
proper 적절한 facility 시설물 inform 알리다 new arrival 새로 도착한 것[사람] safety regulations 안전 규정 follow 따르다
at all times 항상 without exception 예외 없이 lifeguard 구조대
radio 무전기 be in contact with ~와 연락하다
personnel 직원, 인사(부) certify ~을 증명하다 first aid 응급 처치
on duty 근무 중에 first-aid kit 구급상자 in case of ~를 대비해서
unattended 방치된 except ~을 제외하고
in the event of ~하는 경우에 prohibit ~을 금지하다
set an example 모범을 보이다 shift 교체, 교대
instead of ~ 대신에 confident in ~에 자신 있는

155. 회람의 목적을 묻는 문제

이 공지 사항을 작성한 이유는?

(A) 직원들에게 신입 사원을 알리기 위해
(B) 안전 수칙 준수의 중요성을 강조하기 위해
(C) 안전 프로그램의 결점을 지적하기 위해
(D) 직원의 공적을 치하하기 위해

해설 첫 번째 문장 'This notice is a reminder about ~'에서 시설 안전에 대해 상기시키고자 하는 것임을 알 수 있으므로 (B)가 정답이다.

156. 틀린 정보를 찾는 문제

구조요원들은 근무 중에 무엇이 이용 가능하지 않는가?

(A) 직원용 라디오
(B) 청소 도구
(C) MP3 플레이어
(D) 응급처치 상자에 접근

해설 첫 번째 단락이 끝난 후 각각의 사항에서 lifeguard들이 해야 하는 일들을 나열하고 있으므로 쉽게 확인할 수 있다. 그 중 MP3 player는 사용해서는 안 되는(prohibited) 것으로 나와 있으므로 정답은 (C)이다.

〈157-159〉 다음은 이메일에 관한 문제이다.

수신: 로즈마리 하워드 (rosemaryh@Westwood.com)
발신: 조단 겔버 (jgelber@Westwood.com)
날짜: 3월 3일
회신: 언어 특징

하워드 님께,

귀하의 웹 페이지를 살펴본 후, 귀하의 고객들을 위해 회사의 독일어 웹 사이트에서 사용한 코드 프로그래밍에 관해 여쭙고 싶습니다. 저는 고객들이 다수의 언어로 웹 페이지를 보며, 이것이 우리 고객들에게 이상적인 특징이라는 것을 알았습니다. 저는 이러한 기능을 이용하려고 하며, 벨기에 고객들에게 이 기능을 이용 가능하도록 하고 싶습니다. 제게 코드를 보내주시고 어떻게 이 기능을 디자인하는지 알려 주실 수 있으신지요? 그러면 제가 벨기에, 노르웨이, 스웨덴 고객들을 포함한 저희의 목표 시장을 위한 언어 옵션을 바꿀 수 있습니다.

제가 다음 주 베를린의 경영자 워크숍에 참석할 때 귀하를 뵙기를 희망합니다. 독일은 처음 방문하기 때문에 이번 방문이 기대됩니다. 아마도 제가 거기에 있는 동안 프로그램에 관해 추가 문의 사항이 있을 경우, 저희는 또 만날 수 있을 것입니다.

귀하의 시간에 감사드립니다.

조단 겔버

어휘 feature 특징, 특색 function 기능 employ (서비스 등을) 이용하다
alter 변경하다 targeted market 목표 시장 managerial 경영의

157. 글을 쓴 목적을 묻는 문제

이메일을 쓴 이유는 무엇인가?

(A) 번역된 문서의 검사를 요청하기 위해
(B) 기술적인 정보를 요청하기 위해
(C) 워크숍에 등록하기 위해
(D) 프로그램의 결함을 고치기 위해

해설 편지의 목적은 맨 앞에 주로 나와 있다. 'I would like to ask you about the programming codes ~'라고 나와 있으므로 기술적인 정보를 얻기 위해 편지를 보낸 것을 알 수 있다. 그러므로 정답은 (B)이다.

158. 추후 일정을 묻는 문제

겔버 씨는 하워드 씨를 어디에서 만날 것 같은가?

(A) 독일에서
(B) 벨기에에서
(C) 노르웨이에서
(D) 스웨덴에서

해설 두 번째 단락의 'I hope to see you when I attend the managerial workshops in Berlin next week'에서 베를린(독일)임을 알 수 있으므로 정답은 (A)이다.

159. 맥락을 완성시키는 문제

지문에 표시된 [1], [2], [3], 그리고 [4] 중에서 다음의 문장이 들어가기에 가장 좋은 위치가 어디인가?
"저는 이러한 기능을 이용하려고 하며, 벨기에 고객들에게 이 기능을 이용 가능하도록 하고 싶습니다."

(A) [1]
(B) [2]
(C) [3]
(D) [4]

해설 'I noticed that customers could view the Web page in a number of different languages, and a feature which would be ideal for our customer base.'에서 보면 다양한 언어로 웹 페이지를 볼 수 있는 것이

이상적이라는 것을 알게(notice) 되었다고 말하고 있다. 그리고 이후에 이 기능(function)을 얻어서(employ), 이 기능을 디자인(design)하고, 마지막으로 이 기능으로 목표 시장에 맞게 언어를 바꾸도록 (alter) 하겠다고 말하고 있다. 이러한 일련의 논리적인 흐름을 위해서 정답은 (B)이다.

〈160-161〉 다음은 광고에 관한 문제이다.

프로젝트 매니저 구인

적합한 후보를 찾기 위한 아주 좋은 기회입니다. 당신은, 세계 어디서든지 본인의 사무실 안에서 일하며, 내부로부터 승진해 가는, 빠르게 성장하는 회사의 일원이 될 수 있습니다.

요구되는 자격 사항:

- 최소 5년의 프로젝트 관리 경험 필요
- 온라인 뱅킹 또는 많은 전자상거래 업무 경험 선호
- 재정/예산을 계획과 관리, 경과보고를 하는 증명된 능력
- 확립된 프로젝트 방법과 관리 지침에 충실할 수 있는 능력
- 영어와 한국어로 효과적으로 의사소통하는 증명된 능력

아래 이력서를 보내주세요:
executiveplacement@projectmanager.com

어휘 candidate 지원자, 신청자 high volume 다량의 adhere to ~를 준수하다

160. 세부 사항을 묻는 문제

작업 환경으로서 지원자가 예상할 수 있는 것은 무엇인가?

(A) 인터넷으로 일하는 것
(B) 제품 개발을 하는 것
(C) 소매상점에서 일하는 것
(D) 대학교에서 일하는 것

해설 두 번째 문장, 'You could be part of a rapidly growing company, that promotes from within while working from your own office anywhere in the world.'에서 세계 어디서든지 사무실 내에서 일할 수 있다는 것은 다시 말해 인터넷으로 교류 가능하다는 것을 의미한다. 보기 중 위 내용에 적합한 것은 (A)이다.

161. 자격요건을 묻는 문제

이 직업을 위한 자격으로 지원자는 무엇을 꼭 갖추어야 하는가?

(A) 최소 5년의 관리 경험
(B) 온라인 뱅킹 경험
(C) 3개 국어의 유창함
(D) 사람들과 함께 잘 일할 능력

해설 자격 사항 중에서 첫 번째로 'Minimum 5 years' project management experience required'가 언급되었으므로 (A)가 정답이다. (B)의 온라인 뱅킹도 언급되었지만 우대사항(preferred)이므로, 꼭 갖추어야 할 요소는 아니다. 2개 국어를 할 줄 알아야 한다고 했으므로 (C)도 답과 거리가 멀다.

〈162-164〉 다음은 편지에 관한 문제이다.

친애하는 Olivo 씨께,

이 편지는 Speed Access 사와 귀하의 계약이 갱신되었음을 확인하고자 하는 것입니다. 향후 12달 동안 귀하의 가정용 인터넷 제공자로서 우리 회사를 선택하신 데에 다시 한번 깊은 감사를 드립니다. 패키지 안에 9월 2일까지 작성하셔서 본사로 보내 주셔야 할 개인 정보 서류가 첨부되었습니다. 만약 계약 기간 만료일 이전에 서비스를 취소하실 경우 55 달러의 벌금이 있다는 것을 알아 주시기 바랍니다.

귀중한 고객의 한 분으로, 귀하께서는 무제한 초고속 인터넷 서비스와 개인 이메일 계정을 추가 비용 없이 이용하실 수 있습니다.

사용 시 문제점이 발생할 경우 또는 다른 판촉용 패키지를 추가하시길 원하시면 저희 고객서비스 센터, 1-900-544-7878로 연락 주시기 바랍니다. 저희는 고객들에게 고품질의 서비스를 제공하길 약속드리며, Speed Access 사는 귀하와 지속적인 관계를 유지하고자 합니다.

진심을 다해,

Kai Chapman
고객 서비스 팀, 부사장

어휘 confirmation 확인 contract n. 계약(서) v. 계약을 체결하다 renew 갱신하다 provider 제공업체[자] additional 추가의 within ~안에 be required to do ~하도록 요청되다 complete 완성하다 be aware that ~을 인지하다 penalty 벌금 prior to ~앞서 termination 만료 valued 귀중한, 가치있는 unlimited 무제한의 at no additional cost 추가 비용 없이 feel free to do 마음대로 ~하다 customer service center 고객서비스 센터 experience ~을 겪다 add 더하다 promotional 판촉의 be committed to -ing ~하는 것에 전념하다, 헌신하다 provide A with B A에게 B를 제공하다 look forward to -ing ~하기를 고대하다 lasting 지속적인 relationship 관계

162. 동봉 사항을 묻는 문제

이 편지와 함께 Olivo 씨에게 보내진 것은?

(A) 보증서
(B) 팸플릿
(C) 양식
(D) 할인 쿠폰

해설 편지와 함께 동봉한 것을 묻는 문제로, 첫 문단, 두 번째 줄에서 'Within this package, you will find a personal information form, which you are required to complete ~'이 단서이다. 패키지 안에 개인정보 양식이 있으니 이를 기입해서 보내라는 내용이므로 (C)가 정답이다.

163. 세부 사항을 묻는 문제

Olivo 씨는 어떤 상황에서 55 달러의 벌금을 물어야 하는가?

(A) 부가 서비스를 첨가할 경우
(B) 서비스를 일찍 취소할 경우
(C) 개인 이메일 주소를 삭제할 경우
(D) 9월 2일까지 서류를 제출하지 않을 경우

해설 첫 문단, 마지막 줄에서 'Please be aware that there is a penalty of $55 if you cancel the service prior to the termination of your contract'가 정답의 단서로, 계약 종료일 이전에 서비스를 취소할 경우 55달러의 벌금이 있다고 했으므로 (B)가 정답이다.

164. 추후 당부 사항을 묻는 문제

인터넷에 문제가 있을 경우 Olivo 씨는 무엇을 해야 하는가?

(A) 고객 서비스 센터로 전화한다
(B) 서면 요청서를 제출한다
(C) 서비스 불만 양식을 작성한다
(D) 기존의 계약이 만기될 때까지 기다린다

해설 인터넷 사용에 문제가 있거나 판촉용 패키지를 추가하고 싶은 경우 고객 서비스 센터로 연락을 달라고(Feel free to contact our customer service center ~) 언급하고 있으므로 (A)가 정답이다.

〈165-167〉 다음은 기사에 관한 글이다.

일자리를 구할 때 사람들은 노동 시장 특유의 본질을 유념해야 한다. 시장은 피라미드 모양을 하고 있다. 구할 수 있는 많은 일자리들이 신입 직급인 반면 중간급 직위에는 보다 적은 수가, 최고 수준의 자리에는 현저히 적은 수의 일자리가 있다. 이는 곧 고위직에 대한 치열한 경쟁으로 해석된다. 이러한 상위 직책에 관심이 있는 지원자는 자신의 기술과 경력에 부합하는 직업을 구하기 위해 다른 도시나 지역으로 거처를 옮겨야 할 경우도 종종 있다. 대부분의 지원자들은 직장을 위해 그들의 삶의 터전을 바꾸는 것을 원치 않는다고 밝히지만, 지역 내 일자리가 자신의 전문 기술 수준보다 낮다고 보일 경우 이사를 할 가능성이 보다 커진다. 연구에 의하면 자신들의 요건이 너무 출중하다고 생각하는 직원들은 금방 지치고 회사를 그만두는 것으로 나타났다.

어휘 seek ~을 찾다 keep in mind ~을 상기하다 idiosyncratic 특유의 labor market 노동 시장 shaped ~ 모양을 한 available 이용 가능한 entry-level (직급상) 하위의, 신입의 position 직위, 직급 mid-lelve 중간급 considerably 상당히 openings 공석, 빈자리 translate into ~로 해석하다 competition 경쟁, 시합 highranking 고위의, 높은 계급의 candidate 후보자 indicate ~을 나타내다 desire to ~하기 원하다 expertise 전문적 기술 be likely to ~할 것 같다 overqualified 자격 요건을 넘어서는 burn out (기력 등이) 소진되다 quit 그만두다

165. 세부 사항을 묻는 문제

기사에 따르면, 구직자들이 꺼려하는 것은 무엇인가?

(A) 상급 직책에 지원하는 것
(B) 다른 지역으로 이사하는 것
(C) 금방 지치는 것
(D) 중간급 일자리를 받아들이는 것

해설 지문 중반에서 'Most candidates indicate that they do not desire to change their lives for a job'에서 대부분의 취업 희망자들이 직장 때문에 거주지를 변경하는 것을 원하지 않는다고 언급하고 있다. 따라서 (B)가 정답이다. 본문의 most candidates를 jobseekers로, do not desire to change를 are reluctant to do로 바꿔 표현하고 있다.

166. 세부 사항을 묻는 문제

기사에 따르면, 필요 이상으로 자격 요건이 좋은 직원들을 고용한 회사들이 직면하게 되는 것은?

(A) 높은 급여 비용
(B) 많은 신규 지원자들
(C) 많은 수의 이직자
(D) 신입 업무에 대한 지원 증가

해설 본문 하단의 'Studies show that employees who feel overqualified for their jobs burn out quickly and quit their jobs.'에서 키워드인 overqualified employees를 찾을 수 있고, 그들은 빨리 지쳐서 회사를 그만둔다고 언급하고 있다. 그러므로 정답은 (C)이다.

167. 맥락을 완성시키는 문제

지문에 표시된 [1], [2], [3], 그리고 [4] 중에서 다음의 문장이 들어가기에 가장 좋은 위치가 어디인가?

"이는 곧 고위직에 대한 치열한 경쟁으로 해석된다."

(A) [1]
(B) [2]
(C) [3]
(D) [4]

해설 [1] 뒤에서, 'Many available jobs are for entry-level positions while there are a smaller number of mid-level positions and considerably fewer top-level openings.'에서 보면 최고 수준의 자리에는 현저히 적은 수의 일자리가 있으므로 이것은 곧 고위직의 치열한 경쟁으로 해석된다는 맥락이 와야 논리적으로 연결이 된다. 그 이후에는 이러한 상위직책에 관심이 있는 지원자라는 표현으로 맥락을 잇고 있다. 그러므로 정답은 (B)이다.

〈168-171〉 다음은 광고에 관한 글이다.

선셋 비치 리조트 호텔

이국적 풍경의 여행지를 떠올려 보십시오. 현대적 기능성과 고급스러움이 과거의 매력과 함께 어우러져 있는 곳, 관광객들이 한껏 즐길 수 있고 왕처럼 대접 받는 곳, 바로 그곳이 재단장을 마친 선셋 비치 리조트 호텔입니다.
녹음이 우거져서 멋진 열대 정원으로 유명한 저희 호텔은 현대적 감각의 휘트니스 센터와 수영장 근처에 있는 노천카페를 신설했습니다. 호텔에서 조금만 걸어가면 섬 자연 그대로의 모습을 지닌 해변가와 수많은 부티크 그리고 기념품점에 닿을 수 있습니다. 만약 섬 안의 다른 곳을 가고 싶으시다면 저희 호텔에서 무료로 교통편을 마련해 드립니다.
섬의 주요 스포츠 행사로 활용해 보세요. Vivace 철인 3종 경기의 특수를 노리기 위해, 저희는 11월에 대대적인 재개장을 할 예정입니다. 3종 경기 기간 동안 이틀 이상 객실을 예약하는 분들에게는 저희 신설 카페의 음식 할인뿐만 아니라, 객실료 할인 및 근처 동물원과 수족관의 무료입장권까지 제공해 드릴 것입니다.
이 특별 행사는 지금부터 10월 말까지 www.sunsetbeachresort.com 또는 여행사에서 이용 가능하십니다. 온라인 예약을 위해서 환불 불가한 계약금 250달러가 필요합니다.

어휘 exotic 이국적인 matched with ~와 조화를 이룬 pamper 하고 싶은대로 하게 하다 be treated 대접받다 refurbish 재단장하다 boutique 고급 양품점 triathlon 3종 경기

168. 글의 목적을 묻는 문제

이 광고의 목적은 무엇인가?

(A) 스포츠 이벤트를 발표하기 위해
(B) 호텔 패키지를 제공하기 위해
(C) 새로운 편의시설을 설명하기 위해
(D) 손님들에게 계약금을 내라고 설득하기 위해

해설 첫 문단 마지막 부분 'That destination is the refurbished Sunset Beach Resort Hotel'이 선셋 리조트 호텔의 재단장을 언급했으며, 두 번째 문단부터는 여러 새로운 편의시설을 설명하고 있다. 그러므로 정답은 (C)이다.

169. 세부 사항을 묻는 문제

고객이 3종 경기 기간 동안 호텔에 머무를 때 받을 수 있는 혜택은 무엇인가?

(A) 기념품 가게 물품 할인
(B) 섬 무료 관광
(C) 수영장 옆 카페 할인
(D) 그 지방 박물관 무료입장권

해설 'Customers who book rooms for two or more nights during the triathlon will receive room discounts and passes to the local zoo and aquarium as well as discounts on food at our new cafe'에서 3종 경기 기간 동안 신설 카페에서 음식 할인뿐 아니라 객실료 할인, 근처 동물원과 수족관의 무료입장권까지 제공한다고 언급되어 있다. 한편 새로 만들어진 카페의 위치는 두 번째 단락, '~ the hotel has added a modern fitness center and an open-air cafe near the pool'에서 언급됐듯이 수영장 근처이다. 따라서 수영장 옆 카페 할인이라고 한 (C)가 정답이다.

170. 틀린 정보를 찾는 문제

이 광고에서 언급하지 않은 것은?

(A) 계약금은 반환될 수 없다.
(B) 온라인 예약이 가능하다.
(C) 손님은 이틀만 머무를 수 있다.
(D) 특별 이벤트는 10월까지 유효하다.

해설 마지막 문단 'This special promotion is available online at www.sunsetbeachresort.com as well as at travel agencies from now until the end of October. A down payment of 250, which is nonrefundable, is required for online reservations'에서 언급됐듯이 (D) 10월 마지막 날까지 온라인 또는 여행사에서 이용 가능하고, (B) 온라인 예약을 위해서는 250달러가 필요하다고 했으며, 계약금은 반환 불가(nonrefundable)라고 (A)를 언급했다. 세 번째 문단 'Customers who book rooms for two or more nights during the triathlon will receive room discounts ~'에서 이틀만이 아니라 이틀 이상 머물면 여러 가지 혜택이 있다고 언급되었다. 그러므로 정답은 (C)이다.

171. 맥락을 완성시키는 문제

지문에 표시된 [1], [2], [3], 그리고 [4] 중에서 다음의 문장이 들어가기에 가장 좋은 위치가 어디인가?

"만약 섬 안의 다른 곳을 가고 싶으시다면 저희 호텔에서 무료로 교통편을 마련해 드립니다."

(A) [1]
(B) [2]
(C) [3]
(D) [4]

해설 두 번째 문단 첫 줄에서 'Noted for its lush and famous tropical gardens, the hotel has added a modern fitness center and an open-air cafe near the pool.'에서 보면 호텔 내의 부대시설에 대해 알리고 있고, 그 이후는 'Within walking distance of the hotel'로 걸어서 갈 수 있는 호텔 주변을 소개하고 있으므로 이 이후에 바로 섬의 다른 곳(For other destinations on the island)에 대한 설명이 뒷따르는 것이 논리적이다. 그러므로 정답은 (B)이다.

〈172-175〉 다음은 이메일에 관한 문제이다.

수신: Ivan Martin
발신: Adelaide Cho (싱가포르에 있는 MK 배급업자)
주제: W1J-9HG 공기 정화기의 문제

친애하는 Martin 씨에게,

저는 W1J-9HG 공기 정화기에 대해 주의를 끈 문제에 관해 당신에게 알려드리려고 이메일을 보냅니다.
몇몇 소매점에서 이상한 냄새를 내뿜는다는 불평과 함께 정화기기를 되돌려 보내 왔습니다. 우리는 하루에 몇 시간씩 작동시켜 재고로 있는 수십 대의 정화기를 시험했습니다. 단 5일 뒤 그것들 중 6대가 습하고 역한 냄새를 내뿜기 시작했습니다.
각 모델에 있는 필터가 문제의 원인으로 보입니다. 그것들은 빨리 막히고, 더러운 먼지들이 정화된 공기와 함께 재순환하게 하는 것 같아 보입니다. 우리는 필터를 교체해 보았고, 크롬 필터가 이 문제를 완벽하게 해결한 것 같습니다. 물론 우리는 이것이 전체적인 문제라고 확신할 수는 없지만, 당신의 권한으로 우리의 창고에 있는 공기정화기의 정화기들을 교체하기를 원하며, 앞으로 싱가포르에 보내질 공기정화기 전부를 손볼 것을 요청하고 싶습니다.
당신의 빠른 답변을 기대합니다.

친애하는

Adelaide Cho
싱가포르 MK 배급업자

어휘 attention 주의 관심 retail store 소매점, 소매상 complaint 불평 emit 방출하다 damp 습한 pungent 찌르는, 날카로운 clog 막히다, 방해하다 across the board 전반적인, 전체적인 authorization 권한, 권위

172. 글의 목적을 묻는 문제

이메일의 목적은 무엇인가?

(A) 제조업자에게 문제점을 통보하기 위해
(B) 공기 정화기에 대해 문의하기 위해
(C) 싱가포르에 있는 고객과 사업 약속을 하기 위해
(D) 연구 결과물을 논의하기 위해

해설 서두 부분의 Subject에서 주제를 확인한다. "A problem with the W1J-9HG air purifier"라고 언급되어 있다. 그러므로 정답은 (A)이다.

173. 세부 사항을 묻는 문제

W1J-9HG 공기 정화기에 대해 무엇이 보고되었는가?

(A) 싱가포르 시장에서 매우 인기가 있다.
(B) 싱가포르에서 출시하기에 적합할 것이다.
(C) 재검사가 요구된다.
(D) 단기간 사용 후에 악취를 낸다.

해설 두 번째 단락 마지막 문장에 악취가 난다고 "After just five days, six of them began emitting a damp, pungent odor" 언급되어 있다. 그러므로 정답은 (D)이다.

174. 동의어 찾는 문제

세 번째 단락의 네 번째 줄에 있는 'authorization' 단어와 의미상 가장 유사한 것은

(A) 힘
(B) 허가
(C) 도움
(D) 정리

해설 지문에 나온 'authorization'은 "허가, 승인"의 의미이므로 문맥상 permission과 의미가 제일 유사하다. 그러므로 정답은 (B)이다.

175. 추후 당부 사항을 묻는 문제

Adelaide Cho는 무엇을 요청하고 있는가?

(A) 그녀는 특허 사용을 빨리 승인해 달라고 요청했다.
(B) 그녀는 공기 정화기를 항공편으로 보낼 것을 요청했다.
(C) 그녀는 나중에 공기 정화기를 개조할 것을 요청했다.
(D) 그녀는 Martin 씨가 배급업자에게 연락할 것을 요청했다.

해설 세 번째 단락 마지막 문장 중에 "~ request that you alter all the purifiers that are sent to Singapore in the future"라고 언급되어 있듯이 Adelaide Cho는 공기정화기에 있는 문제를 고쳐야 한다는 것을 요청하고 있다는 것을 알 수 있다. 그러므로 정답은 (C)이다.

〈176-180〉 다음은 회람과 정보에 관한 문제이다.

수신: 모든 테크콤 직원들
발신: 레이몬드 카터, 인사부장

우리는 여러분들이 직장에 있을 때 아동들의 보호시설에 대해 얼마나 안심하는지에 여러분들의 생산성이 일부 달려 있다는 사실을 알고 있습니다. 테크콤은 7월에 열리는 현장 탁아소를 발표하게 되어 자랑스럽습니다. 비록 우리가 그 센터의 운영비를 지급하겠지만, 부모들이 조금은 비용을 부담하셔야 합니다.
테크콤의 탁아소는 실비아 존스톤에 의해 관리될 것인데, 그녀는 자격증이 있는 선생님이고 초기 어린이 발달 분야에 박사 학위를 갖고 있습니다. 존스톤 씨는 6년 동안 3학년들을 가르쳤고, 그 후에 그녀는 플레이 하우스 탁아소를 7년간 성공적으로 운영했습니다. 테크콤 빌딩과 남쪽 주차장 사이에는 커다란 풀로 덮인 지역이 있는데 그곳은 울타리로 둘러싸일 것이고 놀이터 장비들이

설치될 것입니다. 실내에서, 아이들은 블록 쌓기, 책, 보드게임, 미술용품, 작업 벤치를 포함해서 다양한 장난감과 게임들을 갖게 될 것입니다. 게다가, 우리는 특별 활동도 제공할 것입니다. 시간과 비용은 부착된 스케줄을 참고하십시오. 종일 탁아소와 함께, 우리는 숙제를 도와줄 수 있는 보증된 선생님들이 있는 방과 후 보호시설도 제공할 것입니다.
테크콤은 우리의 직원들과 그 가족들에게 이 특별 혜택을 제공하게 되어 매우 기쁩니다.

테크콤 탁아소

영업시간: 오전 8:00 - 오후 9:00, 월요일 - 금요일

아이 당 요금

종일 프로그램: 오전 8:00 - 오후 5:00	주당 80달러
방과 후 프로그램 : 오후 3:00 - 오후 6:00	주당 30달러

종일 또는 방과 후 프로그램들의 연장 시간

오후 6:00 - 오후 9:00	시간당 6달러
오전 8:00 - 오후 9:00 방문 시간	시간당 6달러

추가 활동

텀블링과 체조
6주, 한 시간/일주일에 두 번, 현장 — 120달러

초급 음악 또는 중급 음악

4주, 1시간/일주일에 두 번, 현장 — 80달러

수영 레슨

아이들은 YMCA 수영장으로 1블록 도보
4주, 1시간/일주일에 두 번 — 100달러

농구 훈련

아이들은 YMCA 체육관으로 1블록 도보
4주, 1시간/일주일에 두 번 — 100달러

다수의 아이들이 등록하는 가정들에는 수업료가 할인됩니다. 제안사항이나 의견이 있다면, 또는 더 많은 정보를 원하신다면, raymondcarterdhr@techcom.com으로 메일을 보내주십시오. 활동 책자는 원하시면 받으실 수 있습니다. 관심 있는 부모들을 위한 점심식사가 6월 5일, 탁아소에서 마련될 것입니다. 이것은 탁아소 관리인, 실비아 존스톤을 만날 기회가 될 것입니다.

어휘 Human Resources 인사부 productivity 생산성 rely 의지하다, 믿다 in part 일부분, 얼마간 comfortable 편안한, 만족하는 welfare 복지(보호)시설 announce 발표하다 on-site 현장의, 현지의 daycare center 탁아소 subsidize 보조(장려)금을 지급하다 operating cost 운영비 fee 요금 certified 보증된, 면허증을 가진 grassy 풀이 우거진, 풀로 덮인 fence in 둘러(에워)싸다 install 설치하다 playground 놀이터 equipment 장비 indoors 실내에서 array 다량, 다수 refer 참조하다 full-day 종일(반) after-school 방과 후의 benefit 혜택, 이익 extended 연장된 tumbling 텀블링 gymnastics 체조 early 초급 intermediate 중급 tuition 수업료 discounted 할인된 enroll 등록하다 multiple 다수의 suggestion 제안 comment 의견, 평가 brochure 안내 책자 luncheon 점심, 오찬 cater (음식물을)제공하다

176. 틀린 정보를 묻는 문제

탁아소 관리자가 가지고 있지 않은 것은 무엇인가?

(A) 박사 학위
(B) 선생님으로서의 경험
(C) 테크콤 탁아소에서 가르친 경험
(D) 탁아소 관리자로서의 경험

해설 첫 지문, 두 번째 문단에서 'TechCom's childcare will be managed by Sylvia Johnston, who is a certified teacher and has a Ph.D. in early childhood development. Ms. Johnston has taught third grade for 6 years, after which she successfully managed the Play House Daycare Center for 7 years.'에서 탁아소를 관리하게 될 실비아 존스톤에 대해 서술하고 있다. (A), (B), (D) 모두 언급된 내용이지만 (C)는 언급되지 않았다. 테크콤 탁아소는 이번에 새로 생기는 것이므로 거기서 가르친 경험은 있을 수 없다.

177. 세부 사항을 묻는 문제

테크콤은 왜 현장 탁아소를 제공하는가?

(A) 직원 편의를 향상하기 위해
(B) 돈을 벌기 위해
(C) 좋은 탁아 서비스를 제공하기 위해
(D) 아이들에게 그들의 제품을 실험하기 위해

해설 첫 지문 처음에 'We understand that your productivity relies, in part, on how comfortable you are about your child's welfare while you are at work.'라며 탁아소 시설을 발표하고 있다. 즉, 부모들이 아이들의 보호 시설에 대해 안심하고 있어야 생산성이 향상되기 때문에, 회사에서 직접 그 시설을 제공하려는 것이다. 그러므로 정답은 (A)이다. 탁아소 운영으로 돈을 벌려는 것은 아니기 때문에 (B)는 답이 될 수 없다.

178. 세부 사항을 묻는 문제

오전 8시에서 오후 5시에 한 아이의 월별 탁아소 비용은 무엇인가?

(A) 80달러
(B) 100달러
(C) 320달러
(D) 450달러

해설 가격 첫 문단에 'Full-day program 8:00 A.M. - 5:00 P.M. $80/wk'라고 나와 있다. 일주일에 80달러인데 문제에서는 한 달의 비용을 물었으므로, 한 아이의 탁아소 종일반 한달 요금은 (C) 320달러이다.

179. 세부 사항을 묻는 문제

현장에서 제공되는 활동은 무엇인가?

(A) 체조
(B) 수영 레슨
(C) 농구 훈련
(D) 밴드 연습

해설 데이케어 소개를 하고 있는 표에서 현장, 즉 on-site라고 표시된 활동을 찾으면 된다. 텀블링과 체조, 그리고 초급과 중급 음악 수업들이 on-site에서 제공된다. 수영과 농구는 모두 YMCA로 가서 할 것이라고 나와 있으므로 답은 (A)이다. (D)는 언급이 되지 않았다.

180. 통합지문 문제

부모들은 어떻게 더 많은 정보를 받을 수 있는가?

(A) 실비아 존스톤에게 메일을 보냄으로써
(B) 테크콤의 최고 경영자에게 메일을 보냄으로써
(C) 인사부장에게 메일을 보냄으로써
(D) 다른 부모들과 얘기함으로써

해설 정보 하단에 'If you have suggestions or comments or require more information, e-mail raymondcarterdhr@techcom.com'에서 메일 주소를 보면 레이몬드 카터에게 메일을 보내라고 하는 것을 알 수 있다. 레이몬드 카터는 첫 지문인 메일을 보내는 인사부장이다. 따라서 더 많은 정보를 얻을 수 있는 방법으로 (C)가 적절하다.

〈181-185〉 다음은 기사와 안내문에 관한 문제이다.

우리 경제의 나쁜 소식

전문가들이 올해 하반기에 급속한 불경기를 예측한다

4월 6일

여러 전문가들이 현재 불경기가 진행되고 있고 최고점이 10월이 될 것이라고

발표했다. 소비자들이 자신이 무엇을 구매하는지에 대해 더욱 민감해짐으로써, 불경기는 소비자 구매의 하락에 의해 나타났다. 더 알맞은 원인은 경제 성장의 실패이다. 하지만 이 원인은 일반 대중이 추측한 것들이다. 캘리포니아 대학의 앤더슨 센터 전문가인 앤드류 부쉬는 불경기의 원인 3가지를 제시하였다. 그것은 최근 전력 위기, 인플레이션 문제, 세계적 무역의 상당한 불균형이다. 지난주 기자회견에서 그는 이 불경기를 극복하려면 내년에 재정 예산을 줄여야 한다고 발표하였다. 예산에 따르려면 정부가 해야 할 첫 번째 사항은 경제 성장과 발달을 촉진하기 위해 경제의 여러 부문에 최대한 많은 시간과 노력을 투자해야 한다는 것이다. 특정 예측 전문가들이 사용하는 경제 모델에 의하면 더 무시무시한 불경기가 다가올 확률은 90%정도나 높다고 한다. 감소하는 GDP, 증가하는 실업률, 감소하는 투자율, 감원이 이미 예상된다.

감원 발표

최근 불경기로 인하여 앞으로 2년 안에 추가로 500개의 일자리 감축을 발표합니다. 감원은 우리 기업 재건 계획의 일부분입니다. 10% 이상의 인력 감축은 지출을 감소시키고 영업이익률을 더 효율적으로 이끌기 위한 본질적인 계획의 한 국면입니다.

일자리 감축 이외에도, 남아 있는 임원들의 봉급을 줄일 것이며, 지출을 최대한 줄이시길 바랍니다. 경제 침제로 인해 우리 기업도 지금 손해를 보고 있으므로 어느 때보다 현재 만족스러운 금융 상태를 유지해야 합니다.

감사합니다.

어휘 determine 결정하다 recession 경기 하락 peak 꼭대기 estimate 예측하다 sensible 민감한 speculate 추측하다 outline 윤곽을 그리다 list 목록을 작성하다 recent 최근의 crisis 위기 concern 우려 significant 중대한 imbalance 불균형 press conference 기자 회견 tight 빡빡한 overcome 극복하다 priority 우선하는, 상위의 allocate 할당하다 sector 구역 stimulate 자극하다 econometric 계량 경제학의 looming 어렴풋이 나타나는 dwindling 점차 감소하는 job cut 해고 additional 추가적인 essential 본질적인 trim 정돈하다 suffer 고생하다 decent 맞는, 어울리는

181. 세부 사항을 묻는 문제

전문가들은 불경기의 최고점이 언제 나타난다고 예측하는가?

(A) 올해 10월에
(B) 2년 후에
(C) 내년 10월에
(D) 연초에

해설 기사 초반에 경기 하락은 이미 진행 중이고 (a recession in progress) 올해 10월이 되면 최고조에 이를 것으로 전망하고 있다(~ with its peak estimated to be in October). 그러므로 정답은 (A)이다.

182. 틀린 정보를 묻는 문제

예측된 불경기의 원인이 아닌 것은?

(A) 전력 위기
(B) 대기업들의 재건
(C) 전체적인 물가 상승
(D) 무역 불균형

해설 기사 중반에 캘리포니아 대학의 앤더슨 센터의 앤드류 부쉬는 불경기의 원인으로 3가지를 지목했는데, He listed the recent power crisis, inflation concerns, and significant global trade imbalances가 그에 해당한다. 따라서 (B)가 정답이다.

183. 틀린 정보를 묻는 문제

예측되는 불경기의 결과가 아닌 것은?

(A) 실업
(B) 투자율 감소
(C) 일자리 감축
(D) 은행의 파산

해설 기사 후반에 경제학자들은 더 큰 불경기가 도래할 확률을 90% 이상으로 보고, GDP 감소, 실업증가, 투자 감소, 일자리 삭감 등을 결과로 뽑고 있다(A dwindling GDP, increasing unemployment, reduced investments, and job cuts had already predicted). 그러므로 정답은 (D)이다.

184. 세부 사항을 묻는 문제

이 기업은 왜 감원을 하는가?

(A) 직원들의 불만족스러운 근무로 인해
(B) 남아 있는 직원들에게 충분한 관심이 기울여져야 하기 때문에
(C) 새로운 직원을 채용하기 위해
(D) 경제 침체로 인해

해설 경기 하락으로 500개 이상의 일자리를 2년 동안 줄일 것이며, 임원의 10%도 줄인다고 발표했다. 봉급도 줄고 일자리도 줄고, 경제 침체의 영향이다. 그러므로 정답은 (D)이다.

185. 동의어를 찾는 문제

발표의 첫 번째 문단의 세 번째 줄 "aspect"와 뜻이 가장 가까운 것은

(A) 부분
(B) 시도
(C) 수여
(D) 연장

해설 전체의 의미상 계획의 '한 면(= 부분)'이라는 뜻으로 (A) part가 가장 적절하다.

〈186-190〉 다음은 광고, 표 그리고 양식에 관한 문제이다.

AUS 비즈니스 위원회

"맨손으로 시작해서 사업체를 일궈나가는 방법"

자기 자신의 사업을 시작하는 것은 쉽지 않으며 대부분의 사람들에게 예기치 않은 어려운 문제를 야기시킵니다. AUS 비즈니스 위원회는 새로운 사업의 시작과 관련된 여러 가지 문제들에 대해서 바른 결정을 내리기 위해서 필요한 도구들로 신규 기업가들을 준비시킵니다. 9월에 저희는 일련의 세미나를 제공해 드리고, 목록은 저희 웹페이지 www.abc.org.au.에서 보실 수 있습니다.

각 세미나의 비용은 95호주달러이고 등록 마감일은 일정 잡힌 세미나 시작 3일 전입니다. 모든 세미나는 멜버른 다운스뷰가 512번지에 자리한 AUS 비즈니스 위원회 본사에서 개최될 예정입니다. 등록신청 양식은 715-2387번으로 팩스 발송하거나 양식에 나와 있는 주소로 보내실 수 있습니다. 온라인 신청은 www.abc.org.au에서 가능합니다. 등록 링크를 클릭하십시오.

일 정

번호	제목	요일	날짜	시간
C805	숙련된 노동력 고용	월요일	9월 8일	정오 12시 ~ 오후 4시
C806	효과적인 경영 기법	화요일	9월 9일	오후 4시 ~ 오후 8시
C811	회사정책 및 규정 만들기	금요일	9월 19일	오전 9시 ~ 오후 1시
C825	상인 및 납품업체와 협상하기	화요일	9월 23일	오후 4시 ~ 오후 8시

AUS 비즈니스 위원회

다운스뷰 불바르 512 번지 멜버른 오스트레일리아 3831

전화: 715-2323 팩스: 715-238

www.abc.org.au 이메일: jhewitt@www.abc.org.au

등록 신청서

이름: Jacqueline Williams

주소: 엘리자베스가 111번지, 시드니, NSW, 2000, 오스트레일리아

전화: (Phone) 545-2611 (휴대폰) 545-5667

이메일: jwilliams@williamstextiles.au

사명: Jacqueline Williams 텍스타일 주식회사

참석 희망 세미나(번호로 표시): C825

전에 AUS Business Commission 세미나에 참석한 적이 있나요? 아니오

세미나에 참석하기 위해 숙박시설을 요청하시겠습니까? 네

지불수단: (현금 발송하지 마시기 바랍니다, 현금 지불은 본인이 직접 하셔야 합니다.)

신용카드: X 동봉수표: ___

신용카드 종류: 오스텍스___ 수퍼 X 블루카드___

신용카드 번호: 9876-5432-1234-5678

후기/요청: 이메일로 연락 주십시오.

주의: 저희는 참여 부족으로 인하여 세미나를 취소할 권리가 있습니다. 그럴 경우 전액 환불됩니다.

어휘 pose 태도를 취하다 challenge 힘든 일 entrepreneur 사업체, 사업주 sound 견고한 protocol 규정 vendor 소매상인 supplier 공급업체 accommodations 숙박시설 issue 발행하다

186. 전반 내용을 묻는 문제

AUS 비즈니스 위원회는 어떤 종류의 회사인가?

(A) 구인 광고 전문업체
(B) 자산 관리 회사
(C) 섬유 회사
(D) 경영 훈련 전문 기관

해설 광고의 도입부를 보면 'AUS Business Commission provides new entrepreneurs with the tools required to make sound decisions about various issues regarding new business startups. (AUS Business Commission는 새로운 사업의 시작과 관련된 여러 가지 문제들에 대해서 바른 결정을 내리기 위해 필요한 도구들로 새내기 기업가들을 준비시킵니다.)'라고 하므로 새내기 사업가들을 교육시키는 기관임을 알 수 있다. 따라서 정답은 (D)이다.

187. 동의어를 찾는 문제

광고에서 첫 번째 문단 첫 번째 줄의 'poses'와 의미상 가장 가까운 것은

(A) 제시한다
(B) 위치를 정한다
(C) 모양을 만든다
(D) 영향을 미친다

해설 'poses'가 들어가 있는 문장을 보면 'Starting your own business isn't easy and poses unexpected challenges for most people.(자기 자신의 사업을 시작하는 것은 쉽지 않으며 대부분의 사람들에게 예기치 않은 어려운 문제를 야기시킵니다)'라고 하므로 poses는 위 문맥에서 '제시한다, 제기한다'는 뜻을 갖는 presents로 대신할 수 있다. 그러므로 정답은 (A)이다.

188. 사실 정보를 찾는 문제

세미나에 대해서 언급되고 있는 내용은 무엇인가?

(A) 현금 혹은 수표만이 지불 수단이다.
(B) 특정한 상황에서는 할인 혜택이 적용된다.
(C) 경험 있는 기업가들을 위한 세미나이다.
(D) 충분한 수의 사람들이 등록하지 않을 경우에는 취소될 것이다.

해설 양식의 하단을 보면 'Note: We reserve the right to cancel a session due to a lack of interest. In that case a full refund will be issued. (주의: 저희는 참여 부족으로 인하여 세미나를 취소할 권리가 있습니다. 그럴 경우 전액 환불됩니다.)'라고 하므로 인원이 부족할 경우에는 취소될 수 있다는 것을 알 수 있다. 그러므로 정답은 (D)이다.

189. 통합지문 문제

양식에 따르면, Williams 씨는 어떤 날짜에 세미나에 참석할 것인가?

(A) 9월 8일
(B) 9월 9일
(C) 9월 19일
(D) 9월 23일

해설 통합지문 문제로, 등록 신청서를 보면 'Seminar you wish to attend (indicate number): C825(참석 희망 세미나(번호로 표시): C825)'이고 두 번째 지문에서 C825를 찾아보면 'C825/Negotiating with Vendors and Suppliers/Tuesday/September 23/4 P.M. - 8 P.M.(C825/상인 및 납품업체와 협상하기/화요일/9월 23일/오후 4시-오후 8시)'로 되어 있다. C825 세미나는 9월 23일에 개최된다는 것을 알 수 있으므로 정답은 (D)이다.

190. 사실 정보를 찾는 문제

Williams 씨에 대해 어떤 내용이 제시되고 있는가?

(A) 섬유산업에 종사한다.
(B) 과거에 AUS 비즈니스 위원회 사의 고객이었다.
(C) 전화로 연락 받기를 원한다.
(D) 숙박시설을 필요로 하지 않는다.

해설 마지막 지문 신청서 양식에 회사 이름이 'Company Name: Williams Textiles Limited'로 나와 있으므로 Williams 씨는 textile(섬유) 업체에 종사하고 있음을 알 수 있다. 그러므로 정답은 (A)이다.

〈191-195〉 다음은 이메일, 정보, 티켓에 관한 문제이다.

수신: Malcolm Venville <venville@rooksecurity.com>
발신: Judy Greer <greer@rooksecurity.com>
날짜: 10월 6일 목요일 오후 4시 30분
주제: M&G 미팅에 관한 최신 사항

안녕하세요, Malcolm,

저는 M&G의 대표자들과의 미팅 일정을 10월 18일 화요일 오후 3시부터 오후 5시 사이로 조율했습니다. 이것은 전국적으로 건설사들을 선도하는 회사 중 한 곳에 Rook 보안 서비스의 강점을 제대로 소개할 좋은 기회입니다. 우리는 아침에 M&G과의 첫 번째 미팅을 위한 준비사항들에 관해서 이야기해야 합니다.

나는 Rochester로 가는 적절한 열차 스케줄을 확인해 보라고 Carlos에게 요청했고, 당신의 사무실에 한 부를 팩스로 전송하는 것을 상기시켜 주었습니다. 그리고 당신은 10월 18일에 Ashton 사무실에 있을 건가요? 만약 그렇다면, 저는 Carlos에게 우리가 Aston에서 Rochester를 향해 떠날 수 있도록 표를 2장 예약하라고 요청하겠습니다. 만약 당신이 집에서 나가기로 결정한다면, 저는 당신이 Fort Front에서 출발할 것을 권합니다. 그렇게 된다면 당신이 표를 직접 구매하시고 미리 Carlos에게 말씀만 해주세요. M&G은 우리를 Rochester 역에서 오후 2시 45분에 태울 택시를 보내 줄 것입니다. 그들은 또한 우리를 Rochester에 있는 Hot Chilis라고 하는 식당에서 M&G직원과 함께하는 저녁 6시부터 8시까지의 저녁 식사에 초대했습니다. 그 식당은 대략 역에서 30분 떨어져 있어서, 우리가 Ashton으로 돌아오는 기차에 저녁 8시 30분 무렵에 탈 수 있을 것이라 짐작합니다.

Judy

TRAIN LINK

9~11월 운행 시간

Capetown-Lake Park 노선

도착지	135(WE)	205(WD)	115(HD)	495(EX)
Ashton	오후 12:03	오후 12:15	오후 12:03	오후 2:30
Fort Front	오후 12:38	오후 12:50	-	-
Commontown	오후 1:18	오후 1:30	-	-
Kushana	오후 1:55	오후 2:05	오후 1:45	-
Rochester	오후 2:25	오후 2:35	-	-
Laurensville	오후 2:40	오후 2:53	오후 2:20	오후 4:30

EX - 급행; 모든 역마다 정차하지는 않음
WE - 토요일과 일요일에만 운행
WD - 월요일부터 금요일까지만 운행
HD - 휴일 스케줄; 모든 역마다 정차하지는 않음, 9월 18일과 11월 3일 유효

철도청의 자동 응답 서비스가 열차 정보를 안내합니다: 020-1313으로 전화 주세요.

티켓

신용카드 구매
표는 역 출입구에 있는 매표소나 저희 웹사이트 www.trainlink.com/tickets에 들어오셔서 구매 및 출력하실 수 있습니다.

현금 구매
표는 역에 있는 El Plato's 신문가판대, 매표소, 또는 열차에 탑승하셔서 구매하실 수 있습니다.

중요: 열차에 탑승하셔서 구매하시면 추가 요금 3달러가 있습니다.

* 온라인 시스템의 일시적인 점검으로 10월 21까지 Fort Front 역에서는 매표소에서 현금으로만 표 구입이 가능하다는 것을 알아 두십시오.

어휘 representative 대표자 opportunity 기회 strength 강점 nationwide 전국적인 preparation 준비사항 appropriate 적절한 remind (잊지 않도록 상기시켜주다, 생각나게 하다 reserve 예약하다 leave from ~로부터 떠나다 beforehand 미리, 사전에 supposedly 아마 assume 짐작하다 express 고속의 newsstands 신문가판대

191. 추론하는 문제

Greer 씨의 사무실은 아마도 어디에 있을 것인가?

(A) Capetown에
(B) Ashton에
(C) Fort Front에
(D) Lake Park에

해설 첫 지문, 두 번째 문단에서 "In addition, are you going to be at the Ashton office on October 18? If that is the case, I will ask Carlos to reserve two tickets so that we can leave from Ashton to Rochester."에서, Judy는 만약 Malcolm이 10월 18일에 Ashton 사무실에 있을 것이라면 둘이 함께 Rochester 행 열차를 탈 수 있을 것으로 이야기하고 있다. 이를 통해 Judy의 사무실이 (B) Ashton에 있음을 짐작할 수 있다.

192. 사실 정보를 찾는 문제

M&G 사에 대해 나타난 것은?

(A) 가장 가까운 기차역에서 30분 거리에 사무실이 있다.
(B) Rook Security와 다년간 파트너였다.
(C) 가장 최근의 프로젝트는 Hot Chilis를 위한 새로운 건물을 짓는 것이다.
(D) Greer 씨와 Venville 씨의 여행 준비의 일부를 다룬다.

해설 첫 지문, 마지막 문단 하단에 M&G 사가 Greer와 Venville 두 사람이 Rochester 역에 도착하면 이들을 태우기 위해 택시를 보내기로 했으므로, 두 사람의 여행 준비의 일부를 다루는 것이 맞다. 그러므로 정답은 (D)이다.

193. 추론하는 문제

Greer 씨와 Venville 씨가 저녁 8시 이후 돌아와야 하는 이유는 무엇인가?

(A) 그들은 사업상 고객들이 될 사람들과의 저녁 식사에 참석해야 한다.
(B) 그들은 급행열차가 이용 가능한 시간까지 기다리기를 원한다.
(C) 그들은 미팅이 끝난 후에 Rochester를 여행할 예약을 잡았다.
(D) 그들은 휴가를 보낼 것이라서 출발 시간의 선택에 제약이 있다.

해설 이메일 마지막 문단에, 미팅을 가진 후에 저녁 6시부터 8시까지 저녁 식사가 마련되어 있다고(They also have invited us to dinner from 6:00 P.M. to 8:00 P.M.) 했다. 따라서 두 사람이 저녁 8시 이후에 돌아올 여정을 잡는 이유로는 (A)가 알맞다.

194. 통합지문 문제

Greer 씨가 미팅에 참석하기 위해서 타야 하는 열차는?

(A) 115번 열차
(B) 135번 열차
(C) 205번 열차
(D) 495번 열차

해설 첫 지문에서 도착지는 Rochester임을 알 수 있다. 115번과 495번 열차는 Rochester에서 정차하지 않기 때문에 정답에서 제외된다. 또, WE로 표시된 135번 열차는 주말에만 운행하는 열차이다. 미팅은 화요일 오후 3시에 시작하기 때문에 135번 열차는 이용할 수 없다. 따라서, Greer 씨는 205번 열차를 타야 한다. 그러므로 정답은 (C)이다.

195. 통합지문 문제

Venville 씨가 회의 참석을 위해 Fort Front에서 출발한다면 그의 표를 어떻게 구매할 수 있는가?

(A) 철도청의 자동 전화 시스템을 이용하기
(B) El Plato 신문 가판대로 가기
(C) Train Link의 웹 사이트 방문하기
(D) 매표소에서 현금을 지불하기

해설 첫 번째 지문 초반을 보면 M&G과의 미팅이 Rochester에서 10월 18일 오후에 예정되어 있다. 또한 세 번째 지문에서 이 기차가 10월 21일까지 온라인 시스템의 일시적인 점검으로 매표소 현장에서 현금 구매만 된다는 내용을 볼 수가 있다. 이 단서를 조합해 보면 정답은 (D)이다.

〈196-200〉 다음은 공지, 일정표 그리고 신청서에 관한 문제이다.

MTT 메디컬 세미나

웨스트베리 애비뉴 1400번지, 사라소타, 플로리다 60279

다양한 분야로 이루어진 교육 세미나에 참가하셔서 전국의 동료 의사들과 함께하십시오. MTT 세미나는 현재 최고의 의사 선생님 몇 분을 모시고 저희 로우랜드 캠퍼스에서 진행됩니다. 모든 과정은 미국 평생 의료 교육 협회에 의해 인증된 강좌들입니다. 각 세미나 당 참석자 수가 100명으로 제한되므로 조기 등록이 요망됩니다. 온라인 www.mttmedseminars.com으로 등록하시거나 보다 자세한 정보를 원하신다면 703-479-5500으로 발레리 브래드쇼에게 전화 주십시오.

꼭 알아 두세요.
등록 확인 시점까지 아래의 강의료를 지불하셔야 합니다.

8월 10일까지 등록할 경우 130달러
8월 17일까지 등록할 경우 140달러
8월 24일까지 등록할 경우 150달러
현장 등록할 경우 (좌석이 있을 경우) 175달러

세미나 일정

9월 3일 오후 1:00-오후 4:00 응급 의학 Jason Isaacs 박사, 성 마리 병원	9월 9일 오후 3:00- 오후 5:00 1차 진료 및 여성 건강 Lauren Graham 박사, 성 요셉 산부인과
9월 18일 오후 12:00- 오후 3:00 전염병 Jason Kravits 박사, 탐파 종합병원	9월 22일 오후 6:30-오후 9:00 소아과 존 리 박사, 마이애미 대학 의료센터

MTT 온라인 신청서

이름 : Robert Joy
이메일 : rjoy@stlukestexas.com
주소 : 오크몬트 가 427번지, 휴스턴, 텍사스 77030
전화 : 832-640-2900
등록한 세미나 : 9월 22일
신청서 제출일 : 8월 18일

등록해 주셔서 감사합니다. 귀하는 24시간 이내에 이메일로 신청 확인 메일을 받게 됩니다.

어휘 fellow 동료 physician 내과 의사 accredit 승인하다 registration 등록 recommend 추천하다 attendance 참가자 수 primary care 1차 진료 infectious diseases 전염병 general hospital 종합병원 pediatric 소아의 tuition 수업료 pending ~ 까지 confirmation 확인

196. 전반 내용을 묻는 문제

이 광고는 누구를 대상으로 하는가?

(A) 의과 대학생
(B) 간호사
(C) 시설 관리자
(D) 의사

해설 첫 번째 지문의 시작 부분을 보면 '다양한 분야로 이루어진 교육 세미나에 참가하셔서 전국의 동료 의사들과 함께 하십시오. (Join fellow doctors ~ in a variety of fields.)'라고 나와 있으므로 의사들을 대상으로 한 세미나 광고임을 알 수 있다. 그러므로 정답은 (D)이다.

197. 틀린 정보를 찾는 문제

이 세미나에 대해 암시하고 있는 내용이 아닌 것은?

(A) 정원이 찰 것으로 예상된다.
(B) 순서대로 강좌를 들어야 한다.
(C) 최고의 의사들에 의해 진행된다.
(D) 로우랜드 캠퍼스에서 개최될 것이다.

해설 첫 번째 지문의 세 번째 줄을 보면 'Early registration is recommended as attendance is limited to 100 participants per seminar', 그리고 첫 번째 줄 'MTT seminars are led by some of today's top physicians at our Rowland Campus.'에 (A), (C), (D)는 언급되어 있다. 강좌를 순서대로 이수해야 한다는 내용은 없으므로 답은 (B)이다.

198. 세부 사항을 묻는 문제

응급실에서의 치료에 대해 언제 다루게 되는가?

(A) 9월 3일
(B) 9월 9일
(C) 9월 18일
(D) 9월 22일

해설 두 번째 지문의 중반부에 나와 있는 세미나 일정표를 보면 '9월 3일 (September 3)에 응급 의학 (Emergency Medicine)이 다뤄짐을 알 수 있으므로 정답은 (A)이다.

199. 통합지문 문제

Joy 씨는 얼마를 지불하게 되는가?

(A) 130 달러
(B) 140 달러
(C) 150 달러
(D) 175 달러

해설 세 번째 지문의 일정을 보면, '신청서 제출일: 8월 18일(Registration submitted on: August 18)'이라고 되어 있고, 첫 번째 지문을 보면 '8월 24일까지 등록할 경우 150달러 ($150 if registered by August 24)'라고 나와 있으므로 150달러를 지불할 것을 알 수 있다. 따라서 정답은 (C)이다.

200. 통합지문 문제

Joy 씨는 어떤 세미나에 등록했는가?

(A) 소아과
(B) 응급의학
(C) 1차 진료 및 여성 건강
(D) 전염병

해설 세 번째 지문 하단을 보면, '등록한 세미나: 9월 22일 세미나(I am registering for: September 22)'라고 나와 있으며, 두 번째 지문의 세미나 일정표를 보면 '9월 22일 (September 22)/소아과 (Pediatric Medicine)'라고 되어 있으므로 소아과 세미나에 참석한다는 것을 알 수 있다. 그러므로 정답은 (A)이다.

books. english. co. kr

ANSWER SHEET

수험번호						
성명	한글					
	영자					

No.

실전 모의고사

READING (Part V ~ VII)

NO.	ANSWER				NO.	ANSWER				NO.	ANSWER				NO.	ANSWER				NO.	ANSWER			
	A	B	C	D		A	B	C	D		A	B	C	D		A	B	C	D		A	B	C	D
101	Ⓐ	Ⓑ	Ⓒ	Ⓓ	121	Ⓐ	Ⓑ	Ⓒ	Ⓓ	141	Ⓐ	Ⓑ	Ⓒ	Ⓓ	161	Ⓐ	Ⓑ	Ⓒ	Ⓓ	181	Ⓐ	Ⓑ	Ⓒ	Ⓓ
102	Ⓐ	Ⓑ	Ⓒ	Ⓓ	122	Ⓐ	Ⓑ	Ⓒ	Ⓓ	142	Ⓐ	Ⓑ	Ⓒ	Ⓓ	162	Ⓐ	Ⓑ	Ⓒ	Ⓓ	182	Ⓐ	Ⓑ	Ⓒ	Ⓓ
103	Ⓐ	Ⓑ	Ⓒ	Ⓓ	123	Ⓐ	Ⓑ	Ⓒ	Ⓓ	143	Ⓐ	Ⓑ	Ⓒ	Ⓓ	163	Ⓐ	Ⓑ	Ⓒ	Ⓓ	183	Ⓐ	Ⓑ	Ⓒ	Ⓓ
104	Ⓐ	Ⓑ	Ⓒ	Ⓓ	124	Ⓐ	Ⓑ	Ⓒ	Ⓓ	144	Ⓐ	Ⓑ	Ⓒ	Ⓓ	164	Ⓐ	Ⓑ	Ⓒ	Ⓓ	184	Ⓐ	Ⓑ	Ⓒ	Ⓓ
105	Ⓐ	Ⓑ	Ⓒ	Ⓓ	125	Ⓐ	Ⓑ	Ⓒ	Ⓓ	145	Ⓐ	Ⓑ	Ⓒ	Ⓓ	165	Ⓐ	Ⓑ	Ⓒ	Ⓓ	185	Ⓐ	Ⓑ	Ⓒ	Ⓓ
106	Ⓐ	Ⓑ	Ⓒ	Ⓓ	126	Ⓐ	Ⓑ	Ⓒ	Ⓓ	146	Ⓐ	Ⓑ	Ⓒ	Ⓓ	166	Ⓐ	Ⓑ	Ⓒ	Ⓓ	186	Ⓐ	Ⓑ	Ⓒ	Ⓓ
107	Ⓐ	Ⓑ	Ⓒ	Ⓓ	127	Ⓐ	Ⓑ	Ⓒ	Ⓓ	147	Ⓐ	Ⓑ	Ⓒ	Ⓓ	167	Ⓐ	Ⓑ	Ⓒ	Ⓓ	187	Ⓐ	Ⓑ	Ⓒ	Ⓓ
108	Ⓐ	Ⓑ	Ⓒ	Ⓓ	128	Ⓐ	Ⓑ	Ⓒ	Ⓓ	148	Ⓐ	Ⓑ	Ⓒ	Ⓓ	168	Ⓐ	Ⓑ	Ⓒ	Ⓓ	188	Ⓐ	Ⓑ	Ⓒ	Ⓓ
109	Ⓐ	Ⓑ	Ⓒ	Ⓓ	129	Ⓐ	Ⓑ	Ⓒ	Ⓓ	149	Ⓐ	Ⓑ	Ⓒ	Ⓓ	169	Ⓐ	Ⓑ	Ⓒ	Ⓓ	189	Ⓐ	Ⓑ	Ⓒ	Ⓓ
110	Ⓐ	Ⓑ	Ⓒ	Ⓓ	130	Ⓐ	Ⓑ	Ⓒ	Ⓓ	150	Ⓐ	Ⓑ	Ⓒ	Ⓓ	170	Ⓐ	Ⓑ	Ⓒ	Ⓓ	190	Ⓐ	Ⓑ	Ⓒ	Ⓓ
111	Ⓐ	Ⓑ	Ⓒ	Ⓓ	131	Ⓐ	Ⓑ	Ⓒ	Ⓓ	151	Ⓐ	Ⓑ	Ⓒ	Ⓓ	171	Ⓐ	Ⓑ	Ⓒ	Ⓓ	191	Ⓐ	Ⓑ	Ⓒ	Ⓓ
112	Ⓐ	Ⓑ	Ⓒ	Ⓓ	132	Ⓐ	Ⓑ	Ⓒ	Ⓓ	152	Ⓐ	Ⓑ	Ⓒ	Ⓓ	172	Ⓐ	Ⓑ	Ⓒ	Ⓓ	192	Ⓐ	Ⓑ	Ⓒ	Ⓓ
113	Ⓐ	Ⓑ	Ⓒ	Ⓓ	133	Ⓐ	Ⓑ	Ⓒ	Ⓓ	153	Ⓐ	Ⓑ	Ⓒ	Ⓓ	173	Ⓐ	Ⓑ	Ⓒ	Ⓓ	193	Ⓐ	Ⓑ	Ⓒ	Ⓓ
114	Ⓐ	Ⓑ	Ⓒ	Ⓓ	134	Ⓐ	Ⓑ	Ⓒ	Ⓓ	154	Ⓐ	Ⓑ	Ⓒ	Ⓓ	174	Ⓐ	Ⓑ	Ⓒ	Ⓓ	194	Ⓐ	Ⓑ	Ⓒ	Ⓓ
115	Ⓐ	Ⓑ	Ⓒ	Ⓓ	135	Ⓐ	Ⓑ	Ⓒ	Ⓓ	155	Ⓐ	Ⓑ	Ⓒ	Ⓓ	175	Ⓐ	Ⓑ	Ⓒ	Ⓓ	195	Ⓐ	Ⓑ	Ⓒ	Ⓓ
116	Ⓐ	Ⓑ	Ⓒ	Ⓓ	136	Ⓐ	Ⓑ	Ⓒ	Ⓓ	156	Ⓐ	Ⓑ	Ⓒ	Ⓓ	176	Ⓐ	Ⓑ	Ⓒ	Ⓓ	196	Ⓐ	Ⓑ	Ⓒ	Ⓓ
117	Ⓐ	Ⓑ	Ⓒ	Ⓓ	137	Ⓐ	Ⓑ	Ⓒ	Ⓓ	157	Ⓐ	Ⓑ	Ⓒ	Ⓓ	177	Ⓐ	Ⓑ	Ⓒ	Ⓓ	197	Ⓐ	Ⓑ	Ⓒ	Ⓓ
118	Ⓐ	Ⓑ	Ⓒ	Ⓓ	138	Ⓐ	Ⓑ	Ⓒ	Ⓓ	158	Ⓐ	Ⓑ	Ⓒ	Ⓓ	178	Ⓐ	Ⓑ	Ⓒ	Ⓓ	198	Ⓐ	Ⓑ	Ⓒ	Ⓓ
119	Ⓐ	Ⓑ	Ⓒ	Ⓓ	139	Ⓐ	Ⓑ	Ⓒ	Ⓓ	159	Ⓐ	Ⓑ	Ⓒ	Ⓓ	179	Ⓐ	Ⓑ	Ⓒ	Ⓓ	199	Ⓐ	Ⓑ	Ⓒ	Ⓓ
120	Ⓐ	Ⓑ	Ⓒ	Ⓓ	140	Ⓐ	Ⓑ	Ⓒ	Ⓓ	160	Ⓐ	Ⓑ	Ⓒ	Ⓓ	180	Ⓐ	Ⓑ	Ⓒ	Ⓓ	200	Ⓐ	Ⓑ	Ⓒ	Ⓓ

ANSWER SHEET

수험번호						
성명	한글					
	영자					

No.

실전 모의고사

READING (Part V ~ VII)

NO.	ANSWER				NO.	ANSWER				NO.	ANSWER				NO.	ANSWER				NO.	ANSWER			
	A	B	C	D		A	B	C	D		A	B	C	D		A	B	C	D		A	B	C	D
101	Ⓐ	Ⓑ	Ⓒ	Ⓓ	121	Ⓐ	Ⓑ	Ⓒ	Ⓓ	141	Ⓐ	Ⓑ	Ⓒ	Ⓓ	161	Ⓐ	Ⓑ	Ⓒ	Ⓓ	181	Ⓐ	Ⓑ	Ⓒ	Ⓓ
102	Ⓐ	Ⓑ	Ⓒ	Ⓓ	122	Ⓐ	Ⓑ	Ⓒ	Ⓓ	142	Ⓐ	Ⓑ	Ⓒ	Ⓓ	162	Ⓐ	Ⓑ	Ⓒ	Ⓓ	182	Ⓐ	Ⓑ	Ⓒ	Ⓓ
103	Ⓐ	Ⓑ	Ⓒ	Ⓓ	123	Ⓐ	Ⓑ	Ⓒ	Ⓓ	143	Ⓐ	Ⓑ	Ⓒ	Ⓓ	163	Ⓐ	Ⓑ	Ⓒ	Ⓓ	183	Ⓐ	Ⓑ	Ⓒ	Ⓓ
104	Ⓐ	Ⓑ	Ⓒ	Ⓓ	124	Ⓐ	Ⓑ	Ⓒ	Ⓓ	144	Ⓐ	Ⓑ	Ⓒ	Ⓓ	164	Ⓐ	Ⓑ	Ⓒ	Ⓓ	184	Ⓐ	Ⓑ	Ⓒ	Ⓓ
105	Ⓐ	Ⓑ	Ⓒ	Ⓓ	125	Ⓐ	Ⓑ	Ⓒ	Ⓓ	145	Ⓐ	Ⓑ	Ⓒ	Ⓓ	165	Ⓐ	Ⓑ	Ⓒ	Ⓓ	185	Ⓐ	Ⓑ	Ⓒ	Ⓓ
106	Ⓐ	Ⓑ	Ⓒ	Ⓓ	126	Ⓐ	Ⓑ	Ⓒ	Ⓓ	146	Ⓐ	Ⓑ	Ⓒ	Ⓓ	166	Ⓐ	Ⓑ	Ⓒ	Ⓓ	186	Ⓐ	Ⓑ	Ⓒ	Ⓓ
107	Ⓐ	Ⓑ	Ⓒ	Ⓓ	127	Ⓐ	Ⓑ	Ⓒ	Ⓓ	147	Ⓐ	Ⓑ	Ⓒ	Ⓓ	167	Ⓐ	Ⓑ	Ⓒ	Ⓓ	187	Ⓐ	Ⓑ	Ⓒ	Ⓓ
108	Ⓐ	Ⓑ	Ⓒ	Ⓓ	128	Ⓐ	Ⓑ	Ⓒ	Ⓓ	148	Ⓐ	Ⓑ	Ⓒ	Ⓓ	168	Ⓐ	Ⓑ	Ⓒ	Ⓓ	188	Ⓐ	Ⓑ	Ⓒ	Ⓓ
109	Ⓐ	Ⓑ	Ⓒ	Ⓓ	129	Ⓐ	Ⓑ	Ⓒ	Ⓓ	149	Ⓐ	Ⓑ	Ⓒ	Ⓓ	169	Ⓐ	Ⓑ	Ⓒ	Ⓓ	189	Ⓐ	Ⓑ	Ⓒ	Ⓓ
110	Ⓐ	Ⓑ	Ⓒ	Ⓓ	130	Ⓐ	Ⓑ	Ⓒ	Ⓓ	150	Ⓐ	Ⓑ	Ⓒ	Ⓓ	170	Ⓐ	Ⓑ	Ⓒ	Ⓓ	190	Ⓐ	Ⓑ	Ⓒ	Ⓓ
111	Ⓐ	Ⓑ	Ⓒ	Ⓓ	131	Ⓐ	Ⓑ	Ⓒ	Ⓓ	151	Ⓐ	Ⓑ	Ⓒ	Ⓓ	171	Ⓐ	Ⓑ	Ⓒ	Ⓓ	191	Ⓐ	Ⓑ	Ⓒ	Ⓓ
112	Ⓐ	Ⓑ	Ⓒ	Ⓓ	132	Ⓐ	Ⓑ	Ⓒ	Ⓓ	152	Ⓐ	Ⓑ	Ⓒ	Ⓓ	172	Ⓐ	Ⓑ	Ⓒ	Ⓓ	192	Ⓐ	Ⓑ	Ⓒ	Ⓓ
113	Ⓐ	Ⓑ	Ⓒ	Ⓓ	133	Ⓐ	Ⓑ	Ⓒ	Ⓓ	153	Ⓐ	Ⓑ	Ⓒ	Ⓓ	173	Ⓐ	Ⓑ	Ⓒ	Ⓓ	193	Ⓐ	Ⓑ	Ⓒ	Ⓓ
114	Ⓐ	Ⓑ	Ⓒ	Ⓓ	134	Ⓐ	Ⓑ	Ⓒ	Ⓓ	154	Ⓐ	Ⓑ	Ⓒ	Ⓓ	174	Ⓐ	Ⓑ	Ⓒ	Ⓓ	194	Ⓐ	Ⓑ	Ⓒ	Ⓓ
115	Ⓐ	Ⓑ	Ⓒ	Ⓓ	135	Ⓐ	Ⓑ	Ⓒ	Ⓓ	155	Ⓐ	Ⓑ	Ⓒ	Ⓓ	175	Ⓐ	Ⓑ	Ⓒ	Ⓓ	195	Ⓐ	Ⓑ	Ⓒ	Ⓓ
116	Ⓐ	Ⓑ	Ⓒ	Ⓓ	136	Ⓐ	Ⓑ	Ⓒ	Ⓓ	156	Ⓐ	Ⓑ	Ⓒ	Ⓓ	176	Ⓐ	Ⓑ	Ⓒ	Ⓓ	196	Ⓐ	Ⓑ	Ⓒ	Ⓓ
117	Ⓐ	Ⓑ	Ⓒ	Ⓓ	137	Ⓐ	Ⓑ	Ⓒ	Ⓓ	157	Ⓐ	Ⓑ	Ⓒ	Ⓓ	177	Ⓐ	Ⓑ	Ⓒ	Ⓓ	197	Ⓐ	Ⓑ	Ⓒ	Ⓓ
118	Ⓐ	Ⓑ	Ⓒ	Ⓓ	138	Ⓐ	Ⓑ	Ⓒ	Ⓓ	158	Ⓐ	Ⓑ	Ⓒ	Ⓓ	178	Ⓐ	Ⓑ	Ⓒ	Ⓓ	198	Ⓐ	Ⓑ	Ⓒ	Ⓓ
119	Ⓐ	Ⓑ	Ⓒ	Ⓓ	139	Ⓐ	Ⓑ	Ⓒ	Ⓓ	159	Ⓐ	Ⓑ	Ⓒ	Ⓓ	179	Ⓐ	Ⓑ	Ⓒ	Ⓓ	199	Ⓐ	Ⓑ	Ⓒ	Ⓓ
120	Ⓐ	Ⓑ	Ⓒ	Ⓓ	140	Ⓐ	Ⓑ	Ⓒ	Ⓓ	160	Ⓐ	Ⓑ	Ⓒ	Ⓓ	180	Ⓐ	Ⓑ	Ⓒ	Ⓓ	200	Ⓐ	Ⓑ	Ⓒ	Ⓓ

books.english.co.kr

cookie. english. co. kr

entest.co.kr